Index Funds

The 12-Step Program for Active Investors

by Mark T. Hebner

IFA Publishing
Irvine, California

This book is dedicated to Glorianna, Terry, Brie, Kory, Ian, Beth and Tyler.

First edition 2005
Reprinted 2007

This publication is designed to provide accurate and authoritative information in regard to the subject matter covered. It is sold with the understanding that the author is engaged in providing professional investment advisory services, but is not rendering legal, accounting or other professional services.

If legal, accounting or other expert assistance is required, the services of a competent professional person should be sought.

Representations of individuals and/or institutions are not necessarily an endorsement of any investment philosophy or strategy presented in this book. Please see additional disclaimers and disclosures in Appendix D.

ISBN 0-9768023-0-9

Printed in China

ACKNOWLEDGMENTS

Several people have provided encouragement, inspiration, and creative skills to make this book a reality. I want to thank the following people: Scott Simon, Melissa Johnson, Bonnie Bauman, Mary Brunson, Jay David Franklin, Kurt Mackie, Dennie Kuhn, Sam Brunstein, Beth Collins, Brie Hebner, Kory Hebner, Ian Hebner, Jonathan Wang, Gordon Shuler, Dave Mertz, Brendan Connelly, Marsha Koeller, Grace Fritzinger, Thomas Bang, Derrell Thomas, Peter Schumann, Rajiv Patel, Tim Hunold, Laura Gomez, Nicole Trakimas, Paul Karam, Andrew Yang, Matt Moon, Tony Hsu, John Kensey, Ben Barak, Bill Fletcher, Frank Singer, Starr Nowak, Toni Lazane, Steele Nowak, Lloyd Bagtas, Kevin Ohdner, Sonia Lee, Tillie Sita, Amy Brennan, Ken Garner, Kelly Simer, Kathy Gevert, Bob Ewell, George and Nancy Kandel, Lawrence Widarto, Marcel Widarto, Marsallay Spicer, Christine Tang, Mark Nelson, Timothy Wood, Shorty, Susan Kim, Enrique Quinzanos, Cynthia Graff, James Jameson, Dan Solin, Sugeet Wahal, Ara Demirjian, Aftab Alam, who painted the more than 60 water color portraits, Jackson Lin, who designed over 250 figures and tables, and Judith Arisman, who designed the book cover. I would like to give a special thank you to Lala Ragimov for her forty-seven beautiful and creative oil paintings, which are located throughout the book.

ABOUT THE AUTHOR

Mark T. Hebner has been the founder, president and CEO of three companies, one of which became a publicly held corporation. He has made a dozen investments in private companies and has owned a substantial portfolio of stocks and bonds for more than 20 years. He earned an MBA with honors from the University of California, Irvine, and graduated with a degree in nuclear pharmacy from the University of New Mexico. Hebner was a member of the Young Presidents' Organization from 1984 to 2002 and is currently a member of the World Presidents' Organization and the Chief Executive Organization.

Like many other investors, his conversion to the indexing investment philosophy began when he came to realize his investment portfolio was not performing anywhere near market averages. After selling his interest in his public company in 1985, Hebner utilized the services of several stockbrokers at nationally known firms. His primary broker matched Hebner's high-risk capacity with a low-risk exposure portfolio of mostly fixed income and a rotation between oil, gold, blue chip, and technology stocks. After a major loss of investment opportunity through this strategy,

Hebner became so interested in the idea of indexing that he started Index Funds Advisors, a Registered Investment Advisory (RIA) firm in Irvine, California. He and a team of writers, artists, Web designers, statisticians, and researchers have built a very comprehensive Web site, www.ifa.com, which provides elements of this book, numerous videos, several risk capacity surveys, and dynamic charts explaining the advantages and rock solid logic of a tax-managed, globally diversified portfolio of index funds matched to an investor's risk capacity. Hebner hopes to educate investors, so they won't have to look back 15 years from now and discover they did not achieve the return they had the capacity to earn.

PREFACE

The financial services industry has a dark secret, one that costs global investors about $2.5 trillion per year. This secret quietly drains the investment portfolios and retirement pension accounts of almost every worker and retiree. In 1900 French mathematician, Louis Bachelier, unsuspectingly revealed this disturbing fact to the world. Since then, hundreds of academic studies have supported Bachelier's findings. Unfortunately, investors pay little attention to academics and Nobel laureates.

The dark secret is that managers don't beat markets. The fact is that markets outperform managers by a substantial margin over long periods of time. This book offers overwhelming proof of this, while showing investors how to obtain an optimal rate of return by matching their risk capacity to an appropriate risk exposure. That risk exposure is a globally diversified portfolio of index funds.

My own journey to this unsettling truth began in 1985. It was then that I received about $6 million for the sale of a company I had co-founded. I immediately turned my newfound fortune over to a major brokerage firm with a stellar reputation and a fancy office in a towering skyscraper. How could I go wrong?

Like many investors, I didn't take the time to learn how the stock market works. I was completely unaware that since 1930 academic researchers had been applying scientific and statistical analysis to large sets of stock market data. It wasn't until 12 years later that I finally decided to figure out how my investments had performed compared to appropriate benchmarks. As I spent months combing through bookstores and surfing the Internet for information, the knot that had formed in my stomach grew tighter. I was distraught about what I discovered, and didn't sleep well for several nights. It turned out that my lack of understanding of how markets worked had cost me a mind boggling amount of money. When comparing a risk appropriate portfolio of index funds with what I actually achieved in my own portfolio over the last 20 years, I have ended up with at least $30 million less. I repeat, my portfolio earned $30 million less than a simple index fund portfolio. Did I really have to pay $30 million in tuition to finally get my degree from the University of Index Funds (UIF)?

My first course of action was to move my assets into index funds managed by Vanguard. But, after more research, I discovered that despite Vanguard's superiority in the index arena, there was a better firm out there. This firm is Dimensional Fund Advisors (DFA). After this discovery, I started a new business, Index Funds Advisors, to educate and advise others about achieving optimal market rates of returns. Along with a host of other services, my firm offers an extensive and interactive Web site, ifa.com, to educate investors about investing in index funds.

The knowledge I gained through my research enabled me to begin asking the right questions about my risk exposure and the performance of my investments. But, how many others were still in the dark? To answer that question, I spent several weeks asking friends what they knew about the capital markets. I wanted to know how much tuition they themselves had paid to UIF. The more I inquired, the more astounded I became at the lack of knowledge and poor returns achieved by almost everyone I knew. One morning it occurred to me that investors just follow their natural born instincts to trade and to try to predict the future. This behavior, which is akin to a gambling addiction, is driven by the possibility of striking it rich overnight. For its part, the financial services industry is addicted to the massive profits it earns from its clients' gambling. The industry is content to keep its dark secret locked up in the mathematical formulas of *The Journal of Finance* or a university text book. The secret is safe there as the overwhelming majority of investors do not have the time or the inclination to decode the complexities of investing. Riskese, the language of risk, is especially difficult for the average investor to master. Therefore, most continue to place their faith in the mystical powers of market beating gurus.

So, how can investors break these destructive patterns of investing? The same way 30 other addictions are addressed: with a 12-step program. This book explains my program, Active Investors Anonymous, the recommended treatment of choice for wayward investors.

I am passionate about my mission to clear the smoke and mirrors designed to conceal the failure of active management. Ultimately, my goal is to lead investors to a highly efficient, tax-managed, low-cost and risk appropriate index portfolio.

Mark T. Hebner
Index Funds Advisors, Inc.
19100 Von Karman Ave, Suite 450
Irvine, California 92612
888-643-3133
email: info@ifa.com
www.ifa.com

THE SHORT BOOK ON INVESTING

What every investor should know about how capital markets work.

Before learning about the differences between index funds investing and active investing in the *12-Step Program for Active Investors*, it's important to gain an understanding of the following key concepts:

1. The Random Walk Theory: Markets are moved by news. News is unpredictable and random by definition. Therefore, the market's movements are unpredictable and random. This concept is known as "The Random Walk Theory." On the bright side, market randomness carries a positive average of about 10% per year thanks to the success of capitalism. Oftentimes, active managers who claim to outperform a market average or index imply that they have the power to predict tomorrow's news. But, it's impossible to consistently predict the future. The truth is active managers post unpredictable and random results. Louis Bachelier first discussed "The Random Walk Theory" in 1900 in his paper titled "The Theory of Speculation." Since then a large body of academic research has leant credence to the theory. The largest single compilation of this research can be found in Paul Cootner's "The Random Character of Stock Market Prices," a 500-page collection of research papers on the randomness of the market. Next on the list is, "Proof that Properly Anticipated Prices Fluctuate Randomly," a paper written in 1965 by Nobel laureate in Economics and MIT Professor, Paul Samuelson. Also, in 1965, University of Chicago Professor Eugene Fama wrote his highly regarded papers, "Random Walks in Stock Market Prices" and "The Behavior of Stock Market Prices." Once this extensive research is understood, investors will be convinced of the randomness of stock market prices.

2. Skill or Luck: Occasions where actively managed funds beat index funds are attributable to luck, not skill. Time and again research has shown that after costs, the return on the average actively managed dollar will be less than the return on the average passively managed dollar. Actively managed funds may occasionally beat index funds. However, market beating performance in a random market is due to luck, not a skill that is repeatable. Studies show that only about 3% of active managers beat an appropriate index over a 10-year or longer period. It is nearly impossible to predict which manager might get lucky and beat the market. So, investors who have gotten lucky in the past should not expect a continuation of their good fortune.

3. Index Portfolios Best Capture Risk and Return: Actively managed investments are subject to higher risk and lower returns than a globally diversified, tax-managed, and small value tilted portfolio of index funds. Indeed, commissions, management fees, margin costs and taxes all chip away at the returns on actively managed investments and line the pockets of brokers, mutual fund managers, and hedge fund managers. A recent University of California, Davis, study showed that 82% of the 925,000 active traders on the

Taiwanese Stock Exchange lost money. Their losses added up to $8.2 billion a year from 1995 to 1999. In addition, in a 2004 report on investor behavior, Dalbar, Inc. (Dalbar) found that the average equity investor earned a paltry 3.5% annually for the last 20 years, compared to 3.05% inflation and 12.98% for the S&P 500 over that same period.

4. Capitalism Works Because Free Markets are Efficient: Capitalism is a great idea that has worked for centuries. The world's stock exchanges facilitate a free market system that is the cornerstone of capitalism. These capital markets simultaneously price the cost of capital and the expected return from the risk of capitalism. Free markets perform this highly important task in the most effective and efficient manner because the knowledge of all investors exceeds the knowledge of any individual. Therefore, due to the millions of intelligent and highly competitive investors, it is unlikely that any individual investor will consistently profit at the expense of all other investors. From this we can conclude free markets work and current prices reflect the knowledge and expectations of all investors at all times. This concept is known as the Efficient Market Theory. When markets are efficient, active management is not a viable strategy and index funds best capture the market returns. If free markets were not more efficient than controlled markets, like those in communist countries, then it would stand to reason that the communists would be more prosperous than the capitalists.

5. Returns From the Risk of Capitalism Rank Highest: Capitalism has provided an annualized return of about 10% per year since 1926 and has the highest rate of return of all alternative investments tracked over periods of 50 years or more. That rate of return is explained by the difference between the low risk of capital and the high risk of capitalism. It is not the result of speculation in short-term price changes. There is no additional expected return from speculation above the average return. Gains from speculation are offset by losses in any random situation.

6. Expected Returns Equal Cost of Capital: The expected return for an investor (equity buyer) is equal to the cost of capital of the equity seller. A higher cost of capital for the equity seller translates to a higher expected return for the provider of capital (cash). A lower cost of capital for the seller of the equity translates to a lower expected return for the buyer (provider of the capital). Intelligent investors will estimate their expected return based on the risk of the equity, which is tied to the risk of the company. The higher the risk of the company, the higher its cost of capital, and the higher the expected return for the investor. The lower the risk of the company, the lower its cost of capital, and the lower the expected return for the investor. Investors who carefully match their risk capacity with their risk exposure have the best chance of obtaining the long-term historical returns of the global markets. A buy, hold, and rebalanced index portfolio strategy is the best method to capture those returns.

7. Small Value versus Large Growth Companies: Public companies that are unglamorous, small, and relatively cheap (small value) are riskier and have higher costs of capital than those that are glamorous, large and relatively expensive (large growth). To illustrate this point, a dollar invested in a Fama/French Index of small-value companies in 1927 grew to $50,690 by the end of 2006 (14.5% annualized return), and a dollar invested in a Fama/French Index of large growth companies grew to only $1,272 over the same period (9.35% annualized return). When building diversified index portfolios, a tilt towards small value will enhance expected returns.

8. Diversify, Diversify, Diversify: Diversification is an investor's best friend because it reduces the uncertainty of expected returns, otherwise known as risk, without changing the expected return. Concentrating investments only adds risk, and does not increase expected returns. Risk can be defined as the uncertainty of obtaining an expected return. The numbers tell the story best. Any one stock in the S&P 500 has an expected return of about 10% per year plus or minus about 50% two-thirds of the years. However, the S&P 500 Index has the same 10% expected return, but it only has a risk of plus or minus 20% two-thirds of the years. So, 10% plus or minus 20% is far superior to and carries less uncertainty than 10% plus or minus 50%. Highly efficient portfolios of index funds have had returns of 14% per year with risks of 15% over the last 50 years, after fees. (See Index Portfolio 100 in Appendix A, which includes about 16,000 companies from 40 countries.) This is why buying the whole haystack (index) is better than looking for the needle (a stock) in the haystack.

9. Selecting Index Funds: Index fund investors have the option of investing with a handful of world-class companies including Dimensional Fund Advisors (DFA), Barclays Global Investors (BGI), and the Vanguard Group. All three firms offer excellent products for designing index portfolios. For several years, Dalbar has surveyed investment advisors and Dimensional Fund Advisors has been rated the top firm among all mutual fund companies. DFA provides academic-style research, historical risk and return data, extensive investment advisor education and mutual fund products that reflect the leading academic research. It is the only firm that offers no actively managed funds. DFA constructs custom indexes and block trading strategies to capture certain risk factors and to maximize tax-management. They also restrict their shareholders in order to minimize fund turnover and expenses for existing shareholders of their index mutual funds.

10. Peace of Mind: Don't let your retirement years be tainted by the discomfort of poverty. Reliance on family members or government programs for your financial well-being will be a source of unhappiness, insecurity, and low self-esteem. A prudent and intelligently managed investment portfolio of index funds has the highest probability of providing security and peace of mind in the years when it will be needed the most.

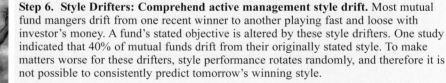

OVERVIEW OF THE 12-STEP PROGRAM FOR ACTIVE INVESTORS

Step 1. Active Investors: Recognize an active investor. Active investors hope to pick winners among the many stocks, times, managers or investment styles. But, the problem with the methods deployed by active investors is that markets are moved by news. News is unpredictable and random. Therefore, the movements of stocks, markets, managers, and styles are unpredictable and random. Markets are also efficient, meaning that news is rapidly reflected in market prices. As a result, active investing is not a viable strategy. The only reliable source of long-term returns is from consistent exposure to economic risk factors that have 80 years of history.

Step 2. Nobel Laureates: Recognize that Nobel Prize winners researched the market. Nobel Prizes have been awarded to academics for their analysis of how stock markets work. The allure of their findings is that they're not biased by a need to earn a commission or sell you an IPO, magazine or newspaper. More than a hundred years of academic research has concluded that index funds are an investor's best investment. Sadly, the great majority of investors have never read these academic studies so they continue as active investors.

Step 3. Stock Pickers: Accept that stock pickers do not beat the market. The primary factor influencing the success of a stock picker is simply luck. In numerous studies, only about 3% of stock pickers beat their benchmark. Most stock pickers invest in stocks that have done well recently; however, those same stocks do poorly in subsequent periods. The performance of stocks is random, just like the news that influences their prices. Therefore, it is not possible to consistently pick stocks that will be top performers in the future.

Step 4. Time Pickers: Understand that no one can pick the right time to be in or out of the market. When 32 market-timing newsletters were compared to the S&P 500 Index over a 10-year period, not one of them beat the broad market index. The primary reason for this inability to time the market is the high concentration of returns and losses that occur in a time period of a few days. In a 10-year period, more than 100% of the total gain was concentrated in just 20 days. It is impossible to pick those 20 days in advance. Professors studied 15,000 predictions by 237 market timers and concluded, "There is no evidence that [market timing] newsletters can time the market."

Step 5. Manager Pickers: Realize that the winning managers were just lucky. The S&P 500 Index consistently outperformed 98% of mutual fund managers over the past three years and 97% over the past 10 years, ending October 2004. In two 30-year studies, the S&P 500 outperformed 97% and 94% of managers. In addition, only about 14% of the top 100 managers repeat their performance in the following years. Therefore, it is not possible to consistently pick next year's hot mutual fund manager. Index portfolios consistently capture the risk and return of markets, which in a high risk index portfolio has been 14% annualized for the past 50 years, compared to 11% for the S&P 500.

Step 6. Style Drifters: Comprehend active management style drift. Most mutual fund mangers drift from one recent winner to another playing fast and loose with investor's money. A fund's stated objective is altered by these style drifters. One study indicated that 40% of mutual funds drift from their originally stated style. To make matters worse for these drifters, style performance rotates randomly, and therefore it is not possible to consistently predict tomorrow's winning style.

Step 7. Silent Partners: Recognize the partners in your returns. There are partners that subtly take a large slice of your investment return. In taxable accounts, over a 15-year period, active investors keep only about 50% of the total return earned by their initial investment. Meanwhile, investors in index funds keep about 85% of the total return by maintaining tight controls over the silent and often invisible partners of high fees, expenses, cash drag, taxes, transaction costs and more. By minimizing the cost of these silent partners investors will increase their expected returns.

Step 8. Riskese: Understand how risk, return and time are related. Lawyers speak legalese and the best investors speak riskese. Learning the language of riskese requires investors to have a basic understanding of the concepts of risk, return, time, and correlation. Understanding riskese is essential for successful investing. Most investors instead chase the short-term returns of stocks, markets, managers or styles, and never truly understand the impact of risk, time, and correlation on their returns. The more fluent you speak riskese, the higher your risk capacity, risk exposure and expected returns.

Step 9. History: Understand the historical risks and returns of indexes. Long-term data is required to estimate the expected risk and return for different stock market indexes. We now have almost 80 years of monthly risk and return data on several important indexes. This mountain of empirical evidence proves that index funds are the most reliable and logical investment choice. Since you can not predict the future based on recent events, the study of long-term stock market data is the only source of probability distributions of the expected risk and return of investments.

Step 10. Risk Capacity: Analyze your five dimensions of risk capacity. A Risk Capacity Survey will help you determine your individual and unique risk capacity. Five dimensions of your risk capacity will be thoroughly measured resulting in a score and corresponding index portfolio.These risk capacity dimensions include time horizon, investment knowledge, net income, net worth, and attitude toward risk.This is your single most important contribution to the investing process, resulting in an Investment Policy Statement that will provide the guidelines for your financial future.

Step 11. Risk Exposure: Analyze your five dimensions of risk exposure. Over 90% of the returns of diversified portfolios of index funds can be explained by their exposure to five dimensions of risk. Those dimensions include market, size, value, term and default. Once investors have determined their risk capacity in Step 10, they will be matched to one of 20 index portfolios. Index funds are utilized to minimize taxes and maximize expected returns. A simulation of a properly designed index portfolio shows an outperformance over the S&P 500 Index by 3% annualized for the last 50 years at the same level of risk and after the deduction of mutual fund fees and investment advisory fees.

Step 12. Invest and Relax: Invest, relax and stay balanced. The road to recovery for active investors ends with a recognition that a strategy of buying, holding, and rebalancing a portfolio of index funds is the best way for investors to maximize the expected returns of their investments. A financial advisor that speaks riskese and understands how markets work can best design, implement, and maintain a risk-appropriate, tax-managed, and highly efficient portfolio of low-cost index funds for investors. After investors implement this prudent investment plan, they can kick back and relax.

INDEX FUNDS: THE 12-STEP PROGRAM FOR ACTIVE INVESTORS

TABLE OF CONTENTS

STEP 3   STOCK PICKERS

STEP 9   HISTORY

STEP 10   RISK CAPACITY

APPENDIXES

[Step 1 ~ Active Investors]

STEP 1
Active Investors

"The investor's chief problem - and even his worst enemy - is likely to be himself."

- Benjamin Graham, legendary American investor, scholar, teacher and co-author of the 1934 classic, *Security Analysis*

"The deeper one delves, the worse things look for actively managed funds."

- William Bernstein, *The Intelligent Asset Allocator*

"The sheer magnitude of the difference we discovered between the total returns earned by funds and the results captured by the average shareholder is shocking and tragic. [Over four years: Funds = 5.7%, Investors = 1%.]"

- Charles Trzcinka, professor of finance, Indiana University. "What Fund Investors Really Need to Know," *Money Magazine*, June 2002

"Over the 10-year period ending 2003, 142 of the largest, smartest pension funds in the USA lost an average 0.3% per year in their active large cap domestic equities programs, relative to simply investing in index funds."

- Keith Ambachtsheer, *The Ambachtsheer Letter*, June 2005

"The common theme unifying this book is that security markets are nearly efficient, meaning most securities are usually priced appropriately given their risk and return attributes," and *"Proponents of the efficient market hypothesis believe that active management is largely a wasted effort and unlikely to justify the expenses incurred. Therefore, they advocate a passive investment strategy [index funds] that makes no attempt to outsmart the market."*

- Zvi Bodie, Alex Kane, and Alan Marcus, *Investments*

"The results of this study are not good news for investors who purchase actively managed mutual funds. No investment style generates positive abnormal returns over the 1965 to 1998 sample period. The sample includes 4,686 funds covering 26,564 fund years."

- James L.Davis, "Mutual Fund Performance and Manager Style," 2001

"Why does indexing outmaneuver the best minds on Wall Street? Paradoxically, it is because the best and brightest in the financial community have made the stock market very efficient. When information arises about individual stocks or the market as a whole, it gets reflected in stock prices without delay, making one stock as reasonably priced as another. Active managers who frequently shift from security to security actually detract from performance [compared to an index fund] by incurring transaction costs."

- Burton G. Malkiel, Chemical Bank Chairman's Professor of Economics, Princeton University, *The Wall Street Journal*

"Most investors are pretty smart. Yet most investors also remain heavily invested in actively managed stock funds. This is puzzling. The temptation, of course, is to dismiss these folks as ignorant fools. But I suspect these folks know the odds are stacked against them, and yet they are more than happy to take their chances."

- Jonathan Clements, *The Wall Street Journal*, February 2001

"[Most investors would] be better off in an index fund."

- Peter Lynch, famous stock picker, *Barron's*, April 1990

"...the best way to own common stocks is through an index fund...," and *"...those index funds that are very low-cost... are investor-friendly by definition and are the best selection for most of those who wish to own equities."*

- Warren Buffett, chairman of Berkshire Hathaway, "Chairman's Letter to Shareholders," 1996 and 2003

1.1 INTRODUCTION

Step 1: Recognize an active investor.

The first step in any recovery program is to recognize that there is a problem. In the 12-Step Program presented in this book, that means identifying the traits of an active investor and specifying why those traits are problematic. The following list describes a number of common behavior patterns of active investors:

- own or plan to own actively managed mutual funds,

- select stocks they think can outperform a market—this is referred to as stock picking,

- think there are times to be in a market and times to be out of a market—this is called time picking, generally known as market timing,

- think that active managers with the best track records are best for managing their investments—this is called manager picking,

- shift in and out of styles or indexes in an effort to chase returns—this is called style drifting,

- are primarily invested in the S&P 500 thinking this provides adequate diversification,

- believe that now is the best time to invest in certain sectors such as healthcare, technology, large cap or small cap,

- invest without considering risk capacity or risk exposure,

- invest without first studying the academic research that explains how and why free markets work,

- keep a stash of Rolaids on hand to cope with short-term market volatility.

1.2 DEFINITIONS

1.2.1 Active Investors

The overwhelming majority of investors are active investors. Extensive research by many academics and investment professionals has shown that investors cannot beat a market in the long run with stock, time, manager or style picking. So, it is disconcerting that about 70% of all institutional money and about 90% of individual investors' assets invested in U.S. stocks are still actively managed. Active investors who claim to outperform a market also claim the power to predict the future. When accurately measured, this is simply impossible. See Table 1-1 for a summary of the differences between the two investment approaches.

As Table 1-1 illustrates, analytical techniques that active investors use are best described as qualitative or speculative. They include predictions of future sales and earnings growth, and are often based on gut feelings and intuition.

The 12-Step Program presented in this book is designed as a recovery program for active investors. Active investing has been shown to be detrimental to investors, and this program is the treatment of choice to cure this problem.

1.2.2 Index Funds Investors

The index funds investing approach is best described as quantitative or scientific. Indexing techniques include the statistical analysis of 78 years worth of risk and return data as well as extensive measurements of numerous performance criteria.

Active vs. Passive

Table 1-1

The Difference Between Two Investment Strategies		
Subject	**Active Investing**	**Index Funds Investing**
Return Objective	Beat a market	Obtain the return of a market, index or asset class
Style Definition	40% drift from classification	Pure and consistent classification
Average Equity Individual Investor Returns over 20 years	3.70% per year according to Dalbar for 20 year period ending 2004	S&P 500 = 13.20% annualized Index Portfolio 100* = 15.32% annualized
Approach	Stock Picking, Time Picking, Manager Picking, or Style Drifting	Buy and hold a globally diversified portfolio of index funds
State of Mind	Stressed	Relaxed
Taxes and Portfolio Turnover	High (20-40% of return over 10 years) Turnover averaged 112% in 2004	Low (less than 8% of the return over 10 years) Turnover averages 10%
Net Performance	Well below the index by the amount of fees, expenses, taxes, and missed opportunities	The index return, less low fees, low taxes, and tracking error
Individual Investors	Currently about 85% of equity funds	Currently about 15% and growing rapidly, since 1999
Institutional Investors	Currently about 56% of domestic stock assets	Currently about 44% and growing
Proponents	Virtually all Brokerage Firms, Mutual Fund Companies, Market Timing Services, Investment Press and Brokerage Training Programs	The Univ. of Chicago, Nobel Prize Recipients, Vanguard Group, Dimensional Fund Advisors, Barclays Global Investors, Warren Buffet, and Charles Schwab & Company
Analytical Techniques	Art - Qualitative, Disregard for Risk, Forecasting, Predicting the Future, Feelings, Intuition, Luck, Betting, Gambling, Speculation	Science - Quantitative, Risk Management, Long Term Statistical Analysis, Accurate Performance Measurements, (like Insurance companies)
*Sources, Updates, and Disclosure: ifa.com/btp, Greenwich Research Associate, John Bogle, and Dalbar, Inc.		

Unlike active managers, managers of index funds are far less active in the buying and selling of stocks. Indeed, managers of index funds do not pick stocks or styles, time markets or make attempts to forecast the future.

Investing in index funds is a growing trend. Approximately 15% of all individual assets and 44% of all institutional assets are currently invested in index funds. In addition, many institutional funds are 100% indexed. Even Charles Schwab & Company in their "Core and Explore" program recommends that investors put 80% of their large-cap assets into index funds. Charles Schwab himself has 75% of his mutual fund investments invested in index funds. Other indexing proponents include Warren Buffett,

Barclays Global Investors, Dimensional Fund Advisors (DFA), the Vanguard Group, numerous academic institutions, Nobel laureates and Index Funds Advisors along with a handful of registered investment advisors. In addition, insurance companies use a similar approach to indexing when setting premiums for the risks they take when insuring against thousands of random events.

Most investors believe that investing in index funds means investing in familiar market indexes such as the Standard & Poor's 500 Index. S&P 500 Index Funds are structured with the aim to provide the same investment performance as the index. By holding all the stocks in the same proportion as the S&P 500 Index, the fund represents about 85% of the market value of all U.S. companies, mostly large blue chip stocks. However, familiar market indexes such as the S&P 500, Russell Indexes, and Wilshire Indexes, were not originally designed as investment vehicles.

In the early 1980s, index funds expanded to customized indexes designed to capture specific risk factors. Originally designed for large pension funds, customized institutional-style index funds are meant to capture various financial risk factors or dimensions of the market. Exposure to a risk factor such as company size or value constitutes a risk dimension of the market. Investors have been compensated with higher returns for risk exposure to these risk factors since 1926. These dimensions of the market can also be referred to as indexes.

Index funds can be defined as groups of stocks that have common risk and return characteristics and comply with specific and clearly defined sets of rules of ownership, which are held constant regardless of market conditions. These groups of stocks include companies from the United States, foreign countries, and emerging markets. There are additional indexes within these markets such as small value, large value, small growth, large growth and real estate securities as well as fixed-income investments such as short-term and long-term treasury bonds, municipal bonds, and corporate bonds. Companies are purchased and held within the index when they meet the index parameters. Stocks are sold when they move outside of these parameters and no longer meet the index rules of construction.

An example of a traditional index fund is Barclays iShare that trades the Russell 2000 Value Index. Generally, the Russell 2000 Value

Index contains the companies with lower price-to-book ratios and lower long-term growth.

An example of a customized index fund is DFA's Micro-Cap Index Fund, which invests in securities whose market capitalization (price per share multiplied by number of shares outstanding) falls within the smallest 4% of the universe of all U.S. companies. This includes all stocks traded on the New York Stock Exchange, the American Stock Exchange, and those listed in the National Association of Securities Dealers Automated Quotation Over-the-Counter (NASDAQ OTC) market. In June 2005, Russell also introduced a micro-cap index. Another example would be DFA's Small-Cap Value Fund. The fund invests in companies ranked in the lowest 8% by size as well as the highest 25% measured by a value measurement known as a book-to-market ratio (BtM). DFA funds are the most highly regarded index funds, and they are now available to individual investors through a small qualified group of independent registered investment advisors who have demonstrated their understanding and commitment to the concepts described in this 12-Step Program. There are no fees of any kind paid by DFA to financial advisors who advise their clients to invest in DFA funds.

1.2.3 Beating the Market

The phrase "beating the market" can be defined as the attempt to obtain a higher net return from a portfolio of stocks, bonds or mutual funds rather than from a relevant index or benchmark. The net return includes adjustments for all commissions, loads, fees, expenses, risks, and federal and state taxes. It is calculated over a reasonable period of at least 10 years, but preferably over 30 years. The net return of an active investor's stock portfolio can then be paralleled to an index fund or a blend of index funds with a comparable risk.

The only way an investor can over perform or underperform an index is to simply invest in something other than the index. But, since the index is the only source of long-term risk and return data, why would investors subject their hard earned savings to anything other than the index? The most basic tenet of all investing is that exposure of money to a higher level of risk should be rewarded with a higher expected return. In contrast, lower levels of risk should correlate to a lower expected return. One of the problems with measuring the performance of stock market investing is the lack of a standardized system of benchmarks from which to measure performance. This lack of available benchmarking is the black hole of investing. If there are no definitive risk benchmarks, it is impossible to determine if the exposure to risk has been properly rewarded. In other words, has an active investor really beaten a market with repeatable skill or can his different results be attributed to an inappropriate benchmark comparison or just luck?

1.2.4 Risk Measurements

There are many measurements used by investment professionals and academics to try to capture and compare risk. These include markets, benchmarks, asset classes, styles, style boxes, investment objectives, risk factors, market dimensions, market segments, categories, market averages, buckets of stocks, rules of ownership, slices of the market, industry classifications, and indexes such as Dow Jones Indexes, Standard & Poor's Indexes, Russell Indexes, Wilshire Indexes, Morgan Stanley Capital Indexes, Fama and French Indexes, CRSP Indexes, and the Wired Index. In addition, diversification and measures of volatility such as standard deviation are also used to capture risk. These are all attempts to identify common risk and return characteristics among groups of stocks or bonds.

Because investment professionals have such an abundance of options, they're likely to use the measurement that best suits their purpose. This tendency can be harmful to investors. To reduce confusion, "market" or "index" will often be used as a substitute for these terms in this book.

An appropriate challenge to the investment industry is a call to action to develop an SEC-approved standard to measure the risk of various investments. The Three-Factor Model, which is explained later in the book, developed by Eugene Fama and Kenneth French in 1992, would be an excellent starting point. Already, it is considered a risk measurement standard by academics. A more widespread use of this method would benefit investors immensely.

1.3 PROBLEMS

1.3.1 Active Investors are Everywhere

About 90% of investors are active investors. The most popular strategies in attempting to beat a market include stock, time, manager, and style picking.

Stock pickers try to pick winning stocks rather than diversify their portfolio. Time pickers try to make money off timing the markets. They think they can strategically pick specific times to get in and out of a market, believing this approach is more profitable than a buy-and-hold strategy. Manager pickers buy stock portfolios or mutual funds managed by money managers who seem to have the best recent performance record. Style pickers identify which style will be the next to perform above and beyond the others. The overwhelming majority of individuals who are invested in stock mutual funds hold shares of an actively managed mutual fund. However, as more information is leaking out to the public, more investors are moving to index funds.

1.3.2 Active Investors are Gamblers

Active investors are commonly under the illusion that they can predict the future direction of market prices. They believe they have a special understanding of the market, a superior edge over other less knowledgeable investors, and are immune to disaster. The truth is that all investors have access to very similar information. Still, many investors believe they are smarter and more sophisticated than the average investor. They fail to realize just how much investment performance depends on luck. Most of them eventually pay dearly for this mistake. Active investing in the stock market is akin to gambling in a casino. Take a look at the numerous comparisons in various news articles below. Note the references to the addictive gambling nature of active investors.

Excerpt from *USA Today*, May 18, 2005, "Could Hedge Funds Cause Market Meltdown?": "When something becomes so popular, you know you're late to the party," says Scott Black, president of investment firm Delphi Management. "A lot of this is gambling with other people's money."

Excerpt from *Times Online*, May 18, 2005, "Investors Beware of 'Lemming' Behavior": "'Investors appear to have been caught up in a whirlwind of speculation and gambling,' says Professor Johnnie Johnson, a researcher from the Center for Risk Research. 'Their appetite for gain led to an explosion of excitement, with rational judgment being one of the first victims.'"

Excerpt from *www.gamblingmagazine.com*, May 19, 2005, "Online Stock Trading Dangers":

"After two months tethered to his computer keyboard, Mr. Anderson says in an interview, 'It only took a few trades to really just wipe me out.' Now deeply in debt and living at home with his parents, he recalls dispiritedly, 'It was sudden. I remember one day I was lying in bed in the fetal position, saying what the hell did I do?'" and "...mental-health professionals say some of today's obsessed day traders...may actually be addicted to online trading."

Excerpt from www.abanet.org, July/August 2001, "Other Bumps in the Road: Gambling": "Paul Good, a clinical psychologist in San Francisco, developed 11 warning signs that may reveal whether an investor is actually a gambler in disguise. Anyone who exhibits five or more of these signs may have a gambling problem. Sign One: High-volume trading in which the action has become more compelling than the objective of the trade."

Paul Samuelson

Paul Samuelson, MIT economist, Nobel laureate and early fan of the indexing technique had this to say about the gambling tendencies of active investors: "My guess is that indexing will have a larger role if you call me 10 years from now than it does now. But it will still be a minority mode of investing. Why? There is something in people; you might even call it a little bit of a gambling instinct. They want to be interested in the process of investing, and it's traditionally been difficult to get too jazzed up about indexing. I tell people investing should be dull. It shouldn't be exciting. Investing should be more like watching paint dry or watching grass grow. If you want excitement, take $800 and go to Las Vegas."

The active investor's addiction to beating the odds is often as strong as any other addiction.

Like gambling, active investing can be extraordinarily exciting for investors who get carried away by the adrenaline of winning. Conversely, it can create significant agony for those who experience the losing side of risk. One of the biggest mistakes made by active investors is they believe there is skill involved when the stock market proves profitable. Many of today's day traders are learning this lesson the hard way. There are an estimated 40 million online accounts in the United States. Stories of mounting losses are becoming more prevalent as the odds of playing the markets take their toll on this new breed of investors. Just like casino gambling, there are more tales about the winners than the losers, and the stories rarely give an accurate accounting of true net profit.

1.3.3　Active Investors Lose

In the June 2002 edition of *Money Magazine*, financial journalist, Jason Zweig, gets to the bottom of annual returns. He describes the difference between the returns that mutual funds report and the actual returns of the average investor in those funds. Active investors chase hot funds. As a consequence, they end up with less than one-

fifth of the funds' annual returns. When inflation and tax estimates are deducted, it is not a pretty picture for active investors. See Figure 1-1.

Table 1-2 enumerates some of the details of a unique study performed by Charles Trzcinka, professor of finance at the University of Indiana. The large gap between the funds' and shareholders' returns was a shock to even the researchers. The reason for this gap is attributed to active investors who followed the destructive behavioral patterns that Dalbar has been describing since 1994. These patterns include waiting for funds to have a good year or two then pouring in a flood of cash just before the fund reaches its peak. Finally, active investors ride the fund to near bottom and sell.

Figure 1-1

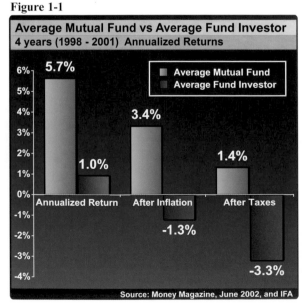

Source: Money Magazine, June 2002, and IFA

Table 1-2

Average Mutual Fund vs Average Fund Investor Annualized Return 1998-2001			
Largest Gaps Among The Largest Funds (Avg Gap = 4.7%)			
Mutual Fund Name	Fund Return	Shareholder Return	Difference
Fidelity Aggressive Growth	2.8%	-24.1%	-26.9%
Vanguard Capital Opportunity Fund	29.2%	5.2%	-23.9%
Invesco Dynamics Inv.	7.0%	-14.4%	-21.4%
Janus Mercury	13.9%	-7.4%	-21.3%
Fidelity Select Electronics	21.7%	7.6%	-14.0%
Van Kampen Emerging Growth	13.2%	-0.7%	-13.9%
Alliance Premier Growth	3.4%	-9.2%	-12.5%
SEI Inst. Mgd. Large Cap Growth	2.5%	-8.3%	-10.8%
Fidelity Growth Company	12.4%	1.9%	-10.5%
Fidelity OTC	7.7%	-2.7%	-10.4%
Narrower Gap Among Index Funds from Dimensional Fund Advisors			
DFA US Large Cap Value	7.7%	7.4%	-0.3%
DFA US Micro Cap	9.8%	8.2%	-1.6%
DFA US Small Cap Value	8.8%	8.6%	-0.2%
DFA US Small Cap	8.1%	7.6%	-0.5%
DFA Large Company	5.5%	1.5%	-4.0%

Source: Money Magazine, June 2002

One encouraging exception is DFA's institutional index funds. DFA investors are limited to either large institutional investors or individuals who have been educated by specially trained investment advisors. Because the shareholders of these funds buy and hold diversified portfolios at all times, they ride out the market gyrations and end up obtaining market rates of returns, as noted in Table 1-2. A study released by Dalbar in 2006 came up with similar results, but over a much longer period. The study indicated that during the 20 years from 1986 to 2005, the average stock fund investor earned returns of only 3.90% per year, while the S&P 500 returned 11.93%. On an inflation adjusted return, the average equity fund investor earned $19,625 on a $100,000 investment made in 1986, while the inflation adjusted return of the S&P 500 would have been $400,938 or 20 times greater, as shown in percentage terms in Figure 1-2 and in dollar terms in Figure 1-3.

The Dalbar studies reveal that the behavior of average fund investors is an obstacle to reaching the published performance of the financial markets in which they are invested. Clearly, investor behavior can have a far more negative impact on investment performance than investors realize.

Some investors can benefit from enlisting an investment educator, coach or mentor who will focus on changing their investing behavior, encouraging long-term investing, and discouraging the gambling practices of trying to beat a market. Active investors are constantly on an emotional roller coaster ride, which leads them to negative returns on average, after all expenses and taxes. The information in Figure 1-4 looks sadly familiar to many investors. As the value of their investments go through their eventual ups and downs, investors wait until they feel excitement that their investments are on the rise. Once

Figure 1-2

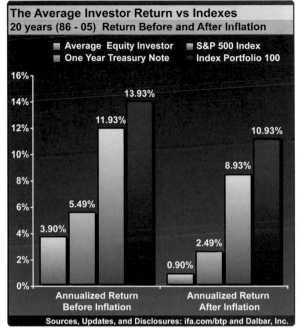

Figure 1-3

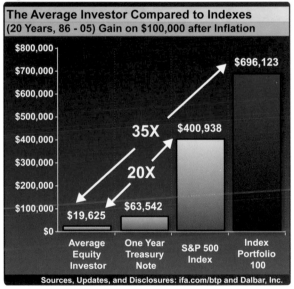

they buy and the price takes a downturn, they then become fearful and sell. This cycle of buying after the price has gone up and selling after it has gone down leaves investors with losses, doubt and regret. The lessons in this 12-Step Program should allow investors to resist the

Figure 1-4

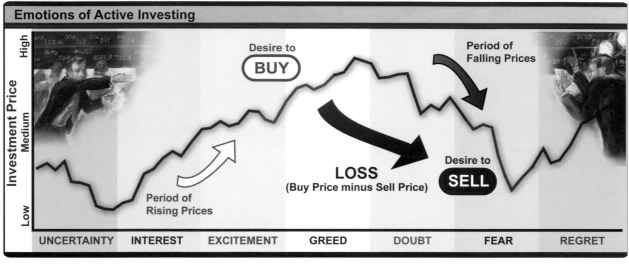

behaviors that have caused them such despair and poor results in the past.

1.3.4 The Poor Accounting of Active Investors

Active investors often do not properly account for their gains and losses. Common mistakes include the exclusion of sales, commissions, taxes, and cash flows in and out of their portfolios. Another common error is quoting the returns of only the portion of their portfolio that performed well or a time period that did well. Then there is the problem of hearing only from the gambling winners and not hearing from the losers, who seem to disappear into thin air. For example, since 1961, 28% of mutual funds have vanished from the database commonly used to analyze them. Consequently, there is no accounting for their almost certain poor performance.

1.3.5 Stock Market Prices are Random

The Random Walk Theory describes the way stock prices change unpredictably as a result of unexpected news appearing in the market. This "random walk" of changing prices has created a misconception among investors that stock prices

change randomly for no rational reason. Investors are actually reacting to news, and thereby creating random movements in the prices.

1.3.6 Stock Markets are Efficient

The Efficient Market Theory explains the process of free and efficient financial markets. First, information about stocks is widely and inexpensively available to all investors. Second, all known and available information is already reflected in current stock prices. Third, the price of a stock agreed on by a buyer and a seller is the best estimate of the true value of that stock. Finally, stock prices change almost instantaneously as new information appears in the market. All of these factors make it nearly impossible to capture returns in excess of a market's return. The only issue of concern is the relationship between risk, return, time, and correlation.

1.3.7 When Risk Capacity is not Matched with Risk Exposure

Risk is the source of investment returns, yet investors prefer to avoid risk. It serves investors well to learn about and embrace risk in accordance with their capacity level. Risk capacity defines the risk level that is appropriate for a particular investor. Many investors invest in portfolios that are mismatched to their risk capacity. A thorough analysis looks at an investor's investment time horizon, net worth, income, investment knowledge, and attitude toward risk. Investors can then review investment choices and make a selection that matches their individual risk capacity.

An investment policy is a statement of the risk capacity assessment and the resulting risk exposure in the form of an asset allocation of indexes. Most investors do not get around to fully assessing their risk capacity, and find themselves without an investment policy for their short-term and long-term investments. Without this policy, they are easily persuaded to change their course. As a result, they lose out on the long-term returns that would result from subjecting their capital to market risk.

1.3.8   The High Cost of Turnover

High turnover creates short-term capital gains in a mutual fund or a portfolio of individual stocks. In taxable accounts this can create an additional insurmountable barrier to beating an index. The average mutual fund turns more than 90% of its stock each year. This high percentage forces the distribution of realized capital gains by mutual funds, which become tax liabilities for the funds' shareholders. Active investors incur far greater federal and state taxes, since almost all of the capital gains are short term and are taxed up to 46%. On the other hand, index fund investors buy and hold, so they rarely incur realized capital gains. When they do, they are long-term gains that are taxed at 15%. Tax managed index funds harvest losses to offset gains and eliminate dividend-paying stocks to reduce taxes paid on dividends. These tax-managed funds nearly elimi-

nate the federal and state taxes associated with actively managed funds.

1.3.9   The Emotional Stress of Active Investing

Investment returns are far more dependent on investor behavior than the performance of the investment. Investors generally make bad decisions under the pressure and stress of trying to outperform a market. These shortfalls are directly attributed to investors overreacting to constantly changing conditions in financial markets, resulting in brief holding periods for mutual funds. The tendency of investors to bail out of stock funds during market downturns and buy back in after the market has recovered obviously harms performance.

When the stock market performs well, as it did for most of the 1980s and 1990s, investors are more prone to believe they can beat a market. When they get lucky and make a profitable investment call more than once, they are lured into thinking they are successful market forecasters. Unfortunately, this false sense of confidence can lead them to the poorhouse.

The media continues to foster and encourage the high emotions of active investing. Many ads lead investors to believe they can beat a market through stock picking and time picking. In a September 1999 advertisement from online broker, Ameritrade, an image of a scowling young woman was displayed. Her quote read as follows: "I don't want to just beat the market. I want to wrestle its scrawny little body to the ground and make it beg for mercy." The ad goes on to say, "Ready to take on the market? The sooner you do, the sooner you can show that lily-livered stock market who's boss." Finally, it ends with, "Believe in yourself." Investing should not be based on beliefs. It should be grounded on a thorough analysis of the extensive body of research performed by conflict-free academics. Then, certain conclusions should be drawn from facts, not beliefs.

1.3.10 More than 1,500 Investors can be Wrong

The lack of investor education has generated a lot of recent interest. Most school systems have not incorporated an educational program for investing. The average investor is unprepared to make decisions about investing. Investors usually receive their education in bits and pieces from advertisements, television, magazines, newspapers or books. These sources are created by an industry that generates huge margin interest, fees, and commissions from the trading of active investors. Most of the promotion and education provided by the investment industry is designed to encourage investors to gamble in the stock market.

Money Magazine and the Vanguard Group conducted a study in 1997, which randomly selected 1,555 investors from across the United States, and asked them 20 basic questions on investing. The respondents received a 67% or an "F" grade! In a 2000 update of the survey, only 37% of the respondents' answers were correct. Why do investors continue to invest in something they do not understand?

1.4 SOLUTIONS

1.4.1 Active Investors Anonymous

Several years ago I learned a painful lesson. After selling a business, I turned about $6 million over to several active managers. What a mistake. I woke up one morning to discover I had lost a $30 million opportunity. After thoroughly researching the science of passive investing and index funds, I concluded I needed to withdraw my investments from those stockbrokers and actively managed mutual funds, and put them into index funds.

As a result of that painful lesson and years of research, I'm now passionate about educating others about the benefits of passively investing in index funds. A 12-step recovery program is critically needed for investors, and this is why I wrote this book and launched Active Investors Anonymous.

1.4.2 The History of 12-Step Recovery Programs

The concept of a 12-step recovery program originated in 1935 and today is used to treat more than 30 addictions, including gambling, alcohol, overeating, drugs, and sex addictions. Millions of people rely on such programs to cure addictions that have taken control of their lives.

Dr. Carl Jung

In the early 1930s an American alcoholic named Rowland H. (only the last initial is used to keep him anonymous) traveled to Switzerland to undergo treatment from the world renowned psychologist, Carl Jung. After a couple of unsuccessful trips, Dr. Jung told Rowland that he needed a "profound spiritual experience" to enable him to stop his drinking. In other words, he needed to find a higher power. Other patients who had taken Dr. Jung's advice had overcome their addictions and changed their behaviors.

The 12-step program is partially based on the replacement of an addiction with a higher power, whatever that may be for a person. For the active investor on the road to recovery, the perfect higher power to turn to is the abundance of academic research available on investing. As investors became more familiar with the Nobel Prize-winning stock market research outlined in this book, many experienced investing epiphanies, and transformed their thinking and investment behaviors. Many "stockaholics" have already been cured.

Rex Sinquefield

Rex Sinquefield, a director at DFA, attended the University of Chicago in the 1970s. Sinquefield said, "Every time one of my professors talked about efficient markets, I thought I was looking at Moses coming down from the mountain, and I took that seriously." Sinquefield went on to create the first S&P 500 Index fund in 1973, and now the firm he cofounded, DFA, is known as the mecca of sophisticated indexing. Maybe Sinquefield had his profound spiritual experience in that classroom.

I had my epiphany while listening to Professor Eugene Fama of the University of Chicago and director of research at DFA discuss the Three-Factor Model at a financial conference.

1.4.3 The Big Book on Investing

When the founder of Alcoholics Anonymous, Bill W., needed a vehicle to carry his message to millions of alcoholics, a book was the only affordable method. So, he wrote *Alcoholics Anonymous* in 1938. That book has become affectionately known as "The Big Book." Coincidentally, 1938 was the same year that Alfred Cowles created what was later to become the Standard & Poor's 500. Cowles did not know that his creation would go on to become the first index used to establish an index fund by Rex Sinquefield.

This book is a modified 12-step program designed to educate investors on how to overcome the emotional desires to actively invest. Some refer to it as the "Big Book on Investing." In 1938, Bill W. was limited to books as an affordable method of communication. But, today we have the Internet. It's a medium I take full advantage of in my mission to lead investors to a highly efficient, tax-managed, low-cost and risk appropriate portfolio. The same material in this book, with additional updates, can be found on Index Funds Advisors' Web site at www.ifa.com.

1.4.4 Top Investors Agree

Billionaire asset allocator Warren Buffett, who is often called "the Oracle of Omaha" for his straightfoward advice, recommended index funds to his own Berkshire Hathaway fellow shareholders. In his 1996 Chairman's letter, dated February 1997, Buffett wrote, "Let me add a few thoughts about your own investments. Most investors, both institutional and individual, will find that the best way to own common stocks is through an index fund that charges minimal fees. Those following this path are sure to beat the net results (after fees and expenses) delivered by the great majority of investment professionals." In February 2003, he wrote, "...those index funds that are very low cost (such as Vanguard's) are investor friendly by definition and are the best selection for most of those who wish to own equities. And, his February 2004 letter states: "Over the [past] 35 years, American business has delivered terrific results. It should therefore have been easy for investors to earn juicy returns: All they had to do was piggyback corporate America in a diversified, low-expense way. An index fund that they never touched would have done the job. Instead many investors have had experiences ranging from mediocre to disastrous." For Berkshire Hathaway vs. IFA Indexes, see Figure 11-5 on page 217.

Even though some professionals outperform a market, it is a different group of professionals that do so each year. A consistent methodology to identify them in advance has yet to be discovered.

Benjamin Graham

Benjamin Graham, the father of fundamental stock analysis, and a man revered by Warren Buffett, also relinquished the idea that investors can expect to beat a market. Shortly before his death in 1976, he said: "I am no longer an advocate of elaborate techniques of security analysis in order to find superior value opportunities. This was a rewarding activity, say, 40 years ago when [the Security Analysis by] Graham and Dodd was first published; but the situation has changed.... [Today] I doubt whether such extensive efforts will generate sufficiently superior selections to justify their cost.... I'm on the side of the 'efficient' market school of thought."

1.4.5 Index Funds Investors Win

Investors in index funds usually win over active investors over long periods of time. The path to recovery for active investors begins with understanding the following steps outlined in this book.

1.5 SUMMARY

More than 90% of investors engage in active investing strategies. A 12-step program can best address the emotional hurdles an active investor needs to clear. The first step of every 12-step recovery program is admitting there is a problem. Hopefully, this first step has helped you rec-ognize active investing behavior, and realize that such harmful behavior can be changed.

1.6 REVIEW QUESTIONS

Questions will appear at the end of each step to affirm the reader's understanding of the information presented in that particular step. At www.ifa.com, you can find a similar test of your knowledge, which will result in a "Certified Indexer" certificate for those with a passing score.

1. Investment managers of index funds engage in:

   a. stock picking

   b. market timing

   c. manager picking

   d. analytical techniques best described as speculative

   e. analytical techniques best described as scientific

2. A Dalbar study showed that the average investor earned $19,625 on a $100,000 investment over a 20-year period, while the S&P 500 gained:

   a. $15,200

   b. $38,613

   c. $591,337

   d. $400,938

   e. $567,239

3. In a February 1997 letter to shareholders, Warren Buffett stated, " the best way to own common stocks is:

   a. to own his company, Berkshire Hathaway.

   b. to have your broker pick 10 growth stocks."

    c. to buy at the bottom of the market and sell at the top."

    d. to own an index fund that charges minimal fees."

4. When 1,555 investors were given a test of 20 basic questions in 2000 regarding investing, the average score was:

    a. none correct

    b. 37% correct

    c. 60% correct

    d. 95% correct

5. PriceWaterhouseCoopers found that one of the largest obstacles warding off investors from investing in index funds was:

    a. the high management fees of index funds

    b. the emotional drive, desire or need to beat a market

    c. the below market performance of index funds

    d. the difficulty in finding an index manager

    e. the high taxes generated by index funds

Step 2 ~ Nobel Laureates

"Sooner than I dared expect, my explicit prayer has been answered. There is coming to market... something called the First Index Investment Trust... offering extremely low portfolio turnover; and best of all, giving the broadest diversification needed to maximize mean return with minimum portfolio variance and volatility." Newsweek magazine, August 1976; Also, "It is not easy to get rich in Las Vegas, at Churchill Downs or at the local Merrill Lynch office."

- Paul A. Samuelson, Nobel Laureate in Economics, 1970, Massachusetts Institute of Technology

"Properly measured, the average actively managed dollar must underperform the average passively managed dollar, net of costs. Empirical analyses that appear to refute this principle are guilty of improper measurement."

- William F. Sharpe, Nobel Laureate in Economics, 1990, "The Arithmetic of Active Management," 1991

"We next consider the rule that the investor does [or should] consider expected return a desirable thing and variance of return an undesirable thing."

- Harry Markowitz, Nobel Laureate in Economics, 1990, "Portfolio Selection," 1952

"Question: ...how do you think people should invest for the future..? Should they buy index funds?

Answer: Absolutely. I have often said, and I know this will get some of your readers mad, that any pension fund manager who doesn't have the vast majority—and I mean 70% or 80% of his or her portfolio—in passive investments is guilty of malfeasance, nonfeasance or some other kind of bad feasance! There's just no sense for most of them to have anything but a passive investment policy."

- Merton Miller, Nobel Laureate in Economics, 1990, *Investment Gurus,* 1990

"Question: So investors shouldn't delude themselves about beating the market? Answer: They're just not going to do it. It's just not going to happen."

- Daniel Kahneman, Nobel Laureate in Economics, 2002, Orange County Register, "Investors Can't Beat Market," 2002

2.1 INTRODUCTION

Step 2: Become aware that Nobel Prize winners researched the market.

Welcome to Step 2 where we discuss the evolution of modern finance and the contribution of Nobel laureates and others.

A review of the collective research of Nobel Prize recipients and other academics shows a sharp contrast between what the average active investor understands about investing and the conclusion of 300 years of unbiased, rigorous, and empirical research conducted by academics. The fact is: that body of research discredits the conventional Wall Street wisdom that a stock picker armed with enough knowledge and research can consistently beat the market. Once active investors accept this fact, they are on the road to recovery. Although this step is titled "Nobel Laureates," numerous academics who have researched the stock market, but have not been awarded a Nobel Prize will also be discussed.

2.2 DEFINITIONS

2.2.1 Nobel Prize in Economic Sciences

Alfred Nobel

The Nobel Prize is an international award given annually since 1901 for achievements in physics, chemistry, medicine, literature and peace. The award is perhaps the most globally recognized honor in each of the fields in which it is presented. Receipt of the prize is the culmination of a rigorous nomination process. Each year category committees send individual proposals to thousands of scientists, academy members, and university professors in numerous countries, asking them to nominate Nobel Prize candidates for the coming year. Nominations received by each committee are then evaluated with the help of specially appointed experts. Once these committees have made their selection among the nominated candidates, and presented their nominations to the prize-awarding institutions, a vote is taken for the final choice of Nobel Prize laureates. It was in 1968 that the Bank of Sweden instituted the Prize in Economic Sciences in Memory of Alfred Nobel, founder of the Nobel Prize. The Nobel Prize in Economic Sciences is awarded to works ranging from methodologies and theories used in studying the efficient use of economic and financial resources to microeconomic performance and economic policy, development economics, and international trade. The prize is subject to the same rigorous nomination process as those awarded in the other Nobel categories.

2.2.2 The University of Chicago, the Center for Research in Security Prices, and the Stock Market Database

In addition to Nobel laureates who have studied the stock market, thousands of academics are also performing market research. The University of Chicago is the premiere institution of learning in stock market research. For years the University has been recognized as a leader in financial research. To be sure, as of 2004, 23 of the 58 Nobel Laureates in Economics attended or taught at the university. This is an impressive 40% of all Nobel Laureates in Economics. (Harvard University boasts the second largest number with four recipients.) Why is the University of Chicago so often an incubator for Nobel Prize laureates?

The answer to this question lies within the historical evolution of stock market research, which received a significant boost at the end of the 1950s. In 1959, Louis Engel, then vice president of Merrill Lynch telephoned Professor James Lorie of the University of Chicago to ask

University of Chicago Hall of Nobel Laureates

him if anyone knew how well most people performed in the stock market relative to other investments. The question so intrigued Lorie that he proposed that Merrill Lynch fund a project with the sole purpose of gathering the prices, dividends, and rates of return of all stocks listed on the New York Stock Exchange. Lorie used the new capabilities offered by computers to develop a database to maintain accurate securities information over time. The project's ultimate goal was to create a complete and accurate database so that researchers would no longer be required to compile their own data.

To that end 1960, the Center for Research in Security Prices (CRSP) was established at the University of Chicago with a $300,000 grant  from Merrill Lynch to house the massive data gathering project. Thankfully, since its creation, the center has received an abundant amount of support. For instance, from 1964 to 1986, it received gifts in excess of $1 million from individuals yearning for stock market information.

Computer Lab, Circa 1960

Lorie was the center's first director, a position he held until 1975. He, along with his colleague, Lawrence Fisher, a former associate professor of finance who became the associate director of CRSP, faced the monumental responsibility of researching the accuracy of each piece of stock information they collected.

The stock market database was completed in 1964 when between two million and three million pieces of information was successfully entered. Lorie and Fisher analyzed total return, dividends received, and changes in capital as a result of price changes of all common stocks listed on the NYSE from 1926 to 1965. The research found that the rate of return on common stocks listed on the NYSE averaged 9%. For the first time in history, an average rate of return could actually be measured. The findings were published in *The Journal of Business* and the front page of *The New York Times's* financial section heralded the pair's results.

However, the research did not really answer Engel's original question. But, a recent study by Dalbar did. The study measured the average investor's performance in the market, and found it to be significantly below the market average.

Over a 20-year period ending in 2004, the average equity investor only earned about 3.7% per year while the S&P 500 gained 13.2% per year. Inflation averaged 3% per year during this period. Active investors also pay about 2.5% of their portfolio value in taxes each year. That equals a loss of about 2% a year for the average equity investor.

For its part, CRSP continues to accumulate data on a regular basis. With a $180,000 grant from Dimensional Fund Advisors (DFA) in 1984, data dating from January 1972 from NASDAQ markets was added. "If I had to rank events, I would say this one (the original CRSP Master Fuel) is probably slightly more significant than the creation of the universe," said Rex Sinquefield, formerly co-chairman and currently a director of DFA. "The entire field of finance has been changed and developed through that database."

In 2003, Professor Eugene Fama was appointed director of CRSP. Fama is famous for his use of CRSP data to determine the dimensions of stock returns. Fama is also on the board of directors and the director of research for DFA.

2.3 PROBLEMS

2.3.1 Investors Rely on Lady Luck

The biggest problem investors face today is their continued reliance on information sources other than empirical research, like the research collected at CRSP, when selecting their investments. Investors often speculate, rely on Lady Luck, market time, and chase recent successes of managers, stocks and investment styles. As opposed to following the expertise of Nobel laureates, they blindly wander into the beckoning arms of active managers who dominate Wall Street walking right past the financial academics, who could offer them the one thing active managers cannot—unbiased, rigorous and empirical research that will guide them to a risk-appropriate, tax-managed, and highly efficient portfolio of low-cost index funds.

2.3.2 Active Investors are Unaware of Academic Studies

Unfortunately, the great majority of investors are unaware of the tremendous amount of academic brain and computer power that has been applied to investing. This lack of awareness makes investors more susceptible to the siren songs of active management.

There is a stark contrast between a peer-reviewed and non-biased academic research paper and an article in *The Wall Street Journal*, *Barron's*, *Forbes*, *Fortune*, *Money Magazine*, an analyst's report or numerous other sources of investment research. Unfortunately, virtually all private investors are unaware of the vast amounts of academic research that points to investing in portfolios of index funds.

2.4 SOLUTION

Nobel Laureates and Academics

The solution to this lack of awareness on the part of investors is for them to take a quick look at the history of modern finance. It's a story that began nearly 350 years ago, and will hopefully lead recovering active investors to a more rational and profitable way to invest. If you are interested in further exploring the academic studies that have impacted modern finance, see the list of supplemental readings in Appendix C.

1654 The Early Attempts to Quantify Risk

Modern finance began with the realization that risk needed to be measured and managed. The intelligent management of risk can be traced to 1654 during the Renaissance Period.

It was a time of great discovery when centuries-old beliefs were constantly under question and reevaluation by intellectuals. This time of rebirth challenged the wizards, mystics, seers, fortunetellers, oracles, and soothsayers that were previously regarded as experts at predicting the future.

Blaise Pascal

In 1654, a French gambler named Chevalier de Mere and a mathematician named Blaise Pascal tried to predict the future outcome of a game of chance. They wanted to determine how to divide up the stakes of an unfinished game when one player was slightly ahead. So, they developed the Theory of Probability.

This theory, which states that future outcomes will have an expected value based on an average and range of deviations from the average, is the basis for the concept of risk management and modern finance. Years later in 1952, Nobel laureate Harry Markowitz embraced what a French gambler questioned in 1654, and converted it into the Theory of Portfolio Selection. His idea revolutionized the investment process.

Who Do You Trust?

1690 Beginning to Understand Risk Management

Edmund Halley

Edmund Halley, the famous English astronomer who discovered Halley's Comet, began work on a series of life tables in early 1690. A probability-based life expectancy could be derived from these tables, which later became the blueprint for the life insurance industry. Techniques of risk management were improved over the years, leading to one of the first commercial applications by the English government. Government officials developed life expectancy tables and sold life annuities, which were soon followed by marine insurance products. Halley's work ultimately led to the founding of Lloyd's of London, which originated in Edward Lloyd's coffee house, a small shop that Halley frequented. Lloyd, who owned the coffee shop, overheard Halley and started the insurance company. The same principles of managing risk were later applied to the stock market.

1730 The Bell-Shaped Curve

Abraham DeMoivre

Abraham de Moivre tutored students in mathematics and served as a resident statistician at Slaughter's Coffee House in London. There, gamblers paid him to calculate their odds. In 1697, the Royal Society elected him a member. De Moivre became friends with Isaac Newton and astronomer-physicist Edmund Halley.

He later pioneered and developed analytic geometry and the Theory of Probability, culminating in his published book, *The Doctrine of Chance* in 1718. Included in the book were problems with dice and other games as well as a definition of statistical independence. With Newton, de Moivre studied the normal distribution curve and found the normal curve was the limit for the binomial curve. The discovery of standard deviation and the bell-shaped curve in 1730 was a critical element in the development of risk management.

1830 The Prudent Man Rule

Judge Samuel Putnum

Judge Samuel Putnum, in a case of the alleged improper management of a trust account, handed down a decision now known as the "Prudent Man Rule." This rule is used today to establish proper guidelines for trustees. Judge Putnum declared, "Do what you will, the capital is at hazard. All that can be required of a trustee to invest is that he shall conduct himself faithfully and exercise a sound discretion. He is to observe how men of prudence, discretion, and intelligence manage their own affairs, considering the probable income as well as the probable safety of the capital to be invested." This was one of the first authoritative and clear statements to convey that risk had to be considered as well as return.

1900 The Birth of the Random Walk Theory

Louis Bachelier

The year 2000 marked the centennial of the Random Walk Theory of stock market prices. Surprisingly, one hundred years after the theory's conception, 90% of investors are still not convinced that the markets move in a random fashion. Many scholars confirmed and refined the research of Louis Bachelier, the seldom recognized hero of financial economics. In 1900 Bachelier published his doctoral thesis titled "The Theory of Speculation," and presented it to the faculty of the Academy of Paris. In his thesis, Bachelier anticipated much of what has become a standard among financial economic theories: the random walk of stock market prices. One of his ground breaking conclusions was "there is no useful information contained in historical price movements of securities."

As is typical with great minds, Bachelier's professors and contemporaries did not appreciate his innovation. His thesis received humiliating marks from his professors casting him into the shadows of the academic underground. After a series of minor posts, he ended up teaching in an obscure French town for much of the rest of his life. His valuable work was largely ignored until the mid-1960s when economist, Paul Samuelson, stumbled upon it in a library in France.

In 1964 MIT Professor Paul Cootner published a 500-page collection of research reprints on the randomness of the market titled "The Random Character of Stock Market Prices." The work contained the first full text English translation of Bachelier's thesis. Cootner said of Bachelier: "So outstanding is his work that we can say that the study of speculative prices has its moment of glory at the moment of its inception."

So, exactly how does the Random Walk Theory apply to modern finance? The theory describes the way stock prices change unpredictably as a result of unexpected information appearing in the market. This "random walk" of changing prices has created a misconception among investors that stock prices change randomly for no rational reason. The reason stock prices are random is because the news that moves the prices is unpredictable and random.

News is inherently unpredictable or it would not be considered news. In reacting rationally to new information, the stock prices look as though they behave in a random fashion. Many other academics including Paul Samuelson, Robert Merton, Eugene Fama, Fischer Black, Myron Scholes, and Burton Malkiel later expanded on Bachelier's work.

1932   The Basis for the Standard & Poor's 500 Index

Alfred Cowles

Alfred Cowles was a wealthy Chicagoan whose father and grandfather had been major stockholders and executives of the Chicago Tribune Company. As a young man, Cowles was struck with tuberculosis. His illness prompted him to move to Colorado Springs to seek treatment. Cowles remained in Colorado for 10 years. During his time there he began to help his father manage the family's finances. To keep up with financial and market news, Cowles subscribed to a number of investment services. After the inability of these services to predict the stock market crash of 1929, Cowles became disillusioned with them. So, he decided to analyze the ability of stock market forecasters to choose a portfolio that succeeded in beating a market average or index. To that end, Cowles reviewed approximately 12,000 recommendations and four years of transactions by 20 leading fire insurance companies. He published his results in a July 1933 article titled "Can Stock Market Forecasters Forecast?" His conclusion: "It is doubtful." Cowles' extensive study of stock mar-

The Cowles Commission, Colorado Springs, CO, 1937
Photo courtesy of the Cowles Foundation

ket data provided an early demonstration of the "random walk" in stock price movements, and the beginning of the Efficient Market Hypothesis. Cowles published a follow-up study in 1944, reviewing 6,900 market forecasts over a period of 15.5 years. Once again, he concluded there was no evidence supporting the ability of the forecaster to predict the future of the market.

In keeping with his newfound realization that market movements cannot be predicted, Cowles founded the Cowles Commission for Research in Economics in 1932. The commission's motto: Science is measurement. The purpose of the commission was to foster the development of logical, mathematical and statistical methods of analysis for application in economics. However, its location in Colorado made it difficult to find a qualified director. So, the commission moved to the University of Chicago in 1939. The commission's move to Chicago ignited a spark in the city that eventually transformed it into a powerhouse of stock market research. Later, the commission moved to Yale University in 1955 where it was renamed the Cowles Foundation. To its credit, almost every U.S. winner of the Nobel Prize in Economics has spent time at the Cowles Foundation.

The Cowles Foundation was just one of the many contributions Cowles made to stock market research. In addition, he created a market index, which became the basis for today's Standard & Poor's 500 Index. His goal was to establish a stock market index to represent the average experience of stock market investors. Cowles determined that despite his research and the research of countless others after him, investors would continue to listen to market forecasters because they wanted to believe that somebody, anybody, could predict the future.

1952　Efficient Diversification

Harry Markowitz

Don't bet the ranch. Get more bang for your buck. Maximize output relative to input. Nothing ventured, nothing gained. Diversify instead of striving to make a killing. Don't put all your eggs in one basket; if it drops, you're in trouble. High volatility is like putting your head in the oven and your feet in the refrigerator.

These common sense sayings capture the essence of Harry Markowitz's brainstorm, which was ignited one afternoon as he sat in the University of Chicago's library reading a book about current theories of stock market investing. Markowitz thought investors should be as concerned with uncertainty or the risk of investments as they were with the return of investments. Thirty-eight years later, this innovative, practical theory earned him the 1990 Nobel Prize in Economics. This landmark contribution to the investment world was first published in 1952 in an essay titled "Portfolio Selection." He later authored a book titled *Portfolio Selection: Efficient Diversification of Investments.*

The book presented a theory for optimal investment in stocks that differs in regard to their expected return and risk. Investment managers and academic economists have long been aware of the necessity of taking both risk and return into account. Markowitz's primary contribution was his development of a rigorously formulated operational theory for portfolio selection under uncertainty. His theory evolved into a foundation for further research in financial economics. Markowitz was the first to place a number on risk relative to investing. Risk was previously discussed in general terms and based more on feeling or intuition. He quantified the "undesirable thing" investors try to avoid by using a range of possible return outcomes based on the past variability of returns.

Under certain conditions, Markowitz showed that an investor's portfolio choice can be reduced to balancing two dimensions: the expected return on the portfolio and its variance or standard deviation. The risk of a diversified portfolio depends not only on the individual variances of the return on different assets, but also on the opposite movement of all assets. When one asset class goes up, another goes down. The opposite movement results in a higher return than if all of the assets go up or down together. "Diversification is both observed and sensible. A rule of behavior, which does not imply the superiority of diversification must be rejected both as a hypothesis and as a maxim," said Markowitz.

In addition, Markowitz made the distinction between the risk of an individual stock and the risk of a portfolio. He showed how individual risky stocks lose much of their risk if combined with less risky stocks in a portfolio. What is remarkable about Markowitz's discovery is that an investor can reduce the volatility of a portfolio and increase its return at the same time.

When Markowitz began to formulate his ideas in the 1950s, leading investment guides recommended that an investor should find one stock with the highest expected return, invest in it, and ignore all the others. If investing involved no amount of risk, holding investments with the highest expected returns would be a highly profitable idea. The experienced investor knows that investing is full of risk. Risk essentially means that there is uncertainty in future outcomes. People do not expect to be in an auto accident, but they invest in auto insurance because of the unpredictable possibilities. People also do not expect a stock in their portfolio to decrease in price, but it will at some point. If an investor's

portfolio is diversified, than the loss incurred from that one stock will be "insured" by other stocks that do not decrease in price. Markowitz knew that in the real world investors are not only interested in return; they are also concerned with risk.

Markowitz concluded that risk is central to the whole process of investing. He then wondered how to measure the appropriate amount of risk investors should undertake. Markowitz came to realize the cruel truth of investing: investors cannot earn higher returns without taking on greater risk, and the greater the risk the greater the possibility of losing. So, he set out to devise ways to help investors apply trade-offs between risk and return. Using mathematics to solve the puzzle, Markowitz discovered a remarkable new way to build an investment portfolio, which he called the "efficient portfolio." The efficient portfolio offers an investor the highest expected return for any given level of risk or the lowest level of risk for any given expected return.

1958   The Separation Theorem

James Tobin

James Tobin contributed the concept of combining risk-free assets, such as cash or low risk bonds, with risky assets such as stocks. His paper titled "Liquidity Preference as Behavior toward Risk" appeared in *The Review of Economic Studies* in February 1958. The paper focuses on the Separation Theorem. This theory claims that Markowitz's approach of selecting stocks for the most efficient risky portfolio is separate from the choice to divide up the total portfolio between risky and risk-free assets. Based on various combinations, investors could have a choice of numerous levels of overall risks in their portfolios, Tobin concluded. (The various index portfolios found in Appendix A offer 20 levels of risk for globally diversified portfolios.) Tobin also performed an analysis of financial markets and their relationship to expenditure decisions, debt decisions, employment, production, and prices.

1958   The Modigliani-Miller Theorems

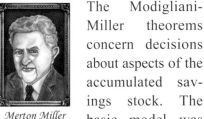

Frank Modigliani   *Merton Miller*

The Modigliani-Miller theorems concern decisions about aspects of the accumulated savings stock. The basic model was formulated in Modigliani and Miller's joint essay titled "The Cost of Capital, Corporation Finance and the Theory of Investment" written in 1958. Using this basic model, Miller and Modigliani derived two so-called invariance theorems, now known as the MM theorems—two letters well-known among financiers.

The main message of the MM theorems is that a firm's value is unrelated to its dividend policy, and that policy is an unreliable guide for stock selection. Additionally, they state that an investor's expected return is equal to a company's cost of capital. The MM theorems have become the comparative norm for theoretical and empirical analysis in corporate finance. When designing strategies for tax-managed portfolios, dividend paying stocks are eliminated and the MM theorems indicate that these criteria should alter expected returns.

1964   The Capital Asset Pricing Model or Risk / Return Model

William Sharpe

The Capital Asset Pricing Model (CAPM) defines risk as volatility relative to the market and states that a stock's cost of capital and an investor's expected return is proportional to the stock's risk relative to the entire stock universe.

In the mid-1960s, several researchers worked independently of one another to contribute to the CAPM. William Sharpe's pioneering achievement in this field is contained in his essay, "Capital Asset Prices: A Theory of Market Equilibrium under Conditions of Risk," published in 1964.

CAPM finds that the expected return of an asset is determined by its beta coefficient—a means of measuring the volatility of a security or portfolio of securities in comparison with the market as a whole. CAPM also measures the similarities between the return on the asset and the return on the market portfolio.

CAPM is the backbone of modern price theory for financial markets. Widely used in empirical analysis, the model allows an abundance of financial statistical data to be utilized systematically and efficiently. It is applied extensively in practical research and has become an important tool for decision making in different areas. Indeed, research often requires information about a firm's cost of capital where the risk premium is an essential component.

1965   Proof That Prices Fluctuate Randomly

Paul Samuelson

Paul Samuelson's findings can be summarized as follows: Market prices are the best estimates of value, price changes follow random patterns, and future stock prices are unpredictable.

Samuelson was the first American to win the Nobel Prize in Economics. His famous textbook titled *Economics*, published in 1948 is now in its 13th edition. Samuelson is considered by some to be the most famous economist of our time. His wisdom is reflected in his own words, "Investing should be dull, like watching paint dry or grass grow. If you want excitement, take $800 and go to Las Vegas. It is not easy to get rich in Las Vegas, at Churchill Downs or at the local Merrill Lynch office."

One of Samuelson's idols was Louis Bachelier, the unappreciated genius who first wrote about random prices over a century ago. Samuelson discovered Bachelier's paper from 1900 in a library in France. Like many others, Samuelson proved, expanded, and refined Bachelier's discovery. In Samuelson's 1965 paper titled "Proof that Properly Anticipated Prices Fluctuate Randomly," he describes "shadow prices" or true values of a security. Samuelson suggests that the best estimate of the true value of a security is the price that is set in the marketplace every minute of every trading day. Although these prices may not be the precise true value, no other estimate is likely to be more accurate than what buyers and sellers agree on in the marketplace.

Some investment professionals disagree with this position. They contend that there are constant differences between the market price and the true value of securities, and that those differ-ences can result in future profits for the skilled money manager. However, Samuelson insists there are no easy pickings and no sure gains. Generally speaking, Samuelson has contributed more than any other contemporary economist to raising the analytical and methodological level in economic science.

1965   Efficient Market Theory

Eugene Fama

As expected from a University of Chicago graduate and professor, Eugene F. Fama is another pillar of modern finance. Building on the ideas of Bachelier, Cowles, Samuelson, and many others, Fama set out to develop a comprehensive theory to explain why stock market prices fluctuate randomly. He also coined the famous phrase "Efficient Market."

Fama worked for a stock market newsletter firm while an undergraduate at Tufts University in Boston. One of his duties at the firm was to find, buy and sell signals based on certain market trends. It was then that he experienced firsthand the difficulty in predicting future market trends. He began to wonder, just as Cowles did before him, why it was so difficult to translate what appeared to be neatly defined past trends into sure methods of making money in the stock market.

These ponderings influenced him enough to attend the University of Chicago, obtain his doctorate, and become a professor teaching classes on the works of Harry Markowitz. Despite the innovative character of Markowitz's writings and his association with Chicago, his work was virtually unknown when Fama first brought it to the attention of the finance department of the University of Chicago. Fama later applied his extensive, world famous research to create numerous index mutual funds at DFA.

In January 1965, *The Journal of Business* published Fama's entire 70-page doctorate dissertation, "The Behavior of Stock Market Prices." The research was summarized nine months later by *The Financial Analysts Journal* and titled "Random Walks in Stock Market Prices." In his dissertation, Fama suggests that by utilizing the tremendous resources that a major brokerage firm can gather for researching industry trends, effects of interest rates and accounting data, and by talking to managers of firms, consulting economists and politicians, a security analyst should be able to consistently outperform a randomly selected portfolio of securities of the same general risk. Since in any given situation, an analyst has a 50% chance of outperforming the random selection, even if his skills are nonexistent, Fama's conclusion was that analysts do not consistently outperform a market.

The Efficient Market Theory explains the workings of free and efficient financial markets. The theory states that information about stocks is widely and cheaply available to all investors and all known and available information is already reflected in current stock prices. The price of a stock agreed on by a buyer and a seller is the best estimate, good or bad, of the investment value of that stock, it says. Stock prices will almost instantaneously change as new unpredictable information about them appears in the market. All of these factors make it almost impossible to capture returns in excess of market returns without taking greater than market levels of risk, the theory holds.

It is relatively rare to find and profit from a mismatch between a stock's price and its value or to identify an undervalued or overvalued stock through fundamental analysis of stocks. This creates efficient financial markets where most stock prices accurately reflect their true underlying investment values. Even when stock prices do not reflect their values, the cost of corrective action is greater than the profit gained from such actions.

The Efficient Market Theory threatens the view that there might be something pinning down the average price of an asset. Deviations of an asset price from this value follow a random walk, the theory asserts. This position annoys those who claim they can anticipate speculative trends in asset prices. The theory clearly states that those individuals can not beat a market because any available information is already incorporated in the price.

However, at a 1968 Institutional Investor conference, one irate money manager insisted that what he and others did for investors had to be worth more than just throwing darts at *The Wall Street Journal*. The "dart board portfolio" soon became a new benchmark for active investors, appearing in newspapers, magazines, and in a 1992 20/20 ABC news segment titled "Who Needs the Experts?" In that segment, a giant wall-sized version of *The Wall Street Journal* was transformed into a dartboard. Reporter John Stossel threw several darts as he described the firms he randomly hit. The results of that portfolio were compared to those of major Wall Street experts. The darts beat 90% of the experts! When ABC requested interviews with several of these experts, none would speak or comment on their humiliating inability to beat the darts.

The Random Walk Theory of stock market prices was detected as early as 1900 by Louis Bachelier and revisited in later studies by Holbrook Working, Alfred Cowles, Clive

Granger with Oskar Morgenstern, and Paul Samuelson. But, it was Fama who took the theory to new heights with enough rigorous statistical analysis to shake up Wall Street.

1965 Active Management Put to the Test

Michael Jensen

Eugene Fama's graduate student, Michael Jensen, published "The Performance of Mutual Funds in the Period 1945-1964" in *The Journal of Finance* in 1965. This was the first study of actively managed mutual funds to document the failure of investment professionals to outperform the appropriate market indexes.

Jensen also added a risk dimension when comparing mutual fund performance. He adjusted returns of funds using Sharpe's volatility measure, beta. This incorporated the idea that investors who take more risk should receive a higher return. Over performance or underperformance of an index may be due to exposure to more or less risk than a comparable index. Jensen found that if investors had held a broadly based portfolio of common stocks at the same risk level as mutual funds, they would have earned 15% more. Only 26 out of 115 funds outperformed the market over the period of the study.

Jensen's dramatic study opened the eyes of both the mutual fund industry and investors. He pointed out that fund managers have access to extensive research, and do their jobs every day with wide ranging contacts and associations in both the business and financial communities. This begs the question: if the experts cannot beat an index, who can?

1971 The First Index Fund

John McQuown joined the Wells Fargo Bank Management Science division in 1964. He was recruited by the division's president to implement modern portfolio theories in the bank's trust department. McQuown had learned of the existence of these new theories from three acquaintances at the University of Chicago—Fisher, Lorie and Fama. Although McQuown had a degree in mechanical engineering, he became more interested in applying computer science to the stock market. While working to revamp the trust department at Wells Fargo, he called on numerous academic consultants, including Markowitz, Sharpe, Fama, Miller, Lorie, Jensen, Scholes, Black and Jack Treynor.

Eventually, McQuown, along with his colleagues James Vertin and William Fouse, developed the first commercial product that actually applied the academic theories developed at the University of Chicago. That product was to become the first index fund.

In 1971, the son of the owner of Samsonite Luggage Corporation completed his graduate studies at the University of Chicago's Department of Finance. When he returned to Denver, he wanted to apply what he had learned to Samsonite's pension fund. His contacts in Chicago put him in touch with Wells Fargo Bank in San Francisco. As a result, Samsonite invested $6 million of its pension fund into the very first index fund. That first index fund was not based on the S&P 500, but comprised of an equal dollar amount of each of the 1,500 stocks on the New York Stock Exchange.

1973   A Random Walk Down Wall Street

Burton Malkiel

In 1973, Burton G. Malkiel published his book, *A Random Walk Down Wall Street*, which clearly lays out several of the principles of the academic research described above. Malkiel's book presents these theories to the private investor. In addition, he calls on institutions to sponsor an index fund. A line in the book's first edition reads, "Fund spokesmen are quick to point out you can't buy the market averages. It's time the public can." Two years later on December 31, 1975, The Vanguard Group, a fledgling mutual fund firm, took Malkiel up on his call when it created the First Index Investment Trust. Malkiel joined Vanguard's board of directors in 1977. Vanguard's founder, John Bogle, has referred to him as the "spiritual leader of the crusade."

1973   The Standard and Poor's Composite Index Funds

Rex Sinquefield

John McQuown at Wells Fargo and Rex Sinquefield at American National Bank in Chicago established the first Standard & Poor's Composite Index Funds in 1973. Both of these funds were established for institutional clients; individual investors were excluded. Wells Fargo invested $5 million from their own pension fund in their index fund, while Illinois Bell invested $5 million of their pension fund assets in the index fund managed by American National Bank.

In 1981, McQuown joined the board of directors of DFA. Benefiting from McQuown's input, DFA further developed index-based investment strategies. For its part, Wells Fargo sold its index operation to Barclays Bank of London, which now operates as Barclays Global Investors and has become one of the world's largest money managers.

1975   The First Index Mutual Fund

John Bogle

John Clifton Bogle graduated from Princeton University in 1951, where his senior thesis included the sentence, "Mutual funds can make no claims of superiority over the market averages." Bogle is best known for launching the first index mutual fund for individual investors. Bogle claims his inspiration to start the fund came from three sources, all of which confirmed his 1951 research - Paul Samuelson's 1974 paper, "Challenge to Judgment," Charles Ellis' 1975 study, "The Loser's Game," and Al Ehrbar's 1975 *Fortune* magazine article on indexing.

Bogle founded The Vanguard Group in 1974; it is now the second largest mutual fund company in the world. Vanguard has 140 mutual funds for U.S. investors, 40 more funds for non-U.S. investors and assets totaling $1.1 trillion. When Bogle started the First Index Investment Trust on December 31, 1975, it was scoffed at by many in the industry, and labeled "Bogle's Folly." It was even regarded as un-American because it sought to achieve the stock market average return rather than insisting that Americans had to play to win. This first index mutual fund, which tracks the Standard & Poor's 500 Index, was later renamed the Vanguard 500 Index Fund. It started with comparatively meager assets of $11 million, but crossed the $100 billion milestone in November 1999, an astonishing growth rate of 50% per year. Bogle predicted in January 1992 that it would very likely surpass the Magellan Fund and become the industry's largest fund before 2001. In 2000, Bogle's prediction became a reality.

1981   A New Frontier of Investing

David Booth

David Booth who graduated from the University of Chicago in 1971 was fortunate enough to be exposed to such great minds as Eugene Fama, Merton Miller, and Kenneth French. In the years before starting his own company, Booth eventually believed that people were missing the importance of the market efficiency story.

After familiarizing himself with 25 years of scientific research, Booth became convinced that academic studies gave investors an advantage. Understanding the vital relationship between risk and return was also facilitated by this academic approach.

So, in 1981, Booth made room in his two-bedroom apartment for a Quotron machine. Determined to explore new frontiers of investing, Booth, along with Rex Sinquefield, founded DFA. Booth continues to head operations as chairman, CEO and CIO of the company. DFA is one of the first in the investment community to impart the idea of equilibrium and the concept that the scientific method proves the direct relationship between risk and return.

The proof of this is in DFA's continued success, which was enjoyed even during the 1980's when small-cap stocks were at their worst. As of December 31, 2006, the firm managed $123 billion in assets.

1990   The Science of Investing is Recognized

On October 16, 1990, the Alfred Nobel Memorial Prize in Economic Sciences was awarded to Harry M. Markowitz of City University of New York, William F. Sharpe of

William Sharpe   *Merton Miller*   *Harry Markowitz*

Stanford University, and Merton H. Miller of the University of Chicago for their pioneering work in the field of financial economics.

It was then that the science of investing was formally recognized marking a milestone by paying homage to the continuing revolution in investment theory and practice that was sparked nearly 40 years ago. All equally deserving, Sharpe was rewarded for the Capital Asset Pricing Model, beta and relative risk; Markowitz for the theory of portfolio selection; and Miller for work on the effect of a firm's capital structure and dividend policy on market price.

1992   The Three-Factor Asset Pricing Model

Eugene Fama   *Kenneth French*

In June 1992, Eugene Fama and Kenneth French of the University of Chicago published an article titled "Size and Book-to-Market Equity: Returns and Economic Fundamentals." Their research improved on William Sharpe's single factor asset-pricing model (CAPM). By identifying market, size, and value factors in returns, the two economists developed the Three-Factor Asset Pricing Model. This model is an invaluable tool for asset allocation and portfolio analysis that revolutionized the way portfolios are constructed and analyzed by identifying independent sources of risk and return. Fama and French introduced the first concentrated, empirical value strategies. The two economists updated their studies in 1998 to include data from as far back as 1929.

2.5 SUMMARY

The tumultuous stock markets contrast dramatically with the quiet academic libraries where dozens of academics created a revolution in investing. This body of academic research deserves to be a superior source of information for making decisions concerning investment portfolios. Random and efficient markets are an underlying theme throughout the bulk of the research.

Historically, the problem with getting this research out to the public was that no one had developed a way to convert it into a practical product. Thus far, the entire investment industry was profiting from the active trading of investment portfolios; even mutual funds, considered the everyman investment vehicle, were just large actively traded portfolios. The good news is: today there are index funds, that incorporate virtually all of the research described in this timeline.

2.6 REVIEW QUESTIONS

1. Who first proposed in 1900 that markets in which stocks are traded are basically random in nature?

   a. William Sharpe
   b. Louis Bachelier
   c. Eugene Fama
   d. Merton Miller

2. Modern Portfolio Theory is not so modern because Harry Markowitz first introduced one of the basic tenets in:

   a. 1654
   b. 1962
   c. 1952
   d. 1933

3. The three factors of Fama and French's Three-Factor Model are:

   a. interest rates, currency risk, and Federal Reserve policy
   b. company growth rates, earnings per share, analyst reports
   c. market, size, and value
   d. company industry, five-year sales growth rates, five-year earnings growth rates

4. Who was the first American to receive a Nobel Prize in Economics?

   a. James Tobin
   b. Paul Samuelson
   c. Harry Markowitz
   d. Merton Miller

5. Most Nobel laureates agree on how investors should invest their money. They recommend:

   a. allocate your portfolio among the top 10 technology stocks from last year
   b. invest in the top 12 mutual funds over the last five years
   c. since markets move randomly and are efficiently priced, diversify among global index funds
   d. buy Treasury bills

Step 3 ~ Stock Pickers

"When some individual made a fortune in the stock market, we have a tendency to assume that that was because he knew something, and of course the individual himself is happy to reinforce that belief - yes, I was a genius or I was very clever or I always said Microsoft was going to make me rich. But what you don't see are the thousands, hundreds of thousands, perhaps millions of people who are going, 'I always said that ABC Company was going to make me rich, and ABC Company went bust.'"

- Professor Zvi Bodie, Boston University, Transcript of the PBS Nova Special, "The Trillion Dollar Bet"

"Very little evidence [was found] that any individual [mutual] fund was able to do significantly better than that which we expected from mere random chance."

- Michael Jensen, "The Performance of Mutual Funds in the Period 1945-1964," *Journal of Finance*, May 1968

"It turns out for all practical purposes there is no such thing as stock picking skill. It's human nature to find patterns where there are none and to find skill where luck is a more likely explanation [particularly if you're the lucky mutual fund manager]. Mutual fund manager performance does not persist and the return of stock picking is zero. We are looking at the proverbial bunch of chimpanzees throwing darts at the stock page. Their 'success' or 'failure' is a purely random affair."

- William Bernstein, *The Intelligent Asset Allocator*

"I have been a stockbroker for five years and have made people money, but I always lose it in the end. I have taken huge risks with my clients. I have lost millions, ... I am tired of looking for new clients."

- Anonymous Stock Broker, ifa.com chat, September 2001

"After taking risk into account, do more managers than you'd see by chance outperform with persistence? Virtually every economist who studied this question answers with a resounding 'no.' Mike Jensen in the sixties and Mark Carhart in the nineties both conducted exhaustive studies of professional investors. They each conclude that in general a manager's fee, and not his skill, plays the biggest role in performance."

- Eugene Fama, Jr.

"If there are 10,000 people looking at the stocks and trying to pick winners, well, one in 10,000 is going to score, by chance alone, a great coup, and that's all that's going on. It's a game, it's a chance operation, and people think they are doing something purposeful... but they're really not."

- Merton Miller, Nobel laureate, Transcript of the PBS Nova Special, "The Trillion Dollar Bet"

"Active management is a little more than a gigantic con game."

- Ron Ross, Ph.D., *The Unbeatable Market*, 2002

"Investment managers sell for the price of a Picasso [what] routinely turns out to be paint-by-number sofa art."

- Patricia C. Dunn, former CEO, Barclays Global Advisors

"The economists arrived at a devastating conclusion: it seemed just as plausible to attribute the success of top traders to sheer luck, rather than skill."

- Transcript of the PBS Nova Special, "The Trillion Dollar Bet"

"The mutual fund industry is now the world's largest skimming operation, a $7 trillion trough from which fund managers, brokers and other insiders are steadily siphoning off an excessive slice of the nation's household, college, and retirement savings."

- Former Illinois Senator Peter Fitzgerald

3.1 INTRODUCTION

Step 3: Accept that stock pickers do not beat the market.

Stock picking is the most common form of active management. On average, stock pickers will always lose by an amount equal to their costs and expenses. Some will do better and some will do worse than an appropriate or blended benchmark of risk factors. Since the average return of the market is the average return of all investors, the average investor earns the average return. Like a coin toss, the markets are random. Thus, the probability of a money manager outperforming other managers each year is approximately equal to turning up heads on the toss of a coin: 50/50.

Academic studies described in this step support this conclusion. The chances of a manager beating a market over the long term (more than 10 years) were one in 36 in one study, one in 39 in another, and one in 41 in yet another. The odds are about the same as betting on one number on a roulette table in Vegas, where odds are one in 38. Over the years, more than 200 articles that measure the performance of active managers have been collected. The results of these studies are conclusively negative for active management.

3.2 DEFINITIONS

3.2.1 Stock Pickers

Stock pickers are active investors who bet they can beat a market by picking stocks they believe will outperform an index or market average. When stock pickers allocate their portfolio differently than the index, they are guaranteed to obtain a different return and risk level.

Sometimes the return is more and sometimes it is less, but the assumption can be made that it will be different when considering both risk and return. Since it takes at least 20 years of risk and return data to indicate skill versus luck, stock pickers are faced with a virtually impossible task in assuring continued success against the appropriate market index. However, most indexes are a source of 20-year risk and return data. As a result, they are the only logical choice for establishing efficient portfolios of various levels of expected risks and returns.

3.2.2 Adjusted Performance

The performance of stock pickers must be examined on an adjusted basis. This means that all factors must be considered before determining if the stock picker has achieved a benefit over an appropriate index or benchmark. Therefore, when comparing active management to an index, investors must:

1. make sure they are talking about the entire portfolios for the exact same period or time,

2. confirm proper accounting of the returns, including the cash flows in and out of the account,

3. consider the state and federal taxes paid on short and long-term capital gains and dividends,

4. consider all fees when assessing net return—many funds report gross performance before deduction of fees and or loads and commissions,

5. adjust for the portfolios' exposure to market risk, size risk and value risk factors,

6. consider the level of diversification of the two portfolios,

7. analyze the standard deviations or volatility measurements,

The Big Casino

8. consider if the over and underperformance is within the bounds of what would be expected randomly, and be sure to compare results to an appropriate benchmark as proper benchmark specification avoids inflated performance reports. If looking at a group of stock pickers, be sure to include the returns of those pickers that did not survive the duration of the period, usually due to significant losses, and check to make sure the stock picking manager did not style drift during the period in question.

Making these comparisons requires a high degree of understanding of each of the concepts listed above. The truth is that the only way to end up with performance that is different from an index is to own investments that differ from those found in an index. But, since an index is the only source of consistent 20-year risk and return data, it would be foolish for an investor to choose anything other than the index. Therefore, the only important question for an investor to consider is: What mix of indexes is appropriate for me?

3.3 PROBLEMS

3.3.1 Why Stock Pickers Fail

The main reason that stock pickers fail is that stock prices are moved by news, and news is unpredictable and random in nature. Therefore, the movements of stock prices are unpredictable and random.

This simple logic makes it impossible for any human being to consistently pick stocks that outperform the averages of a market.

Secondly, the news that moves stock prices is incorporated into the new price within minutes of its release. This adds a major hurdle for stock pickers. It means they must compete with thousands of highly intelligent and well-informed traders on a minute-by-minute basis.

John Stossel of ABC's 20/20, reported a story on the perils of picking stocks. Stossel interviewed Professor Burton Malkiel of Princeton University, author of the book, *A Random Walk down Wall Street*. In the interview, Professor Malkiel said that stock markets historically deliver a performance of 9.5% to 10% compounded per year over the long haul. Inquired Stossel: "To beat that average, should an investor listen to the Wall Street professionals?"

"No," replied Professor Malkiel. "All the information an analyst can learn about a company, from balance sheets to marketing material, is already built into the stock price, because all of the other thousands of analysts have the same information. What they don't have is the knowledge that will move the stock, knowledge such as a news event, which is unpredictable and impossible to forecast."

Indeed, an analyst can only guess about a future event, which is no different than throwing a dart at a newspaper while blindfolded to find a stock. Both events are unpredictable. The main purpose of the financial research industry is to try to predict the future course of events since that is the only thing that will drive future stock prices. If thousands of highly intelligent, sophisticated analysts with degrees from top universities and access to the best computing power available can't predict the future, what use are they? How can one company or research analyst have more knowledge than another without it being inside information, which would be illegal?

Stock Pickers' Graveyard

3.3.2 The Stock Picker's Graveyard

"Survivorship bias" is one of the many reasons that stock pickers' returns look better than they actually are. Survivorship bias is when mutual fund managers tout their fund's performance based on comparisons with an "average" mutual fund. This average is calculated from a list of funds that have survived during a particular period. Funds that did not survive the period are not included in the calculation. According to the Center for Research on Securities Prices (CRSP) at the University of Chicago, if only data from surviving funds is considered, the growth of a dollar for the surviving funds appears to be 19% better since 1962. If only "live growth and income funds" are considered over this period, $100 appears to grow to about $2,500. However, the only way to properly account for all active managers is to include those mutual funds that did not survive. When taking these dead funds into account, CRSP found that the average stock picker's $100 investment grew to only about $2,100.

CRSP has the only complete database of both live and dead mutual funds. Mark M. Carhart developed this unique database for his 1995 Ph.D. dissertation at the University of Chicago's Graduate School of Business. Carhart noted that the explosion in new mutual funds has been "accompanied by a steady disappearance of many other funds through merger, liquidation and other means. This data is not reported by mutual fund data services or financial periodicals, and in most cases is electronically purged from current databases. This imposes a selection bias on the mutual fund data available to researchers, since only survivors are included."

In estimating the performance of an equal-weight index of equity mutual funds, Carhart found that analyzing only surviving funds biases annual performance upward by about 1% per year.

The CRSP database includes 16,979 mutual funds from 1961 to 2000. In that time, 4,816 of the 16,979 mutual funds died. That means 28.4% of mutual fund data is not included in the average returns of active managers. The active managers who ran the data happily buried most of the information about dead funds. Is it possible that the 4,816 dead mutual funds had high returns for their investors? Table 3-1 shows a list of the top 20 worst performing dead mutual funds dating back to 1961.

3.3.3 Incubator Funds

In addition to funds that die, there is an indeterminable number of funds that are aborted. These funds are referred to as incubator funds, and are basically experiments within a fund firm that never develop into a publicly available mutual fund.

Upon their inception, the funds are not available to the public; therefore, they are safe from public scrutiny. After a time, the fund shop rolls out only the best performing funds.

The stock picking managers of these incubator funds tried something new and ended up with a failure. This little known fact has yet to be quantified in the average returns of stock pickers.

Finally, there are the revolving doors of stockbrokers who are churning through clients and constantly rotating from one firm to another. Their records are quickly extinguished, never to be counted in the average of stock pickers.

The financial press will always go to great lengths to advertise the active managers who had good luck in articles hawking the hot funds

Incubator Bias

Table 3-1

	Top 20 Worst Performing Dead Mutual Funds				
Rank	Mutual Fund Name	Total Loss Over the Life of the Fund	Born	Died	Last Fund Objective
1	Harwick Fund	-96.5%	12/1/70	12/31/72	Max. Capital Gains
2	S&P/InterCapital Dynamics	-95.7%	12/1/69	12/31/74	Not Available
3	Chase Frontier Capital Fund of Boston	-92.6%	12/1/68	12/31/80	Max. Capital Gains
4	Steadman Technology & Growth Fund	-91.1%	5/1/68	6/30/98	Max. Capital Gains
5	Mutual Securities Fund of Boston	-90.1%	2/1/61	12/31/72	Growth
6	Doll Fund	-88.6%	12/1/68	12/31/78	Max Capital Gains
7	Investment/Indicators Fund	-85.8%	12/1/67	12/21/73	Max. Capital Gains
8	First Sierra Fund	-84.4%	2/1/61	12/31/72	Growth
9	E & E Mutual Fund	-83.7%	12/1/61	12/31/74	Growth
10	CitiFunds Emerging Asian Markets Equity Prt	-82.5%	8/1/95	9/30/98	International Stocks
11	de Vegh Mutual Fund	-81.3%	12/1/61	12/31/86	Growth
12	Directors Capital Fund	-81.0%	12/1/70	12/31/82	Max. Capital Gains
13	All American Fund	-80.8%	12/1/63	12/31/74	Growth
14	Astron Fund	-80.7%	12/1/68	12/31/72	Not Available
15	Warren (Ted) Fund	-80.3%	12/1/67	12/31/72	Growth
16	Morgan Stanley Instl Fd: Gold/B	-79.4%	1/1/96	3/31/98	Precious Metals
17	Capital Investors Growth Fund	-77.9%	12/1/61	12/31/73	Growth
18	Admiralty Fund - Growth Series	-77.7%	12/1/61	12/31/75	Growth
19	Channing American Fund	-76.6%	12/1/61	12/31/74	Growth-Income
20	Market Growth Fund	-75.5%	12/1/65	12/31/72	Max. Capital Gain

Source : CRSP

investors should buy "Now!" Of course data is omitted concerning those funds that lost money by taking their chances in the market, only to shut their doors and bury their bad returns.

In addition to dead mutual funds, there is a large graveyard full of dead companies. Table 3-2 lists the largest bankruptcies from 1980 to the present.

Two examples of bankruptcy filings help remind investors how easy it is to pick the wrong stock. The first example is Bethlehem Steel. Bethlehem Steel was founded by legendary steel tycoon Charles Schwab in 1904 in Bethlehem, Pennsylvania. The company produced some of the nation's first steel railroad rails, revolution-

ized high-rise building construction with the introduction of structural I-beams in 1908, and built the country's first aircraft carrier in 1925. Landmarks such as the Golden Gate Bridge, the Chicago Merchandise Mart, Rockefeller Center and the U.S. Supreme Court were constructed with Bethlehem steel. Peacetime employment reached a peak of 157,000 workers in 1957, and profits hit a record $426 million in 1988 and in 2001 the mammoth steel company filed for Chapter 11 bankruptcy.

Bethlehem was one of the stocks in the Dow Jones Industrial Average for nearly 70 years until its replacement by Johnson & Johnson in 1997. Its stock price reached a peak of nearly $60 in late 1959, and remained in a broad trading range

Stocks in a Box

Table 3-2

The Largest Bankruptcies 1980 - 2006		
Company	Date	Total Assets Pre-Bankruptcy
Worldcom, Inc.	07/21/2002	$103,914,000,000
Enron Corp.	12/02/2001	$63,392,000,000
Conseco, Inc.	12/18/2002	$61,392,000,000
Texaco, Inc.	4/12/1987	$35,892,000,000
Financial Crp. of America	9/09/1988	$33,864,000,000
Refco Inc.	10/17/2005	$33,333,172,000
Global Crossing Ltd.	1/28/2002	$30,185,000,000
Pacific Gas & Electric Co.	4/06/2001	$29,770,000,000
Capline Corp.	12/20/2005	$27,216,088,000
UAL Corp.	12/09/2002	$25,197,000,000
Delta Air Line, Inc.	9/14/2005	$21,801,000,000
Adelphia Comm.	6/25/2002	$21,499,000,000
MCorp	3/31/1989	$20,228,000,000
Mirant Corporation	7/14/2003	$19,415,000,000
First Executive Corp.	5/13/1991	$15,193,000,000
Gibraltar Financial Corp.	2/08/1990	$15,011,000,000
Kmart Corp.	1/22/2002	$14,600,000,000
FINOVA Group, Inc.,(The)	3/07/2001	$14,050,000,000
Northwest Airlines Corp.	9/14/2005	$14,042,000,000
HomeFed Corp.	10/22/1992	$13,885,000,000
Southeast Banking Corp.	9/20/1991	$13,390,000,000
NTL, Inc.	5/08/2002	$13,003,000,000
Reliance Grp Holdings	6/12/2001	$12,598,000,000
Imperial Corp. of America	2/28/1990	$12,263,000,000
Total Business Bankruptcies	2004	34,317
Total Business Bankruptcies	2005	39,201

Source: New Generation Research, Inc.

over the next 40 years as the firm struggled to improve its competitive position through various acquisitions, divestitures, and cost cuts.

Indeed, only three members of the original 30-stock Dow Average established in October 1928 are still included today: General Electric, General Motors, and Standard Oil of New Jersey, now ExxonMobil.

Another example is Polaroid Corp., which was founded in 1937 by 28-year old Harvard dropout Edwin Land. Land was a brilliant physicist and tireless inventor who accumulated 535 patents by the time of his death in 1991 (second only to Thomas Edison). An early quest to solve the problem of headlight glare led to a patented process for polarized glass, and a variety of optical products for military and commercial use. The self-developing Polaroid Land camera he ultimately developed was a marketing sensation when introduced for $89.50 in 1948. A steady stream of improvements including instant color film stoked consumer interest in the 1950s and 1960s.

Polaroid shares were a favorite among aggressive investors, soaring more than 40 fold from their initial public offering in 1957 to an all-time high of $149.50 in 1972 ($74.75 adjusted for a subsequent two-for-one split). The SX-70 camera, which ejected prints that developed externally, was introduced the same year. In addition, there was talk of a forthcoming instant movie system.

What's more, in 1991, a successful patent infringement lawsuit against Eastman Kodak appeared to vanquish the sole competitive threat in instant photography. But Polaroid was unable to capitalize on the $925 million judgment, and struggled to broaden its product line amidst the proliferation of inexpensive 35mm cameras, one-hour photo kiosks and digital photography. Eventually Polaroid filed for bankruptcy in 2001.

The moral of these stories is that success today does not ensure survival tomorrow; therefore, investors need to diversify so that these kinds of events will not destroy their portfolio.

In the book *Creative Destruction*, McKinsey & Company consultants Richard Foster and

Sarah Kaplan researched the original S&P 500, which was created in 1957. The survival of companies is similar to the survival of mutual fund managers. Figure 3-1 shows that in the 41 years from 1957 to 1998, only 74 of the original 500 companies were still in existence and only 12 of those outperformed the S&P 500 Index over the 1957 to 1998 period. The study found that the odds of picking a winning stock that beat the S&P 500 Index was one in 42.

3.3.4 Studies and Observations that Show the Daunting Odds of Stock Picking

If the average index fund charges 0.4% and the average active mutual fund charges 1.6%, there is already an innate cost disadvantage with active management even before taking into account that active management underperforms the respective index. What exactly are investors paying for? According to hundreds of studies, it appears that investors are paying for nothing more than false hope or promises.

A survey of both the popular and academic literature provides a crystal clear picture of the daunting odds of stock picking.

Robert Jeffrey and Robert Arnott published a study titled "Is your Alpha Big Enough to cover its Taxes?" In the study, 71 large cap growth and growth and income active mutual fund managers were compared to the S&P 500 over a period of 10 years from 1982 to 1991. Most invested in styles that closely represented the S&P 500, but none were exact. Only two out of these 71 managers beat the index. That is a mere 3%! Had they all just invested in the S&P 500, they would have equaled its return. For those investors who were invested in either of the two funds that did beat the S&P 500, very few enjoyed the full returns of these funds. This is because huge cash inflows showed up in the last year of the time

Figure 3-1

period, a typical sign indicative of manager or stock picking. See Figure 3-2.

The odds of throwing a two (snake eyes) at the craps table are the same as the results of this study, one in 36. The least likely rolls of a pair of dice are two and 12. The odds in roulette are one in 38 for picking a one-number winner. Gambling in Las Vegas may lead to more success than trying to find a manager who beats a chosen index at the beginning of the period. Says John Bogle, founder of Vanguard: "Investors earn a net return, after all of the costs of our system of financial intermediation. Just as gambling in a casino is a zero-sum game before the croupiers rake in their share and a loser's game thereafter, so beating the stock and bond markets is a zero-sum game before the intermediation costs, and a loser's game thereafter."

Listed below are several more studies that reflect the daunting odds of stock picking.

Alfred Cowles conducted one of the first recorded studies of stock pickers' performance in a July 1933 article titled "Can Stock Market

Figure 3-2

Can you find the two mutual fund managers who beat their benchmark?*

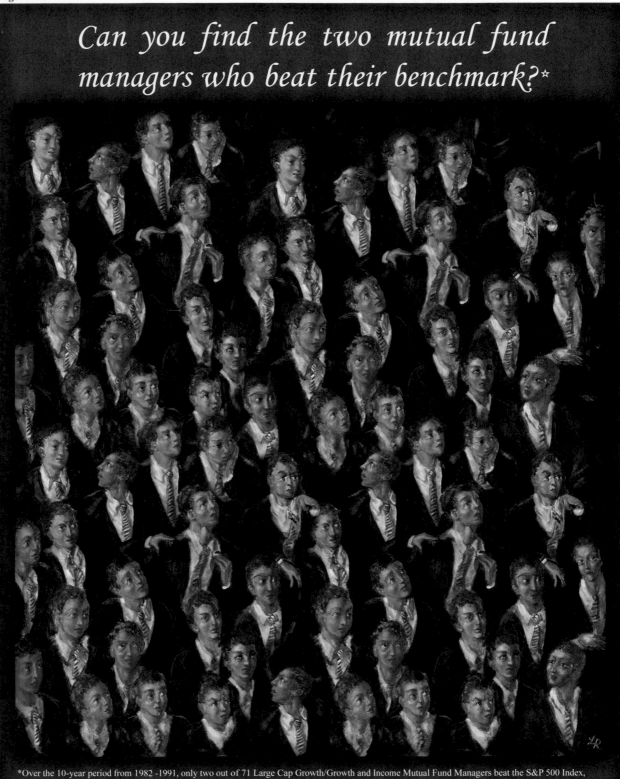

*Over the 10-year period from 1982 -1991, only two out of 71 Large Cap Growth/Growth and Income Mutual Fund Managers beat the S&P 500 Index, (adjusted for loads, fees, and federal taxes, but not adjusted for risk or state taxes). Source: "Is Your Alpha Big Enough to Cover Your Taxes," *The Journal of Portfolio Management*, (Spring 1993, pp. 15-25), by Robert D. Arnott, Robert Jeffrey, with load adjust by W. Scott Simon in *Index Mutual Funds, Profiting from an Investment Revolution (Namborn Publishing Co., Camarillo, CA., 1998).*

Forecasters Forecast?" He concluded that it was "doubtful."

In another study titled "Bogle on Equity Fund Selection," Bogle determined that only nine out of 355 equity funds beat their benchmark over a period of 30 years. Interestingly, that is 2.5% or a one in 39 chance of choosing the correct mutual fund in advance. Another study using CRSP data showed similar results. See Figures 3-3 and 3-4.

A study by Brad Barber of the University of California, Davis, titled "Who Gains from Trade? Evidence from Taiwan," showed that 82% of the 925,000 active traders on the Taiwan stock exchange lost $8.2 billion per year from 1995 to 1999.

Another stock picking study titled "The Importance of Investment Policy," conducted by Ronald Surz, Dale Stevens, and Mark Wimer found that the market timing and stock picking done by active managers had a predictably negative effect on returns. These findings indicate that asset allocation contributed to more than 100% of the expected return of an actively managed portfolio. Active management created a negative drag compared to a portfolio of index funds that most closely replicated the active manager's asset allocation. Adjustments were not made for taxes in taxable accounts.

The case against active management is clearly and logically spelled out by Nobel laureate William Sharpe in an article titled "The Arithmetic of Active Management." In the article, Sharpe clearly states that before costs, the return on the average actively managed dollar will equal the return on the average passively managed dollar, and after costs the return on the average actively managed dollar will be less than the return on the average passively managed dollar.

The findings of another study by Sharpe titled "Asset Allocation: Management Style and Performance Measurement, an Asset Class Factor Model can Help Make Order out of Chaos" supported the hypothesis that the average mutual fund cannot beat the market before costs. That's because such funds constitute a large and presumably representative part of the market. Annualized, the mean underperformance is approximately 0.89% per year—an amount that is approximately equal to the costs incurred by a typical mutual fund.

In a study titled "Are Investors Reluctant to Realize their Losses?" Terrance Odean, using 10,000 random discount brokerage accounts, demonstrates that the trading volume of discount brokerage clients is excessive. Overconfident investors overestimate the amount of profit they can make and will thus engage in costly trading, even though the profits will not cover the associated costs. Overconfident investors also believe they have discreet, useful information when in reality they have no such knowledge. Odean found that stocks that investors purchased underperformed securities they sold!

In a follow-up study titled "Trading is Hazardous to Wealth: The Common Investment Performance of Individual Investors," Odean along with Barber analyzed 66,465 individual trading accounts. They found that from 1991 to 1996, investors that traded the most earned an annual return of 11.4%. In the same time period, the market returned 17.9%. The simple conclusion: Active investment strategies will underperform passive or indexed investment strategies.

In another study by Odean and Barber titled "Too Many Cooks Spoil the Profits: The

Figure 3-3

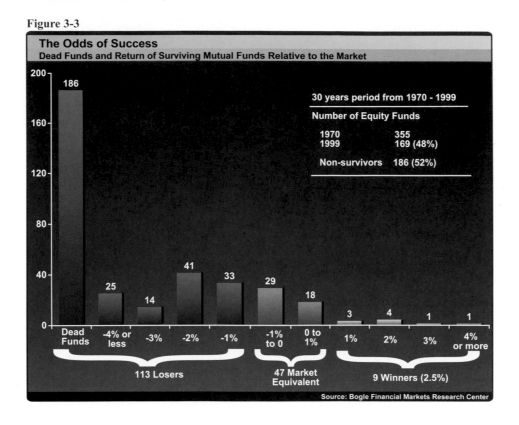

The Odds of Success
Dead Funds and Return of Surviving Mutual Funds Relative to the Market

30 years period from 1970 - 1999

Number of Equity Funds

1970	355
1999	169 (48%)
Non-survivors	186 (52%)

113 Losers · 47 Market Equivalent · 9 Winners (2.5%)

Source: Bogle Financial Markets Research Center

Figure 3-4

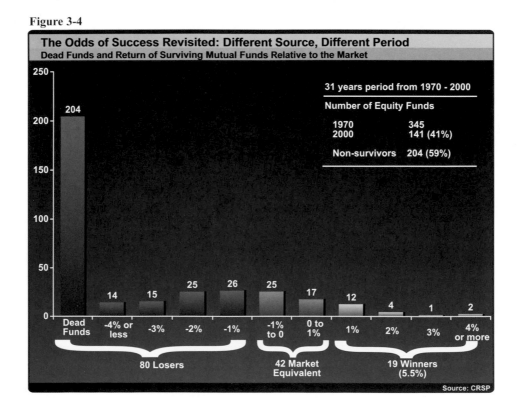

The Odds of Success Revisited: Different Source, Different Period
Dead Funds and Return of Surviving Mutual Funds Relative to the Market

31 years period from 1970 - 2000

Number of Equity Funds

1970	345
2000	141 (41%)
Non-survivors	204 (59%)

80 Losers · 42 Market Equivalent · 19 Winners (5.5%)

Source: CRSP

Performance of Investment Clubs," 166 investment clubs were followed from February 1991 through December 1996. Many people belong to investment clubs, which are touted as a valuable way for investors to learn about the markets. Of the total investment clubs, 57% underperformed the market. See Figure 3-5.

In a study titled "The Performance of Mutual Funds in the Period 1945 to 1964," Michael C. Jensen tested the predictive ability of 115 mutual fund managers in the period 1945 to 1964. He was interested in gauging their ability to earn higher returns than those that would be expected given the level of risk of each of the portfolios. What he found was that on average the 115 mutual funds were not able to predict security prices well enough to outperform a buy-the-market-and-hold policy. In addition, there was very little evidence that any individual fund was able to do significantly better than that which was expected from mere random chance. Jensen's conclusions held up even when fund returns gross of management expenses were measured.

In a study titled "Mutual Fund Performance and Manager Style," James Davis looked at the relationship between fund performance and manager style. Two specific issues were addressed. First, did any particular investment style reliably deliver abnormal performance? Second, when funds with similar styles were compared, was there any evidence of performance persistence? The results of the study were not good news for investors who purchased actively managed mutual funds. According to the findings, no investment style generated positive abnormal returns over the 1965 to 1998 sample period.

Edwin Elton, Martin Gruber, M. Hlavka and Sanjiv Das studied all 143 equity mutual funds that survived from 1965 to 1984. These funds were compared to a set of indexes comprised of

Figure 3-5

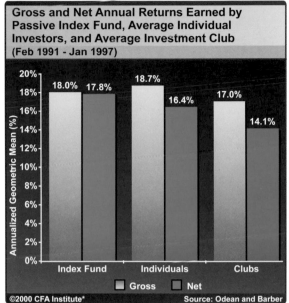

Gross and Net Annual Returns Earned by Passive Index Fund, Average Individual Investors, and Average Investment Club (Feb 1991 - Jan 1997)

©2000 CFA Institute*   Source: Odean and Barber

large cap, small cap, and fixed income, that most closely matched the actual investment choices of the funds. The result: on average these funds underperform the indexes by a whopping 1.6% per year, before federal and state taxes. Not a single fund generated a positive performance that was statistically significant.

A far more comprehensive study of 1,892 funds that existed in any period between 1961 and 1993 became the dissertation of Mark Carhart while he was earning his Ph.D from the University of Chicago. The study titled "On Persistence in Mutual Fund Performance" found that when adjusted for the common factors in returns, an equal-weighted portfolio of the funds underperformed the proper benchmark by 1.8% per year, before federal and state taxes.

In the first major study of bonds funds, Christopher Blake, Edwin Elton and Martin Gruber examined 361 bonds funds for the period starting in 1977. They compared the actively managed bond funds to a simple index alternative. The result: the actively managed bond funds underperformed the proper benchmark by 0.85% per year, before federal and state taxes.

A study by Brad Barber, Reuven Lehavy, Maureen McNichols and Brett Trueman titled "Prophets and Losses: Reassessing the Returns to Analysts' Stock Recommendations" analyzed the returns to analysts' stock recommendations over the 1996 to 2000 period. The period was one of growing doubt about the value of these recommendations, as analysts became increasingly involved in the investment banking side of their business. The study showed that the more highly recommended stocks earned greater market-adjusted returns during the 1996 to 1999 period than did those that were less highly recommended. However, the opposite was true for 2000, as the least favorably rated stocks earned the highest returns. These missed predictions of stock pickers prevailed during most of 2000 while the market was rising and as it was falling.

DFA looked at 31 institutional pension plans with $70 billion in total assets. The firm found that when the returns were properly risk adjusted using the Fama/French Three-Factor Model, 97% of the returns were explained by the three risk factors, and the value added by active management was statistically insignificant, even before fees.

When Jeff Brown of TwinCities.com wrote an article titled "Beating Index Funds Takes Rare Luck or Genius," he asked Morningstar to look at the record of mutual funds. The independent investment research firm determined that there are 1,446 large-cap blend funds that invest in a similar asset class to the S&P 500. Over the 10-year period ending October 2004, only 35 mutual funds matched or beat the performance of the S&P 500. That's only 2.4% or one in 41. See Figure 3-6. Morningstar also looked at the last three years, and only 22 out of the 1,446 funds consistently beat the S&P 500. Brown's sobering conclusion was that "if such a small percentage beat the index, many of them do it with luck, and there's no way to identify those that really are

Figure 3-6

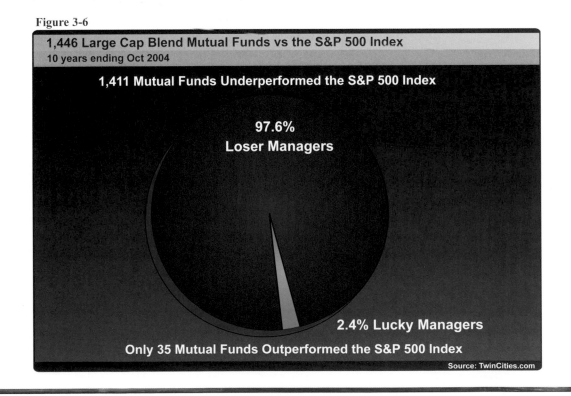

brilliantly managed...well that's why index fund investing is so attractive."

Another sobering observation comes from Bill Miller, portfolio manager of Legg Mason Value Trust, who outperformed the S&P 500 for the fourteenth consecutive year in 2004. Miller is a philosophy major who has this to say about the irony of his record in a January 6, 2005 *Wall Street Journal* article titled "Bill Miller Dishes on his Streak and his Strategy": "As for the so-called streak, that's an accident of the calendar. If the year ended on different months it wouldn't be there and at some point the mathematics will hit us. We've been lucky. Well, maybe it's not 100% luck—maybe 95% luck." Based on that comment, it might be a good idea to put a warning on the Legg Mason Value Trust prospectus reminding investors that luck is not a reliable source of returns in the future– maybe something along the lines of the health warning on a package of cigarettes.

The studies mentioned above represent only a sampling of the mountain of research that have been stockpiled over the years. The impact of the research can best be summed up in the words of Henry Blodget, former securities analyst turned financial journalist: "Academics have essentially proved that active fund management for the fund customer is a loser's game. The vast majority of active funds underperform passive benchmarks. So, the vast majority of customers of active funds pay billions of dollars in exchange for, at best, nothing."

3.3.5 Stock Pickers and Coin Flippers

The attempt to predict the outcome of a coin toss is a futile endeavor. Unless the coin is rigged, the only way to make a correct prediction is to guess blindly. Unfortunately, it is with the same disregard for investors' financial health that the financial institutions and media perpetuate the false idea that some people have a gift or method for predicting future stock price gyrations.

In a study by Walter Good and Roy Hermansen, a hypothetical coin flipping experiment was compared to mutual fund manager performance. Three-hundred college students were asked to guess the outcome of 10 coin tosses. Their guesses were tabulated and charted. The performances of 300 mutual fund managers were then tabulated for 10 years (1987 to 1996) from Morningstar® Principia®. See Figure 3-7.

The number of years that the mutual fund managers were rated in the top 50% of fund managers was then counted and compared to the ability of college students to correctly guess the outcome of the flip of a coin. The results were nearly identical.

Figure 3-7

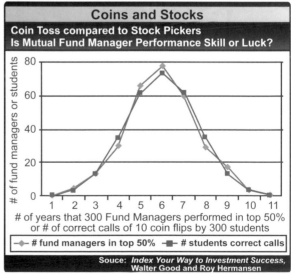

An interesting point was raised by a hypothetical nationwide coin toss. In this example proposed by Warren Buffett, 225 million Americans are given one silver dollar and expected to flip it once per day, with heads winning and tails losing. After 25 consecutive days, the statistical result would be comparable to six people flipping heads for 25 days in a row. These people would be regarded as geniuses for being so masterful at flipping coins. This is nonsense, of course, but it would do well for investors to see mutual fund managers as the six masterful coin flippers rather than geniuses, gurus or all star analysts.

3.3.6 Stock Pickers are Focused on Short Term

Charles Ellis

"The average long-term experience in investing is never surprising, but the short-term experience is always surprising," - Charles D. Ellis - *Winning the Loser's Game.*

The confusion of most investors is derived from their inability to look at large sets of data about stocks, times, managers or styles. Here is the reason for the confusion. With a small set of data, such as the 50 rolls of three dice shown in Figure 3-8, the assumption is that the chances of getting a six on the next roll was the best of all combinations. This poor representation of the long-term characteristics of the three dice is known as random drift, (in the casino they call it luck). This is similar to saying that an investor feels confident about a certain stock, time period, manager or style based on a recent short-term experience.

However, if one looks at the long-term or a thousand rolls of three dice (see Figure 3-9), a far better representation of the risk and return characteristics of the dice is demonstrated, which

reduces or eliminates the confusion caused by random drift or luck. Rolling a six is just as likely as rolling a 15 and a lot less likely than rolling a 10 or 11. The population characteristics for any

Figure 3-8

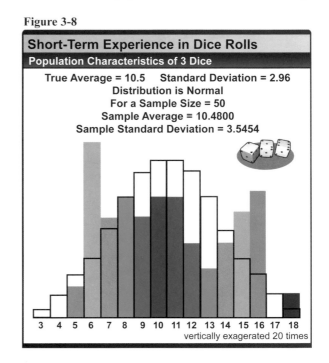

Figure 3-9

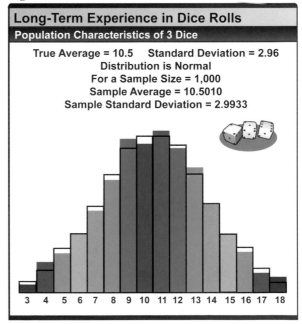

large data set are best described by the average and the standard deviation, which represents the variance around the average.

The approximate distributions of times and stock returns in Figures 3-11 to 3-15 on the following pages look strikingly similar to the roll of the three dice above. Investors, who think they see a pattern in monthly or quarterly returns are experiencing random drift, just like 50 rolls of the dice. They are being fooled by randomness.

The mutual fund managers' returns and the students' ability to guess a coin flip both look strikingly similar to the distribution of the dice and the annual stock returns of the S&P 500 stocks, all of which are driven by random and unpredictable events.

3.3.7 Stock Pickers are Style Drifters

One of the most difficult problems in confirming stock pickers' skill is that they are constantly changing the criteria, ownership rules or style of their investments. Since their style is constantly changing, it is very difficult to track and compare them to the proper index. In fact, one study found that 40% of mutual funds are invested outside of their stated styles. This will alter their performance and result in different risk and return characteristics, which is sort of like changing the number of dice in the dice roll example.

In fact, every portfolio that differs from the stated benchmark or style will result in a different return. Since these portfolios that have drifted from a benchmark have no long-term characteristics, investors have no idea what to expect from the manager's newly created style. In the absence of expectations, an investor becomes a speculator, and the expected return of speculation is zero.

Figure 3-11

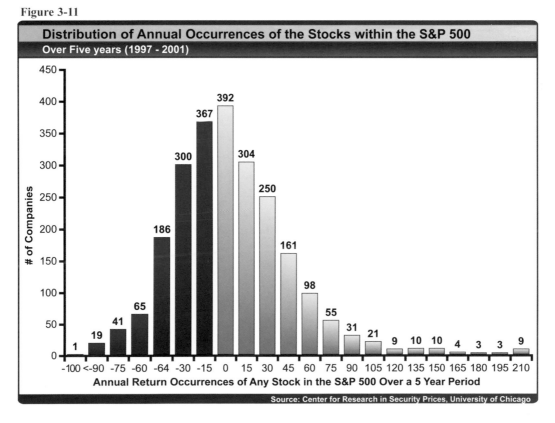

55

Figure 3-11

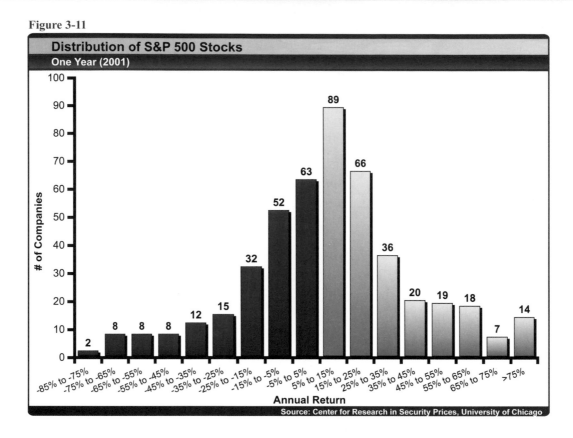

Distribution of S&P 500 Stocks

One Year (2001)

Source: Center for Research in Security Prices, University of Chicago

Figure 3-12

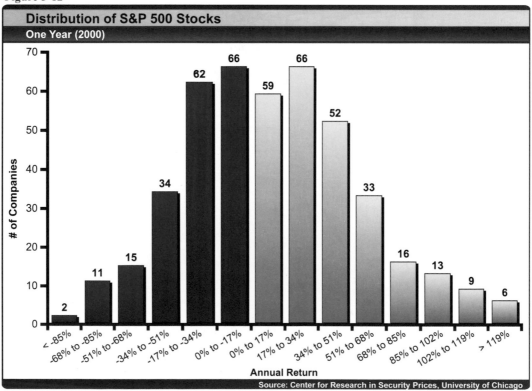

Distribution of S&P 500 Stocks

One Year (2000)

Source: Center for Research in Security Prices, University of Chicago

Figure 3-13

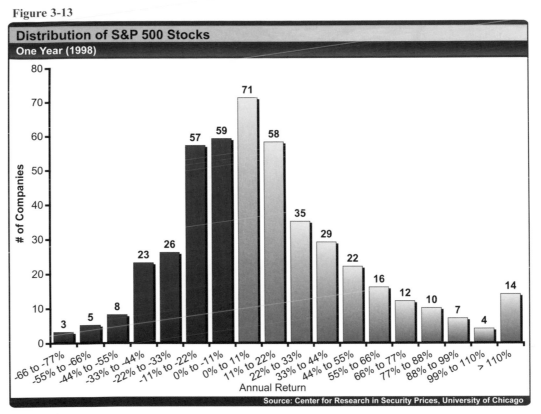

Distribution of S&P 500 Stocks

One Year (1998)

Source: Center for Research in Security Prices, University of Chicago

Figure 3-14

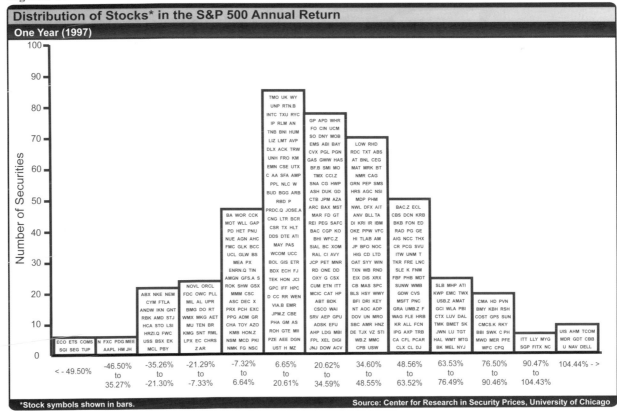

Distribution of Stocks* in the S&P 500 Annual Return

One Year (1997)

*Stock symbols shown in bars.

Source: Center for Research in Security Prices, University of Chicago

3.3.8 Stock Pickers are Looking for a Needle in a Haystack

John Bogle accurately described stock picking as looking for a needle in a haystack (see page 65). The top 10 stocks perform 20 times better in their first three years than they do in the following three years, according to a study by Ibbotson and Associates. Stock pickers are often surprised when they purchase what they think have been winners, only to be grossly disappointed in the period after purchase.

Many investors invest in blue chip companies, believing they are reliable and true blue. See Table 3-3 for less than favorable outcomes of 10 of these blue chip companies.

The solution is to buy the haystack rather than pick and choose certain stocks. This will guarantee market returns at a much lower cost.

Table 3-3

Stories from 10 Blue Chips From 1959 to 1985	
Blue Chip Companies	**Outcomes & Time Periods**
General Electric Company	Price appreciation from 1965 to 1980 = zero.
IBM	For the 19 years from 1961 to 1979 market value drops 65%.
Proctor & Gamble	1973 high price not exceeded until 1985.
Polaroid Corp.	1998 stock price one-third of the price from 1968.
Gillette	Stock buyer in 1961 reaches break-even in 1984. 65% decline over 19 years from 1961 to 1979.
Coca Cola Co.	1973 price peaks at $75, drops 60% over nine years to below $30 in 1982.
Black & Decker Corp.	Shares up 500 times in 15 years. 1972 peak price not seen again until 1998.
Aluminum Co. of America	From 1959 to 1983, zero growth for investors.
Digital Equipment Corp.	Shares went up 1,000 fold from 1967 to 1987. Lost 85% of value in next five years.
Campbell Soup Co.	Investors lost appetite from 1961 until 1982, with no price appreciation.
Source: Standard & Poor's; Securities Research Corp.	

The only valid question is: Which haystack or index, and in what proportions?

3.3.9 Stock Pickers Play a Zero Sum Game

All financial markets are zero sum games. This is a mathematical fact. In any financial market it is mathematically impossible for the average investor in that market to outperform the average of the market. This is because in any market, the pre-cost returns earned by good, bad, and average stock pickers combined together must be the same as the total market return. The after-cost returns will be less than the total market return. All investors as a group are mathematically obligated to underperform the market by the amount of their costs of investing.

There are occasional active investors who outperform a given market, even after costs and taxes. The market-beating returns they generate must then counterbalance the inferior returns of those who underperform the market. That is, the amount of the outperformance must be offset to the same degree as the amount of the underperformance for reasons none other than simple arithmetic!

3.3.10 Stock Pickers in International Markets

Many investors agree that the U.S. financial markets are highly efficient. But are other markets outside the United States efficient? Are there profitable investments that can be made that might outperform their respective index? Many investors believe that these "underdeveloped" markets are inferior to our own, and that analysts are better at choosing stocks in international markets that outperform the appropriate index. Evidence shows that this is not the case.

Several studies have proven that the indexes of these smaller markets, on average, will perform better than an active fund. If one investment manager has an idea about an international country or company, it would only be logical to have numerous other firms investigating the profitable possibilities, with only one conclusion available—that none of the firms will outperform the index average over any lengthy period of time.

In fact, there have been studies that show higher costs associated with international investing make it even harder for active investors to beat their benchmarks. In a research paper by Garret Quigley and Rex Sinquefield titled "Performance of UK Equity Unit Trusts," the authors concluded that UK money managers were unable to outperform markets in any meaningful sense.

3.3.11   Stock Pickers in Small-Cap Markets

Many people are led to believe that active managers can provide a greater advantage and higher value to investors in the small-cap versus large-cap market, thus resulting in a larger alpha. A large alpha infers that the stock or mutual fund has performed better than would be expected based on its volatility or risk, suggesting that active management is the reason for the better than expected performance.

A study by Cambridge Associates looked at U.S. Small-Cap manager performance form 1995 to 2004. Specifically, the survey looked at the persistence of U.S. small- cap manager performance across two five-year periods: 1995 to 1999 and 2000 to 2004. Of the managers in the top quintile of performance in the first period, 59% landed in the bottom quintile in the following period. A full 97% ended up in the bottom two quintiles. In addition, more than half of the

managers in the second best quintile in the 1995 to 1999 period dropped to the bottom two quintiles in 2000 to 2004. The point: there is no evidence to suggest consistency in manager performance. A couple of managers post great performance over an extended period of time. But, the reason is most certainly luck.

Richard M. Ennis and Michael D. Sebastian of Ennis Knupp + Associates, one of the 10 largest pension consulting firms, published a paper titled "The Small-Cap-Alpha Myth," in September 2001. In the study, the firm constructed a sample of 128 small-cap managers from the Mobius Group M-Search database, a small-cap database of institutional commingled funds and composites of separate accounts. The researchers concluded that this so-called small-cap-alpha advantage is actually the "small-cap-alpha myth." At first blush, it appears that a small-cap-alpha advantage does exist. But when looking at the 10-year period ending June 30, 2001, their research showed that the median portfolio in their sample outperformed the Russell 2000 Index by 4.04%. A more accurate picture formed when they delved deeper.

When three important performance evaluation methods were considered, the alpha diminished to virtually zero. These performance evaluation errors include (1) neglecting to account for management fees, (2) comparing the portfolio to an inappropriate benchmark, and (3) overlooking survivorship bias.

Error #1: Ninety percent of the products in the sample reported performance before fees. When fees were included in the equation, the stock picker's advantage dropped from 4.04% to 3.09%.

Error #2: To derive an accurate net return, appropriate benchmarks must be used for comparison. A single index, such as the Russell 2000, cannot be used for proper comparison if the portfolios being compared are not exactly the same in style and make-up as that index. Ennis and Sebastian created effective style mixes (ESMs) for the products being studied. Based on a type of multiple regression, ESMs are a more precise way to benchmark. Now accounting for errors #1 and #2, the adjusted alpha dropped from 4.04% to 1.2%.

Error #3: Many databases do not include the records of stock pickers that went out of business, which hyper-inflates the performance reports of active managers and funds. This survivorship bias does not accurately reflect the true performance of all managers that started at the beginning of the period.

When considering all three performance evaluation errors, Ennis and Sebastian concluded that the true median alpha in their sample is "likely to be zero or negative, not 4%." In conclusion they found "no support for the claim that active management of small-cap portfolios is any more fruitful than it is for large-cap portfolios." In other words, forget about it! Focus on the only important question of investing: What allocation of index funds is most appropriate for you?

3.3.12 Stock Pickers Pay More Taxes

Stock pickers manage their portfolios as if taxes do not matter. The average active manager has approximately a 100% turnover rate per year, while index funds range from 5% to 35%. The cost of turnover is detrimental to the overall performance of the portfolio.

There is a substantial incentive for investors to hold their stocks for a year or more. For stock sales with holding periods of less than one year, the gain is treated as ordinary income and subject to the full federal and state tax rate.

Depending on the tax bracket and state of residence, this could be 39.6% for federal taxes and 11% for state taxes, and can have a dramatic impact on actual returns. For holding periods of one year or more, the tax rate is reduced to the long-term capital gains rate of 15%.

3.3.13 Stock Picking Gurus and their Real Records

The dangers of stock picking become crystal clear when we focus on the best, brightest, and most famous stars of the investment industry.

Jack Grubman was touted as king of the telecom stock industry in the mid-to-late 1990s. As Salomon Smith Barney's appointed telecom analyst, Grubman was regarded as the most influential power broker in the industry. He was rated number one in Institutional Investor's annual analyst rankings and was profiled by *The Wall Street Journal*, *BusinessWeek*, and *New York Magazine*. When Grubman talked, people listened. If he said, "buy," people bought; if he said, "sell," people sold. One broker likened Grubman's advice to a narcotic. Everybody wanted it. Salomon Smith Barney's 13,000 brokers passed along his stock picks to their clients. His many monikers included, "Telecom god," "Consigliore," and "Ax." At the height of the telecom industry, he gave advice on 40 stocks with a combined market value of more than $1 trillion. He himself made $20 million a year.

Most everyone knows the rest of the story. The glamorous telecom sector soared beyond imagination, and then went bust with enormous consequences. Grubman's top 10 picks in March, 2001, all plummeted to the lowest of lows a year later. As of May 2002, five of the 10 were trading under $1 a share. Three of the 10 had filed for bankruptcy including Global Crossing, McLeodUSA, and Winstar Communications. Along with the Global Crossing bankruptcy went $55 billion of paper wealth down the drain.

Investors lost millions relying on Grubman's supposed wisdom. The "King of Kings" lost his seat on the analyst throne and no longer wears the stock picker's crown. When asked what he learned from this disaster, he said, "You learn that even good management teams and macro-industry trends being favorable do not always translate into equity returns being positive." Spoken by the fallen stock picking hero himself.

Here's another example of a stock picking guru who fell from grace: On March 30, 2000, Tiger Management LLC confirmed that it was closing all six of its hedge funds. The legendary value investment manager, Julian Robertson Jr., stated that he could no longer understand this irrational market. For the first two months of the year, the funds were down 13%. Robertson wrote, "What I do know is that there is no point in subjecting our investors to risk in a market, which I frankly do not understand." This quote comes from the head of 1999s second-largest hedge fund group in the world. If he and his numerous high priced analysts and strategists cannot comprehend how to beat the market, how can anyone?

In another tale of misfortune from the financial industry's elite, the famous George Soros' $14.2 billion investment firm lost two top managers when the world's largest hedge fund lost approximately $5 billion during March and April of 2000. Here's how the story unfolded: Stanley Druckenmiller and Nicholas Roditi were two of the top managers in charge of developing and implementing investment strategies for the firm.

Druckenmiller managed the $8.2 billion Quantum Fund, which was down 22% for the first four months of 2000, while Roditi managed the $1.2 billion Quota Fund, which plunged 33% during the same period.

Although the Soros funds survived, albeit with new managers, how much of this poor performance can be blamed on the managers when no one can outperform a market over a long period of time? "I think there is going to be more fallout within the hedge fund industry," stated a chief executive of Tass Investment Research. This is not the first case of a trader whose market calls have severely underperformed the markets. For many years, Victor Niederhoffer was one of Soros' best traders. He later ran his own fund but was forced to close it in 1997 due to extremely heavy losses. History is littered with discarded, former legendary investors and strategists who eventually succumbed to the random and efficient markets, underperforming so dramatically that they were rarely heard from again.

Michael Murphy has been hailed as the number one Technology Stock advisor. He offers his "Six Secrets to Successful Technology Investing." However, his record is not so successful. For the five years ending March 1999 his Monterey Murphy Technology Fund had a mere 0.9% annualized return. An approximate index for technology stocks would be the NASDAQ 100 Index Fund, which had an annualized return of 41.3% over the same five-year period. The technology mutual fund average was only 25.5% and the S&P 500 over this period was 26.2%, (Table 3-4).

The financial industry has finally begun investigating the results of poor manager performances. In an article published in *The Financial Analysts' Journal* in 1996, three top investment officers at Washington State

Table 3-4

Technology Stock Picker	
Five Years - Ending March 1999	
Funds	**Annualized Retun**
NASDAQ 100 (Rydex OTC index fund)	41.3%
S&P 500	26.2%
Technology Mutual Fund Average	25.5%
Monterey Murphy Technology Fund	**0.9%**

Investment Board analyzed some of the information discovered by financial academia. One of the studies performed by Ronald Kahn and Andrew Rudd came to two main conclusions: (1) no persistence of returns can be found among U.S. equity managers, and (2) some persistence can be found among U.S. fixed-income managers, but not enough to justify the payment of active manager fees.

According to this and other information, the Washington State Investment Board, which had investment responsibilities in 1996 for more than $30 billion, restructured its investments. In 1993 it allocated approximately 70% of its U.S. equity portfolio to large-capitalization stocks, the bulk of which is invested passively in an S&P 500 Index fund. Their internal findings and newly developed and refined investment philosophy dictates that in the case of efficient markets, the best investment style is passive. Even quasi-active or enhanced strategies that take active bets in addition to a passive style will not add value. The board doubted that any value could be added to a passive investment strategy.

The Washington State Investment Board is one of the enlightened investment organizations whose principals realize there is no value to being an active manager. They know that active management lowers the overall value of the portfolio and that all efforts to increase the performance of the fund are futile. According to a study performed from 1987 to 1993, only one out of 28 major pension funds beat a portfolio consisting

of a 60/40 split between the S&P 500 Index and the Lehman Bond Index.

Financial services firms make money through trading. They take a slice of the pie with every trade. With discount brokerages now in fierce competition, they have reduced their profit margins per trade. In order to maintain the same or greater profit, they must increase the number of trades individuals make. Trading frequently is a high cost activity, not only because of the trade commission paid to the broker, but also because of the spread between the bid and the ask, and the fact that most individuals buy stocks with low expected returns and sell stocks with high expected returns. Brokerage firms are similar to casinos, in that the longer and more often a person plays or trades in the market, the greater the chances that the brokerage firm will make money. The investor's odds of losing unfortunately increase with the frequency of trading. In other words, trading can be hazardous to your wealth.

3.3.14 Stock Pickers don't Want You to Know the Truth

For many mutual fund managers, analysts, traders, stockbrokers and various other individuals associated with the financial industry, the idea of index funds strikes fear in their hearts. This is because stock pickers and analysts charge very high fees on mutual funds, and these fees pay for a lot of the jobs in the industry. It is in the interest of these stock, time, manager, and style pickers to imply that a market can be beat by listening to their strategist or by risking money with their manager. Who will pay for their cars, houses and yachts? Thousands of jobs in the industry are redundant and completely useless to an investor. As one book from the 1940s asks, "Where are the Customers' Yachts?"

If investors consciously want to gamble, then that is a different story. They can try to outperform the index and their fellow investors if they wish. But, they must realize they will not be able to outperform the indexes for any lengthy period of time. Although they may win a few times at the roulette wheel, they will count themselves lucky, but hardly skillful. After all, if a majority of the gamblers in Vegas actually won, who would pay for all the fancy lights?

3.4 SOLUTION

Stock prices move randomly and reflect the daily fair market value of each stock. Therefore, the only hope of success for stock pickers is luck or chance. Time and money are too precious to waste on stock picking. The best investment strategy is to own a global, tax-managed, and diversified portfolio of index funds matched to risk capacity. If investments are not on the optimal returns line between risk capacity and risk exposure, then the appropriate market rate of return will not be achieved.

3.5 SUMMARY

Simply put, stock picking is expensive speculation with negative expected returns relative to a blended benchmark. The best advice is to just let go of it, forget about it, stay away from it, and find something more productive to do.

3.6 REVIEW QUESTIONS

1. The performance of stock pickers must be examined on an adjusted basis. When comparing a stock picker's portfolio to an index, which factors must be considered before determining if the stock picker has beat the index?

   a. proper accounting of returns, including cash flows in and out of the account

   b. the exposure to market risk, size risk, and value risk of both portfolios

   c. level of diversification of the two portfolios

   d. standard deviations or volatility measurements

   e. all of the above

2. Stock pickers pay more taxes than indexers because:

   a. their annual returns are higher

   b. the average actively managed portfolio has a 45% turnover rate, while index funds range from 5% - 35%

   c. the average actively managed portfolio has a nearly 100% turnover rate, while index funds range from 5% - 35%

   d. they don't pay fees or commissions to their brokers, thereby offsetting the higher taxes

3. There are many studies that analyze the percentages of stock prices that outperform an appropriate benchmark. The average percentage of winners is about:

   a. 85%

   b. 30%

   c. 0%

   d. 5%

   e. 60%

4. Stock pickers are often compared to:

   a. chimpanzees throwing darts at the stock page

   b. someone looking for a needle in a haystack

   c. gamblers at the roulette table

   d. tax generators for the government

   e. all of the above

A Devastating Conclusion

Needle in the Haystack

Step 4 ~ Time Pickers

"Market Timing is a wicked idea. Don't try it — ever."

- Charles D. Ellis, author of *Winning the Loser's Game*

"There are two kinds of investors, be they large or small: those who don't know where the market is headed, and those who don't know that they don't know. Then again, there is a third type of investor - the investment professional, who indeed knows that he or she doesn't know, but whose livelihood depends upon appearing to know."

- William Bernstein, *The Intelligent Asset Allocator*

"Statistical research has shown that, to a close approximation, stock prices seem to follow a random walk with no discernible predictable patterns that investors can exploit. Such findings are now taken to be evidence of market efficiency, that is, evidence that market prices reflect all currently available information. Only new information will move stock prices, and this information is equally likely to be good or bad news."

- *Investments*, Fifth Edition, p. 374, Zvi Bodie, Professor of Finance, Boston University School of Management, Ph.D. MIT. Co-authors include Alex Kane and Alan Marcus

"October is one of the peculiarly dangerous months to speculate in stocks. The others are July, January, September, April, November, May, March, June, December, August and February." Also, *"There are two times when a man shouldn't speculate: when he can't afford it, and when he can."*

- Mark Twain, (1835-1910), *Following the Equator, Pudd'nhead Wilson's New Calendar*

"O Fortuna! Like the moon everchanging, rising first then declining."

- Carmina Burana, Lyrics from O Fortuna [The Goddess of Luck - *the active investors' only hope*]

"If I have noticed anything over these 60 years on Wall Street, it is that people do not succeed in forecasting what's going to happen to the stock market."

- Benjamin Graham, Legendary investor and author, Warren Buffett's Mentor, *Security Analysis*, 1934

"... most [stock pickers and market timers] should go out of business - take up plumbing, teach Greek..."

- Paul A. Samuelson, Nobel Laureate, "Challenge to Judgement," *The Journal of Portfolio Management*, Fall 1974, p. 17-19 1974

"Hulbert's conclusion: None of the newsletter timers beat the market [over a ten year period]. The average return was 11.06%. During the same period, Standard & Poor's 500-stock index earned 18.06% annually..."

- Jeffrey M. Laderman - "Market Timing: A Perilous Ploy," *Business Week*, March 9, 1998, Table of Results

"I tell investors to put a large portion of their stock investments in index funds."

- Mark Hulbert, *Hulbert Financial Digest*, taken from an interview by Benjamin Mark Cole in *The Pied Pipers of Wall Street*

"The market is like watching a drunk walk a tight rope. You never know what's going to happen next."

- Arthur Cashin, CNBC Commentary, CNBC Television, November 21, 2003

4.1 INTRODUCTION

Step 4: Understand that no one can pick the right time to be in or out of the market.

Time pickers, also known as market timers, believe they can predict the future direction of the market. In their efforts to time the market, they attempt to invest in stocks when the market is up and shelter their investments in cash, Treasury bills or bonds when the market hits a downturn.

Nobel laureate Robert Merton wanted to estimate what a clairvoyant time picker would earn. To that end, he calculated the value of being invested in the market during upturns and Treasury bills during market downturns. His findings show that investors who stayed invested in T-bills from 1927 through 1978 would have seen their $1,000 investments grow to $3,600. Meanwhile, in the broad market of the New York Stock Exchange (NYSE) Index, a $1,000 investment would have grown to $67,500 during the same period. A time picker with the vision to forecast all the months that the NYSE outperformed T-bills during the 52-year period would naturally invest in the market at the beginning of each of these months. According to this timing system, $1,000 would have grown to $5.36 billion. Now that is a real incentive to figure out how to pick the right times to invest. It also proves that if timers really had psychic powers that allowed them to see next month's market trends, they would grace the covers of *Forbes*, *Fortune*, *BusinessWeek* and *The Wall Street Journal*. But, they do not.

Is it possible that there are a few visionary timers out there? Sorry, but they just don't exist.

In 1978, the wealthiest individual on record didn't come close to these numbers. Wealth is not created by purposeful market timing. There may be cases where one got lucky for a while, but that is not a reliable strategy for long-term investors.

There are numerous time-picking purveyors who offer their visions of tomorrow through tele-marketing, fax broadcasting, newsletters, e-mails, and Web sites. However, investors should be aware that these market-timing newsletters are not regulated by the SEC, whose job it is to protect investors. Estimates show that investors who flock like sheep to follow the market predictions of "expert timers" lose millions of dollars each month.

The landmark and definitive study of time pickers was conducted by John Graham of the University of Utah and Campbell Harvey of Duke University. The professors painstakingly tracked and analyzed more than 15,000 predictions by 237 market timing investment newsletters from June 1980 through December 1992. By the end of the 12.5 year period, 94.5% of the newsletters had gone out of business, with an average length of operations of about four years! The conclusion of this 51-page analysis could not have been stated more clearly. "There is no evidence that newsletters can time the market. Consistent with mutual fund studies, 'winners' rarely win again and 'losers' often lose again." This clearly indicates that the market's signals are inaudible to the thousands of time pickers claiming to clearly hear them. Any investment professional who speculates on the market's future should be relegated to the fortune telling parlor.

Jeffrey Lauderman wrote a *BusinessWeek* article dispelling the myth of market timing, a practice he called "a perilous ploy" and "a guessing game." His 1998 analysis included an interview with Mark Hulbert, publisher of a service that objectively monitors investment newsletter performance. Hulbert's conclusion provided a knockout blow to all 25 newsletters he tracked. None of the newsletter timers beat the market. For the 10-year period from 1988 to 1997, the time pickers' average return was 11.06% annually, while the S&P 500 Stock Index earned 18.06% annually and the Wilshire 5000 earned 17.57% annually. Figure 4-1 tells the story.

The truth is, time pickers vacillate from near zero risk to high risk and then back to zero risk again. A more rational approach for investors is to match their risk exposure to their risk capacity. Once that match is established, the right time to be in the market is when an investor has money, and the right time to get out of the market is when an investor needs their money.

4.2 DEFINITIONS

The underlying assumption of all forms of time picking is that the pickers know news or information not known to millions of other market participants. For continued success, the picker must have a never-ending source of information not available to all other traders. No one can single-handedly possess such incredibly powerful and immensely valuable information.

Two concepts that support the idea that timers are unable to pick the right times to invest are the Random Walk Theory and the Efficient Market Hypothesis.

4.2.1 Random Walk Theory

The Random Walk Theory states that there are no discernible patterns in stock market prices. The logic behind the theory is that news moves the markets. News is both unpredictable and random

by definition. At the moment of public discovery, news rapidly becomes old. Since free financial markets are free of constraints, new information is continuously reflected in the prices of relevant financial instruments. Therefore, the world's markets move in a random and unpredictable manner. As an example of randomness, look at these market summaries from *The Wall Street Journal*:

- **JULY 24, 2002**: The Dow Jones Industrial Average soared 488.95 points, or 6.4%, to 8191.29 Wednesday — their second-highest point gain ever — as bargain-hunting and short-covering provided a powerful antidote for the persistent sell off. The Nasdaq Composite surged 60.96, or 5%, to 1290.01.

- **SEPTEMBER 19, 2002:** U.S. stocks slid Thursday as investors were bombarded by bad news from EDS, Morgan Stanley and Merrill Lynch. Few analysts saw the EDS news coming. The Dow Jones Industrial Average fell below 8000, dropping 230.06, or 2.8%, to 7942.39, while the Nasdaq Composite Index sank 35.70 or 2.9%, to 1216.43.

- **SEPTEMBER 27, 2002:** U.S. stocks moved lower Friday, weighed down by concerns about corporate profits and somber economic news. In late-afternoon trading, the Dow Jones Industrial Average fell 250 points, or 3.1%, to 7745, while the Nasdaq Composite Index slipped 13 to 1208.

- **NOVEMBER 27, 2002:** U.S. stocks rebounded Wednesday, with an abundance of upbeat economic data helping push the Dow Jones Industrial Average up 255.26, or nearly 3%, to end at 8931.68. The Nasdaq Composite Index jumped 43.51, or 3.1%, to 1487.94.

Figure 4-1

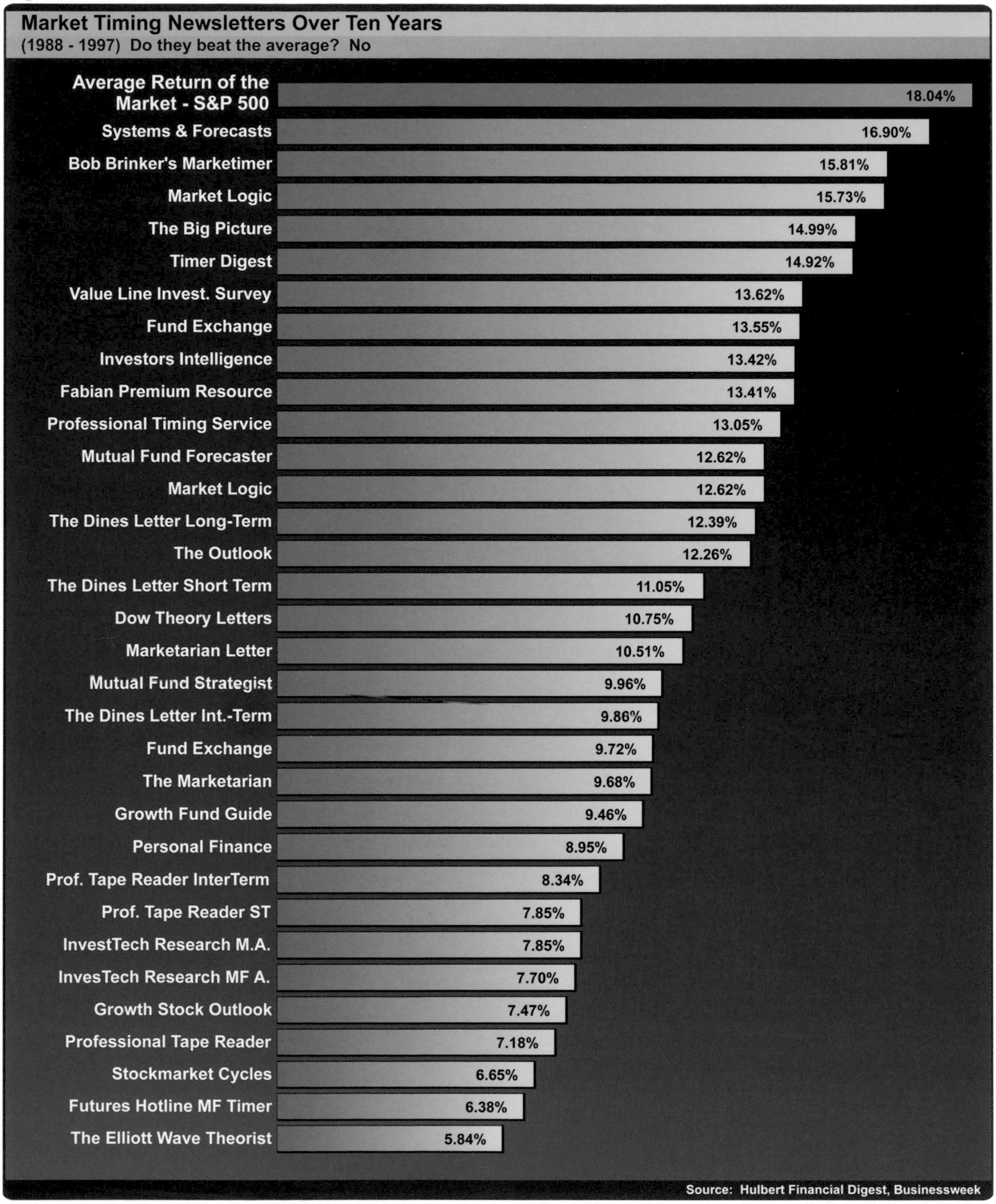

Market Timing Newsletters Over Ten Years
(1988 - 1997) Do they beat the average? No

Average Return of the Market - S&P 500	18.04%
Systems & Forecasts	16.90%
Bob Brinker's Marketimer	15.81%
Market Logic	15.73%
The Big Picture	14.99%
Timer Digest	14.92%
Value Line Invest. Survey	13.62%
Fund Exchange	13.55%
Investors Intelligence	13.42%
Fabian Premium Resource	13.41%
Professional Timing Service	13.05%
Mutual Fund Forecaster	12.62%
Market Logic	12.62%
The Dines Letter Long-Term	12.39%
The Outlook	12.26%
The Dines Letter Short Term	11.05%
Dow Theory Letters	10.75%
Marketarian Letter	10.51%
Mutual Fund Strategist	9.96%
The Dines Letter Int.-Term	9.86%
Fund Exchange	9.72%
The Marketarian	9.68%
Growth Fund Guide	9.46%
Personal Finance	8.95%
Prof. Tape Reader InterTerm	8.34%
Prof. Tape Reader ST	7.85%
InvestTech Research M.A.	7.85%
InvesTech Research MF A.	7.70%
Growth Stock Outlook	7.47%
Professional Tape Reader	7.18%
Stockmarket Cycles	6.65%
Futures Hotline MF Timer	6.38%
The Elliott Wave Theorist	5.84%

Source: Hulbert Financial Digest, Businessweek

MARCH 13, 2003: Major U.S. stock indexes logged their biggest gains of the year on hopes for a delay in a possible war with Iraq. The Dow Jones Industrial Average surged 269.68, or 3.6%, to 7821.75 in heavy trading, while the Nasdaq Composite Index had jumped 61.54, or 4.8%, to 1340.78.

MARCH 17, 2003: U.S. stocks surged Monday on signs the U.S. will go to war with Iraq, a move some say will remove a level of uncertainty in the market. The Dow Jones Industrial Average was up about 239 points in late-afternoon trading, while the Nasdaq Composite Index was ahead roughly 3.2%.

MARCH 24, 2003: The Dow Industrials tumbled 307.29 points, or 3.6%, to 8214.68 Monday as investors began to worry that the war in Iraq could drag out longer than anticipated. The Nasdaq composite lost 52.06, or 3.7%, to 1369.78.

JULY 7, 2003: U.S. stocks surged Monday, with the S&P 500-stock index rising above 1000 as investors pinned hopes on a strong second-quarter earnings season. By midmorning, the Dow Jones Industrial Average was up 179 points, or 2%, to 9251. The Nasdaq Composite Index jumped 45 points, or 2.7%, to 1708.20, and the S&P 500 rose 18.20, or 1.9%, to 1003.90.

As a side note, the reason markets trend upward is that the sun shines on capitalism, as investors' cash provides the fuel to fund profitable ventures. Cash is injected into the market through the purchase of products, services, debts or equities. On average, this free market system works better than a central government controlled system. Communism still exists in only a few countries where there is a mentality similar to that of active investors. This mentality is based on the falsehood that free markets do not reflect all information. Market speculators and communists both think they know more than the collective opinion of millions of voting market participants. They assume that they possess information that has not yet been picked up by the radar of all traders throughout the world. On the other hand, those who invest in index funds invest under the assumption that markets properly price assets and risk.

Rex Sinquefield is a director of Dimensional Fund Advisors (DFA) and one of the world's foremost experts on the stock market. In 1995 he was asked to represent index funds investing in a debate with an active manager at a Schwab conference. After an eloquent review of the history of capital markets from Adam Smith to Eugene Fama, he threw down the gauntlet to a room full of active managers: "So who still believes that markets don't work? Apparently it is only the North Koreans, the Cubans, and the active managers," he said.

4.2.2 Efficient Market Hypothesis

The efficiency of communication has progressed as follows: horseback, slow boat, smoke signals, homing pigeons, flashing lights on navy ships, Morse code, telegraphs, telephones, radios, televisions, computer networks, and finally the Internet. With each step, information and news became cheaper, more accurate, and more rapidly disseminated.

The Efficient Market Hypothesis simply states that market prices accurately reflect all available information at all times. This leads to the conclusion that it is impossible to consistently beat the market averages. As Bachelier stated in 1900, the expected return of speculation is zero. The most recent studies by Richard Roll, a professor of finance at the University of

California, indicate that new information is reflected in market prices within five to 60 minutes. Within that 60 minutes there are hundreds or thousands of traders all competing to profit from the information. If you are in charge of $1 billion, a 0.1% annual gain is worth $1 million per year. Consequently, managers of those funds are applying considerable resources to squeeze out every little gain from new information. For this reason alone, there is an absence of opportunities for one trader to consistently profit from all other traders who have access to the same information at the same time! In short, it is impossible for one person to consistently possess more knowledge than all the other traders combined.

Analysis for Financial Management, a book written by Robert C. Higgins, paints a vivid picture of how information is devoured by market participants: "Market efficiency is a description of how prices in competitive markets respond to new information. The arrival of new information to a competitive market can be likened to the arrival of a lamb chop to a school of flesh-eating piranhas, where investors are—plausibly enough—the piranhas. The instant the lamb chop hits the water, there is turmoil as the fish devour the meat. Very soon the meat is gone, leaving only the worthless bone behind, and the water returns to normal. Similarly, when new information reaches a competitive market there is much

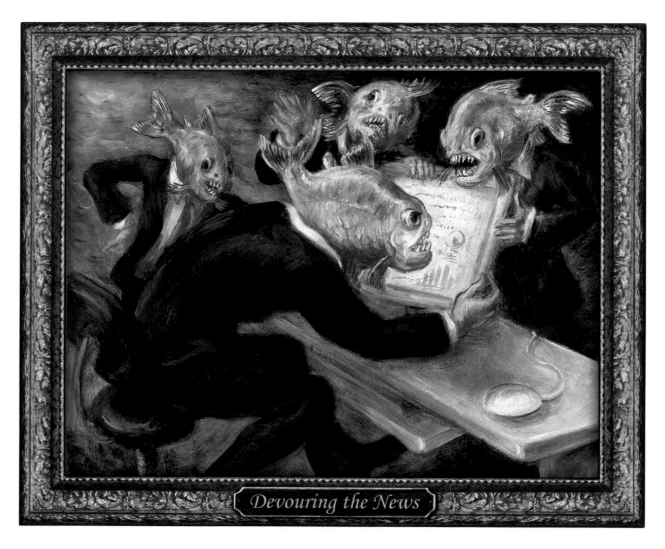

Devouring the News

turmoil as investors buy and sell securities in response to the news, causing prices to change. Once prices adjust, all that is left of the information is the worthless bone. No amount of gnawing on the bone will yield any more meat, and no further study of old information will yield any more valuable intelligence."

4.3 PROBLEMS

4.3.1 Time Pickers are Fooled by Randomness

An important point for investors to understand about time picking is the Random Walk Theory, which states that nobody can consistently see what tomorrow will bring. Remember that news moves the market and is random and unpredictable by definition; therefore, the markets move in a random and unpredictable fashion—period, end of story.

This simple and easy to understand concept about the markets was first published more than one hundred years ago. Since then, virtually all subsequent academic studies detailing actual stock market data conclude that time picking is not likely to be a successful investment strategy. Unless, of course, the Goddess Fortuna is whispering stock tips in your ear. She may be the only antidote to market randomness and the active investors' only hope. You can make your own luck by staying in the market at all times and owning a globally diversified portfolio of indexes.

From 1901 to 1990, the stock market return was approximately 9.5% per year. SEI Corp. completed a study in 1992 that showed in order to just equal this average annual return over this 90-year period, a time picker needed to correctly select about 70% of the ups and downs of the market.

The study also showed that if time pickers called 100% of the declining markets and only 50% of the rising markets, they still were not able to exceed the return of the overall market during this period. To add a final blow, there was no consideration for the high short-term capital gains taxes or transaction costs involved in this highly flawed strategy. No wonder 95% of market-timing newsletters go out of business.

There's more bad news for time pickers. For one thing, most of the gain achieved in a rising market is often concentrated at the beginning of its rise in highly concentrated surges. Because the markets go up on average, there are greater benefits to be in the rising markets than there are to avoid the falling markets. This additional tidbit is garnered from a New York University study completed in 1986. The study's clincher was that it found no evidence that time pickers could successfully time either the beginning of a rising market or the end of a falling market.

Another IFA study examined the 2,516 stock market trading days over ten years from 1997 through 2006. The data shows that during this period, the S&P 500 Index produced an annualized return of 8.4%. Therefore, a smart and prudent investor who invested $10,000 in the S&P 500 at the beginning of 1997, and stayed fully invested was handsomely rewarded with a $12,444 gain by the end of the 10 years.

However, if just 10 trading days with the largest gains were missed, the annualized return would have dropped from 8.4% to 3.4%. Instead of gaining by $12,444, the investor would have ended with only a $3,992 gain.

Active Investors' Only Hope

Figure 4-2

Out of these 2,516 Trading days, could you have found the 20 days that made up 100% of the returns?*

*According to data from Standard & Poors, for the ten-year period 1997-2006, the 20 days with the biggest gains acccounted for 100% of the total gain.

Table 4-1

The Real Problem with Market Timing: Missing the Big Days 10 Year Period (1997 - 2006)				
$10,000 Invested in the S&P 500 from 1997-2006	S&P 500 Annualized Return	Value at the End of the Period	Gain	Contribution of Missing Days
All 2,516 Trading Days	8.4%	$22,444	$12,444	0.0%
Less the 5 days with the biggest gains	5.7%	$17,360	$7,360	40.9%
Less the 10 days with the biggest gains	3.4%	$13,992	$3,992	67.9%
Less the 15 days with the biggest gains	1.4%	$11,546	$1,546	87.6%
Less the 20 days with the biggest gains	-0.4%	$9,640	$-360	102.9%

Source: Yahoo! Fiance

If the best 20 trading days were missed, which is less than 1% of the total number of trading days, the annualized return would have dropped to a minus 0.4%, yielding a loss of $360. Thus, more than 100% of the return would have been lost in just 20 days, or an average of 2 days per year (see Table 4-1 and Figure 4-2). A random walk of any of the world's markets is impossible to predict.

The odds against success in picking the right times are overwhelming, and the odds become worse over time with the high taxes and fees associated with frequent trading.

4.3.2 Academic Studies Prove that Time Picking doesn't Work

Studies fill literature confirming the failure of market timing. All these peer-reviewed research papers share the same conclusion—forget timing the market.

In the paper titled "Selectivity and Market Timing Performance of Fidelity Sector Mutual Funds," Wilfred Dellva, Andrea Demaskey and Colleen Smith concluded that there was negative timing ability among the Fidelity sector funds during the period from 1989 to 1998.

In 1998, Professors Connie Becker, Wayne Ferson, David Myers, and Michael Schill studied market timing in their paper titled "Conditional Market Timing with Benchmark Investors." The academics found no evidence supporting the claim that funds have significant market timing ability.

Professor Wei Jiang presented his market timing studies in his 2001 paper, "A Nonparametric Test of Market Timing." After spending countless hours combing through the results of 1,557 retail mutual funds and 210 institutional funds, Jiang concluded that timing ability on average is negative. Just as a side note, this paper lists 41 other academic studies in the reference section, providing further corroboration that market timing doesn't work.

Superstar academic William Goetzmann, along with Jonathan Ingersoll and Zoran Ivkovich, contributed their two cents with a paper titled "Monthly Measurement of Daily Timers." The professors performed four tests of timing skill on a sample of 558 mutual funds, and concluded that very few funds exhibit statistically significant timing skill.

In another paper written in 2002 by Professors Michael Johannes, Nicholas Polson and Jonathan Stroud market timing was once again put to the test. The simple yet powerful conclusion of this paper was that market timing strategies performed worse than the buy-and-hold strategy in all cases examined.

Meanwhile, to illustrate the extreme concentration of stock market returns, Professor H. Nejat Seyhun carefully analyzed the 7,802 trading days for the 30 years from 1963 to 1993. Seyhun is the chairman of finance at the University of Michigan School of Business Administration, a position that is only obtained by highly dedicated and intelligent individuals who have spent many years learning how capital markets work. His conclusion provides a crushing blow to timers who think they can outsmart the market. A mere 90 days over 30 years contained 95% of all the market gains. That is an average of three days per year.

The academic evidence described above overwhelmingly proves that time pickers cannot consistently know where the market is headed. The idea that time pickers can predict market movements is nothing more than a fairy tale.

4.3.3 Time Picking Gurus

Even though financial academics widely accept the concept of market efficiency, Wall Street firms continue to pander their market timing predictions through their appointed gurus. Their strategy is to encourage their clients to trade more, even though academics conclude that trading is hazardous to the client's wealth.

The pied pipers of Wall Street do not have a good batting average. No Babe Ruths there. Smartmoney.com has been tracking these pundits dating back to 1997. Table 4-2 summarizes

Table 4-2

Batting Averages of Time Pickers	
Market Pundits	**Batting Average**
Abby Joseph Cohen	0.128
Edward Kerschner	0.136
Jeffrey Applegate	0.147
Thomas Galvin	0.147
Edward Yardeni	0.152
Laszlo Birinyi	0.157
David Jones	0.164
Richard Bernstein	0.183
Bill Gross	0.189
Tobias Levkovich	0.200
Edward Hyman	0.236
Average of all 11 forecasters	**0.167**

Source: Smartmoney.com

some of their batting averages. You can see that Ed Hyman, who is considered one of the best economists, has the best batting average with a 0.236. That is the equivalent of hitting an average double each time at bat or in the scoring system, a call that may win plaudits for accuracy, but not for insight and strong feeling. For example, the forecaster made a correct, but obvious and wishy-washy call about the direction of interest rates. For those who scored lower, it generally means a true dud of a pick or a mostly inaccurate prediction that might have one redeeming feature but that likely fails the degree of difficulty and or confidence tests. A batting average of 0.400 would indicate an accurate forecast that was difficult to make but still uttered with the utmost confidence.

Here are the averages as reported by Smartmoney.com, where the average batting average for all 12 forecasters was somewhere between first and second base, 0.166. Since an accurate call would yield an average of 0.400, the most respected and well-known market forecaster falls on the side of inaccuracy about 60% of the time and accuracy about 40% of the time.

For further evidence of the heavy fog in crystal balls, let's take a look at results from 2003 and predictions about them. In that year, stock prices rose in almost every global market. Returns for U.S. small company stocks were particularly strong; the total return for the Russell 2000 Index was 47.25%, the highest annual return since inception of the index in 1979, according to Russell Analytic Service; and the total return for the CRSP 9-10 Micro Cap Index was in excess of 70%, the highest annual return since 1967, according to the Center for Research in Security Prices, University of Chicago.

However, investors seeking to capture market rates of return in 2003 would have had to ignore a large body of opinion, a sample of which appears below, suggesting that stocks were unattractive. Most of the quotations listed appeared during the first quarter of 2003 when stock prices were slumping and the outlook most uncertain. Year-to-date returns for the S&P 500 and Russell 2000 Indices did not turn positive until mid-April.

"It's going to be a difficult environment for stock investors. Don't count on the market to move up. To make money, you've got to select the right names." - Quotation attributed to David J. Winters. Source: Franklin Mutual Advisers LLC, "Brainwork from the Experts," *BusinessWeek,* December 30, 2002, p. 102. [From December 2002 to December 2006, the return of the S&P 500 was 62.46%, and for Index Portfolio (IP) 100 (see Appendix A) it was 145.54%.]

"I suspect that 2003 will end up being the fourth consecutive down year for the first time since 1932." - Quotation attributed to Jeremy Grantham of Grantham, Mayo, Van Otterloo & Co. Source: "Is the Bear Market over?" *Smart Money*, January 2003, p. 71. [From January 2003 to December 2006, the return of the S&P 500 was 72.62%, and IP 100 was 153.66%.]

"Many investors have become skeptics, inclined to sell and take profits when stocks rise, rather than buy in hopes of more gains." - Source: E.S. Browning, "Euphoric Burst, then it's Back to Usual Blahs," *The Wall Street Journal*, January 6, 2003, p. C1. [From January 2003 to December 2006, the return of the S&P 500 was 72.62%, and IP 100 was 121.91%.]

"War worries also are driving money back into Treasury bonds and even into the money market, despite the fact that both of those investments feature some of the lowest interest rates in years." - Source: E.S. Browning, "Stocks Drop, Wiping out January's Gains," *The Wall Street Journal*, January 23, 2003. [From February 2003 to December 2006, the return of the S&P 500 was 77.30%, and IP 100 was 158.81%.]

"I do not believe a long-term investor will make money in this market because it is a secular bear market." - Quotation attributed to Felix Zuelauf of Zuelauf Asset Management. Source: "On the Money — Roundtable Part II," *Barron's* (January 27, 2003). [From February 2003 to December 2006, the return of the S&P 500 was 77.30%, and IP 100 was 158.81%.]

"The fear is that it could be a long war and we could have a sustained sell-off because of it." - Quotation attributed to Tim Heekin of Thomas Weisel Partners. Source: "Fears of War with Iraq Send Blue Chips below 8000," *The Wall Street Journal*, January 28, 2003, p. C1. [From February 2003 to December 2006, the return of the S&P was 77.30%, and IP 100 was 158.81%.]

"According to a monthly survey by Merrill Lynch, global money managers are more risk-averse than at any time since the days following the terrorist attacks of September 2001." - Source: E. S. Browning, "Investment Pros Want No Part of Current Risk," *The Wall Street Journal*, February 24, 2003, p. C1 [From February 2003 to December 2006, the return of the S&P 500 was 77.30%, and IP 100 was 158.81%.]

"Soaring energy costs, the threat of terrorism, and a stagnant job market have sent consumers' spirits plunging to levels normally seen only in recessions. The Conference Board's index of consumer confidence fell to 64 in February, the lowest since 1993." - Source: Greg Ip, "Consumer Spirits Decline to Levels last Seen in '93," *The Wall Street Journal*, February 26, 2003, p. A3. [From February 2003 to December 2006, the return of the S&P 500 was 77.30%, and IP 100 was 158.81%.]

"Mr. Grantham's study of bubbles suggests that it takes them about as long to deflate as it did to inflate.... He says the Standard & Poor's 500-stock index could fall more than an additional 20% from its current level." - Quotation attributed to Jeremy Grantham of Grantham, Mayo, Van Otterloo & Co. Source: E.S. Browning, "A Party so Wild, the Cleanup Goes on," *The Wall Street Journal*, March 3, 2003, p. C1. [From March 2003 to December 2006, the return on the S&P 500 was 80.02%, and IP 100 was 164.36%.]

"U.S. moves toward war against Iraq sent nervous Asian stock markets to lows not seen in years, even decades, threatening an already shaky regional economy." - Source: Martin Fackler, "Nikkei Declines to Lowest Level in Two Decades," *The Wall Street Journal*, March 10, 2003, p. C14. [From March 2003 to December 2006, the return on the S&P 500 was 80.02%, and IP 100 was 164.36%.]

"Investors continue to sour on stocks. So far this year, investors have made net withdrawals of $11.3 billion from their stock mutual funds —

including a hefty $3.7 billion just last week — according to AMG Data Services. - Source: Gregory Zuckerman, "Investors Rush to Buy Bonds, Fleeing Stocks," *The Wall Street Journal*, March 11, 2003, p. C1. [From March 2003 to December 2006, the return of the S&P 500 was 80.02%, and IP 100 was 164.36%.]

"No rally may be enough to entice some investors back. 'I don't trust it anymore,' says Polly Sveda of the market, 'I never should have trusted it.' There is plenty of evidence that a growing number of individual investors are shunning stocks." - Source: Tom Petruno, "After the Fall," *Los Angeles Times*, March 16, 2003, p. C1. [From March 2003 to December 2006, the return of the S&P 500 was 80.02%, and IP 100 was 164.36%.]

"This quarter is shaping up to have the worst ratio of negative warnings to positive outlooks since the third quarter of 2001." - Source: Jesse Eisinger, Ahead of the Tape, *The Wall Street Journal*, March 31, 2003, p. C1. [From March 2003 to December 2006, the return of the S&P 500 was 80.02%, and IP 100 was 164.36%.]

"If we see 8% this year, that will be good." - Quotation attributed to Edgar Peters of PanAgora Asset Management. - Source: E.S. Browning, "Trading Ranges Keep the Bulls in." *The Wall Street Journal*, April 21, 2003. [From April 2003 to December 2006, the return on the S&P 500 was 78.29%, and IP 100 was 164.76%.]

"These stocks still are way ahead of themselves. I am not at all sure we have seen the bottom; I think we could see new, lower lows." - Quotation attributed to John Rutledge of Evergreen Investments. Source: E.S. Browning, "Experts Duel over Fate of Bellwether Rally," *The Wall Street Journal*, June 16, 2003, p. C1. [From June 2003 to December 2006, the return on the S&P 500 was 56.47%, and IP 100 was 121.91%.]

"Several important signals suggest that prices at best have topped out for the time being, and at worst are primed to move back down. Such signals 'are classic signs of a market top,' says Charles Biderman, president of market-research firm Trimtabs.com."- Source: Jeff Opdyke, "Four Signs Stocks May Be Near a Peak," *The Wall Street Journal*, June 26, 2003, p. D1. [From June 2003 to December 2006, the return on the S&P 500 was 56.47%, and IP 100 was 121.91%.]

"In our view, the quality of earnings of the S&P 500 from an accounting standpoint is the worst it has been in more than a decade." - Quotation attributed to David Bianco of UBS Financial Services. Source: Henny Sender, "At Earnings Halftime, Stocks Hear Mixed Messages," *The Wall Street Journal*, July 28, 2003, p. C1. [From July 2003 to December 2006, the return on the S&P 500 was 54.57%, and IP 100 was 114.82%.]

"Even some bears now acknowledge that, when they warned people to stay away from stocks one year ago they were wrong. But they insist that now, after the market's big gains, it is too late to buy." - Source: E.S. Browning, "Stocks are Defying the Critics," *The Wall Street Journal*, October 13, 2003, p. C1. [From October 2003 to December 2006, the return of the S&P 500 was 50.62%, and IP 100 was 94.93%.]

Figure 4-3

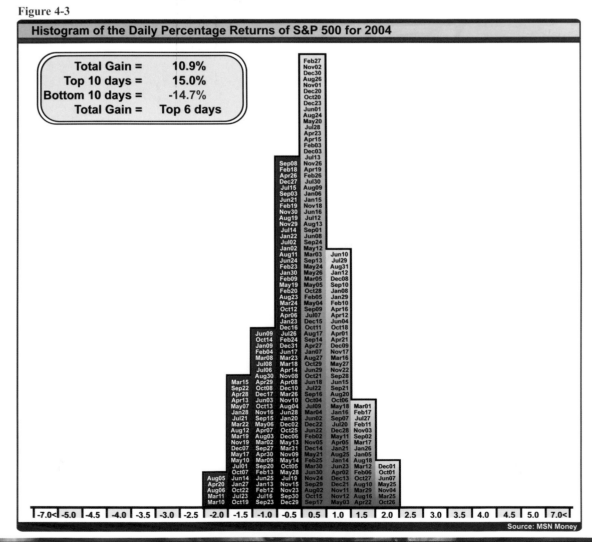

Figure 4-4

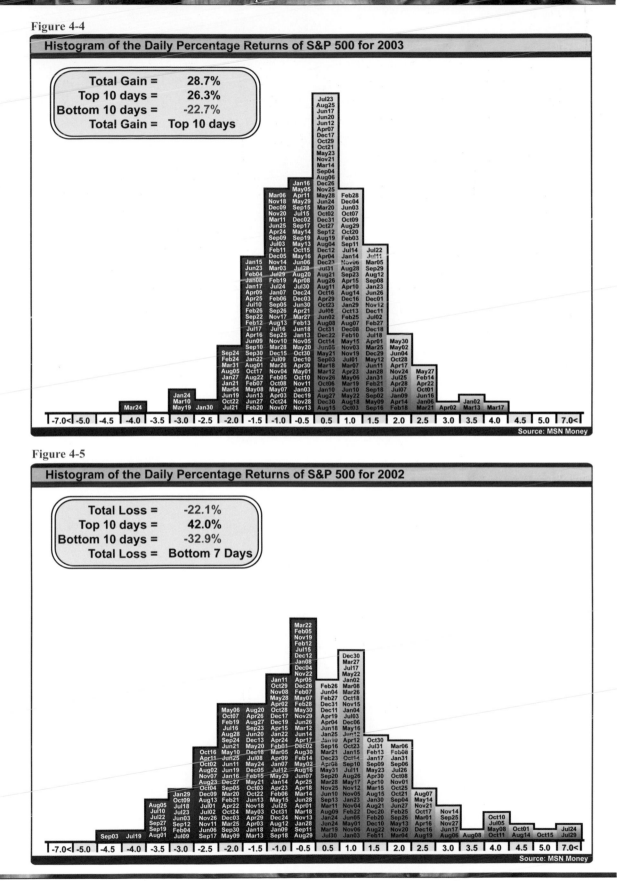

Figure 4-6

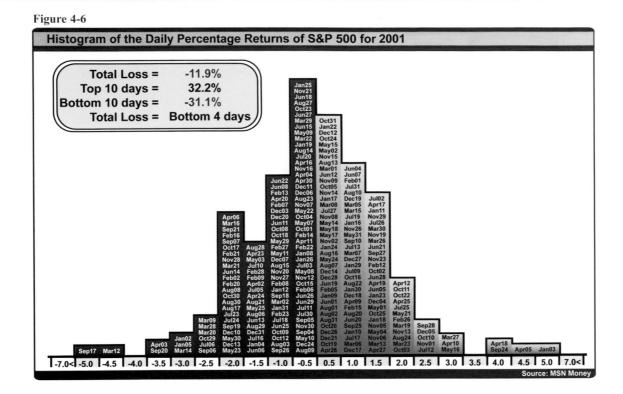

Histogram of the Daily Percentage Returns of S&P 500 for 2001

Total Loss =	-11.9%
Top 10 days =	32.2%
Bottom 10 days =	-31.1%
Total Loss =	Bottom 4 days

Figure 4-7

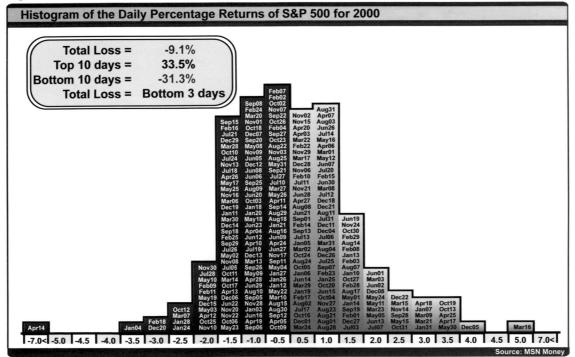

Histogram of the Daily Percentage Returns of S&P 500 for 2000

Total Loss =	-9.1%
Top 10 days =	33.5%
Bottom 10 days =	-31.3%
Total Loss =	Bottom 3 days

Figure 4-8

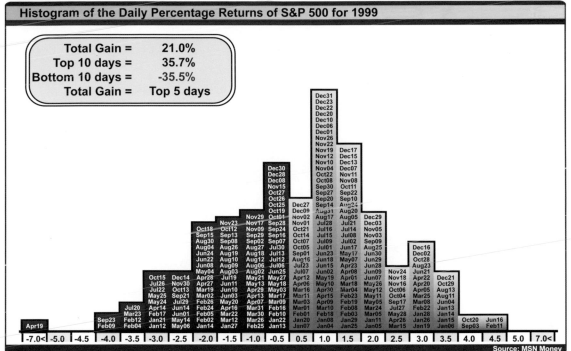

Histogram of the Daily Percentage Returns of S&P 500 for 1999

Total Gain =	21.0%
Top 10 days =	35.7%
Bottom 10 days =	-35.5%
Total Gain =	Top 5 days

Source: MSN Money

Figure 4-9

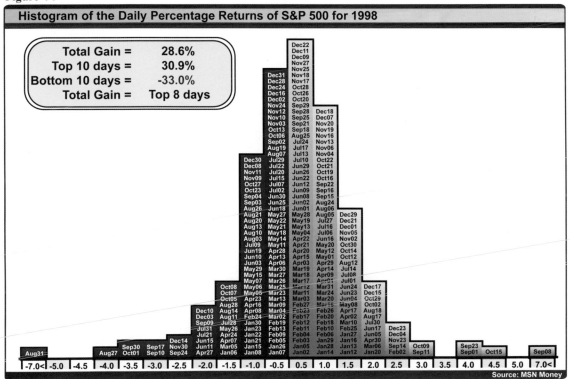

Histogram of the Daily Percentage Returns of S&P 500 for 1998

Total Gain =	28.6%
Top 10 days =	30.9%
Bottom 10 days =	-33.0%
Total Gain =	Top 8 days

Source: MSN Money

Figure 4-10

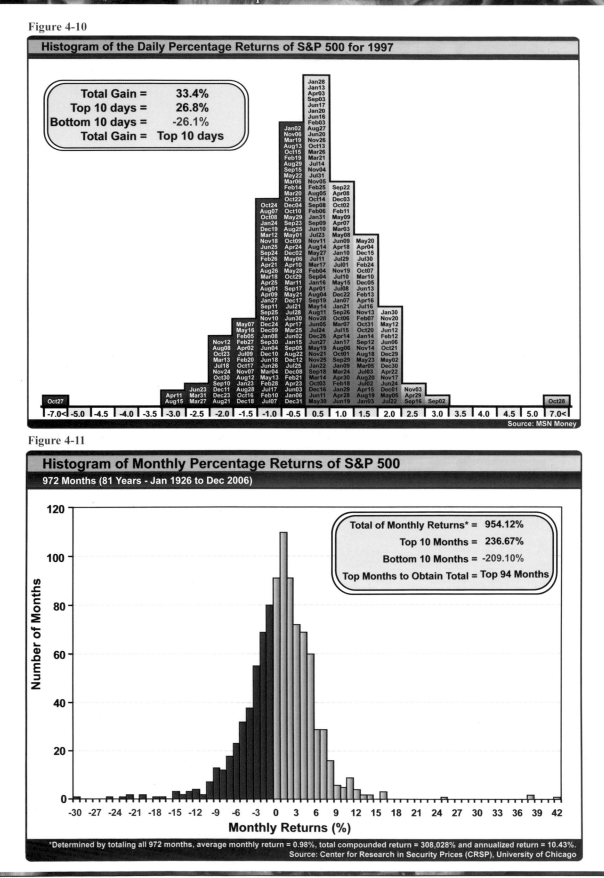

Figure 4-11

Figure 4-12

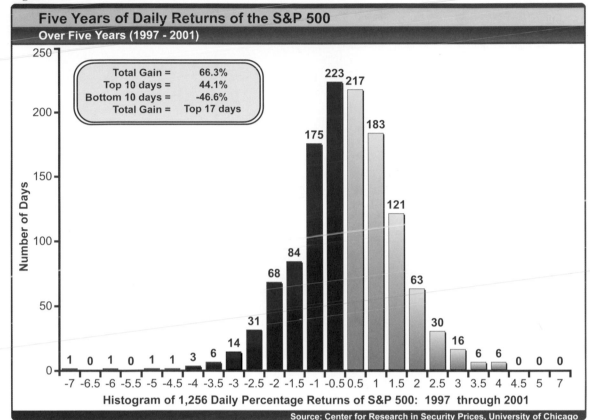

Five Years of Daily Returns of the S&P 500

Over Five Years (1997 - 2001)

Total Gain = 66.3%
Top 10 days = 44.1%
Bottom 10 days = -46.6%
Total Gain = Top 17 days

Histogram of 1,256 Daily Percentage Returns of S&P 500: 1997 through 2001

Source: Center for Research in Security Prices, University of Chicago

If the experts cannot get it right, then who can predict the direction of markets? Nobody.

4.3.4 Gains and Losses are Impossible to Identify in Advance

Figures 4-3 through 4-10 show the distribution of daily returns of the S&P 500 Index from 2004 back to 1997, obtained from the MSN Money Web site. The red days equal losses and the orange days equal gains. Note that every histogram is quite evenly distributed, which is to be expected from a random distribution. The display of a central distribution around the average is indicative of the randomness of the news that generates the random and unpredictable movements of the S&P 500 or any other index.

Figure 4-13

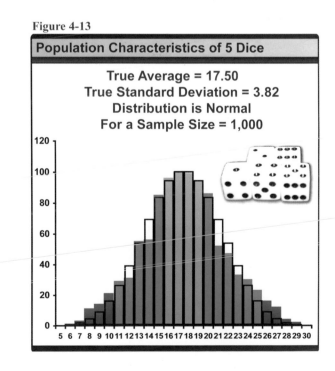

Population Characteristics of 5 Dice

True Average = 17.50
True Standard Deviation = 3.82
Distribution is Normal
For a Sample Size = 1,000

Based on these histograms, investors can see how difficult it is to find the randomly distributed days with gains or to avoid the days with losses. For each period, the large gains or major losses for the entire period are highly concentrated at the right and left tails, making it impossible to consistently identify them in advance. In other words, it is impossible for time pickers to consistently outperform the market.

Figure 4-11 shows the distribution of monthly returns of the S&P 500 for the 81years (972 months) from January 1926 through December 2006. Figure 4-12 is a histogram of 1,256 days of S&P 500 returns for the period 1997 through 2001.

The distribution of five dice being rolled is seen in Figure 4-13. The characteristics of the average and standard deviation of a five dice roll are not the same as the S&P 500, but the concept of a central distribution around the mean is similar, as defined by the Central Limit Theorem.

Whether you are looking at daily returns over one year, 972 monthly returns, 1,256 daily returns, or 1,000 rolls of five dice, the distributions all look like bell-shaped curves generated by random events. Such distributions are indicative of random variables, such as the news that moves the markets or a roll of the dice. In both situations it is impossible to predict the sequence of future outcomes. However, the average and range of outcomes (standard deviations) provide valuable information for both wise investors and casino statisticians.

4.3.5   Time Pickers Pay More Taxes

Time pickers usually charge clients an annual fee of 2% to 3% of the value of their investment portfolios. These timers are nothing more than highly paid gamblers who bet with your money.

Some investors who time markets invest in market timing mutual funds, which often produce high trading costs. This timing strategy also generates short-term taxable capital gains for existing fund shareholders due to the liquidation of fund stock positions needed to pay off departing shareholders. This assumes they make a gain, which is certainly not guaranteed. Investors can avoid cost-generating, tax-creating moves made by managers and shareholders of active mutual funds by remaining fully invested in index funds at all times, especially mutual fund companies that restrict their shareholders to those who understand how the market works. DFA is one firm that restricts access to their funds. Only large institutional investors and clients of pre-approved investment advisors are allowed to invest in their funds. You might call it a group of really smart investors.

When investors move in and out of investments, they also create the possibility of paying a huge portion of their gains in taxes. For short-term gains, taxes can exceed 40% in some states. Even when time pickers are lucky enough to win, taxes significantly reduce their return.

4.4   SOLUTION

Here's the bottom line: the right time to be in the market is when an investor has money, and the right time to get out of the market is when an investor needs the money. The longer an investor can stay invested, the better. The investor who stays fully invested throughout market swings is there to capture those five to 10 days per year that contain the entire return of the year. There is no reason to believe that professional market timers can correctly identify those few days in advance.

Even though a buy-and-hold investor most likely experiences losses about one out of every three years over the long run, the losses of these fewer "down" years are far outweighed by the gains of the more numerous "up" years. For the 80 years from 1927 to 2006, the S&P 500 has averaged an excellent annual compound return of 10.3% with a range of plus or minus 19% two-thirds of the years.

 4.5 SUMMARY

The goal of a time picker is to obtain upswings of the market and avoid downswings. In other words, the goal is to get return without risk. But, risk is the source of returns; therefore, investors must subject their capital to risk. How else would they expect to make a profit? It is only a question of how much risk is right for each investor.

Time picking is beneficial only to financial firms who make money trading shares and selling this useless advice. The firms that charge top dollar for this advice ironically end up with sub-market returns. Market strategists, even those considered successful, have eventually fallen out of the limelight. The industry has created a world in which complicated ratios and mathematical formulas are paraded in front of the unsuspecting public in hopes of impressing investors with superior knowledge and skills. This elevates the analysts in the public's eye and ultimately influences investors' decisions on which firm to choose to handle their investments. Those engaging in time picking are sure to underperform the market average over the long term.

The stock market has experienced a healthy upward climb in value over the long run, which is precisely what makes time picking unnecessary. The best way for an investor to capture these returns is to remain fully invested at all times, holding a globally diversified portfolio of index funds.

John Bogle

John Bogle notes, "In 30 years in this business, I do not know anybody who has done [market timing] successfully and consistently, nor anybody who knows anybody who has done it successfully and consistently. Indeed, my impression is that trying to do market timing is likely not only not to add value to your investment program, but to be counterproductive."

In the end, time pickers have two critical decisions to make: when to get in the market and when to get out. Data now conclusively shows that there is no reliable timing method to help make either decision. It is time, not timing, that determines an investor's return.

4.6 REVIEW QUESTIONS

1. What percentage of accuracy must a time picker maintain in order to be successful?

   a. 60%

   b. 40%

   c. 70%

   d. 30%

   e. 15%

2. Who was the only successful time picker ever recorded?

   a. John C. Bogle

   b. William F. Sharpe

   c. There are hundreds of successful time pickers.

   d. There are no successful time pickers.

   e. Harry Markowitz

3. The S&P 500 produced an annualized return of 8.4% in the 10-year period from 1997 through 2006. A $10,000 investment that stayed fully invested throughout the entire decade grew to $22,444. What would the end value be if an investor had missed the best 20 trading days?

   a. 12.6% return or $32,763

   b. 9.3% return or $24,333

   c. 6.5% return or $18,771

   d. 3.9% return or $14,661

   e. a minus 0.4% return or $9,640

4. The best lesson to learn from market timing pundits is:

   a. Time pickers have no way of predicting the market, and are therefore valueless.

   b. Be choosy when selecting time pickers and research their records thoroughly.

   c. Companies do not report their earnings on a timely basis.

   d. It is timing that determines an investor's return.

   e. The largest brokerage firms have the best stock market predictors.

5. When 32 market-timing newsletter recommendations were tracked over a period of 10 years, how many of them beat the average return of the market?

   a. 27

   b. 13

   c. 0

   d. 19

   e. 5

Step 5 ~ Manager Pickers

"I have become increasingly convinced that the past records of mutual fund managers are essentially worthless in predicting future success. The few examples of consistently superior performance occur no more frequently than can be expected by chance."

- Professor Burton G. Malkiel, *A Random Walk Down Wall Street*

"History shows that in the long run a thoughtfully designed, diversified strategy of 'passive' funds typically beats all but a few active managers. It's not easy to structure and maintain such a strategy. It requires some initial research and discipline to stay the course. But it's much easier than predicting which active managers will randomly beat this approach."

- Eugene Fama, Jr.

"Studies show either that most managers cannot outperform passive strategies, or that if there is a margin of superiority, it is small."

- Zvi Bodie, *Investments*

"By day we write about 'Six Funds to Buy NOW!'... By night, we invest in sensible index funds. Unfortunately, pro-index fund stories don't sell magazines."

- Anonymous *Fortune* magazine writer, *Fortune* Magazine, 4/26/99

"People exaggerate their own skills. They are overoptimistic about their prospects and overconfident about their guesses, including which [investment] managers to pick."

- Richard Thaler, *Investment Titans*, by Jonathan Burton

"Wall Street's favorite scam is pretending that luck is skill."

- Ron Ross, Ph.D. *The Unbeatable Market*

"Statisticians will tell you that you need twenty years worth of data - that's right, two full decades - to draw statistically meaningful conclusions [about mutual funds]. Anything less, they say, and you have little to hang your hat on. But here's the problem for fund investors. After twenty successful years of managing a mutual fund, most managers are ready to retire. In fact, only twenty-two U.S. stock funds have had the same manager on board for at least two decades - and I wouldn't call all the managers in that bunch skilled."

- Susan Dziubinski, Morningstar, Inc.

"All the time and effort people devote to picking the right fund, the hot hand, or the great manager have, in most cases, led to no advantage."

- Peter Lynch, *Beating the Street*

"Most depressing of all, the 'superstar' fund managers I encountered in the early 1990s had a disconcerting habit of fading from supernova to black hole: Rod Linafelter, ..., Richard Fontaine, John Hartwell, John Kaweske, Heiko Thieme. I soon realized that if you thought they were great, you had only to wait a year and look again: Now they were terrible."

- Jason Zweig, "I don't know, I don't care, Indexing lets you say those magic words." *CNNMoney.com*

"Yet even the smartest, most determined fund picker can't escape a host of nasty surprises. Next time you're tempted to buy anything other than an index fund, remember this — and think again."

- Robert Barker, "It's Tough to Find Fund Whizzes," *BusinessWeek.com*

"... skepticism about past returns is crucial. The truth is, as much as you may wish you could know which funds will be hot, you can't - and neither can the legions of advisers and publications that claim they can. That's why building a portfolio around index funds isn't really settling for average. It's just refusing to believe in magic."

- Bethany McLean, "The Skeptic's Guide to Mutual Funds," *Fortune*

5.1 INTRODUCTION

Step 5: Manager Pickers: Realize that the winning managers were just lucky.

Like stock and time picking, manager picking is a worthless endeavor; however, there are still investors out there who believe they can select an all-star manager or financial guru who can beat the odds. To be sure, there is no shortage of managers out there who are willing to try to beat the odds for their clients or mutual fund shareholders—for a hefty fee. Like all speculators, these managers do win occasionally, attracting lots of media attention and new clients. Truth be told, the majority of expenses and fees in the investment industry go toward money managers who gamble with other peoples' money. Investors would be wise to pose the following questions to their money managers:

1. Do you have skill or were you just lucky?

2. Were you the beneficiary of the market's random walk or did you really know tomorrow's news and how it would affect the investments you picked for your clients?

3. Will there be persistence in your performance?

4. Is a three to five-year time period long enough to judge your success?

5. Statisticians say we need 20 years of data to judge success. Have you ever managed a mutual fund for 20 years or more or do you know anyone who has?

So-called star money managers attract about 75% of new mutual fund investors. This is despite the fact that what are considered "today's top 10 mutual funds" often tank within three years.

Typically, investors first invest in a "star" fund run by a "star" manager when they read about the "latest and greatest funds." Then they sell their investments within a few years when they become disenchanted by the fund's shoddy performance. This trend supports the findings of the 2004 Dalbar study on investor behavior, which shows that investors hold mutual funds for an average of 4.2 years, buying at the highs and selling at the lows. This results in the average investor greatly underperforming a market.

Manager picking has become so popular among investors that an entire industry has sprung up to help identify future winners based on past performance. Media advertisements feature winning mutual fund managers boasting of their recent success. The performance histories of mutual funds regularly appear in such publications as *Barron's*, *BusinessWeek*, *Fortune*, *Money*, and *Consumer Reports*. Even highly sophisticated consultants retained by multi-billion dollar pension plans use recent fund performance as the most important criterion in selecting "the best" money managers.

But, as Figure 5-1 clearly shows, that top performance rarely repeats in following years. Only about 14% of the top 100 managers from the one-year periods repeated their top 100 performance in the second year. In 1999, only one of the top 100 managers made the list in 2000.

5.2 DEFINITION

5.2.1 Manager Ratings

Since more than 95% of mutual funds are actively managed, the various mutual fund ratings exist primarily for manager pickers. However, a recent review of these ratings show a wide variation in rating methods and results. For example, the

Figure 5-1

Top 100 Mutual Fund Managers That Remained in the Top 100 the Following Year
11 Years (1996-2006) Only an average of 14% of fund managers repeat their performance in the following year.

First Year (All of Top 100)　Second Year (Repeat Performance)

* The Morningstar universe of 23,148 funds was used in this analysis.　Source: Morningstar® Principia® January 2007

Table 5-1

Mutual Fund Manager Ratings				
	Mutual Funds Managers			
Publications:	Mutual Fund A	Mutual Fund B	Mutual Fund C	Mutual Fund D
Forbes (12/00)	C	A	A+	D
U.S.News & World Report (12/00)*	34	50	10	93
Wall Street Journal (1/01)	E	C	A	B
Business Week (1/01)	A	No Ranking	B+	C
* 100 is highest rating; 1 is lowest rating.				

same four funds were rated according to four different publications. Table 5-1 reveals the results.

On this table, funds A, B, C, and D are actual mutual funds. They are not identified because the purpose of this illustration is not to sell a particular security. It is to emphasize that ratings, in and of themselves, do not provide enough information for making an investment decision.

These systems measure criteria about managers that is about as useful as a tipster giving advice at the race track. To make matters worse, there are countless stockbrokers, money managers, hedge fund managers, investment advisors, private money managers, and newsletter publishers, who do not operate publicly traded mutual funds. They are not required to report the same detailed information that is required of mutual fund managers. These managers are often criticized for the smoke and mirrors they have created to mask their results.

Luckily, investors received a gift from the SEC that blew away some of the smoke. In 2001 the SEC adopted a rule that requires mutual funds to disclose after-tax returns in their prospectuses.

This requirement equipped investors with a more accurate report on returns.

The ruling also helped open the eyes of investors, especially those using actively managed funds in taxable accounts.

5.3 PROBLEMS

5.3.1 Past Performance is No Guarantee of Future Results

Unlike the 20-year characteristic of an index, the past performance of money managers has no bearing on their future performance. Every reputable study of mutual fund performance over the past 30 years has found there is no reliable way to know if past superior managers will win again in the future. This is why some variation of the disclaimer "past performance is no guarantee of future results" must appear in all mutual fund advertisements and prospectuses, even though the SEC allows it to be written in very small print.

Studies show that those who have outperformed some past benchmark are more likely to underperform it in the future. Burton Malkiel, author of the long-time investment best seller, *A Random Walk Down Wall Street*, conducted a study in 1995. In the study's conclusion, he states, "It does not appear that one can fashion a dependable strategy of generating excess returns based on a belief that long-run mutual fund returns are persistent."

Investment experts give several reasons why past performance is no guarantee of future results. The most frequently cited is that any outstanding track record turned in by a money manager is the result of the market favoring his particular investment style. One implication of this is that any such performance is entirely unpredictable—as is the time period that such good fortune may or may not last. Since market returns are correlated to risk factors (not to managers), there is no reason to expect that one manager will do better than another.

In addition, outstanding performance is often achieved when a mutual fund is small. This performance usually fuels an exponential growth in the amount of money that must be invested by the fund. The trading and other costs generated by the investment of this much larger amount of money can neutralize or even outweigh the margin by which a mutual fund manager may beat the market in the future.

These factors alone are all that is needed to prove that manager picking doesn't work and is not a good basis on which to invest money.

5.3.2 Persistence in Track Records

Once again you can see that manager picking is virtually impossible. As Bob Dylan said in the last verse of his tune, "The Times they are a Changin," "the first one now will later be last, for the times they are a changin'."

There happens to be one correlation between the past and the future, which seems to ring true for some mutual funds. Past poor performance tends to persist in the future, primarily because of the high costs charged by many funds. A 1996 study by Mark Carhart concluded, "Persistence in mutual fund performance does not reflect superior stock picking skill. Rather, common factors in stock returns and persistent differences in mutual fund expenses and transaction costs explain almost all of the predictability in mutual fund returns. While the popular press will no doubt continue to glamorize the best performing mutual fund managers, the mundane explana-

Pick Your Manager

tions of strategy and investment costs account for almost all of the important predictability in mutual fund returns."

Any predictability in performance has little to do with the stock picking skills of a specific mutual fund manager. A better way to determine which funds will do better over the long run is to find those that have captured the appropriate risk factors, are low cost, and generate minimal taxes. Index mutual funds fit these criteria very well.

An analysis of the Morningstar database of 800 domestic equity funds with 10 years of returns is shown in Figure 5-2. The top graph shows the rankings of 800 managers from best to

worst for the first five year period from 1991 to 1995, and then maintains the first period ranking for the subsequent five years, from 1996 to 2000, to see if manager performance persisted. It came as no surprise to the researchers that what appears to be a sorting of skilled and unskilled managers in the first period turns into randomness in the subsequent period. The second study shown in Figures 5-3 looks at another five-year period from 1995 to 1999. The second period of 2000 to 2004 also shows total randomness of manager performance. Figure 5-4 is a similar analysis, but for three-year periods and only 100 managers so the lines are more visible. As can be seen, there is no useful information in three-year returns either. Whether it is five-year or three-year track records, the conclusion is the same: managers' track records of returns are of no value to manager pickers.

An example showing how the performance of actively managed mutual funds can be the result of luck rather than skill is illustrated in Table 5-2. Data in the center column represent returns at the end of five-year periods from 1971 to 2000 for the top 30 mutual funds. Contrast those returns with the column to the right, which shows the performance of the same top 30 mutual funds in a subsequent period. The Table shows that the so-called "great 30 funds" did worse than the S&P 500 in subsequent years. If the performance were due to skill, one would expect returns that continued to beat the S&P 500 Index in the subsequent period, which was not the case.

An investment strategy that focuses on investing in index funds using an asset allocation

method does not require chasing the recent performance of a particular money manager or index because that index is already known to be a winner over the long term.

Seventy-five percent of mutual fund inflows typically follow the previous year's "winners," usually based on the Morningstar Rating for funds. As already stated, a Dalbar study concluded that the average investor holds a mutual fund for 4.2 years. The result of this short-term holding pattern is a phenomenon called "investor whipsaw."

Please look several pages forward for Tables 5-3 through 5-15. These tables provide an interesting analysis of managers' performance over time. They track the rankings of the top 10 mutual funds from one year into subsequent years. The total number of mutual funds for each year is listed at the bottom of each column. The managers are tracked up to 2006 to see how those

Figure 5-2

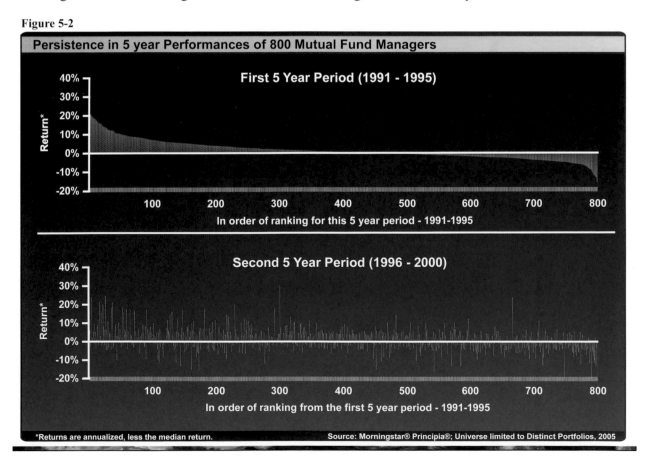

Figure 5-3

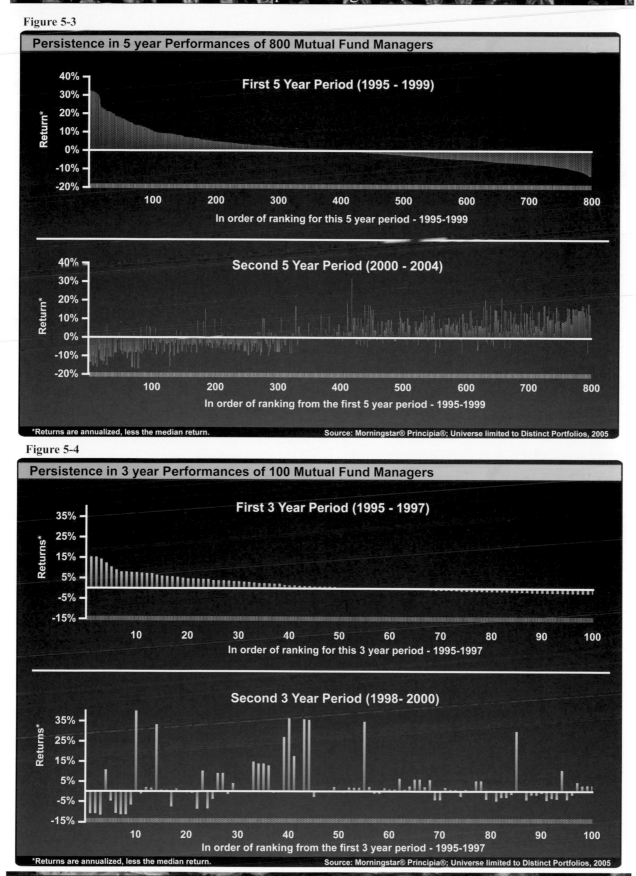

Persistence in 5 year Performances of 800 Mutual Fund Managers

First 5 Year Period (1995 - 1999)

In order of ranking for this 5 year period - 1995-1999

Second 5 Year Period (2000 - 2004)

In order of ranking from the first 5 year period - 1995-1999

*Returns are annualized, less the median return.   Source: Morningstar® Principia®; Universe limited to Distinct Portfolios, 2005

Figure 5-4

Persistence in 3 year Performances of 100 Mutual Fund Managers

First 3 Year Period (1995 - 1997)

In order of ranking for this 3 year period - 1995-1997

Second 3 Year Period (1998- 2000)

In order of ranking from the first 3 year period - 1995-1997

*Returns are annualized, less the median return.   Source: Morningstar® Principia®; Universe limited to Distinct Portfolios, 2005

Table 5-2

Subsequent Performance of Top 30 Mutual Funds		
Jan 1971 - Dec 2002		
	Annualized Return 1971-1975	Annualized Return 1976-2002
Top 30 funds 1971-1975	6.81%	13.21%
All Funds	1.31%	9.00%
S&P 500 Index	3.21%	12.54%
	Annualized Return 1976-1980	Annualized Return 1981-2002
Top 30 funds 1976-1980	34.33%	9.85%
All Funds	15.83%	7.74%
S&P 500 Index	13.95%	12.23%
	Annualized Return 1981-1985	Annualized Return 1986-2002
Top 30 funds 1981-1985	21.72%	9.71%
All Funds	10.93%	7.99%
S&P 500 Index	14.72%	11.50%
	Annualized Return 1986-1990	Annualized Return 1991-2002
Top 30 funds 1986-1990	14.91%	10.14%
All Funds	8.09%	8.89%
S&P 500 Index	13.16%	10.82%
	Annualized Return 1991-1995	Annualized Return 1996-2002
Top 30 funds 1991-1995	39.78%	2.05%
All Funds	16.27%	4.68%
S&P 500 Index	16.59%	6.88%
	Annualized Return 1996-2000	Annualized Return 2001-2002
Top 30 funds 1996-2000	30.97%	-22.83%
All Funds	15.23%	-17.21%
S&P 500 Index	18.34%	-17.15%
		Source: Morningstar® Principia®

Figure 5-5

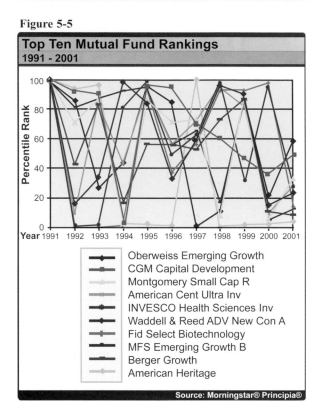

Top Ten Mutual Fund Rankings 1991 - 2001

- Oberweiss Emerging Growth
- CGM Capital Development
- Montgomery Small Cap R
- American Cent Ultra Inv
- INVESCO Health Sciences Inv
- Waddell & Reed ADV New Con A
- Fid Select Biotechnology
- MFS Emerging Growth B
- Berger Growth
- American Heritage

Source: Morningstar® Principia®

"great funds" from the first years did in subsequent periods. The results are similar, whether looking at all funds or one asset class. Tables 5-13 through 5-15 show the top ten managers of specific asset classes and their subsequent performance. As the tables show, those funds that were the winners in one year performed poorly in subsequent years. For the top ten managers from 1996 (Table 5-12), the highest ranked from that group fell to 4,695 out of 6,348 in 2006. And the number eight performer from 1996 came in at 5,330 out of 6,348, and was outperformed by 84% of his peers--quite a tumble indeed.

Figure 5-5 illustrates how investors can get whipsawed after buying a top fund. It lists the top 10 mutual funds in 1991, then tracks them by decile rankings through 2001. A 100th percentile rank means that those funds performed in the top one-hundredth of all funds that year. Note continued randomness of future percentile rankings. After wildly bouncing around, eight of the 10 funds ended up in the lower 50th percentile at the end of the 10 years. The other two landed in the lower 60th percentile. The long-term performance of each fund was neither consistently good nor consistently poor.

5.3.3 Sources of Information Used by Manager Pickers

Morningstar, *Forbes'* "Mutual Fund Honor Roll," and mutual fund advertisements are some of the most well-known sources of investment information used by manager pickers. Examining these sources shows why superior performance cannot be correlated to past superior performance; because the future cannot be predicted.

Table 5-3

2005 Top Ten Managers and Subsequent Performance			
Fund Name	**Manager Name**	**Annual Rankings**	
		2005	2006
ProFunds UltraJapan Inv	Petit/Banke/Joshi/Ames/Rubin/Croll	1	2,337
ING Russia A	Mignon/Derks/Oubadia	2	7
Fidelity Adv Korea A	Urquhart, David	3	2,813
Gartmore Global Nat Res A	Kotik/Gerlach	4	994
Guiness Atkinson Glb Eng	Guiness/Harris	5	6,273
T. Rowe Price Latin Amer	Pangaro, Gonzalo	6	15
T. Rowe Price Em EurMedi	Alderson, Christopher	7	156
Matthews Korea	Matthews/Headley/oh	8	2,610
BlackRock Glb Res Inv A	Rice III/Walsh III	9	4,695
iOhares SP Latin 40	Leung/O'Connor	10	53
Total Number of Mutual Funds:		**5,852**	**6,348**
Source: Morningstar® Principia®; Universe limited to "Distinct Portfolios" and Indexes, Jan. 2007 Disc			

Table 5-4

2004 Top Ten Managers and Subsequent Performance				
Fund Name	**Manager Name**	**Annual Rankings**		
		2004	2005	2006
iShares Austria Index	O'Connor/Chen	1	250	126
Pro Funds Ult Mobile Inv	Foster/Najarian/Neches/Fleites	2	1,402	6,250
Bruce Fund	Bruce/Bruce	3	2,062	1,399
Metzler/Payden EuroEmMkts	Brueck, Markus	4	75	28
US Global Inv East Euro	Bottcher/Wiles	5	54	206
Eastern European Equity	Faschang, Guenter	6	305	297
iShares Mexico Index	O'Connor/Chen	7	33	38
BlackRock Glb Res Inv A	Rice, III/Walsh, III	8	9	4,695
Morgan Stan Ins IntlR/E A	Paske/Kemenade/Ho/Bigman	9	560	12
Pro Funds Ultra Oil&Gas Iv	Foster/Najarian/Neches/Fleites	10	29	421
Total Number of Mutual Funds:		**5,492**	**5,852**	**6,348**
Source: Morningstar® Principia®; Universe limited to "Distinct Portfolios" and Indexes, Jan. 2007 Disc				

Table 5-5

2003 Top Ten Managers and Subsequent Performance					
Fund Name	**Manager Name**	**Annual Rankings**			
		2003	2004	2005	2006
Apex Mid Cap Growth	Bhirud, Suresh L.	1	5,444	5,848	5,690
ProFunds Sem UltSec Inv	Najarian/Neches/Hanson	2	5,491	1,190	6,333
ProFunds Int UltSec Inv	Najarian/Neches/Hanson	3	139	1,572	6,260
Reynolds	Reynolds, Frederick I	4	5,419	5,845	4,577
Eaton Vance Grtr India A	Mehta, Samir	5	975	35	104
iShares Brazil Index	Leung/O'Connor	6	72	18	37
Oberweis Micro-Cap	Oberweis, James W.	7	5,015	930	6,133
Schneider Small Cap Val	Schneider III, Arnie	8	219	1,466	884
iShares GS Network	Leung/O'Connor	9	2,745	4,526	5,767
ProFunds UltraOTC Inv	Petit/Benke/Joshi/Ames	10	1,414	5,741	4,588
Total Number of Mutual Funds:		**5,192**	**5,492**	**5,852**	**6,348**
Source: Morningstar® Principia®; Universe limited to "Distinct Portfolios" and Indexes, Jan. 2007 Disc					

Table 5-6

2002 Top Ten Managers and Subsequent Performance		Annual Rankings				
Fund Name	Manager Name	2002	2003	2004	2005	2006
First Eagle Gold A	Eveillard/de Vaulx	1	1,009	5,438	187	863
OCM Gold	Orrell, Greg	2	480	5,473	188	96
Van Eck Intl Gold A	Foster, Joseph M.	3	678	5,452	87	32
Gabelli Gold	Bryan, Caesar	4	441	5,465	109	222
US Global Inv Wld PrecMin	Management Team	5	20	5,292	138	14
Tocqueville Gold	Hathaway, John c.	6	312	5,443	144	61
US Global Inv Gold Shrs	Management Team	7	103	5,446	115	17
AmCent Global Gold Inv	Martin/Schniedwind/Sterling	8	555	5,453	154	435
Evergreen Prec Metals B	Gunn, Gilman C.	9	123	5,447	98	136
USAA Precious Metals&Min	Johnson, Mark W.	10	74	5,463	62	44
Total Number of Mutual Funds:		4,916	5,192	5,492	5,852	6,348

Source: Morningstar® Principia®; Universe limited to "Distinct Portfolios" and Indexes, Jan. 2007 Disc

Table 5-7

2001 Top Ten Managers and Subsequent Performance		Annual Rankings					
Fund Name	Manager Name	2001	2002	2003	2004	2005	2006
ING Russia A	Management Team	1	35	54	3,725	2	7
Matthews Korea	Matthew/Headley	2	856	1,683	386	8	2,610
Corbin Small-Cap Value	Corbin, David A.	3	2,642	424	1,989	1,223	1,509
Wasatch Micro Cap	Gardiner/Chace	4	3,134	112	2,084	197	2,075
CGM Focus	Heebner, G. Keeneth	5	2,906	336	1,217	2,074	1,852
Robeco Boston Part Sm Cp II Inv	Dabora/Rosenbluth	6	1,266	1,628	914	12	3,088
iShares S. Korea Indx	Leung/O'Connor	7	1,590	1,404	1,807	3,560	1,381
Aegis Value	Barbee, Scott .	8	1,436	1,344	1,302	1,010	1,042
Third Millenium Russia	Connor, John	9	33	62	667	21	122
Satuit Capital Micro Cap	Sullivan, Robert J.	10	2,667	154	719	708	2,480
Total Number of Mutual Funds:		4,605	4,916	5,192	5,492	5,852	6,348

Source: Morningstar® Principia®; Universe limited to "Distinct Portfolios" and Indexes, Jan. 2007 Disc

Table 5-8

2000 Top Ten Managers and Subsequent Performance		Annual Rankings						
Fund Name	Manager Name	2000	2001	2002	2003	2004	2005	2006
Evergreen Health Care A	McCormick, Walter T.	1	2,042	3,952	493	3,241	1,384	3,072
Manning & Napier Life Scn	Andreach/Donlon/Gambill	2	309	3,153	2,236	4,747	715	2,723
Munder Health Y	Wald/Rajogopal	3	4,013	4,743	459	2,076	2,020	6,240
BlackRock Glb Res Inv A	Rice, III/Walsh III	4	2,459	1,371	185	8	9	4,695
Allianz RCM Biotech D	Tsuboi/Dauchot	5	4,225	4,785	962	1,366	5,758	6,264
Eaton Vance Wld Health A	Isaly/Hsu/Borho/Klemm	6	2,810	4,219	2,053	3,549	2,021	6,215
ICON Energy	Waller, J.C.	7	2,512	1,906	1,750	32	46	3,539
JennDry Jenn Health A	Chan/Del Balso	8	2,333	4,605	810	154	233	3,951
Allianz RCM Health D	Dauchot, Michael	9	3,544	4,267	2,319	1,995	4,886	6,178
Fidelity Sel Natural Gas	McElligott, James	10	4,116	2,178	2,351	22	30	4,616
Total Number of Mutual Funds:		4,140	4,605	4,916	5,192	5,492	5,852	6,348

Source: Morningstar® Principia®; Universe limited to "Distinct Portfolios" and Indexes, Jan. 2007 Disc

Table 5-9

1999 Top Ten Managers and Subsequent Performance

Fund Name	Manager Name	Annual Rankings							
		1999	2000	2001	2002	2003	2004	2005	2006
Van Wagoner Emerging Gr	Van Wagoner, Garrett R.	1	3,826	4,598	4,911	532	5,482	5,847	3,182
Brown Advisory Opp Instl	Chew/Hathaway/Berrie	2	3,921	4,562	4,877	50	5,420	5,762	5,913
Credit Suisse Jpn Eq Comm	Tomiyama, Kunio	3	4,137	4,253	4,370	883	3,420	199	6,305
Old Mutual Col Cir TechZ	Rizza, Anthony	4	4,117	4,586	4,900	639	3,874	1,594	5,330
Fidelity Japan Small Co	Mizushita, Kenichi	5	4,126	3,942	1,603	177	483	49	6,341
ProFunds UltraOTC Inv	Petit/Benke/Joshi/Ames	6	4,138	4,601	4,914	10	1,414	5,741	4,588
BlackRock US Opps Inv A	Callan/Rosenbaum	7	3,137	3,586	4,767	535	978	719	1,309
Kinetics Internet	Stahl/Tuen/Boyle/Larsson	8	4,128	3,047	3,953	955	2,756	5,693	1,641
Firsthand Tech Value	Landis, Kevin M.	9	3,317	4,558	4,906	60	5,446	992	3,710
WF Adv Enterprise Inv	Slingerlend/Wilson	10	4,008	4,062	4,395	1,281	1,587	1,753	2,907
Total Number of Mutual Funds:		**3,837**	**4,140**	**4,605**	**4,916**	**5,192**	**5,492**	**5,852**	**6,348**

Source: Morningstar® Principia®; Universe limited to "Distinct Portfolios" and Indexes, Jan. 2007 Disc

Table 5-10

1998 Top Ten Managers and Subsequent Performance

Fund Name	Manager Name	Annual Rankings								
		1998	1999	2000	2001	2002	2003	2004	2005	2006
Kinetics Internet	Stahl/Tuen/Boyle	1	8	4,128	3,047	3,953	955	2,756	5,693	1,641
ProFunds UltraOTC Inv	Petit/Benke/Joshi/Ames	2	6	4,138	4,601	4,914	10	1,414	5,741	4,588
Fidelity Adv Korea A	Urquhart, David	3	50	4,135	23	1,504	2,242	993	3	2,813
Direxion NASDAQ Bull I	Smyth/King/Murray	4	62	4,124	4,554	4,689	203	2,510	5,649	4,474
Berkshire Focus	Fobes III, Malcolm R	5	41	3,632	4,604	4,909	106	4,515	553	5,253
Dreyfus Prem Tech Gr A	Herskovitz, Mark	6	25	3,980	4,493	4,782	354	5,369	3,575	5,761
Munder Internet A	Lebovitz/Woodley/Smith	7	20	4,132	4,577	4,854	96	1,677	1,903	6,186
Fidelity Sel Computers	Lawrence, Heather	8	218	4,018	4,322	4,823	156	5,417	4,263	3,584
Matthews Korea	Matthews/Headley/Oh	9	106	4,130	2	856	1,683	386	8	2,610
Rydex OTC Inv	Dellapa/Byrum/King	10	129	4,098	4,492	4,756	578	2,883	5,258	4,345
Total Number of Mutual Funds:		**3,472**	**3,837**	**4,140**	**4,605**	**4,916**	**5,192**	**5,492**	**5,852**	**6,348**

Source: Morningstar® Principia®; Universe limited to "Distinct Portfolios" and Indexes, Jan. 2007 Disc

Table 5-11

1997 Top Ten Managers and Subsequent Performance

Fund Name	Manager Name	Annual Rankings									
		1995	1996	1997	1998	1999	2000	2001	2002	2003	2004
American Heritage	Thieme, Heiko H.	1	3,471	3,835	4,028	4,593	2,447	2,367	83	5,849	6,325
Munder Micro-Cap Eqty A	Hollinshead	2	3,167	256	3,527	183	3,706	136	463	1,143	4,280
FMI Focus	Lane/Primack	3	160	458	256	2,007	3,751	490	3,489	3,004	2,664
ING Russia A	Mignon/Derks	4	3,472	24	3,722	315	35	54	3,725	1,976	7
ING Financial Services A	Kloss/Rayner	5	3,061	3,821	176	3,003	2,574	1,799	1,884	146	1,478
Fidelity Sel Brokerage	Taylor, Yolanda	6	2,369	895	175	3,716	3,064	1,334	1,923	685	870
Baron Partners	Baron, Ronald	7	1,287	1,265	2,222	75	3,223	1,512	19	5,686	836
FBR Small Cap Financial	Ellison, David	8	3,312	3,611	101	62	68	890	1,295	1,491	2,924
Alpine U.S. Real Est Y	Lieber, Samuel A.	9	3,382	3,817	280	2,820	1,488	37	25	6,231	1,851
Hartford Cap Apprec A	Catrickes/Pannell	10	2,845	318	1,731	2,820	3,870	934	970	598	1,851
Total Number of Mutual Funds:		**3,092**	**3,472**	**3,837**	**4,140**	**4,605**	**4,916**	**5,192**	**5,492**	**5,852**	**6,348**

Source: Morningstar® Principia®; Universe limited to "Distinct Portfolios" and Indexes, Jan. 2007 Disc

Table 5-12

1996 Top Ten Managers and Subsequent Performance

Fund Name	Manager Name	Annual Rankings										
		1996	1997	1998	1999	2000	2001	2002	2003	2004	2005	2006
BlackRock Glb Res Inv A	Rice, III/Walsh, III	1	2,763	3,469	1,560	4	2,459	1,371	185	8	9	4,695
GMO Emerging Ctry DbtIII	Nemerever/Cooper	2	354	3,438	857	249	232	62	1,349	803	525	2,103
Van Kampen Mid Cap Gr A	Lynch/Norton	3	613	555	399	2,761	3,922	4,142	2,572	593	380	3,704
Firsthand Tech Value	Landis, Kevin M.	4	2,659	539	14	3,317	4,558	4,906	60	5,448	992	3,710
First Amer Sm Cp Gr Opp Y	McDougal/McLeod	5	1,437	3,079	47	949	1,201	4,195	197	5,317	1,514	4,682
BlackRock Aurora Inv A	Archambo/O'Conner	6	24	3,323	816	68	194	3,420	429	1,518	4,099	2,669
Phoenix Emerging Mkt Bd A	Gagliardi/Marber	7	1,449	3,447	684	2,450	1,157	137	1,848	3,098	1,520	3,763
Old Mutual Col Cir TechZ	Rizza, Anthony	8	2,856	450	4	4,117	4,586	4,900	639	3,874	1,594	5,330
Phoenix Small-Cp Growth A	Lipsker/Holtz	9	667	1,058	199	3,554	4,404	4,545	481	3,230	1,477	4,569
Needham Growth	Kloppenburg	10	1,334	688	224	1,904	297	4,399	527	3,672	666	1,342
Total Number of Mutual Funds:		**2,749**	**3,092**	**3,472**	**3,837**	**4,140**	**4,605**	**4,916**	**5,192**	**5,492**	**5,852**	**6,348**

Source: Morningstar® Principia®; Universe limited to "Distinct Portfolios" and Indexes, Jan. 2007 Disc

Table 5-13

1996 Top Ten Large Growth Mutual Fund Managers and Subsequent Performance

Fund Name	Manager Name	Annual Rankings										
		1996	1997	1998	1999	2000	2001	2002	2003	2004	2005	2006
Rydex OTC Inv	Dellapa, Byrum	1	57	3	272	312	19	384	28	156	415	308
Morgan Stan Ins Foc Eq A	Norton, Cohen	2	193	223	200	159	254	253	151	270	6	423
Fidelity Ewp & Multinatl	Victor Thay	3	77	201	176	40	369	44	113	45	22	200
Buffalo USA Global	Dornitzer, Gasaway	4	37	247	157	14	327	179	66	263	299	63
Aston/Montag Growth N	Ronald Canakaris	5	193	121	65	112	292	94	405	382	263	214
AXA Ent Growth A	Ronald Canakaris	6	176	128	58	120	291	113	411	391	281	246
White Oak Select Growth	Oelschlager, Barton	7	84	52	215	31	8	388	265	432	460	469
Morgan St Ins US LgCpGr A	Lynch, Norton	8	154	211	169	158	261	223	409	233	13	403
W.P. Stewart & Co. Growth	John Mahler Jr.	9	92	111	10	64	296	28	9	11	260	274
Franklin Flex Cap Gr A	Herman, Moberg	10	21	241	266	107	121	164	40	51	226	331
Total Nember of Mutual Funds:		**198**	**219**	**255**	**279**	**316**	**376**	**397**	**414**	**433**	**463**	**499**

Source: Morningstar® Principia®; Universe limited to "Distinct Portfolios" and Indexes based on Morningstar Category of Large Growth, Jan. 2007 Disc

Table 5-14

1996 Top Ten Small Value Mutual Fund Managers and Subsequent Performance

Fund Name	Manager Name	Annual Rankings										
		1996	1997	1998	1999	2000	2001	2002	2003	2004	2005	2006
FPA Capital	Rodriguez, Robert	1	40	11	18	73	4	18	71	106	3	133
Evergreen Special Val A	Tringas, James M.	2	25	14	28	45	34	30	88	66	19	21
Morgan Stan InsUSSmVallns	Yaggy/Glass	3	19	12	9	66	79	71	70	65	34	3
Heartland Value Plus	Nasgovitz/Hathaway	4	20	40	40	74	5	17	18	91	106	96
Longleaf Partners Sm-Cap	Hawkins/Cates	5	26	1	36	50	73	16	37	99	18	12
Skyline Spec Equities	Fiedler/Odegard	6	6	34	70	17	50	32	57	93	16	58
Mainstay Small Cap Opp I	Samoilovich	7	10	5	38	75	51	15	16	11	13	106
DWS Dreman Sm Val A	Woodward/Roach	8	39	42	44	72	48	49	47	16	21	6
CornerCap Small Cap Val	Quinn/Bean	9	13	39	39	54	18	56	43	98	117	113
Allianz NFJ Sm Cap Val I	Magnuson/Mckinney	10	8	38	60	29	31	3	95	27	17	53
Total Number of Mutual Funds:		**35**	**41**	**47**	**70**	**75**	**81**	**87**	**101**	**110**	**124**	**135**

Source: Morningstar® Principia®; Universe limited to "Distinct Portfolios" and Indexes based on Morningstar Category of Small Value, Jan. 2007 Disc

Table 5-15

1996 Top Ten Large Value Mutual Fund Managers and Subsequent Performance												
Fund Name	**Manager Name**	**Annual Rankings**										
		1996	**1997**	**1998**	**1999**	**2000**	**2001**	**2002**	**2003**	**2004**	**2005**	**2006**
Dreyfus Prem Strat Val A	Ferguson, Brian	1	159	117	73	25	131	285	9	45	94	111
Sound Shore	Burn III/DeGulis	2	5	161	156	31	99	103	79	95	135	284
Legg Mason P Inv Val A	McAllister/Feitler	3	122	53	46	60	156	227	83	266	166	239
Ivy Value A	Norris, Matthew T.	4	161	169	157	215	231	108	202	143	266	297
Primary Trend	Arnold/Gust	5	169	180	179	24	69	44	203	316	336	266
Muhlenkamp	Muhlenkamp	6	15	164	47	12	16	198	4	2	107	386
First Amer Lg Cap Val A	Earley/Mellum	7	157	123	76	202	207	215	248	186	128	207
DWS Dreman HiRetEqA	Hutchinson/Dreman	8	28	89	208	3	79	167	90	167	110	252
T. Rowe Price Value	Linehan, John	9	64	146	64	55	73	129	115	93	160	120
WF Adv US Val Z	Costomiris, Robert	10	35	12	27	211	239	136	111	147	328	172
Total Number of Mutual Funds:		**158**	**173**	**190**	**210**	**231**	**262**	**294**	**310**	**333**	**355**	**387**
Source: Morningstar® Principia®; Universe limited to "Distinct Portfolios" and Indexes based on Morningstar Category of Large Value, Jan. 2007 Disc												

Is a Highly Rated Fund a Good Thing?

Morningstar, a well-known independent investment research firm, is one of the many sources of information used by manager pickers. Mutual funds are currently assigned stars based on three, five and 10-year performances, risks and fees. When available, the 10-year performance has a 50% weighting, while the three year has a 30% and the two year has a 20% weight. While the long-term overall star rating formula seems to give the most weight to the 10-year period, the most recent three-year period actually has the greatest impact because it is included in all three rating periods. Morningstar holds that the star ratings are designed to be a starting point for investors and that the ratings themselves are not predictive of future performance. Its goal is to help the individual investor make better decisions. Nonetheless, since they are commonly contained in mutual fund advertisements, it is my belief that many investors look to the stars as a guide.

In a July 15, 2003 report on investor behavior, Dalbar stated that, "Motivated by fear and greed, investors pour money into equity funds on market upswings and are quick to sell on downturns. Most investors are unable to profitably time the market and are left with equity fund returns lower than inflation." The report goes on to state that the average holding period for equity mutual funds was a little more than two years. The average manager picker is not grasping the concept that past performance has nothing to do with future performance.

An April 5, 2005 report by John Waggoner, of USATODAY.com, illustrates the problem Dalbar has identified. Waggoner tracked the asset flows into the then highly rated Fidelity Aggressive Growth Fund, which had $23 billion in assets in March 2000. Investors poured 65% of those assets, $15.1 billion, into the fund the 12 months before the S&P 500 peaked in March of 2000. So, a $10,000 investment back in March 2000 would be worth $2,697 in April 2005—that's a 73% loss.

Other once hot funds that have subsequently performed badly include Janus Worldwide, once a $13-billion fund that fell 45% over the five years; Nasdaq 100 Trust, once a $10- billion fund that has fell 67%, and Janus Global Technology, a $10-billion fund in March 2000 that plummeted 73%.

In total, investors put $228 billion into the 50 best-selling stock funds in the 12 months before the market peaked, yet only two of the top 50 funds had a gain over the next five years: American Funds New Perspectives, up 2.3%, and Vanguard Capital Opportunity, up 1.5%. In total, the active investors who plowed money into the 50 hottest-selling funds in March 2000 are down an average 42%, by March 2005, according to Lipper Analytical Services, a well-known mutual fund data firm. (Further details of this active investor madness are recounted in the book *American Sucker*, by David Denby.)

Another example of the difficulty of picking a winning fund manager is found in "Selling the Future: Concerns About the Misuse of Mutual Fund Ratings," a May 16, 1994 study conducted by Lipper Analytical Services, a well-known mutual fund data firm. In the study, Lipper selected highly rated mutual funds from Morningstar at the beginning of a year and then measured their performances in the following 12 months against mutual fund averages. This study was conducted in four subsequent one-year periods: 1990, 1991, 1992, and 1993. The study found that the majority of highly rated stock mutual funds underperformed mutual fund averages in each of the four subsequent years. This means that investors who select mutual funds from the list of highly rated funds can often end up in the wrong mutual funds at the wrong time. This not only demonstrates the unreliability of investing based on past performance over a period as short as one year, it also shows how consistently unpredictable mutual funds can be in outperforming the market. The results of the Lipper study are depicted in Table 5-16.

The study also found that at the end of 1990, after a long period of superior performance by foreign-oriented mutual funds, only 32% (25 out of 77) of the total number of highly rated stock funds were listed in the "international" and "global" fund categories. Predictably, many investors jumped into these funds, believing that their past superior performance would be repeated in the future. Not surprisingly, every one of these 25 international and global funds subse-

Table 5-16

The Percentage of Morningstar's Five-Star Stock Mutual Funds Subsequently Underperforming Stock Mutual Fund Averages		
Beginning Year	**Subsequent Year**	**Percentage Subsequently Underperforming**
1990	1991	52.6
1991	1992	71.1
1992	1993	56.0
1993	1994	63.6
		Source: Lipper Analytical Services, Inc.

quently underperformed the average stock fund in the following 12 months. At the end of 1992, after foreign-oriented mutual funds performed poorly for a year, no international or global funds appeared on a highly rated funds' list. Few investors were attracted to these international and global funds because they were at the bottom of the pile. The result: investors missed the superior performance of international and global mutual funds that began at the end of 1992.

Morningstar, for its part, released a new star-rating system in July of 2002. The old system compared the historic risk and returns from a mutual fund with the risk and returns of a broad group of funds. The new star system attempts to compare a fund with a much smaller group of funds of a similar style. According to a March 2004 paper published in *The Journal of Financial Planning* by William Reichenstein, Ph.D., Morningstar's decision to change rating systems reflects a decade of studies on the importance of investment style in explaining stock returns. As discussed several times in this book, a Fama and French study in 1992 concluded that stock returns vary systematically across two dimensions: size and value-growth. Actually, Fama and French came to this conclusion after completing two different studies. First, the researchers focused on returns from a period from 1963 to 1990. In a later study they conducted along with their colleague Jim Davis, the researchers looked at returns from a longer period—1929 to 1997. The researchers discovered that stock returns can best be explained when stocks are separated into portfolios based on size as measured by market capitalization and value-growth as measured by book/market ratios. Many studies over the past decade have confirmed and reinforced Fama and French's conclusion that returns vary systematically across size and value-growth dimensions. This type of fund analysis was pioneered by Dimensional Fund Advisors (DFA), where Fama is the director of research. Fama also has written extensively on the random walk and efficient market theories and is one of the world's most cited economists. DFA uses a Fama/French designed factor regression analysis to show that active managers' returns are attributable not to skill, but to exposure to these risk factors. Consistent with the Fama and French research, DFA offers no actively managed funds, but has a complete assortment of passively managed index funds.

The *Forbes* Mutual Fund Honor Roll

The *Forbes* Mutual Fund Honor Roll is hailed by the media as a dependable way to find superior performing mutual funds. Each year since 1973, the highly respected *Forbes* magazine has singled out 15 to 30 stock mutual funds and elevated them to *Forbes* Honor Roll status. These funds are selected on the basis of their total returns over at least a 10-year period, the stability of their investment management over at least seven years, and their relative performance in both bull markets and bear markets over several market cycles.

A comprehensive 1992 study by John Bogle titled "Selecting Equity Mutual Funds" examined the record of the *Forbes* Honor Roll covering the period of 1974 to 1990. The study sought to answer two questions: (1) did Honor Roll mutual funds continue to beat comparable non-Honor Roll funds in subsequent years during the 1974 to 1990 time period and (2) did Honor Roll funds continue to beat the market in the ensuing years during this time period?

To answer the first question, the study found that there was a virtual tie in performance between the Honor Roll funds and the average stock mutual fund in subsequent years during this time period. To answer the second question, the study found that after commission loads were taken into account, the Honor Roll funds subsequently underperformed the market by a significant amount over the 1974 to 1990 period. The cumulative returns of the Honor Roll funds was 439.7% and the cumulative return of the market was 633.4%. That's a difference of 193.7%.

The study found that mutual fund winners from the past significantly underperformed the market in the future for several reasons. For one thing, the superior performance generated by an active fund manager's investment style is dependent on the time period in which the market favors that style. Since the stock market unpredictably favors different investment styles for different time periods, a manager's past superior performance is closely tied to a past time period in which the market happened to favor his or her kind of investment style.

A good example of the link between superior performance and a certain time period is found in the 1983 *Forbes* Honor Roll. In that year it contained a large number of small company stock mutual funds because small company stocks had generally outperformed large company stocks over the previous six or seven years. In the following years beginning in 1984, small company stocks began a dismal run in performance relative to large company stocks. As a result, small company stock funds began to drop out of the Honor Roll after 1983. Although the small company stock funds in the 1983 Honor Roll had outstanding performance histories, their returns in 1984 and in the following years were inferior on average to the market and to the average stock mutual fund.

The *Forbes* Honor Roll study reached two conclusions: (1) investors can't pick a future winning mutual fund based on its past performance and (2) over the long run, even highly rated active funds underperform their respective benchmark.

Mutual Fund Advertisements

Mutual fund advertisements are another source investors turn to when manager picking. Unfortunately, they convey this false message: "Since these funds have done well in the past, they will do well in the future, so buy them today."

Mutual fund advertisements carry an SEC mandated disclaimer stating: "Past performance is no guarantee of future results." There is a reason why the SEC requires this—it's true! According to Dalbar it appears that many investors act as if this disclaimer is not true at all. They continue to buy and sell mutual funds based on short-term past performance falling for the implied message of mutual fund advertising.

5.3.4 Markets Make Managers

There is one other point regarding the futility of attempting to identify skillful money managers. An old investment proverb observes that "markets make managers." This means that if the market favors a money manager's particular investment style anyone can achieve outstanding performance.

Markets can make a money manager look good or bad—a factor that's independent of their "skillful" stock picking or market-timing abilities. An active money manager that an investor selects will usually turn out to be a winning or a losing manager because of the behavior of the market itself, rather than the manager's skill at picking stocks or timing markets. Active money managers play a game that's almost entirely random in conferring long-term investment success among them.

5.3.5 Irrelevant Benchmarks

There are at least three other problems associated with manager picking. For one thing, investors are seldom aware that active funds or separate portfolios that have good performance histories are always riskier than the indexes they outperform. According to the Modern Portfolio Theory, any portfolio of investments that hold fewer stocks than the index in which it is invested must be, by definition, underdiversified relative to that index portfolio. It follows then that any mutual fund or separate portfolio that has turned in a market-beating performance achieved it by holding investments that somehow were different in kind or amount from those of the relevant index. Any mutual fund or separate portfolio that boasts a superior performance history must therefore be riskier.

A mutual fund manager with recent performance success has bet money and concentrated it in specific stocks or bonds. The bet may pay off, but people are too blinded by the "brilliant investment insight" to understand that the bet was too risky in the first place. Peter Lynch, the legendary manager of Fidelity's Magellan mutual fund, concentrated about 25% of the fund's holdings in foreign stocks in the 1980s. These stocks turned out to be top performers, and Magellan widely outpaced the S&P 500. The irony is that these stocks weren't even represented in the S&P 500.

Lynch's performance was not measured against an appropriate benchmark comprised of a proportionately weighted mix of U.S. and foreign stocks. It was measured against the wrong benchmark, the S&P 500. Using an appropriate benchmark would have reduced, perhaps even eliminated, his successful performance during this period. Lynch's bet was nevertheless deemed a winner by popular acclaim, and he was widely hailed as the leading investment guru of the decade.

Had Lynch's bet turned out wrong and Magellan underperformed, Lynch would have been widely criticized as a fool for making such a risky bet. Right or wrong, it was still a risky bet because Magellan had a greater amount of diversifiable risk than was represented in the benchmark by which it was measured.

There are two lessons to be learned from this. First, any active investment strategy is inherently risky, but is not considered risky in hindsight if it turns out to be a winner. Second, a mutual fund's outstanding performance history is nothing more than the market's reward for exposure to excessive investment risk. Due to the unpredictable nature of the market, the same excessive risk that produces outstanding performance today can turn and produce miserable performance in the future. Once the market begins to favor sectors other than those a manager is invested in, his or her luck has run out.

Yet another problem with manager picking is that outstanding performance histories can be surprisingly fragile. Few investors realize that the most important factor separating a winning performance history from a losing one is the choice of starting and ending dates. Fidelity's

Magellan beat the S&P 500 for the decade ending in mid-1995. Lengthening the ending date by one year to mid-1996 would have painted a very different picture. Fidelity's Magellan underperformed the S&P 500 for that 11-year period.

Lastly, outstanding performance histories don't always reflect taxes or commission loads. Published mutual fund ratings are often pre-tax returns that disguise their true after-tax performance in taxable accounts. Fidelity's Magellan generated an average annual pre-tax return of 18.3% over the 10-year period from mid-1985 to mid-1995. Once the taxes and commission loads were factored in, the net return dropped to 12.7%. At first glance, this fund appeared to widely outperform the market. A closer look reveals that Fidelity's Magellan came very close to underperforming it. However, an investor may never know this because mutual fund advertisements often feature only pre-tax and/or pre-commission load returns. Tax-adjusted returns are now available from Morningstar on the Internet at www.morningstar.com. Morningstar's tax-adjusted returns only account for federal income taxes, but not state income taxes. Investors should also consider that state income taxes need to be deducted in order to see a complete picture of how all taxes impact investment performance, especially relative to a tax-efficient index fund.

5.4 SOLUTION

The solution for manager pickers is to stop being fooled by randomness, stop believing in Santa Claus, and give up the hope that a fund manager can be selected in advance to consistently beat a market in the future.

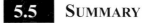

5.5 SUMMARY

Statisticians have stated their case saying they need at least 20 years worth of risk and return data to establish skill in a manager. The real problem is choosing those managers at the beginning of the period. Therefore, index funds are a far better choice for investors because of their nearly 80-year track records.

5.6 REVIEW QUESTIONS

1. Statisticians tell you that you need a minimum number of years of performance data on mutual funds to draw conclusions about future risks and returns. How many years are required?

    a. 1 year
    b. 5 years
    c. 10 years
    d. 20 years

2. The problem with picking a manager to beat the appropriate index is that:

    a. they can't pick next year's winning stocks
    b. they can't pick the best time to be in or out of the market
    c. they can't determine which style of investing is the best
    d. there is no persistence in manager performance
    e. all of the above

3. A Dalbar study found manager pickers changed their managers every:

    a. 7 months
    b. 5.3 years
    c. 2.6 years
    d. 15.5 years

4. There are overlooked factors when investors review the past performance of managers. They include:

    a. improper benchmarks
    b. after-tax returns in taxable accounts
    c. exact same time periods
    d. commission charged on the purchase of the fund
    e. all of the above

5. According to the mutual fund tracking service, Lipper, the top 50 hottest selling mutual funds in March 2000 were reviewed again in March 2005. On average, the top 50 funds had a total change in value of:

    a. up 83%
    b. down 42%
    c. up 5%
    d. down 10%
    e. up 22%

Step 6 ~ Style Drifters

"Style drift is a serious problem for [investors] because it distorts asset allocation and undermines performance when styles rotate. Value managers who have drifted over the past three years [1998-2000] toward more favored growth stocks are regretting those moves, but not as much as their [investors]."

- Ron Surz, President, PPCA Inc., *Get the Drift*, 2001

"If a fund is drifting to a style that is dramatically different, your potential returns, volatility, and risk are going to change."

- Rosanne Pane, Director, S&P Fund Services Group, "Spotting Style Creep, When a fund starts to wander, returns can suffer," *BusinessWeek Online*

"One thing is clear. Style drift happens to a sizable percentage of mutual funds...For [investors or] planners seeking to create portfolios tapping into consistently different equity styles, style drift presents a significant concern."

- Craig L. Israelsen, PhD, "Drift Happens," *Financial Planning Interactive*

"The SEC deems it a fraud if performance results are compared to an inappropriate index, without disclosing the material differences between the index and the accounts under management."

- Robert J. Zutz, *Compliance Review*, Schwab Institutional

"But beyond asset allocation, style drift also may have an effect on a fund's returns. Recent studies, including a 2001 study by Keith Brown and W.V. Harlow, have found that funds that are consistent in their investment style produce better returns that those with style drift. Style-consistent funds also have lower portfolio turnover, which means lower costs."

- Stephen Schurr, Senior Editor, TheStreet.com, *The Case for Index Funds*, 4/10/2003

6.1 INTRODUCTION

Step 6: Comprehend active management style drift.

Style drift happens when an active manager drifts from a specific style, asset class or index that is described as the investment purpose of a portfolio or mutual fund. For example, a manager may drift from small-cap value to small-cap growth. This is a substantial problem if you have carefully determined your risk capacity and matched it to a risk exposure.

Mutual fund managers are pushed to outperform other fund managers and their proper benchmarks. The temptation to dabble outside the scope of their fund's stated style in order to enhance the fund's performance sets all actively managed funds adrift.

To avoid style drift, it is best to implement your asset allocation with "pure style" index funds. Index funds are invested using clearly defined rules of ownership. Forty percent of the time, actively managed funds follow a manager's drift to a market the manager thinks will keep his shareholders happy and save his own hide. Unfortunately, the shareholders suffer in the long run. As we have seen in previous steps, this predicting or chasing of returns has resulted in "below market" performance.

6.2 DEFINITIONS

6.2.1 Investment Style

Investment professionals and academics use many terms to define risk including markets, benchmarks, asset classes, styles, style boxes, investment objectives, risk factors, market dimensions, market segments, buckets of stocks, rules of ownership, slices of the market, industry classifications, and indexes such as Dow Jones Indexes, Standard & Poor's Indexes, Russell Indexes, Wilshire Indexes, Morgan Stanley Capital Indexes, the Wired Index, and many more. Style, just one of many terms used, is simply a classification of an investment's risk characteristics.

Stocks of a particular style generally share long-term risk, return, and correlation characteristics. This helps investors and financial planners decide how to allocate their assets. An equity fund's style refers to the types of stocks the fund holds.

Active mutual fund managers define their own investment style, which guides them in picking individual stocks. For example, a fund manager may manage a growth fund that reflects a style preference of growth stocks.

The problem with investment style is that it is not consistently defined within the industry. Terms such as large, small, value, and growth have a wide range of definitions. This lack of specificity makes it difficult for investors to measure their risks and rewards, and easier for active managers to claim market-beating returns over a nebulous benchmark.

A growth style includes stocks that are experiencing rapid growth in earnings, sales or return on equity. Growth stocks tend to carry low book-to-market ratios, high price earnings ratios, and usually offer no dividend yields. Growth stocks are priced much higher than their book values, indicating that a large portion of the purchase price goes to goodwill. Goodwill is basically the difference between the price and the book value. Growth is somewhat of a misnomer. The price paid for goodwill is often deflated by the news of lower than expected earnings growth of a company. Growth stocks are expected to under perform value stocks and the total market.

A value style includes stocks that tend to carry high book-to-market ratios, low price earnings ratios, high dividend yields, and is often described as being in distress. It is perceived by investors to be of higher risk. But, investors need to remember that higher risk equates to higher expected return. The shareholders of value stocks have a high cost of capital, which equates to a higher expected return for the capital provider. The capital provider is the investor or the capitalist. Value stocks have the potential to receive a lot of negative publicity and experience a downturn in their business.

The styles of large, small, and micro are based on a company's share price multiplied by the total number of shares. Companies are ranked and grouped into categories that vary substantially within the investment industry. For example, as of March 2005, the Russell 2000 Index of small-cap stocks had a weighted average market cap of $1.06 billion, while the Dimensional Fund Advisor's (DFA's) small-cap index had $862 million, and the DFA Micro-cap index had $426 million. Morningstar, Russell,

Lipper, Barra, Wilshire Associates, DFA, Morgan Stanley Capital Indexes, and Standard and Poor's are all considered reliable sources of style criteria. Each has its own set of rules for measuring value, growth, large, small, international or emerging markets. So it's no surprise that the active investor is dazed and confused.

6.2.2 Style Drift

Style drift refers to the tendency of active managers and actively managed mutual funds to deviate from their stated or expected investment style. This drift can occur gradually over time such as when "small-cap" managers buy larger and larger companies as the asset base of their funds grow. Style drift can also occur abruptly if an active manager perceives opportunities for higher returns from a different style. For example, a U.S. large company fund may purchase a high percentage of Mexican stocks, changing the fund's style.

6.3 PROBLEMS

6.3.1 Style Drift Alters Risk Exposure

Style drift creates numerous problems for active investors. For instance, it keeps them from maintaining reliable asset allocations for their portfolios. This results in inconsistent exposure to risk and the resulting variations in expected average returns.

The importance of style affecting the risk of mutual funds was crystallized when the highly respected members of the Financial Economists Round Table provided their "Statement on Risk Disclosure by Mutual Funds" in 1996. They stated, "To better communicate the sources of risk associated with mutual fund investments, fund managers should provide estimates of the principal risk fac-

tors that are likely to influence fund returns in the future. Specifically, fund managers should describe and quantify the expected relationship between their funds' future returns and relevant security market indexes as well as the likely extent of divergence (style drift) of their returns from such indexes and the probable sources of such divergence. In subsequent periods, actual fund returns should be compared with the portfolio of market indexes previously selected by a fund."

Experts widely agree that over time, asset allocation is on average the single most important determinant of variance in investment performance. The best way to design a portfolio's asset allocation is to use historical index data.

However, active investors design their portfolios by relying on style labels that are carried by active mutual funds such as "value," "growth," "large" or "small." An active fund usually does not relate to the risk and return potential of any single index. It is unclear how the reliance on labels that supposedly identify these indexes can help active investors design asset allocations for their portfolios. This task can prove even more difficult for an active investor who invests in a separate portfolio of individual stocks and bonds. It is essentially impossible to rationally design a portfolio's asset allocation when the building blocks of the investment strategy used to implement it are active mutual funds or individual stocks, bonds or both.

Style drift prevents an active investor from optimally reducing diversifiable risk because the manager of a typical active fund does not remain consistently invested in the same asset class. On the surface, this does not seem to be much of a problem, but investors who reduce diversifiable risk get a bonus. The bonus is increased return.

Style drift heightens the uncertainty felt by active investors who have little idea how their investments will perform and how their performance will relate to a discrete index. Unnecessary costs and taxes are generated in efforts to maintain consistency between a portfolio's asset allocation and the various investments used to implement it.

The considerable latitude given to managers by active mutual fund prospectuses often results in style drift. Style labels assigned to active mutual funds by fund rating services are not particularly helpful to active investors who rely on them to design asset allocations for their portfolios. For example, an active investor who wants to design an asset allocation that includes the asset class of U.S. large company stocks may find an entire list of labeled "U.S. large company" (active) mutual funds. The problem is that the investments held by an active fund can change over time. Investors in the Fidelity Magellan Fund found this out the hard way when money manager Jeffrey Vinik shifted 30% of the fund's assets from stocks to bonds and cash. This must have been an unwelcome surprise to investors who had chosen Magellan to earn the returns of stocks, not bonds or cash, and based their asset allocations on that expectation.

That is precisely the problem with style drift. It introduces a lot of needless uncertainty as to whether investors can implement their asset allocations, since it is likely that active funds will drift from their benchmarks. Even worse, there is no way to know which active mutual funds will survive in the future, much less which ones will be winners or losers.

6.3.2 Style Drifters

Money manager Jeffrey Vinik's notorious fall from grace after tinkering with the popular Fidelity Magellan Fund in 1996 is one of the most publicized examples of style drift. Fidelity's Magellan was the world's largest mutual fund, and had been a popular equity investment. In February 1996, Magellan's asset allocation was only 70% equity. Vinik, the fund's manager at the time, had invested 20% of the fund in bonds and 10% in short-term marketable securities, betting they would outperform the equities market. Instead, the market soared to new heights, bonds fell in value, and Vinik left Fidelity. The key issue was not the outcome of Vinik's decision, but the investor's loss of control of the asset allocation process.

In March 1999, Fidelity was once again criticized for misrepresenting its funds. Steven Syre and Steve Bailey, columnists for *The Boston Globe*, took the company to task for including stocks of mammoth companies like Microsoft and MCI WorldCom in its Fidelity Emerging Growth Fund. The fund markets itself as one that invests in small and mid-sized companies. Thomas Edison, Fidelity's senior vice president and director of corporate affairs, conceded that Syre and Bailey had made a legitimate point.

Fidelity touted the fund's returns by comparing them to the performance of small and medium company stocks. In 1998, they performed dramatically worse than large company stocks. "It's not that uncommon for a fund to beat its competition by a few points if you're comparing apples to apples," Syre said in an interview with *Brill's Content*. "But this thing was blowing them away."

The SEC agreed with the journalists. Consequently, Fidelity changed the fund's name to the "Aggressive Growth Fund" and eliminated language in its prospectus that suggested a focus on smaller stocks. Since then style drift has been

Figure 6-1

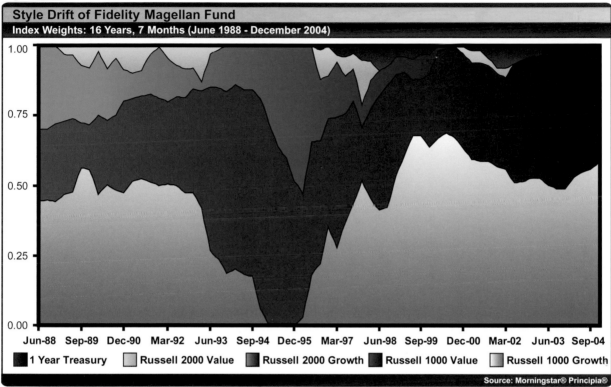

Figure 6-2

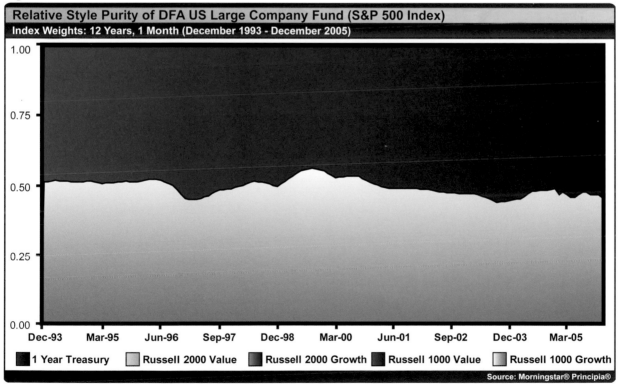

Figure 6-3

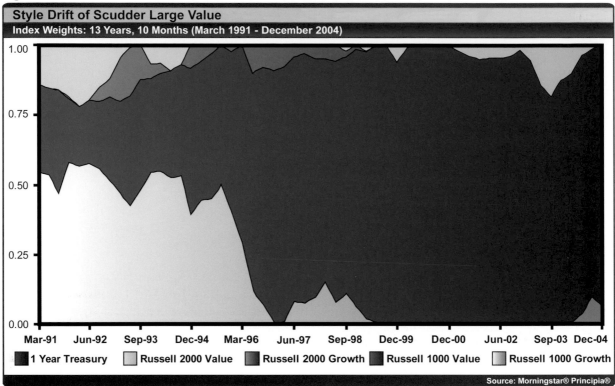

Figure 6-4

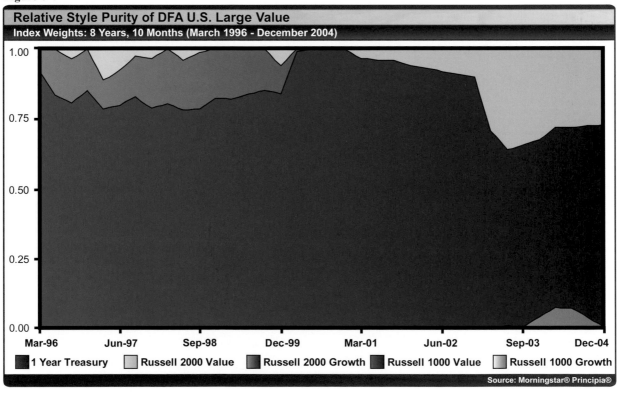

Figure 6-5

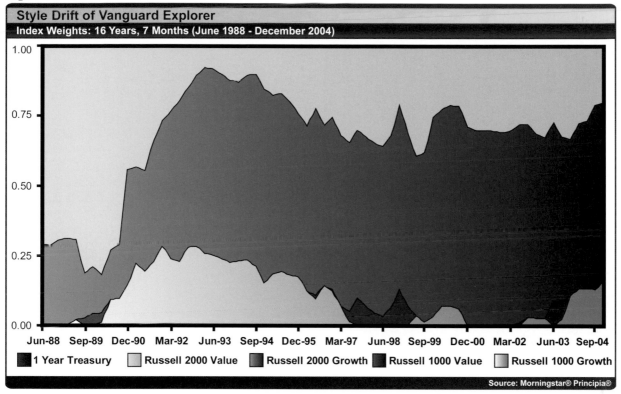

Figure 6-6

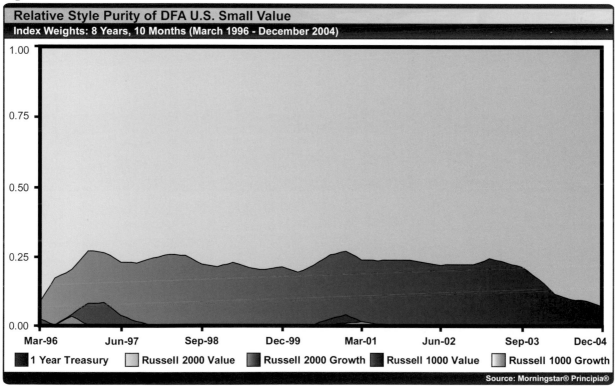

Figure 6-7

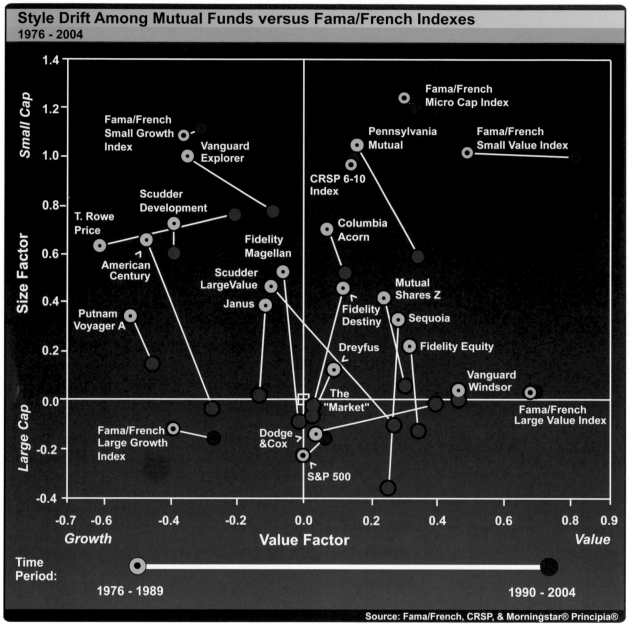

a practice the SEC has been focusing its examinations on.

A study by the Association for Investment Management found that approximately 40% of actively managed funds are classified inaccurately based on the stated goals versus actual investments. Fund managers are drifting along, chasing the latest hot trend. All actively managed funds drift from their benchmark to varying degrees. On the other hand, index funds adhere to the same rules of ownership, regardless of market conditions.

One way to analyze style drift is to measure the exposure to different indexes at sequential times. Figure 6-1 illustrates the drifting styles of the Fidelity Magellan Fund from June 1988 to December 2004. The scale on the left designates the relative exposure to different styles. Note that the dark blue zone is a large value index and the light blue is a large growth index. In June of 1995, it would have been better to classify the fund as a large value fund, while in February 2000 it would have been a large growth fund. Style drifters, like the managers of the Magellan Fund, are altering their styles in their quest for the next winner. Over the last 15 years, Magellan's style drifting has resulted in returns below that of the steady hand of the S&P 500 Index Fund. As a contrast, see Figure 6-2, which illustrates the style purity of a S&P 500 Index Fund. In looking at the chart you can see a contrast equal to the exposure between the large growth and large value as represented by the Russell 1000 Value and Russell 1000 Growth.

Figure 6-3 compares the styles of the Scudder Large Value Fund over time to a DFA Large Value passively managed index fund in Figure 6-4. Finally, Figure 6-5 compares the Vanguard Explorer Fund, which is described by Morningstar as a small growth fund. As a comparison, see the DFA Small Value Index Fund in Figure 6-6. Because of the undesirable characteristics of small growth, DFA does not offer a small growth index fund. In each comparison the bottom index fund provides more consistent and style pure risk exposure.

6.3.3 Style Drift and the Fama/French Risk Factors

Style drift is caused by competition within the mutual fund industry. If active mutual fund managers think they cannot get sufficient performance from the stocks in which they are supposed to be investing, they buy other types of instruments, such as bonds, if they believe bonds will

outperform stocks over the short run. When small company stocks are in a slump, the manager of an active small company stock fund may start buying large company stocks in hopes of enhancing performance. This has been a widespread practice among active money managers over the last decade as U.S. large company, blue chip stocks have outperformed small company stocks.

Fama and French identified risk factors in 1992 that highly correlate with long-term historical returns, namely company size and value orientation. Style drift among these two factors for two periods of approximately 14 years each can be seen in Figure 6-7. On the horizontal axis, value is a high book-to-market ratio (BtM) and growth is a low BtM. On the vertical axis, small and large cap are companies with small and large market capitalization, respectively. The numbers on the axes are measures of market exposure to each of these risk factors. The 0,0 point (the crossing of the axes) represents the total stock market. It reflects all of the stocks in the Center for Research in Security Prices (CRSP) database and is the reference for the other measurements. The CRSP 1-10 refers to the 10 deciles of stocks classified by market capitalization.

The yellow points reflect the average exposure of the funds during the period between 1976 and 1989. The red points reflect average exposure during the period between 1990 and 2004. Note how far some funds moved from their starting point. This movement reflects style drift and is often an unannounced change in investment objectives. Other funds barely moved. It should be noted that the data fails to reveal the many additional shifts in positions that these funds made within each of the years depicted. These additional shifts drive up trading costs, generate higher taxes, alter risk, and lower returns.

Style Picking

Before discussing the next set of tables, please refer to Figure 6-8, which provides a legend for the portfolio and index buttons on Tables 6-1, 6-2, 6-3 and 6-4. For further information about these buttons see Appendices A and B.

One of the reasons it is so dangerous to style drift is because future style winners are as unpredictable as stocks, times or managers. Table 6-1 shows the annual returns of the S&P 500 and 20 index portfolios of different style over the last 80 years. Some investment managers use a strategy referred to as tactical asset allocation. This is a form of style picking where a manager alters the allocation of styles based on their prediction of the future style winners. To illustrate how difficult it is to predict the next winning asset allocation of styles, refer to Table 6-2, which is ranked each year with the highest return for that year on the left and the lowest return on the right. The random rotation of styles from left to right illustrate the difficulty style drifters have in picking the next winning style.

Table 6-3 provides the annual returns of the 15 IFA Indexes and the total market index from CRSP for the last 80 years. In Table 6-4, the returns are sorted so that the highest is on the left. Note the random rotation of individual indexes

or styles from year to year is virtually impossible for managers to predict. It is no wonder that both professional and amateur investors are whipsawed into investing in different styles. But, investors who hold onto diversified portfolios obtain the returns and losses of all top performing asset classes over time. This method has been shown to substantially improve your returns.

6.4 SOLUTIONS

Asset allocation with pure index funds can be implemented to avoid style drift. Index funds are invested using clearly defined rules of ownership. Investors cannot control the style drift that so often negatively impacts the performance of the actively managed mutual funds they have chosen.

The simple solution to style drift is to relinquish active investing and invest in index funds. An indexing investment strategy is the most reliable way to implement a portfolio's asset allocation. The manager of an index fund keeps it constantly invested solely in all (or a representative sample) of the investments that comprise a discrete asset class. For example, the manager of the DFA Tax-Managed Small-Cap Value Fund has established specific criteria for the stocks that the

Figure 6-8

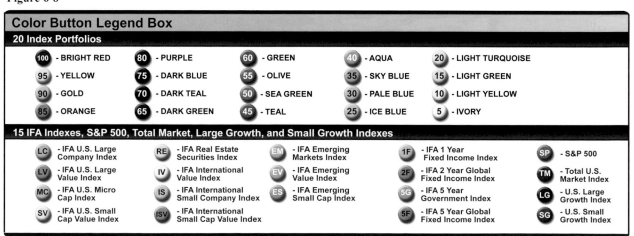

Table 6-1

Annual Returns of 20 Index Portfolios and S&P 500

80 years (1927 - 2006)

Year	SP	100	95	90	85	80	75	70	65	60	55	50	45	40	35	30	25	20	15	10	5
1927	37.3	31.1	31.3	31.4	30.0	28.6	27.2	25.8	24.3	22.9	21.5	20.1	18.6	17.2	15.8	14.4	13.0	11.5	10.1	8.7	7.3
1928	43.4	37.2	36.3	35.5	33.7	32.0	30.2	28.5	26.7	25.0	23.2	21.4	19.7	17.9	16.2	14.4	12.7	10.9	9.1	7.4	5.6
1929	-8.5	-33.7	-30.0	-26.3	-24.8	-23.2	-21.7	-20.1	-18.6	-17.1	-15.5	-14.0	-12.4	-10.9	-9.4	-7.8	-6.3	-4.7	-3.2	-1.7	-0.1
1930	-25.0	-43.6	-42.7	-41.8	-39.5	-37.2	-34.9	-32.5	-30.2	-27.9	-25.6	-23.3	-21.0	-18.7	-16.4	-14.0	-11.7	-9.4	-7.1	-4.8	-2.5
1931	-43.4	-53.0	-53.2	-53.4	-50.8	-48.3	-45.8	-43.2	-40.7	-38.1	-35.6	-33.1	-30.5	-28.0	-25.4	-22.9	-20.4	-17.8	-15.3	-12.7	-10.2
1932	-8.3	-1.7	-2.6	-3.6	-3.1	-2.7	-2.2	-1.7	-1.3	-0.8	-0.4	0.1	0.6	1.0	1.5	2.0	2.4	2.9	3.3	3.8	4.3
1933	53.8	130.4	122.2	114.0	108.3	102.6	96.9	91.2	85.5	79.9	74.2	68.5	62.8	57.1	51.5	45.8	40.1	34.4	28.7	23.0	17.4
1934	-1.6	4.9	2.1	-0.7	-0.4	0.0	0.3	0.6	0.9	1.2	1.5	1.8	2.2	2.5	2.8	3.1	3.4	3.7	4.0	4.3	4.7
1935	47.5	53.9	52.4	50.9	48.6	46.2	43.9	41.6	39.2	36.9	34.5	32.2	29.9	27.5	25.2	22.8	20.5	18.1	15.8	13.5	11.1
1936	33.8	65.3	62.0	58.6	55.7	52.9	50.0	47.1	44.3	41.4	38.5	35.6	32.8	29.9	27.0	24.2	21.3	18.4	15.5	12.7	9.8
1937	-35.1	-48.2	-46.7	-45.1	-42.9	-40.6	-38.3	-36.1	-33.8	-31.5	-29.3	-27.0	-24.8	-22.5	-20.2	-18.0	-15.7	-13.5	-11.2	-8.9	-6.7
1938	31.0	29.0	29.1	29.1	27.9	26.6	25.3	24.0	22.7	21.4	20.2	18.9	17.6	16.3	15.0	13.7	12.5	11.2	9.9	8.6	7.3
1939	-0.5	-6.4	-6.9	-7.4	-6.9	-6.5	-6.0	-5.5	-5.0	-4.5	-4.1	-3.6	-3.1	-2.6	-2.1	-1.6	-1.2	-0.7	-0.2	0.3	0.8
1940	-9.9	-10.9	-10.7	-10.4	-9.8	-9.2	-8.7	-8.1	-7.5	-6.9	-6.4	-5.8	-5.2	-4.7	-4.1	-3.5	-2.9	-2.4	-1.8	-1.2	-0.7
1941	-11.7	-8.5	-8.1	-7.7	-7.4	-7.0	-6.7	-6.3	-6.0	-5.6	-5.3	-4.9	-4.6	-4.2	-3.9	-3.5	-3.2	-2.8	-2.5	-2.2	-1.8
1942	20.2	37.0	35.8	34.5	32.8	31.1	29.4	27.6	25.9	24.2	22.5	20.8	19.1	17.4	15.7	14.0	12.3	10.6	8.9	7.2	5.5
1943	25.8	73.6	67.5	61.5	58.5	55.5	52.4	49.4	46.4	43.4	40.3	37.3	34.3	31.3	28.2	25.2	22.2	19.2	16.2	13.1	10.1
1944	19.6	46.4	44.2	42.0	39.9	37.9	35.8	33.7	31.6	29.5	27.4	25.3	23.3	21.2	19.1	17.0	14.9	12.8	10.7	8.6	6.6
1945	36.3	62.5	59.1	55.7	53.0	50.2	47.5	44.7	42.0	39.2	36.4	33.7	30.9	28.2	25.4	22.7	19.9	17.1	14.1	11.6	8.9
1946	-8.2	-12.0	-11.5	-11.1	-10.6	-10.0	-9.5	-8.9	-8.4	-7.9	-7.3	-6.8	-6.2	-5.7	-5.2	-4.6	-4.1	-3.5	-3.0	-2.5	-1.9
1947	5.6	2.4	2.9	3.4	3.2	3.0	2.9	2.7	2.5	2.3	2.1	1.9	1.7	1.5	1.4	1.2	1.0	0.8	0.6	0.4	0.2
1948	5.4	-4.2	-3.1	-2.0	-1.8	-1.7	-1.6	-1.5	-1.4	-1.2	-1.1	-1.0	-0.9	-0.8	-0.6	-0.5	-0.4	-0.3	-0.2	0.0	0.1
1949	18.7	17.7	17.3	16.9	16.1	15.3	14.5	13.7	12.9	12.1	11.3	10.5	9.7	8.9	8.1	7.3	6.5	5.7	4.9	4.1	3.3
1950	31.6	47.2	47.1	46.9	44.6	42.2	39.9	37.5	35.1	32.8	30.4	28.0	25.7	23.3	21.0	18.6	16.2	13.9	11.5	9.1	6.8
1951	23.9	11.3	12.1	12.8	12.2	11.5	10.8	10.2	9.5	8.8	8.2	7.5	6.8	6.2	5.5	4.8	4.2	3.5	2.8	2.2	1.5
1952	18.2	9.2	10.4	11.6	11.0	10.5	9.9	9.4	8.8	8.3	7.7	7.2	6.6	6.1	5.5	5.0	4.5	3.9	3.4	2.8	2.3
1953	-1.1	-7.3	-7.1	-6.8	-6.4	-6.0	-5.5	-5.1	-4.7	-4.3	-3.9	-3.5	-3.1	-2.6	-2.2	-1.8	-1.4	-1.0	-0.6	-0.2	0.3
1954	52.5	63.7	64.0	64.3	61.1	58.0	54.8	51.6	48.5	45.3	42.2	39.0	35.8	32.7	29.5	26.3	23.2	20.0	16.9	13.7	10.5
1955	31.4	21.7	21.7	21.7	20.5	19.4	18.3	17.1	16.0	14.9	13.7	12.6	11.5	10.3	9.2	8.1	6.9	5.8	4.6	3.5	2.4
1956	6.4	2.7	2.5	2.3	2.1	2.0	1.9	1.8	1.6	1.5	1.4	1.3	1.2	1.0	0.9	0.8	0.7	0.5	0.4	0.3	0.2
1957	-10.9	-16.9	-16.5	-16.2	-15.2	-14.1	-13.1	-12.1	-11.0	-10.0	-8.9	-7.9	-6.9	-5.8	-4.8	-3.8	-2.7	-1.7	-0.6	0.4	1.4
1958	43.2	64.3	62.7	61.1	58.0	54.9	51.8	48.7	45.5	42.4	39.3	36.2	33.1	30.0	26.9	23.8	20.6	17.5	14.4	11.3	8.2
1959	11.8	16.8	17.4	18.0	17.1	16.2	15.3	14.5	13.6	12.7	11.8	10.9	10.0	9.2	8.3	7.4	6.5	5.6	4.8	3.9	3.0
1960	0.3	-6.6	-6.5	-6.3	-5.6	-5.0	-4.3	-3.6	-3.0	-2.3	-1.6	-0.9	-0.3	0.4	1.1	1.7	2.4	3.1	3.8	4.4	5.1
1961	26.7	26.9	26.1	25.4	24.1	22.9	21.7	20.5	19.3	18.1	16.9	15.6	14.4	13.2	12.0	10.8	9.6	8.4	7.1	5.9	4.7
1962	-8.8	-11.1	-10.3	-9.5	-8.8	-8.2	-7.6	-7.0	-6.3	-5.7	-5.1	-4.4	-3.8	-3.2	-2.6	-1.9	-1.3	-0.7	0.0	0.6	1.2
1963	22.6	20.4	20.8	21.2	20.2	19.2	18.2	17.2	16.3	15.3	14.3	13.3	12.3	11.3	10.3	9.3	8.3	7.3	6.3	5.3	4.3
1964	16.4	17.8	17.1	16.5	15.8	15.1	14.4	13.8	13.1	12.4	11.7	11.0	10.4	9.7	9.0	8.3	7.6	7.0	6.3	5.6	4.9
1965	12.3	31.1	28.8	26.5	25.2	24.0	22.7	21.5	20.2	18.9	17.7	16.4	15.2	13.9	12.6	11.4	10.1	8.8	7.6	6.3	5.1
1966	-10.2	-9.8	-9.9	-10.1	-9.4	-8.7	-8.0	-7.3	-6.6	-5.8	-5.1	-4.4	-3.7	-3.0	-2.3	-1.6	-0.9	-0.2	0.5	1.2	1.9
1967	23.8	64.6	58.7	52.9	50.3	47.8	45.2	42.6	40.1	37.5	34.9	32.4	29.8	27.2	24.7	22.1	19.5	17.0	14.4	11.8	9.3
1968	11.0	39.1	36.5	33.9	32.4	30.9	29.4	27.9	26.4	24.9	23.4	21.9	20.4	19.0	17.5	16.0	14.5	13.0	11.5	10.0	8.5
1969	-8.6	-24.9	-22.9	-20.8	-19.7	-18.5	-17.4	-16.2	-15.1	-13.9	-12.8	-11.7	-10.5	-9.4	-8.2	-7.1	-5.9	-4.8	-3.6	-2.5	-1.4
1970	3.9	-4.8	-3.7	-2.6	-1.9	-1.1	-0.3	0.4	1.2	2.0	2.7	3.5	4.2	5.0	5.7	6.5	7.3	8.0	8.8	9.5	10.3
1971	14.2	26.4	25.7	25.0	24.1	23.1	22.2	21.2	20.3	19.4	18.4	17.5	16.5	15.6	14.6	13.7	12.7	11.8	10.8	9.9	8.9
1972	18.8	20.4	21.1	21.9	21.0	20.1	19.1	18.2	17.3	16.4	15.5	14.5	13.6	12.7	11.8	10.9	9.9	9.0	8.1	7.2	6.3
1973	-14.8	-24.0	-21.9	-19.9	-18.7	-17.5	-16.3	-15.1	-13.8	-12.6	-11.4	-10.2	-9.0	-7.8	-6.6	-5.4	-4.1	-2.9	-1.7	-0.5	0.7
1974	-26.6	-25.5	-25.1	-24.8	-23.2	-21.6	-20.0	-18.4	-16.8	-15.2	-13.6	-12.0	-10.4	-8.8	-7.2	-5.6	-4.0	-2.4	-0.8	0.8	2.4
1975	37.1	51.3	48.4	45.6	43.6	41.7	39.7	37.8	35.9	33.9	32.0	30.0	28.1	26.2	24.2	22.3	20.3	18.4	16.5	14.5	12.6
1976	23.7	34.0	32.3	30.6	29.4	28.3	27.2	26.0	24.9	23.8	22.6	21.5	20.4	19.2	18.1	16.9	15.8	14.7	13.5	12.4	11.3
1977	-7.3	23.7	20.6	17.5	16.8	16.1	15.3	14.6	13.9	13.1	12.4	11.6	10.9	10.2	9.4	8.7	8.0	7.2	6.5	5.8	5.0
1978	6.5	26.2	24.1	22.0	21.0	20.1	19.2	18.3	17.4	16.4	15.5	14.6	13.7	12.8	11.9	10.9	10.0	9.1	8.2	7.3	6.3
1979	18.3	21.2	20.0	18.7	18.2	17.6	17.1	16.5	16.0	15.4	14.9	14.3	13.7	13.2	12.6	12.1	11.5	11.0	10.4	9.9	9.3
1980	32.3	26.0	25.5	25.0	24.2	23.4	22.6	21.8	21.0	20.2	19.4	18.6	17.8	17.0	16.2	15.4	14.6	13.9	13.1	12.3	11.5
1981	-5.0	6.4	5.9	5.5	5.9	6.3	6.7	7.1	7.5	7.9	8.3	8.7	9.1	9.5	9.9	10.3	10.7	11.1	11.5	11.9	12.3
1982	21.3	17.9	16.9	16.0	16.2	16.3	16.5	16.7	16.9	17.0	17.2	17.4	17.6	17.7	17.9	18.1	18.3	18.4	18.6	18.8	18.9
1983	22.4	34.9	33.2	31.6	30.4	29.2	28.0	26.8	25.5	24.3	23.1	21.9	20.7	19.5	18.3	17.1	15.9	14.7	13.4	12.2	11.0
1984	6.1	4.3	5.6	6.8	7.0	7.3	7.5	7.8	8.0	8.2	8.5	8.7	9.0	9.2	9.5	9.7	10.0	10.2	10.5	10.7	10.9
1985	32.0	36.7	36.4	36.1	34.9	33.8	32.6	31.4	30.3	29.1	27.9	26.8	25.6	24.5	23.3	22.1	21.0	19.8	18.6	17.5	16.3
1986	18.3	25.8	27.1	28.5	27.5	26.6	25.7	24.8	23.9	23.0	22.1	21.2	20.2	19.3	18.4	17.5	16.6	15.7	14.8	13.9	12.9
1987	5.1	9.2	9.8	10.4	10.1	9.8	9.6	9.3	9.0	8.7	8.4	8.1	7.8	7.5	7.3	7.0	6.7	6.4	6.1	5.8	5.5
1988	16.7	25.7	24.9	24.1	23.2	22.3	21.4	20.5	19.6	18.7	17.8	16.9	16.0	15.1	14.2	13.3	12.4	11.5	10.6	9.7	8.8
1989	31.3	26.4	26.6	26.8	25.8	24.9	23.9	23.0	22.0	21.1	20.1	19.1	18.2	17.2	16.3	15.3	14.4	13.4	12.4	11.5	10.5
1990	-3.2	-18.0	-17.3	-16.6	-15.4	-14.2	-13.0	-11.9	-10.7	-9.5	-8.3	-7.1	-5.9	-4.7	-3.6	-2.4	-1.2	0.0	1.2	2.4	3.6
1991	30.1	32.6	31.3	30.0	29.1	28.1	27.2	26.2	25.3	24.3	23.4	22.4	21.5	20.5	19.6	18.6	17.7	16.7	15.8	14.8	13.8
1992	7.3	11.8	10.5	9.3	9.1	8.9	8.7	8.5	8.3	8.1	7.9	7.7	7.5	7.3	7.0	6.8	6.6	6.4	6.2	6.0	5.8
1993	9.6	31.9	30.1	28.3	27.2	26.1	25.0	23.9	22.8	21.7	20.6	19.5	18.4	17.3	16.2	15.2	14.1	13.0	11.9	10.8	9.7
1994	1.3	2.1	1.5	0.9	0.8	0.6	0.5	0.3	0.2	0.0	-0.1	-0.3	-0.4	-0.6	-0.7	-0.8	-1.0	-1.1	-1.3	-1.4	-1.6
1995	37.1	21.5	21.9	22.3	21.7	21.0	20.4	19.7	19.1	18.4	17.8	17.2	16.5	15.9	15.2	14.6	13.9	13.3	12.7	12.0	11.4
1996	22.6	15.7	16.2	16.8	16.3	15.8	15.3	14.8	14.2	13.7	13.2	12.7	12.2	11.7	11.2	10.7	10.2	9.7	9.2	8.7	8.2
1997	33.1	12.5	13.2	13.9	13.5	13.1	12.7	12.3	11.9	11.5	11.1	10.6	10.2	9.8	9.4	9.0	8.6	8.2	7.8	7.3	6.9
1998	28.7	1.2	3.5	5.7	5.7	5.7	5.7	5.7	5.7	5.7	5.7	5.7	5.7	5.6	5.6	5.6	5.6	5.6	5.6	5.6	5.6
1999	20.8	24.4	22.1	19.9	19.1	18.2	17.4	16.6	15.7	14.9	14.1	13.2	12.4	11.6	10.7	9.9	9.1	8.2	7.4	6.6	5.7
2000	-9.3	-2.9	-1.9	-0.9	-0.6	-0.3	0.1	0.4	0.7	1.1	1.4	1.7	2.1	2.4	2.7	3.0	3.4	3.7	4.0	4.4	4.7
2001	-12.1	5.5	3.1	0.7	0.9	1.1	1.4	1.6	1.8	2.1	2.3	2.5	2.7	3.0	3.2	3.4	3.7	3.9	4.1	4.3	4.6
2002	-22.2	-10.1	-10.5	-10.9	-10.0	-9.1	-8.2	-7.3	-6.4	-5.6	-4.7	-3.8	-2.9	-2.0	-1.1	-0.2	0.7	1.6	2.4	3.3	4.2
2003	28.5	51.6	48.4	45.1	43.0	40.8	38.6	36.4	34.2	32.0	29.8	27.6	25.5	23.3	21.1	18.9	16.7	14.5	12.3	10.1	7.9
2004	10.7	22.6	22.2	21.7	20.7	19.6	18.6	17.5	16.5	15.5	14.4	13.4	12.3	11.3	10.3	9.2	8.2	7.1	6.1	5.1	4.0
2005	4.9	11.5	11.4	11.3	10.8	10.3	9.7	9.2	8.7	8.2	7.6	7.1	6.6	6.0	5.5	5.0	4.5	3.9	3.4	2.9	2.4
2006	15.7	22.3	22.6	23.0	22.0	21.0	20.0	19.1	18.1	17.1	16.1	15.2	14.2	13.2	12.3	11.3	10.3	9.3	8.4	7.4	6.4
Annualized Return (%)	10.27	12.74	12.45	12.14	11.89	11.63	11.34	11.04	10.71	10.38	10.02	9.65	9.26	8.85	8.43	7.99	7.54	7.07	6.58	6.07	5.55
Standard Deviation (%)	19.23	26.59	25.69	24.85	23.58	22.32	21.08	19.85	18.63	17.42	16.21	15.01	13.82	12.63	11.44	10.26	9.08	7.91	6.74	5.60	4.49
Growth of $1	$2,483	$14,652	$11,947	$9,568	$8,016	$6,622	$5,395	$4,337	$3,439	$2,692	$2,079	$1,585	$1,193	$886	$649	$470	$335	$236	$164	$112	$75.38

* See Appendix A for Index Portfolio Button Definitions

Sources, Updates, and Disclosures: ifa.com/btp

Table 6-2

Annual Returns of 20 Index Portfolios and S&P 500 Over 80 Years (1927 - 2006)

Legend*: SP, 100, 95, 90, 85, 80, 75, 70, 65, 60, 55, 50, 45, 40, 35, 30, 25, 20, 15, 10, 5

Year	Highest Return									Sorted in Order of Returns for Each Year										Lowest Return
1927	37.3	31.4	31.3	31.1	30.0	28.6	27.2	25.8	24.3	22.9	21.5	20.1	18.6	17.2	15.8	14.4	13.0	11.5	10.1	8.7	7.3
1928	43.4	37.2	36.3	35.5	33.7	32.0	30.2	28.5	26.7	25.0	23.2	21.4	19.7	17.9	16.2	14.4	12.7	10.9	9.1	7.4	5.6
1929	-0.1	-1.7	-3.2	-4.7	-6.3	-7.8	-8.5	-9.4	-10.9	-12.4	-14.0	-15.5	-17.1	-18.6	-20.1	-21.7	-23.2	-24.8	-26.3	-30.0	-33.7
1930	-2.5	-4.8	-7.1	-9.4	-11.7	-14.0	-16.4	-18.7	-21.0	-23.3	-25.0	-25.6	-27.9	-30.2	-32.5	-34.9	-37.2	-39.5	-41.8	-42.7	-43.6
1931	-10.2	-12.7	-15.3	-17.8	-20.4	-22.9	-25.4	-28.0	-30.5	-33.1	-35.6	-38.1	-40.7	-43.2	-43.4	-45.8	-48.3	-50.8	-53.0	-53.2	-53.4
1932	4.3	3.8	3.3	2.9	2.4	2.0	1.5	1.0	0.6	0.1	-0.4	-0.8	-1.3	-1.7	-1.7	-2.2	-2.6	-2.7	-3.1	-3.6	-8.3
1933	130.4	122.2	114.0	108.3	102.6	96.9	91.2	85.5	79.9	74.2	68.5	62.8	57.1	53.8	51.5	45.8	40.1	34.4	28.7	23.0	17.4
1934	4.9	4.7	4.3	4.0	3.7	3.4	3.1	2.8	2.5	2.2	2.1	1.8	1.5	1.2	0.9	0.6	0.3	0.0	-0.4	-0.7	-1.6
1935	53.9	52.4	50.9	48.6	47.5	46.2	43.9	41.6	39.2	36.9	34.5	32.2	29.9	27.5	25.2	22.8	20.5	18.1	15.8	13.5	11.1
1936	65.3	62.0	58.6	55.7	52.9	50.0	47.1	44.3	41.4	38.5	35.6	33.8	32.8	29.9	27.0	24.2	21.3	18.4	15.5	12.7	9.8
1937	-6.7	-8.9	-11.2	-13.5	-15.7	-18.0	-20.2	-22.5	-24.8	-27.0	-29.3	-31.5	-33.8	-35.1	-36.1	-38.3	-40.6	-42.9	-45.1	-46.7	-48.2
1938	31.0	29.1	29.1	29.0	27.9	26.6	25.3	24.0	22.7	21.4	20.2	18.9	17.6	16.3	15.0	13.7	12.5	11.2	9.9	8.6	7.3
1939	0.8	0.3	-0.2	-0.5	-0.7	-1.2	-1.6	-2.1	-2.6	-3.1	-3.6	-4.1	-4.5	-5.0	-5.5	-6.0	-6.4	-6.5	-6.9	-6.9	-7.4
1940	-0.7	-1.2	-1.8	-2.4	-2.9	-3.5	-4.1	-4.7	-5.2	-5.8	-6.4	-6.9	-7.5	-8.1	-8.7	-9.2	-9.8	-9.9	-10.4	-10.7	-10.9
1941	-1.8	-2.2	-2.5	-2.8	-3.2	-3.5	-3.9	-4.2	-4.6	-4.9	-5.3	-5.6	-6.0	-6.3	-6.7	-7.0	-7.4	-7.7	-8.1	-8.5	-11.7
1942	37.0	35.8	34.5	32.8	31.1	29.4	27.6	25.9	24.2	22.5	20.8	20.2	19.1	17.4	15.7	14.0	12.3	10.6	8.9	7.2	5.5
1943	73.6	67.5	61.5	58.5	55.5	52.4	49.4	46.4	43.4	40.3	37.3	34.3	31.3	28.2	25.8	25.2	22.2	19.2	16.2	13.1	10.1
1944	46.4	44.2	42.0	39.9	37.9	35.8	33.7	31.6	29.5	27.4	25.3	23.3	21.2	19.6	19.1	17.0	14.9	12.8	10.7	8.6	6.6
1945	62.5	59.1	55.7	53.0	50.2	47.5	44.7	42.0	39.2	36.4	36.3	33.7	30.9	28.2	25.4	22.7	19.9	17.1	14.4	11.6	8.9
1946	-1.9	-2.5	-3.0	-3.5	-4.1	-4.6	-5.2	-5.7	-6.2	-6.8	-7.3	-7.9	-8.2	-8.4	-8.9	-9.5	-10.0	-10.6	-11.1	-11.5	-12.0
1947	5.6	3.4	3.2	3.0	2.9	2.9	2.7	2.5	2.4	2.3	2.1	1.9	1.7	1.5	1.4	1.2	1.0	0.8	0.6	0.4	0.2
1948	5.4	0.1	0.0	-0.2	-0.3	-0.4	-0.5	-0.6	-0.8	-0.9	-1.0	-1.1	-1.2	-1.4	-1.5	-1.6	-1.7	-1.8	-2.0	-3.1	-4.2
1949	18.7	17.7	17.3	16.9	16.1	15.3	14.5	13.7	12.9	12.1	11.3	10.5	9.7	8.9	8.1	7.3	6.5	5.7	4.9	4.1	3.3
1950	47.2	47.1	46.9	44.6	42.2	39.9	37.5	35.1	32.8	31.6	30.4	28.0	25.7	23.3	21.0	18.6	16.2	13.9	11.5	9.1	6.8
1951	23.9	12.8	12.2	12.1	11.5	11.3	10.8	10.2	9.5	8.8	8.2	7.5	6.8	6.2	5.5	4.8	4.2	3.5	2.8	2.2	1.5
1952	18.2	11.6	11.0	10.5	10.4	9.9	9.4	9.2	8.8	8.3	7.7	7.2	6.6	6.1	5.5	5.0	4.5	3.9	3.4	2.8	2.3
1953	0.3	-0.2	-0.6	-1.0	-1.1	-1.4	-1.8	-2.2	-2.6	-3.1	-3.5	-3.9	-4.3	-4.7	-5.1	-5.5	-6.0	-6.4	-6.8	-7.1	-7.3
1954	64.3	64.0	63.7	61.1	58.0	54.8	52.5	51.6	48.5	45.3	42.2	39.0	35.8	32.7	29.5	26.3	23.2	20.0	16.9	13.7	10.5
1955	31.4	21.7	21.7	21.7	20.5	19.4	18.3	17.1	16.0	14.9	13.7	12.6	11.5	10.3	9.2	8.1	6.9	5.8	4.6	3.5	2.4
1956	6.4	2.7	2.5	2.3	2.1	2.0	1.9	1.8	1.6	1.5	1.4	1.3	1.2	1.0	0.9	0.8	0.7	0.5	0.4	0.3	0.2
1957	1.4	0.4	-0.6	-1.7	-2.7	-3.8	-4.8	-5.8	-6.9	-7.9	-8.9	-10.0	-10.9	-11.0	-12.1	-13.1	-14.1	-15.2	-16.2	-16.5	-16.9
1958	64.3	62.7	61.1	58.0	54.9	51.8	48.7	45.5	43.2	42.4	39.3	36.2	33.1	30.0	26.9	23.8	20.6	17.5	14.4	11.3	8.2
1959	18.0	17.4	17.1	16.8	16.2	15.3	14.5	13.6	12.7	11.8	11.8	10.9	10.0	9.2	8.3	7.4	6.5	5.6	4.8	3.9	3.0
1960	5.1	4.4	3.8	3.1	2.4	1.7	1.1	0.4	0.3	-0.3	-0.9	-1.6	-2.3	-3.0	-3.6	-4.3	-5.0	-5.6	-6.3	-6.5	-6.6
1961	26.9	26.7	26.1	25.4	24.1	22.9	21.7	20.5	19.3	18.1	16.9	15.6	14.4	13.2	12.0	10.8	9.6	8.4	7.1	5.9	4.7
1962	1.2	0.6	0.0	-0.7	-1.3	-1.9	-2.6	-3.2	-3.8	-4.4	-5.1	-5.7	-6.3	-7.0	-7.6	-8.2	-8.8	-8.8	-9.5	-10.3	-11.1
1963	22.6	21.2	20.8	20.4	20.2	19.2	18.2	17.2	16.3	15.3	14.3	13.3	12.3	11.3	10.3	9.3	8.3	7.3	6.3	5.3	4.3
1964	17.8	17.1	16.5	16.4	15.8	15.1	14.4	13.8	13.1	12.4	11.7	11.0	10.4	9.7	9.0	8.3	7.6	7.0	6.3	5.6	4.9
1965	31.1	28.8	26.5	25.2	24.0	22.7	21.5	20.2	18.9	17.7	16.4	15.2	13.9	12.6	12.3	11.4	10.1	8.8	7.6	6.3	5.1
1966	1.9	1.2	0.5	-0.2	-0.9	-1.6	-2.3	-3.0	-3.7	-4.4	-5.1	-5.8	-6.6	-7.3	-8.0	-8.7	-9.4	-9.8	-9.9	-10.1	-10.2
1967	64.6	58.7	52.9	50.3	47.8	45.2	42.6	40.1	37.5	34.9	32.4	29.8	27.2	24.7	23.8	22.1	19.5	17.0	14.4	11.8	9.3
1968	39.1	36.5	33.9	32.4	30.9	29.4	27.9	26.4	24.9	23.4	21.9	20.4	19.0	17.5	16.0	14.5	13.0	11.5	11.0	10.0	8.5
1969	-1.4	-2.5	-3.6	-4.8	-5.9	-7.1	-8.2	-8.6	-9.4	-10.5	-11.7	-12.8	-13.9	-15.1	-16.2	-17.4	-18.5	-19.7	-20.8	-22.9	-24.9
1970	10.3	9.5	8.8	8.0	7.3	6.5	5.7	5.0	4.2	3.9	3.5	2.7	2.0	1.2	0.4	-0.3	-1.1	-1.9	-2.6	-3.7	-4.8
1971	26.4	25.7	25.0	24.1	23.1	22.2	21.2	20.3	19.4	18.4	17.5	16.5	15.6	14.6	14.2	13.7	12.7	11.8	10.8	9.9	8.9
1972	21.9	21.1	21.0	20.4	20.1	19.1	18.8	18.2	17.3	16.4	15.5	14.5	13.6	12.7	11.8	10.9	9.9	9.0	8.1	7.2	6.3
1973	0.7	-0.5	-1.7	-2.9	-4.1	-5.4	-6.6	-7.8	-9.0	-10.2	-11.4	-12.6	-13.8	-14.8	-15.1	-16.3	-17.5	-18.7	-19.9	-21.9	-24.0
1974	2.4	0.8	-0.8	-2.4	-4.0	-5.6	-7.2	-8.8	-10.4	-12.0	-13.6	-15.2	-16.8	-18.4	-20.0	-21.6	-23.2	-24.8	-25.1	-25.5	-26.6
1975	51.3	48.4	45.6	43.6	41.7	39.7	37.8	37.1	35.9	33.9	32.0	30.0	28.1	26.2	24.2	22.3	20.3	18.4	16.5	14.5	12.6
1976	34.0	32.3	30.6	29.4	28.3	27.2	26.0	24.9	23.8	23.7	22.6	21.5	20.4	19.2	18.1	16.9	15.8	14.7	13.5	12.4	11.3
1977	23.7	20.6	17.5	16.8	16.1	15.3	14.6	13.9	13.1	12.4	11.6	10.9	10.2	9.4	8.7	8.0	7.2	6.5	5.8	5.0	-7.3
1978	26.2	24.1	22.0	21.0	20.1	19.2	18.3	17.4	16.4	15.5	14.6	13.7	12.8	11.9	10.9	10.0	9.1	8.2	7.3	6.5	6.3
1979	21.2	20.0	18.7	18.3	18.2	17.6	17.1	16.5	16.0	15.4	14.9	14.3	13.7	13.2	12.6	12.1	11.5	11.0	10.4	9.9	9.3
1980	32.3	26.0	25.5	25.0	24.2	23.4	22.6	21.8	21.0	20.2	19.4	18.6	17.8	17.0	16.2	15.4	14.6	13.9	13.1	12.3	11.5
1981	12.3	11.9	11.5	11.1	10.7	10.3	9.9	9.5	9.1	8.7	8.3	7.9	7.5	7.1	6.7	6.4	6.3	5.9	5.9	5.5	-5.0
1982	21.3	18.9	18.8	18.6	18.4	18.3	18.1	17.9	17.9	17.7	17.6	17.4	17.2	17.0	16.9	16.9	16.7	16.5	16.3	16.2	16.0
1983	34.9	33.2	31.6	30.4	29.2	28.0	26.8	25.5	24.3	23.1	22.4	21.9	20.7	19.5	18.3	17.1	15.9	14.7	13.4	12.2	11.0
1984	10.9	10.7	10.5	10.2	10.0	9.7	9.5	9.2	9.0	8.7	8.5	8.2	8.0	7.8	7.5	7.3	7.0	6.8	6.1	5.6	4.3
1985	36.7	36.4	36.1	34.9	33.8	32.6	32.0	31.4	30.3	29.1	27.9	26.8	25.6	24.5	23.3	22.1	21.0	19.8	18.6	17.5	16.3
1986	28.5	27.5	27.1	26.6	25.8	25.7	24.8	23.9	23.0	22.1	21.2	20.2	19.3	18.4	18.3	17.5	16.6	15.7	14.8	13.9	12.9
1987	10.4	10.1	9.8	9.8	9.6	9.3	9.2	9.0	8.7	8.4	8.1	7.8	7.5	7.3	7.0	6.7	6.4	6.1	5.8	5.5	5.1
1988	25.7	24.9	24.1	23.2	22.3	21.4	20.5	19.6	18.7	17.8	16.9	16.7	16.0	15.1	14.2	13.3	12.4	11.5	10.6	9.7	8.8
1989	31.3	26.8	26.6	26.4	25.8	24.9	23.9	23.0	22.0	21.1	20.1	19.1	18.2	17.2	16.3	15.3	14.4	13.4	12.4	11.5	10.5
1990	3.6	2.4	1.2	0.0	-1.2	-2.4	-3.2	-3.6	-4.7	-5.9	-7.1	-8.3	-9.5	-10.7	-11.9	-13.0	-14.2	-15.4	-16.6	-17.3	-18.0
1991	32.6	31.3	30.1	30.0	29.1	28.1	27.2	26.2	25.3	24.3	23.4	22.4	21.5	20.5	19.6	18.6	17.7	16.7	15.8	14.8	13.8
1992	11.8	10.5	9.3	9.1	8.9	8.7	8.5	8.3	8.1	7.9	7.7	7.5	7.3	7.3	7.0	6.8	6.6	6.4	6.2	6.0	5.8
1993	31.9	30.1	28.3	27.2	26.1	25.0	23.9	22.8	21.7	20.6	19.5	18.4	17.3	16.2	15.2	14.1	13.0	11.9	10.8	9.7	9.6
1994	2.1	1.5	1.3	0.9	0.8	0.6	0.5	0.3	0.2	0.0	-0.1	-0.3	-0.4	-0.6	-0.7	-0.8	-1.0	-1.1	-1.3	-1.4	-1.6
1995	37.1	22.3	21.9	21.7	21.5	21.0	20.4	19.7	19.1	18.4	17.8	17.2	16.5	15.9	15.2	14.6	13.9	13.3	12.7	12.0	11.4
1996	22.6	16.8	16.3	16.2	15.8	15.7	15.3	14.8	14.2	13.7	13.2	12.7	12.2	11.7	11.2	10.7	10.2	9.7	9.2	8.7	8.2
1997	33.1	13.9	13.5	13.2	13.1	12.7	12.5	12.3	11.9	11.5	11.1	10.6	10.2	9.8	9.4	9.0	8.6	8.2	7.8	7.3	6.9
1998	28.7	5.7	5.7	5.7	5.7	5.7	5.7	5.7	5.7	5.7	5.7	5.6	5.6	5.6	5.6	5.6	5.6	5.6	5.6	3.5	1.2
1999	24.4	22.1	20.8	19.9	19.1	18.2	17.4	16.6	15.7	14.9	14.1	13.2	12.4	11.6	10.7	9.9	9.1	8.2	7.4	6.6	5.7
2000	4.7	4.4	4.0	3.7	3.4	3.0	2.7	2.4	2.1	1.7	1.4	1.1	0.7	0.4	0.1	-0.3	-0.6	-0.9	-1.9	-2.9	-9.3
2001	5.5	4.6	4.3	4.1	3.9	3.7	3.4	3.2	3.1	3.0	2.7	2.5	2.3	2.1	1.8	1.6	1.4	1.1	0.9	0.7	-12.1
2002	4.2	3.3	2.4	1.6	0.7	-0.2	-1.1	-2.0	-2.9	-3.8	-4.7	-5.6	-6.4	-7.3	-8.2	-9.1	-10.0	-10.1	-10.5	-10.9	-22.2
2003	51.6	48.4	45.1	43.0	40.8	38.6	36.4	34.2	32.0	29.8	28.5	27.6	25.5	23.3	21.1	18.9	16.7	14.5	12.3	10.1	7.9
2004	22.6	22.2	21.7	20.7	19.6	18.6	17.5	16.5	15.5	14.4	13.4	12.3	11.3	10.7	10.3	9.2	8.2	7.1	6.1	5.1	4.0
2005	11.5	11.4	11.3	10.8	10.3	9.7	9.2	8.7	8.2	7.6	7.1	6.6	6.0	5.5	5.0	4.9	4.5	3.9	3.4	2.9	2.4
2006	23.0	22.6	22.3	22.0	21.0	20.0	19.1	18.1	17.1	16.1	15.7	15.2	14.2	13.2	12.3	11.3	10.3	9.3	8.4	7.4	6.4
Annualized Return (%)	21.78	19.11	18.03	17.10	16.09	15.04	13.99	12.98	11.91	10.85	9.82	8.79	7.69	6.63	5.69	4.60	3.45	2.33	1.20	0.08	-1.82
Standard Deviation (%)	23.12	22.24	21.37	20.74	20.09	19.47	18.87	18.32	17.78	17.32	16.89	16.44	16.06	15.71	15.39	15.13	14.87	14.64	14.45	14.19	14.33
Growth of $1	$7,034K	$1,195K	$574K	$304K	$152K	$73,566	$35,418	$17,328	$8,093	$3,791	$1,798	$843	$375	$170	$83.90	$36.53	$15.07	$6.29	$2.59	$1.07	$0.23

* See Appendix A for Index Portfolio Button Definitions

Sources, Updates, and Disclosures: ifa.com/btp

Table 6-3

Annual Returns of 15 Indexes
80 years (1927 - 2006)

Year	LC	LV	MC	SV	RE	IV	IS	ISV	EM	EV	ES	1F	2F	5G	5F
1927	37.3	31.3	30.8	33.2	32.1	31.3	26.1	33.2	31.2	33.2	30.8	2.9	4.3	4.3	4.3
1928	43.4	25.2	44.2	39.0	41.8	25.2	40.0	39.0	34.9	39.0	44.2	3.0	0.7	0.7	0.7
1929	-8.5	-6.7	-51.4	-41.8	-46.7	-6.7	-30.9	-41.8	-32.1	-41.8	-51.4	4.5	5.8	5.8	5.8
1930	-25.0	-45.2	-46.1	-47.7	-46.8	-45.2	-32.3	-47.7	-45.2	-47.7	-46.1	2.2	6.5	6.5	6.5
1931	-43.4	-60.8	-50.3	-53.8	-52.0	-60.8	-48.5	-53.8	-55.4	-53.8	-50.3	0.8	-2.6	-2.6	-2.6
1932	-8.3	-6.4	8.9	-2.0	3.7	-6.4	-8.7	-2.0	3.2	-2.0	8.9	0.7	8.6	8.6	8.6
1933	53.8	90.8	185.3	141.2	162.9	90.8	120.4	141.2	137.8	141.2	185.3	0.1	1.6	1.6	1.6
1934	-1.6	-21.8	23.4	7.4	15.3	-21.8	19.5	7.4	-1.0	7.4	23.4	-0.1	8.7	8.7	8.7
1935	47.5	42.6	69.6	49.2	59.2	42.6	75.3	49.2	56.6	49.2	69.6	-0.1	6.7	6.7	6.7
1936	33.8	50.8	83.7	76.7	80.4	50.8	48.0	76.7	67.8	76.7	83.7	-0.1	2.8	2.8	2.8
1937	-35.1	-38.2	-53.1	-53.0	-53.0	-38.2	-49.0	-53.0	-45.9	-53.0	-53.1	0.1	1.3	1.3	1.3
1938	31.0	29.7	23.8	33.5	28.6	29.7	42.9	33.5	27.4	33.5	23.8	-0.3	6.0	6.0	6.0
1939	-0.5	-15.0	-0.2	-7.7	-3.8	-15.0	0.6	-7.7	-7.3	-7.7	-0.2	-0.2	4.3	4.3	4.3
1940	-9.9	-7.4	-12.5	-11.2	-11.8	-7.4	-2.4	-11.2	-9.7	-11.2	-12.5	-0.3	2.7	2.7	2.7
1941	-11.7	-0.5	-14.0	-4.0	-9.1	-0.5	-11.5	-4.0	-7.2	-4.0	-14.0	-0.2	0.3	0.3	0.3
1942	20.2	36.0	50.2	37.5	43.8	36.0	27.0	37.5	43.3	37.5	50.2	0.0	1.7	1.7	1.7
1943	25.8	39.0	97.8	98.9	98.5	39.0	54.0	98.9	66.8	98.9	97.8	0.1	2.6	2.6	2.6
1944	19.6	41.7	59.4	52.6	56.0	41.7	39.5	52.6	50.5	52.6	59.4	0.1	1.6	1.6	1.6
1945	36.3	43.8	80.9	72.0	76.4	43.8	50.2	73.0	61.3	71.0	80.9	0.1	2.0	2.0	2.0
1946	-8.2	-8.2	-13.5	-12.2	-12.8	-8.2	-10.1	-12.2	-10.7	-12.2	-13.5	0.1	0.8	0.8	0.8
1947	5.6	7.7	-3.5	7.3	1.8	7.7	-2.7	7.3	2.1	7.3	-3.5	0.3	0.7	0.7	0.7
1948	5.4	3.8	-7.0	-6.6	-6.8	3.8	-7.6	-6.6	-1.7	-6.6	-7.0	0.6	1.6	1.6	1.6
1949	18.7	13.9	20.6	19.5	20.1	13.9	22.1	19.5	17.3	19.5	20.6	0.9	2.1	2.1	2.1
1950	31.6	58.7	44.9	55.0	49.9	58.7	31.6	55.0	51.8	55.0	44.9	1.0	0.5	0.5	0.5
1951	23.9	13.3	8.6	10.4	9.5	13.3	14.3	10.4	11.0	10.4	8.6	1.3	0.1	0.1	0.1
1952	18.2	18.3	5.7	6.6	6.2	18.3	9.5	6.6	11.9	6.6	5.7	1.4	1.9	1.4	1.4
1953	-1.1	-7.1	-6.4	-9.1	-7.8	-7.1	-1.8	-9.1	-6.7	-9.1	-6.4	1.6	2.1	3.0	3.0
1954	52.5	77.1	64.1	64.2	64.2	77.1	60.4	64.2	70.7	64.2	64.1	0.6	2.3	2.5	2.5
1955	31.4	20.3	21.4	25.0	23.2	9.8	19.8	25.0	20.9	25.0	21.4	1.3	-0.1	-0.9	-0.9
1956	6.4	1.7	2.9	5.3	4.1	-6.5	7.1	5.3	2.4	5.3	2.9	2.2	1.9	-0.7	-0.7
1957	-10.9	-23.0	-15.7	-18.2	-16.9	-1.4	-15.7	-18.2	-19.4	-18.2	-15.7	2.9	3.9	7.6	7.6
1958	43.2	71.6	69.4	73.8	71.7	44.0	56.6	73.8	70.6	73.8	69.4	1.3	0.8	-1.5	-1.5
1959	11.8	14.7	17.6	14.1	15.9	56.7	19.1	14.1	16.2	14.1	17.6	2.7	3.6	-0.6	-0.6
1960	0.3	-9.1	-5.6	-7.4	-6.5	-6.3	-1.5	-7.4	-7.3	-7.4	-5.6	2.4	6.8	11.5	11.5
1961	26.7	27.2	30.0	31.1	30.6	4.7	30.2	31.1	28.7	31.1	30.0	1.9	2.8	1.6	1.6
1962	-8.8	-1.7	-16.6	-9.5	-13.1	-1.3	-15.8	-9.5	-9.3	-9.5	-16.6	2.5	3.0	5.3	5.3
1963	22.6	29.5	11.3	28.8	19.8	17.3	15.8	28.8	20.2	28.8	11.3	3.1	3.2	1.4	1.4
1964	16.4	21.6	17.7	24.3	21.0	-4.9	17.2	24.3	19.7	24.3	17.7	3.8	3.9	3.8	3.8
1965	12.3	22.5	37.2	43.2	40.2	11.5	32.5	43.2	29.8	43.2	37.2	3.7	3.5	0.8	0.8
1966	-10.2	-12.5	-8.8	-8.4	-8.6	-5.0	-6.4	-8.4	-10.4	-8.4	-8.8	6.2	4.9	4.4	4.4
1967	23.8	32.3	102.1	72.0	86.6	16.2	70.8	72.0	64.0	72.0	102.1	4.7	3.7	0.8	0.8
1968	11.0	21.4	49.4	50.1	49.9	46.2	39.4	50.1	35.2	50.1	49.4	5.5	5.8	4.3	4.3
1969	-8.6	-17.6	-32.8	-30.0	-31.4	2.3	-23.7	-30.0	-25.4	-30.0	-32.8	6.9	7.1	-1.0	-1.0
1970	3.9	9.7	-17.2	-1.5	-9.6	-10.9	0.3	0.3	-5.4	-5.4	-5.4	10.2	11.0	16.6	16.6
1971	14.2	19.0	17.4	15.2	16.4	30.6	67.3	67.3	48.1	48.1	48.1	5.4	5.9	8.5	8.5
1972	18.8	18.9	-1.6	4.4	1.4	37.0	63.3	63.3	49.7	49.7	49.7	3.9	3.9	4.9	4.9
1973	-14.8	-4.4	-41.1	-32.4	-36.8	-14.6	-14.2	-14.2	-14.3	-14.3	-14.3	6.7	6.1	3.1	5.3
1974	-26.6	-17.4	-29.7	-20.7	-25.3	-22.5	-29.1	-29.1	-25.8	-25.8	-25.8	8.5	9.1	6.8	8.1
1975	37.1	47.1	68.9	66.0	34.2	38.3	49.0	49.0	43.7	43.7	43.7	7.2	7.9	8.1	7.8
1976	23.7	50.3	53.6	56.6	38.7	2.8	10.8	10.8	6.8	6.8	6.8	6.1	8.9	11.5	8.8
1977	-7.3	-6.1	21.4	20.9	17.6	29.4	73.1	73.1	50.1	50.1	50.1	4.7	3.7	2.8	3.7
1978	6.5	3.1	21.1	21.5	9.0	42.0	64.6	64.6	53.1	53.1	53.1	6.1	5.5	2.0	4.5
1979	18.3	22.9	43.4	33.1	32.8	5.5	-1.4	-1.4	2.1	2.1	2.1	9.1	10.4	6.3	8.6
1980	32.3	16.0	33.9	21.9	29.2	18.2	34.7	34.7	26.3	26.3	26.3	9.7	14.1	6.4	10.1
1981	-5.0	16.1	7.1	16.0	5.8	8.5	-0.5	1.8	4.1	4.1	4.1	14.3	18.9	10.5	14.5
1982	21.3	20.2	28.8	37.0	27.8	-2.7	-0.6	-3.1	-1.6	-1.6	-1.6	17.0	19.5	25.1	20.5
1983	22.4	34.5	39.7	48.4	29.1	28.8	35.3	36.1	32.1	32.1	32.1	8.5	8.6	8.0	8.4
1984	6.1	9.0	-6.7	3.1	21.4	8.5	11.0	10.9	9.8	9.8	9.8	11.2	12.8	14.0	12.7
1985	32.0	30.6	24.7	27.2	11.5	54.4	66.6	72.5	60.4	60.4	60.4	10.5	13.2	17.7	13.8
1986	18.3	19.8	6.9	4.5	24.4	64.6	58.6	55.7	62.2	62.2	62.2	8.9	11.9	12.8	11.2
1987	5.1	3.5	-9.3	-5.4	-6.4	34.4	39.8	52.8	37.2	37.2	37.2	6.4	6.0	3.5	6.6
1988	16.7	23.6	22.9	30.0	14.1	38.0	25.2	33.6	37.4	37.4	37.4	7.4	5.9	6.3	8.7
1989	31.3	27.0	10.2	10.9	6.3	17.6	30.0	37.2	116.1	53.2	82.6	9.6	8.7	9.5	6.8
1990	-3.2	-22.8	-21.6	-26.6	-16.3	-22.0	-18.5	-17.7	-8.4	1.1	5.6	9.1	8.9	10.8	3.5
1991	30.1	34.3	44.6	42.1	39.8	9.2	5.2	4.5	69.0	39.8	24.3	9.8	10.7	14.6	12.7
1992	7.3	15.6	23.4	34.2	27.9	-10.3	-21.1	-21.9	2.9	-5.4	9.3	5.2	5.7	7.3	6.5
1993	9.6	17.0	21.0	26.3	15.5	44.7	33.6	44.6	89.2	105.8	89.5	4.4	5.1	8.3	11.6
1994	1.3	-4.5	3.1	1.2	-8.4	8.8	15.2	21.1	-10.6	13.8	2.5	2.5	0.5	-3.2	-4.3
1995	37.1	38.4	34.5	29.3	12.1	11.5	2.1	1.2	2.2	-8.3	-10.1	8.0	8.1	9.6	16.1
1996	22.6	20.2	17.6	22.3	33.8	7.8	3.4	0.9	11.4	11.5	4.8	5.8	7.2	6.6	10.8
1997	33.1	28.1	22.8	30.8	19.4	-3.1	-23.7	22.7	-18.9	-15.7	-22.6	6.0	5.9	6.4	8.3
1998	28.7	12.0	-7.3	-7.3	-15.4	14.9	8.2	5.3	-9.4	-5.7	-3.8	5.7	6.5	5.4	8.4
1999	20.8	4.8	29.8	13.0	-2.0	16.3	21.9	19.0	71.7	84.3	85.3	4.6	4.6	3.8	3.7
2000	-9.3	10.2	-3.6	9.0	20.4	-0.2	-5.4	-3.1	-29.2	-34.2	-31.8	6.7	6.5	6.8	6.7
2001	-12.1	3.9	22.8	22.6	13.2	-15.3	-10.5	-4.6	-6.8	-1.0	-2.6	5.8	6.1	7.1	5.9
2002	-22.2	-14.9	-13.3	-9.3	4.2	-8.5	1.9	5.8	-9.4	-1.7	-0.2	3.9	5.3	11.8	10.4
2003	28.5	34.4	60.7	59.4	35.6	49.9	58.8	66.5	60.2	76.2	72.8	1.6	1.9	2.7	3.0
2004	10.7	18.3	18.4	25.4	32.1	28.8	30.9	34.8	29.9	39.5	28.9	0.9	0.7	2.8	2.9
2005	4.9	10.2	5.7	7.8	13.2	15.3	22.0	23.2	29.9	30.8	25.7	2.3	1.9	0.8	1.7
2006	15.7	20.2	16.2	21.5	35.3	34.1	24.9	28.4	29.2	37.9	37.3	4.8	4.5	4.5	3.9
Annualized Return (%)	10.27	11.53	12.83	13.92	12.44	11.35	13.97	15.05	15.22	15.99	15.90	4.06	5.10	4.95	5.10
Standard Deviation (%)	19.23	25.74	32.98	29.63	30.02	25.86	24.35	28.96	28.73	29.80	32.08	1.55	2.13	3.66	3.25
Growth of $1	$2,483	$6,182	$15,621	$33,621	$11,816	$5,419	$35,007	$74,335	$83,846	$142,461	$133,843	$24.22	$53.38	$48.73	$53.40

* See Appendix B for Index Portfolio Button Definitions

Sources, Updates, and Disclosures: ifa.com/btp

Table 6-4

Annual Returns of 15 Indexes Over 80 Years (1927 - 2006)

Legend*: LC LV MC SV RE IV IS ISV EM EV ES 1F 2F 5G 5F

Year	← Highest Return				Sorted in Order of Returns for Each Year									Lowest Return →	
1927	37.3	33.2	33.2	33.2	32.1	31.3	31.3	31.2	30.8	30.8	26.1	4.3	4.3	4.3	2.9
1928	44.2	44.2	43.4	41.8	40.0	39.0	39.0	39.0	34.9	25.2	25.2	3.0	0.7	0.7	0.7
1929	5.8	5.8	5.8	4.5	-6.7	-6.7	-8.5	-30.9	-32.1	-41.8	-41.8	-41.8	-46.7	-51.4	-51.4
1930	6.5	6.5	6.5	2.2	-25.0	-32.3	-45.2	-45.2	-45.2	-46.1	-46.1	-46.8	-47.7	-47.7	-47.7
1931	0.8	-2.6	-2.6	-2.6	-43.4	-48.5	-50.3	-50.3	-52.0	-53.8	-53.8	-53.8	-55.4	-60.8	-60.8
1932	8.9	8.9	8.6	8.6	8.6	3.7	3.2	0.7	-2.0	-2.0	-2.0	-6.4	-6.4	-8.3	-8.7
1933	185.3	185.3	162.9	141.2	141.2	141.2	137.8	120.4	90.8	90.8	53.8	1.6	1.6	1.6	0.1
1934	23.4	23.4	19.5	15.3	8.7	8.7	8.7	7.4	7.4	7.4	-0.1	-1.0	-1.6	-21.8	-21.8
1935	75.3	69.6	69.6	59.2	56.6	49.2	49.2	49.2	47.5	42.6	42.6	6.7	6.7	6.7	-0.1
1936	83.7	83.7	80.4	76.7	76.7	76.7	67.8	50.8	50.8	48.0	33.8	2.8	2.8	2.8	-0.1
1937	1.3	1.3	1.3	0.1	-35.1	-38.2	-38.2	-45.9	-49.0	-53.0	-53.0	-53.0	-53.0	-53.1	-53.1
1938	42.9	33.5	33.5	33.5	31.0	29.7	29.7	28.6	27.4	23.8	23.8	6.0	6.0	6.0	-0.3
1939	4.3	4.3	4.3	0.6	-0.2	-0.2	-0.2	-0.5	-3.8	-7.3	-7.7	-7.7	-7.7	-15.0	-15.0
1940	2.7	2.7	2.7	-0.3	-2.4	-7.4	-7.4	-9.7	-9.9	-11.2	-11.2	-11.2	-11.8	-12.5	-12.5
1941	0.3	0.3	0.3	-0.2	-0.5	-0.5	-4.0	-4.0	-7.2	-9.1	-11.5	-11.7	-14.0	-14.0	-14.0
1942	50.2	50.2	43.8	43.3	37.5	37.5	37.5	36.0	36.0	27.0	20.2	1.7	1.7	1.7	0.0
1943	98.9	98.9	98.9	98.5	97.8	97.8	66.8	54.0	39.0	39.0	25.8	2.6	2.6	2.6	0.1
1944	59.4	59.4	56.0	52.6	52.6	52.6	50.5	41.7	41.7	39.5	19.6	1.6	1.6	1.6	0.1
1945	80.9	80.9	76.4	72.0	72.0	72.0	61.5	59.2	43.8	43.8	36.3	2.0	2.0	2.0	0.1
1946	0.8	0.8	0.8	0.1	-8.2	-8.2	-8.2	-10.1	-10.7	-12.2	-12.2	-12.2	-12.8	-13.5	-13.5
1947	7.7	7.7	7.3	7.3	7.3	5.6	2.1	1.8	0.7	0.7	0.7	0.3	-2.7	-3.5	-3.5
1948	5.4	3.8	3.8	1.6	1.6	1.6	0.6	-1.7	-6.6	-6.6	-6.6	-6.8	-7.0	-7.0	-7.6
1949	22.1	20.6	20.6	20.1	19.5	19.5	19.5	18.7	17.3	13.9	13.9	2.1	2.1	2.1	0.9
1950	58.7	58.7	55.0	55.0	55.0	51.8	49.9	44.9	44.9	31.6	31.6	1.0	0.5	0.5	0.5
1951	23.9	14.3	13.3	13.3	11.0	10.4	10.4	10.4	9.5	8.6	8.6	1.3	0.1	0.1	0.1
1952	18.3	18.3	18.2	11.9	9.5	6.6	6.6	6.6	6.2	5.7	5.7	1.9	1.4	1.4	1.4
1953	3.0	3.0	2.1	1.6	-1.1	-1.8	-6.4	-6.4	-6.7	-7.1	-7.1	-7.8	-9.1	-9.1	-9.1
1954	77.1	77.1	70.7	64.2	64.2	64.2	64.2	64.1	64.1	60.4	52.5	2.5	2.5	2.3	0.6
1955	31.4	25.0	25.0	25.0	23.2	21.4	21.4	20.9	20.3	19.8	9.8	1.3	-0.1	-0.9	-0.9
1956	7.1	6.4	5.3	5.3	5.3	4.1	2.9	2.9	2.4	2.2	1.9	1.7	-0.7	-0.7	-6.5
1957	7.6	7.6	3.9	2.9	-1.4	-10.9	-15.7	-15.7	-15.7	-16.9	-18.2	-18.2	-18.2	-19.4	-23.0
1958	73.8	73.8	73.8	71.7	71.6	70.6	69.4	69.4	56.6	44.0	43.2	1.3	0.8	-1.5	-1.5
1959	56.7	19.1	17.6	17.6	16.2	15.9	14.7	14.1	14.1	14.1	11.8	3.6	2.7	-0.6	-0.6
1960	11.5	11.5	6.8	2.4	0.3	-1.5	-5.6	-5.6	-6.3	-6.5	-7.3	-7.4	-7.4	-7.4	-9.1
1961	31.1	31.1	31.1	30.6	30.2	30.0	30.0	28.7	27.2	26.7	4.7	2.8	1.9	1.6	1.6
1962	5.3	5.3	3.0	2.5	-1.3	-1.7	-8.8	-9.3	-9.5	-9.5	-9.5	-13.1	-15.8	-16.6	-16.6
1963	29.5	28.8	28.8	28.8	22.6	20.2	19.8	17.3	15.8	11.3	11.3	3.2	3.1	1.4	1.4
1964	24.3	24.3	24.3	21.6	21.0	19.7	17.7	17.7	17.2	16.4	3.9	3.8	3.8	3.8	-4.9
1965	43.2	43.2	43.2	40.2	37.2	37.2	32.5	29.8	22.5	12.3	11.5	3.7	3.5	0.8	0.8
1966	6.2	4.9	4.4	4.4	-5.0	-6.4	-8.4	-8.4	-8.4	-8.6	-8.8	-8.8	-10.2	-10.4	-12.5
1967	102.1	102.1	86.6	72.0	72.0	72.0	70.8	64.0	32.3	23.8	16.2	4.7	3.7	0.8	0.8
1968	50.1	50.1	50.1	49.9	49.4	49.4	46.2	39.4	35.2	21.4	11.0	5.8	5.5	4.3	4.3
1969	7.1	6.9	2.3	-1.0	-1.0	-8.6	-17.6	-23.7	-25.4	-30.0	-30.0	-30.0	-31.4	-32.8	-32.8
1970	16.6	16.6	11.0	10.2	9.7	3.9	0.3	0.3	-1.5	-5.4	-5.4	-5.4	-9.6	-10.9	-17.2
1971	67.3	67.3	48.1	48.1	48.1	30.6	19.0	17.4	16.4	15.2	14.2	8.5	8.5	5.9	5.4
1972	63.3	63.3	49.7	49.7	49.7	37.0	18.9	18.8	4.9	4.9	4.4	3.9	3.9	1.4	-1.6
1973	6.7	6.1	5.3	3.1	-4.4	-14.2	-14.2	-14.3	-14.3	-14.3	-14.6	-14.8	-32.4	-36.8	-41.1
1974	9.1	8.5	8.1	6.8	-17.4	-20.7	-22.5	-25.3	-25.8	-25.8	-25.8	-26.6	-29.1	-29.1	-29.7
1975	68.9	66.0	49.0	49.0	47.1	43.7	43.7	43.7	38.3	37.1	34.2	8.1	7.9	7.8	7.2
1976	56.6	53.6	50.3	38.7	23.7	11.5	10.8	10.8	8.9	8.8	6.8	6.8	6.8	6.1	2.8
1977	73.1	73.1	50.1	50.1	50.1	29.4	21.4	20.9	17.6	4.7	3.7	3.7	2.8	-6.1	-7.3
1978	64.6	64.6	53.1	53.1	53.1	42.0	21.5	21.1	9.0	6.5	6.1	5.5	4.5	3.1	2.0
1979	43.4	33.1	32.8	22.9	18.3	10.4	9.1	8.6	6.3	5.5	2.1	2.1	2.1	-1.4	-1.4
1980	34.7	34.7	33.9	32.3	29.2	26.3	26.3	26.3	21.9	18.2	16.0	14.1	10.1	9.7	6.4
1981	18.9	16.1	16.0	14.5	14.3	10.5	8.5	7.1	5.8	4.1	4.1	4.1	1.8	-0.5	-5.0
1982	37.0	28.8	27.8	25.1	21.3	20.5	20.2	19.5	17.0	-0.6	-1.6	-1.6	-1.6	-2.7	-3.1
1983	48.4	39.7	36.1	35.3	34.5	32.1	32.1	32.1	29.1	28.8	22.4	8.6	8.5	8.4	8.0
1984	21.4	14.0	12.8	12.7	11.2	11.0	10.9	9.8	9.8	9.8	9.0	8.5	6.1	3.1	-6.7
1985	72.5	66.6	60.4	60.4	60.4	54.4	32.0	30.6	27.2	24.7	17.7	13.8	13.2	11.5	10.5
1986	64.6	62.2	62.2	62.2	58.6	55.7	24.4	19.8	18.3	12.8	11.9	11.2	8.9	6.9	4.5
1987	52.8	39.8	37.2	37.2	37.2	34.4	6.6	6.4	6.0	5.1	3.5	3.5	-5.4	-6.4	-9.3
1988	38.0	37.4	37.4	37.4	33.6	30.0	25.2	23.6	22.9	16.7	14.1	8.7	7.4	6.3	5.9
1989	116.1	82.6	53.2	37.2	31.3	30.0	27.0	17.6	10.9	10.2	9.6	9.5	8.7	6.8	6.3
1990	10.8	9.1	8.9	3.5	1.5	1.1	-3.2	-8.4	-16.3	-17.7	-18.5	-21.6	-22.0	-22.8	-26.6
1991	69.0	44.6	42.1	39.8	39.8	34.3	30.1	24.3	14.6	12.7	10.7	9.8	9.2	5.2	4.5
1992	34.2	27.9	23.4	15.6	9.3	7.3	7.3	6.5	5.7	5.2	2.9	-5.4	-10.3	-21.1	-21.9
1993	105.8	89.5	89.2	44.7	44.6	33.6	26.3	21.0	17.0	15.5	11.6	9.6	8.3	5.1	4.4
1994	21.1	15.2	13.8	8.8	3.1	2.5	2.5	1.3	1.2	0.5	-3.2	-4.3	-4.5	-8.4	-10.6
1995	38.4	37.1	34.5	29.3	16.1	12.1	11.5	9.6	8.1	8.0	2.2	2.1	1.2	-8.3	-10.1
1996	33.8	22.6	22.3	20.2	17.6	11.5	11.4	10.8	7.8	7.2	6.6	5.8	4.8	3.4	0.9
1997	33.1	30.8	28.1	22.8	19.4	8.3	6.4	6.0	5.9	-3.1	-15.7	-18.9	-22.6	-22.7	-23.7
1998	28.7	14.9	12.0	8.4	8.2	6.5	5.7	5.4	5.3	-3.8	-5.7	-7.3	-7.3	-9.4	-15.4
1999	85.3	84.3	71.7	29.8	21.9	20.8	19.0	16.3	13.0	4.8	4.6	4.6	3.8	3.7	-2.0
2000	28.4	10.2	9.0	6.8	6.7	6.7	6.5	-0.2	-3.1	-3.6	-5.4	-9.3	-29.2	-31.8	-34.2
2001	22.8	22.6	13.2	7.1	6.1	5.9	5.8	3.9	-1.0	-2.6	-4.6	-6.8	-10.5	-12.1	-15.3
2002	11.8	10.4	5.8	5.3	4.2	3.9	1.9	-0.2	-1.7	-8.5	-9.3	-9.4	-13.3	-14.9	-22.2
2003	76.2	72.8	66.5	60.7	60.2	59.4	58.8	49.9	35.6	34.4	28.5	3.0	2.7	1.9	1.6
2004	39.5	34.8	32.1	30.9	29.9	28.9	28.8	25.4	18.4	18.3	10.7	2.9	2.8	0.9	0.7
2005	30.8	29.9	25.7	23.2	22.0	15.3	13.2	10.2	7.8	5.7	4.9	2.3	1.9	1.7	0.8
2006	37.9	37.1	35.3	34.1	29.2	28.4	24.9	21.5	20.2	16.2	15.7	4.8	4.5	4.5	3.9
Annualized Return (%)	36.51	33.00	29.87	26.44	21.55	18.17	14.37	11.77	8.65	5.56	2.59	-4.13	-5.84	-7.83	-9.53
Standard Deviation (%)	33.28	32.28	29.09	26.40	29.52	29.77	28.34	27.01	24.12	23.57	20.52	13.73	14.59	15.09	14.94
Growth of $1	$65B	$8.1B	$1.2B	$141M	$6M	$632K	$46,331	$7,358	$764	$75.74	$8.00	$0.03	$0.00	$0.00	$0.00

* See Appendix B for Index Portfolio Button Definitions

Sources, Updates, and Disclosures: ifa.com/btp

fund will hold. This fund virtually duplicates the investment performance of the asset class in a very cost and tax-efficient way.

Indexers avoid style drift and its problems. An index fund remains invested in a discrete asset class. Indexers understand the volatility of their investments, thus are more patient and less likely to sell their funds. Actively managed mutual funds eventually experience unwanted volatility or under perform their benchmarks. This encourages active investors to sell the fund, causing the fund to either go out of business or merge into other active funds. Another tombstone is then added to the mutual fund graveyard.

6.5 SUMMARY

An active investment strategy complicates a portfolio's asset class allocation with style drift. Indexing is the only solution to the problems caused by style drift in active investing because asset class allocation is always on target.

6.6 REVIEW QUESTIONS

1. What percent of actively managed mutual funds engage in some degree of style drift?

   a. 5%

   b. 30%

   c. 40%

   d. 50%

   e. 100%

2. Style drift is best described as:

   a. money managers who stop wearing pin-striped suits

   b. ETFs

   c. index mutual funds

   d. change in investment objective

e. casual Friday on Wall Street

3. Actively managed funds tend to "drift" from their defined investment style because:

   a. fund managers go on vacation

   b fund managers retire

   c. fund managers chase the hot asset class

   d fund managers stick to their described objectives

   e. fund investors force fund managers to drift

4. Jeffrey Vinik is important in the history of style drift because he:

   a. discovered it

   b. developed the style system

   c. was the most publicized style drifter

   d. cured style drift

   e. wrote a book about style drift

5. Index fund managers avoid problems with style drift by:

   a. purchasing stocks outside their investment criteria

   b. selling stocks that meet their investment criteria

   c. selling stocks that no longer meet their funds objectives

   d. purchasing stocks that fit their investment criteria

   e. both c and d

Step 7 ~ Silent Partners

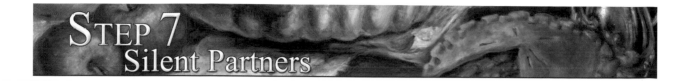

"None of my clients are taxable... Once you introduce taxes, active management probably has an insurmountable hurdle. We've been asked to manage taxable money - and declined."

- Theodore Aronson of Aronson+Partners, *Institutional Money Manager*

"It is difficult to systematically beat the market. But it is not difficult to systematically throw money down a rat hole by generating commissions (and other costs)."

- Michael C. Jensen, Harvard University

"Inflation is the one form of taxation that can be imposed without legislation."

- Milton Friedman, 1976 Nobel Prize for Economics

"It's not brains or brawn that matter in taxable investing; it's efficiency. Taxable investing is a loser's game. Those who lose the least — to taxes and fees — stand to win the most when the game's all over."

- James P. Garland, President of the Jeffrey Company

"The art of taxation consists in so plucking the goose as to get the most feathers with the least hissing."

- Jean Baptiste Colbert

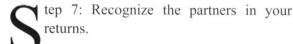

7.1 INTRODUCTION

Step 7: Recognize the partners in your returns.

The term "Silent Partners" refers to the parties who silently share in the realized and unrealized gains on an investment. Fees, expenses, taxes, and inflation are silent partners that can set an investor back before returns even begin. Investment costs alone for the average active fund can consume nearly 55% of its gross wealth. By investing in index funds however, high costs and high taxes can be avoided. In this case, the only uncontrollable partner is inflation.

One illustration over a 15-year period demonstrates that 40% of total return is allocated to silent partners. On a $10,000 investment, this translates to $41,000 of compounded return. An index fund limits the partners' take to only 13%. In tax-managed index funds, the percentage is even lower. This step discusses the unnecessary partners involved in your returns and how to keep them from eating slices of your "returns pie."

7.2 DEFINITION

Silent Partners

There are several silent partners that take a bite out of realized and unrealized gains on investments. These partners include:

- The sales agent or stockbroker who earns a commission or load for individual stock and mutual fund trades

- Federal and state income tax agencies that tax realized gains

- The fund manager who actively invests the stocks in a mutual fund

- Accountants that determine the tax ramifications of active investing

- Firms that charge investment advisory fees

- Market makers who earn a bid-ask spread on transactions

- Transfer agents who handle the share transfers for all those trades

- Mutual fund distributors

- If applicable, the brokerage firm that earns interest on margin accounts

7.3   PROBLEMS

7.3.1   Active Investors are Unaware of all the Costs

Each partner's bite adds up to claim a significant share of an investor's return. The tax effects on actively managed mutual funds are rarely evident from the reported data. Since investors do not feel the tax bite until the following April 15th, most investors do not consider the more than 17% of their pre-tax returns as lost to taxes. The effect reinforces the substantial value of passively buying and holding stocks in an index fund. Table 7-1 demonstrates that on an after-tax basis, the S&P 500 Index Fund outperformed most of the funds that routinely claim superior performance.

According to a study conducted by John Bogle, the founder of Vanguard, over a 15-year period, investors only get to keep 47% of the cumulative return of the average actively managed mutual fund, but they keep 87% in a market index fund. This means $10,000 invested in the index fund grew to $90,000 versus $49,000 in the average actively managed stock mutual fund, see Figure 7-1 and Table 7-2. That's a 40% gain from the reduction in the portion that goes to silent partners. Everyone should be interested in that!

Table 7-1

Value Lost to Taxes for the Top 15 Funds with the Highest Net Assets				
Annualized Returns (%) 10 years (1997 to 2006)			(Sorted by value lost to taxes from greatest to least)	
Fund Name	Pre-Tax Return	After-Tax Return	Difference	Value lost to taxes on $100,000 over 10 years
Amer Funds CapWrldGl A	13.79%	11.19%	2.60%	$75,109
Dodge & Cox Stock	14.23%	11.75%	2.48%	$74,549
Amer Funds CpIncBldr A	11.26%	8.36%	2.90%	$67,466
Amer Funds Inc Fund A	10.12%	6.99%	3.13%	$65,686
Amer Funds WashingtonA	9.88%	7.36%	2.52%	$53,124
Amer Funds Inv Co Am A	10.47%	8.09%	2.38%	$52,974
Amer Funds Grth Fund A	12.94%	11.04%	1.90%	$52,692
Amer Funds EuroPac A	11.23%	9.27%	1.96%	$47,214
PIMCO Total Ret Instl	6.84%	4.29%	2.55%	$41,589
Fidelity Contrafund	11.01%	9.48%	1.53%	$36,828
Fidelity Diversified Int	13.16%	12.26%	0.90%	$26,423
Fidelity Magellan	6.99%	5.73%	1.26%	$21,956
SPDR Trust Series 1	8.30%	7.70%	0.60%	$11,995
Vanguard Inst Index	8.47%	7.91%	0.56%	$11,374
Vanguard 500 Index	8.34%	7.83%	0.51%	$10,268

Source: Morningstar® Principia®, December 31, 2006

Figure 7-1

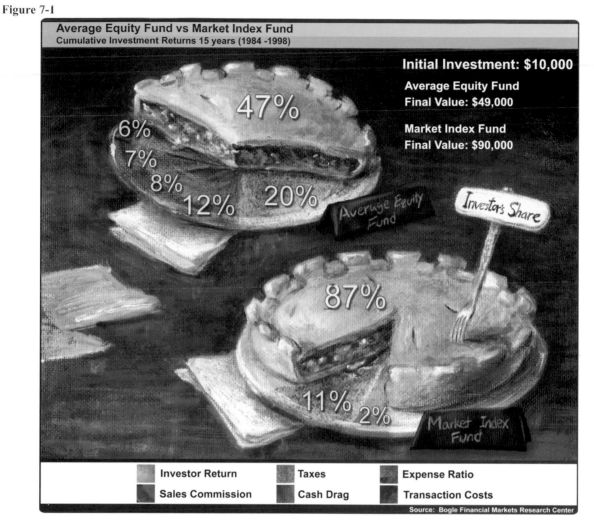

Average Equity Fund vs Market Index Fund
Cumulative Investment Returns 15 years (1984 -1998)

Initial Investment: $10,000

Average Equity Fund
Final Value: $49,000

Market Index Fund
Final Value: $90,000

| Investor Return | Taxes | Expense Ratio |
| Sales Commission | Cash Drag | Transaction Costs |

Source: Bogle Financial Markets Research Center

7.3.2 Taxes

Now let's take a look at how the tax-managed index funds can almost eliminate Uncle Sam's big bite out of your returns in taxable accounts. No wonder he looks so sad.

As indicated above, most index funds are very tax efficient. However, some indexes can be further tax managed to squeeze out even more taxes. Tax-managed index funds make an already tax efficient investment even more tax efficient by offsetting realized gains with a realized loss then deferring the realization of net capital gains and minimizing the receipt of dividend income. The result is minimal taxable distributions to investors.

Table 7-2

Average Equity Fund vs Market Index Fund Annual Investment Returns over 15 Years (1984-1998)	Average Mutual Fund	Wilshire 5000 Index Fund
Equity Return	16.9%	16.9%
Sales Commission 6% (annual impact)	-0.5%	-
Cash Drag	-0.5%	-
Fund Return	15.8%	16.9%
Transaction Costs	-0.7%	-
Expense Ratio	-1.2%	-0.2%
Investor Return	13.9%	16.7%
Tax	-2.7%	-0.9%
Investor Return	11.2%	15.8%
Reduction in Equity Return	-5.7%	-1.1%

Source: Bogle Financial Markets Research Center

Sad Uncle Sam

In a telephone survey by the Dreyfus Corporation, one thousand mutual fund investors were questioned about their tax knowledge. Eighty-five percent of respondents claimed taxes play an important role in investment decisions, but only 33% felt that they were knowledgeable about the tax implications of investing. Eighty-two percent were unable to identify the maximum rate for long-term capital gains.

Taxes on realized (distributed) capital gains, dividends, and interest can be significant. It is estimated that the average active mutual fund investor loses about three percentage points of return to taxes every year. The more an investor earns in active mutual funds, the higher the taxes. This reduces the potential for wealth, which defeats the purpose of investing. A study conducted by Stanford University measured the performance of 62 equity funds for the period from 1963 through 1992. It found that although each dollar invested in this group of funds would have grown to $21.89 in a tax-deferred account, the same amount of money invested in a taxable account would have produced only $9.87 for a high-tax-bracket investor. Taxes cut returns by 57.5%! Index funds, however, have low portfolio turnover and their capital gains distributions are also very low, thereby reducing the impact of taxes. Table 7-3 lists eleven funds and their annual turnover for 2006.

Managers of Active Funds Seem to Manage Money as if Taxes do not Matter

Historically, many active mutual fund managers managed pension plans and other tax-free pools of money, so they did not have to worry about the tax impact of their investment trades. As a result, managers of active funds today often disregard the high taxes generated by their stock picks and market timing, not to mention the adverse effect on fund performance. Realized

Table 7-3

Turnover Ratio of Various Funds January to December 2006	
Fund	**Turnover**
Schwab S&P 500 In e.Sh	3%
Vanguard 500 Index	7%
Dimensional US LgCpVal	9%
Morgan Stanley Growth C	21%
Dimensional US SmCpVal	27%
Vanguard Windsor	38%
Fidelity Contrafund	60%
Fidelity Magellan	74%
Fidelity Growth and Income	120%
Brandywine Advisors	207%
Rock Canyon Top Flight	1,635%
Source: Morningstar® Principia®, Dec. 31, 2006	

capital gains taxes are not reflected in active mutual fund performance ratings thereby catching the average active mutual fund investor by surprise.

Imagine an active fund, such as Invesco's Asian Growth Fund. At the end of 1997, this company distributed 21% of its net asset value, but lost over 38% throughout the year. An investment of $10,000 at the beginning of 1997 lost $3,800 before the $2,100 gain on which taxes must be paid. Realized capital gains can be taxed in two ways: long-term (12 months or longer) capital gains or short-term dividends. The federal tax code ensures that long-term capital gains are taxed at nearly half the tax rate of short-term dividends whose maximum taxes are about 40%!

Taxes do Matter

Instead of being distributed and taxed, unrealized capital gains are profits that have not yet been realized for tax purposes; taxes need not be paid on these gains. Unrealized capital gains remain a growing part of the net asset value of a fund's share rather than being distributed to the investor. The index fund manager minimizes portfolio turnover, and so maximizes unrealized capital gain. When stocks in an active fund increase in value and are sold for a profit by the fund's manager, the result is that the fund actually realizes gains as opposed to simply reporting an increase in the value of the portfolio, and investors pay both ordinary income and capital gains taxes on those distributions. On the other hand, by the time an investor is ready to realize an investment in an index fund, it will be a long-term capital gain, untaxed for years. Realized long-term capital gains have a much lower tax rate.

As might be expected, taxes affect active fund performance, not only earnings. Stanford University released the results of a 30-year study in 1993 that examined the difference between the average pre-tax, after-tax, and liquidation performance of 62 actively managed stock mutual funds. Pre-tax performance assumes reinvestment of all distributions, after-tax assumes reinvestment of distributions left after taxes have been paid, and liquidation is selling out completely and paying all taxes, rather than reinvesting in the fund. The study also took into account differing tax brackets, whether high (55% taxes paid), medium (41%) or low (25%). According to the study's results, between 1963 and 1992 it was found that a high tax bracket investor who reinvested after-tax distributions ended up with an accumulated wealth of 45% of the fund's published performance. Investors in a middle tax bracket realized 55% of published performance.

As mentioned earlier, actively managed mutual fund advertisements and published ratings feature only pre-tax returns, often misleading investors. In fact, Robert Jeffrey and Robert Arnott proved with their 10-year study titled "Is Your Alpha Big Enough to Cover its Taxes?" that on an after-tax basis, index funds outperformed 97% of active mutual funds. They also found that although 71 active funds tried to beat the market

with high turnover efforts, the added returns did not outweigh the resulting taxes.

7.3.3 Inflation

Unlike investment costs and taxes, nothing can be done about inflation.

Inflation is an equal opportunity destroyer of an investment's purchasing power. A certain amount of loss from inflation is incurred whether an investment is in stocks or bonds, but investing as large a portion of a portfolio in stocks for as long as possible is the best way to outpace inflation. Stocks have grown in value much more than bonds over the years and have been the best antidote for inflation.

Inflation has averaged 2.7% per year over the last five years, which does not seem too significant. Therein lies the jeopardy! The investment media, politicians, and others may convince investors that a 2.7% inflation rate is insignificant, but this rate can cut purchasing power by 26% in 10 years, 45% within 20 years, and 59% within 30 years! A 2.7% inflation rate is only negligible in very short terms; an investment purchased for $10,000 in 1970 would cost $26,094 in 2006, so it is best to buy as soon as possible and not touch that money until the last possible moment. Not even tax-deferred retirement plans can escape inflation, the most inevitable partner.

7.4 SOLUTIONS

7.4.1 Index Funds and Tax-Managed Index Funds

Unless an actively managed mutual fund states that it focuses on after-tax returns, an investor should never assume that it is managed with tax considerations in mind. A tax efficient or tax-managed mutual fund usually means that the published return and the after-tax return are close to each other.

Index funds can be tax-managed as well. Index funds have natural advantages from a tax standpoint. Managers of index funds employ tax-managed trading strategies, while managers of active funds manage money as though taxes do not matter.

Critics of tax-managed funds warn that an investor should not let tax considerations outweigh investment judgment. As author Charles Ellis said in his book, *Investment Policy*, "Never do anything for tax reasons." This is excellent advice, but when faced with taxes of 15% to 40%, any tax-managed strategy a fund manager uses takes on great importance.

One strategy used by an index fund manager is to identify and "harvest losses" by selling stocks at a loss to offset other realized capital gains. Another is to sell the stocks with the highest cost basis. As a result of these strategies, a fund will incur losses before any gains are realized. This helps an index fund maximize net after-tax return. By nature, index fund managers attempt to defer realization of short-term capital gains until they become long term. Also, a tax-managed index fund seeks to discourage short-term trading among its investors by assessing redemption fees.

7.4.2 Reduce Taxes and Turnover Costs with Index Funds

Index funds tracking the S&P 500 or Wilshire 5000 use a buy and hold approach. Capital gains are minimized, with the exception of adding and deleting stocks from these indexes. Highly liquid U.S. large company stocks dominate these index-es, and index funds tracking these stocks have a natural tax advantage.

Other index funds, however, are generally less tax efficient. Some funds sponsored by Dimensional Fund Advisors (DFA) are invested in small company stocks or value stocks. Any stocks in these index funds that become larger or seem to be growing quickly must be sold by DFA so that the funds can remain exposed to small stock or value stock risk factors. This results in higher turnover and greater realized capital gains than other indexing strategies, whereas attempting to avoid taxes by not selling these stocks would reduce exposure to small company or value risk factors. Index funds that invest in higher expected return indexes are not very tax efficient.

To help with this dilemma, DFA launched three new tax-managed index funds in 1998 and one new tax-managed fund in 2001. They are the DFA Tax-Managed U.S. Small-Cap Portfolio, the Tax-Managed U.S. Small-Cap Value Portfolio, the Tax-Managed U.S. Marketwide Value Portfolio and the Tax-Managed U.S. Equity Portfolio. DFA's research shows that the increase in after-tax returns associated with these funds can range from 1% to 1.5% per year. DFA has also run simulations with its tax-managed U.S. Market Wide Value Fund, which show that if the fund dropped 20% from its value, it could sell nearly 40% of its assets without realizing any net capital gains. Vanguard, for its part, has a handful of tax-managed funds including its Tax-Managed Balanced Fund, Tax-Managed Growth and Income Fund, Tax-Managed Capital Appreciation Fund, Tax-Managed Small-Cap Fund and Tax-Managed International Fund.

The Feast

7.5   SUMMARY

There are many silent partners eating a piece of investment returns. The best solution to this problem is to buy and hold a diversified portfolio of index funds, including tax managed funds in taxable accounts.

7.6   REVIEW QUESTIONS

1. The only uncontrollable partner in investing is:

    a. income tax

    b. inflation

    c. commissions

    d. margin account interest

    e. transaction costs

2. What is the difference between realized and unrealized gains?

    a. realized are taxed and unrealized are not

    b. old money and new money

    c. fund based and investor based

    d. IRS only reviews unrealized gains

    e. realized gains are the only real gain

3. What are the advantages of low portfolio turnover?

    a. lower taxes

    b. fewer trading costs

    c. maximum capital gain

    d. less cash drag on returns

    e. all of the above

4. Tax managed index funds add to after-tax returns because:

    a. they minimize dividend paying stocks

    b. tax loss harvest among stocks in the portfolio

    c. they generate large amounts of short-term capital gains

    d. they distribute more dividends then the regular index fund

    e. both a and b

5. According to a study by Vanguard, the average equity fund investor kept about 47% of the cumulative investment return over a 15-year period. A market index fund kept:

    a. 23%

    b. 48%

    c. 87%

    d. 13%

    e. 59%

Step 8 ~ Riskese

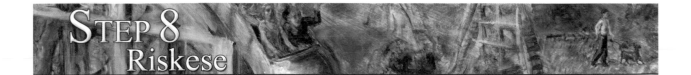

"The probable is what usually happens."

- Aristotle, *Lady Luck, The Theory of Probability* by Warren Weaver

"Probability is the very guide of life."

- Cicero, *Lady Luck, The Theory of Probability* by Warren Weaver

"The most important questions of life are, for the most part, really only problems of probability."

- Marquis de Laplace, Theorie Analytique des Probabilites, *Lady Luck, The Theory of Probability* by Warren Weaver

"The average long-term experience in investing is never surprising, but the short-term experience is always surprising. We now know to focus not on rate of return, but on the informed management of risk."

- Charles Ellis, *Investment Policy*, 1985

"If your broker [or investment advisor] is not familiar with the concept of standard deviation of returns, get a new one."

- William Bernstein, *The Intelligent Asset Allocator*

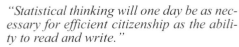

"Statistical thinking will one day be as necessary for efficient citizenship as the ability to read and write."

- H.G. Wells, *Lady Luck, The Theory of Probability* by Warren Weaver

"Investors must keep in mind that there's a difference between a good company and a good stock. After all, you can buy a good car but pay too much for it."

- Richard Thaler, *Upside*, July 6, 1999

"Odds are you don't know what the odds are."

- Gary Belsky and Thomas Gilovich, *Why Smart People Make Big Money Mistakes*

"In investing, what is comfortable is rarely profitable."

- Robert Arnott, Investment Manager

"Since the dawn of capitalism, there has been one golden rule: If you want to make money, you have to take risks."

- Opening line of the Nova Special, "The Trillion Dollar Bet"

"The record of a month's roulette playing at Monte Carlo can afford us material for discussing the foundations of knowledge."

- Karl Pearson, *Lady Luck, The Theory of Probability* by Warren Weaver

"There ain't no such thing as a free lunch."

- Acronym TANSTAAFL by Robert Heinlein, *The Moon is a Harsh Mistress*

"One of the most striking and fundamental things about probability theory is that it leads to an understanding of the otherwise strange fact that events which are individually capricious and unpredictable can, when treated en masse, lead to very stable average performances."

- Warren Weaver, *Lady Luck, The Theory of Probability*

8.1 INTRODUCTION

Step 8: Understand how risk, return, and time are related.

Do you speak riskese? Residents of China speak Chinese, citizens of Japan speak Japanese, lawyers speak legalese and top-notch investment advisors, casino statisticians, and insurance underwriters speak riskese. Riskese is the language that's used to discuss topics of risk, return, time, and correlation.

Risk, return and time are all intertwined. Higher exposure to the right risk factors leads to higher expected returns. The longer you hold a risky investment, the more likely you will obtain the long-term expected return. However, because of "random drift," risk is very unpredictable in the short run, but it can be quantified far more accurately than gut feelings and intuition in the long run. For example, you can flip 10 heads in a row with a coin, but there is still a 50/50 chance that you will flip heads the next time and in the long run. Remember that if there is no risk, there is no reason that you can expect a higher return than Treasury bills, which have paid an annualized return of 3.8% per year for the last 70 years, just 0.5% over inflation.

High risk exposure is like a scream inducing roller coaster, with soaring highs and stomach churning lows. On the roller coaster, the greater the ups and downs, the greater the returns... measured in thrills. The same thing applies to investing. However, not everyone has the "capacity" for such "exposure" to risk. In this step the concepts of risk, return and time will be explained.

8.2 DEFINITIONS

8.2.1 Standard Deviation

Standard deviation, as used by investors, is a statistical measure of the historical volatility of a stock, mutual fund or portfolio, usually computed using a minimum of 36 monthly returns. More specifically, it is a measure of the extent to which numbers are spread around their average. It also quantifies the uncertainty in a random variable, such as historical stock market returns.

Figure 8-1 explains standard deviation. One standard deviation away from the average in both directions on the horizontal axis (the green area) accounts for approximately 68% of the annual returns in the time period. Two standard deviations away from the mean (the green and blue areas) account for approximately 95% of the annual returns. And three standard deviations (the green, blue, and red areas) account for approximately 99% of the annual returns.

An investment like Index Portfolio 90, see Appendix A, is highly volatile. Figure 8-2 shows

Figure 8-1

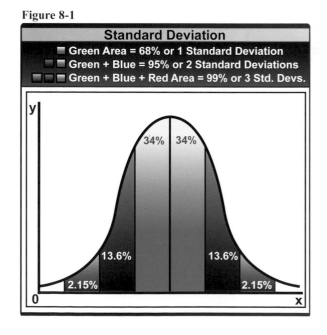

Figure 8-2

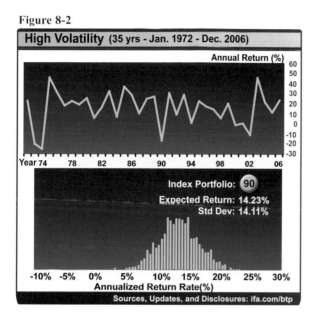

High Volatility (35 yrs - Jan. 1972 - Dec. 2006)

Index Portfolio: 90
Expected Return: 14.23%
Std Dev: 14.11%

Figure 8-3

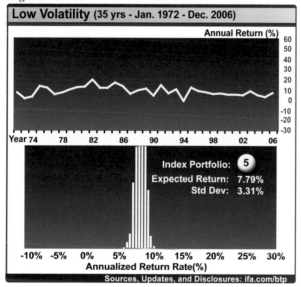

Low Volatility (35 yrs - Jan. 1972 - Dec. 2006)

Index Portfolio: 5
Expected Return: 7.79%
Std Dev: 3.31%

Figure 8-4

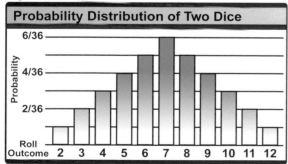

Probability Distribution of Two Dice

the annual returns over 35 years in the top graph and a histogram based on the average return and standard deviation on the bottom graph. Figure 8-3 shows a low standard deviation investment, Index Portfolio 5. Note the lack of volatility over the 35 years on the top graph and the narrow distribution of the bell curve on the bottom graph.

8.2.2 Probability Distributions and Histograms

A probability distribution is a mathematical function that describes the probabilities of possible outcomes. For example, if two dice are rolled, the range of possible outcomes or the possible results of the dice toss are two through 12. The corresponding probability distribution for the dice toss is reflected in Figure 8-4.

The mean of a probability distribution is its average or expected value. Figure 8-5 shows a distribution of 780 monthly returns of Index Portfolio 90, which is a histogram of simulated past results over the last 65 years from 1942 to 2006. The average monthly return was 1.28% and the standard deviation was 4.32%. Based on the average return and standard deviation of long-term historic data, a probability distribution of future outcomes can be estimated. Figure 8-6 provides a comparison of a more narrow histogram of monthly returns. The lower risk level of Index Portfolio 25 is illustrated in the narrower range of past monthly returns.

8.2.3 Mean Reversion

Mean reversion is a tendency for certain random variables to remain at or return over time to a long-run average level. For example, interest rates and broadly diversified indexes tend to be mean reverting. Individual stock prices, mutual fund manager performances, and short-term market performance tend not to be mean reverting.

Figure 8-5

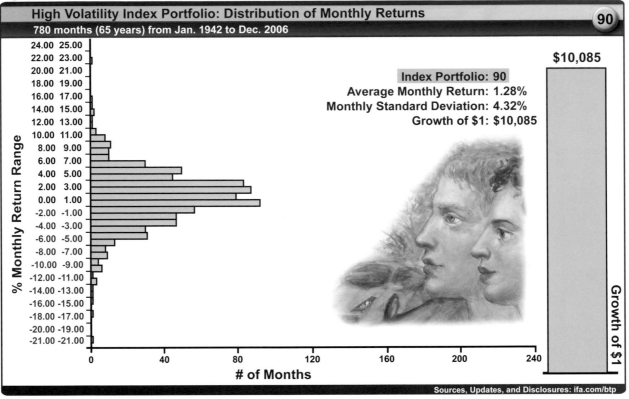

High Volatility Index Portfolio: Distribution of Monthly Returns — 90

780 months (65 years) from Jan. 1942 to Dec. 2006

Index Portfolio: 90
Average Monthly Return: 1.28%
Monthly Standard Deviation: 4.32%
Growth of $1: $10,085

$10,085

Growth of $1

% Monthly Return Range / # of Months

Sources, Updates, and Disclosures: ifa.com/btp

Figure 8-6

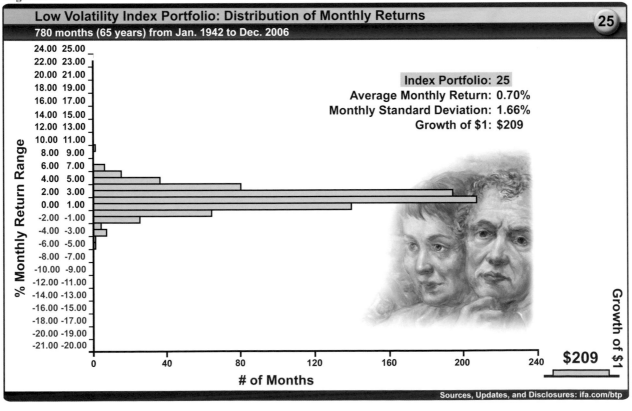

Low Volatility Index Portfolio: Distribution of Monthly Returns — 25

780 months (65 years) from Jan. 1942 to Dec. 2006

Index Portfolio: 25
Average Monthly Return: 0.70%
Monthly Standard Deviation: 1.66%
Growth of $1: $209

$209

Growth of $1

% Monthly Return Range / # of Months

Sources, Updates, and Disclosures: ifa.com/btp

Large diversified portfolios of stocks, such as the CRSP 1-10 Total Market Index or the S&P 500 Index rates of return tend to be mean reverting. They may be high or low from one year to the next. However, over 80 years, the rate of return of the S&P 500 has tended to average in the 10% range plus or minus 20% two-thirds of the time.

It is impossible to tell for certain if a variable is mean reverting by looking at its performance over any short period of time, such as a three or five-year track record of a stock, time, manager or style. This is because a tendency toward mean reversion may only reveal itself over very long horizons of 20 years or more. Figure 8-7 illustrates the difference between mean reverting and non-mean reverting outcomes.

Figure 8-7

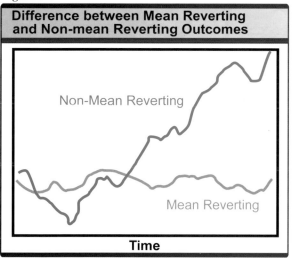

Difference between Mean Reverting and Non-mean Reverting Outcomes

Non-Mean Reverting

Mean Reverting

Time

8.2.4　Expected Return

Expected return refers to the expected or average rate of return of an investment. The term refers to a theoretical future performance, and it is definitely not a guarantee. The expected return of an index can only be derived from its very long-term historical past performance. Because returns are full of uncertainty, higher variables and the actual return for short periods of time is unpredictable, but the expected return remains

the same. Only the uncertainty or standard deviation of expected returns changes with time.

An investment's expected return is simply the middle value of the probability distribution or bell-shaped curve, which is shown as 5% in Figure 8-8. Investors are constantly surprised by short-term results, which will look nothing like the distribution below. In practice, sophisticated investors often base their expected return and volatility assumptions on historical returns of 20 years or more of an index or asset class.

Figure 8-8

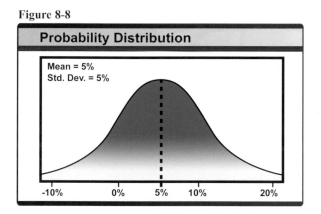

Probability Distribution

Mean = 5%
Std. Dev. = 5%

-10%　　0%　5%　10%　　20%

8.2.5 Rolling Period Returns

One problem for investors is the high level of error when drawing conclusions from the small sample of stock market data. One way to get an improvement in the number of observed periods is to create rolling periods with monthly or annual data that overlap from one period to the next. The overlapping period returns do have some statistical problems because each period contains a substantial amount of the same data. But, since monthly returns are random and have no correlation to each other, a rolling period of 144 consecutive months out of 600 months should be similar to a random sample of 144 months out of 600 months. This random sampling is another methodology of looking at returns called bootstrapping. A third method that is used to increase sample size is Monte Carlo simulations, which simulate future outcomes of portfolios based on the historical average and standard deviation.

Figure 8-9 illustrates how rolling periods are obtained using monthly frequency. For example, Period #1 includes the 12 years from January 1957 to December 31, 1968. Period #2 starts one month later on February 1, 1957 to January 31, 1969. Imagine this happening 457 times. This analysis helps capture the various experiences of 12-year investors who start their investments in July 1957, January 1963 or just about any month within the last 50 years.

Table 8-1 is a rolling period analysis of Index Portfolio 100. If you look at the red highlighted row, you will see that it covers 12-year rolling periods (144 months each) and in the period from January 1957 to December 2006, there are 457 12-year rolling periods. As you read across the red highlighted row, you can see lots of interesting data about those rolling periods. You may notice that those investors who started in January 1963 experienced the single lowest 12-year annualized return of 7.44%.

8.2.6 Risk

What is risk? In the following definition from Webster's Dictionary risk is defined in terms of loss: "Exposure to the chance of injury or loss; a hazard or dangerous chance." But, a more appropriate definition of risk for investors is "uncertainty of expected returns." Most investors think of risk as some sort of loss. To the surprise of many investors, the potential for loss is also the reason they earn a return. "Loss aversion" refers to the concept that the pain of losing a sum of money is greater than the pleasure of gaining the same amount of money. This is incorporated into the optimization process that uses risk and return trade-offs of different asset classes to build portfolios. Research shows that investors are about

twice as sensitive to investment losses as to gains.

Risk is most commonly measured in terms of standard deviation or the volatility around a given average. Prior to the groundbreaking Fama/French research, stock market risk was measured as volatility around the average return of the total stock market. However, Fama and French added two more dimensions to the measurement of investment risk — size and value.

Investors envision risk in several different ways. One way would be the worst case probability of a loss, such as the chance of not achieving an expected rate of return, not being able to readily obtain an expected amount of money at a specific time or the need to withdraw funds from investments when they are in a cumulative negative return position.

Risk is one of the most avoided, least quantified and misunderstood subjects by those working in the financial services industry. This is unfortunate because the primary purpose of investment professionals is the intelligent management of financial risks and the alignment of an investor's risk capacity with the appropriate exposure to financial risk or uncertainty.

One dimension of Risk Capacity™ is an investor's knowledge about risk, the more they understand it, the more capacity they have for risk. We face risk because nobody can consistently predict the future. After all, if we could see the future, there would be no risk. Wouldn't it be nice to get next year's *Wall Street Journal* today!

Risk, return, and time are all interconnected. Higher exposure to the right risk factors leads to higher expected returns. In accordance with the law of numbers, the longer an investor holds a broadly diversified risky investment, the more

Figure 8-9

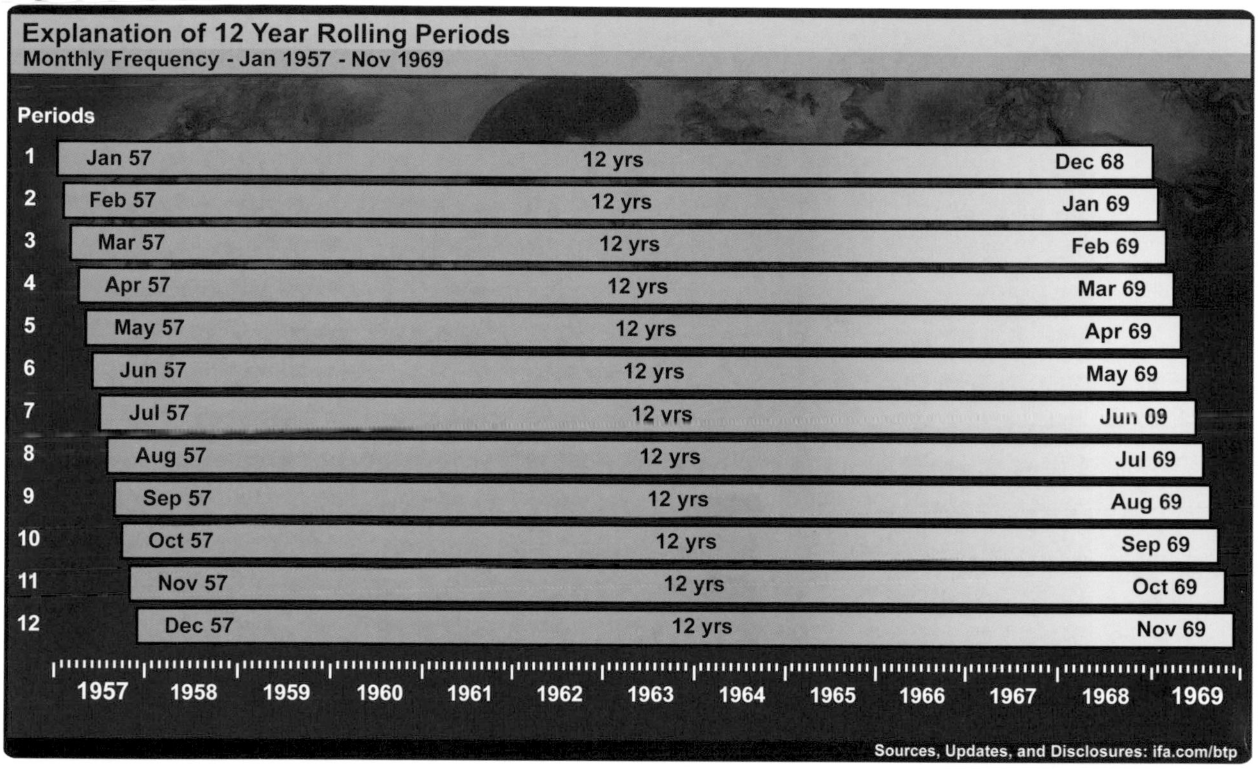

Explanation of 12 Year Rolling Periods
Monthly Frequency - Jan 1957 - Nov 1969

Periods

#	Start	Duration	End
1	Jan 57	12 yrs	Dec 68
2	Feb 57	12 yrs	Jan 69
3	Mar 57	12 yrs	Feb 69
4	Apr 57	12 yrs	Mar 69
5	May 57	12 yrs	Apr 69
6	Jun 57	12 yrs	May 69
7	Jul 57	12 vrs	Jun 09
8	Aug 57	12 yrs	Jul 69
9	Sep 57	12 yrs	Aug 69
10	Oct 57	12 yrs	Sep 69
11	Nov 57	12 yrs	Oct 69
12	Dec 57	12 yrs	Nov 69

1957 1958 1959 1960 1961 1962 1963 1964 1965 1966 1967 1968 1969

Sources, Updates, and Disclosures: ifa.com/btp

Table 8-1

Monthly Rolling Period Analysis
Based on 50 years (600 months) of Monthly Data (Jan 1957 - Dec 2006)

Index Portfolio 100: Bright Red

Per Period Number of: Yrs	Months	# of Rolling Periods	Average Ann'lzd Return	Std. Dev. of Avg. Ann'lzd Return	Lowest Rolling Period Date	Lowest Rolling Period Return	Growth of $1 in Lowest Period	Highest Rolling Period Date	Highest Rolling Period Return	Growth of $1 in Highest Period	Average Growth of $1
1	12	589	15.85%	18.57%	10/73-9/74	-35.02%	$0.65	4/03-3/04	69.39%	$1.69	$1.16
2	24	577	14.96%	11.79%	1/73-12/74	-24.74%	$0.57	12/66-11/68	52.03%	$2.31	$1.62
3	36	565	14.49%	8.95%	1/72-12/74	-11.99%	$0.68	8/84-7/87	36.02%	$2.52	$1.53
4	48	553	14.28%	7.42%	1/71-12/74	-3.66%	$0.86	10/74-9/78	34.53%	$3.28	$1.75
5	60	541	14.12%	6.70%	11/69-10/74	-4.18%	$0.81	8/82-7/87	32.62%	$4.10	$2.00
6	72	529	14.15%	6.00%	1/69-12/74	-7.75%	$0.62	1/75-12/80	30.03%	$4.83	$2.30
7	84	517	14.23%	5.34%	1/68-12/74	-2.18%	$0.86	8/82-7/89	26.64%	$5.22	$2.65
8	96	505	14.28%	4.81%	12/68-11/76	1.72%	$1.15	1/75-12/82	25.26%	$6.06	$3.05
9	108	493	14.34%	4.55%	1/66-12/74	2.71%	$1.27	1/75-12/83	26.30%	$8.18	$3.53
10	120	481	14.41%	4.24%	1/65-12/74	5.25%	$1.67	9/77-8/87	24.20%	$8.73	$4.09
11	132	469	14.45%	4.06%	1/64-12/74	6.33%	$1.06	1/75-12/85	25.02%	$11.66	$4.74
12*	144	457	14.42%	3.85%	1/63-12/74	7.44%	$2.37	1/75-12/86	25.08%	$14.66	$5.45
13	156	445	14.42%	3.72%	1/62-12/74	5.89%	$2.10	10/74-9/87	25.43%	$19.02	$6.27
14	168	433	14.50%	3.51%	1/61-12/74	7.26%	$2.67	1/75-12/88	23.92%	$20.14	$7.26
15	180	421	14.55%	3.34%	1/60-12/74	6.28%	$2.49	1/75-12/89	24.08%	$25.44	$8.39
20	240	361	15.08%	2.04%	1/57-12/76	11.00%	$8.06	1/75-12/94	20.50%	$41.66	$17.65
30	360	241	15.08%	0.87%	10/68-9/98	12.88%	$37.89	1/75-12/04	17.96%	$141.92	$69.29
40	480	121	14.34%	0.44%	4/63-3/03	13.48%	$157.32	1/58-12/97	15.47%	$315.33	$215.38
50	600	1	14.22%	0.00%	1/57-12/06	14.22%	$771.09	1/57-12/06	14.22%	$771.09	$771.09

Sources, Updates, and Disclosures: ifa.com/btp

*12 years represents the estimated average holding period for investors who score 100 on the Risk Capacity Survey at ifa.com.

likely a long-term expected return will be obtained. However, because of random drift, risk is very unpredictable in the short run, yet more accurately quantifiable than gut feelings and intuition in the long run. Random drift can be illustrated by flipping a coin and obtaining 10 heads in a row. There is still a 50/50 chance of heads the next time and every time in the future.

Risk and Return Correlate Closely

Investment risk and return correlate closely and are tightly intertwined. The bottom line is that risk must be taken to achieve a return. Risk is the currency of return. A greater return can be considered as payment for investors subjecting themselves to greater uncertainty of those returns. Without the uncertainty of gain or loss, why would there be any logical reason for investors to earn money? This correlation is evident in virtually all stock market historical data. There are ways to refine risk and return, but at the end of the day, risk is the currency used to purchase returns.

With that clarification, the question then arises as to what denominations and values can be identified. In other words, what are the risk factors, and how are they priced? These questions were addressed by Eugene Fama and Kenneth French.

Systematic and Unsystematic Risk

When Nobel laureate William Sharpe published his Capital Asset Pricing Model (CAPM) in 1964, he decomposed a portfolio's risk into systematic or nonspecific risk and nonsystematic or specific risk.

Systematic risk refers to the risks of the entire market as opposed to the risks specific to one stock. These market-wide risks are tied to large scale risks like the risk of capitalism being a viable economic social system. Other risks not specific to one stock include war, recession, inflation, and government policies.

Nonsystematic risk refers to those risks that are specific to individual companies. Examples include lawsuits, fraud, competition and other unique circumstances related to a company. The important fact for investors to understand is that there is no added expected return for nonsystematic risk above the expected return for systematic risk. This is a very big idea that essentially says that all stocks have an expected return that is the same as the market or a market index fund return. However, those stocks have more uncertainty of the expected return.

The incremental risk of one stock (nonsystematic risk) is unrewarded risk, and therefore should be avoided by investors. However, the systematic risk of capitalism is essentially the market risk and has earned an annualized return of about 10% per year for 80 years. But, in periods of less than 10 years, the annualized returns can be very volatile and uncertain. In periods longer than 20 years, the annualized returns of each period are far more consistent than one to five-year periods.

Concentration Risk

Individual stocks and bonds contain both systematic and nonsystematic risk. If investors hold the market portfolio of stocks like the Wilshire 5000, they have eliminated nonsystematic risk and they have not concentrated their portfolio on fewer stocks than the market. Concentration risk occurs when investors try to pick stocks and bonds that they think will outperform the market. Concentration of investments is akin to speculation and adds risk, but provides no additional expected return.

Figure 8-10

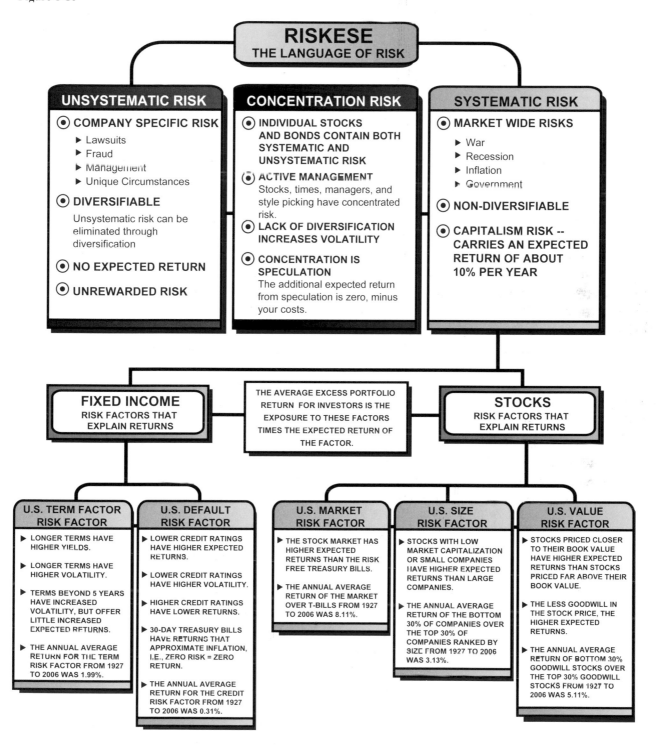

RISKESE
THE LANGUAGE OF RISK

UNSYSTEMATIC RISK

- ⊙ COMPANY SPECIFIC RISK
  - ▶ Lawsuits
  - ▶ Fraud
  - ▶ Management
  - ▶ Unique Circumstances
- ⊙ DIVERSIFIABLE

  Unsystematic risk can be eliminated through diversification
- ⊙ NO EXPECTED RETURN
- ⊙ UNREWARDED RISK

CONCENTRATION RISK

- ⊙ INDIVIDUAL STOCKS AND BONDS CONTAIN BOTH SYSTEMATIC AND UNSYSTEMATIC RISK
- ⊙ ACTIVE MANAGEMENT

  Stocks, times, managers, and style picking have concentrated risk.
- ⊙ LACK OF DIVERSIFICATION INCREASES VOLATILITY
- ⊙ CONCENTRATION IS SPECULATION

  The additional expected return from speculation is zero, minus your costs.

SYSTEMATIC RISK

- ⊙ MARKET WIDE RISKS
  - ▶ War
  - ▶ Recession
  - ▶ Inflation
  - ▶ Government
- ⊙ NON-DIVERSIFIABLE
- ⊙ CAPITALISM RISK -- CARRIES AN EXPECTED RETURN OF ABOUT 10% PER YEAR

FIXED INCOME
RISK FACTORS THAT EXPLAIN RETURNS

THE AVERAGE EXCESS PORTFOLIO RETURN FOR INVESTORS IS THE EXPOSURE TO THESE FACTORS TIMES THE EXPECTED RETURN OF THE FACTOR.

STOCKS
RISK FACTORS THAT EXPLAIN RETURNS

U.S. TERM FACTOR
RISK FACTOR

- ▶ LONGER TERMS HAVE HIGHER YIELDS.
- ▶ LONGER TERMS HAVE HIGHER VOLATILITY.
- ▶ TERMS BEYOND 5 YEARS HAVE INCREASED VOLATILITY, BUT OFFER LITTLE INCREASED EXPECTED RETURNS.
- ▶ THE ANNUAL AVERAGE RETURN FOR THE TERM RISK FACTOR FROM 1927 TO 2006 WAS 1.99%.

U.S. DEFAULT
RISK FACTOR

- ▶ LOWER CREDIT RATINGS HAVE HIGHER EXPECTED RETURNS.
- ▶ LOWER CREDIT RATINGS HAVE HIGHER VOLATILITY.
- ▶ HIGHER CREDIT RATINGS HAVE LOWER RETURNS.
- ▶ 30-DAY TREASURY BILLS HAVE RETURNS THAT APPROXIMATE INFLATION, I.E., ZERO RISK = ZERO RETURN.
- ▶ THE ANNUAL AVERAGE RETURN FOR THE CREDIT RISK FACTOR FROM 1927 TO 2006 WAS 0.31%.

U.S. MARKET
RISK FACTOR

- ▶ THE STOCK MARKET HAS HIGHER EXPECTED RETURNS THAN THE RISK FREE TREASURY BILLS.
- ▶ THE ANNUAL AVERAGE RETURN OF THE MARKET OVER T-BILLS FROM 1927 TO 2006 WAS 8.11%.

U.S. SIZE
RISK FACTOR

- ▶ STOCKS WITH LOW MARKET CAPITALIZATION OR SMALL COMPANIES HAVE HIGHER EXPECTED RETURNS THAN LARGE COMPANIES.
- ▶ THE ANNUAL AVERAGE RETURN OF THE BOTTOM 30% OF COMPANIES OVER THE TOP 30% OF COMPANIES RANKED BY SIZE FROM 1927 TO 2006 WAS 3.13%.

U.S. VALUE
RISK FACTOR

- ▶ STOCKS PRICED CLOSER TO THEIR BOOK VALUE HAVE HIGHER EXPECTED RETURNS THAN STOCKS PRICED FAR ABOVE THEIR BOOK VALUE.
- ▶ THE LESS GOODWILL IN THE STOCK PRICE, THE HIGHER EXPECTED RETURNS.
- ▶ THE ANNUAL AVERAGE RETURN OF BOTTOM 30% GOODWILL STOCKS OVER THE TOP 30% GOODWILL STOCKS FROM 1927 TO 2006 WAS 5.11%.

Figure 8-11

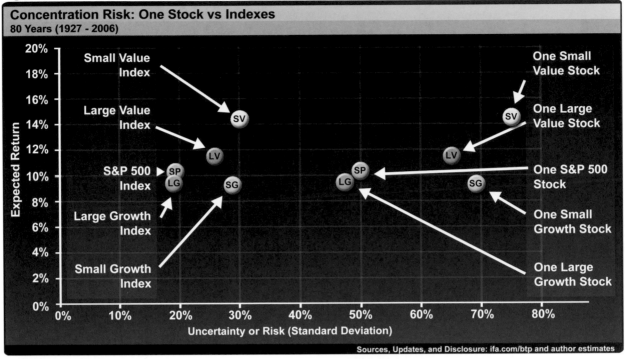

Concentration Risk: One Stock vs Indexes
80 Years (1927 - 2006)

Sources, Updates, and Disclosure: ifa.com/btp and author estimates

Concentration risk comes from all active management strategies such as stocks, timers, managers or style picking. The opposite of concentration is diversification and therefore diversification is often referred to as the antidote to uncertainty. Figure 8-10 summarizes these concepts of riskese in a flow diagram. Figures 8-11 and 8-12 explain the reasons to avoid concentration risk.

Index Funds Reduce Uncertainty of Expected Returns

Portfolios of index funds shield investors from diversifiable risk better than portfolios of active funds. Yet no portfolio, whether active or index, can reduce the systematic risk or non-diversifiable risk that is inherent in all portfolios. This is the market risk that a person's investments, however conservative, will decline in value because of a market downturn.

Figure 8-12

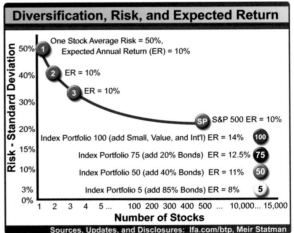

Diversification, Risk, and Expected Return

Sources, Updates, and Disclosures: Ifa.com/btp, Meir Statman

8.2.7 The Dimensions of Stock Return

Researchers did not have a very good idea about what sources of investment risk actually produced higher returns until 1992. They previously only had Sharpe's One-Factor Model to explain how investment returns were derived as seen in Figure 8-13. However, Sharpe's One-Factor Model explained only about 70% of the returns of the stock market.

Figure 8-13

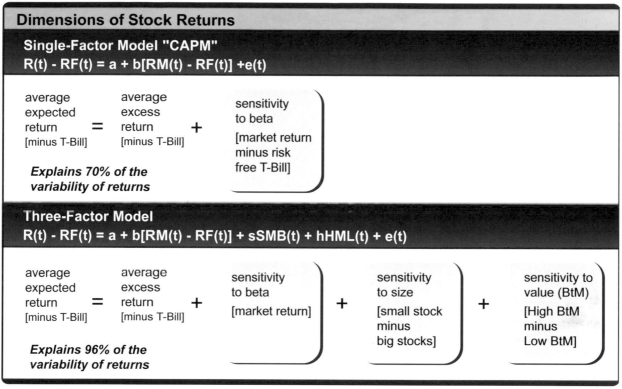

Dimensions of Stock Returns

Single-Factor Model "CAPM"
$R(t) - RF(t) = a + b[RM(t) - RF(t)] + e(t)$

average expected return [minus T-Bill] = average excess return [minus T-Bill] + sensitivity to beta [market return minus risk free T-Bill]

Explains 70% of the variability of returns

Three-Factor Model
$R(t) - RF(t) = a + b[RM(t) - RF(t)] + sSMB(t) + hHML(t) + e(t)$

average expected return [minus T-Bill] = average excess return [minus T-Bill] + sensitivity to beta [market return] + sensitivity to size [small stock minus big stocks] + sensitivity to value (BtM) [High BtM minus Low BtM]

Explains 96% of the variability of returns

Figure 8-14

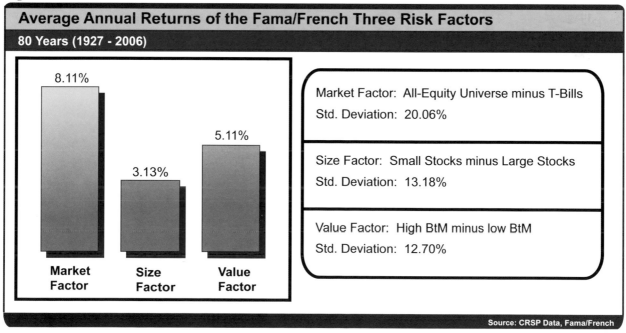

Average Annual Returns of the Fama/French Three Risk Factors

80 Years (1927 - 2006)

- Market Factor: 8.11%
- Size Factor: 3.13%
- Value Factor: 5.11%

Market Factor: All-Equity Universe minus T-Bills
Std. Deviation: 20.06%

Size Factor: Small Stocks minus Large Stocks
Std. Deviation: 13.18%

Value Factor: High BtM minus low BtM
Std. Deviation: 12.70%

Source: CRSP Data, Fama/French

In 1992, Eugene F. Fama of the University of Chicago and Kenneth R. French of Yale University developed a three-factor model to characterize and describe the relationship between risk and return for stocks. Their model is essentially an extension of Sharpe's One-Factor Model. Sharpe said that the amount of a portfolio invested in stocks is the most important determinant of return. The Fama/French model added two other fundamental determinants. Fama and French sought to determine the factors that best describe why there are differences among the returns of stock asset classes over long periods of time. They first studied the period starting in 1964, the year that reliable computer data was available. It was later updated and confirmed with data dating back to 1926. In short, they tried to identify the factors that explained the remaining 30% of returns left unexplained by Sharpe.

Fama and French concluded that exposure to three risk factors—market, size, and value (book-to-market)—collectively do the best job pinpointing the sources of investment risk that account for stock market returns. Risk factors are sources of risk that the stock market seems to reward over the long run. Based on the Fama/French findings, these three risk factors constitute the dimensions of stock returns. To review the average annual returns for the last 80 years, see Figure 8-14.

These three risk factors combined explain up to 95% of the returns of the market in U.S. and foreign stock markets. These findings suggest that an investor's investment performance in comparison to the stock market or other investors depends almost entirely on the percentage of stocks (market factor) held in a portfolio, and more specifically, the amount of small stocks (size factor) and high book-to-market ratio stocks (value factor) held.

Figure 8-15 illustrates the three dimensions of market, size, and value in 20 different index portfolios, as seen in Appendix A. Each colored circle represents one index portfolio, with the red button representing the highest exposure to market, small size stocks and value stocks.

Figure 8-15

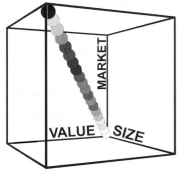

Market Risk Factor

The first risk factor in the Fama/French Three-Factor Model is the amount of exposure to the overall stock market or the market risk factor. Exposure to this factor is determined by the amount of a portfolio that's invested in or exposed to stocks. The greater this exposure, the higher the return in comparison to U.S. Treasury bills.

Size Risk Factor

The second risk factor in the Fama/French model is the amount of exposure to small company stocks or the size risk factor. Exposure to this factor is determined by the amount of a portfolio that is invested in small company stocks. The greater this exposure, the higher the return in comparison to large company stocks.

Small company stocks have small market capitalization. The market cap is determined by multiplying the total number of shares times the price per share. These stocks are generally perceived as riskier than large company stocks because small companies have fewer financial resources and more uncertain earnings than large companies. Small companies are also less able to survive prolonged periods of economic downturns. Even when small companies have good track records, these track records aren't very long, adding more uncertainty and greater risk to their stocks. Because investing in small company stocks is riskier, investors demand a higher rate of return.

It's important to understand that the average return of small-cap company stocks have significantly outperformed large company stocks over the last 80 years by 3.13% per year. But, to get higher returns, investors must accept a step up in the uncertainty of those returns. Figure 8-16 plots the deciles (one-tenth buckets) of U.S. companies sorted by size over the last 80 years. Note that a fairly clear line exists between the less risky large-cap stocks in decile 1 and the very risky microcap stocks in decile 10.

However, in shorter time periods they don't always outperform large company stocks. In fact, the size risk factor fluctuates unpredictably. This is consistent with the Random Walk Theory of changes in stock prices.

Value Risk Factor

The third risk factor in the Fama/French model is the amount of exposure to low priced stocks, which is measured by a book-to-market (BtM) value ratio. The book value of a company is just an accounting term for its net worth, its assets minus its liabilities. The market value of a company is its price per share times the number of shares outstanding. This risk factor is known by several different designations. It has been referred to as the value factor, BtM factor, style factor and price factor. Note that charts referring to it may have any of these designations. The most current designation is the value factor, referring to the low prices of these stocks compared to a company's book value or to other stocks.

Exposure to the value factor is determined by the amount of a portfolio exposure to high BtM stocks. In other words, when a stock's market price is less than its book value, the BtM ratio is greater than one. The greater the exposure to

Figure 8-16

the value factor, the higher the historic and expected return in comparison to low BtM stocks. High BtM companies usually have low earnings and experience other signs of financial distress. Investors don't like these stocks for these reasons. As a result of their poor track records, the market drives down the prices of these stocks. This naturally makes them riskier to investors.

Stocks with a low BtM ratio have low book values relative to their market prices and are termed growth stocks. Investors favor growth stocks because they're perceived to be great companies and therefore are less risky. They represent successful companies with strong track records and healthy earnings.

The Nobel Prize-winning contribution made by Merton Miller provides a framework for better understanding the connection between the value risk factor and stock returns. Miller set forth a simple but profound notion: the cost of capital to a company equals the expected return to an investor who holds its stock. In other words, a company's cost of capital equals the future returns it is foregoing in order to obtain capital from investors.

For example, suppose that a value company and a growth company each approach a bank for a loan. Which company will have to pay the higher cost of capital (the higher interest rate) on its loan? The value company will pay the higher cost because its future is less certain and the bank will need to charge extra interest for taking the extra risk that the company won't be able to pay back its loan. Thus, the riskier the company's stock, the higher the cost of capital paid by a company.

Because the market perceives a value stock to be riskier, it drives down their price so that the expected return is high enough to make it worthwhile for investors to hold, in spite of the extra risk they take when buying it. In this way, stock prices adjust, (the market sets the price at a discount, so its expected return is higher) to reflect the perceived riskiness of the stock. This ensures that the stock will be purchased, even though growth companies have better earnings prospects and generally seem safer.

The key to understanding the connection between the value risk factor and stock returns lies in focusing on the market price of a stock. A high BtM ratio suggests that the market values the stock less than the stock's accountants. This is usually because the stock has poor earnings as well as other indications of financial distress. This makes the stock riskier. As a result, investors demand a higher rate of return to compensate them for the risk that a high BtM stock will do worse than expected, go bankrupt, and end up as one of the "stocks in a box."

A 1987 study compared the investment performance of a portfolio of 29 growth stocks to one with 29 value stocks. The growth stocks represented companies that were stronger and healthier than value stocks by every economic measure, including return on total capital, return on equity, and return on sales. The value stocks represented companies that had little profitability, terrible management, and a bad image. Yet, the study found that the value stocks outperformed the growth stocks, 298% to 182%, over the five-year period of 1981 to 1985.

This means that investors earned higher returns by owning the stocks of companies that did poorly. That seems counterintuitive to most investors, since they tend to think that healthy stocks are better investments than distressed stocks. After all, if investors ask for a stock tip, they want to hear the name of the next Microsoft, not a stock with poor earnings. The fact is that investors should be interested in great investments (value stocks), not great companies (growth stocks).

Figure 8-17 illustrates the relationship between expected return and the three factors of market, size, and value. Since we are only discussing stocks, the market exposure is not shown on this plot. The higher the investment plots in the top right quadrant, the higher the expected return. The full page Figure 8-18 actually puts values of average expected returns of various

Figure 8-17

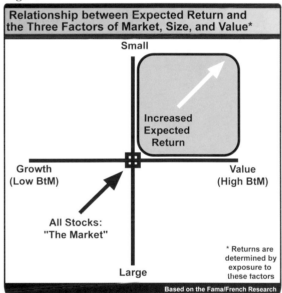

indexes over the market return. The blue circles on the plot represent various indexes. The total market index is plotted at the center of the cross hatch, which is a 0,0 on the scale of size and value. The return in the top right corner is the highest return on the plot. The dotted diagonal line represents indexes that would have the same return as the market return. Also note that large growth stocks have negative average returns relative to the total market return, with the bottom left corner value being -4.71%. Large and safe companies have lower risk associated with them and therefore have lower returns compared to

smaller companies. Note that a portfolio similar to Index Portfolio 90 (see Appendix A) plots with an expected average return of about 3.8% over the total market return. Because Index Portfolio 90 has international indexes in the mix, this is not entirely accurate, but does give us an idea of how this type of analysis works.

8.2.8 Implications of the Fama/French Three-Factor Model

Structuring Index Funds

Most investors are really only guessing which managers or asset classes will outperform the market. They encounter vast inefficiencies in trying to pick winners from among thousands of money managers and mutual funds. However, with the introduction of the Fama/French model, these costly efforts can be entirely eliminated by investing in Fama/French designed index funds.

Some mutual fund companies such as Dimensional Fund Advisors (DFA) have taken advantage of the Fama/French research by offering a full assortment of index funds, including low price and small company index funds. Investing in these funds is the most efficient and effective way to maximize exposure to the three risk factors that generate 95% of the market returns. For example, DFA offers investors value index funds that are structured to (1) maximize exposure to the size and value risk factors and (2) diversify that exposure as much as possible. This building block approach to building portfolios is a cleaner and more consistent way of managing money.

How a portfolio is structured for optimal exposure to the three risk factors determines how well the portfolio performs relative to other portfolios. Portfolio structure refers to the indexes the portfolio holds and in what proportions. The

Figure 8-18

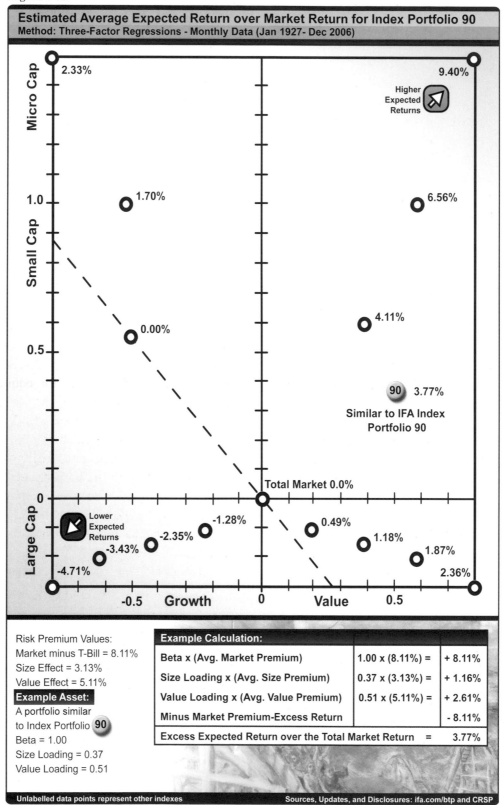

Estimated Average Expected Return over Market Return for Index Portfolio 90
Method: Three-Factor Regressions - Monthly Data (Jan 1927- Dec 2006)

Micro Cap — 2.33%   9.40%

Higher Expected Returns

Small Cap — 1.70% — 1.0 — 6.56%

0.00% — 0.5 — 4.11%

90 3.77%
Similar to IFA Index Portfolio 90

Total Market 0.0%

Large Cap — 0

Lower Expected Returns — -1.28% — 0.49%

-2.35% — 1.18%

-3.43% — 1.87%

-4.71% — 2.36%

-0.5   **Growth**   0   **Value**   0.5

Risk Premium Values:
Market minus T-Bill = 8.11%
Size Effect = 3.13%
Value Effect = 5.11%
Example Asset:
A portfolio similar to Index Portfolio **90**
Beta = 1.00
Size Loading = 0.37
Value Loading = 0.51

Example Calculation:		
Beta x (Avg. Market Premium)	1.00 x (8.11%) =	+ 8.11%
Size Loading x (Avg. Size Premium)	0.37 x (3.13%) =	+ 1.16%
Value Loading x (Avg. Value Premium)	0.51 x (5.11%) =	+ 2.61%
Minus Market Premium-Excess Return		- 8.11%
Excess Expected Return over the Total Market Return =		3.77%

Unlabelled data points represent other indexes

Sources, Updates, and Disclosures: ifa.com/btp and CRSP

Fama/French findings offer guidelines to investors for effectively allocating indexes within a portfolio. The allocation decision is crucial, since the degree of exposure to the three risk factors for equities and two additional factors for bonds accounts for nearly all the returns earned by diversified portfolios of stocks and bonds. That's why investors should focus on properly structuring their portfolios rather than trying to pick winning stocks or managers.

Measuring the Performance of Active Managers

Indexes such as the S&P 500 or Wilshire 5000 are often used to evaluate the performances of active money managers. Given the Fama/French findings, the use of such benchmarks is often misleading. Because these indexes are weighted heavily towards large company stocks and high priced stocks, the performances of managers investing more heavily in small company stocks or low priced stocks won't be accurately measured by them. Instead, customized benchmarks are needed to provide accurate measurements of the contributions to performances made by active money managers.

The Fama/French Three-Factor Model is a superior way to evaluate the performances of active money managers. It shows whether a manager achieves returns in excess of index returns. After all, an active manager shouldn't be rewarded just for buying value stocks—that's something that can be done inexpensively with an indexing strategy.

The place where a portfolio is positioned or structured on the crosshair map in Figure 8-18 determines the vast majority of its return. The crosshair map doesn't plot the market risk factor since all stock portfolios take similar market risk and are plotted relative to the stock market. So,

there's no need for a separate axis; instead, the stock market sits right at the crosshairs of the map. The crosshair map has two dimensions. The size dimension is plotted along the vertical axis, and the BtM dimension is plotted along the horizontal axis. The axes represent exposure to these two risk factors. Portfolios that take on a lot of size risk appear higher along the size axis, and portfolios that take on a lot of value risk appear further along to the right on the growth/value axis.

Changing the Definition of "Alpha"

The Fama/French Three-Factor (Five Factors with bonds) Model changes the definition of alpha, as seen in Figure 8-19. According to the one-factor CAPM, alpha is the amount by which an active money manager outperforms a broad market index. The Fama/French Three-Factor Model defines alpha for equities more precisely as the return an active manager achieves above the sum of the portfolio's expected return due to all three equity risk factors. Alpha measures a manager's skill in earning a return that couldn't have been achieved by indexing the same exact risk exposure as the portfolio run by the manager. In short, did the money manager earn anything above the indexed return?

A portfolio can be plotted anywhere on the crosshair map, and it's easy to calculate its expected return. For example, a small-cap manager may overweight value stocks relative to a benchmark, such as the Russell 2000 Small-Cap Index. As a result, the manager outperforms it. But if the extra return was simply compensation for taking additional non-diversifiable market risk, why should the manager get credit? The job of an active manager is to consistently outsmart the millions of other traders who get the same news at the same second, and through this

Figure 8-19

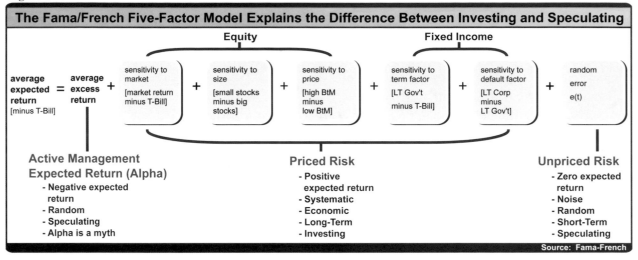

The Fama/French Five-Factor Model Explains the Difference Between Investing and Speculating

process provide additional returns that can't be achieved through indexing. This is exactly what the alpha is in the Three-Factor Model. Investors should insist that a manager outperforms a three factor risk adjusted benchmark before crediting him with an alpha return. After all, active manager fees are supposed to pay for predicting the future of stock prices, not for taking additional market risk from low cost index funds.

So, what "positive alpha" managers have been doing with the one-factor CAPM measurement model is just systematically subjecting their clients to two additional risk factors - size (small company) and high BtM value (distress). Thus, what's showing up as alpha (skill) is nothing more than a measurement error. If the performances of active managers are compared between CAPM and the Fama/French model, there are radical changes in the outcomes. Any evidence of manager skill just vanishes under the Fama/French model. The formula for this type of analysis is summarized in Figure 8-19.

Even though active managers focus on alpha, the amount of return due to alpha from stock picking or market timing is random, and on average is expected to be negative. It turns out that

alpha is nothing more than a myth perpetuated by the improper measurement of a manager's performance.

Higher Expected Returns of Value and Small Company Stocks

Long-term investment data makes it clear that value stocks outperform growth stocks and small company stocks outperform large company stocks, as seen in the 80 years of returns data seen in Figure 8-20.

But there has been some debate as to what causes these stocks to outperform large company stocks. Why are there differences in the expected returns of these indexes?

In one corner of the ring are those who say that value and small company stocks outperform because investors mistakenly price the value of the future earnings of distressed companies too low. This is the "market inefficiency" view. That is, investors see the poor earnings and high risks of value and small company stocks and decide that they are worse investments than they really are. As a result, the market sets erroneously low prices for these stocks. In effect, the combination

Figure 8-20

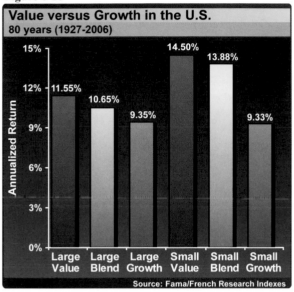

Value versus Growth in the U.S.
80 years (1927-2006)

Annualized Return

- Large Value: 11.55%
- Large Blend: 10.65%
- Large Growth: 9.35%
- Small Value: 14.50%
- Small Blend: 13.88%
- Small Growth: 9.33%

Source: Fama/French Research Indexes

of all market participants' opinions is wrong, and they agreed on a price that undervalues these stocks. When value and small company stocks then go up, the market is surprised. If investors guessed wrong in the past, presumably they should learn from their mistakes and guess right in the future. But, according to the market inefficiency point of view, investors will continue to repeat these mistakes in the future, thereby allowing other investors such as certain professional stock pickers to outperform them and the market. The market inefficiency view holds that the value and size risk factors turned up by Fama and French aren't really fundamental sources of risk, just opportunities for stock picking.

The field of behavioral finance would add that these mispriced stocks are over or under reactions of investors to market news. A study by Eugene Fama titled "Market Efficiency, Long-Term Returns, and Behavioral Finance," indicates that this may be the case, but such reactions are random and therefore not a viable investment strategy. That paper and many other academic papers can be found on the Internet at www.ssrn.com.

Eugene Fama and other proponents of efficient markets say that the higher expected returns of small and value stocks are compensation for bearing the greater risk.

According to this "market efficiency" view, greater risk and cost of capital of these firms creates higher expected return for investors, reflected in the lower prices relative to book value for value stocks, and the lower market capitalizations of small company stocks. Quite simply, there are differences in expected returns because there are differences in risk. If value and size truly are risk factors, their expected return premiums shouldn't disappear, even when more investors are informed about the favorable risk/return relationships. As a result, there shouldn't be a predictable decline over long periods of time in the probability distributions of future returns generated by these stocks, compared to the safer overall market returns. Remember that the expected returns for these risk factors have standard deviations of about 13%, (see again Figure 8-14) so an expected return of about 4%, plus or minus 13% two-thirds of the time, is a very wide probability distribution.

Regardless of whether an investor thinks that the higher returns of value and small company stocks are a result of habitual mispricing (market inefficiency) or rational risk compensation (market efficiency), the conclusion is the same. It would behoove investors to include value and small company stock indexes in their diversified portfolios.

The Dimensions of Bond Returns

Bonds are a component of investment portfolios because they dampen the volatility of stocks due to their low correlations to movements of stock prices. Bonds also provide short-term liquidity to investors with cash needs over a two to four-year period.

There are two primary risk factors that explain bond returns. The first is the term factor, which is the difference between the returns of long-term government bonds and short-term Treasury bills. The annual average return for the term risk factor has been 1.99% for the 80 years from 1927 to 2006.

The second risk factor is the default factor. It measures the difference between long-term corporate bonds and long-term government bonds, assuming that governments are less likely to default than corporations. The annual average return for the default risk factor has been 0.31% for the 80 years from 1927 to 2006.

While the term provides higher expected returns, the excess returns diminish significantly beyond a term of five years as can be seen in Figure 8-21, so bonds with terms of more than five years should be avoided.

If investors keep terms or maturities short and default risk relatively low, they have more opportunity to capture the much higher expected returns from the size and value risk factors of stocks.

The Five Dimensions of Risk Exposure

Now that we have the three risk factors of stocks and the two risk factors of bonds, we can look at the explanation of returns for balanced portfolios that include stocks and bonds. Take another look at Figure 8-19 for a verbal equation that explains all five of the risk factors of stocks and bonds.

The Trade-offs between Risk and Return

Risk and return are inseparable. This means that investors must often face bedeviling trade-offs between risk and return. There's no way around these decisions, since they're required in order to build portfolios. For example, sometimes investors look at short-term CD rates. They like the certainty and stability of CD returns, but they feel they need to obtain higher returns. So, these investors turn to stocks. But, when they focus on the years of negative returns, they become uncomfortable because of their aversion to losses.

The result of all this is the "eat well/sleep well dilemma." That is, if investors want to eat well and earn higher returns with stocks, they need to be prepared to take more risk and go through the volatile roller coaster ride of fluctuations in the value of their portfolio. But if they want to sleep well, they must take less risk; that is invest in fixed-income investments such as bonds, and accept that they'll earn lower returns. Thus, the price of obtaining greater long-term accumulation of wealth with stocks is frightening fluctuations in the value of a portfolio. There

Figure 8-21

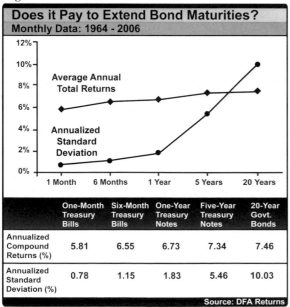

	One-Month Treasury Bills	Six-Month Treasury Bills	One-Year Treasury Notes	Five-Year Treasury Notes	20-Year Govt. Bonds
Annualized Compound Returns (%)	5.81	6.55	6.73	7.34	7.46
Annualized Standard Deviation (%)	0.78	1.15	1.83	5.46	10.03

Figure 8-22

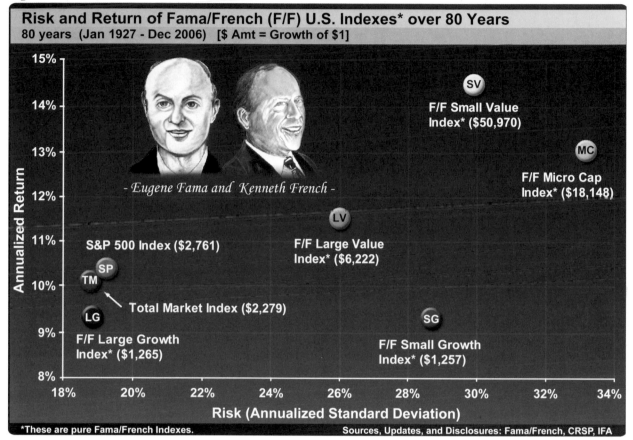

Risk and Return of Fama/French (F/F) U.S. Indexes* over 80 Years
80 years (Jan 1927 - Dec 2006) [$ Amt = Growth of $1]

- Eugene Fama and Kenneth French -

F/F Small Value Index* ($50,970) — SV

F/F Micro Cap Index* ($18,148) — MC

F/F Large Value Index* ($6,222) — LV

S&P 500 Index ($2,761) — SP

Total Market Index ($2,279) — TM

F/F Large Growth Index* ($1,265) — LG

F/F Small Growth Index* ($1,257) — SG

Annualized Return (vertical axis): 8% – 15%
Risk (Annualized Standard Deviation) (horizontal axis): 18% – 34%

*These are pure Fama/French Indexes.   Sources, Updates, and Disclosures: Fama/French, CRSP, IFA

really is no free lunch in investing. It's the same old story of risk and return trade-offs identified by Markowitz.

Investors can select from a wide array of risk and return combinations when building efficient portfolios. Figure 8-22 shows the risk and return trade-offs for various Fama/French indexes over an 80-year period from January 1927 to December 2006.

High risk exposure is like a scream inducing roller coaster with soaring highs and stomach churning lows. Investors should hop on a milder ride if they don't like the extreme rush of the one they're on. On the roller coaster, the greater the ups and downs, the greater the returns, which can be measured in thrills. The same concept applies

to investing. However, not everybody has the capacity for such exposure to risk. Figure 8-23 shows the roller coaster like returns of five different index portfolios. The gold colored Index Portfolio 90 has higher highs and lower lows than the other lower risk portfolios. Also, note that the growth of $100,000 over 35 years is higher for the higher risk Index Portfolio 90. Figure 8-24 shows what the one index of small value stocks looks like on the same scale. These graphs provide a vivid illustration of the concepts of risk, return, and time. They are available in dynamic versions that allow movement and selection options at www.ifa.com.

Figure 8-23

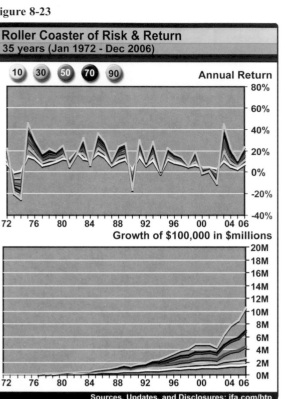

Figure 8-24

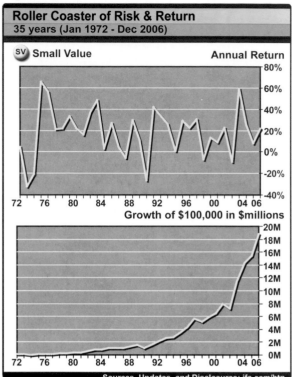

8.2.9   Time Diversification of Risk

Charles Ellis

Charles D. Ellis said, "The average long-term experience in investing is never surprising, but the short-term experience is always surprising."

Figures 8-25 through 8-29 illustrate this famous quote by Ellis, one of the first proponents of indexing. These charts show 50 years of returns on monthly, quarterly, annual, five-year rolling, and ten-year rolling periods, and will help investors better understand the time element of riskese. These are clear indicators of the reversion to the mean concept already described. Does time reduce risk? For many years, this question has generated a hot debate among academic researchers and investment professionals.

On one side are those who believe that the risk involved in holding stocks is reduced the longer the investment time horizon. This belief is based on two facts.

First, as the investment time horizon lengthens, the actual average annual compound return achieved by a stock portfolio converges to its expected returns. As the period of measurement changes from monthly to every ten years, the volatility of returns reduces, and the existence of a losing period diminishes.

Figures 8-25 through 8-29 show that the chance of incurring a negative total return declines as the time horizon lengthens. In fact, here the chance of negative returns nearly disappeared as returns were graphed every five years. The long-term horizon phenomenon occurs because the risk or standard deviation of an all equity portfolio drops by 67% (from 19.2% to

Figure 8-25

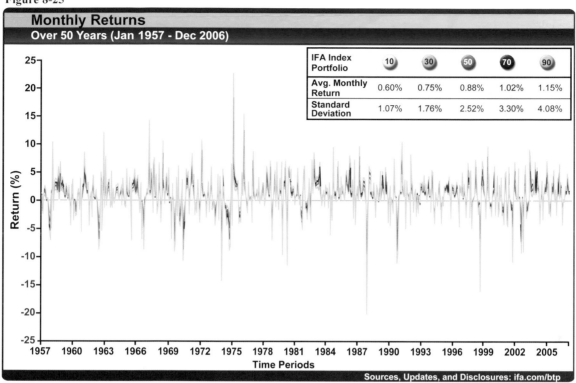

Monthly Returns
Over 50 Years (Jan 1957 - Dec 2006)

IFA Index Portfolio	10	30	50	70	90
Avg. Monthly Return	0.60%	0.75%	0.88%	1.02%	1.15%
Standard Deviation	1.07%	1.76%	2.52%	3.30%	4.08%

Sources, Updates, and Disclosures: ifa.com/btp

Figure 8-26

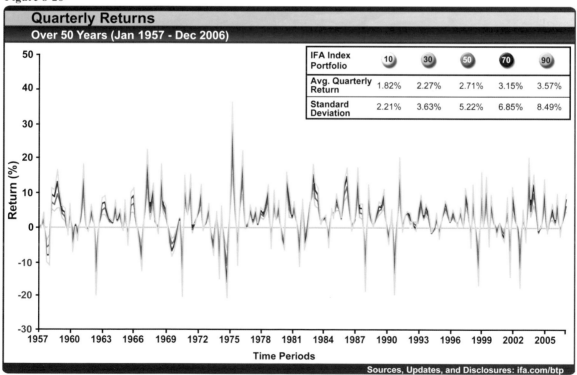

Quarterly Returns
Over 50 Years (Jan 1957 - Dec 2006)

IFA Index Portfolio	10	30	50	70	90
Avg. Quarterly Return	1.82%	2.27%	2.71%	3.15%	3.57%
Standard Deviation	2.21%	3.63%	5.22%	6.85%	8.49%

Sources, Updates, and Disclosures: ifa.com/btp

Figure 8-27

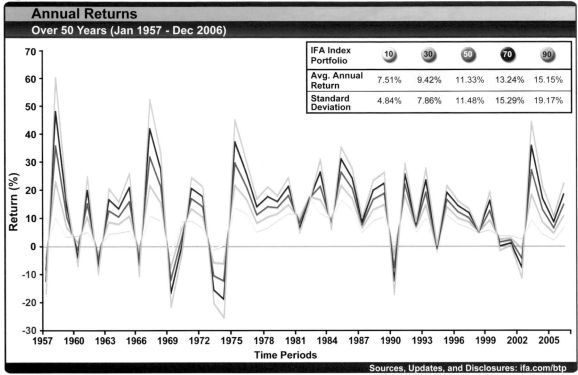

Annual Returns

Over 50 Years (Jan 1957 - Dec 2006)

IFA Index Portfolio	10	30	50	70	90
Avg. Annual Return	7.51%	9.42%	11.33%	13.24%	15.15%
Standard Deviation	4.84%	7.86%	11.48%	15.29%	19.17%

Sources, Updates, and Disclosures: ifa.com/btp

Figure 8-28

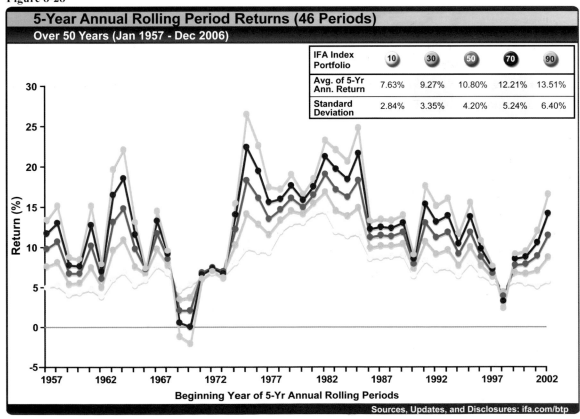

5-Year Annual Rolling Period Returns (46 Periods)

Over 50 Years (Jan 1957 - Dec 2006)

IFA Index Portfolio	10	30	50	70	90
Avg. of 5-Yr Ann. Return	7.63%	9.27%	10.80%	12.21%	13.51%
Standard Deviation	2.84%	3.35%	4.20%	5.24%	6.40%

Sources, Updates, and Disclosures: ifa.com/btp

Figure 8-29

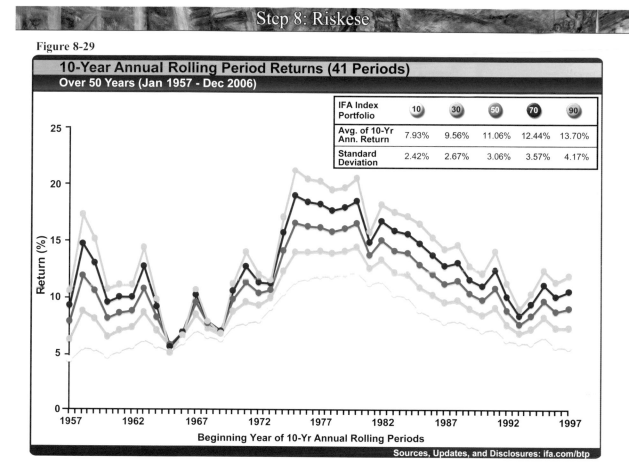

10-Year Annual Rolling Period Returns (41 Periods)
Over 50 Years (Jan 1957 - Dec 2006)

IFA Index Portfolio	10	30	50	70	90
Avg. of 10-Yr Ann. Return	7.93%	9.56%	11.06%	12.44%	13.70%
Standard Deviation	2.42%	2.67%	3.06%	3.57%	4.17%

Sources, Updates, and Disclosures: ifa.com/btp

6.4%) when extending the investment time horizon from one year to five years. After 10 years, 78% of the risk (now down to 4.2%) has been eliminated. See Appendix A for the 50-year rolling period analysis of these index portfolios.

However, as the investment time horizon lengthens, the dispersion of expected total accumulated wealth increasingly diverges from expected total accumulated wealth because the compounding grows faster than the risk reduces. This can be a little confusing. The bottom line is that an investor must carefully measure the five dimensions of personal risk capacity and invest in a risk exposure that is appropriate at all times.

James K. Glassman summarizes the investor's dilemma: "In the stock market (as in much of life), the beginning of wisdom is admitting your own ignorance. One of the many things you cannot know about stocks is exactly when

they will [go] up or go down. Over periods of days, weeks and months, no one has any idea what they will do. Still, nearly all investors think they are smart enough to divine such short-term movements. This hubris frequently gets them into trouble."

8.3 PROBLEMS

8.3.1 Active Investors don't Understand Risk and Return

One of the primary deterrents to investors earning market rates of returns is their lack of understanding of the relationship between risk and return. The natural tendency is to want returns without risk.

Because risk is the source of returns, investors would be better served to be more concerned with the risk level of their investments.

8.3.2 Investors like Comfort and Dislike Uncertainty

The notion of loss aversion forms the basis for how investors make trade-offs between risk and return. The pricing system that's at the heart of free market capitalism, reflects this trade-off as the market sets prices for different risk factors.

As is evident in Figure 8-30, it's uncomfortable to remain invested in a fund that hasn't performed well, as doubt and fear play into investors' emotions. It's also uncomfortable to pull money out of a fund that has performed well. Greed takes over. It's even more uncomfortable to switch money from a fund that's done well to the uncertainty and fear of the investment that hasn't done so well.

Based on these simple observations, it's easy to see that investors like comfort and excitement of investments that have done well and dislike the uncertainty, doubt and fear of those that are not doing well. Since this is the case, the likely

Figure 8-31

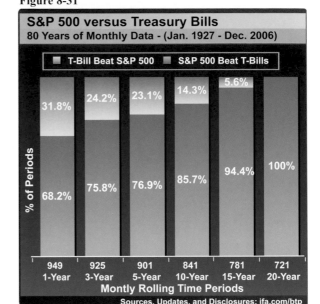

conclusion would be that all investors would simply hold Treasury bills, but you can see in the second column of Figure 8-31, the S&P 500 has beat T-bills 75.8% of the time in 925 monthly rolling 3-Year Periods. Investors who want more return must incur more risk.

The financial market will price asset classes according to its comfort level. That is, uncomfortable and riskier asset classes are priced low enough so that their expected returns are high

Figure 8-30

enough to compensate investors for the higher risk of holding them. If the market didn't price riskier asset classes relatively lower, no one would buy them. Conversely, those who invest in more comfortable and less risky asset classes such as Treasury bills or even large growth companies, have lower expected returns, since financial markets tend to offer less reward to investors who seek comfort. Huge conglomerates like General Electric are near the safety level of holding many government debt instruments, consequently, GE has a low cost of capital and investors should expected a lower return relative to other smaller, riskier companies.

In short, comfortable investments should produce less return, and uncertain and uncomfortable investments should produce more return. The prices of asset classes will reflect this risk/return relationship to ensure that all securities are held by someone.

8.3.3 Stock Pickers Dilute the Two Most Important Risk Factors

The primary role in the life of active money managers is to pick winning stocks, but they usually avoid picking high BtM value (distressed) and small company stocks. Why? Because investing in value and small company stocks is about investing in companies with some degree of financial distress that's often evidenced by poor earnings.

So when a manager goes through the lists of eligible stocks, he often throws out value and small company stocks because they're so undesirable. Even when a money manager specializes in picking value stocks, he typically leans toward picking the largest, most "growth-like" (lower BtM) stocks. Similarly, if he picks small company stocks, he tends to pick the largest small company stocks with the highest earnings.

The problem with this approach is that it dilutes the size and value risk factors identified by Fama and French. An active manager investing in a portfolio of value and small company stocks with favorable prospects holds a portfolio biased towards growth and large company stocks. But it's not growth and large company stocks that have the highest expected returns. It's value and small company stocks — companies with the highest costs of capital. That's why active managers consistently avoid exposure to these risk factors that generate higher returns. In doing so, they attempt to achieve higher returns through speculation and the avoidance of the risk factors that explain returns.

Structured investing with index funds is just the opposite. It's about an investor's willingness to take risk in order to earn commensurate return. As seen in Figure 8-32, there is a clear correlation of higher returns with higher risks along the line of the 20 index portfolios. Also note that large growth stocks similar to those on NASDAQ (represented in IFA/NSDQ), have lots of risk, but very low returns. This is evidence of the lower expected returns of the growth stocks.

Figure 8-32

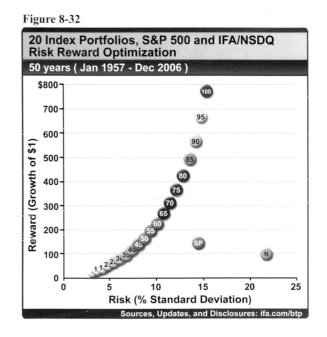

Index Portfolio 100 has a fairly high tilt toward small and value stocks and as you see, investors have been rewarded for holding those risk factors over the last 50 years. The growth of $1 in Index Portfolio 100 is about $771, while the mostly large growth companies on IFA/NSDQ grew to only about $97.

An active manager who picks value and small company stocks often must explain to their clients the reasons he bought "doggy" value and small company stocks with bad earnings. Usually the explanation falls on deaf ears. In order to retain the client's business, the money manager, more often than not, must invest in large company and growth stocks — stocks with good earnings, but lower expected returns.

8.3.4 The Myth of the Ideal Investment

Investors clearly like return and dislike risk. So, an ideal investment would be something that provides a 40% return year after year, isn't volatile, is liquid, and is tax-free. Unfortunately, such an investment doesn't exist. Markowitz's insight that investors should be concerned with risk as well as return is the next best thing to a riskless, high return investment because it's the basis on which investors can build their portfolios using the clear risk and return trade-offs of different asset classes.

8.4 SOLUTION

If an executive has business to do in China but does not speak Chinese, he hires an interpreter. If a businesswoman is engaged in a complicated transaction, she hires a lawyer who is fluent in legalese. The same is true for investing. Few investors understand that knowledge of riskese, the language of risk, is extremely important in investing and actually correlates with returns.

The higher the knowledge, the higher the expected returns. It would be advantageous for investors to learn as much as they can about risk and work with an investment advisor who has a strong statistics and risk knowledge base.

8.5 SUMMARY

With risk as the currency of returns, investors need to understand the denominations or dimensions of risk. Once these are more clearly understood, investors will welcome the dimensions of risk in the proper doses.

8.6 REVIEW QUESTIONS

1. When academics study the stock market, they apply the principle of:

    a. statistics

    b. probabilities

    c. intuition

    d. both a and b

    e. a crystal ball

2. Standard deviation is a critical concept for investors because:

    a. it identifies the deviant personalities of investors.

    b. it explains the standard rule of securities analysis.

    c. it describes the uncertainty of obtaining an expected return.

    d. it explains 100% of stock market returns.

    e. it standardizes stock selection

3. Risk factors are the most important concept for investors to understand because:

a. they help them time the market

b. they tell them which active managers are best

c. they identify the source of returns

d. they tell investors what to avoid in their portfolios

e. they eliminate risk in portfolios

4. If you look at 721 monthly rolling 20-Year Periods from 1926 to 2006, how often do treasury bills underperform the S&P 500?

a. 26% of the time

b. 54% of the time

c. 48% of the time

d. 3% of the time

e. 100% of the time

5. Eugene Fama and Kenneth French looked at stocks on two key dimensions of risk and return. They concluded that the highest returns for investors come from:

a. large value stocks

b. small growth stocks

c. large growth stocks

d. small value stocks

e. market neutral stocks

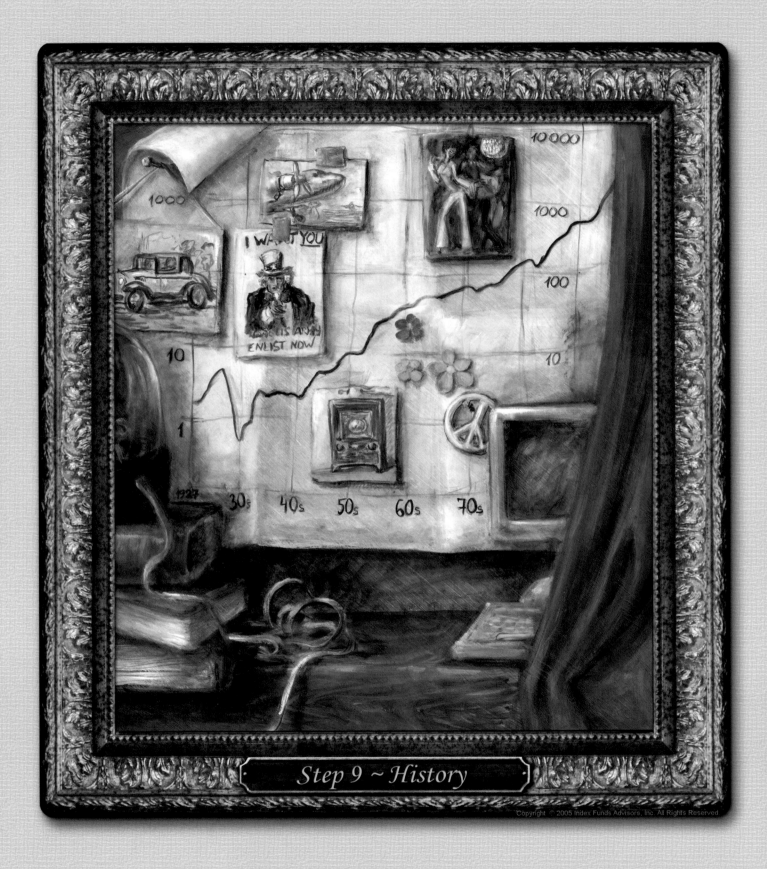

Step 9 ~ History

"The only new thing in the world is the history you don't know."

  - Harry S. Truman

"Those who are ignorant of investment history are bound to repeat it. Historical investment returns and risks of various asset classes should be studied. Investment results for an asset over a long enough period (greater than 20 years) are a good guide to the future returns and risks of that asset. Further, it should be possible to approximate the future long-term return and risk of a portfolio consisting of such assets."

  - William Bernstein, *The Intelligent Asset Allocator*

"While much has changed over the years, some things remain the same. There is still a strong relation between risk and expected return, and price-scaled fundamental variables (such as book-to-market) still have explanatory power for stock returns. Some things have stood the test of time."

  - James L. Davis, *Digging the Panama Canal*

"Data! Data! Data!" he cried impatiently. "I can't make bricks out of clay!"

  - Sherlock Holmes, *The Adventures of the Copper Beeches*

"It takes between 20 and 800 years of monitoring performance to statistically prove that a money manager is skillful rather than lucky — which is a lot more than most people have in mind when they say 'long-term' [track record]."

  - Ted Aronson, "Confessions of a Fund Pro," *Money*

"I know of no way of judging the future but by the past."

  - Patrick Henry, March 23, 1775, Virginia Convention Speech

"... statisticians will tell you that you need 20 years worth of data — that's right, two full decades — to draw statistically meaningful conclusions. Anything less, they say, and you have little to hang your hat on."

  - Susan Dziubinski, Morningstar, Inc.

"The four most dangerous words in investing are, It's different this time."

  - Sir John Templeton, legendary investor. *Money Magazine*

"Those who forget the past are condemned to repeat it."

  - George Santanya, Philosopher

"History teaches everything including the future."

  - Lamartine

"Whoever wishes to foresee the future must consult the past; for human events ever resemble those of preceding times. This arises from the fact that they are produced by men who ever have been, and ever shall be, animated by the same passions, and thus they necessarily have the same results."

  - Machiavelli

"History, in brief, is an analysis of the past in order that we may understand the present and guide our conduct into the future."

  - Sidney E. Mead

"If a man dwells on the past, then he robs the present; but if a man ignores the past, he may rob the future. The seeds of our destiny are nurtured by the roots of our past."

  - Master Po, Kung Fu Television Series

9.1 INTRODUCTION

Step 9: Understand the historical risks and returns of indexes.

The decision of how and where to invest is important. This decision cannot be made wisely without having a good sense of the historical long-term risk and returns of different indexes. Gaining this understanding involves identifying the universe of indexes that are available for investment. Ideally, investors invest in index portfolios that provide the highest rate of return at a level of risk that matches their risk capacity.

Only a good understanding of the long-term historical risk and return of various indexes will enable investors to know how to allocate indexes in accordance with their personal risk capacity. This step provides data on the risk and return characteristics of both size and value subsets of markets around the world. For many indexes, data dates as far back as 1926.

Before proceeding, it's important to understand that a big difference exists between track records of active mutual funds and the historical returns of indexes. The most obvious distinction is the difference in time periods or in statistical terms, the sample size. Statisticians are quick to remind you that the smaller the sample size, the more error there is in information obtained from the sample.

As previously mentioned, manager picking occurs when an investor identifies an investment, such as a mutual fund with an outstanding track record, and invests in it because of the fund manager's past performance. This involves picking out specific funds with the best track records from among thousands. A manager picker assumes that a mutual fund with a great track record will continue its excellent performance into the future.

However, the track record of any given active mutual fund or its manager rarely exceeds 10 years and is notoriously unreliable in predicting future returns. That's because the typical active fund manager doesn't hold investments that comprise a single discrete index. To complicate matters, the manager randomly moves in and out of different types of stocks and holds them in inexplicably different proportions for unpredictably different times because of attempts to outperform the market. Many active mutual funds eventually go out of business and simply disappear from the mutual fund databases. Some funds merge into other active funds or the manager gets fired, retires or moves on to run other funds. Thus, not only are the track records of active funds uncertain over any time period, so is the continued survival of the funds and the continued existence of their managers.

Examining the historical risk and return data of indexes is a completely different exercise than examining the track records of specific active mutual funds. In sharp contrast to the unclear investment methods of active funds and their managers, index funds deploy an understandable and clear strategy.

The best index fund managers have identified the risk factors that generate higher stock returns and structure the construction rules of their indexes for maximum exposure to those factors. This is really nothing more than taking advantage of a fundamental principle of investing—the relationship between risk and return. This isn't to say that the actual returns earned by any given index in the future are known today. But, an indexer can be quite sure that an index fund will efficiently capture the performance of the index. It's simply more reliable.

9.2 DEFINITIONS

9.2.1 Historical Databases and Studies

Several different historical databases are used to study the market. One of the first was the Cowles Commission's Common-Stock Indexes, spearheaded by Alfred Cowles. The Common-Stock Indexes were created in order to portray the average experience of investors who invested in those securities from 1871 to 1938. The compilation of the data was no easy task. Remember, it was assembled without the help of modern computer technology. The data, which was published in August 1938, was the product of years of research and data collection. According to Cowles, more than 1.5 million worksheet entries were made (and we're not talking about Excel worksheets!).

The premier source of historical data used by the academic and corporate community comes from the Center for Research in Security Prices (CRSP). CRSP, which is housed at the University of Chicago Graduate School of Business was established in 1960 with the goal of building and maintaining historical databases for stock (NASDAQ, AMEX, NYSE), indexes, bond, and mutual fund securities. Part of the goal of the center was to unite the common interests between the academic and financial communities by providing a better understanding of the operations of the market. Since computer technology was in its infancy, no machine-readable, historical stock data files were in existence at the time CRSP was launched. Initially, CRSP was formed to accurately measure the returns from investing in common stocks listed on the New York Stock Exchange for the period 1926 to 1960. It took the researchers at CRSP four years to complete this initial study. Since its inception CRSP has developed a host of new data resources. The data housed at CRSP is used extensively for financial,

economic, and accounting research. Currently, Eugene Fama, a well respected professor of finance at the Graduate School of Business at the University of Chicago and director of research at DFA, is the chairman of CRSP. DFA bases several of its investment products on Fama's findings from that database.

The prestigious University of Chicago publication, *The Journal of Business*, caused the academic equivalent of an earthquake in an article published in January 1964 titled "Rates of Return on Investments in Common Stocks." In the article, James Lorie and Lawrence Fisher, two business professors at the school, made the first comprehensive measurement of the performance of all common stocks listed on the New York Stock Exchange from 1926 through 1960. They obtained and compiled their data from CRSP.

The study presented a mind-boggling accumulation of statistical calculations. Both academic researchers and investment professionals were astonished at Fisher and Lorie's discoveries. For instance, the study showed that an investor who invested $1,000 in the stock market in 1926, reinvested all dividends, paid no taxes, and remained fully invested until the end of 1960 would have accumulated nearly $30,000 or a gain of about 9% a year. In light of the fact that many investors in 1964 still had vivid memories of the Great Depression and its stock market crash, 9% a year was a great deal of money. In addition, this return was far greater than the amount an investor would have earned from bonds or savings bank deposits during that time period. For the first time, investors had comprehensive historical investment data that gave them a sense of how common stocks performed compared to other investments.

Roger G. Ibbotson and Rex A. Sinquefield, two graduates of the business school at the

Rex Sinquefield   *Roger Ibbotson*

University of Chicago, released a study that was published in *The Journal of Business* titled "Stocks, Bonds, Bills and Inflation." The two researchers were the first to compile and present in an organized way historical investment data that covered not only stocks, but bonds as well. They even reported data on inflation. As was the case with Lorie and Fisher's study, their data went back to 1926, and was obtained from CRSP. The Ibbotson-Sinquefield data, now updated annually in what has come to be known as the "Stocks, Bonds, Bills and Inflation (SBBI) Yearbook," is widely used in the investment world.

In 1990, G. William Schwert of the University of Rochester published an article in *The Journal of Business* titled "Indexes of U.S. Stock Prices from 1802 to 1987." Schwert pointed out that the data compiled by CRSP launched an explosion of research in finance in the 1960s to 1970s. However, notes Schwert, a major drawback of the CRSP database is that it starts in 1926, a time right before the Great Depression. Consequently, the behavior of the stock market and stock returns was unusual in the 1929 to 1939 decade. Therefore, an empirical study based on the data could be "suspect." So, Schwert set his sights on pre-CRSP stock return data. His article compares and contrasts all of the major indexes of stock prices or returns that were available monthly from 1802 to 1925 or daily from 1885 to 1962. The outcome of the comparison is a series of monthly stock portfolio returns from 1802 to 1925, and daily returns from 1885 to 1962. This important study included many refinements of the concept of "stitching" together several different index data series to obtain a longer term prospective.

9.2.2 Time Series Construction

A time series construction is the stitching together of indexes through history so that researchers and investors can better characterize the risk and return of their investments. See Figure 9-1 for an example of the time series construction of indexes. As seen in the graph, indexes are stitched together to increase the sample size of the data. All indexes have been taken back to 1927 through this process. A substitution process is used to extend current indexes back in time. This process is far from perfect, but provides the best information available for extending current indexes and mixes of those indexes back in time. Table 9-1 is the annual returns of these stitched together indexes with corresponding color buttons, and a total market index for comparisons. This is an interesting assembly of the per-year annual returns for each index going all the way back to 1927! These indexes are described in further detail in Appendix B.

9.3 PROBLEM

A lack of quality long-term data of stock market returns presents a hurdle for many investors. Furthermore, many are largely unaware that long-term data is more valuable than short-term data. When looking at 80 years of data, many investors think it is irrelevant because they do not have 80 years to live. This point of view negates the importance of sample size and the issue of sample error. When characterizing the risk and return of capitalism, the more quality data you have, the more accurate your conclusions. Any subset of the data, such as five years' worth, is bound to contain significant errors in its attempt to describe the risk and return of an index. For example, for the five-year period from 2000 to 2004, the S&P 500 had a total loss of 12%. Based on that negative total

Figure 9-1

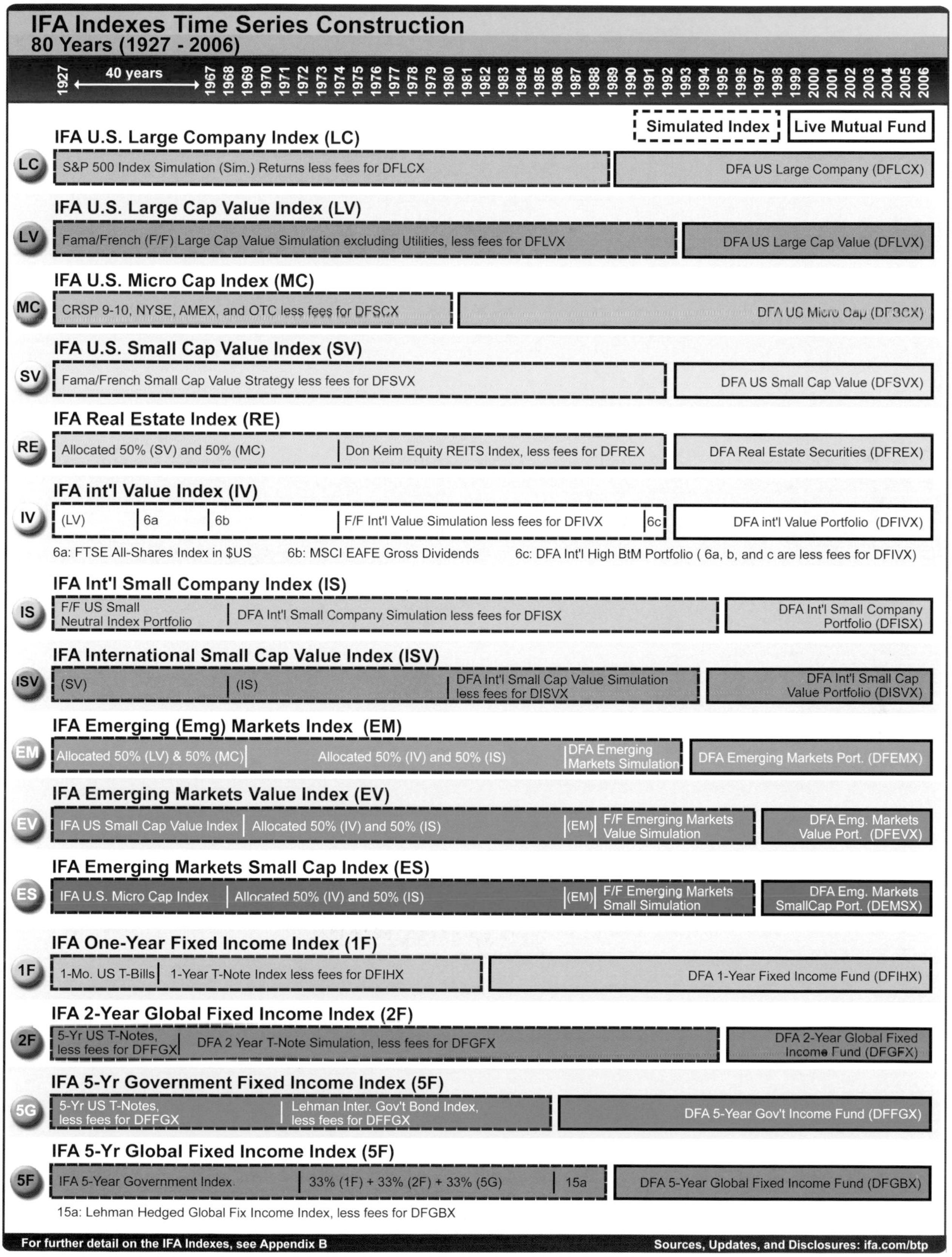

IFA Indexes Time Series Construction
80 Years (1927 - 2006)

1927 ← 40 years → 1967 1968 1969 1970 1971 1972 1973 1974 1975 1976 1977 1978 1979 1980 1981 1982 1983 1984 1985 1986 1987 1988 1989 1990 1991 1992 1993 1994 1995 1996 1997 1998 1999 2000 2001 2002 2003 2004 2005 2006

Simulated Index | Live Mutual Fund

IFA U.S. Large Company Index (LC)
LC — S&P 500 Index Simulation (Sim.) Returns less fees for DFLCX | DFA US Large Company (DFLCX)

IFA U.S. Large Cap Value Index (LV)
LV — Fama/French (F/F) Large Cap Value Simulation excluding Utilities, less fees for DFLVX | DFA US Large Cap Value (DFLVX)

IFA U.S. Micro Cap Index (MC)
MC — CRSP 9-10, NYSE, AMEX, and OTC less fees for DFSCX | DFA US Micro Cap (DFSCX)

IFA U.S. Small Cap Value Index (SV)
SV — Fama/French Small Cap Value Strategy less fees for DFSVX | DFA US Small Cap Value (DFSVX)

IFA Real Estate Index (RE)
RE — Allocated 50% (SV) and 50% (MC) | Don Keim Equity REITS Index, less fees for DFREX | DFA Real Estate Securities (DFREX)

IFA int'l Value Index (IV)
IV — (LV) | 6a | 6b | F/F Int'l Value Simulation less fees for DFIVX | 6c | DFA int'l Value Portfolio (DFIVX)
6a: FTSE All-Shares Index in $US   6b: MSCI EAFE Gross Dividends   6c: DFA Int'l High BtM Portfolio (6a, b, and c are less fees for DFIVX)

IFA Int'l Small Company Index (IS)
IS — F/F US Small Neutral Index Portfolio | DFA Int'l Small Company Simulation less fees for DFISX | DFA Int'l Small Company Portfolio (DFISX)

IFA International Small Cap Value Index (ISV)
ISV — (SV) | (IS) | DFA Int'l Small Cap Value Simulation less fees for DISVX | DFA Int'l Small Cap Value Portfolio (DISVX)

IFA Emerging (Emg) Markets Index (EM)
EM — Allocated 50% (LV) & 50% (MC) | Allocated 50% (IV) and 50% (IS) | DFA Emerging Markets Simulation | DFA Emerging Markets Port. (DFEMX)

IFA Emerging Markets Value Index (EV)
EV — IFA US Small Cap Value Index | Allocated 50% (IV) and 50% (IS) | (EM) | F/F Emerging Markets Value Simulation | DFA Emg. Markets Value Port. (DFEVX)

IFA Emerging Markets Small Cap Index (ES)
ES — IFA U.S. Micro Cap Index | Allocated 50% (IV) and 50% (IS) | (EM) | F/F Emerging Markets Small Simulation | DFA Emg. Markets SmallCap Port. (DEMSX)

IFA One-Year Fixed Income Index (1F)
1F — 1-Mo. US T-Bills | 1-Year T-Note Index less fees for DFIHX | DFA 1-Year Fixed Income Fund (DFIHX)

IFA 2-Year Global Fixed Income Index (2F)
2F — 5-Yr US T-Notes, less fees for DFFGX | DFA 2 Year T-Note Simulation, less fees for DFGFX | DFA 2-Year Global Fixed Income Fund (DFGFX)

IFA 5-Yr Government Fixed Income Index (5F)
5G — 5-Yr US T-Notes, less fees for DFFGX | Lehman Inter. Gov't Bond Index, less fees for DFFGX | DFA 5-Year Gov't Income Fund (DFFGX)

IFA 5-Yr Global Fixed Income Index (5F)
5F — IFA 5-Year Government Index | 33% (1F) + 33% (2F) + 33% (5G) | 15a | DFA 5-Year Global Fixed Income Fund (DFGBX)
15a: Lehman Hedged Global Fix Income Index, less fees for DFGBX

For further detail on the IFA Indexes, see Appendix B | Sources, Updates, and Disclosures: ifa.com/btp

Table 9-1

Annual Returns of 15 Indexes
80 years (1927 - 2006)

Year	LC	LV	MC	SV	RE	IV	IS	ISV	EM	EV	ES	1F	2F	5G	5F
1927	37.3	31.3	30.8	33.2	32.1	31.3	26.1	33.2	31.2	33.2	30.8	2.9	4.3	4.3	4.3
1928	43.4	25.2	44.2	39.0	41.8	25.2	40.0	39.0	34.9	39.0	44.2	3.0	0.7	0.7	0.7
1929	-8.5	-6.7	-51.4	-41.8	-46.7	-6.7	-30.9	-41.8	-32.1	-41.8	-51.4	4.5	5.8	5.8	5.8
1930	-25.0	-45.2	-46.1	-47.7	-46.8	-45.2	-32.3	-47.7	-45.2	-47.7	-46.1	2.2	6.5	6.5	6.5
1931	-43.4	-60.8	-50.3	-53.8	-52.0	-60.8	-48.5	-53.8	-55.4	-53.8	-50.3	0.8	-2.6	-2.6	-2.6
1932	-8.3	-6.4	8.9	-2.0	3.7	-6.4	-8.7	-2.0	3.2	-2.0	8.9	0.7	8.6	8.6	8.6
1933	53.8	90.8	185.3	141.2	162.9	90.8	120.4	141.2	137.8	141.2	185.3	0.1	1.6	1.6	1.6
1934	-1.6	-21.8	23.4	7.4	15.3	-21.8	19.5	7.4	-1.0	7.4	23.4	-0.1	8.7	8.7	8.7
1935	47.5	42.6	69.6	49.2	59.2	42.6	75.3	49.2	56.6	49.2	69.6	-0.1	6.7	6.7	6.7
1936	33.8	50.8	83.7	76.7	80.4	50.8	48.0	76.7	67.8	76.7	83.7	-0.1	2.8	2.8	2.8
1937	-35.1	-38.2	-53.1	-53.0	-53.0	-38.2	-49.0	-53.0	-45.9	-53.0	-53.1	0.1	1.3	1.3	1.3
1938	31.0	29.7	23.8	33.5	28.6	29.7	42.9	33.5	27.4	33.5	23.8	-0.3	6.0	6.0	6.0
1939	-0.5	-15.0	-0.2	-7.7	-3.8	-15.0	0.6	-7.7	-7.3	-7.7	-0.2	-0.2	4.3	4.3	4.3
1940	-9.9	-7.4	-12.5	-11.2	-11.8	-7.4	-2.4	-11.2	-9.7	-11.2	-12.5	-0.3	2.7	2.7	2.7
1941	-11.7	-0.5	-14.0	-4.0	-9.1	-0.5	-11.5	-4.0	-7.2	-4.0	-14.0	-0.2	0.3	0.3	0.3
1942	20.2	36.0	50.2	37.5	43.8	36.0	27.0	37.5	43.3	37.5	50.2	0.0	1.7	1.7	1.7
1943	25.8	39.0	97.8	98.9	98.5	39.0	54.0	98.9	66.8	98.9	97.8	0.1	2.6	2.6	2.6
1944	19.6	41.7	59.4	52.6	56.0	41.7	39.5	52.6	50.5	52.6	59.4	0.1	1.6	1.6	1.6
1945	36.3	43.8	80.9	72.0	76.4	43.8	59.2	72.0	61.5	72.0	80.9	0.1	2.0	2.0	2.0
1946	-8.2	-8.2	-13.5	-12.2	-12.8	-8.2	-10.1	-12.2	-10.7	-12.2	-13.5	0.1	0.8	0.8	0.8
1947	5.6	7.7	-3.5	7.3	1.8	7.7	-2.7	7.3	2.1	7.3	-3.5	0.3	0.7	0.7	0.7
1948	5.4	3.8	-7.0	-6.6	-6.8	3.8	-7.6	-6.6	-1.7	-6.6	-7.0	0.6	1.6	1.6	1.6
1949	18.7	13.9	20.6	19.5	20.1	13.9	22.1	19.5	17.3	19.5	20.6	0.9	2.1	2.1	2.1
1950	31.6	58.7	44.9	55.0	49.9	58.7	31.6	55.0	51.8	55.0	44.9	1.0	0.5	0.5	0.5
1951	23.9	13.3	8.6	10.4	9.5	13.3	14.3	10.4	11.0	10.4	8.6	1.3	0.1	0.1	0.1
1952	18.2	18.3	5.7	6.6	6.2	18.3	9.5	6.6	11.9	6.6	5.7	1.4	1.9	1.4	1.4
1953	-1.1	-7.1	-6.4	-9.1	-7.8	-7.1	-1.8	-9.1	-6.7	-9.1	-6.4	1.6	2.1	3.0	3.0
1954	52.5	77.1	64.1	64.2	64.2	77.1	60.4	64.2	70.7	64.2	64.1	0.6	2.3	2.5	2.5
1955	31.4	20.3	21.4	25.0	23.2	9.8	19.8	25.0	20.9	25.0	21.4	1.3	-0.1	-0.9	-0.9
1956	6.4	1.7	2.9	5.3	4.1	-6.5	7.1	5.3	2.4	5.3	2.9	2.2	1.9	-0.7	-0.7
1957	-10.9	-23.0	-15.7	-18.2	-16.9	-1.4	-15.7	-18.2	-19.4	-18.2	-15.7	2.9	3.9	7.6	7.6
1958	43.2	71.6	69.4	73.8	71.7	44.0	56.6	73.8	70.6	73.8	69.4	1.3	0.8	-1.5	-1.5
1959	11.8	14.7	17.6	14.1	15.9	56.7	19.1	14.1	16.2	14.1	17.6	2.7	3.6	-0.6	-0.6
1960	0.3	-9.1	-5.6	-7.4	-6.5	-6.3	-1.5	-7.4	-7.3	-7.4	-5.6	2.4	6.8	11.5	11.5
1961	26.7	27.2	30.0	31.1	30.6	4.7	30.2	31.1	28.7	31.1	30.0	1.9	2.8	1.6	1.6
1962	-8.8	-1.7	-16.6	-9.5	-13.1	-1.3	-15.8	-9.5	-9.3	-9.5	-16.6	2.5	3.0	5.3	5.3
1963	22.6	29.5	11.3	28.8	19.8	17.3	18.8	28.8	20.2	28.8	11.3	3.1	3.2	1.4	1.4
1964	16.4	21.6	17.7	24.3	21.0	-4.9	17.2	24.3	19.7	24.3	17.7	3.8	3.9	3.8	3.8
1965	12.3	22.5	37.2	43.2	40.2	11.5	32.5	43.2	29.8	43.2	37.2	3.7	3.5	0.8	0.8
1966	-10.2	-12.5	-8.8	-8.4	-8.6	-5.0	-6.4	-8.4	-10.4	-8.4	-8.8	6.2	4.9	4.4	4.4
1967	23.8	32.3	102.1	72.0	86.6	16.2	70.8	72.0	64.0	72.0	102.1	4.7	3.7	0.8	0.8
1968	11.0	21.4	49.4	50.1	49.9	46.2	39.4	50.1	35.2	50.1	49.4	5.5	5.8	4.3	4.3
1969	-8.6	-17.6	-32.8	-30.0	-31.4	2.3	-23.7	-30.0	-25.4	-30.0	-32.8	6.9	7.1	-1.0	-1.0
1970	3.9	9.7	-17.2	-1.5	-9.6	-10.9	0.3	0.3	-5.4	-5.4	-5.4	10.2	11.0	16.6	16.6
1971	14.2	19.0	17.4	15.2	16.4	30.6	67.3	67.3	48.1	48.1	48.1	5.4	5.9	8.5	8.5
1972	18.8	18.9	-1.6	4.4	1.4	37.0	63.3	63.3	49.7	49.7	49.7	3.9	3.9	4.9	4.9
1973	-14.8	-4.4	-41.1	-32.4	-36.8	-14.6	-14.2	-14.2	-14.3	-14.3	-14.3	6.7	6.1	3.1	5.3
1974	-26.6	-17.4	-29.7	-20.7	-25.3	-22.5	-29.1	-29.1	-25.8	-25.8	-25.8	8.5	9.1	6.8	8.1
1975	37.1	47.1	68.9	66.0	34.2	38.3	49.0	49.0	43.7	43.7	43.7	7.2	7.9	8.1	7.8
1976	23.7	50.3	53.6	56.6	38.7	2.8	10.8	10.8	6.8	6.8	6.8	6.1	8.9	11.5	8.8
1977	-7.3	-6.1	21.4	20.9	17.6	29.4	73.1	73.1	50.1	50.1	50.1	4.7	3.7	2.8	3.7
1978	6.5	3.1	21.1	21.5	9.0	42.0	64.6	64.6	53.1	53.1	53.1	6.1	5.5	2.0	4.5
1979	18.3	22.9	43.4	33.1	32.8	5.5	-1.4	-1.4	2.1	2.1	2.1	9.1	10.4	6.3	8.6
1980	32.3	16.0	33.9	21.9	29.2	18.2	34.7	34.7	26.3	26.3	26.3	9.7	14.1	6.4	10.1
1981	-5.0	16.1	7.1	16.0	5.8	8.5	-0.5	1.8	4.1	4.1	4.1	14.3	18.9	10.5	14.5
1982	21.3	20.2	28.8	37.0	27.8	-2.7	-0.6	-3.1	-1.6	-1.6	-1.6	17.0	19.5	25.1	20.5
1983	22.4	34.5	39.7	48.4	29.1	28.8	35.3	36.1	32.1	32.1	32.1	8.5	8.6	8.0	8.4
1984	6.1	9.0	-6.7	3.1	21.4	8.5	11.0	10.9	9.8	9.8	9.8	11.2	12.8	14.0	12.7
1985	32.0	30.6	24.7	27.2	11.5	54.4	66.6	72.5	60.4	60.4	60.4	10.5	13.2	17.7	13.8
1986	18.3	19.8	6.9	4.5	24.4	64.6	58.6	55.7	62.2	62.2	62.2	8.9	11.9	12.8	11.2
1987	5.1	3.5	-9.3	-5.4	-6.4	34.4	39.8	52.8	37.2	37.2	37.2	6.4	6.0	3.5	6.6
1988	16.7	23.6	22.9	30.0	14.1	38.0	25.2	33.6	37.4	37.4	37.4	7.4	5.9	6.3	8.7
1989	31.3	27.0	10.2	10.9	6.3	17.6	30.0	37.2	116.1	53.2	82.6	9.6	8.7	9.5	6.8
1990	-3.2	-22.8	-21.6	-26.6	-16.3	-22.0	-18.5	-17.7	-8.4	1.1	1.5	9.1	8.9	10.8	3.5
1991	30.1	34.3	44.6	42.1	39.8	9.2	5.2	4.5	69.0	39.8	24.3	9.8	10.7	14.6	12.7
1992	7.3	15.6	23.4	34.2	27.9	-10.3	-21.1	-21.9	2.9	-5.4	9.3	5.2	5.7	7.3	6.5
1993	9.6	17.0	21.0	26.3	15.5	44.7	33.6	44.6	89.2	105.8	89.5	4.4	5.1	8.3	11.6
1994	1.3	-4.5	3.1	1.2	-8.4	8.8	15.2	21.1	-10.6	13.8	2.5	2.5	0.5	-3.2	-4.3
1995	37.1	38.4	34.5	29.3	12.1	11.5	2.1	1.2	2.2	-8.3	-10.1	8.0	8.1	9.6	16.1
1996	22.6	20.2	17.6	22.3	33.8	7.8	3.4	0.9	11.4	11.5	4.8	5.8	7.2	6.6	10.8
1997	33.1	28.1	22.8	30.8	19.4	-3.1	-23.7	-22.7	-18.9	-15.7	-22.6	6.0	5.9	6.4	8.3
1998	28.7	12.0	-7.3	-7.3	-15.4	14.9	8.2	5.3	-9.4	-5.7	-3.8	5.7	6.5	5.4	8.4
1999	20.8	4.8	29.8	13.0	-2.0	16.3	21.9	19.0	71.7	84.3	85.3	4.6	4.6	3.8	3.7
2000	-9.3	10.2	-3.6	9.0	28.4	-0.2	-5.4	-3.1	-29.2	-34.2	-31.8	6.7	6.5	6.8	6.7
2001	-12.1	3.9	22.8	22.6	13.2	-15.3	-10.5	-4.6	-6.8	-1.0	-2.6	5.8	6.1	7.1	5.9
2002	-22.2	-14.9	-13.3	-9.3	4.2	-8.5	1.9	5.8	-9.4	-1.7	-0.2	3.9	5.3	11.8	10.4
2003	28.5	34.4	60.7	59.4	35.6	49.9	58.8	66.5	60.2	76.2	72.8	1.6	1.9	2.7	3.0
2004	10.7	18.3	18.4	25.4	32.1	28.8	30.9	34.8	29.9	39.5	28.9	0.9	0.7	2.8	2.9
2005	4.9	10.2	5.7	7.8	13.2	15.3	22.0	23.2	29.9	30.8	25.7	2.3	1.9	0.8	1.7
2006	15.7	20.2	16.2	21.5	35.3	34.1	24.9	28.4	29.2	37.9	37.3	4.8	4.5	4.5	3.9
Annualized Return (%)	10.27	11.53	12.83	13.92	12.44	11.35	13.97	15.05	15.22	15.99	15.90	4.06	5.10	4.95	5.10
Standard Deviation (%)	19.23	25.74	32.98	29.63	30.02	25.86	24.35	28.96	28.73	29.80	32.08	1.55	2.13	3.66	3.25
Growth of $1	$2,483	$6,182	$15,621	$33,621	$11,816	$5,419	$35,007	$74,335	$83,846	$142,461	$133,843	$24.22	$53.38	$48.73	$53.40

* See Appendix B for Index Portfolio Button Definitions

Sources, Updates, and Disclosures: ifa.com/btp

return, many investors would conclude that the S&P 500 was not a good investment. But when considering 80 years from 1927 to 2006, we see that the annualized return over that period is about 10% per year, and it would be within normal limits for it to fluctuate that much over five year periods. Therefore, it is still an important component of diversified index portfolios. That is a very different conclusion and is far more accurate than the conclusion many investors make based on the last five years.

9.4 SOLUTIONS

9.4.1 Long-term History Characterizes Risk and Return

The history of several U.S. stock markets are captured in Figure 9-2. In essence this chart captures the effectiveness of capitalism over the last 80 years. The numbered events in Figure 9-2 are taken from the historical events in Table 9-2 below it, titled "Market Turmoil and the Dow Jones Industrial Average." Despite several set backs, capitalism continues to work. Also note that the value of a dollar scale is a log scale, so each unit increases by a factor of 10. These are indexes and therefore the growth of a dollar does not reflect any fees or transaction costs. This long-term history of quality data allows investors to create the best set of probabilistic estimates of future performances of these indexes.

The global history of the size and value effect on stocks is made even more clear by reviewing Figure 9-3. Next, Table 9-4 provides a thorough analysis of many indexes over the 1927 to 2006 period. Both the chart and table indicate that over the 80-year period, small-value has outperformed the S&P 500 and large-cap growth. Also, it is clear that value has higher returns in international and emerging markets,

even though available data only dates back to 1975 for international and 1988 for emerging markets.

To expand the range of asset classes to include art, farmland and gold, let's take a look at Table 9-3.

Table 9-3

Various Asset Class Returns		
Annualized Returns over 48 years - (1945 to 1992)		
Asset Class	**Return %**	**Risk Index**
Emerging Markets Equities	16.0	29.6
Venture Capital	15.9	35.4
Japanese Stocks	15.9	29.2
U. S. Small-Cap Stocks	13.5	25.7
S&P 500	11.7	16.5
U.S. Farmland	9.9	7.4
Art	8.5	15.0
U.S. Real Estate (commercial)	7.6	5.7
U.S. Real Estate (residential)	7.3	4.0
Corporate Bonds	5.4	6.2
Long-term Government Bonds	4.9	9.7
Gold	4.9	26.0
U. S. Treasury Bills	4.8	3.2
Silver	4.2	56.2
Inflation	4.5	1.7
Source: Morgan Stanley Capital International		

It is interesting that over the 48-year period emerging market public equities outperformed venture capital, and at a lower risk level. In addition, the S&P 500 outperformed real estate by more than 50%, although the S&P 500 had about three times the risk. Figure 9-4 graphs the data from Table 9-3 on the Markowitz risk/return plot and adds in index portfolios 5, 50 and 100 for comparison. Note where venture capital and emerging markets sit on the plot. Gold and silver are also interesting, reinforcing the idea that they have lots of risk and returns pretty close to T-bills and bonds.

Venture Economics, an information provider for equity professionals, compiled a 20-year data series of various types of private equity strategies for the period ending September 30, 2001. According to the survey, venture and private

Table 9-2

Market Turmoil and the Dow Jones Industrial Average

	Date	Event	First Trading Session Response to Event				Subsequent Market Behavior		
			DJIA Close Previous Day	DJIA Close	DJIA Change	DJIA % Change	One Month Change	Six Months Change	One Year Change
①	3/19/03	Operation Iraqi Freedom	8194.23	8265.45	71.22	0.87%	0.77%	16.69%	23.24%
②	9/11/01	World Trade Center Towers Destroyed	9605.51	8920.70	-684.81	-7.13%	3.50%	18.58%	-7.99%
③	4/19/95	Oklahoma Bombing	4179.13	4207.49	28.36	0.68%	3.18%	14.14%	31.56%
④	1/16/91	US Launches Bombing Attack on Iraq	2490.59	2508.91	18.32	0.74%	16.87%	18.93%	28.53%
⑤	8/2/90	Iraq Invades Kuwait	2899.26	2864.60	-34.66	-1.20%	-8.74%	-3.22%	4.95%
⑥	10/25/83	Crisis in Grenada	1248.98	1252.44	3.46	0.28%	2.00%	-7.10%	-3.31%
⑦	3/30/81	President Reagan Shot	994.78	992.16	-2.62	-0.26%	0.56%	-14.33%	-16.90%
⑧	11/4/79	Iran Hostage Crisis	818.94	812.63	-6.31	-0.77%	1.51%	0.45%	17.29%
⑨	8/9/74	President Nixon Resigns	784.89	777.30	-7.59	-0.97%	-14.71%	-8.87%	5.98%
⑩	2/26/65	Vietnam Conflict	899.90	903.48	3.58	0.40%	-1.31%	-0.81%	5.37%
⑪	11/22/63	President Kennedy Assassinated	732.65	711.49	-21.16	-2.89%	6.58%	15.37%	25.19%
⑫	10/22/62	Cuban Missile Crisis	573.29	568.60	-4.69	-0.82%	13.41%	25.05%	31.41%
⑬	9/24/55	President Eisenhower Heart Attack	487.45	455.56	-31.89	-6.54%	1.15%	12.62%	7.06%
⑭	6/25/50	North Korea Invades South Korea	224.35	213.91	-10.44	-4.65%	-4.71%	9.49%	14.67%
⑮	12/7/41	Japan Attacks Pearl Harbor, Hawaii	115.90	112.52	-3.38	-2.92%	-0.86%	-6.19%	2.88%

Sources: djindexes.com and Yahoo! Finance

Figure 9-2

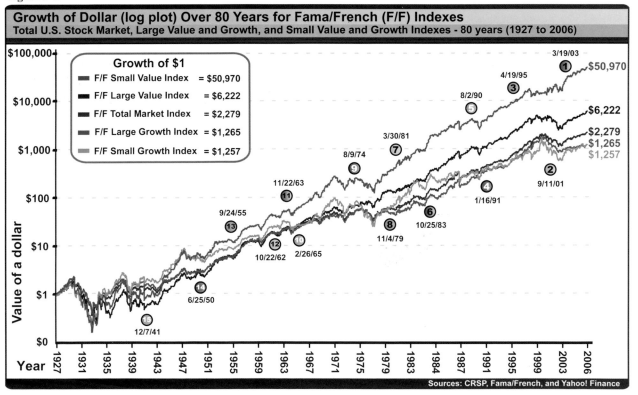

Growth of Dollar (log plot) Over 80 Years for Fama/French (F/F) Indexes
Total U.S. Stock Market, Large Value and Growth, and Small Value and Growth Indexes - 80 years (1927 to 2006)

Growth of $1
- F/F Small Value Index = $50,970
- F/F Large Value Index = $6,222
- F/F Total Market Index = $2,279
- F/F Large Growth Index = $1,265
- F/F Small Growth Index = $1,257

Sources: CRSP, Fama/French, and Yahoo! Finance

Figure 9-3

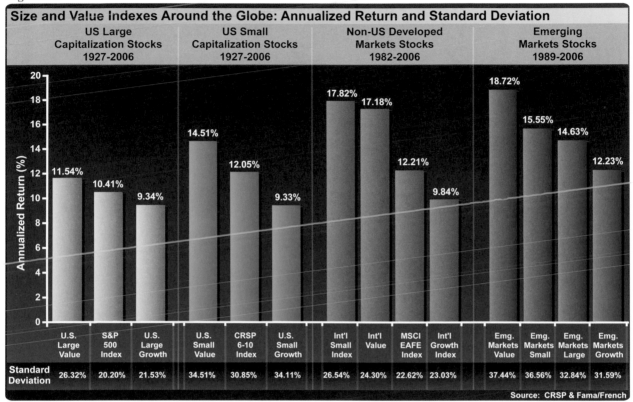

Size and Value Indexes Around the Globe: Annualized Return and Standard Deviation

	US Large Capitalization Stocks 1927-2006			US Small Capitalization Stocks 1927-2006			Non-US Developed Markets Stocks 1982-2006				Emerging Markets Stocks 1989-2006			
	U.S. Large Value	S&P 500 Index	U.S. Large Growth	U.S. Small Value	CRSP 6-10 Index	U.S. Small Growth	Int'l Small Index	Int'l Value	MSCI EAFE Index	Int'l Growth Index	Emg. Markets Value	Emg. Markets Small	Emg. Markets Large	Emg. Markets Growth
Annualized Return	11.54%	10.41%	9.34%	14.51%	12.05%	9.33%	17.82%	17.18%	12.21%	9.84%	18.72%	15.55%	14.63%	12.23%
Standard Deviation	26.32%	20.20%	21.53%	34.51%	30.85%	34.11%	26.54%	24.30%	22.62%	23.03%	37.44%	36.56%	32.84%	31.59%

Source: CRSP & Fama/French

Figure 9-4

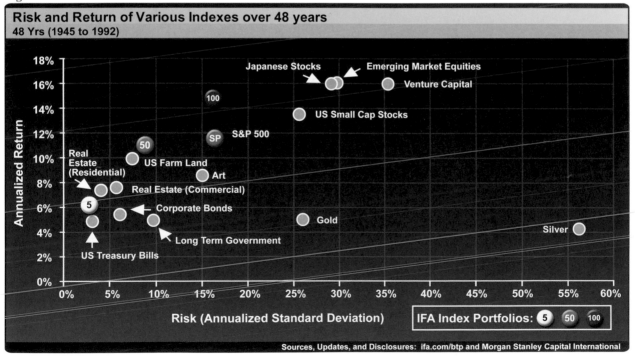

Risk and Return of Various Indexes over 48 years
48 Yrs (1945 to 1992)

Sources, Updates, and Disclosures: ifa.com/btp and Morgan Stanley Capital International

Table 9-4

Fama/French, IFA, and Other Indexes - Annualized Rates of Returns (%)
80 years (1927 to 2006)

Indexes	1 Yr 2006	1 Yr 2005	1 Yr 2004	1 Yr 2003	5 Yr 2002-2006	10 Yr 1997-2006	25 Yr 1982-2006	35 Yr 1972-2006	50 Yr 1957-2006	80 Yr 1927-2006
LC IFA U.S. Large Company Index	15.71	4.85	10.72	28.49	6.07	8.28	13.19	11.19	10.47	10.27
TM Fama/French Total US Market Index	15.28	6.13	11.88	31.76	7.29	8.63	13.05	11.32	10.70	10.15
MC IFA U.S. Micro Cap Index	16.17	5.69	18.39	60.70	15.16	13.48	14.07	13.57	13.13	12.83
LV IFA U.S. Large Cap Value Index	20.18	10.24	18.25	34.43	12.38	11.93	14.69	14.14	13.30	11.53
LG Fama/French US Large Growth	6.54	3.39	5.27	17.77	1.29	5.38	11.79	9.56	9.42	9.35
SV IFA U.S. Small Cap Value Index	21.55	7.79	25.38	59.39	18.89	15.84	16.63	16.14	15.66	13.92
SG Fama/French US Small Growth	9.32	6.01	11.16	54.72	5.44	5.68	7.91	8.36	8.93	9.33
RE IFA U.S. Real Estate REIT Index	35.25	13.16	32.06	35.58	23.34	15.17	14.68	12.60	12.83	12.44
IV IFA International Value Index	34.15	15.29	28.79	49.94	22.26	11.58	14.95	14.20	13.40	11.35
IS IFA International Small Cap Index	24.89	21.96	30.91	58.77	26.40	10.63	14.11	15.76	15.69	13.97
ISV IFA International Small Cap Value Index	28.39	23.24	34.80	66.46	30.31	12.90	16.39	17.48	17.51	15.05
EM IFA Emerging Markets Index	29.17	29.85	29.90	60.18	25.89	10.16	21.19	19.76	17.85	15.22
EV IFA Emerging Markets Value Index	37.93	30.80	39.54	76.18	34.23	15.32	21.96	20.30	19.05	15.99
ES IFA Emerging Markets Small Cap Index	37.31	25.74	28.88	72.81	30.82	13.37	20.82	19.50	18.10	15.90
N IFA NSDQ/FF Small Growth Index	9.51	1.38	5.43	53.29	4.37	6.47	10.57	9.11	9.58	9.74
1F IFA One-Year Fixed Income Index	4.77	2.30	0.88	1.63	2.69	4.20	6.60	6.88	6.07	4.06
2F IFA Two-Year Global Fixed Income Index	4.47	1.89	0.73	1.92	2.84	4.35	6.98	7.48	6.62	5.10
5F IFA Five-Year Global Fixed Income Index	3.90	1.73	2.90	2.97	4.33	5.45	7.89	7.80	6.68	5.10
5G IFA Five-Year Government Index	4.51	0.78	2.77	2.68	4.43	5.15	7.97	7.46	6.44	4.95
Long Term Government Bonds Index	1.42	7.81	9.34	1.44	7.40	7.94	11.20	8.73	6.82	5.42
Long Term Corporate Bonds Index	3.45	5.87	8.72	5.27	7.84	7.74	11.15	8.76	7.10	5.85
One Month Treasury Bills Index	4.82	3.42	1.19	1.02	2.32	3.60	5.33	6.02	5.36	3.72
Inflation (Consumer Price Index)	3.06	2.98	3.25	1.88	2.80	2.49	3.14	4.68	4.08	3.10
5 IFA Index Portfolio 05	6.40	2.35	4.03	7.95	4.97	5.23	7.84	7.79	6.94	5.55
10 IFA Index Portfolio 10	7.38	2.88	5.07	10.14	5.72	5.68	8.30	8.23	7.40	6.07
15 IFA Index Portfolio 15	8.35	3.41	6.11	12.32	6.46	6.11	8.76	8.65	7.85	6.58
20 IFA Index Portfolio 20	9.32	3.93	7.15	14.51	7.20	6.55	9.22	9.07	8.29	7.07
25 IFA Index Portfolio 25	10.30	4.46	8.19	16.70	7.92	6.97	9.67	9.48	8.72	7.54
30 IFA Index Portfolio 30	11.27	4.99	9.22	18.89	8.64	7.39	10.11	9.89	9.14	7.99
35 IFA Index Portfolio 35	12.25	5.52	10.26	21.07	9.35	7.81	10.56	10.28	9.55	8.43
40 IFA Index Portfolio 40	13.22	6.04	11.30	23.26	10.05	8.21	10.99	10.68	9.95	8.85
45 IFA Index Portfolio 45	14.19	6.57	12.34	25.45	10.74	8.62	11.42	11.06	10.35	9.26
50 IFA Index Portfolio 50	15.17	7.10	13.38	27.64	11.42	9.01	11.85	11.44	10.73	9.65
55 IFA Index Portfolio 55	16.14	7.63	14.42	29.82	12.10	9.41	12.27	11.81	11.11	10.02
60 IFA Index Portfolio 60	17.12	8.16	15.46	32.01	12.77	9.79	12.69	12.18	11.48	10.38
65 IFA Index Portfolio 65	18.09	8.68	16.50	34.20	13.42	10.17	13.11	12.54	11.84	10.71
70 IFA Index Portfolio 70	19.06	9.21	17.54	36.39	14.07	10.55	13.51	12.89	12.19	11.04
75 IFA Index Portfolio 75	20.04	9.74	18.58	38.58	14.72	10.92	13.92	13.24	12.54	11.34
80 IFA Index Portfolio 80	21.01	10.27	19.62	40.76	15.35	11.28	14.32	13.58	12.87	11.63
85 IFA Index Portfolio 85	21.99	10.79	20.66	42.95	15.98	11.64	14.71	13.91	13.20	11.89
90 IFA Index Portfolio 90	22.96	11.32	21.70	45.14	16.59	11.99	15.10	14.23	13.51	12.14
95 IFA Index Portfolio 95	22.63	11.42	22.17	48.38	17.26	12.36	15.37	14.61	13.88	12.45
100 IFA Index Portfolio 100	22.30	11.51	22.64	51.63	17.92	12.71	15.62	14.97	14.22	12.74

IFA Index Portfolios shown net of IFA fees.   Sources, Updates, and Disclosures: ifa.com/btp, CRSP, and Fama/French

equity strategies generally performed well over the period. But, the premium relative to public securities appears rather small considering the higher risk, investment concentration, absence of liquidity, transparency and daily pricing. The results are shown in Table 9-5.

Table 9-5

Private Equity Strategies 20 Years - Jan. 1986 - Dec. 2005	
Asset Class	**Return %**
IFA Emerging Markets Value Index	**21.0%**
IFA Emerging Markets Index	**20.5%**
Early/Seed Venture Capital	20.4%
All Venture Capital	16.5%
IFA U.S. Small Value Index	**14.3%**
All Private Equity	14.2%
IFA Index Portfolio 100	**13.9%**
Later Stage Venture Capital	13.5%
Buyouts	13.3%
IFA U.S. Micro Cap Index	**12.8%**
IFA U.S. Large Value Index	**12.8%**
IFA U.S. Large Company Index	**11.7%**
Mezzanine Financing	8.9%
Source: Thomson Finanacial/National Venture Capital Association Sources, Updates, and Disclosures: ifa.com/btp	

9.4.2 Cross Correlation among Indexes

In addition to the long-term risk and return of indexes, a third input used to create optimal portfolios is cross correlation. Cross correlation refers to the extent to which performances of different asset classes move in relation to each other. The lower the correlation among different indexes in a portfolio, the greater the diversification, which means lower volatility of returns.

If indexes are highly correlated, then their prices are responding to market news in the same direction at the same time. Market news that affects prices in all markets, include the overall strength of the U.S. economy, consumer confidence, the level of interest rates and expectations for inflation rates. A low correlation means that market prices of different indexes react in different directions to the same news. These indexes have market price movements that are not connected, showing a low similarity in movement to each other.

For example, large company stocks and small company stocks historically have a low

Figure 9-5

Correlation Matrix for 15 IFA Indexes 80 years (Jan 1927 to Dec 2006 - Monthly Data)		LC	LV	MC	SV	RE	IV	IS	ISV	EM	EV	ES	1F	2F	5G	5F
IFA U.S. Large Company Index	LC	1.00														
IFA U.S. Large Value Index	LV	0.86	1.00													
IFA U.S. Micro Cap Index	MC	0.68	0.62	1.00												
IFA U.S. Small Cap Value Index	SV	0.73	0.79	0.93	1.00											
IFA Real Estate Securities Index	RE	0.42	0.51	0.49	0.59	1.00										
IFA International Value Index	IV	0.58	0.56	0.48	0.55	0.33	1.00									
IFA International Small Company Index	IS	0.44	0.42	0.46	0.48	0.23	0.87	1.00								
IFA International Small Cap Value Index	ISV	0.43	0.43	0.43	0.47	0.25	0.88	0.99	1.00							
IFA Emerging Markets Index	EM	0.57	0.57	0.55	0.59	0.35	0.56	0.51	0.51	1.00						
IFA Emerging Value Index	EV	0.57	0.56	0.56	0.59	0.32	0.60	0.57	0.56	0.91	1.00					
IFA Emerging Small Cap Index	ES	0.54	0.54	0.56	0.59	0.31	0.60	0.57	0.57	0.90	0.96	1.00				
IFA One-Year Fixed Income Index	1F	0.08	0.01	-0.10	-0.13	0.02	-0.09	-0.09	-0.09	0.01	-0.07	-0.10	1.00			
IFA Two-Year Global Fixed Income Index	2F	-0.01	-0.05	-0.15	-0.17	0.03	-0.12	-0.09	-0.10	-0.04	-0.12	-0.16	0.88	1.00		
IFA Five-Year Government Index	5G	0.00	-0.05	-0.12	-0.14	0.11	-0.08	-0.03	-0.04	-0.04	-0.10	-0.14	0.74	0.87	1.00	
IFA Five-Year Global Fixed Income Index	5F	0.07	0.04	-0.09	-0.10	0.15	0.00	0.02	0.00	-0.02	-0.05	-0.09	0.60	0.75	0.82	1.00

Sources, Updates, and Disclosures: ifa.com/btp

correlation. As seen in Figure 9-5, large company stocks and one-year fixed income stocks have a very low correlation of 0.01, which means that there's almost no correlation between the market price movements of these two asset classes.

The next best diversifier of risk is low positive correlation among asset classes in a portfolio. By designing the proper mix of low correlation index funds, it is possible to lower a portfolio's risk and increase its risk-adjusted return at the same time. More historical data on the correlation among indexes found in the global financial markets appears in Figure 9-5.

The data in Figures 9-6, 9-7 and 9-8 is attributable to the three risk factors documented by Eugene Fama, Kenneth French, and Jim Davis. These factors are used in a multiple regression analysis to risk adjust returns of other investments and to establish the cost of capital of firms that sell their equity. Remember that a firm's cost of capital is equal to the investor's expected return. The Fama/French data indicates that these three factors explain 95% of stock returns in diversified portfolios. In those calculations, average instead of annualized returns are used. The average annual returns of these risk factors are known as the risk premiums.

A Comparative History of Several Indexes using Rolling Periods

At times investors doubt whether the fundamentals of capitalism and the relationship between risk and return will hold up in the future. For example, the August 13, 1979 issue of *BusinessWeek* featured this question on the cover: "Are Equities Dead?" After 10 years of lousy performance, it really must have appeared that way. For the 11-year period of 1969 to 1979, the S&P 500 average annual compound return

Figures 9-6, 9-7, 9-8

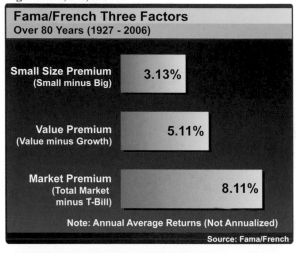

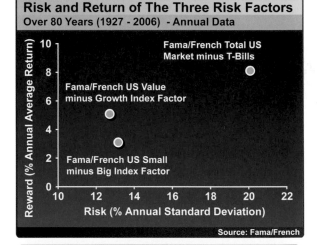

U.S. Indexes	Growth of $1	Annualized Return	Annualized Standard Deviation
Fama/French US Small Cap Value Index	$50,970	14.51%	29.94%
Fama/French US Micro Cap Index	$18,148	13.04%	33.22%
Fama/French US Large Cap Value Index	$6,222	11.54%	25.99%
Fama/French US Large Company Index	$2,761	10.41%	19.24%
Fama/French Small Cap Growth Stock Index	$1,257	9.33%	28.68%
Fama/French Large Cap Growth Stock Index	$1,265	9.34%	18.90%
One-Month Treasury Bills	$18.61	3.72%	0.88%
Inflation (US Consumer Price Index)	$0.09	3.10%	1.85%

Sources, Updates, and Disclosures: Fama/French and CRSP

was only 4.5%. And, it was even worse, 3.2%, for the more than seven-year period of 1973 to 1979, just before the article. These kinds of returns made it seem as if stocks were no longer a viable investment. Thus, many investors decided to invest only in Treasury bills, which outperformed stocks for both periods, and avoid the risk of stocks. Of course, the concern that the fundamental relationship between risk and return wouldn't hold up was as ridiculous then as it is now.

An analysis of multiple year rolling periods offers an interesting way to sort out these kinds of concerns. For example, if you look at Figure 9-11 you will see that we have 841 ten-year periods shifting one month at a time, over the 80 years from 1927 to 2006. Of those 841 periods the S&P 500 Index outperformed T-bills 85.7% of the time. In the 721 twenty-year periods it out performed T-bills 100% of the time. And in the 949 one-year periods, it outperformed only 68.2% of the time. This brings to mind Benjamin Graham's famous observation that, "In the short run, the market is a voting machine, but in the long run it is a weighing machine."

Figures 9-9 through 9-16 offer numerous comparisons of this kind of data and they are very helpful in understanding the comparisons of various indexes. Figure 9-16 shows that large value does not always outperform large growth stocks. In fact, the size and value risk factors come and go unpredictably. This is consistent with the Random Walk Theory of changes in stock prices. In addition, the cycle of good or bad returns for small company stocks compared to large company stocks can last for many years.

A Comparative History of Market Cap Deciles

Figure 9-17 clearly lays out the history of the size effect. The several charts break out a number of time periods in history to illustrate the diversifying power of small-cap stocks. This chart is created using CRSP market capitalization data broken down into one-tenth size buckets, referred to as deciles. All 10 deciles are then measured and charted in different time periods. It illustrates that especially in shorter periods, small company stocks don't always outperform large company stocks, but as seen in the top left chart, over the whole time period of 1927 to 2006, there is a clear advantage to have some exposure to small companies. But, in shorter periods anything can happen. For example, during the five-year period of 2002 to 2006, small company stocks widely outperformed large company stocks, while during the seven-year period of 1984 to 1990, and six years from 1994 to 1999, large-cap stocks were the king of the hill.

The Returns Matrix

The use of a returns matrix is yet another interesting way to look at long-term data. Figures 9-18 and 9-19 bring together annual and annualized returns covering every combination from 1927 to 2006 for an Index Portfolio 90 (see Appendix A). Because the matrix is so large, it is spread out over two pages. This big triangle identifies the years along all three borders. The intersection of any two years shows the annualized return over that period. The diagonal lines show one year returns on the first diagonal and rolling period returns can be found on each diagonal line below the first one. For example, the second gray diagonal shows five year rolling periods from 1927 to 2006. The very bottom left hand corner shows the annualized return over the entire 80-year period, which is 12.1% for Index Portfolio 90.

Figure 9-9

Small Value versus Small Growth
80Years of Monthly Data - Jan. 1927 to Dec. 2006

- Small Growth Beats Small Value
- Small Value Beats Small Growth

% of Periods

| 37.1% | 26.5% | 22.4% | 10.3% | 8.6% | 6.2% |
| 62.9% | 73.5% | 77.6% | 89.7% | 91.4% | 93.8% |

| 949 1-Year | 925 3-Year | 901 5-Year | 841 10-Year | 781 15-Year | 721 20-Year |

Monthly Rolling Time Periods

Sources, Updates, and Disclosures: ifa.com/btp

Figure 9-10

Large Growth versus Small Growth
80 Years of Monthly Data - Jan. 1927 to Dec. 2006

- Small Growth Beats Large Growth
- Large Growth Beats Small Growth

% of Periods

| 48.3% | 44.5% | 46.4% | 45.1% | 51.7% | 48.8% |
| 51.7% | 55.5% | 53.6% | 54.9% | 48.3% | 51.2% |

| 949 1-Year | 925 3-Year | 901 5-Year | 841 10-Year | 781 15-Year | 721 20-Year |

Monthly Rolling Time Periods

Sources, Updates, and Disclosures: ifa.com/btp

Figure 9-11

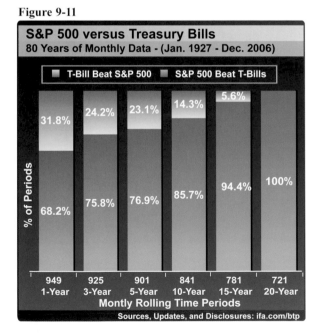

S&P 500 versus Treasury Bills
80 Years of Monthly Data - (Jan. 1927 - Dec. 2006)

- T-Bill Beat S&P 500
- S&P 500 Beat T-Bills

% of Periods

| 31.8% | 24.2% | 23.1% | 14.3% | 5.6% | |
| 68.2% | 75.8% | 76.9% | 85.7% | 94.4% | 100% |

| 949 1-Year | 925 3-Year | 901 5-Year | 841 10-Year | 781 15-Year | 721 20-Year |

Montly Rolling Time Periods

Sources, Updates, and Disclosures: ifa.com/btp

Figure 9-12

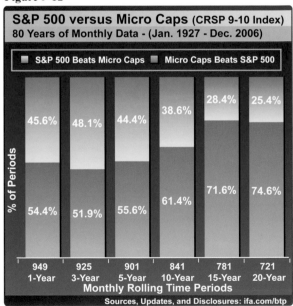

S&P 500 versus Micro Caps (CRSP 9-10 Index)
80 Years of Monthly Data - (Jan. 1927 - Dec. 2006)

- S&P 500 Beats Micro Caps
- Micro Caps Beats S&P 500

% of Periods

| 45.6% | 48.1% | 44.4% | 38.6% | 28.4% | 25.4% |
| 54.4% | 51.9% | 55.6% | 61.4% | 71.6% | 74.6% |

| 949 1-Year | 925 3-Year | 901 5-Year | 841 10-Year | 781 15-Year | 721 20-Year |

Montly Rolling Time Periods

Sources, Updates, and Disclosures: ifa.com/btp

Figure 9-13

Small Value versus Large Growth
80 Years of Monthly Data - Jan. 1927 to Dec. 2006

Figure 9-14

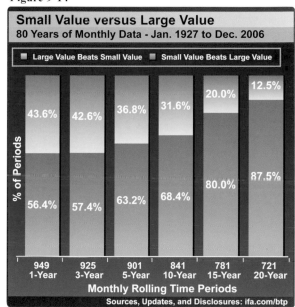

Small Value versus Large Value
80 Years of Monthly Data - Jan. 1927 to Dec. 2006

Figure 9-15

Large Value versus Small Growth
80 Years of Monthly Data - Jan. 1927 to Dec. 2006

Figure 9-16

Large Value versus Large Growth
80 Years of Monthly Data - Jan. 1927 to Dec. 2006

Figure 9-17

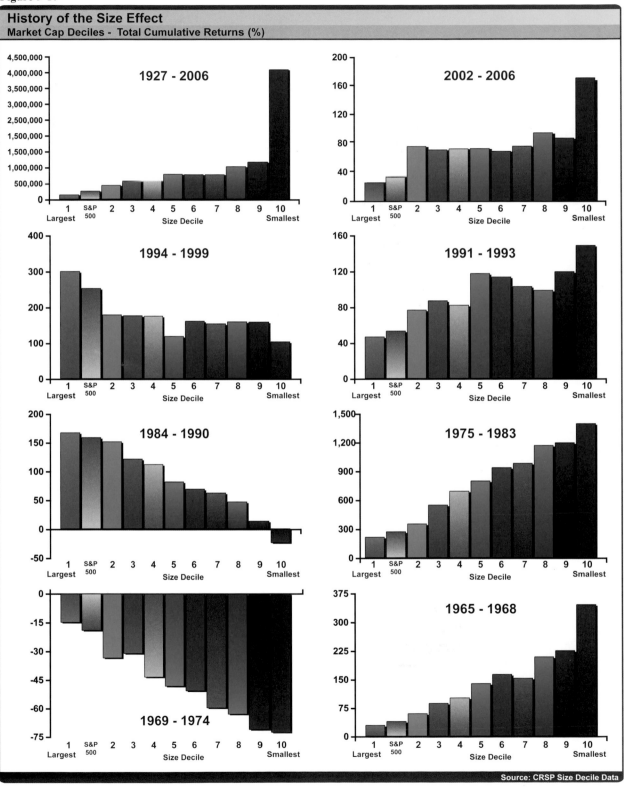

History of the Size Effect
Market Cap Deciles - Total Cumulative Returns (%)

Source: CRSP Size Decile Data

180

Figure 9-18

Index Portfolio 90 Gold

Annualized Returns Matrix (%)
80 Years of IFA Index Portfolio 90 (1927 - 2006)
Returns Net of IFA and DFA fees

Part A

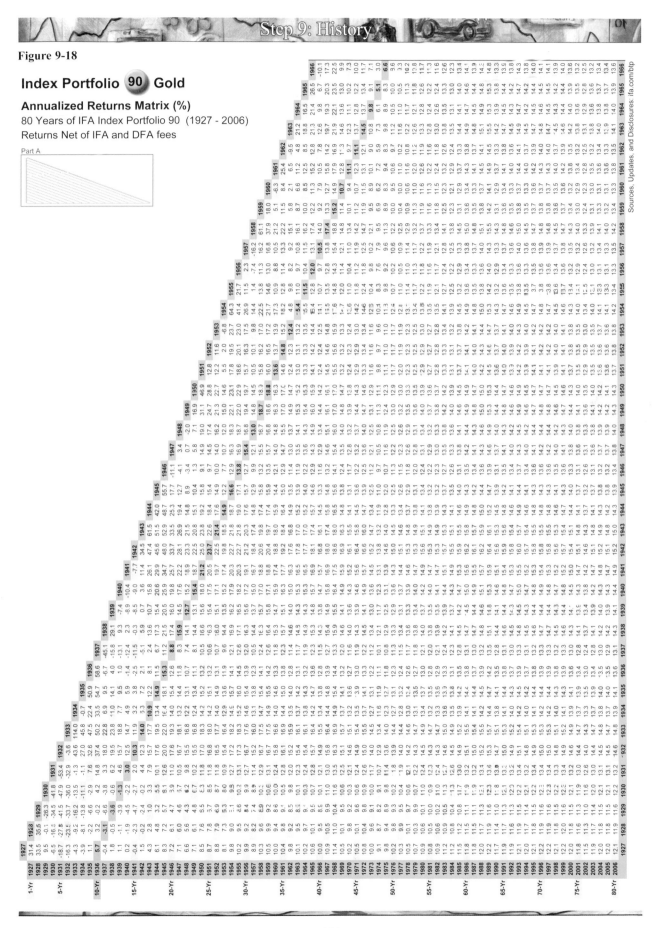

Figure 9-19

Index Portfolio 90 Gold

Annualized Returns Matrix (%)

80 Years of IFA Index Portfolio 90 (1927 - 2006)

Returns Net of IFA and DFA fees

Part B

		1967	1968	1969	1970	1971	1972	1973	1974	1975	1976	1977	1978	1979	1980
1-Yr	1967	52.9													
	1968	43.1	33.9												
	1969	17.5	3.0	-20.8											
	1970	12.1	1.1	-12.2	-2.6										
5-Yr	1971	14.6	6.6	-1.2	10.3	25.0									
	1972	15.8	9.5	4.1	14.1	23.4	21.9								
	1973	9.8	3.9	-1.2	4.4	6.9	-1.2	-19.9							
	1974	4.7	-0.8	-5.6	-2.2	-2.1	-9.8	-22.4	-24.8						
	1975	8.6	4.1	0.4	4.5	6.0	1.7	-4.3	4.6	45.6					
10-Yr	1976	10.7	6.8	3.8	7.9	9.7	6.9	3.4	12.6	37.9	30.6				
	1977	11.3	7.8	5.2	9.0	10.8	8.6	6.1	13.8	30.7	23.9	17.5			
	1978	12.1	9.0	6.8	10.4	12.1	10.4	8.6	15.4	28.5	23.2	19.7	22.0		
	1979	12.6	9.8	7.8	11.2	12.9	11.4	10.0	16.0	26.5	22.1	19.4	20.3	18.7	
	1980	13.5	10.9	9.2	12.4	14.0	12.8	11.8	17.2	26.2	22.7	20.8	21.9	21.8	25.0
15-Yr	1981	12.9	10.5	8.9	11.8	13.2	12.1	11.0	15.7	23.0	19.6	17.5	17.5	16.1	14.8
	1982	13.1	10.8	9.4	12.1	13.4	12.4	11.5	15.7	22.1	19.1	17.3	17.2	16.1	15.2
	1983	14.1	12.0	10.7	13.4	14.7	13.9	13.2	17.2	23.1	20.6	19.2	19.5	19.0	19.1
	1984	13.7	11.7	10.5	12.9	14.1	13.4	12.7	16.2	21.4	19.0	17.6	17.6	16.9	16.5
	1985	14.8	13.0	11.8	14.3	15.5	14.8	14.3	17.8	22.7	20.6	19.5	19.8	19.5	19.6
20-Yr	1986	15.4	13.7	12.7	15.1	16.3	15.7	15.3	18.5	23.1	21.3	20.4	20.7	20.5	20.8
	1987	15.2	13.6	12.6	14.8	15.9	15.4	14.9	17.9	22.1	20.3	19.4	19.6	19.4	19.5
	1988	15.6	14.0	13.1	15.3	16.4	15.9	15.5	18.4	22.2	20.6	19.8	20.0	19.8	20.0
	1989	16.0	14.6	13.7	15.8	16.9	16.4	16.1	18.9	22.5	21.0	20.3	20.6	20.5	20.6
	1990	14.4	13.0	12.2	14.0	14.9	14.4	14.0	16.4	19.6	18.1	17.2	17.2	16.8	16.7
25-Yr	1991	15.0	13.7	12.9	14.7	15.6	15.2	14.8	17.1	20.2	18.8	18.0	18.1	17.8	17.7
	1992	14.8	13.5	12.7	14.5	15.3	14.9	14.5	16.7	19.6	18.2	17.5	17.5	17.2	17.0
	1993	15.3	14.0	13.3	15.0	15.8	15.4	15.1	17.3	20.0	18.7	18.1	18.1	17.9	17.8
	1994	14.7	13.5	12.8	14.4	15.2	14.8	14.5	16.4	19.0	17.7	17.1	17.0	16.7	16.6
	1995	15.0	13.8	13.1	14.7	15.5	15.1	14.8	16.7	19.1	18.0	17.3	17.3	17.1	16.9
30-Yr	1996	15.0	13.9	13.3	14.8	15.5	15.1	14.9	16.7	19.0	17.9	17.3	17.3	17.0	16.9
	1997	15.0	13.9	13.3	14.8	15.4	15.1	14.8	16.6	18.8	17.7	17.1	17.1	16.9	16.8
	1998	14.7	13.6	13.0	14.4	15.1	14.7	14.5	16.1	18.2	17.2	16.6	16.6	16.3	16.2
	1999	14.9	13.8	13.2	14.6	15.3	14.9	14.7	16.3	18.3	17.3	16.7	16.7	16.5	16.3
	2000	14.4	13.4	12.8	14.1	14.7	14.3	14.1	15.6	17.5	16.5	15.9	15.9	15.6	15.5
35-Yr	2001	13.9	13.0	12.4	13.6	14.2	13.8	13.6	15.0	16.8	15.8	15.3	15.2	14.9	14.7
	2002	13.2	12.2	11.6	12.8	13.3	12.9	12.7	14.0	15.7	14.7	14.2	14.0	13.7	13.5
	2003	13.9	13.0	12.5	13.6	14.2	13.8	13.6	14.9	16.6	15.7	15.2	15.1	14.8	14.7
	2004	14.1	13.2	12.7	13.9	14.4	14.1	13.8	15.1	16.8	15.9	15.4	15.3	15.1	14.9
	2005	14.1	13.2	12.7	13.8	14.3	14.0	13.8	15.0	16.6	15.7	15.3	15.2	14.9	14.8
40-Yr	2006	14.3	13.4	12.9	14.0	14.5	14.2	14.0	15.2	16.8	16.0	15.5	15.4	15.2	15.1
		1967	1968	1969	1970	1971	1972	1973	1974	1975	1976	1977	1978	1979	1980

	1981	1982	1983	1984	1985	1986	1987	1988	1989	1990	1991	1992	1993
1981	5.5												
1982	10.6	16.0											
1983	17.2	23.5	31.6										
1984	14.5	17.7	18.5	6.8									
1985	18.5	22.0	24.1	20.5	36.1								
1986	20.1	23.3	25.2	23.1	32.2	28.5							
1987	18.7	21.0	22.1	19.8	24.5	19.1	10.4						
1988	19.4	21.5	22.4	20.7	24.4	20.7	17.1	24.1					
1989	20.2	22.1	23.0	21.7	24.9	22.2	20.2	25.5	26.8				
1990	15.9	17.1	17.2	15.3	16.8	13.2	9.7	9.5	2.8	-16.6			
1991	17.1	18.3	18.6	17.0	18.6	15.9	13.5	14.3	11.2	4.1	30.0		
1992	16.4	17.5	17.6	16.1	17.4	14.9	12.8	13.3	10.7	5.8	19.2	9.3	
1993	17.3	18.3	18.5	17.3	18.5	16.5	14.9	15.7	14.0	11.0	22.1	18.4	28.3
1994	16.0	16.9	17.0	15.7	16.6	14.7	13.0	13.4	11.7	8.9	16.5	12.3	13.8
1995	16.4	17.3	17.4	16.2	17.1	15.4	14.0	14.5	13.2	11.1	17.6	14.7	16.6
1996	16.5	17.2	17.3	16.3	17.1	15.5	14.3	14.7	13.6	11.9	17.5	15.1	16.6
1997	16.3	17.0	17.1	16.1	16.9	15.4	14.3	14.7	13.7	12.1	17.0	14.9	16.1
1998	15.7	16.3	16.3	15.4	16.0	14.6	13.5	13.8	12.8	11.4	15.5	13.6	14.3
1999	15.9	16.5	16.5	15.7	16.3	15.0	14.0	14.3	13.5	12.2	16.0	14.3	15.1
2000	15.0	15.5	15.5	14.6	15.1	13.9	12.9	13.1	12.2	10.9	14.2	12.5	12.9
2001	14.3	14.7	14.7	13.8	14.2	13.0	12.0	12.1	11.3	10.1	12.9	11.3	11.5
2002	13.0	13.4	13.2	12.3	12.7	11.4	10.4	10.4	9.5	8.3	10.7	9.1	9.0
2003	14.2	14.6	14.6	13.8	14.2	13.1	12.2	12.3	11.6	10.6	13.0	11.7	11.9
2004	14.5	14.9	14.9	14.2	14.5	13.5	12.7	12.9	12.2	11.3	13.6	12.4	12.7
2005	14.4	14.8	14.7	14.0	14.4	13.4	12.7	12.8	12.1	11.3	13.4	12.3	12.6
2006	14.7	15.1	15.1	14.4	14.8	13.8	13.1	13.3	12.7	11.9	14.0	13.0	13.3
	1981	1982	1983	1984	1985	1986	1987	1988	1989	1990	1991	1992	1993

	1994	1995	1996	1997	1998	1999	2000	2001	2002	2003	2004	2005	2006
1994	0.9												
1995	11.1	22.3											
1996	13.0	19.5	16.8										
1997	13.2	17.6	15.3	13.9									
1998	11.7	14.5	12.0	9.8	5.7								
1999	13.0	15.6	14.0	13.0	12.6	19.9							
2000	10.9	12.7	10.8	9.4	7.9	9.0	-0.9						
2001	9.6	10.9	9.1	7.6	6.0	6.1	-0.1	0.7					
2002	7.1	7.9	6.0	4.3	2.4	1.6	-3.9	-5.3	-10.9				
2003	10.4	11.5	10.2	9.3	8.5	9.1	6.6	9.2	13.7	45.1			
2004	11.4	12.5	11.4	10.8	10.3	11.1	9.4	12.2	16.3	32.9	21.7		
2005	11.4	12.4	11.4	10.8	10.5	11.1	9.8	12.0	15.1	25.3	16.4	11.3	
2006	12.2	13.2	12.4	12.0	11.8	12.6	11.5	13.8	16.6	24.7	18.5	17.0	23.0
	1994	1995	1996	1997	1998	1999	2000	2001	2002	2003	2004	2005	2006

Sources, Updates, and Disclosures: ifa.com/btp

How to read the Annualized Returns Matrix: You can locate the annualized compounded rate of return for this simulated Index Portfolio for a designated time period by following these easy instructions: Locate the column for the beginning year of the period. Years are labeled at the top and the bottom of each column. Then, locate the ending year of the period on the left-most vertical column. The annualized return can be found where the first year's column intersects with the ending year's row. IFA advisory fees of 0.9% per year and DFA mutual fund expense ratios have been deducted from these results. The 10-Yr diagonal (highlighted, starting from far left column) represents the estimated average holding period for investors who score 90 on the Risk Capacity Survey at ifa.com. Sources, Updates, and Disclosures: ifa.com/btp.

9.5 SUMMARY

A good understanding of the long-term historical risk and return of various indexes enables an investor to know how to construct an efficient asset allocation according to risk capacity. Risk and return will work themselves out or revert to the mean over the long run. In the meantime, the best bet is to diversify among index funds that are structured for optimal exposure to risk factors that history has shown to be most rewarding.

9.6 REVIEW QUESTIONS

1. Stock markets are best characterized when looking at:

   a. one-year periods

   b. five-year periods

   c. eighty-year periods

   d. three-year periods

2. The long-term characteristics of indexes are important because:

   a. they better reflect the differences between capital and capitalism

   b. margin rules are the same throughout history

   c. favored industries change with time

   d. the law of large numbers is not applicable to market returns

3. Many high net worth investors try to get allotments of venture capital partnerships. According to Morgan Stanley, over a 48-year period venture capital had a 16% return and a 35.4 risk index. Emerging market equities over the same period had the following:

   a. 4.9% return, 26 risk

   b. 16% return, 29.6 risk

   c. 5.4% return, 6.2 risk

   d. 12.7% return, 8.2 risk

4. Many people look at 80-year risk and return data and say that it is not relevant to them because they don't have 80 years to invest. This is faulty logic because:

   a. the basic concept of sampling error means short-term data is worse than long-term data.

   b. three years of data contains a large sampling error.

   c. one year of data has no predictive value on the following year's data.

   d. five years of data have little predictive value on the following year's data.

   e. all of the above

5. The index with the highest return since 1927 is:

   a. large growth index

   b. large value index

   c. small growth index

   d. small value index

   e. total market index

Step 10 ~ Risk Capacity

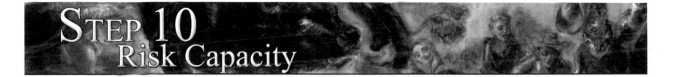

STEP 10
Risk Capacity

"Design a portfolio you are not likely to trade... akin to pre-marital counseling advice; try to build a portfolio that you can live with for a long, long time."

-*Is Your Beta Big Enough to Cover Your Taxes?* Robert D. Arnott, president, First Quadrant Corp.

"Investment Policy [asset allocation] is the foundation upon which portfolios should be constructed and managed."

-Charles D. Ellis, *Investment Policy*, 1985

"Rip Van Winkle would be the ideal stock market investor. Rip could invest in the market before his nap and when he woke up 20 years later, he'd be happy. He would have been asleep through all the ups and downs in between. But few investors resemble Mr. Van Winkle. The more often an investor counts his money — or looks at the value of his mutual funds in the newspaper — the lower his risk tolerance."

-Richard Thaler, a University of Chicago economist, *MSN Money.com*

10.1 INTRODUCTION

Step 10: Analyze your five dimensions of risk capacity.

Now that we have investigated the pitfalls of active investing, learned the language of riskese, and reviewed the history of various indexes, we are ready to move into the implementation phase of the 12-Step Program. This next step is what we call "CEO Investing." CEO, which stands for "Capacity Exposure Optimization," is the process that best matches people with portfolios. At the intersection of risk capacity and risk exposure sits a portfolio that will be optimal for each investor, and will therefore generate optimal returns for that investor. Figure 10-1 illustrates this concept.

Investors are entitled to a level of return that is commensurate with their risk capacity. Based on this logic, the measurement of risk capacity can be elevated to a very high level of importance in the investing process.

The reason investors only earn approximately a very small fraction of market rate of returns is that their risk exposure rarely matches their capacity. For example, if an investor has a risk capacity of 65% and selects a risk exposure of 35%, he is being overly conservative. When stock market returns start taking off, this investor feels he should further increase his risk exposure by moving it up to 95%. The problem is at a higher exposure of 95%, the portfolio is expected to have high volatility, which ultimately scares the investor back down to a 35% exposure.

The optimal scenario for this investor is to choose a 65% exposure to match his 65% risk capacity and ride out the volatility at a level that is comfortable and minimizes the urge to move. The market is like a wild bull trying to buck investors off its back. The objective of CEO investing is to find the bull each investor can stick with and ride until the buzzer sounds. In this analogy, the buzzer represents an investor's need to withdraw funds from his account.

Figure 10-1

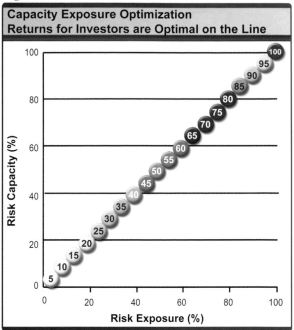

Capacity Exposure Optimization
Returns for Investors are Optimal on the Line

There are five dimensions of risk capacity. Each one can be carefully measured by having the investor answer a properly designed survey consisting of 49 questions. Then the answers are scored and matched to five dimensions of risk exposure.

In addition, the investor should consult with an expert in CEO investing. This thorough analysis is critical, and allows investors to pinpoint an optimal portfolio of index funds, which will in turn provide them with optimal returns.

Since all long-term returns are determined by asset allocation or risk exposure, it is essential that each investor thoroughly understand the individual components of risk capacity.

 10.2 DEFINITIONS

The five dimensions for determining risk capacity, which are discussed in this step, are defined below.

Dimension One: Time Horizon and Liquidity Needs

The "Time Horizon and Liquidity Needs" dimension estimates how rapidly investors may need to withdraw money from their investments. A low score in a survey indicates that an investor may need money in less than two years. A higher score indicates that an investor may not need to withdraw money for 10 years or more. The longer an investor holds onto a risky asset with at least a 20 year record of associated returns, the less chance there is of obtaining poor cumulative returns.

Dimension Two: Attitude toward Risk

The "Attitude toward Risk" dimension estimates aversion or attraction to risk. Risk is defined as "the possibility of loss," and this category addresses an investor's ability to stomach the inevitable decline of any investment subject to risk. If the investment never declines, there is no risk and therefore no reason for it to earn a return. However, high returns are not available

Figure 10-2

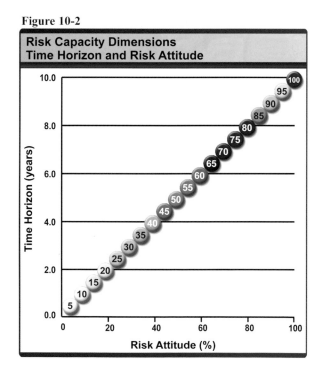

Risk Capacity Dimensions
Time Horizon and Risk Attitude

without accepting high risk. A high score suggests a capacity for tolerating high risk investing to obtain the potential for higher returns, which is required. A low score indicates a risk aversion and the need to invest more conservatively. High risk attitudes are derived from a number of factors including an individual's personality, experience and gaming inclinations. Of all the five risk capacity dimensions, this one is the most difficult to quantify because it's an intangible quality. Figure 10-2 shows the relationship between risk attitude, time horizon, and optimal portfolios.

Dimension Three: Net Worth

The "Net Worth" dimension estimates capacity to take various levels of risk with investments. A high net worth provides a cushion for the uncertainty of future cash needs. Because life is a random walk, we are never certain of tomorrow's requirements. However, the more assets one has in reserve, the higher one's capacity for risk. The higher the net worth, the higher the capacity for risk.

Dimension Four: Income and Savings Rate

The "Income and Savings Rate" dimension estimates excess income and ability to add to savings. A high score here indicates that a large percentage of an investor's income is discretionary and is available for investing. A low score indicates that all or almost all of an investor's income is being used for ordinary expenses and not being added to annual investments. A higher income also adds to the cushion set up for surprise or emergency cash requirements. Figure 10-3 shows the relationship between net worth, net income, and optimal portfolios.

Figure 10-3

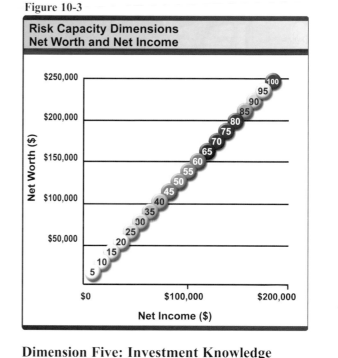

Figure 10-4

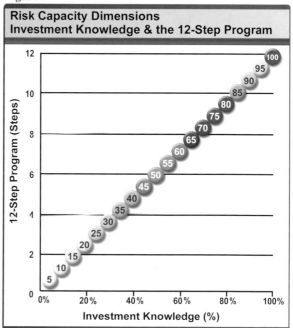

Dimension Five: Investment Knowledge

The "Investment Knowledge" dimension estimates an investor's understanding of the 12-Step Program for Active Investors. See Figure 10-4.

A high score indicates a good understanding of the Modern Portfolio Theory and the failure of active management. A low score indicates that a review of this 12-Step Program may be needed.

10.3 PROBLEMS

10.3.1 Investors do not Properly Assess Risk Capacity.

The problem many investors face is an improper measurement of their risk capacity. Each dimension has to be carefully examined and then quantified. Finally, some dimensions are more important than others, so they must carry more weight in the determination of a final score. As in any survey, the questions must be carefully designed, and the investor must be totally honest and accurate.

10.3.2 Risk Capacity Changes over Time

The second problem investors face is that their risk capacity changes with time and circumstances, and they fail to recalibrate their capacity on an annual basis. Just as a portfolio needs rebalancing to maintain consistent risk exposure, the dimensions of risk capacity need to be remeasured to maintain a consistent risk capacity that matches changing circumstances.

10.4 SOLUTIONS

10.4.1 The Risk Capacity Survey

The five dimensions of risk capacity are measured through a risk capacity survey that poses several questions to the investor. This survey is the single most important step of the investment planning process. Index Funds Advisors offers three surveys on their Web site at www.ifa.com.

The complete survey includes 49 questions, the 401(k) survey has 19 questions, and the quick survey is comprised of five questions. Based on the answers from the two longer surveys, a thorough analysis is generated. The quick survey is designed to provide an overview of the five dimensions and should not be relied on for determining asset allocation, unless the answers are discussed with an investment advisor. The survey contains the following questions:

1. Assume your investments do not increase in value. Within how many years do you plan to withdraw more than 20% of all your investments?

   a. less than 2 years

   b. more than 2, but less than 5 years

   c. more than 5, but less than 7 years

   d. more than 7, but less than 10 years

   e. more than 10 years

2. What is the current value of your long-term investments? Please include your retirement savings plan with your employer and your individual retirement accounts (IRAs).

   a. less than $25,000

   b. $25,000 to $49,999

   c. $50,000 to $99,999

   d. $100,000 to $249,999

   e. $250,000 or more

3. What is your total annual income after the deduction of taxes?

   a. Less than $50,000

   b. $50,000 to $74,999

   c. $75,000 to $99,999

   d. $100,000 to $199,999

   e. $200,000 or more

4. What is the worst 12 month unrealized percentage loss you would tolerate for your long-term investments?

   a. 35%

   b. 27%

   c. 19%

   d. 10%

   e. Zero; any loss is unacceptable to me.

5. How would you rate your knowledge about investing in general and more specifically, the relationship between risk, return, and time?

   a. significantly below average

   b. below average

   c. average

   d above average

   e. expert

The total score of a survey is the sum of the scores in each category, each weighted by its estimated contribution to overall capacity. Higher scores point toward higher risk, higher returns, higher volatility, lower-liquidity, and longer-term investments. These would include a larger allocation of small capitalization, value, international and emerging market indexes. A weighted total score of 100 indicates the highest capacity for risk. On the other hand, lower scores would match up to portfolios with lower risk, lower returns, lower volatility and higher liquidity. These would include shorter-term investments such as fixed-income.

10.4.2 The 10 Dimensions of Risk

The 10 dimensions of risk are shown in Figure 10-5 and the method of measuring and weighting the categories are depicted in the investment

Figure 10-5

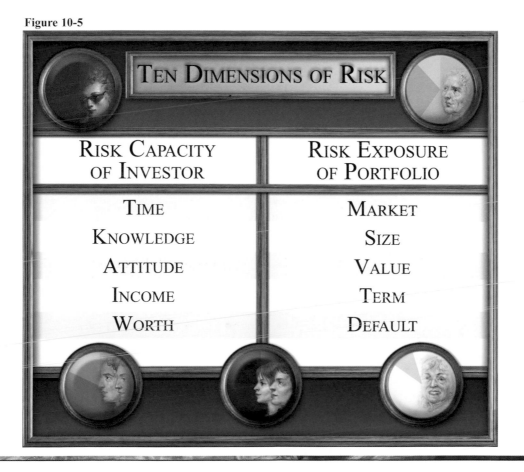

Figure 10-6

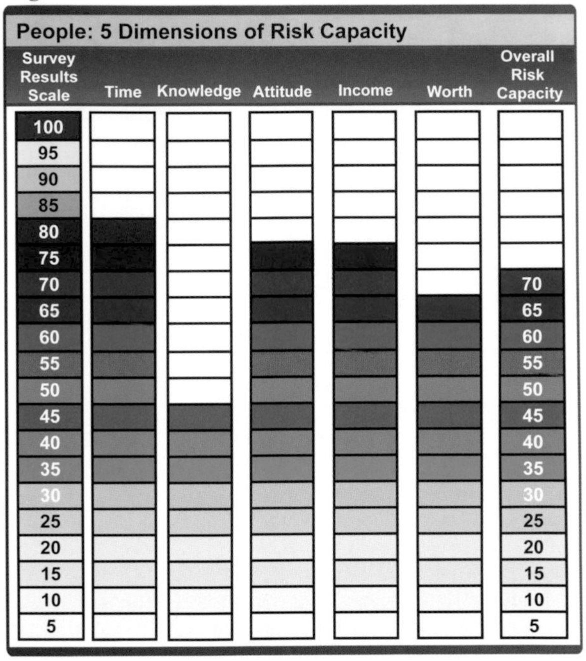

People: 5 Dimensions of Risk Capacity						
Survey Results Scale	Time	Knowledge	Attitude	Income	Worth	Overall Risk Capacity
100						
95						
90						
85						
80						
75						
70						70
65						65
60						60
55						55
50						50
45						45
40						40
35						35
30						30
25						25
20						20
15						15
10						10
5						5

Figure 10-7

Portfolios: 5 Dimensions of Risk Exposure						
Factor Loading Scale	Market Risk	Size Risk	Value Risk	Term Risk	Default Risk	Overall Risk Exposure
100						
95						
90						
85						
80						
75						
70						70
65						65
60						60
55						55
50						50
45						45
40						40
35						35
30						30
25						25
20						20
15						15
10						10
5						5

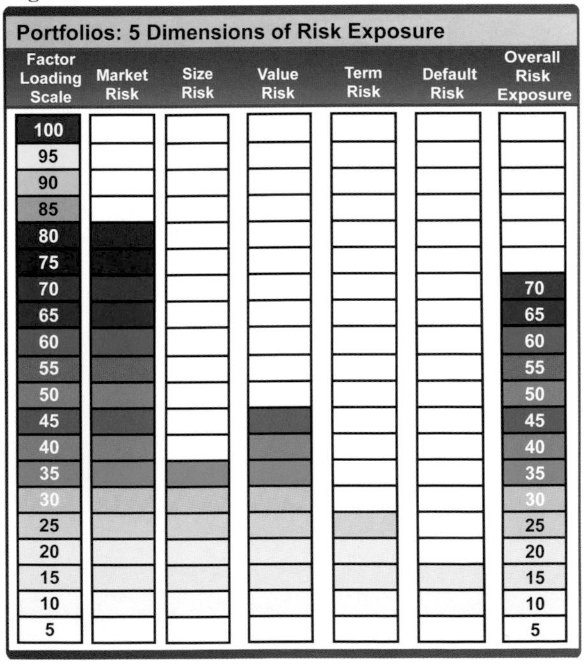

meters in Figures 10-6 and 10-7. In Figure 10-6, an individual's five dimensions of capacity are shown with a meter depicting the scores obtained in a hypothetical risk capacity survey. The scale of measurement is on the left and the weighted average of each category is displayed in the column titled Overall Risk Capacity. Each category is assigned a numerical weight according to its contribution to risk capacity, and a weighted total score is then derived. In this case, it is a capacity level of 70. Table 10-1 is the allocation of indexes in Portfolio 70. This portfolio could now be regarded as this investor's personal benchmark or the bull that can be ridden for the long run.

10.4.3 The Color of Risk Spectrum

The "color of risk spectrum" was created to correlate with various levels of risk and return. The light and cool colors are at the low risk level and the darker, brighter and warmer colors are in the

Table 10-1

Index Portfolio 70 - Dark Teal	
IFA Indexes	**Index Allocation (%)**
IFA US Large Company Index	16
IFA US Large Cap Value Index	16
IFA US Micro Cap Index	8
IFA US Small Value Index	8
IFA Real Estate Index	8
IFA International Value Index	8
IFA International Small Company Index	4
IFA International Small Value Index	4
IFA Emerging Markets Index	2.4
IFA Emerging Markets Value Index	2.4
IFA Emerging Markets Small Cap Index	3.2
IFA One-Year Fixed Income Index	5
IFA Two-Year Global Fixed Income Index	5
IFA Five-Year Gov't Income Index	5
IFA Five-Year Global Fixed Income Index	5
Total	100%

Figure 10-8

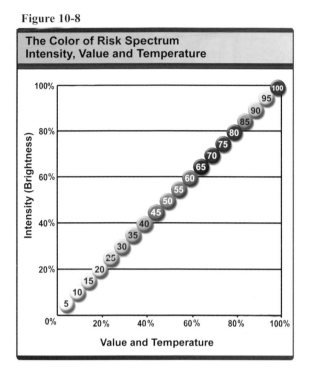

The Color of Risk Spectrum
Intensity, Value and Temperature

Figure 10-9

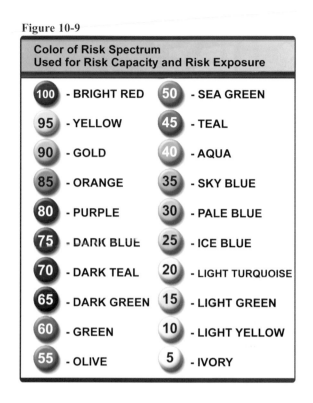

Color of Risk Spectrum
Used for Risk Capacity and Risk Exposure

middle and high end of the risk scale. See Figures 10-8 and 10-9.

10.4.4   Twenty Risk Capacities

The results of the risk capacity survey are rounded off to the nearest increment of five, creating 20 different risk capacity levels. In an effort to capture the 20 levels of risk capacity in images, Lala Ragimov, a Russian artist, created the paintings found on the following pages. See Figures 10-10 through 10-29. Each are colored to represent a risk spectrum. The collages depicted in each present images that convey age, family makeup, activities, careers, retirement and overall lifestyles.

10.4.5   Capacity Adjusted Risk

The time horizon of an investment is one dimension of Risk Capacity. The longer investors hold a portfolio, the more likely it is that they will obtain the expected annualized return. Risk can

be defined as the uncertainty of obtaining the expected return and quantified with the standard deviation measurement. As each year passes the standard deviation of annualized returns over the time period is reduced. If you look at Figure 10-30, you will see that as the time increases along the bottom scale, the uncertainty of expected annualized returns reduces over time on the left scale.

An average holding period for all 20 levels of risk capacity can be estimated. Figure 10-31 indicates that investors who score a 100 on the survey have a holding period of a minimum of 12 years. Risk capacity scores of 50 have average holding periods of about seven years and at levels of five, the period is around four years. People scoring a 90 on the survey have about a 10-year average time horizon. For that reason, investors who fall within the 90 risk capacity score range should concentrate on the uncertain-

Figures 10-10 through 10-29 (p.192 - p.196)

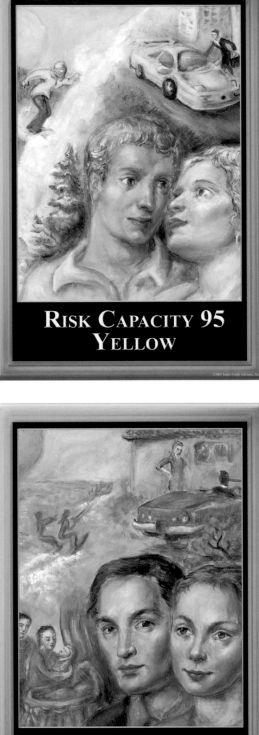

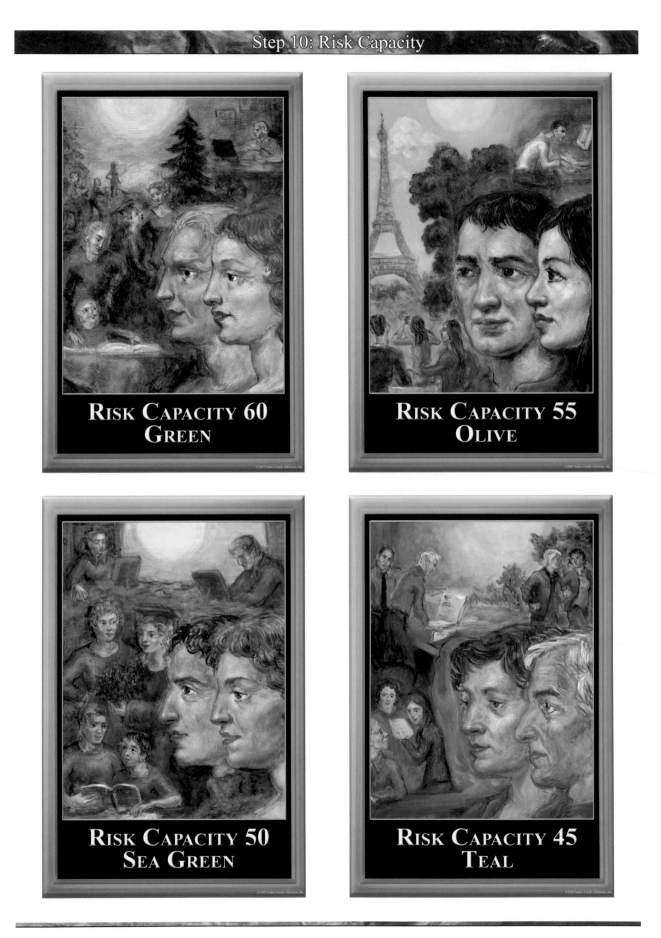

RISK CAPACITY 20
LIGHT TURQUOISE

RISK CAPACITY 15
LIGHT GREEN

RISK CAPACITY 10
LIGHT YELLOW

RISK CAPACITY 5
IVORY

Figure 10-30

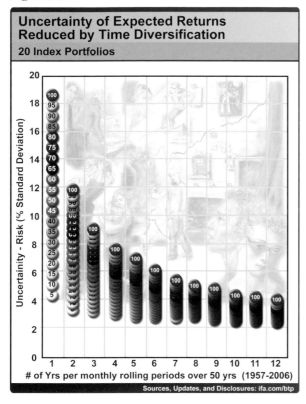

Uncertainty of Expected Returns Reduced by Time Diversification
20 Index Portfolios

Uncertainty - Risk (% Standard Deviation)

# of Yrs per monthly rolling periods over 50 yrs (1957-2006)

Sources, Updates, and Disclosures: ifa.com/btp

Figure 10-31

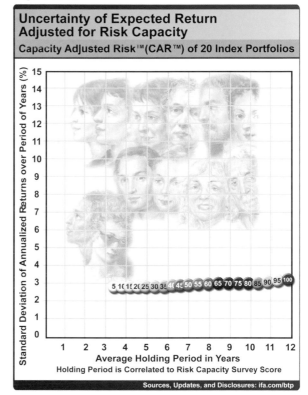

Uncertainty of Expected Return Adjusted for Risk Capacity
Capacity Adjusted Risk™(CAR™) of 20 Index Portfolios

Standard Deviation of Annualized Returns over Period of Years (%)

Average Holding Period in Years
Holding Period is Correlated to Risk Capacity Survey Score

Sources, Updates, and Disclosures: ifa.com/btp

Figure 10-32

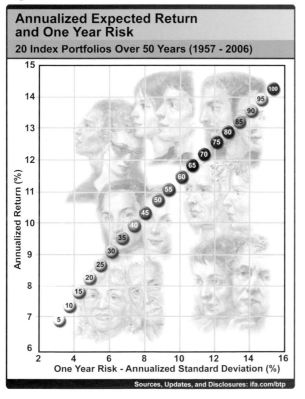

Annualized Expected Return and One Year Risk
20 Index Portfolios Over 50 Years (1957 - 2006)

Annualized Return (%)

One Year Risk - Annualized Standard Deviation (%)

Sources, Updates, and Disclosures: ifa.com/btp

Figure 10-33

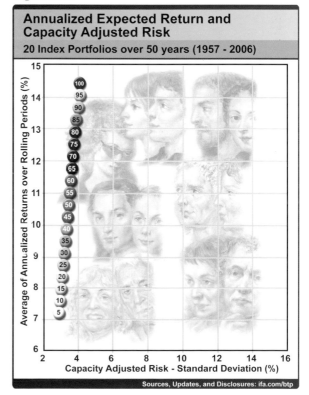

Annualized Expected Return and Capacity Adjusted Risk
20 Index Portfolios over 50 years (1957 - 2006)

Average of Annualized Returns over Rolling Periods (%)

Capacity Adjusted Risk - Standard Deviation (%)

Sources, Updates, and Disclosures: ifa.com/btp

Figure 10-34

INDEX PORTFOLIO 90: GOLD

Annualized Returns Matrix (%)
35 years of Index Portfolio 90 (1972–2006)
Returns Net of IFA and DFA Fees

Period	End \ Begin	1972	1973	1974	1975	1976	1977	1978	1979	1980	1981	1982	1983	1984	1985	1986	1987	1988	1989	1990	1991	1992	1993	1994	1995	1996	1997	1998	1999	2000	2001	2002	2003	2004	2005	2006
1-Yr	1972	21.9																																		
	1973	-1.2	-19.9																																	
	1974	-9.8	-22.4	-24.8																																
	1975	1.7	-4.3	4.6	45.6																															
5-Yr	1976	6.9	3.4	12.6	37.9	30.6																														
	1977	8.6	6.1	13.8	30.7	23.9	17.5																													
	1978	10.4	8.6	15.4	28.5	23.2	19.7	22.0																												
	1979	11.4	10.0	16.0	26.5	22.1	19.4	19.7	17.5																											
	1980	12.8	11.8	17.2	26.2	22.7	20.3	20.8	21.8	25.0																										
10-Yr	1981	12.1	11.0	15.7	23.0	19.6	17.5	17.3	17.2	14.8	5.5																									
	1982	12.4	11.5	15.7	22.1	19.1	17.3	17.2	17.2	15.2	10.6	16.0																								
	1983	13.9	13.2	17.2	23.1	20.6	19.2	19.5	19.0	18.7	17.2	23.5	31.6																							
	1984	13.4	12.7	16.2	21.4	19.0	17.6	17.9	16.1	16.5	14.5	17.2	18.0	6.8																						
	1985	14.8	14.3	17.8	22.7	20.6	19.8	20.0	19.6	18.5	17.7	20.7	22.2	20.5	36.1																					
15-Yr	1986	15.7	15.3	18.6	23.1	21.3	20.5	20.7	20.8	20.1	19.8	23.1	25.2	24.4	32.2	28.5																				
	1987	15.4	14.9	17.9	22.1	20.3	19.4	19.6	19.5	18.7	18.2	20.8	21.8	19.8	24.5	19.1	10.4																			
	1988	15.9	15.5	18.4	22.2	20.6	19.8	20.0	20.0	19.4	19.1	21.4	22.4	20.8	24.4	20.8	17.1	24.1																		
	1989	16.1	15.9	18.9	22.5	21.0	20.3	20.6	20.6	20.0	19.8	22.1	23.0	21.7	24.9	22.2	20.7	24.1	26.8																	
	1990	14.4	14.0	16.4	19.6	18.1	17.2	17.2	16.8	15.9	15.3	16.8	16.5	14.9	15.7	13.2	9.7	9.5	13.2	-16.6																
20-Yr	1991	15.2	14.8	17.1	20.2	18.8	18.0	18.1	17.7	17.1	16.7	18.6	17.0	18.6	19.1	15.9	13.5	14.3	11.2	4.1	30.0															
	1992	14.9	14.5	16.7	19.6	18.2	17.5	17.2	16.9	16.4	16.1	17.6	16.1	14.9	16.5	14.9	12.8	13.3	10.7	5.8	19.2	9.3														
	1993	15.1	15.1	17.3	20.0	18.7	18.1	17.9	17.8	17.3	17.0	18.5	17.3	16.5	17.3	16.5	14.0	15.7	14.3	11.0	22.1	18.4	28.3													
	1994	14.8	14.5	16.4	19.0	17.7	17.1	17.0	16.6	16.2	15.7	17.0	16.3	14.7	16.5	14.7	13.0	13.4	11.7	8.9	16.5	12.3	13.8	0.9												
25-Yr	1995	15.1	14.8	17.1	18.0	17.3	17.1	17.0	16.5	16.4	16.2	17.4	16.2	15.4	17.1	15.4	14.0	14.5	13.2	11.1	17.6	14.7	16.6	11.1	22.3											
	1996	15.1	15.1	16.7	18.1	17.9	17.3	16.9	16.5	16.3	16.1	17.3	16.3	15.5	17.1	15.5	14.3	14.8	13.6	11.9	17.5	15.1	16.6	13.0	19.5	16.8										
	1997	15.1	14.8	16.6	17.9	17.7	17.1	16.9	16.3	16.2	16.1	17.0	16.1	15.4	16.9	15.4	13.7	14.7	13.6	12.1	16.1	14.9	16.1	13.2	17.6	15.3	13.9									
	1998	14.9	14.7	16.3	17.7	17.3	16.6	16.3	16.2	15.7	15.5	16.3	15.5	14.6	16.0	14.6	13.8	13.7	12.1	11.4	14.5	13.6	14.3	11.7	14.5	13.2	9.8	5.7								
	1999	14.9	14.7	16.3	17.3	17.0	16.5	16.3	15.9	15.7	15.6	16.6	15.7	15.0	16.3	15.0	14.3	13.8	12.8	12.2	16.0	14.3	14.3	13.0	15.6	14.0	13.0	12.6	19.9							
30-Yr	2000	14.3	14.1	15.6	16.5	15.9	15.5	15.6	15.5	15.0	14.7	15.5	14.6	13.9	15.0	13.9	12.9	13.1	12.2	10.9	14.2	12.5	12.9	10.8	12.7	10.9	9.4	9.0	9.0	-0.9						
	2001	13.8	13.6	15.0	15.8	15.3	14.9	14.7	14.7	14.2	13.8	14.6	13.8	12.9	13.9	12.9	12.0	12.1	11.3	10.1	12.9	11.5	11.5	9.6	10.9	9.1	7.6	6.0	6.1	-0.1	0.7					
	2002	13.0	12.7	14.0	14.7	14.2	13.5	13.4	13.2	12.7	12.3	13.2	12.3	11.4	12.3	11.4	10.4	10.4	9.5	8.3	10.7	9.0	9.1	7.1	7.9	6.0	4.3	2.4	1.6	-3.8	-5.3	-10.9				
	2003	13.8	13.6	14.9	15.7	15.2	14.7	14.6	14.3	13.8	13.8	14.6	13.8	13.1	14.2	13.1	12.2	12.3	11.6	10.6	13.0	11.7	11.9	10.2	11.5	10.2	9.3	8.5	9.2	6.6	9.2	13.7	45.1			
	2004	14.1	13.8	15.1	15.9	15.4	14.8	14.7	14.2	13.8	14.2	14.9	14.2	13.5	14.5	13.5	12.7	12.9	12.2	11.3	13.6	12.4	12.7	11.1	12.5	11.4	10.3	11.1	9.4	6.6	9.2	13.7	32.9	21.7		
	2005	14.0	13.8	15.0	15.7	15.3	14.9	14.8	14.4	14.0	14.4	14.7	14.0	13.4	14.4	13.4	12.8	12.7	12.1	11.3	13.4	12.3	12.6	10.8	12.4	11.4	10.5	10.8	9.8	9.4	12.0	16.6	25.3	16.4	11.3	
35-Yr	2006	14.2	14.0	15.2	16.0	15.7	15.5	15.1	14.8	14.7	14.4	15.1	14.4	13.8	14.8	13.8	13.1	13.3	12.7	11.9	14.0	13.0	13.2	11.8	13.2	12.4	12.0	12.0	11.5	11.5	13.8	16.6	24.7	18.5	17.0	23.0

How to read the Annualized Returns Matrix: You can locate the annualized compounded rate of return for this simulated Index Portfolio for a designated time period by following these easy instructions: Locate the column for the beginning year of the period. Then, locate the ending year of the period on the left-most vertical column. The annualized return can be found where the first year's column intersects with the ending year's row. IFA advisory fees of 0.9% per year and DFA mutual fund expense ratios have been deducted from these results. The 10-Yr diagonal (highlighted, starting from far left column) represents the estimated average holding period for investors who score 90 on the Risk Capacity Survey at ifa.com. Sources, Updates, and Disclosures: ifa.com/btp.

Figure 10-35

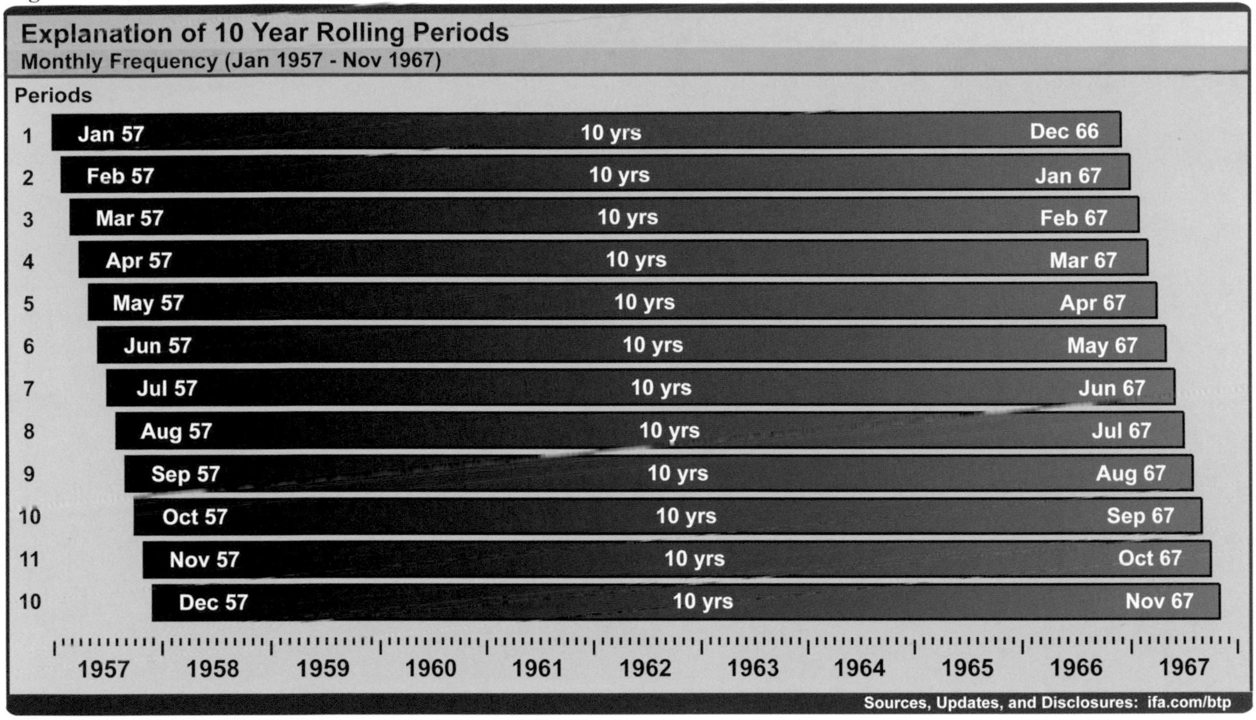

Explanation of 10 Year Rolling Periods
Monthly Frequency (Jan 1957 - Nov 1967)

Periods

1	Jan 57	10 yrs	Dec 66
2	Feb 57	10 yrs	Jan 67
3	Mar 57	10 yrs	Feb 67
4	Apr 57	10 yrs	Mar 67
5	May 57	10 yrs	Apr 67
6	Jun 57	10 yrs	May 67
7	Jul 57	10 yrs	Jun 67
8	Aug 57	10 yrs	Jul 67
9	Sep 57	10 yrs	Aug 67
10	Oct 57	10 yrs	Sep 67
11	Nov 57	10 yrs	Oct 67
10	Dec 57	10 yrs	Nov 67

1957 1958 1959 1960 1961 1962 1963 1964 1965 1966 1967

Sources, Updates, and Disclosures: ifa.com/btp

Figure 10-36

Monthly Rolling Period Analysis
Based on 50 years (600 months) of Monthly Data (Jan 1957 - Dec 2006)

IFA Index Portfolio 90 Gold

Per Period Number of: Yrs	Months	# of Rolling Periods	Average Anualized Return	Std. Dev. of Avg. Anualized Return	Lowest Rolling Period Date	Lowest Rolling Period Return	Growth of $1 in Lowest Period	Highest Rolling Period Date	Highest Rolling Period Return	Growth of $1 in Highest Period	Average Growth of $1
1	12	589	14.87%	16.85%	10/73-9/74	-34.51%	$0.65	1/58-12/58	61.10%	$1.61	$1.15
2	24	577	14.13%	10.74%	1/73-12/74	-22.39%	$0.60	12/66-11/68	44.00%	$2.07	$1.59
3	36	565	13.70%	8.13%	1/72-12/74	-9.79%	$0.73	8/84-7/87	37.25%	$2.59	$1.49
4	48	553	13.51%	6.72%	1/71-12/74	-2.12%	$0.92	7/82-6/86	32.16%	$3.05	$1.69
5	60	541	13.37%	6.09%	10/69-9/74	-2.47%	$0.88	8/82-7/87	32.81%	$4.13	$1.93
6	72	529	13.42%	5.50%	1/69-12/74	-5.59%	$0.71	10/81-9/87	26.88%	$4.17	$2.20
7	84	517	13.50%	4.93%	1/68-12/74	-0.76%	$0.95	8/82-7/89	26.79%	$5.27	$2.52
8	96	505	13.56%	4.47%	12/68-11/76	2.69%	$1.24	8/82-7/90	23.85%	$5.54	$2.89
9	108	493	13.63%	4.27%	1/66-12/74	2.98%	$1.30	1/75-12/83	23.13%	$6.51	$3.32
10*	120	481	13.70%	4.03%	1/65-12/74	5.12%	$1.65	9/77-8/87	23.05%	$7.96	$3.82
11	132	469	13.73%	3.88%	1/64-12/74	6.11%	$1.92	1/75-12/85	22.66%	$9.46	$4.40
12	144	457	13.71%	3.70%	1/63-12/74	7.29%	$2.33	10/75-9/87	23.18%	$12.20	$5.03
13	156	445	13.72%	3.59%	1/62-12/74	5.90%	$2.11	10/74-9/87	23.81%	$16.06	$5.76
14	168	433	13.80%	3.40%	1/61-12/74	7.18%	$2.64	1/75-12/88	22.25%	$16.65	$6.63
15	180	421	13.85%	3.24%	1/60-12/74	6.23%	$2.48	1/75-12/89	22.54%	$21.09	$7.62
20	240	361	14.34%	2.00%	1/57-12/76	10.59%	$7.49	10/74-9/94	19.05%	$32.70	$15.45
30	360	241	14.33%	0.73%	4/73-3/03	12.63%	$35.45	1/75-12/04	16.78%	$104.97	$56.57
40	480	121	13.63%	0.44%	4/63-3/03	12.75%	$121.52	4/58-3/98	14.80%	$249.85	$168.09
50	600	1	13.51%	0.00%	1/57-12/06	13.51%	$564.55	1/57-12/06	13.51%	$564.55	$564.55

Source, Updates, and Disclosures: ifa.com/btp

*10 years represents the estimated average holding period for investors who score 90 on the Risk Capacity Survey at ifa.com.

Figure 10-37

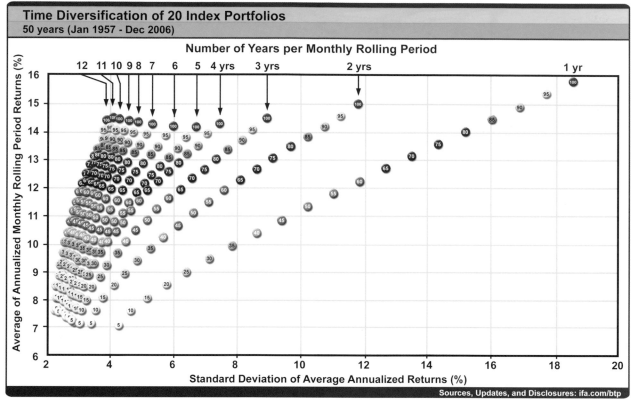

ty of 10-year returns, not one year returns. So, instead of looking at the traditional efficient frontier of one year returns as seen in Figure 10-32, investors can capacity adjust their risk and stand the efficient frontier nearly straight up as seen on Figure 10-33.

The Annualized Return Matrix shown in Figure 10-34 reinforces the concept of capacity adjusted risk. Investors who score a 90 on the Risk Capacity Survey should focus their time horizon on the 10-year diagonal, which is highlighted in the gold color on the return matrix presented in Figure 10-34. When comparing the variation of 10-year annualized returns with the variation of one-year annual returns along the top diagonal, you can easily see that time diversifies returns, as the markets goes through its random gyrations from year to year. Of course the gyra-

tions can be constrained by the level of risk exposure in the index portfolio.

Figure 10-35 explains the concept of rolling period returns, which was also covered in Step 8. Note that the figure captures the experiences of different investors, such as those who may have invested on January 1957 (period #1) or in August 1957 (period 8). This method allows us to review 481 ten-year rolling periods from January 1957 to December 2006, as seen in the gold highlighted row in Figure 10-36. The data in this table represents rolling periods as shown in Figure 10-35. Note that in one-year rolling periods, the standard deviation of returns is 16.85% in column five, but in 10-year rolling periods the standard deviation of annualized returns drops significantly to 4.03%, as seeen in the gold highlighted row. Also shown is the lowest 10-year rolling period over that 50 years, which was

January 1, 1965 to December 31, 1974, where the annualized return was 5.12%, which meant that one dollar grew to about $1.65 over that period. The highest annualized return of the 481 periods occurred on September 1, 1977 to August 31, 1987, where each dollar grew to $7.96 over the period.

If we look at how uncertainty of annualized returns are reduced over time for all 20 risk capacity levels and plot all this data on one big honkin' chart, you get Figure 10-37. Appendix A provides an abundant amount of data about the 20 risk exposures that match the 20 risk capacities shown in this step. Figure 10-37 summarizes the entire concept and the enormous amounts of data contained in Appendix A.

Capacity adjusted risk is an entirely new way for investors to look at the uncertainty of their investments. One of its primary benefits is that it starts to get investors focused on a longer term prospective and not the daily, monthly, annual, or even three-year returns that detract investors from staying the course on their investment plan.

For investors who accurately answer the questions in the Risk Capacity Survey, the risk of their investments can now be seen in a new perspective, adjusted for their capacity. Essentially, risk is held fairly constant for all investors as long as they adhere to the average time horizon of their risk capacity score. As explained above, that score measures dimensions beyond just time horizon, so that time is not the only consideration.

10.5 SUMMARY

Matching people with portfolios is a key component in assuring optimal returns. It is highly recommended that an investor hold a portfolio that matches their personal risk capacity. Risk capacity can be determined by answering the questions in the Risk Capacity Survey at www.ifa.com, preferably on an annual basis or when there are major changes in an investor's financial situation. Risk capacity can be measured and determined through five dimensions: time horizon and liquidity needs, attitude toward risk, net worth, income and savings rate, and investment knowledge. The larger the capacity for holding on to risk, the greater the expected returns.

10.6 REVIEW QUESTIONS

Please answer the following questions before proceeding to Step 11.

1. A high score in the "Time Horizon and Liquidity Needs" dimension indicates that an investor:

   a. needs immediate cash

   b. won't need to withdraw money for six months to one year

   c. won't need to withdraw money for one to three years

   d. won't need to withdraw money for 10 years or more

2. A low score in the "Attitude toward Risk" dimension indicates that an investor:

   a. is willing to take a lot of risk

   b. most likely has a tendency to gamble

   c. is averse to risk and can't stomach the thought of any loss

3. In addition to the "Time Horizon and Liquidity Needs" and "Attitude Toward Risk" dimensions, the other risk dimensions are:

   a. age, fund amount in a 401(k), and investment knowledge

b. net worth, amount of equity in real estate, and investment knowledge

c. net worth, income and savings rate, and investment knowledge

d. income and savings rate, number of children in college, and net worth

4. What percentage of long-term returns does asset allocation determine:

a. 25%

b. 50%

c. 15%

d. 100%

5. What is the single most important step of the investment planning process for individual investors?

a. signing your check

b. completing a risk capacity survey

c. researching stocks on the Internet

d. signing a margin agreement with a financial advisor at local brokerage office

Step 11 ~ Risk Exposure

"We can extrapolate from the study that for the long-term individual investor, who maintains a consistent asset allocation and leans toward index funds, asset allocation determines about 100% of performance."

- Roger Ibbotson, Ibbottson Associates, *The True Impact of Asset Allocation on Returns*

"A rising tide may lift all boats, but every year some vessels in the stock market spring a leak. Broad diversification ensures they won't sink the whole portfolio."

- Weston Wellington

"Investment Policy [asset allocation] is the foundation upon which portfolios should be constructed and managed."

- Charles D. Ellis, author of *Investment Policy*, 1985

"Diversification is your buddy."

- Merton Miller, Nobel laureate

"The essence of effective portfolio construction is the use of a large number of poorly correlated assets."

- William Bernstein, *The Intelligent Asset Allocator*

"Most people want candy, when what they really need is a balanced meal."

- John J. Bowen, Jr., *The Prudent Investor's Guide to Beating Wall Street at Its Own Game*

"You get rewarded for taking the risk of doing badly in bad times."

- William F. Sharpe, Nobel Laureate in Economics, 1990, *Investment Advisor*, December 6, 2004

"'Tis the part of a wise man to keep himself today for tomorrow, and not venture all his eggs in one basket."

- Miguel de Cervantes

11.1 INTRODUCTION

Step 11: Match your risk capacity to five dimensions of risk exposure.

Now that you understand risk capacity, the next step is to match the results of the risk capacity survey with a specific risk exposure. By doing this, investors position themselves to achieve personalized optimal returns. Not all investors have the capacity to expose their investments to high levels of risk; therefore, a continuum of risk exposures is needed to meet the unique risk

capacities of each investor. This concept extends to larger institutional investments, such as fire and police pension plans, church funds, college endowments, and any other funds governed by committees.

Numerous studies including those by Gary Brinson, Ron Surz, and Roger Ibbotson have determined there is essentially only one decision that investors need to make: Which mix of indexes is best for them.

There are 20 premixed portfolios of indexes presented in this step. These portfolios have a

Figure 11-1

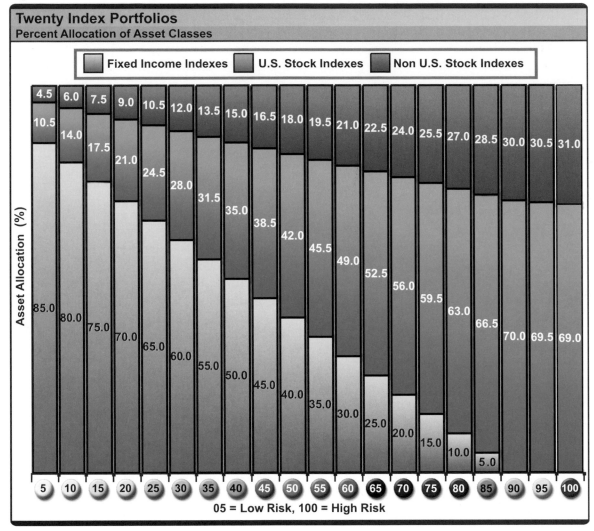

Twenty Index Portfolios
Percent Allocation of Asset Classes

specific percentage allocation of asset classes that match the 20 specific Risk Capacities. Figure 11-1 shows the asset class allocations of the 20 IFA Index Portfolios, labeled 5 through 100 in five-point increments. Each one is coupled with a specific risk capacity. Investors can be matched to one of these based on the results of Step 10's Risk Capacity Survey.

Once investors determine their best mix, they or their investment advisor can determine which available index funds will best represent the chosen mix of indexes.

11.2   DEFINITIONS

11.2.1   Modern Portfolio Theory

One day in the early 1950s, a Ph.D. candidate in economics sat in the library at the University of Chicago. The young man, Harry Markowitz, was studying leading investment guides used by professional money managers. The guides seemed to recommend that an investor should invest in stocks with the highest expected return and ignore all the rest. After awhile, it suddenly occurred to Markowitz that investors should consider risk as well as return.

It was a simple conclusion; however, it spawned one of the most important investment ideas of the 20th Century, and has generated a whole body of scholarly work known as "Modern Portfolio Theory." Thirty-eight years later it earned Markowitz a Nobel Prize in Economics. The fact that trillions of dollars around the globe are now invested and managed according to the principle proposed by Markowitz is testament to its central importance in the investment process. This revolutionary insight has not only transformed the investment world of corporate and government pension plans, insurance companies, banks and other large institutional investors, it has also changed the way individual investors invest.

Markowitz, for his part, knew that no one had really tried to systematically understand the importance of risk in the investment process. Up to that time, investors had focused on an investment's return, but if they believed it contained some arbitrary, undefined notion of risk, then the investment wasn't included in the portfolio. Markowitz understood quite clearly that risk and return are related. After all, investors like return and want to increase it, and they dislike risk and want to reduce it. On that day in the library, Markowitz set out to show investors how they could improve their investment performance by optimizing trade-offs between risk and return.

Because it seems so obvious, it's hard to appreciate how truly profound Markowitz's idea was. Of course both risk and return should be considered. In spite of the evident nature of this idea, the investment media continues to spread the "good news" of returns, while downplaying the "bad news" of risk.

In Figure 11-2 you can see a 10-year annualized return of efficient index portfolios compared

Figure 11-2

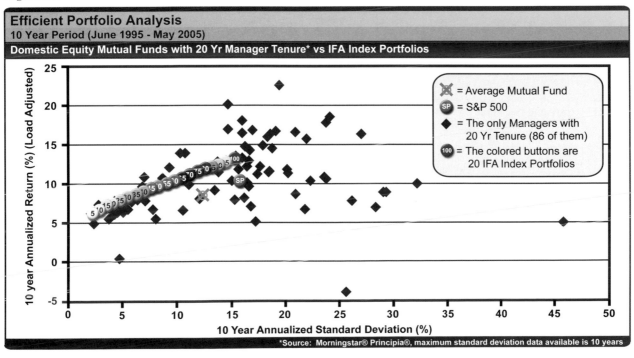

to the average mutual fund (the green X), the S&P 500, and the only 86 managers in the Morningstar database with 20 years of managing the same fund. Morningstar® Principia® risk data does not go beyond 10 years, so the chart is shown using the 10 years from 1996 to 2005. About 10 actively managed funds are shown to be more efficient than the line of index portfolios. That means they are in the top left quadrant above the colorful line of buttons. Keep in mind that to have selected those funds 20 years ago would have been a near impossible task. Hindsight is 20/20. But index portfolios are always a better choice because they are consistent in their strategies.

11.2.2 Diversification

Diversification in investing refers to the spreading out risk. Look at a single stock in an index versus the entire index, as seen in Figure 11-3. Because of the random nature of risk, no one knows what is going to happen in the short term to a subset of stocks in the index.

A subset of the index would actually be another index altogether with different risk and return characteristics. At an extreme, one stand alone stock represents its own index, but it has a very high risk and offers no additional expected return over the asset class to which it belongs.

Look at one small value stock in Figure 11-3. It has a risk of about 75% and an expected return that's the same as the small value index. However, the index only has a risk of 30%. So, why buy just one stock? Or better yet, why buy any stocks with an expected risk higher than the index? There is no logical answer, other than to speculate on the random outcomes of a higher risk investment. What is the expected return of speculation? Answer: Zero minus your costs.

When investors concentrate their investments, they are increasing their risk with no

Figure 11-3

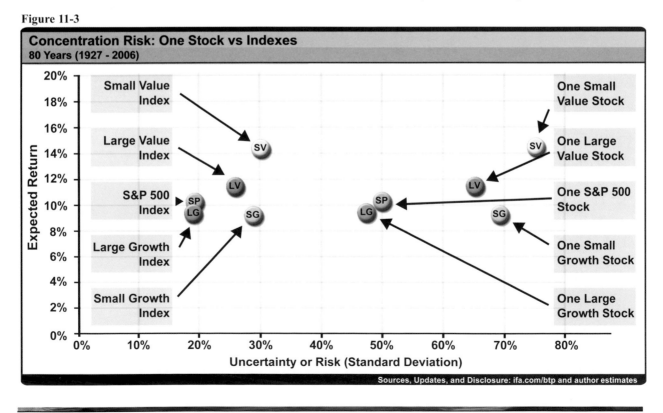

added benefit of higher expected return. In other words, investors are not rewarded for taking the higher risk of concentrating their investments such as selecting just a handful of stocks for their portfolio. The result is that over a period of 20 years or so the risk or volatility of an individual stock is about 2.5 times that of a market index with no expected extra payoff.

The most prudent approach to minimize risk and maximize the probability of achieving a market rate of return is to hold the entire index. The optimal approach is to find an index with desirable risk and return characteristics and then adhere to the index rules of ownership, which is the job of the index mutual fund manager. This way the specific risk of each stock in the index is diversified down to near zero. This leaves investors with the systematic risk of the market the index is designed to track. Anything less than this optimal approach will cause the portfolio's risk to exceed the risk of the index as a whole.

Harry Markowitz

When Harry Markowitz wrote his Nobel Prize-winning paper in 1952 titled "Portfolio Selection," he laid out the mathematics of diversification and the foundation of the design of risk exposure. He set out to apply his engineering background to investing, so, his thesis could be referred to as "portfolio engineering." In his paper he indicated that it's best to engineer a portfolio to include stocks that do not act like each other or move together.

For example, stock A and stock B move in opposite directions. When stock A goes up, stock B goes down and vice versa. This is called a low correlation of the two investments. If each stock yields returns with the exact same average, investors actually earn a diversification benefit of lower volatility and higher returns if they hold these stocks in the same portfolio. This is a good thing! As Markowitz stated in 1952, investors should consider expected returns desirable and variance of returns undesirable.

Unfortunately, many investors still do not get this important point. One diversification detractor is the book, *The Battle for Investment Survival*, written by Gerald Loeb in 1935. Loeb expressed a conventional investing idea that became popular in the 1950s. He claimed that an investor who diversifies is basically admitting a lack of knowledge and trying only to strike an average. Loeb recommended that one, two or at most three or four securities should be bought. He said that competent investors will never be satisfied beating the averages by a few small percentage points. Broad diversification was considered undesirable, and he suggested that investors analyze securities one by one, focus on picking winners, and concentrate holdings to maximize returns.

Fortunately, there is now ample evidence to counter and debunk Loeb's theories. This 12-Step Program was created to educate those investors who still insist on practicing futile investment strategies, such as non-diversification of portfolios.

11.2.3 Global Diversification

Global diversification is a good idea because the international market is increasingly important in the world economy. The United States used to be a much larger percentage of the world market. It declined from 68% of the global equity value to 49% in 2006, as seen in Figure 11-4. Now, there are more risk factors in international markets that can both smooth out your volatility and increase your expected returns. To be effective, a portfo-

Figure 11-4

lio cannot afford to ignore international investments.

11.2.4 Portfolio Rebalancing

One idea built into the long-term buy and hold strategy of risk exposure is the concept of maintaining consistent exposure to risk as the individual indexes that comprise a portfolio change along the way. For example, an original mix may include 10% of a U.S. small value index. If that grows to 15% of the overall mix, the portfolio now has a different overall risk exposure. In this case, it would be important to trim the 15% back down to 10% by investing the proceeds in other indexes that have gone down or not grown as much. Then, the original mix is restored to its proper allocation.

11.2.5 Whole Portfolios

Most investors end up with at least three accounts. They have a 401(k) or 403(b) at work,

an IRA or Roth IRA, and a regular taxable investment account. The risk capacity analysis applies to an investor's total investable assets, so the resultant risk exposure represents all accounts as if they were one whole portfolio.

This is where the mixing process gets tricky. A hybrid tax strategy must be applied to optimize the tax deferred and taxable nature of different accounts. A spreadsheet that combines the assets of each account and verifies overall risk exposure is a required tool for determining the dollar amount to be invested in each mutual fund and to optimize future cash outflows, inflows, rebalancing, and tax loss harvesting. This is where an index funds advisor adds substantial value to an investor's portfolio. Since risk is the source of returns, and too little or too much risk is undesirable, the maintenance of proper risk exposure and the optimization of a tax-hybrid strategy is a highly rewarded effort that leads to optimal returns unique to each investor.

11.2.6 The Prudent Investor Act

Index funds are an ideal way to implement risk exposure making them the best way to achieve an investor's goals. This concept is even incorporated into legal guidelines under the American Law Institute's so-called "Restatement of the Law, Trust, Prudent Investor Rule."

The rule, published in 1992, was written as a guideline for the prudent management of trust assets and many states passed it into law. In California it passed into law in 1996 under the title "The Uniform Prudent Investor Act." This rule points out the value of the Modern Portfolio Theory. It essentially tells trustees that index funds are the prudent way to invest trust assets. The rule acts as a legal road map for estate planning attorneys, trustees of all types of trusts, and investment advisors.

The following reporter's notes on the Prudent Investor Rule points out the problems with active management. "Economic evidence shows that from a typical investment perspective, the major capital markets of this country are highly efficient, in the sense that available information is rapidly digested and reflected in the market prices of securities. As a result, fiduciaries and other investors are confronted with potent evidence that the application of expertise, investigation, and diligence in efforts to 'beat the market' in these publicly traded securities ordinarily promises little or no payoff or even a negative payoff after taking research and transaction costs into account. Empirical research supporting the theory of efficient markets reveals that in such markets skilled professionals have rarely been able to identify underpriced securities, (that is, to outguess the market with respect to future return) with any regularity. In fact, evidence shows that there is little correlation between fund managers' earlier successes and their ability to produce above-market returns in subsequent periods."

Five Principles of Prudence

1. Sound diversification is fundamental to risk management and is therefore ordinarily required of trustees.

2. Risk and return are so directly related that trustees have a duty to analyze and make conscious decisions concerning the levels of risk appropriate to the purposes, distribution requirements, and other circumstances of the trusts they administer.

3. Trustees have a duty to avoid fees, transaction costs and other expenses that are not justified by the needs and realistic objectives of the trust's investment program.

4. The fiduciary duty of impartiality requires a balancing of the elements of return between production of current income and the protection of purchasing power.

5. Trustees may have a duty as well as the authority to delegate as prudent investors would.

11.3 PROBLEMS

11.3.1 How Much Risk is There?

It is extremely rare for any stockbroker, investment advisor or mutual fund manager to quote the risk level of a client's whole portfolio or any part of it. This is one of the many reasons investors do so poorly. So where do investors obtain this rare and important data? The most convenient and accessible measurement is the standard deviation, and the data becomes more reliable the longer the time frame is considered.

The standard deviation quantifies the variation of the returns around the average return. A larger variation or standard deviation often goes hand in hand with a higher risk that an investor may sell the investment out of fear or panic when it goes down. This obviously is an undesirable outcome. Ideally, a high risk exposure is accompanied by a high expected return. That is not always the case. Clearly there are high risks with low expected returns such as small growth and large growth indexes.

Statisticians require a minimum of 20 years of data to reduce the error and increase the confidence to an acceptable level of the reported risk and return characteristics of any investment. This dramatically reduces the investments options to index mutual funds and ETFs, since the indexes they track provide more than 20 years of data. There are currently only 86 active managers in the Morningstar database with 20 years or more tenure.

As with anything, the best strategies are useless without quality input— "garbage in." A minimum of 20 years of data is necessary to generate quality output. So how much risk is in a fund or portfolio? A globally diversified portfolio of indexes with a 50-year history holds a risk with a standard deviation of 14.7% and a simulated return of 13.9%. However, in order to handle this level of risk exposure, an investor must score at least a 90% on The Risk Capacity Survey located at www.ifa.com.

11.3.2   Where is the Data?

Virtually all reliable data about the stock market originates from the University of Chicago's Center for Research of Security Prices (CRSP). CRSP is a descendant of the Cowles Commission, which was created out of the deep pain caused by the 1929 stock market crash.

Today, many firms and research organizations obtain new data from CRSP and crunch numbers. Among them are Dimensional Fund Advisors (DFA), Ibbotson and Associates, and Standard and Poor's Micropal. Other data sources include Morningstar and Lipper.

Of all the mutual fund companies, DFA stands alone in providing its pool of unique financial advisors with a complete data set on numerous indexes, going back to 1927. This allows index funds advisors to perform analysis that is normally only available to academic researchers. DFA is the only company that provides several seminars per year, offering the best and brightest of academia to lecture and interact with practicing professional advisors. The term "professional" here is important. Genuine professional advisors use index funds to construct portfolios.

David Booth

So, where is the data? DFA houses the best source of meaningful long-term data, including the unique indexes or rules of ownership established by Eugene Fama, Kenneth French, Merton Miller, Myron Scholes, David Booth (CEO), and Rex Sinquefield. On a Web site that offers peer-reviewed academic research in the social sciences, (www.ssrn.com), Fama is the number one downloaded business author from more than 70,688 authors. Out of 13.4 million downloads, Fama has 3 of the top 10 downloaded articles, as of January 2007. Besides his Ph.D., Fama has received honorary degrees and numerous awards and is Director of CRSP.

11.3.3   Investors Want to Avoid Risk

Another problem related to risk exposure is that most investors do not like risk, but they do want returns. Unfortunately, it just does not work that way. To avoid risk is to avoid returns. If an investor is feeling uncomfortable taking a risk, not much return can be expected.

The desire to avoid risk is at the very core of the poor performance many investors experience. Investors like to invest after the market has already gone up. They like to invest in companies that are best described as glamour stocks, otherwise known as large growth stocks. They like to turn their hard earned money over to the fund manager with favorable three to five years of market beating returns — the manager that appears on the cover of *Money Magazine*. All these tendencies feel good, safe, and less risky. The fact is: these featured funds are all relatively expensive due to their popularity. These funds provide their sellers a low cost of acquiring an investor's capital. Here's the big lesson: an investor's expected return is the same as the seller's cost of capital. A low cost of capital exists in all high priced investments; therefore, investors end up with a low return, hence the adages, "No risk, no return. Nothing ventured, nothing gained. Buy low and risky, sell high and safe." Simply put, risk is good. Embrace it.

11.3.4 Risk is Good in Proper Doses

Investors must learn to relish risk and to realize it is the source of their returns, not their nemesis. It's all a matter of matching people with portfolios or risk capacity with risk exposure. This process results in the arrival of a risk exposure that each investor can hang onto through thick and thin, sickness and health, bull or bear markets, for richer or poorer or until there is a need to withdraw the money.

In proper doses, risk is a beautiful thing. This concept is brought to investors by the brilliant minds of academics and Nobel laureates.

11.3.5 Portfolios Get Out of Balance

Another concern for investors is the maintenance of risk exposure or portfolio rebalancing. As discussed in the definition of rebalancing, this procedure is far more complex than it appears, especially when it is conducted across several investment accounts with different tax considerations. There is also a balance between the transaction costs and capital gains generated by rebalancing. A trade-off between risk exposure maintenance and transaction costs must be carefully weighed and include the changes in risk capacity since the previous measurement.

11.3.6 Selecting Index Funds

How is the wheat sorted from the chaff? Since index funds are the only funds that use risk and return data that deploy a constant set of rules of ownership, they are the first level to screen over

23,000 existing mutual funds in the Morningstar database.

This process of elimination limits the choices down to about 1,000 index funds and exchange traded funds (ETF's). ETF's are essentially index funds that trade like stocks, but like individual stocks, they usually have commissions and spreads between bids and asks. Most importantly, investors need to consider the net expected return of each index fund representing a unique set of rules of ownership. A sorting of index mutual funds, loads, fees, and expenses will quickly eliminate all but Vanguard and DFA index funds. Then another problem arises.

DFA funds require a minimum trade amount of $2 million per fund purchase unless the purchase is made through a DFA approved fee-only advisor. Most advisors require minimum account sizes of around $250,000. However, Index Funds Advisors' (IFA) minimum account size is $100,000. The primary difference between DFA and Vanguard is that they use different indexes to design their index mutual funds. DFA custom designs its indexes to capture the risk factors that explain 95% of stock market returns. Those factors include company size (market capitalization) and value (book to market ratio or BtM).

There are smaller size and higher value oriented stocks in DFA indexes. Based on the higher long-term returns of these factors, there are higher expected returns for long-term investors with DFA index funds. However, past performance is not a guarantee of future performance. Vanguard is now a fairly aggressive proponent of "tandem investing," which is a post-Bogle slogan that encourages Vanguard investors to mix in some actively managed funds in their portfolios.

It is as if the dark force has encroached on this champion of investor protection and low

Table 11-1

Overall Ratings of Mutual Fund Companies by Registered Investment Advisors 1997 - 2004

1997 Rankings	
Company	Rating (max = 4.0)
Dimensional Fund Advisors	3.86
Vanguard Group	3.82
Oakmark Funds	3.79
T. Rowe Price	3.79
American Funds	3.79
Janus Funds	3.72
MFS Funds	3.62
SEI Financial	3.61
PIMCO Advisors	3.60
Franklin/Templeton Funds	3.58
Strong Funds	3.48
Putnam Investments	3.42
Fidelity Investments	3.33

2000 Rankings	
Company	Rating (max = 4.0)
Dimensional Fund Advisors	3.81
Janus Funds	3.76
PIMCO	3.71
American Skandia	3.70
INVESCO	3.67
Oppenheimer Funds	3.66
Vanguard	3.66
American Funds	3.65
AIM	3.63
MFS Funds	3.62
Sunamerica	3.57
BenchMark	3.51
Schwab	3.50

2002 Rankings	
Company	Rating (max = 4.0)
Dimensional Fund Advisors	3.93
American Funds	3.84
Artisan Funds	3.82
Oakmark Funds	3.73
State Street Research	3.71
PIMCO Advisors	3.64
SEI Financials	3.64
Smith Barney Mutual Funds	3.64
WM Group	3.64
Calvert	3.58
Hartford Life	3.58
Lord Abbett	3.56
Vanguard	3.56

2004 Rankings	
Company	Rating (max = 4.0)
General Opinion Top 5	
Dodge and Cox Funds	3.96
Dimensional Fund Advisors	3.93
American Funds	3.84
Pacific Funds	3.82
Russell Investment Group	3.80
Investment Management Top 6	
Dimensional Fund Advisors	3.96
First Eagle Funds	3.91
Dodge and Cox Funds	3.90
Calamos	3.89
American Funds	3.88
Davis Funds	3.86

Source: Dalbar, Inc., and "Changing of the Guard" by David J. Drucker Research, Nov. 2004

costs. There is no conceivable or logical reason for Vanguard to do this, other than it can make higher fees off uneducated and unsophisticated investors.

DFA, for its part, is the purest among all mutual fund companies in their application of the Efficient Market Theory and low-cost structure. They have an added benefit of providing substantial index data going as far back as 1926.

As proof of DFA's unique position in the investment product industry, Dalbar surveyed investment advisors four times between 1997 and 2004. The study was titled "The Professionals' Pick." Dalbar rated DFA the best overall no-load mutual fund company in 1997, 2000, 2002, and number two in 2004. DFA rated highest in the "Investment Management" and "Current Use" categories in the 2004 survey. See Table 11-1. These funds are low cost, style pure and well diversified.

One unique advantage of DFA is their innovative execution of small capitalization stock trades. Because of the low liquidity in these stocks, the trading cost can be very high. DFA's board members and consultants include some of the world's most distinguished academic theorists: Eugene Fama, Kenneth French, Roger Ibbotson, Donald Keim, and Nobel laureates Myron Scholes and Robert Merton.

It is normal for investors to be suspicious when an author or advisor leans so heavily toward one mutual fund company. Indeed, it is wise to be cautious of loads or 12b-1 fees that may be kicked back to the advisor. This is not the case with DFA. DFA has no loads or trailing fees for advisors and they provide the absolute best education of any fund company, including monthly updates on risk and return data and a

software package to analyze the data. Simply put, they are the best in the business.

11.4 SOLUTIONS

11.4.1 Twenty Index Portfolios

The answer to the investor's dilemma is to design the most efficient portfolios of available investable indexes. (See Table 11-2 and Appendix A for a listing of the portfolios and data concerning them.) Input into efficient analysis must be based on at least 20 years of risk and return data. But, thanks to DFA, there are now 80 years of reasonably good index simulations. Figures 11-5 through 11-8 show the risk and reward plots for all 20 portfolios and the component indexes for several different time periods.

We have assembled a continuum of risk exposures as summarized in Figures 11-9 through 12. These are depictions of both the risk and return of all 20 index portfolios. They are numbered and color coded to denote their risk level beginning with Portfolio 100 — Bright Red at the highest risk, down to Portfolio 5 — Ivory at the lowest risk. These charts show a histogram of 780 months of returns data on the left and the growth of one dollar on the right. The risk capacity painting is also included to give an idea of the age appropriateness of each portfolio.

Table 11-3 shows the risk and simulated returns of all 20 portfolios. An investor's actual returns will vary from these asset class allocations due to differences in asset allocations, timing of withdrawals and contributions, index tracking errors, rebalancing strategies and costs, fees, and other factors. Table 11-4 shows the simulated annual returns for all 20 portfolios going back to 1927. The annualized returns shown in both tables are net of an advisor fee of 0.90% per

Table 11-2

Twenty Index Portfolios
Percent Allocations of IFA Indexes

Indexes		5	10	15	20	25	30	35	40	45	50	55	60	65	70	75	80	85	90	95	100
IFA U.S. Large Company Index	LC	3.00	4.00	5.00	6.00	7.00	8.00	9.00	10.00	11.00	12.00	13.00	14.00	15.00	16.00	17.00	18.00	19.00	20.00	16.00	12.00
IFA U.S. Large Value Index	LV	3.00	4.00	5.00	6.00	7.00	8.00	9.00	10.00	11.00	12.00	13.00	14.00	15.00	16.00	17.00	18.00	19.00	20.00	16.00	12.00
IFA U.S. Micro Cap Index	MC	1.50	2.00	2.50	3.00	3.50	4.00	4.50	5.00	5.50	6.00	6.50	7.00	7.50	8.00	8.50	9.00	9.50	10.00	15.00	20.00
IFA U.S. Small Cap Value Index	SV	1.50	2.00	2.50	3.00	3.50	4.00	4.50	5.00	5.50	6.00	6.50	7.00	7.50	8.00	8.50	9.00	9.50	10.00	15.00	20.00
IFA Real Estate Securities Index	RE	1.50	2.00	2.50	3.00	3.50	4.00	4.50	5.00	5.50	6.00	6.50	7.00	7.50	8.00	8.50	9.00	9.50	10.00	7.50	5.00
IFA International Value Index	IV	1.50	2.00	2.50	3.00	3.50	4.00	4.50	5.00	5.50	6.00	6.50	7.00	7.50	8.00	8.50	9.00	9.50	10.00	8.00	6.00
IFA International Small Company Index	IS	0.75	1.00	1.25	1.50	1.75	2.00	2.25	2.50	2.75	3.00	3.25	3.50	3.75	4.00	4.25	4.50	4.75	5.00	5.50	6.00
IFA International Small Cap Value Index	ISV	0.75	1.00	1.25	1.50	1.75	2.00	2.25	2.50	2.75	3.00	3.25	3.50	3.75	4.00	4.25	4.50	4.75	5.00	5.50	6.00
IFA Emerging Markets Index	EM	0.45	0.60	0.75	0.90	1.05	1.20	1.35	1.50	1.65	1.80	1.95	2.10	2.25	2.40	2.55	2.70	2.85	3.00	3.50	4.00
IFA Emerging Value Index	EV	0.45	0.60	0.75	0.90	1.05	1.20	1.35	1.50	1.65	1.80	1.95	2.10	2.25	2.40	2.55	2.70	2.85	3.00	3.50	4.00
IFA Emerging Small Cap Index	ES	0.60	0.80	1.00	1.20	1.40	1.60	1.80	2.00	2.20	2.40	2.60	2.80	3.00	3.20	3.40	3.60	3.80	4.00	4.50	5.00
IFA One-Year Fixed Income Index	1F	21.25	20.00	18.75	17.50	16.25	15.00	13.75	12.50	11.25	10.00	8.75	7.50	6.25	5.00	3.75	2.50	1.25	0.00	0.00	0.00
IFA Two-Year Global Fixed Income Index	2F	21.25	20.00	18.75	17.50	16.25	15.00	13.75	12.50	11.25	10.00	8.75	7.50	6.25	5.00	3.75	2.50	1.25	0.00	0.00	0.00
IFA Five-Year Government Index	5G	21.25	20.00	18.75	17.50	16.25	15.00	13.75	12.50	11.25	10.00	8.75	7.50	6.25	5.00	3.75	2.50	1.25	0.00	0.00	0.00
IFA Five-Year Global Fixed Income Index	5F	21.25	20.00	18.75	17.50	16.25	15.00	13.75	12.50	11.25	10.00	8.75	7.50	6.25	5.00	3.75	2.50	1.25	0.00	0.00	0.00

20 IFA Index Portfolios

See Appendices A and B for button descriptions

Sources, Updates, and Disclosures: ifa.com/btp

Figure 11-5

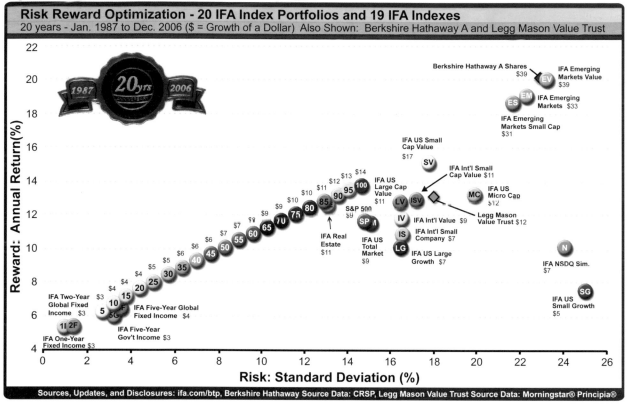

Risk Reward Optimization - 20 IFA Index Portfolios and 19 IFA Indexes
20 years - Jan. 1987 to Dec. 2006 ($ = Growth of a Dollar) Also Shown: Berkshire Hathaway A and Legg Mason Value Trust

Sources, Updates, and Disclosures: ifa.com/btp, Berkshire Hathaway Source Data: CRSP, Legg Mason Value Trust Source Data: Morningstar® Principia®

Figure 11-6

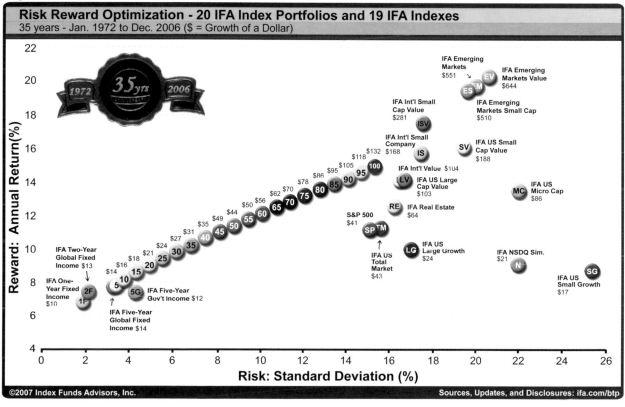

Risk Reward Optimization - 20 IFA Index Portfolios and 19 IFA Indexes
35 years - Jan. 1972 to Dec. 2006 ($ = Growth of a Dollar)

Sources, Updates, and Disclosures: ifa.com/btp

Figure 11-7

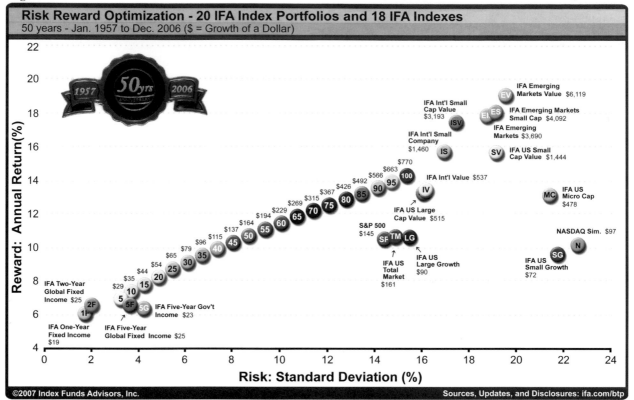

Risk Reward Optimization - 20 IFA Index Portfolios and 18 IFA Indexes
50 years - Jan. 1957 to Dec. 2006 ($ = Growth of a Dollar)

©2007 Index Funds Advisors, Inc. — Sources, Updates, and Disclosures: ifa.com/btp

Figure 11-8

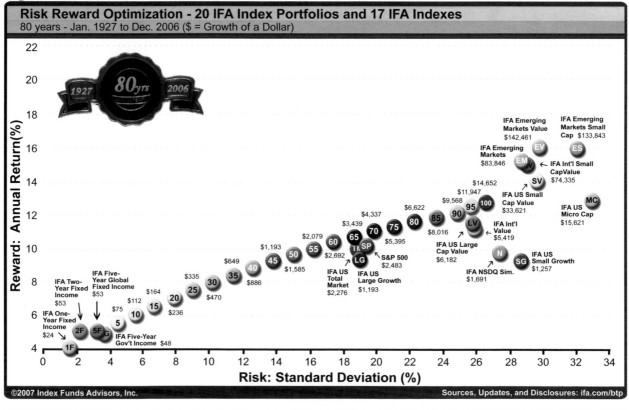

Risk Reward Optimization - 20 IFA Index Portfolios and 17 IFA Indexes
80 years - Jan. 1927 to Dec. 2006 ($ = Growth of a Dollar)

©2007 Index Funds Advisors, Inc. — Sources, Updates, and Disclosures: ifa.com/btp

Figure 11-9

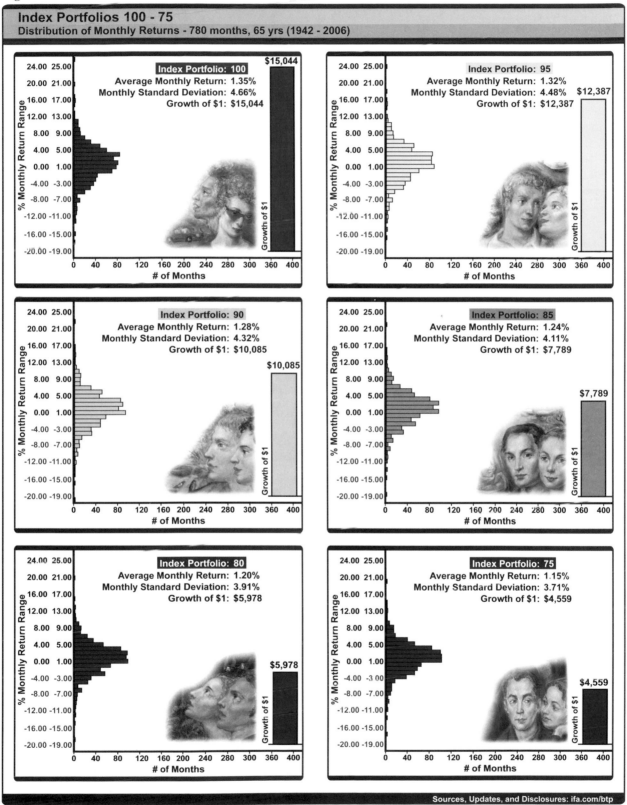

Index Portfolios 100 - 75
Distribution of Monthly Returns - 780 months, 65 yrs (1942 - 2006)

Index Portfolio: 100
Average Monthly Return: 1.35%
Monthly Standard Deviation: 4.66%
Growth of $1: $15,044 — $15,044

Index Portfolio: 95
Average Monthly Return: 1.32%
Monthly Standard Deviation: 4.48%
Growth of $1: $12,387 — $12,387

Index Portfolio: 90
Average Monthly Return: 1.28%
Monthly Standard Deviation: 4.32%
Growth of $1: $10,085 — $10,085

Index Portfolio: 85
Average Monthly Return: 1.24%
Monthly Standard Deviation: 4.11%
Growth of $1: $7,789 — $7,789

Index Portfolio: 80
Average Monthly Return: 1.20%
Monthly Standard Deviation: 3.91%
Growth of $1: $5,978 — $5,978

Index Portfolio: 75
Average Monthly Return: 1.15%
Monthly Standard Deviation: 3.71%
Growth of $1: $4,559 — $4,559

Sources, Updates, and Disclosures: ifa.com/btp

Figure 11-10

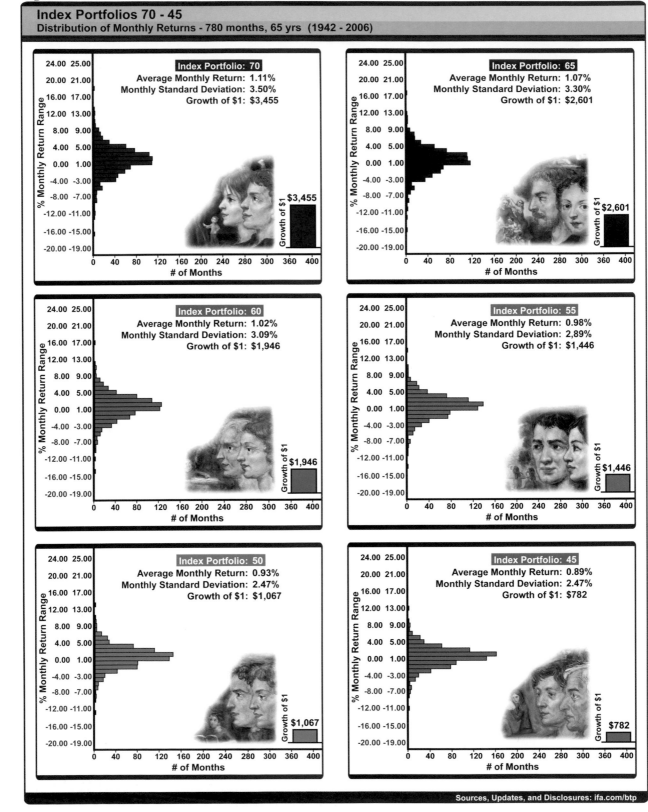

Index Portfolios 70 - 45
Distribution of Monthly Returns - 780 months, 65 yrs (1942 - 2006)

Index Portfolio: 70
Average Monthly Return: 1.11%
Monthly Standard Deviation: 3.50%
Growth of $1: $3,455

Index Portfolio: 65
Average Monthly Return: 1.07%
Monthly Standard Deviation: 3.30%
Growth of $1: $2,601

Index Portfolio: 60
Average Monthly Return: 1.02%
Monthly Standard Deviation: 3.09%
Growth of $1: $1,946

Index Portfolio: 55
Average Monthly Return: 0.98%
Monthly Standard Deviation: 2,89%
Growth of $1: $1,446

Index Portfolio: 50
Average Monthly Return: 0.93%
Monthly Standard Deviation: 2.47%
Growth of $1: $1,067

Index Portfolio: 45
Average Monthly Return: 0.89%
Monthly Standard Deviation: 2.47%
Growth of $1: $782

Figure 11-11

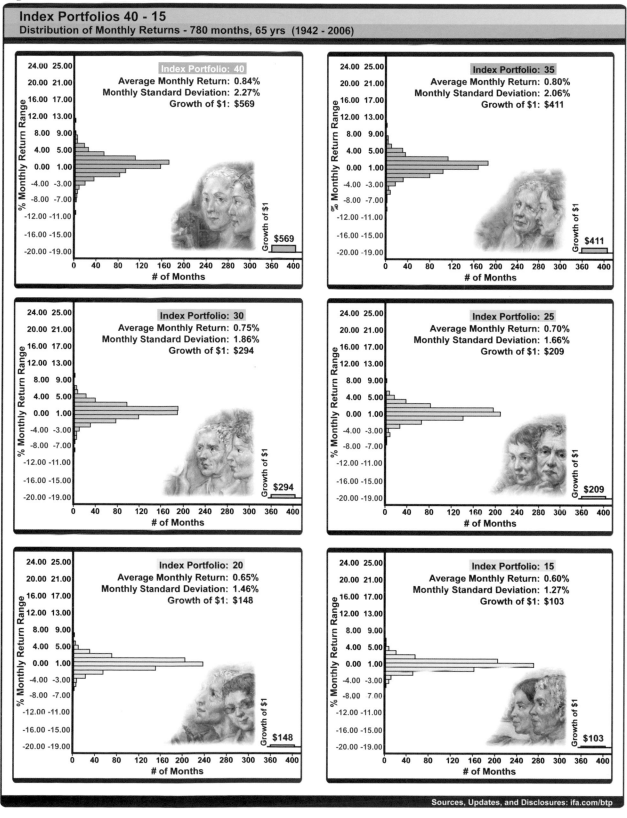

Index Portfolios 40 - 15
Distribution of Monthly Returns - 780 months, 65 yrs (1942 - 2006)

Index Portfolio: 40
Average Monthly Return: 0.84%
Monthly Standard Deviation: 2.27%
Growth of $1: $569

Index Portfolio: 35
Average Monthly Return: 0.80%
Monthly Standard Deviation: 2.06%
Growth of $1: $411

Index Portfolio: 30
Average Monthly Return: 0.75%
Monthly Standard Deviation: 1.86%
Growth of $1: $294

Index Portfolio: 25
Average Monthly Return: 0.70%
Monthly Standard Deviation: 1.66%
Growth of $1: $209

Index Portfolio: 20
Average Monthly Return: 0.65%
Monthly Standard Deviation: 1.46%
Growth of $1: $148

Index Portfolio: 15
Average Monthly Return: 0.60%
Monthly Standard Deviation: 1.27%
Growth of $1: $103

Sources, Updates, and Disclosures: ifa.com/btp

Figure 11-12

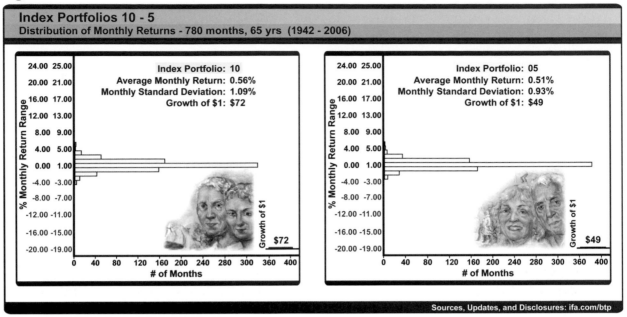

Index Portfolios 10 - 5
Distribution of Monthly Returns - 780 months, 65 yrs (1942 - 2006)

Index Portfolio: 10
Average Monthly Return: 0.56%
Monthly Standard Deviation: 1.09%
Growth of $1: $72

Index Portfolio: 05
Average Monthly Return: 0.51%
Monthly Standard Deviation: 0.93%
Growth of $1: $49

Sources, Updates, and Disclosures: ifa.com/btp

year. However, the DFA and S&P 500 Index Fund is shown with no advisor fee deducted. Asset class or index returns do not represent actual mutual fund performance and are for illustration purposes only. Past performance does not guarantee future performance. In fact, the risk (SD) in each portfolio illustrates this lack of predictability. The higher the historical standard deviation, the higher the risk and the wider the range of future probable outcomes. Please see the Data and Sources information in Appendix C. Also visit ifa.com/btp for a complete explanation on back tested performance information.

11.4.2 Index Mutual Funds Earn more Return and Eliminate more Risk

Investing in index funds assures a higher return with less risk than the average active fund. According to the tenets of Modern Portfolio Theory, indexing is inherently less risky than active investing. Because an index fund holds all of the investments that comprise a discrete asset class, it maximally reduces risk within that asset class. Although it's not possible to entirely rid

diversifiable risk from investment portfolios, index portfolios come very close. An indexer therefore incurs virtually no diversifiable risk.

While it's true that most risk is eliminated with a portfolio of 100 stocks, this is not always the case. The amount of risk not eliminated is what active money managers "leave on the table" as seemingly small amounts of diversifiable risk. Yet this risk can have a substantially negative impact on investment performance over the long run. Even the expected return of an active portfolio containing as many as 200 stocks can diverge one percentage point on either side of the market's expected return. Although this differential is certainly not substantial in any one year, it can represent enormous differences in accumulated wealth when compounded over extended periods of time.

In short, the diversification advantage offered by indexing can't be matched by any actively managed portfolio, whether it holds mutual funds or individual stocks and or bonds or some combination thereof.

Table 11-3

20 Index Portfolios and S&P 500
Growth of Dollar, Annualized Return % (net of fees*), and Risk (Standard Deviation %)

20 Index Portfolios and S&P 500	Data Labels	YTD ending March 2007	1 Yr ending 2006	1 Yr ending 2005	1 Yr ending 2004	1 Yr ending 2003	3 Yrs 2004-2006	5 Yrs 2002-2006	10 Yrs 1997-2006	15 Yrs 1992-2006	25 Yrs 1982-2006	35 Yrs 1972-2006	50 Yrs 1957-2006	80 Yrs 1927-2006
SP	Growth $1	1.01	1.16	1.05	1.11	1.28	1.34	1.34	2.22	4.44	22.14	40.94	145.34	2,483
	Return %	1.13	15.73	4.85	10.72	28.49	10.34	6.07	8.28	10.44	13.19	11.19	10.47	10.27
	Risk - SD	-	5.61	7.88	7.29	11.42	6.89	12.39	15.33	13.45	14.80	15.10	14.38	19.23
100	Growth $1	1.03	1.22	1.12	1.23	1.52	1.67	2.28	3.31	7.00	37.66	132.03	770.26	14,652
	Return %	3.39	22.30	11.51	22.63	51.63	18.70	17.92	12.71	13.85	15.62	14.97	14.22	12.74
	Risk - SD	-	11.08	11.18	11.89	13.62	11.14	13.87	15.57	13.70	14.13	15.30	15.37	26.59
95	Growth $1	1.03	1.23	1.11	1.22	1.48	1.67	2.22	3.21	6.63	35.67	118.29	663.00	11,947
	Return %	3.26	22.63	11.42	22.17	48.38	18.62	17.26	12.36	13.45	15.37	14.61	13.88	12.45
	Risk - SD	-	10.26	10.55	11.23	13.05	10.46	13.25	14.77	13.00	13.62	14.67	14.73	25.69
90	Growth $1	1.03	1.23	1.11	1.22	1.45	1.67	2.15	3.10	6.27	33.68	105.40	565.71	9,568
	Return %	3.13	22.96	11.32	21.70	45.14	18.54	16.59	11.99	13.02	15.10	14.23	13.51	12.14
	Risk - SD	-	9.44	9.95	10.62	12.50	9.81	12.67	14.10	12.42	13.20	14.11	14.15	24.85
85	Growth $1	1.03	1.22	1.11	1.21	1.43	1.63	2.10	3.01	5.95	30.93	95.39	491.76	8,016
	Return %	3.03	21.95	10.79	20.66	42.95	17.70	15.98	11.64	12.62	14.71	13.91	13.20	11.89
	Risk - SD	-	8.99	9.44	10.15	11.89	9.35	12.01	13.38	11.80	12.57	13.44	13.47	23.58
80	Growth $1	1.03	1.21	1.10	1.20	1.41	1.60	2.04	2.91	5.64	28.37	86.12	425.67	6,622
	Return %	2.93	21.01	10.27	19.62	40.76	16.87	15.35	11.28	12.22	14.32	13.58	12.87	11.63
	Risk - SD	-	8.54	8.93	9.69	11.28	8.89	11.35	12.66	11.18	11.94	12.77	12.79	22.32
75	Growth $1	1.03	1.20	1.10	1.19	1.39	1.56	1.99	2.82	5.34	25.99	77.56	366.91	5,395
	Return %	2.82	20.04	9.74	18.58	38.57	16.03	14.72	10.92	11.81	13.92	13.24	12.54	11.34
	Risk - SD	-	8.09	8.42	9.22	10.68	8.42	10.68	11.94	10.56	11.32	12.10	12.11	21.08
70	Growth $1	1.03	1.19	1.09	1.18	1.36	1.53	1.93	2.73	5.05	23.78	69.69	314.91	4,337
	Return %	2.72	19.06	9.21	17.54	36.39	15.19	14.07	10.55	11.40	13.51	12.89	12.19	11.04
	Risk - SD	-	7.63	7.91	8.76	10.07	7.96	10.03	11.22	9.94	10.69	11.43	11.43	19.85
65	Growth $1	1.03	1.18	1.09	1.16	1.34	1.50	1.88	2.63	4.77	21.73	62.46	269.12	3,439
	Return %	2.62	18.09	8.68	16.50	34.20	14.35	13.42	10.17	10.98	13.11	12.54	11.84	10.71
	Risk - SD	-	7.17	7.40	8.29	9.47	7.49	9.37	10.50	9.32	10.06	10.77	10.76	18.63
60	Growth $1	1.03	1.17	1.08	1.15	1.32	1.46	1.82	2.54	4.51	19.83	55.84	229.00	2,692
	Return %	2.51	17.12	8.16	15.46	32.01	13.51	12.77	9.79	10.56	12.69	12.18	11.48	10.38
	Risk - SD	-	6.71	6.90	7.82	8.86	7.03	8.71	9.78	8.70	9.43	10.10	10.08	17.42
55	Growth $1	1.02	1.16	1.08	1.14	1.30	1.43	1.77	2.46	4.26	18.07	49.81	194.00	2,079
	Return %	2.41	16.14	7.63	14.42	29.82	12.67	12.10	9.41	10.14	12.27	11.81	11.11	10.02
	Risk - SD	-	6.24	6.39	7.36	8.26	6.56	8.06	9.07	8.09	8.81	9.43	9.41	16.21
50	Growth $1	1.02	1.15	1.07	1.13	1.28	1.40	1.72	2.37	4.02	16.44	44.32	163.63	1,585
	Return %	2.31	15.17	7.10	13.38	27.63	11.83	11.42	9.01	9.71	11.85	11.44	10.73	9.65
	Risk - SD	-	5.77	5.89	6.89	7.66	6.09	7.41	8.35	7.47	8.18	8.77	8.74	15.01
45	Growth $1	2.20	1.14	1.07	1.12	1.25	1.37	1.67	2.29	3.79	14.94	39.33	137.40	1,193
	Return %	1.02	14.19	6.57	12.34	25.45	10.99	10.74	8.62	9.28	11.42	11.06	10.35	9.26
	Risk - SD	-	5.30	5.38	6.43	7.07	5.63	6.77	7.64	6.86	7.56	8.11	8.07	13.82
40	Growth $1	1.02	1.13	1.06	1.11	1.23	1.34	1.61	2.20	3.57	13.56	34.82	114.85	885.98
	Return %	2.10	13.22	6.04	11.30	23.26	10.15	10.05	8.21	8.85	10.99	10.68	9.95	8.85
	Risk - SD	-	4.83	4.88	5.97	6.48	5.17	6.13	6.93	6.26	6.94	7.45	7.41	12.63
35	Growth $1	1.02	1.12	1.06	1.10	1.21	1.31	1.56	2.12	3.36	12.29	30.75	95.57	649.35
	Return %	2.00	12.25	5.52	10.26	21.07	9.30	9.35	7.81	8.41	10.56	10.28	9.55	8.43
	Risk - SD	-	4.35	4.39	5.52	5.91	4.71	5.50	6.23	5.66	6.32	6.80	6.76	11.44
30	Growth $1	1.02	1.11	1.05	1.09	1.19	1.28	1.51	2.04	3.16	11.12	27.09	79.15	469.57
	Return %	1.89	11.27	4.99	9.22	18.88	8.46	8.64	7.39	7.97	10.11	9.89	9.14	7.99
	Risk - SD	-	3.87	3.90	5.08	5.35	4.26	4.89	5.53	5.06	5.71	6.16	6.11	10.26
25	Growth $1	1.02	1.10	1.04	1.08	1.17	1.25	1.46	1.96	2.97	10.05	23.81	65.24	335.01
	Return %	1.79	10.30	4.46	8.18	16.70	7.62	7.92	6.97	7.52	9.67	9.48	8.72	7.54
	Risk - SD	-	3.39	3.42	4.65	4.82	3.81	4.29	4.84	4.48	5.11	5.53	5.47	9.08
20	Growth $1	1.02	1.09	1.04	1.07	1.15	1.22	1.42	1.89	2.78	9.06	20.87	53.52	235.73
	Return %	1.69	9.32	3.93	7.14	14.51	6.78	7.20	6.55	7.07	9.22	9.07	8.29	7.07
	Risk - SD	-	2.91	2.95	4.24	4.32	3.38	3.71	4.17	3.91	4.53	4.92	4.86	7.91
15	Growth $1	1.02	1.08	1.04	1.06	1.12	1.19	1.37	1.81	2.61	8.17	18.24	43.69	163.56
	Return %	1.58	8.35	3.41	6.10	12.32	5.93	6.46	6.11	6.61	8.76	8.65	7.85	6.58
	Risk - SD	-	2.42	2.51	3.85	3.87	2.97	3.18	3.52	3.37	3.97	4.33	4.27	6.74
10	Growth $1	1.01	1.07	1.03	1.05	1.10	1.16	1.32	1.74	2.45	7.35	15.91	35.49	111.86
	Return %	1.48	7.38	2.88	5.06	10.13	5.09	5.72	5.68	6.15	8.30	8.23	7.40	6.07
	Risk - SD	-	1.93	2.10	3.50	3.50	2.59	2.71	2.90	2.87	3.45	3.79	3.72	5.60
5	Growth $1	1.01	1.06	1.02	1.04	1.08	1.13	1.27	1.67	2.29	6.60	13.83	28.68	75.38
	Return %	1.38	6.40	2.35	4.03	7.94	4.25	4.97	5.23	5.68	7.84	7.79	6.94	5.55
	Risk - SD	-	1.45	1.75	3.20	3.23	2.25	2.36	2.36	2.43	2.99	3.31	3.24	4.49

*Returns net of IFA and DFA fees.

Sources, Updates, and Disclosures: ifa.com/btp

Table 11- 4

Annual Returns of 20 Index Portfolios and S&P 500

80 years (1927 - 2006)

Year	SP	100	95	90	85	80	75	70	65	60	55	50	45	40	35	30	25	20	15	10	5
1927	37.3	31.1	31.3	31.4	30.0	28.6	27.2	25.8	24.3	22.9	21.5	20.1	18.6	17.2	15.8	14.4	13.0	11.5	10.1	8.7	7.3
1928	43.4	37.2	36.3	35.5	33.7	32.0	30.2	28.5	26.7	25.0	23.2	21.4	19.7	17.9	16.2	14.4	12.7	10.9	9.1	7.4	5.6
1929	-8.5	-33.7	-30.0	-26.3	-24.8	-23.2	-21.7	-20.1	-18.6	-17.1	-15.5	-14.0	-12.4	-10.9	-9.4	-7.8	-6.3	-4.7	-3.2	-1.7	-0.1
1930	-25.0	-43.6	-42.7	-41.8	-39.5	-37.2	-34.9	-32.5	-30.2	-27.9	-25.6	-23.3	-21.0	-18.7	-16.4	-14.0	-11.7	-9.4	-7.1	-4.8	-2.5
1931	-43.4	-53.0	-53.2	-53.4	-50.8	-48.3	-45.8	-43.2	-40.7	-38.1	-35.6	-33.1	-30.5	-28.0	-25.4	-22.9	-20.4	-17.8	-15.3	-12.7	-10.2
1932	-8.3	-1.7	-2.6	-3.6	-3.1	-2.7	-2.2	-1.7	-1.3	-0.8	-0.4	0.1	0.6	1.0	1.5	2.0	2.4	2.9	3.3	3.8	4.3
1933	53.8	130.4	122.2	114.0	108.3	102.6	96.9	91.2	85.5	79.9	74.2	68.5	62.8	57.1	51.5	45.8	40.1	34.4	28.7	23.0	17.4
1934	-1.6	4.9	2.1	-0.7	-0.4	0.0	0.3	0.6	0.9	1.2	1.5	1.8	2.2	2.5	2.8	3.1	3.4	3.7	4.0	4.3	4.7
1935	47.5	53.9	52.4	50.9	48.6	46.2	43.9	41.6	39.2	36.9	34.5	32.2	29.9	27.5	25.2	22.8	20.5	18.1	15.8	13.5	11.1
1936	33.8	65.3	62.0	58.6	55.7	52.9	50.0	47.1	44.3	41.4	38.5	35.6	32.8	29.9	27.0	24.2	21.3	18.4	15.5	12.7	9.8
1937	-35.1	-48.2	-46.7	-45.1	-42.9	-40.6	-38.3	-36.1	-33.8	-31.5	-29.3	-27.0	-24.8	-22.5	-20.2	-18.0	-15.7	-13.5	-11.2	-8.9	-6.7
1938	31.0	29.0	29.1	29.1	27.9	26.6	25.3	24.0	22.7	21.4	20.2	18.9	17.6	16.3	15.0	13.7	12.5	11.2	9.9	8.6	7.3
1939	-0.5	-6.4	-6.9	-7.4	-6.9	-6.5	-6.0	-5.5	-5.0	-4.5	-4.1	-3.6	-3.1	-2.6	-2.1	-1.6	-1.2	-0.7	-0.2	0.3	0.8
1940	-9.9	-10.9	-10.7	-10.4	-9.8	-9.2	-8.7	-8.1	-7.5	-6.9	-6.4	-5.8	-5.2	-4.7	-4.1	-3.5	-2.9	-2.4	-1.8	-1.2	-0.7
1941	-11.7	-8.5	-8.1	-7.7	-7.4	-7.0	-6.7	-6.3	-6.0	-5.6	-5.3	-4.9	-4.6	-4.2	-3.9	-3.5	-3.2	-2.8	-2.5	-2.2	-1.8
1942	20.2	37.0	35.8	34.5	32.8	31.1	29.4	27.6	25.9	24.2	22.5	20.8	19.1	17.4	15.7	14.0	12.3	10.6	8.9	7.2	5.5
1943	25.8	73.6	67.5	61.5	58.5	55.5	52.4	49.4	46.4	43.4	40.3	37.3	34.3	31.3	28.2	25.2	22.2	19.2	16.2	13.1	10.1
1944	19.6	46.4	44.2	42.0	39.9	37.9	35.8	33.7	31.6	29.5	27.4	25.3	23.3	21.2	19.1	17.0	14.9	12.8	10.7	8.6	6.6
1945	36.3	62.5	59.1	55.7	53.0	50.2	47.5	44.7	42.0	39.2	36.4	33.7	30.9	28.2	25.4	22.7	19.9	17.1	14.4	11.6	8.9
1946	-8.2	-12.0	-11.5	-11.1	-10.6	-10.0	-9.5	-8.9	-8.4	-7.9	-7.3	-6.8	-6.2	-5.7	-5.2	-4.6	-4.1	-3.5	-3.0	-2.5	-1.9
1947	5.6	2.4	2.9	3.4	3.2	3.0	2.9	2.7	2.5	2.3	2.1	1.9	1.7	1.5	1.4	1.2	1.0	0.8	0.6	0.4	0.2
1948	5.4	-4.2	-3.1	-2.0	-1.8	-1.7	-1.6	-1.5	-1.4	-1.2	-1.1	-1.0	-0.9	-0.8	-0.6	-0.5	-0.4	-0.3	-0.2	0.0	0.1
1949	18.7	17.7	17.3	16.9	16.1	15.3	14.5	13.7	12.9	12.1	11.3	10.5	9.7	8.9	8.1	7.3	6.5	5.7	4.9	4.1	3.3
1950	31.6	47.2	47.1	46.9	44.6	42.2	39.9	37.5	35.1	32.8	30.4	28.0	25.7	23.3	21.0	18.6	16.2	13.9	11.5	9.1	6.8
1951	23.9	11.3	12.1	12.8	12.2	11.5	10.8	10.2	9.5	8.8	8.2	7.5	6.8	6.2	5.5	4.8	4.2	3.5	2.8	2.2	1.5
1952	18.2	9.2	10.4	11.6	11.0	10.5	9.9	9.4	8.8	8.3	7.7	7.2	6.6	6.1	5.5	5.0	4.5	3.9	3.4	2.8	2.3
1953	-1.1	-7.3	-7.1	-6.8	-6.4	-6.0	-5.5	-5.1	-4.7	-4.3	-3.9	-3.5	-3.1	-2.6	-2.2	-1.8	-1.4	-1.0	-0.6	-0.2	0.3
1954	52.5	63.7	64.0	64.3	61.1	58.0	54.8	51.6	48.5	45.3	42.2	39.0	35.8	32.7	29.5	26.3	23.2	20.0	16.9	13.7	10.5
1955	31.4	21.7	21.7	21.7	20.5	19.4	18.3	17.1	16.0	14.9	13.7	12.6	11.5	10.3	9.2	8.1	6.9	5.8	4.6	3.5	2.4
1956	6.4	2.7	2.5	2.3	2.1	2.0	1.9	1.8	1.6	1.5	1.4	1.3	1.2	1.0	0.9	0.8	0.7	0.5	0.4	0.3	0.2
1957	-10.9	-16.9	-16.5	-16.2	-15.2	-14.1	-13.1	-12.1	-11.0	-10.0	-8.9	-7.9	-6.9	-5.8	-4.8	-3.8	-2.7	-1.7	-0.6	0.4	1.4
1958	43.2	64.3	62.7	61.1	58.0	54.9	51.8	48.7	45.5	42.4	39.3	36.2	33.1	30.0	26.9	23.8	20.6	17.5	14.4	11.3	8.2
1959	11.8	16.8	17.4	18.0	17.1	16.2	15.3	14.5	13.6	12.7	11.8	10.9	10.0	9.2	8.3	7.4	6.5	5.6	4.8	3.9	3.0
1960	0.3	-6.6	-6.5	-6.3	-5.6	-5.0	-4.3	-3.6	-3.0	-2.3	-1.6	-0.9	-0.3	0.4	1.1	1.7	2.4	3.1	3.8	4.4	5.1
1961	26.7	26.9	26.1	25.4	24.1	22.9	21.7	20.5	19.3	18.1	16.9	15.6	14.4	13.2	12.0	10.8	9.6	8.4	7.1	5.9	4.7
1962	-8.8	-11.1	-10.3	-9.5	-8.8	-8.2	-7.6	-7.0	-6.3	-5.7	-5.1	-4.4	-3.8	-3.2	-2.6	-1.9	-1.3	-0.7	0.0	0.6	1.2
1963	22.6	20.4	20.8	21.2	20.2	19.2	18.2	17.2	16.3	15.3	14.3	13.3	12.3	11.3	10.3	9.3	8.3	7.3	6.3	5.3	4.3
1964	16.4	17.8	17.1	16.5	15.8	15.1	14.4	13.8	13.1	12.4	11.7	11.0	10.4	9.7	9.0	8.3	7.6	7.0	6.3	5.6	4.9
1965	12.3	31.1	28.8	26.5	25.2	24.0	22.7	21.5	20.2	18.9	17.7	16.4	15.2	13.9	12.6	11.4	10.1	8.8	7.6	6.3	5.1
1966	-10.2	-9.8	-9.9	-10.1	-9.4	-8.7	-8.0	-7.3	-6.6	-5.8	-5.1	-4.4	-3.7	-3.0	-2.3	-1.6	-0.9	-0.2	0.5	1.2	1.9
1967	23.8	64.6	58.7	52.9	50.3	47.8	45.2	42.6	40.1	37.5	34.9	32.4	29.8	27.2	24.7	22.1	19.5	17.0	14.4	11.8	9.3
1968	11.0	39.1	36.5	33.9	32.4	30.9	29.4	27.9	26.4	24.9	23.4	21.9	20.4	19.0	17.5	16.0	14.5	13.0	11.5	10.0	8.5
1969	-8.6	-24.9	-22.9	-20.8	-19.7	-18.5	-17.4	-16.2	-15.1	-13.9	-12.8	-11.7	-10.5	-9.4	-8.2	-7.1	-5.9	-4.8	-3.6	-2.5	-1.4
1970	3.9	-4.8	-3.7	-2.6	-1.9	-1.1	-0.3	0.4	1.2	2.0	2.7	3.5	4.2	5.0	5.7	6.5	7.3	8.0	8.8	9.5	10.3
1971	14.2	26.4	25.7	25.0	24.1	23.1	22.2	21.2	20.3	19.4	18.4	17.5	16.5	15.6	14.6	13.7	12.7	11.8	10.8	9.9	8.9
1972	18.8	20.4	21.1	21.9	21.0	20.1	19.1	18.2	17.3	16.4	15.5	14.5	13.6	12.7	11.8	10.9	9.9	9.0	8.1	7.2	6.3
1973	-14.8	-24.0	-21.9	-19.9	-18.7	-17.5	-16.3	-15.1	-13.8	-12.6	-11.4	-10.2	-9.0	-7.8	-6.6	-5.4	-4.1	-2.9	-1.7	-0.5	0.7
1974	-26.6	-25.5	-25.1	-24.8	-23.2	-21.6	-20.0	-18.4	-16.8	-15.2	-13.6	-12.0	-10.4	-8.8	-7.2	-5.6	-4.0	-2.4	-0.8	0.8	2.4
1975	37.1	51.3	48.4	45.6	43.6	41.7	39.7	37.8	35.9	33.9	32.0	30.0	28.1	26.2	24.2	22.3	20.3	18.4	16.5	14.5	12.6
1976	23.7	34.0	32.3	30.6	29.4	28.3	27.2	26.0	24.9	23.8	22.6	21.5	20.4	19.2	18.1	16.9	15.8	14.7	13.5	12.4	11.3
1977	-7.3	23.7	20.6	17.5	16.8	16.1	15.3	14.6	13.9	13.1	12.4	11.6	10.9	10.2	9.4	8.7	8.0	7.2	6.5	5.8	5.0
1978	6.5	26.2	24.1	22.0	21.0	20.1	19.2	18.3	17.4	16.4	15.5	14.6	13.7	12.8	11.9	10.9	10.0	9.1	8.2	7.3	6.3
1979	18.3	21.2	20.0	18.7	18.2	17.6	17.1	16.5	16.0	15.4	14.9	14.3	13.7	13.2	12.6	12.1	11.5	11.0	10.4	9.9	9.3
1980	32.3	26.0	25.5	25.0	24.2	23.4	22.6	21.8	21.0	20.2	19.4	18.6	17.8	17.0	16.2	15.4	14.6	13.9	13.1	12.3	11.5
1981	-5.0	6.4	5.9	5.5	5.9	6.3	6.7	7.1	7.5	7.9	8.3	8.7	9.1	9.5	9.9	10.3	10.7	11.1	11.5	11.9	12.3
1982	21.3	17.9	16.9	16.0	16.2	16.3	16.5	16.7	16.9	17.0	17.2	17.4	17.6	17.7	17.9	18.1	18.3	18.4	18.6	18.8	18.9
1983	22.4	34.9	33.2	31.6	30.4	29.2	28.0	26.8	25.5	24.3	23.1	21.9	20.7	19.5	18.3	17.1	15.9	14.7	13.4	12.2	11.0
1984	6.1	4.3	5.6	6.8	7.0	7.3	7.5	7.8	8.0	8.2	8.5	8.7	9.0	9.2	9.5	9.7	10.0	10.2	10.5	10.7	10.9
1985	32.0	36.7	36.4	36.1	34.9	33.8	32.6	31.4	30.3	29.1	27.9	26.8	25.6	24.5	23.3	22.1	21.0	19.8	18.6	17.5	16.3
1986	18.3	25.8	27.1	28.5	27.5	26.6	25.7	24.8	23.9	23.0	22.1	21.2	20.2	19.3	18.4	17.5	16.6	15.7	14.8	13.9	12.9
1987	5.1	9.2	9.8	10.4	10.1	9.8	9.6	9.3	9.0	8.7	8.4	8.1	7.8	7.5	7.3	7.0	6.7	6.4	6.1	5.8	5.5
1988	16.7	25.7	24.9	24.1	23.2	22.3	21.4	20.5	19.6	18.7	17.8	16.9	16.0	15.1	14.2	13.3	12.4	11.5	10.6	9.7	8.8
1989	31.3	26.4	26.6	26.8	25.8	24.9	23.9	23.0	22.0	21.1	20.1	19.1	18.2	17.2	16.3	15.3	14.4	13.4	12.4	11.5	10.5
1990	-3.2	-18.0	-17.3	-16.6	-15.4	-14.2	-13.0	-11.9	-10.7	-9.5	-8.3	-7.1	-5.9	-4.7	-3.6	-2.4	-1.2	0.0	1.2	2.4	3.6
1991	30.1	32.6	31.3	30.0	29.1	28.1	27.2	26.2	25.3	24.3	23.4	22.4	21.5	20.5	19.6	18.6	17.7	16.7	15.8	14.8	13.8
1992	7.3	11.8	10.5	9.3	9.1	8.9	8.7	8.5	8.3	8.1	7.9	7.7	7.5	7.3	7.0	6.8	6.6	6.4	6.2	6.0	5.8
1993	9.6	31.9	30.1	28.3	27.2	26.1	25.0	23.9	22.8	21.7	20.6	19.5	18.4	17.3	16.2	15.2	14.1	13.0	11.9	10.8	9.7
1994	1.3	2.1	1.5	0.9	0.8	0.6	0.5	0.3	0.2	0.0	-0.1	-0.3	-0.4	-0.6	-0.7	-0.8	-1.0	-1.1	-1.3	-1.4	-1.6
1995	37.1	21.5	21.9	22.3	21.7	21.0	20.4	19.7	19.1	18.4	17.8	17.2	16.5	15.9	15.2	14.6	13.9	13.3	12.7	12.0	11.4
1996	22.6	15.7	16.2	16.8	16.3	15.8	15.3	14.8	14.2	13.7	13.2	12.7	12.2	11.7	11.2	10.7	10.2	9.7	9.2	8.7	8.2
1997	33.1	12.5	13.2	13.9	13.5	13.1	12.7	12.3	11.9	11.5	11.1	10.6	10.2	9.8	9.4	9.0	8.6	8.2	7.8	7.3	6.9
1998	28.7	1.2	3.5	5.7	5.7	5.7	5.7	5.7	5.7	5.7	5.7	5.7	5.7	5.6	5.6	5.6	5.6	5.6	5.6	5.6	5.6
1999	20.8	24.4	22.1	19.9	19.1	18.2	17.4	16.6	15.7	14.9	14.1	13.2	12.4	11.6	10.7	9.9	9.1	8.2	7.4	6.6	5.7
2000	-9.3	-2.9	-1.9	-0.9	-0.6	-0.3	0.1	0.4	0.7	1.1	1.4	1.7	2.1	2.4	2.7	3.0	3.4	3.7	4.0	4.4	4.7
2001	-12.1	5.5	3.1	0.7	0.9	1.1	1.4	1.6	1.8	2.1	2.3	2.5	2.7	3.0	3.2	3.4	3.7	3.9	4.1	4.3	4.6
2002	-22.2	-10.1	-10.5	-10.9	-10.0	-9.1	-8.2	-7.3	-6.4	-5.6	-4.7	-3.8	-2.9	-2.0	-1.1	-0.2	0.7	1.6	2.4	3.3	4.2
2003	28.5	51.6	48.4	45.1	43.0	40.8	38.6	36.4	34.2	32.0	29.8	27.6	25.5	23.3	21.1	18.9	16.7	14.5	12.3	10.1	7.9
2004	10.7	22.6	22.2	21.7	20.7	19.6	18.6	17.5	16.5	15.5	14.4	13.4	12.3	11.3	10.3	9.2	8.2	7.1	6.1	5.1	4.0
2005	4.9	11.5	11.4	11.3	10.8	10.3	9.7	9.2	8.7	8.2	7.6	7.1	6.6	6.0	5.5	5.0	4.5	3.9	3.4	2.9	2.4
2006	15.7	22.3	22.6	23.0	22.0	21.0	20.0	19.1	18.1	17.1	16.1	15.2	14.2	13.2	12.3	11.3	10.3	9.3	8.4	7.4	6.4
Annualized Return (%)	10.27	12.74	12.45	12.14	11.89	11.63	11.34	11.04	10.71	10.38	10.02	9.65	9.26	8.85	8.43	7.99	7.54	7.07	6.58	6.07	5.55
Standard Deviation (%)	19.23	26.59	25.69	24.85	23.58	22.32	21.08	19.85	18.63	17.42	16.21	15.01	13.82	12.63	11.44	10.26	9.08	7.91	6.74	5.60	4.49
Growth of $1	$2,483	$14,652	$11,947	$9,568	$8,016	$6,622	$5,395	$4,337	$3,439	$2,692	$2,079	$1,585	$1,193	$886	$649	$470	$335	$236	$164	$112	$75.38

* See Appendix A for Index Portfolio Button Definitions

Sources, Updates, and Disclosures: ifa.com/btp

11.4.3 The Most Efficient Funds on the Market

DFA has created index mutual funds to capture all risk factors, and their funds are hands down the best, most efficient index mutual funds available. The following information describes their various investment strategies.

Small-Cap Strategy

DFA has been a pioneer in small stock research since the firm's start in 1981. Their research has found that small companies worldwide form an asset class with higher expected returns than large companies. Small stocks allow investors to achieve large diversification benefits. DFA's objective is to deliver the small company effect. To accomplish this, DFA provides index mutual funds that invest in a broadly diversified cross section of small companies in the United States and major international markets.

Small companies are defined by market capitalization (price times shares outstanding). DFA defines small companies as those companies whose market capitalization comprise the smallest 12.5% of the total market universe. The total market universe is defined as the aggregate capitalization of the NYSE, AMEX and NASDAQ National Market System firms.

U.S. Small-Cap Strategy

The small-cap strategy invests in securities of U.S. companies whose size (market capitalization) falls within the smallest 8% of the total market universe. Their goal is to be fully invested in equities at all times. They limit themselves to publicly traded companies that meet the size criteria of the applicable portfolio. Additional screening criteria is also employed. These criteria include eliminating REIT's, investment companies, limited partnerships, companies in bank-

ruptcy, ADRs, companies with qualified financial statements, OTC stocks with fewer than four market makers or those not included on the National Market System. They are aggressive in keeping cash levels low, generally under 2%.

New cash flow is controlled so portfolios may remain fully invested. On a quarterly basis, the market capitalization ranking of eligible stocks are examined to determine which issues are eligible for purchase and which issues are sale candidates. A hold or buffer range for sales minimizes transaction costs and keeps portfolio turnover low. Issues that migrate above the hold range are sold, and proceeds are reinvested in the portfolio. Individual small companies worldwide are thinly traded. As a result they follow unique trading procedures, which have been developed and refined to effectively and economically trade small companies.

U.S. Micro-Cap Strategy

The micro-cap strategy invests in securities of U.S. companies whose size (market capitalization) falls within the smallest 4% of the total market universe.

Value Strategies

Studies conducted by Professors Eugene Fama at the University of Chicago and Kenneth French, currently at the Tuck School of Business, Dartmouth College, established that the three economic factors of size, book-to-market (BtM), and the performance of the market as a whole explain most of the variation of equity portfolio average returns. DFA's value strategies incorporate the Fama/French research in multifactor portfolios designed to capture the return premiums associated with high BtM and market capitalization.

U.S. Small-Cap Value Strategy

The small-cap value strategy invests in companies whose market capitalization is in the size range of the smallest 8% of the total market universe. After identifying the 8% of aggregate market capitalization that would determine size, a value screen is then applied to this universe. For the small-cap value strategy, value stocks must have BtM ratios in the upper 25th percentile of the value-weighted universe ranked by BtM. This BtM sort excludes firms with negative or zero book values. Book value is reconstructed for each eligible issue based on the interpretation of how accounting charges affect "real" book value.

U.S. Large-Cap Value Strategy

The U.S. large-cap value strategy invests in companies that have a market capitalization in the largest 90% of the total market universe. After identifying the 90% of the aggregate market capitalization that would determine size, a value screen is then applied to this universe. For the U.S. large-cap value strategy, value stocks must have BtM ratios in the upper 10th percentile of the value-weighted universe ranked by BtM. This BtM sort excludes those firms with negative or zero book values.

Real Estate Securities Strategy

DFA's objective is to capture real estate market returns. This strategy is based on rigorously back-tested research and uses a disciplined approach designed to achieve its objective. DFA's real estate securities strategy has the advantage of providing market-based pricing and daily liquidity. The strategy is based on original research conducted by Professors Donald Keim and Joseph Gyourko at The Wharton School. The Gyourko and Keim research analyzed the risk return characteristics of different types of real estate-related firms traded on the New York and American stock exchanges. This research indicates that returns from the real estate series correlate with the actual performance of the real estate market as measured by the Wilshire REIT-only Index.

The portfolio is market-cap weighted and diversified. Investments are made in all eligible publicly traded REITs. The portfolio consists of shares of equity and hybrid real estate investment trusts, (to the extent that at least 75% of the REITs' assets are equity investments). The stocks in the portfolio represent more than $123 billion in market capitalization and pro rate ownership of several thousand properties. On at least a semi-annual basis, DFA reviews all eligible companies to assure that their principal line of business is real estate related. Their screening process also excludes health care REITs, prison REITs, REITs in extreme financial difficulty, REITs involved in a merger or consolidation and REITs that are the subject of an acquisition, which could result in a company no longer being considered principally in the real estate business. Since real estate issues can be classified as small companies, DFA's considerable small-cap trading experience can be used to keep transaction costs and portfolio turnover low.

U.S. Large Company Strategy

DFA provides access to U.S. large companies in a portfolio structured to approximate the investment performance of the S&P 500 Index. Currently, the S&P 500 Index is comprised of investments in large-capitalization U.S. stocks, representing approximately 80% of the total market capitalization of U.S. publicly traded stocks. DFA's portfolio invests in all the stocks that comprise the S&P 500 Index in approximatcly the same proportions as they are represented in the index. The portfolio may also invest in index futures and index options. Annual portfolio turnover is expected to be approximately 10%.

Developed International Markets

The developed markets portfolios invest in countries included in the MSCI EAFE (Morgan Stanley Capital International Inc. and Europe, Australia and Far East) Index. However, some of DFA's international equity portfolios invest in asset classes not represented or are only partially represented by the standard EAFE index. These include DFA's international small company and international value strategies.

DFA has managed small capitalization equities in the international markets since 1986 when they created regional portfolios in Japan and the United Kingdom. Since then, the firm has added small company portfolios in Continental Europe and the Pacific Rim and now offers a single mutual fund that provides exposure to small capitalization stocks in all four regions. In the standalone international small cap portfolio, DFA utilizes a regional weighting scheme to ensure diversification among the four regions. Within multi-country regions, countries are weighted proportionately by the size of their respective small-cap markets.

DFA defines small capitalization by region, setting a maximum market capitalization based on the bottom portion of a major regional market index. This methodology, which mimics the U.S. small company portfolios, allows flexibility to adjust the size break with market fluctuations and avoids size drift. As a result, DFA's international small cap portfolios typically have a lower average market cap than competitors or benchmarks

DFA trades small company stocks through its London and Sydney offices. Where possible, the firm leverages its expertise in trading U.S. small-cap stocks, adopting a similar patient and careful style of trading. In the United Kingdom's stock market in particular, DFA uses a block trading strategy to add value.

DFA also offers both large company and small company portfolios designed to capture the value effect. Value in their international portfolios is defined by individual country. In the International Large Value Portfolio, countries are weighted by market capitalization. The International Small Value Portfolio uses a regional weighting strategy similar to the International Small Company Portfolio.

Emerging Markets

The emerging markets portfolios include Argentina, Brazil, Chile, Greece, Hungary, Indonesia, Israel, Malaysia, Mexico, Philippines, Poland, South Korea, Thailand, and Turkey. Like DFA's other strategies, the emerging markets portfolios are constructed to represent categories of asset risk. Therefore, DFA offers large capitalization, small capitalization, and value portfolios as they do in domestic and developed international markets.

Before adding a country in the emerging markets portfolio, DFA undertakes a rigorous review, including a visit by a member of its investment committee. First, the country must meet certain criteria, including a market capitalization of at least $10 billion, sufficient liquidity and a delivery versus payment system. DFA also applies subjective requirements, including fair treatment of foreign investors, well-developed property rights and a commitment to free markets. As in DFA's other international strategies, DFA gains exposure to companies in emerging markets mainly by investing in the local market in ordinary common equity. Where advantageous, it may also invest in American Depository Receipts (ADRs) traded in the United States to gain exposure to an emerging markets country. For example, DFA purchases ADR's in Chile because they provide broad coverage of the stock market and allows U.S. investors to avoid repatriation restrictions. In emerging markets, individual countries are characterized by a high degree of volatility and a low degree of cross-correlation among countries. DFA weights the countries in its emerging markets portfolios equally, maximizing diversification and minimizing overall portfolio volatility. DFA believes that a diversified portfolio of emerging markets' equities complements a well-structured asset allocation.

Fixed Income

Many studies have been done regarding the question of bond market efficiency. Much of this research is similar in nature to efficient market studies performed on the stock market. The conclusions are similar - there is no reliable method of forecasting future bond prices, and therefore future interest rates. The bond market is efficient.

Investors seeking short-term, non-forecasting strategies are not limited to "buy and hold" or indexing strategies. Investors can increase their risk-adjusted returns with an alternative approach developed by Professor Fama of the University of Chicago.

This variable maturity strategy shifts the maturities of the portfolio as yield-curve changes create the possibility for lower risk with higher expected return outcomes. In recognizing the bond market as being highly efficient, the variable maturity approach does not anticipate changes in the yield curve; rather it seeks to max-

imize the risk-adjusted returns present in the current curve. Investors can further expand their opportunity set by also considering global bonds. If currency exposure is fully hedged, globally managed fixed income portfolios can provide higher expected returns and lower standard deviations.

For extra reading on DFA principals, several papers authored by Fama and French are available for download at ssrn.com through the Social Science Research Network. Titles include "Market Efficiency, Long-Term Returns and Behavioral Finance," "Value Versus Growth: The International Evidence," and "The Equity Premium." DFA's impressive academic affiliates are listed in Table 11-5.

11.4.4 Matching People and Portfolios

The process of prudent investing is the intelligent management of risk. At the most fundamental level, this process matches each investor's capacity to expose his assets to risk. The measurement of capacity, is both an event and a process because this capacity slowly erodes as an investor closes in on the need to withdraw money from the account. Investors should revisit the Risk Capacity Survey at least once a year. Since knowledge of investing is an important component of risk capacity, investors should allocate some time to read about the Modern Portfolio Theory.

11.5　SUMMARY

There is only one risk exposure question that needs to be posed. What mix of indexes provides the highest expected return at each level of risk? Getting to that answer involves concepts discovered by academics who methodically applied the

Table 11-5

Dimensional Fund Advisors and their Academic Affiliates			
Professor	**University**	**Dimensional Affiliation**	**Best Known For**
George M. Constantinides Leo Melamed Professor of Finance	University of Chicago Graduate School of Business	Board Member, Dimensional's Mutual Funds	Asset Pricing, Capital Markets Research
James L. Davis Assistant Professor	Kansas State University	Vice President Dimensional Fund Advisors Inc.	Asset Pricing, Value Stock Research
Eugene F. Fama Robert R. McCormick Distinguished Service Professor of Finance	University of Chicago Graduate School of Business	Director of Research; Board Member, Dimensional Fund Advisors; Fixed Income and Value Stocks	Efficient Markets Hypothesis; Random Walk Hypothesis; Capital Markets Research; Multifactor Model; Definitive Finance Text; World's Most Cited Economist
Kenneth R. French Heidt Professor of Finance	Dartmouth College Tuck School of Business	Director of Investment Strategy, Consultant	Capital Markets Research, Multifactor Model, Tax Research
John P. Gould Steven G. Rothmeier Distinguished Service Professor of Economics	University of Chicago Graduate School of Business	Board Member, Dimensional's Mutual Funds	
Roger G. Ibbotson Professor in the Practice of Finance	Yale University School of Management	Board Member, Dimensional's Mutual Funds	Capital Markets Research; Comprehensive SBBI database (with Sinquefield); Data consultant firm
Donald B. Keim Professor of Finance	University of Pennsylvania The Wharton School	Consultant, Real Estate Securities; Trading Cost Research	Capital Markets Research; Small Stock "January Effect"
Myron S. Scholes Nobel Laureate Frank E. Buck Professor Emeritus of Finance and Law	Stanford University Graduate School of Business	Board Member of Dimensional's US Mutual Funds	Capital Markets Research, Options Pricing Model
Robert C. Merton Nobel Laureate John and Natty McArthur University Professor	Harvard University Harvard Business School	Board Member of Dimensional's US Mutual Funds	Asset Pricing Theory, Valuation of Derivative Securities
Abbie J. Smith Boris and Irene Stern Professor of Accounting	University of Chicago Graduate School of Business	Board Member of Dimensional's US Mutual Funds	Capital Markets Research, Financial Accounting Information, Corporate Restructuring, Corporate Governance
Marvin Zonis Professor	University of Chicago Graduate School of Business	Consultant for International Economics	Capital Markets Research, World Political Affairs, Foreign Policy Analysis

scientific method to this problem. See the list below for examples of these concepts.

1. Obtain data with acceptable confidence levels. This requires at least 20 years of risk and return characteristics of indexes.

2. Select several indexes that best capture the three factors that explain 95% of stock market returns. Those include indexes from the United States, international, and emerging markets. Within each area, select indexes that focus on total market, small cap, and value stocks.

3. Assemble those indexes in such a manner that you obtain global diversification, tax management where applicable, and high expected returns at each level of risk.

4. Considering the taxable status of each account, allocate the index mutual funds that best match the indexes. In taxable accounts, use tax-managed index funds. In tax deferred accounts, use standard index funds.

11.6   REVIEW QUESTIONS

1. What is the minimum number of years of risk and return data of an index needed to design an efficient portfolio?

   a. 1
   b. 20
   c. 3
   d. 10
   e. 5

2. Dimensional Fund Advisors (DFA) and Vanguard both offer a broad selection of index funds. Why does DFA consistently rank higher?

   a. Vanguard promotes actively managed funds in addition to index funds

   b. DFA has indexes that are more concentrated in small and value stocks

   c. DFA provides high-level education and data to its advisors

   d. DFA restricts "hot" money investors by channeling through approved index investment advisors

   e. All of the above

3. Tax-managed index funds:

   a. have very high distributions of short-term capital gains

   b. include a loss harvesting strategy

   c. minimize the dividend paying stocks in the tracked index

   d. are used in tax-deferred accounts

   e. b and c

4. The 20 portfolios of indexes:

   a. allow investors to match their risk capacity score to a risk exposure

   b. were designed based on five years of risk and return data

   c. include companies that are only located in the United States

   d. have fixed income added to some portfolios to increase the risk exposure

   e. include small growth and large growth indexes

5. The long-term expected return of a portfolio can best be estimated by:

   a. the track record of the stock pickers

   b. the track record of the time pickers or market timers

   c. the track record of the advisor selecting other money managers

   d. the selection of indexes used in asset allocation

   e. the track record of a manager using style or sector timing

Step 12 ~ Invest & Relax

STEP 12
Invest & Relax

"Most of the mutual fund investments I have are index funds, approximately 75%."

- Charles Schwab, Author, Guide to Financial Independence, Random House, Inc.*

"A decade ago, I really did believe that the average investor could do it himself. After all, the flesh was willing, the vehicles were available, and the math wasn't that hard. I was wrong. Having emailed and spoken to thousands of investors over the years, I've come to the sad conclusion that only a tiny minority, at most one percent, are capable of pulling it off. Heck, if Helen Young Hayes, Robert Sanborn, Julian Robertson, and the nation's largest pension funds can't get it right, what chance does John Q. Investor have?"

- William Bernstein, "The Probability of Success,"efficientfrontier.com/ef/103/probable.htm

"So passive investing may not be the most exciting method of investing or the most talked-about method, but it's certainly the most prudent. So keep your investments passive, and save the active behavior for your retirement lifestyle."

- Charles Massimo, *Plan, Diversify and Relax Your Way To a More Profitable Retirement*, www.moldmakingtechnology.com/articles/090405.html

"Most institutional and individual investors will find the best way to own common stock is through an index fund that charges minimal fees. Those following this path are sure to beat the net results (after fees and expenses) delivered by the great majority of investment professionals."

- Warren Buffett, 1996 Shareholder Letter

12.1 INTRODUCTION

Step12: Invest, relax and stay balanced.

It is possible to invest and relax without fretting over the ups and downs of the market. This 12-Step Program has explained many advantages of passive indexing over active investing. Investing in this passive approach provides freedom from stress, anguish and the panic of active investing. Remember, indexing is not designed to be a quick fix and does not carry the seductive quality of gambling or day trading. This approach neither has the sizzle the media likes nor does it feed the adrenaline rush of chasing leads or returns. Active investing often leads to lost opportunity. Like most things of value in life, passive investing takes discipline and time to reap the rewards.

It is the most intelligent and prudent way to build wealth over the long run. Indexing is a journey, a lifestyle, a process based on a solid academic foundation of empirical research. Look again at this quick review of the 12-Step Program. It substantiates the case for passive indexing by demonstrating the following:

- It is virtually impossible to beat a market over time through active investing.

- Indexing is backed by Nobel laureates who have provided unbiased, rigorous, empirical research, most notably Modern Portfolio Theory.

- Stock pickers are analogous to gamblers who rely on feelings and emotions when making bets.

- Time pickers or market timers move money in and out of different investments in an attempt to profit from short-term cyclical events, which is a futile endeavor.

• Manager picking is not a reliable practice because the past performance of money managers does not predict their future performance. Star money managers fall from their stature sooner or later, since their stellar performance is attributed to Lady Luck rather than skill.

• Style drift is detrimental in maintaining an efficient portfolio because it changes the portfolio's risk exposure. This is a problem when risk exposure has carefully been chosen based on an investor's predetermined risk capacity.

• Silent partners in active management diminish an investor's wealth by eating large slices of the investment pie.

• Understanding riskese, the language used to discuss the relationship between risk, return, and time is essential to engaging in the ownership of risk.

• To achieve above average returns, assets must be exposed to above average risk over a long period of time because of the relationship between time, risk, and return.

• Index funds are based on a long history of data dating back to 1926. Knowledge and understanding of this long-term historical data helps investors make intelligent decisions on portfolio asset allocation.

• Each investor has a personal risk capacity, a key component in choosing a portfolio.

• The mixture of indexes in a portfolio or the asset allocation accounts for 100% of the variance of long-term return. Asset allocation is the most important decision an investor can make.

• The most efficient way to invest is to hold a portfolio comprised of global diversified index funds.

• Dimensional Fund Advisors (DFA) offers the highest rated, most efficient and lowest cost institutional funds, now available to individual investors through registered investment advisors.

12.2 DEFINITIONS

12.2.1 Registered Investment Advisors

An understanding of the 12-Step Program for Active Investors may lead investors to believe they can do it on their own. They absolutely can if they wish, but working with an investment advisor is still recommended. Taking the steps to gain a knowledge base of what works and what doesn't work in the market is critically important, and every investor owes it to himself to learn this information. Knowing that money managers cannot beat the market over the long run is essential when choosing an investment method. Many investors decide to manage their own investments through the no-load index funds now available on the market through various mutual funds.

Although indexing can be done on one's own, there is a high value to working with a qualified registered investment advisor (RIA). Many RIA's have been registered with the SEC and can provide valuable ongoing advice and education. A study by Dalbar found that active investors who invest on their own are more apt to attempt market timing and less inclined to stay invested in a mutual fund for an average of 2.6 years. This is where an investment advisor can help. A good investment advisor supports the process of indexing, encourages long-term buy and hold and rebalancing strategies, advises prudent investing through the ups and downs of the market, and builds a long-term relationship with the client.

There are many advisory options available to today's investor. This abundance of resources can be confusing and disconcerting for the average investor, making it difficult to know whom to trust. Many investors seek advice from stockbrokers, insurance sales reps, or commissioned financial planners. These types of advisors are customarily paid to sell products rather than help investors make wise investment decisions. Investors often question whose best interest these advisors have in mind — the investors' or their own? Further, a commissioned based pay structure often sets up a conflict of interest for the investment advisor.

In contrast, a fee-only advisor keeps the best interests of the client in mind, because neither the advisor nor any related party receives compensation that is contingent upon the purchase or sale of any financial products. These advisors provide investors with comprehensive and objective financial advice for a set fee that reflects a percentage of the market value of a managed client portfolio (often 1%). Since the fee is dependent on the size of the portfolio, both the advisor and the client make more money as the portfolio grows.

12.2.2 Dimensional Fund Advisors

DFA now makes their low cost, institutional index funds available to individual investors through approved registered financial advisors. This is a great opportunity for investors because these funds were previously available only to institutional investors. DFA's funds are designed based on the principles of efficient markets, diversification, asset allocation, and the relationship between risk and return. DFA works with many of the top academic financial economists who provide findings and strategies based on empirical research. They also minimize trading

costs that adversely impact portfolio performance.

DFA funds provide investors with the following benefits:

- Engineered exposure to risk factors that generate higher expected returns
- Low expenses
- Low taxes, including tax-managed index funds
- Improved trading and engineering, adding value to portfolio construction
- Low turnover rates due to the passive investing approach
- Asset class persistence; no style drift

Index Funds Advisors (IFA) at ifa.com is one of the select RIA's approved to offer DFA funds to individual investors. IFA provides special online services and resources that educate clients on the principles of investing, including a risk capacity survey that matches individual investors with specific portfolios that yield optimal returns. This matching is achieved by carefully measuring an investor's risk capacity and risk exposure. A portfolio simulator and calculator are also provided to compare the risk and returns of all 20 portfolios to alternative investments.

12.2.3 Rebalancing Portfolios

Rebalancing a portfolio is one of the most important factors involved in achieving long-term investment goals. As explained in this 12-Step Program, it is best for an investor to hold a portfolio that matches personal risk capacity, a component that can best be measured through a risk capacity survey. For optimal returns, asset allocation within a portfolio should be based on an investor's capacity for risk. Matching investors with portfolios is a critical element to optimal investment performance.

To maintain a portfolio's asset allocation, periodic rebalancing must be done to ensure that the portfolio continues to reflect the level of risk an investor is willing or able to take. After a thorough evaluation of risk capacity, an investor may be directed to an investment allocation of 65% stocks, 35% fixed income. After a year of bull market conditions, the stock's allocation value rises to 75% with fixed-income at 25%.

This shift in asset allocation is to be expected, as asset class values change and grow at different rates. Rebalancing back to the initial allocation keeps the portfolio in balance for consistent risk exposure. In this example, the allocation would balance back to 65% stocks, 35% fixed income. Rebalancing in this particular case would entail selling some stock and buying more fixed income. The purchase of fixed income could also be accomplished by using the proceeds of the stocks sold, which may result in capital gains taxes or using additional cash on hand to invest.

Selling stocks that are performing well and buying more of the asset classes that are performing poorly is often difficult for investors, as it seems to contradict common sense. This resistance to rebalancing often leads investors to either do nothing or to sell the perceived losers and buy more of the winners, going completely against the prudent principle of rebalancing. Rebalancing often involves buying low and selling high. Many investors make the costly mistake of doing the opposite, buying high and selling low, resulting in lower returns in the long run.

In the face of a fluctuating market, it is important to maintain a portfolio's target asset allocation in order to control two important factors discussed throughout the 12-Step Program. These two factors are risk and return. Without rebalancing, portfolios will tend to become over weighted with some indexes, creating a change in risk. Rebalancing allows investors to take advantage of favorable time periods for each asset class, resulting in a steadier, less volatile performance.

A portfolio that becomes more or less risky due to lack of rebalancing also leads to less optimal returns, defeating the purpose of investing in a risk appropriate portfolio in the first place.

There are certain times when it is wise to consider changing a portfolio's target asset allocation because of a change in an investor's capacity for risk. These times include:

a. when investment goals change

b. when income level significantly changes

c. when number of dependents changes

d. at retirement

e. when life conditions change - medical emergencies, etc

f. when short-term vs. long-term expenses change

12.2.4 Rebalancing Formula

The logic behind rebalancing is that it maintains a consistent level of risk exposure. There are several rebalancing formulas that are used in the investment industry. Although rebalancing is necessary to maintain an optimal portfolio, it can incur transaction fees and expenses.

Rebalancing is recommended either, (1) annually, (2) when opportunities for new investments arise or (3) when a portfolio significantly shifts out of balance.

The Rebalancing Act

What is considered a "significant imbalance" depends on what formula is used. One common approach is the 5%/25% variance trigger. This rule states that it is time to rebalance when an asset class either, (a) moves an absolute 5% or (b) 25% from its original allocation percentage, whichever comes first.

Rebalancing among several taxable and tax-deferred accounts is a very complicated process. A highly sophisticated spreadsheet is required with many factors to be considered, such as the need for liquidity versus the need for reduced volatility. This information has a significant impact on tax liabilities generated by the placement of indexes in different accounts. Rebalancing is required each time assets are added or subtracted from the overall portfolio.

A good rule of thumb is to test a portfolio quarterly and rebalance when necessary, generally on an annual basis. In addition, an investor's risk capacity should be measured annually or when a significant life event occurs, such as a loss of a job, purchase of a home, marriage or divorce.

12.3 PROBLEMS

12.3.1 Active Investors Procrastinate

It is often said that investors procrastinate when it comes to changing their investments. Once a prudent strategy has been identified, investors need to take action and move their investments to the new strategy that meets the four acid tests of expected risk, expected return, expenses, and taxes.

12.3.2 Active Investors "Go It Alone"

A second problem is that investors get in their own way of success. As the legendary investor Benjamin Graham stated, "The investor's chief problem, and even his worst enemy, is likely to be himself." An investor may want to consider the fees paid to an index fund advisor as a casualty insurance premium, insuring the investor against himself.

12.3.3 The Media Wants Investors to Worry

The media has a propensity to alarm investors with hyped messages of gloom and doom and make people feel they need to rely on financial news shows and investment gurus for minute-to-minute updated information on the stock market. It benefits the media to have investors hooked on financial and economic news stories and articles.

This 12-Step Program teaches investors that index funds investing does not require constant vigilance, following daily returns or listening to today's star money managers. Readers have learned that prudent investing means not worrying about the ups and downs of the market. It means being able to invest and relax.

Invest in Index Mutual Funds

The primary reason to invest in index funds is that in the long run, an indexer will achieve greater risk-adjusted portfolio performance with less stress than active investors. This 12-Step Program has demonstrated how and why indexers outperform the average active investor after fees and taxes. The following reasons provide a review of the benefits of indexing.

Asset Allocation

Research has shown that asset class allocation is the most important factor in determining a portfolio's expected return level. In fact, asset allocation is 100% responsible for the variance in investment performance. Since an index fund is invested solely in the securities or fixed income positions that comprise a discrete asset class, it possesses the same rules of ownership, characteristics, and expected performance of the comparable index.

Indexing makes it easier to rebalance and maintain a consistent asset allocation over time, rather than participate in the style drift of active management. An actively managed fund generally does not stay invested in the same asset class, so it cannot reliably capture the performance of any particular asset class. Active managers often buy and sell their fund's securities due to the pressure to outperform the market, which results in high trading costs and the adverse effects of style drift.

Minimization of Investment Costs

Index funds have minimal investment costs. They do not have the high annual operating expenses of active funds. These consist mainly of investment advisory fees that compensate an active fund for its manager's efforts at stock picking and 12b-1 fees that reimburse it for its sales and marketing costs. Index funds also do not have the high trading costs characteristic of many active funds. Most of these costs are due to the efforts of active fund managers to implement their stock picking ideas to beat the market. Finally, very few index funds charge commission loads, while most active funds carry some type of load.

The investment costs associated with active funds have generally increased over the last decade, while those of index funds have decreased steadily. Although there is always the possibility that this gap will narrow in the future,

all evidence indicates just the opposite. The investment advantages of low costs do not depend on Lady Luck.

Minimization of Taxes

By maintaining low portfolio turnover, index funds minimize realized capital gains, which keep capital gains taxes low. Minimization of capital gains taxes results in a comparatively small difference between an index fund's pre-tax and after-tax performance. This makes an index fund a tax efficient investment. In fact, investing in index funds, especially tax-managed index funds, results in such low taxation that it is almost like putting your entire portfolio into an IRA. The best way for a taxable-basis investor to minimize taxes and thus more efficiently compound investment wealth is to assemble a portfolio of index funds and keep it for life.

Managers of active mutual funds typically manage money as if taxes don't matter. However, as a number of studies have shown taxes do matter. They actually have an enormous negative impact on investment performance. Investors who ignore this and invest in active funds are relinquishing money to Uncle Sam that could otherwise be available to compound into future wealth.

Reliable Investment Performance

An investor who holds a portfolio of index funds is assured of the reliable investment performance of free and efficient financial markets. An index fund invested in an asset class will always earn the returns of that asset class. Thus, indexing is an investment strategy that delivers what it promises to investors.

In comparison, the returns of active funds are erratic and less reliable than index funds, sometimes outperforming the market and sometimes underperforming it. These variations in performance are caused by the market's unpredictability. They can also result from style drift, when the fund manager modifies the fund's asset class mix.

Both U.S. and international financial markets are becoming more efficient, which indicates that investors and money managers who engage in stock picking and time picking must take greater and greater risks to beat the market. The more educated investors can gain from the efficiency of markets, the more that active money managers need to defend their investment strategies to try to beat the market.

A Simple and Understandable Investment Strategy

Because indexers recognize they cannot beat the market, they focus on building wealth over the long run by holding efficient, globally diversified portfolios. Passive investors stay with their investments and rebalance only when necessary in comparison to active investors who constantly seek ways to beat the market, spending a lot of valuable time reading investment newsletters, reports, magazines, and other media-driven publications.

An Easier Way to Track Investment Performance

Tracking the performance of index fund portfolios against their respective benchmarks is simple, since the return earned by an index fund reflects the return of the comparable index. On the other hand, the performance of active funds is more difficult to track against benchmarks. Although many funds are compared to the S&P 500, it is not an accurate comparison.

Increased Leverage and Compounding of Investment Wealth

Indexers can leverage their funds and thus more efficiently compound investment wealth. Since index funds carry no cash reserves, indexers are invested 100% in the market at all times. Indexers are also better able to leverage their funds because they can hang onto the money invested that an active investor would need to pay the commissions and high annual expenses and taxes associated with active mutual funds. Seemingly small amounts of money continually compounds through the years and helps to accelerate the accumulation of wealth for indexers.

Invest like Institutional Investors

Large institutional investors such as corporate pension plans and educational endowment funds that invest billions of dollars, can certainly afford to hire any money manager in the world. Yet, they continue to index a significant portion of their investments. Individual investors can follow the example of these institutions and reap the same benefits by investing in DFA funds.

12.4 SOLUTIONS

The 12-Step Program explained in this book has been written for investors who are engaged in any active investing practices, including stock picking, time picking, manager picking or style picking. The intention is to transform the active investors of yesterday into indexers of today through education and motivation.

This program has provided research and education about the advantages of indexing over active investing. The information that has been presented shows clearly why index funds are best for achieving investors' goals.

12.5 SUMMARY

With index funds, the stress and pressure of investing melts away, allowing the investor to receive the market returns of a diversified portfolio that is matched to risk capacity, all at a very low cost. Stepping off the emotional roller coaster of active investing, a recovering or reformed active investor experiences a new peace of mind. Instead of panicking, an indexer can calmly invest without fear or tension.

Just like with the original 12-step program, the first step is to admit you're powerless and your life has become unmanageable. In this case, the admission of powerlessness is over the market. By surrendering to the program, a walk through the 12 steps leads investors to the light of intelligent risk management and a realization that active investing is a losing game. When investors reach this pinnacle of investing insight, they are well on their way to entering what we like to call "Tradeless Nirvana" (see page 242).

Congratulations on completing the 12-Step Program! It's now time to take action, so you can invest and relax.

12.6 REVIEW QUESTIONS

1. Which is not a fundamental principle of prudent investing?

    a. stock picking
    b. the need to build efficient portfolios
    c. the importance of long-term investments
    d. passive investing with index funds
    e. diversification of assets and time.

2. Why should a portfolio be rebalanced?

    a. to keep risk exposure matched with risk capacity

    b. market changes may change the balance of the portfolio
    c an investor's financial situation or investment goals may change
    d. because all the day traders think it's a good idea
    e. a, b, and c

3. The most efficient way to invest is:

    a. pick your 5-10 favorite stocks and trade on these as frequently as possible
    b. buy the stocks that have performed the best over the last six months
    c. join an investment club
    d. invest in a globally diversified portfolio of index funds and invest for the long run
    e. invest only in Treasury bills and Certificates of Deposit

4. As opposed to relaxing, active investors:

    a. monitor the financial media
    b. worry about market declines
    c. search for the next market gain
    d. search for the next hot stock
    e. all of the above

5. By maintaining low portfolio turnover, index funds:

    a. maximize realized capital gains
    b. keep capital gains low
    c. minimize realized capital gains
    d. miss out on "hot" stocks
    e. both b and c

Tradeless Nirvana

Appendix A

TWENTY INDEX PORTFOLIOS

Matching People with Portfolios

Congratulations, you've successfully made it through the 12-Step Program for Active Investors. As this book shows, the best investment is a globaly diversified, tax-managed mix of index funds matched to an investor's unique risk capacity. An index portfolio's best long-term asset allocations for investing are divided among three broad asset classes: fixed income, U.S. stocks and foreign stocks. The simple fact is: the asset allocation of a portfolio of index funds explains virtually all of an investor's long-term expected risk and return. As was explained in Step 11, there is only one decision for investors to make: which mix of indexes is best for them?

This appendix provides supplemental information that coincides with Step 11. Twenty pre-mixed portfolios of indexes are presented here. The portfolios are labeled 5 through 100 in five-point increments. Each of the 20 portfolios can be matched with a specific risk capacity score. For example, Index Portfolio 5, which has the lowest expected risk and return, is tilted toward fixed income with a moderate investment in stocks. Conversely, Index Portfolio 100, which has the highest expected risk and return, has no fixed income and the stock indexes are tilted toward small companies and value companies in the U.S, international, and emerging markets.

The data for each portfolio consists of a list of the indexes contained in each portfolio, simulated returns and volatility data, charts that represent annual returns and growth of $1 from 1957 to 2006, annualized returns and growth of $1 matrices, 50-year rolling period analysis, and a histogram of monthly rolling periods for the time intervals matched to the average holding period for each level of risk capacity.

RISK CAPACITY 100
BRIGHT RED

Index Portfolio 100: Bright Red

Index Allocations

General Asset Class		Specific Index	
24%	US Large	12%	IFA US Large Company Index
		12%	IFA US Large Cap Value Index
40%	US Small	20%	IFA US Micro Cap Index
		20%	IFA US Small Cap Value Index
5%	Real Estate	5%	IFA Real Estate Index
18%	International	6%	IFA International Value Index
		6%	IFA International Small Company Index
		6%	IFA International Small Cap Value Index
13%	Emerging Markets	4%	IFA Emerging Markets Index
		4%	IFA Emerging Markets Value Index
		5%	IFA Emerging Markets Small Cap Index
0%	Fixed Income	0%	IFA One-Year Fixed Income Index
		0%	IFA Two-Year Global Fixed Income Index
		0%	IFA Five-Year Gov't Income Index
		0%	IFA Five-Year Global Fixed Income Index

Index Portfolio - Simulated Returns and Volatility Data*

	1yr ending 2006	1yr ending 2005	1yr ending 2004	1yr ending 2003	3yrs 2004-2006	5yrs 2002-2006	10yrs 1996-2006	25yrs 1982-2006	35yrs 1972-2006	50yrs 1957-2006	80yrs 1927-2006
Growth of $1	1.22	1.12	1.23	1.52	1.67	2.28	3.31	37.66	132.03	770.26	14,652
Annualized Return %	22.30	11.51	22.63	51.63	18.70	17.92	12.71	15.62	14.97	14.22	12.74
Annualized Volatility (Standard Deviation %)	11.08	11.18	11.89	13.62	11.14	13.87	15.57	14.13	15.30	15.37	26.59

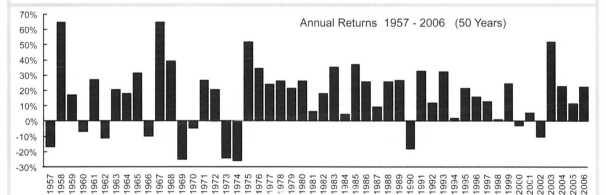

Annual Returns 1957 - 2006 (50 Years)

Growth of $1 1957 - 2006 (50 Years)
logarithmic scale

*Sources, Updates, and Disclosures: ifa.com/btp. Returns net of IFA & DFA fees. Past performance does not guarantee future results.

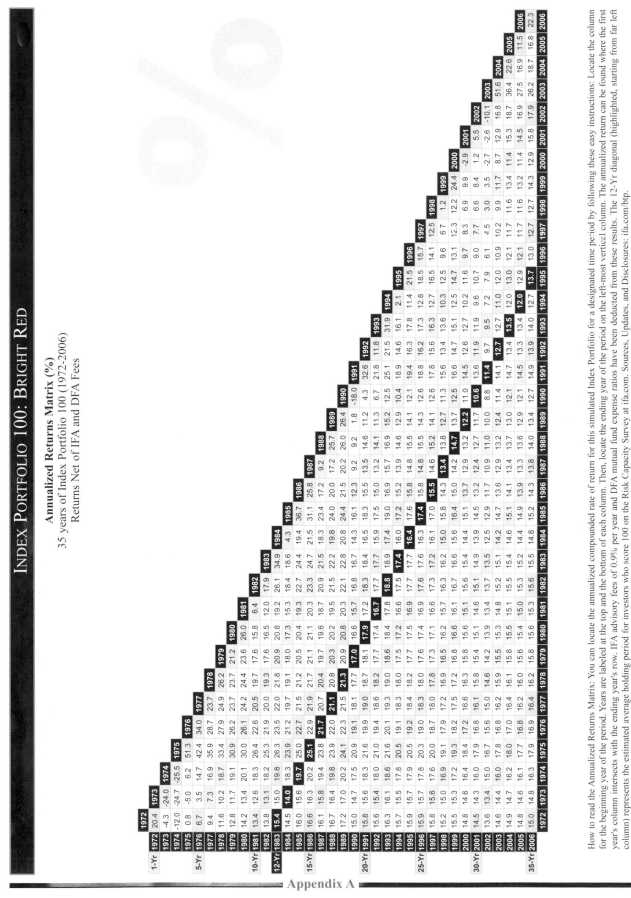

INDEX PORTFOLIO 100: BRIGHT RED

Annualized Returns Matrix (%)
35 years of Index Portfolio 100 (1972-2006)
Returns Net of IFA and DFA Fees

How to read the Annualized Returns Matrix: You can locate the annualized compounded rate of return for this simulated Index Portfolio for a designated time period by following these easy instructions: Locate the column for the beginning year of the period. Years are labeled at the top and the bottom of each column. Then, locate the ending year of the period on the left-most vertical column. The annualized return can be found where the first year's column intersects with the ending year's row. IFA advisory fees of 0.9% per year and DFA mutual fund expense ratios have been deducted from these results. The 12-Yr diagonal (highlighted, starting from far left column) represents the estimated average holding period for investors who score 100 on the Risk Capacity Survey at ifa.com. Sources, Updates, and Disclosures: ifa.com/btp.

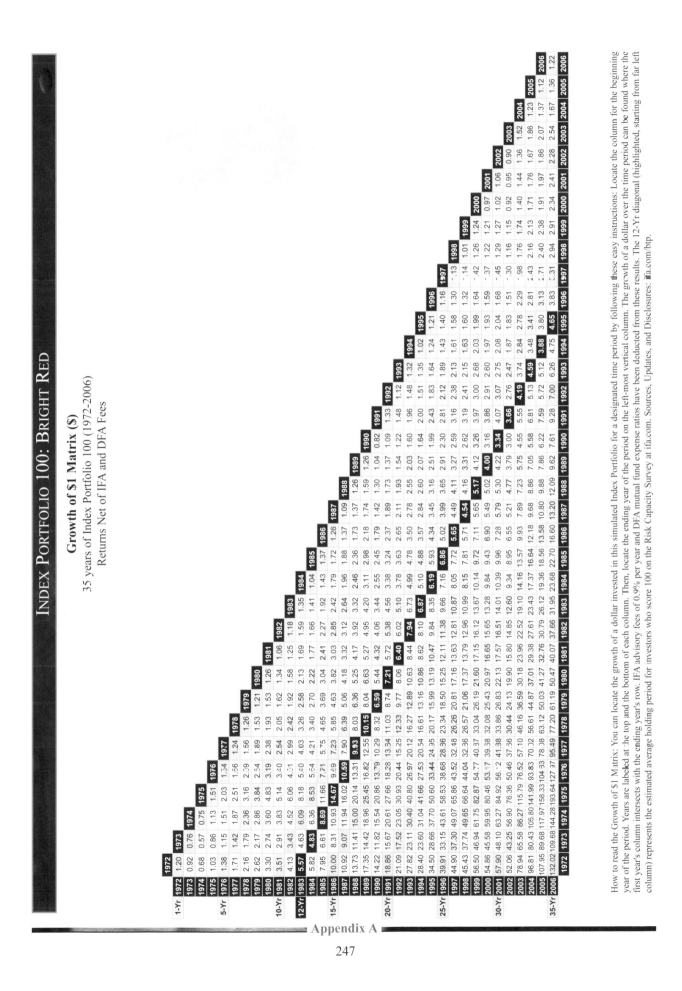

Growth of $1 Matrix ($)

35 years of Index Portfolio 100 (1972-2006)

Returns Net of IFA and DFA Fees

How to read the Growth of $1 Matrix: You can locate the growth of a dollar invested in this simulated Index Portfolio for a designated time period by following these easy instructions: Locate the column for the beginning year of the period. Years are labeled at the top and the bottom of each column. Then, locate the ending year of the period on the left-most vertical column. The growth of a dollar over the time period can be found where the first year's column intersects with the ending year's row. IFA advisory fees of 0.9% per year and DFA mutual fund expense ratios have been deducted from these results. The 12-Yr diagonal (highlighted, starting from far left column) represents the estimated average holding period for investors who score 100 on the Risk Capacity Survey at ifa.com. Sources, Updates, and Disclosures: ifa.com/btp.

Index Portfolio 100: Bright Red
Monthly Rolling Period Analysis*
Based on 50 Years (600 months) of Monthly Data
Jan 1957 to Dec 2006

Examples of 12 Year Monthly Rolling Periods**

Periods

1	Jan 57	◄— 12 Years —►	Dec 68
2	Feb 57	◄— 12 Years —►	Jan 69
3	Mar 57	◄— 12 Years —►	Feb 69
4	Apr 57	◄— 12 Years —►	Mar 69

457

Year 1957 1958 1959 1960 1961 1962 1963 1964 1965 1966 1967 1968 1969

Per Period Number of: Yrs	Months	# of Rolling Periods	Average Ann'lzd Rtn. %*	Std. Dev. of Avg. Ann'lzd Rtn. %*	Lowest Rolling Period Date	Lowest Rolling Period Return	Growth of $1 in Lowest Period	Highest Rolling Period Date	Highest Rolling Period Return	Growth of $1 in Highest Period	Average Growth of $1
0.08	1	600	1.21*	4.44*	10/87-10/87	-21.79	$0.78	1/75-1/75	26.20	$1.26	$1.01
0.25	3	598	3.76*	8.78*	9/87-11/87	-24.32	$0.43	1/75-3/75	42.21	$1.42	$1.04
0.5	6	595	7.63*	12.93*	4/74-9/74	-28.27	$0.72	1/75-6/75	59.00	$1.59	$1.08
1	12	589	15.85	18.57	10/73-9/74	-35.02	$0.65	4/03-3/04	69.39	$1.69	$1.16
2	24	577	14.96	11.79	1/73-12/74	-24.74	$0.57	12/66-11/68	52.03	$2.31	$1.62
3	36	565	14.49	8.95	1/72-12/74	-11.99	$0.68	8/84-7/87	36.02	$2.52	$1.53
4	48	553	14.28	7.42	1/71-12/74	-3.66	$0.86	10/74-9/78	34.53	$3.28	$1.75
5	60	541	14.12	6.70	11/69-10/74	-4.18	$0.81	8/82-7/87	32.62	$4.10	$2.00
6	72	529	14.15	6.00	1/69-12/74	-7.75	$0.62	1/75-12/80	30.03	$4.83	$2.30
7	84	517	14.23	5.34	1/68-12/74	-2.18	$0.86	8/82-7/89	26.64	$5.22	$2.65
8	96	505	14.28	4.81	12/68-11/76	1.72	$1.15	1/75-12/82	25.26	$6.06	$3.05
9	108	493	14.34	4.55	1/66-12/74	2.71	$1.27	1/75-12/83	26.30	$8.18	$3.53
10	120	481	14.41	4.24	1/65-12/74	5.25	$1.67	9/77-8/87	24.20	$8.73	$4.09
11	132	469	14.45	4.06	1/64-12/74	6.33	$1.96	1/75-12/85	25.02	$11.66	$4.74
12**	**144**	**457**	**14.42**	**3.85**	**1/63-12/74**	**7.44**	**$2.37**	**1/75-12/86**	**25.08**	**$14.66**	**$5.45**
13	156	445	14.42	3.72	1/62-12/74	5.89	$2.10	10/74-9/87	25.43	$19.02	$6.27
14	168	433	14.50	3.51	1/61-12/74	7.26	$2.67	1/75-12/88	23.92	$20.14	$7.26
15	180	421	14.55	3.34	1/60-12/74	6.28	$2.49	1/75-12/89	24.08	$25.44	$8.39
20	240	361	15.08	2.04	1/57-12/76	11.00	$8.06	1/75-12/94	20.50	$41.66	$17.65
30	360	241	15.08	0.87	10/68-9/98	12.88	$37.89	1/75-12/04	17.96	$141.92	$69.29
40	480	121	14.34	0.44	4/63-3/03	13.48	$157.32	1/58-12/97	15.47	$315.33	$215.38
50	600	1	14.22	0.00	1/57-12/06	14.22	$771.09	1/57-12/06	14.22	$771.09	$771.09

12 Year Monthly Rolling Periods** - Jan 1957 to Dec 2006 - 457 Monthly Rolling Periods Over 50 Years

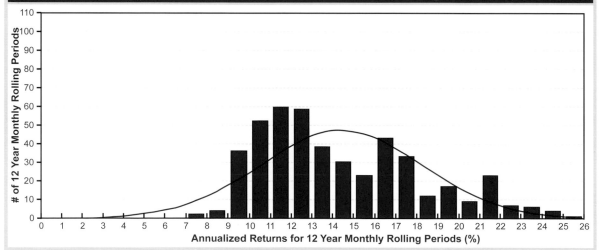

Annualized Returns for 12 Year Monthly Rolling Periods (%)

*Sources, Updates, and Disclosures: ifa.com/btp. Returns are net of IFA & DFA fees. The returns and standard deviation shown for 1, 3, and 6 month periods are not annualized. Past performance does not guarantee future results. **12 years represents the estimated average holding period for investors who score 100 on the Risk Capacity Survey at ifa.com.

RISK CAPACITY 95
YELLOW

Index Allocations

General Asset Class		Specific Index	
32%	US Large	16%	IFA US Large Company Index
		16%	IFA US Large Cap Value Index
30%	US Small	15%	IFA US Micro Cap Index
		15%	IFA US Small Cap Value Index
7.5%	Real Estate	7.5%	IFA Real Estate Index
19%	International	8%	IFA International Value Index
		5.5%	IFA International Small Company Index
		5.5%	IFA International Small Cap Value Index
11.5%	Emerging Markets	3.5%	IFA Emerging Markets Index
		3.5%	IFA Emerging Markets Value Index
		4.5%	IFA Emerging Markets Small Cap Index
0%	Fixed Income	0%	IFA One-Year Fixed Income Index
		0%	IFA Two-Year Global Fixed Income Index
		0%	IFA Five-Year Gov't Income Index
		0%	IFA Five-Year Global Fixed Income Index

Index Portfolio - Simulated Returns and Volatility Data*

	1yr ending 2006	1yr ending 2005	1yr ending 2004	1yr ending 2003	3yrs 2004-2006	5yrs 2002-2006	10yrs 1996-2006	25yrs 1982-2006	35yrs 1972-2006	50yrs 1957-2006	80yrs 1927-2006
Growth of $1	1.23	1.11	1.22	1.48	1.67	2.22	3.21	35.67	118.29	663.00	11,947
Annualized Return %	22.63	11.42	22.17	48.38	18.62	17.26	12.36	15.37	14.61	13.88	12.45
Annualized Volatility (Standard Deviation %)	10.26	10.55	11.23	13.05	10.46	13.25	14.77	13.62	14.67	14.73	25.69

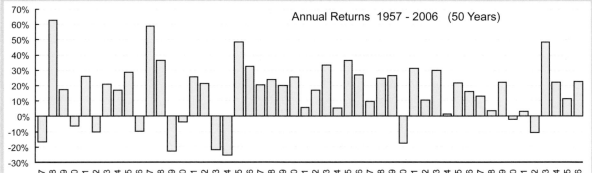

Annual Returns 1957 - 2006 (50 Years)

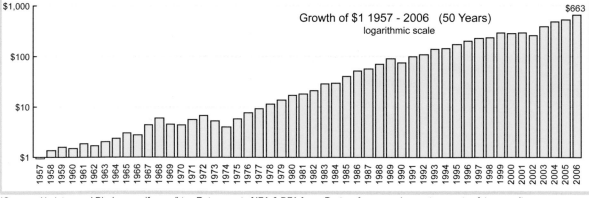

Growth of $1 1957 - 2006 (50 Years)
logarithmic scale

$663

*Sources, Updates, and Disclosures: ifa.com/btp. Returns net of IFA & DFA fees. Past performance does not guarantee future results.

INDEX PORTFOLIO 95: YELLOW

Annualized Returns Matrix (%)
35 years of Index Portfolio 95 (1972–2006)
Returns Net of IFA and DFA Fees

Each ending-year row lists the annualized return for the beginning years 1972 up to that ending year (left = begin 1972, right = 1-year return for that year).

Period	End Yr	Values (beginning year 1972 → ending year)
1-Yr	1972	21.1
	1973	-2.8 | -21.9
	1974	-10.9 | -23.6 | -25.1
	1975	1.2 | -4.6 | 5.4 | 48.4
5-Yr	1976	6.8 | 3.5 | 13.7 | 40.1 | 32.3
	1977	9.0 | 6.7 | 15.4 | 33.3 | 26.3 | 20.6
	1978	11.0 | 9.4 | 17.1 | 30.9 | 25.6 | 22.3 | 24.1
	1979	12.1 | 10.9 | 17.6 | 28.7 | 24.1 | 21.5 | 22.5 | 20.0
	1980	13.5 | 12.6 | 18.7 | 24.7 | 24.4 | 22.5 | 23.1 | 22.7 | 25.5
10-Yr	1981	12.7 | 11.8 | 17.0 | 23.1 | 21.1 | 19.0 | 18.7 | 18.3 | 15.3 | 5.9
11-Yr	1982	13.1 | 12.3 | 17.0 | 23.7 | 22.0 | 20.6 | 20.6 | 18.6 | 16.9 | 11.3 | 16.9
	1983	14.7 | 14.1 | 18.5 | 24.7 | 22.0 | 20.6 | 20.6 | 20.0 | 18.2 | 15.8 | 24.8 | 33.2
	1984	13.9 | 13.4 | 17.3 | 22.7 | 20.0 | 18.6 | 18.4 | 17.4 | 16.9 | 14.9 | 18.0 | 18.6 | 5.6
	1985	15.4 | 15.0 | 18.8 | 23.8 | 21.6 | 20.5 | 20.5 | 20.0 | 18.9 | 16.6 | 20.0 | 24.2 | 20.0 | 36.4
15-Yr	1986	16.2 | 15.8 | 19.4 | 24.1 | 21.6 | 21.1 | 21.2 | 20.8 | 20.2 | 18.7 | 23.3 | 25.0 | 23.9 | 31.7 | 27.1
	1987	15.8 | 15.8 | 18.7 | 22.3 | 21.0 | 20.1 | 20.0 | 19.6 | 19.5 | 18.2 | 21.0 | 21.8 | 19.1 | 23.9 | 18.2 | 9.8
	1988	16.3 | 16.0 | 19.1 | 23.1 | 21.3 | 20.5 | 20.4 | 20.1 | 20.1 | 19.4 | 21.5 | 22.3 | 20.2 | 24.2 | 20.4 | 17.1 | 24.9
	1989	16.8 | 16.6 | 19.5 | 23.3 | 21.7 | 20.9 | 20.7 | 20.1 | 20.7 | 20.2 | 22.1 | 22.9 | 21.3 | 24.7 | 21.9 | 20.2 | 25.7 | 26.6
	1990	14.7 | 14.4 | 17.0 | 20.3 | 18.6 | 17.7 | 17.5 | 16.9 | 16.6 | 15.8 | 17.0 | 17.0 | 14.8 | 16.4 | 12.8 | 9.5 | 11.2 | 2.3 | -17.3
20-Yr	1991	15.5 | 15.2 | 17.7 | 20.9 | 19.4 | 18.5 | 18.4 | 18.0 | 17.8 | 17.1 | 18.3 | 18.5 | 16.7 | 18.4 | 15.7 | 13.5 | 14.5 | 11.2 | 4.2 | 31.3
	1992	15.3 | 15.0 | 17.3 | 20.3 | 18.8 | 18.0 | 17.9 | 17.4 | 17.1 | 16.6 | 17.6 | 17.7 | 16.0 | 17.4 | 13.0 | 13.7 | 13.1 | 6.3 | 11.8 | 20.5 | 9.8
	1993	15.9 | 15.6 | 17.9 | 20.8 | 19.4 | 18.7 | 18.6 | 18.2 | 18.1 | 17.6 | 18.6 | 18.7 | 17.4 | 18.8 | 16.3 | 15.3 | 16.3 | 14.6 | 11.8 | 23.6 | 19.9 | 30.1
	1994	15.2 | 15.0 | 17.1 | 19.7 | 18.4 | 17.7 | 17.5 | 17.1 | 16.9 | 16.3 | 17.2 | 17.2 | 15.8 | 16.9 | 14.9 | 13.5 | 14.0 | 12.3 | 9.6 | 17.7 | 13.4 | 14.9 | 1.5
	1995	15.5 | 15.3 | 17.3 | 19.9 | 18.6 | 17.9 | 17.7 | 17.4 | 17.2 | 16.7 | 17.5 | 17.5 | 16.3 | 17.4 | 15.6 | 14.4 | 15.0 | 13.6 | 11.6 | 18.5 | 15.5 | 17.2 | 11.2 | 21.9
25-Yr	1996	15.5 | 15.3 | 17.3 | 19.7 | 18.5 | 17.8 | 17.7 | 17.4 | 17.2 | 16.7 | 17.4 | 17.3 | 16.3 | 17.3 | 15.5 | 14.6 | 15.0 | 13.6 | 12.3 | 18.5 | 15.6 | 17.2 | 12.9 | 19.0 | 16.2
	1997	15.4 | 15.2 | 17.1 | 19.4 | 18.2 | 17.6 | 17.4 | 17.2 | 16.7 | 16.5 | 17.2 | 17.2 | 16.1 | 17.0 | 15.4 | 14.6 | 14.9 | 13.9 | 12.4 | 18.1 | 15.6 | 16.2 | 12.9 | 19.0 | 16.2 | 13.2
	1998	15.0 | 14.7 | 16.5 | 18.7 | 17.5 | 16.9 | 16.7 | 16.3 | 16.2 | 15.7 | 16.3 | 16.3 | 15.2 | 15.9 | 14.5 | 13.5 | 13.8 | 12.8 | 11.3 | 15.6 | 13.5 | 14.0 | 11.0 | 13.5 | 10.8 | 14.7 | 3.5
	1999	15.2 | 15.0 | 16.7 | 18.8 | 17.7 | 17.1 | 17.0 | 16.6 | 16.5 | 16.0 | 16.6 | 16.6 | 15.6 | 16.3 | 15.0 | 14.1 | 14.5 | 13.6 | 12.4 | 16.3 | 14.5 | 15.1 | 12.8 | 15.2 | 13.6 | 12.7 | 8.2 | 22.1
	2000	14.6 | 14.4 | 16.0 | 17.9 | 17.0 | 16.3 | 16.1 | 15.7 | 15.5 | 15.1 | 15.6 | 15.5 | 14.5 | 15.0 | 13.8 | 12.9 | 13.1 | 12.2 | 11.0 | 14.3 | 12.6 | 12.8 | 10.6 | 12.1 | 10.3 | 8.8 | 7.4 | 9.5 | -1.9
30-Yr	2001	14.2 | 13.9 | 15.5 | 17.4 | 16.1 | 15.7 | 15.5 | 15.2 | 14.5 | 14.5 | 15.0 | 14.9 | 13.8 | 14.4 | 13.1 | 12.2 | 12.4 | 11.5 | 10.3 | 13.2 | 11.6 | 11.7 | 9.6 | 10.8 | 9.1 | 7.7 | 6.3 | 7.3 | 0.6 | 3.1
	2002	13.3 | 13.0 | 14.6 | 16.2 | 15.2 | 14.6 | 14.3 | 13.9 | 13.7 | 13.2 | 13.5 | 13.4 | 12.4 | 12.8 | 11.6 | 10.7 | 10.7 | 9.8 | 8.6 | 11.1 | 9.4 | 9.3 | 7.2 | 7.9 | 6.0 | 4.4 | 2.7 | 2.5 | -3.3 | -3.9 | -10.5
	2003	14.2 | 14.0 | 15.7 | 17.2 | 15.5 | 15.7 | 15.5 | 15.2 | 15.0 | 14.5 | 14.8 | 14.8 | 14.0 | 13.3 | 12.6 | 12.6 | 12.8 | 12.0 | 11.0 | 13.6 | 12.2 | 12.3 | 10.7 | 11.8 | 10.6 | 9.8 | 9.2 | 10.4 | 7.7 | 11.1 | 15.3 | 48.4
	2004	14.5 | 14.3 | 15.7 | 17.4 | 16.4 | 15.7 | 15.4 | 15.2 | 14.8 | 14.5 | 15.2 | 14.4 | 14.0 | 13.8 | 13.1 | 13.3 | 13.3 | 12.6 | 11.7 | 14.1 | 12.9 | 13.1 | 11.7 | 12.8 | 11.8 | 11.3 | 11.0 | 12.3 | 10.4 | 13.7 | 17.5 | 34.6 | 22.2
	2005	14.4 | 14.2 | 15.6 | 17.2 | 15.3 | 15.7 | 15.3 | 15.1 | 14.7 | 14.3 | 15.0 | 14.2 | 14.2 | 13.7 | 13.0 | 13.2 | 13.2 | 12.5 | 11.7 | 14.0 | 13.0 | 13.0 | 11.7 | 12.6 | 11.8 | 11.3 | 11.0 | 12.2 | 10.6 | 13.3 | 16.0 | 26.4 | 16.7 | 11.4
35-Yr	2006	14.6 | 14.4 | 15.8 | 16.5 | 16.0 | 15.5 | 15.3 | 15.0 | 14.7 | 14.0 | 15.4 | 14.6 | 14.2 | 14.0 | 13.5 | 13.7 | 13.7 | 12.3 | 12.3 | 14.5 | 13.4 | 13.7 | 12.5 | 13.4 | 12.7 | 12.4 | 12.3 | 13.4 | 12.2 | 14.8 | 17.3 | 25.5 | 18.6 | 16.9 | 22.6

Column labels (beginning/ending year) run: 1972 1973 1974 1975 1976 1977 1978 1979 1980 1981 1982 1983 1984 1985 1986 1987 1988 1989 1990 1991 1992 1993 1994 1995 1996 1997 1998 1999 2000 2001 2002 2003 2004 2005 2006

How to read the Annualized Returns Matrix: You can locate the annualized compounded rate of return for this simulated Index Portfolio for a designated time per od by following these easy instructions: Locate the column for the beginning year of the period. Years are labeled at the top and the bottom of each column. Then, locate the row for the ending year of the period on the left-most vertical column. The annualized return can be found where the first year's column intersects with the ending year's row. IFA adv sory fees of 0.9% per year and DFA mutual fund expense ratios have been deducted from these results. The 11-Yr diagonal (highlighted, starting from far left column) represents the estimated average holding period for investors who score 95 on the Risk Capacity Survey at ifa.com. Sources, Updates, and Disclosures: ifa.com/btp.

INDEX PORTFOLIO 95: YELLOW

Growth of $1 Matrix ($)
35 years of Index Portfolio 95 (1972-2006)
Returns Net of IFA and DFA Fees

	Yr	1972	1973	1974	1975	1976	1977	1978	1979	1980	1981	1982	1983	1984	1985	1986	1987	1988	1989	1990	1991	1992	1993	1994	1995	1996	1997	1998	1999	2000	2001	2002	2003	2004	2005	2006
1-Yr	1972	1.21																																		
	1973	0.95	0.78																																	
	1974	0.71	0.58	0.75																																
	1975	1.05	0.87	1.11	1.48																															
5-Yr	1976	1.39	1.15	1.47	1.96	1.32																														
	1977	1.68	1.38	1.77	2.37	1.60	1.21																													
	1978	2.08	1.72	2.20	2.94	1.98	1.50	1.24																												
	1979	2.50	2.06	2.64	3.53	2.37	1.80	1.49	1.20																											
	1980	3.13	2.58	3.31	4.42	2.98	2.25	1.87	1.51	1.25																										
10-Yr	1981	3.32	2.74	3.51	4.69	3.16	2.39	1.98	1.59	1.33	1.06																									
11-Yr	1982	3.88	3.20	4.10	5.48	3.69	2.79	2.31	1.86	1.55	1.24	1.17																								
	1983	5.17	4.27	5.46	7.30	4.92	3.72	3.08	2.48	2.07	1.65	1.56	1.33																							
	1984	5.45	4.50	5.77	7.71	5.19	3.92	3.25	2.62	2.19	1.74	1.64	1.41	1.06																						
	1985	7.44	6.14	7.87	10.51	7.08	5.35	4.44	3.58	2.98	2.38	2.24	1.92	1.44	1.36																					
15-Yr	1986	9.46	7.81	10.00	13.36	9.00	6.80	5.64	4.55	3.79	3.02	2.85	2.44	1.83	1.73	1.27																				
	1987	10.38	8.57	10.98	14.67	9.88	7.47	6.19	4.99	4.16	3.32	3.13	2.68	2.01	1.90	1.40	1.10																			
	1988	12.97	10.71	13.72	18.33	12.35	9.33	7.74	6.24	5.20	4.14	3.91	3.34	2.51	2.38	1.74	1.37	1.25																		
	1989	16.42	13.56	17.37	23.20	15.63	11.81	9.80	7.90	6.58	5.25	4.95	4.23	3.18	3.01	2.21	1.74	1.58	1.27																	
	1990	13.58	11.21	14.36	19.18	12.92	9.77	8.10	6.53	5.44	4.34	4.09	3.50	2.63	2.49	1.83	1.44	1.31	1.05	0.83																
20-Yr	1991	17.83	14.72	18.86	25.19	16.97	12.83	10.64	8.57	7.15	5.70	5.38	4.60	3.45	3.27	2.40	1.89	1.72	1.37	1.09	1.31															
	1992	19.71	16.27	20.84	27.84	18.76	14.18	11.76	9.48	7.90	6.30	5.94	5.08	3.81	3.61	2.65	2.08	1.90	1.52	1.20	1.45	1.11														
	1993	25.64	21.17	27.12	36.22	24.40	18.45	15.29	12.33	10.27	8.19	7.73	6.61	4.96	4.70	3.45	2.71	2.47	1.98	1.56	1.89	1.44	1.30													
	1994	26.03	21.49	27.53	36.77	24.77	18.72	15.52	12.51	10.43	8.31	7.85	6.71	5.04	4.77	3.50	2.75	2.51	2.01	1.58	1.92	1.46	1.32	1.02												
	1995	31.72	26.19	33.55	44.82	30.19	22.82	18.92	15.25	12.71	10.13	9.57	8.18	6.14	5.82	4.26	3.36	3.05	2.45	1.93	2.34	1.78	1.61	1.24	1.22											
25-Yr	1996	36.87	30.44	39.00	52.09	35.09	26.53	21.99	17.73	14.78	11.78	11.12	9.51	7.14	6.76	4.96	3.90	3.55	2.84	2.25	2.72	2.07	1.87	1.44	1.42	1.16										
	1997	41.75	34.47	44.16	58.98	39.74	30.04	24.90	20.07	16.73	13.34	12.59	10.77	8.08	7.66	5.61	4.42	4.02	3.22	2.54	3.07	2.34	2.12	1.63	1.60	1.32	1.13									
	1998	43.20	35.66	45.68	61.03	41.11	31.08	25.77	20.77	17.31	13.80	13.02	11.14	8.36	7.92	5.81	4.57	4.16	3.33	2.63	3.18	2.42	2.19	1.68	1.66	1.36	1.17	1.03								
	1999	52.76	43.56	55.80	74.54	50.21	37.96	31.47	25.37	21.14	16.85	15.91	13.60	10.21	9.67	7.09	5.58	5.08	4.07	3.21	3.89	2.96	2.68	2.06	2.03	1.66	1.43	1.26	1.22							
	2000	51.75	42.72	54.73	73.11	49.25	37.23	30.87	24.88	20.74	16.53	15.60	13.34	10.01	9.49	6.96	5.47	4.98	3.99	3.15	3.81	2.90	2.63	2.02	1.99	1.63	1.40	1.24	1.20	0.98						
30-Yr	2001	53.36	44.05	56.43	75.38	50.78	38.39	31.83	25.65	21.38	17.04	16.09	13.76	10.33	9.78	7.17	5.64	5.14	4.11	3.25	3.93	2.99	2.71	2.08	2.05	1.68	1.45	1.28	1.24	1.01	1.03					
	2002	47.76	39.43	50.51	67.48	45.46	34.36	28.49	22.97	19.14	15.26	14.40	12.32	9.24	8.76	6.42	5.05	4.60	3.68	2.91	3.52	2.68	2.42	1.86	1.84	1.51	1.30	1.14	1.11	0.91	0.92	0.90				
	2003	70.87	58.51	74.95	100.13	67.45	50.99	42.27	34.08	28.40	22.64	21.37	18.27	13.72	12.99	9.53	7.50	6.82	5.46	4.32	5.22	3.97	3.60	2.76	2.72	2.23	1.92	1.70	1.64	1.34	1.37	1.33	1.48			
	2004	86.58	71.48	91.57	122.32	82.41	62.29	51.65	41.63	34.70	27.66	26.11	22.33	16.76	15.88	11.64	9.16	8.34	6.67	5.27	6.38	4.86	4.39	3.38	3.33	2.73	2.35	2.07	2.00	1.64	1.67	1.62	1.81	1.22		
	2005	96.47	79.64	102.03	136.29	91.82	69.41	57.55	46.39	38.66	30.82	29.09	24.88	18.67	17.69	12.97	10.20	9.29	7.44	5.87	7.10	5.41	4.89	3.76	3.71	3.04	2.62	2.31	2.23	1.83	1.86	1.81	2.02	1.36	1.11	
35-Yr	2006	118.30	97.67	125.12	167.14	112.59	85.11	70.57	56.88	47.41	37.79	35.67	30.51	22.89	21.69	15.90	12.51	11.39	9.12	7.20	8.71	6.64	6.00	4.61	4.55	3.73	3.21	2.83	2.74	2.24	2.29	2.22	2.48	1.67	1.37	1.23
		1972	1973	1974	1975	1976	1977	1978	1979	1980	1981	1982	1983	1984	1985	1986	1987	1988	1989	1990	1991	1992	1993	1994	1995	1996	1997	1998	1999	2000	2001	2002	2003	2004	2005	2006

How to read the Growth of $1 Matrix: You can locate the growth of a dollar invested in this simulated Index Portfolio for a designated time period by following these easy instructions: Locate the column for the beginning year of the period. Years are labeled at the top and the bottom of each column. Then, locate the ending year of the period on the left-most vertical column. The growth of a dollar over the time period can be found where the first year's column intersects with the ending year's row. IFA advisory fees of 0.9% per year and DFA mutual fund expense ratios have been deducted from these results. The 11-Yr diagonal (highlighted, starting from far left column) represents the estimated average holding period for investors who score 95 on the Risk Capacity Survey at ifa.com. Sources, Updates, and Disclosures: Ifa.com/btp.

Index Portfolio 95: Yellow

Monthly Rolling Period Analysis*
Based on 50 years (600 months) of Monthly Data
Jan 1957 to Dec 2006

Examples of 11 Year Monthly Rolling Periods**

Periods

1	Jan 57	← 11 Years →	Dec 67
2	Feb 57	← 11 Years →	Jan 68
3	Mar 57	← 11 Years →	Feb 68
4	Apr 57	← 11 Years →	Mar 68

469

Year 1957　1958　1959　1960　1961　1962　1963　1964　1965　1966　1967　1968　1969

Per Period Number of: Yrs	Months	# of Rolling Periods	Average Ann'lzd Rtn. %*	Std. Dev. of Avg. Ann'lzd Rtn. %*	Lowest Rolling Period Date	Lowest Rolling Period Return	Growth of $1 in Lowest Period	Highest Rolling Period Date	Highest Rolling Period Return	Growth of $1 in Highest Period	Average Growth of $1
0.08	1	600	1.18*	4.25*	10/87-10/87	-21.01	$0.79	1/75-1/75	24.38	$1.24	$1.01
0.25	3	598	3.65*	8.35*	9/87-11/87	-23.75	$0.76	1/75-3/75	39.22	$1.39	$1.04
0.5	6	595	7.40*	12.33*	4/74-9/74	-28.03	$0.72	1/75-6/75	54.78	$1.55	$1.07
1	12	589	15.36	17.67	10/73-9/74	-34.74	$0.65	4/03-3/04	65.06	$1.65	$1.15
2	24	577	14.55	11.23	1/73-12/74	-23.56	$0.58	12/66-11/68	48.02	$2.19	$1.60
3	36	565	14.10	8.50	1/72-12/74	-10.88	$0.71	8/84-7/87	36.64	$2.55	$1.51
4	48	553	13.90	7.03	1/71-12/74	-2.88	$0.89	7/82-6/86	32.46	$3.08	$1.72
5	60	541	13.76	6.36	11/69-10/74	-3.28	$0.85	8/82-7/87	32.72	$4.12	$1.96
6	72	529	13.79	5.72	1/69-12/74	-6.67	$0.66	1/75-12/80	28.12	$4.42	$2.25
7	84	517	13.87	5.11	1/68-12/74	-1.46	$0.90	8/82-7/89	26.72	$5.25	$2.59
8	96	505	13.93	4.62	12/68-11/76	2.21	$1.19	8/82-7/90	23.84	$5.53	$2.97
9	108	493	13.99	4.40	1/66-12/74	2.87	$1.29	1/75-12/83	24.72	$7.30	$3.43
10	120	481	14.06	4.12	1/65-12/74	5.21	$1.66	9/77-8/87	23.63	$8.34	$3.96
11**	**132**	**469**	**14.10**	**3.96**	**1/64-12/74**	**6.24**	**$1.95**	**1/75-12/85**	**23.84**	**$10.51**	**$4.57**
12	144	457	14.08	3.77	1/63-12/74	7.38	$2.35	1/75-12/86	24.11	$13.36	$5.24
13	156	445	14.08	3.64	1/62-12/74	5.91	$2.11	10/74-9/87	24.62	$17.48	$6.02
14	168	433	14.16	3.45	1/61-12/74	7.24	$2.66	1/75-12/88	23.09	$18.33	$6.94
15	180	421	14.21	3.28	1/60-12/74	6.27	$2.49	1/75-12/89	23.32	$23.20	$8.00
20	240	361	14.72	2.00	1/57-12/76	10.81	$7.79	10/74-9/94	19.75	$36.77	$16.53
30	360	241	14.71	0.80	10/68-9/98	12.81	$37.19	1/75-12/04	17.38	$122.41	$62.75
40	480	121	14.00	0.43	4/63-3/03	13.13	$139.03	1/58-12/97	15.13	$280.25	$190.93
50	600	1	13.88	0.00	1/57-12/06	13.88	$664.31	1/57-12/06	13.88	$664.31	$664.31

11 Year Monthly Rolling Periods** - Jan 1957 to Dec 2006 - 469 Monthly Rolling Periods Over 50 Years

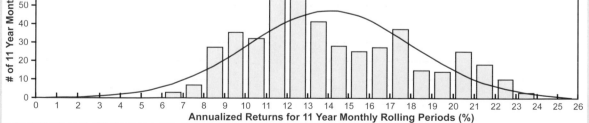

Annualized Returns for 11 Year Monthly Rolling Periods (%)

*Sources, Updates, and Disclosures: ifa.com/btp. Returns are net of IFA & DFA fees. The returns and standard deviation shown for 1, 3, and 6 month periods are not annualized. Past performance does not guarantee future results. **11 years represents the estimated average holding period for investors who score 95 on the Risk Capacity Survey at ifa.com.

RISK CAPACITY 90
GOLD

Index Portfolio 90: Gold

Index Allocations

General Asset Class		Specific Index	
40%	US Large	20%	IFA US Large Company Index
		20%	IFA US Large Cap Value Index
20%	US Small	10%	IFA US Micro Cap Index
		10%	IFA US Small Cap Value Index
10%	Real Estate	10%	IFA Real Estate Index
		10%	IFA International Value Index
20%	International	5%	IFA International Small Company Index
		5%	IFA International Small Cap Value Index
		3%	IFA Emerging Markets Index
10%	Emerging Markets	3%	IFA Emerging Markets Value Index
		4%	IFA Emerging Markets Small Cap Index
		0%	IFA One-Year Fixed Income Index
0%	Fixed Income	0%	IFA Two-Year Global Fixed Income Index
		0%	IFA Five-Year Gov't Income Index
		0%	IFA Five-Year Global Fixed Income Index

Index Portfolio - Simulated Returns and Volatility Data*

	1yr ending 2006	1yr ending 2005	1yr ending 2004	1yr ending 2003	3yrs 2004-2006	5yrs 2002-2006	10yrs 1996-2006	25yrs 1982-2006	35yrs 1972-2006	50yrs 1957-2006	80yrs 1927-2006
Growth of $1	1.23	1.11	1.22	1.45	1.67	2.15	3.10	33.68	105.40	565.71	9,568
Annualized Return %	22.96	11.32	21.70	45.14	18.54	16.59	11.99	15.10	14.23	13.51	12.14
Annualized Volatility (Standard Deviation %)	9.44	9.95	10.62	12.50	9.81	12.67	14.10	13.20	14.11	14.15	24.85

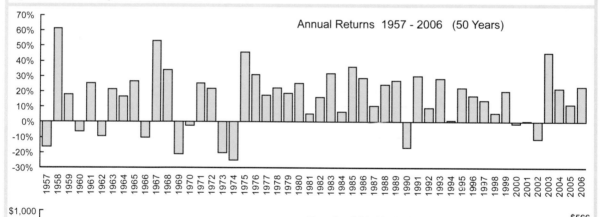

Annual Returns 1957 - 2006 (50 Years)

Growth of $1 1957 - 2006 (50 Years)
logarithmic scale

$566

*Sources, Updates, and Disclosures: ifa.com/btp. Returns net of IFA & DFA fees. Past performance does not guarantee future results.

INDEX PORTFOLIO 90: GOLD

Annualized Returns Matrix (%)
35 years of Index Portfolio 90 (1972–2006)
Returns Net of IFA and DFA Fees

%

End \ Begin	1972	1973	1974	1975	1976	1977	1978	1979	1980	1981	1982	1983	1984	1985	1986	1987	1988	1989	1990	1991	1992	1993	1994	1995	1996	1997	1998	1999	2000	2001	2002	2003	2004	2005	2006
1-Yr 1972	21.9																																		
1973	-1.2	-19.9																																	
1974	-9.8	-22.4	-24.8																																
1975	1.7	-4.3	4.6	45.6																															
5-Yr 1976	6.9	3.4	12.6	37.9	30.6																														
1977	8.6	6.1	13.8	30.7	23.9	17.5																													
1978	10.4	8.6	15.4	28.5	23.2	19.7	22.0																												
1979	11.4	10.0	16.0	26.5	22.1	19.4	20.3	18.7																											
1980	12.8	11.8	17.2	26.2	22.7	20.8	21.9	21.8	25.0																										
10-Yr 1981	12.1	11.0	15.7	23.0	19.6	17.5	17.6	16.1	14.8	5.5																									
1982	12.4	11.5	15.7	22.1	19.1	17.3	17.2	16.1	15.2	10.6	16.0																								
1983	13.9	13.2	17.2	23.1	20.6	19.2	19.5	19.0	19.1	17.2	23.3	31.6																							
1984	13.4	12.7	16.2	21.4	19.0	17.6	17.6	16.9	16.5	14.5	17.7	18.5	6.8																						
1985	14.8	14.3	17.8	22.7	20.6	19.5	19.8	19.5	19.6	18.5	22.0	24.1	20.5	36.1																					
15-Yr 1986	15.7	15.3	18.6	23.1	21.3	20.4	20.7	20.6	20.8	20.1	23.3	25.2	23.1	32.2	28.5																				
1987	15.4	14.9	17.9	22.1	20.3	19.4	19.6	19.4	19.5	18.7	22.1	22.1	19.1	24.5	19.1	10.4																			
1988	15.9	15.5	18.2	22.3	20.6	19.8	20.0	19.8	20.0	19.4	22.4	22.4	20.7	24.4	20.8	14.3	24.1																		
1989	16.4	16.1	18.9	22.5	21.0	20.3	20.5	20.4	20.6	20.1	22.2	23.0	22.2	24.9	22.2	17.1	25.5	26.6																	
1990	14.4	14.0	16.4	19.6	18.1	17.2	17.2	16.8	16.6	15.8	17.1	17.2	15.3	16.7	13.2	9.7	9.5	2.8	-16.6																
20-Yr 1991	15.2	14.8	17.1	20.2	18.8	18.0	18.1	17.8	17.7	17.1	18.3	18.6	17.0	18.5	15.9	13.5	14.3	11.1	4.1	30.0															
1992	14.9	14.5	16.7	19.6	18.2	17.5	17.5	17.2	17.0	16.4	17.2	17.6	16.1	17.3	14.9	12.8	13.3	10.7	5.8	19.2	9.3														
1993	15.4	15.1	17.3	20.0	18.7	18.1	17.9	17.9	17.8	17.3	18.3	18.5	17.3	18.5	16.5	14.9	15.7	14.0	11.0	22.1	18.4	28.3													
1994	14.8	14.5	16.4	19.0	17.7	17.1	17.0	16.7	16.6	16.0	16.9	17.0	15.7	16.6	14.7	13.0	13.4	11.7	8.9	16.5	12.3	13.8	0.9												
1995	15.1	14.8	16.7	19.1	18.0	17.3	17.3	17.0	16.9	16.4	17.0	17.1	16.2	17.1	15.4	14.0	14.5	13.2	11.1	17.6	14.7	16.6	11.1	22.3											
25-Yr 1996	15.1	14.9	16.7	19.0	17.9	17.3	17.3	17.0	16.9	16.4	17.1	17.1	16.3	17.1	15.5	14.3	14.8	13.6	11.9	17.5	15.1	16.6	13.0	19.5	16.8										
1997	15.1	14.8	16.6	18.8	17.7	17.1	17.1	16.9	16.8	16.3	17.0	17.1	16.1	16.9	15.4	14.3	14.6	13.6	12.1	17.0	14.9	16.1	13.2	17.6	15.3	13.9									
1998	14.7	14.5	16.1	18.2	17.2	16.6	16.5	16.3	16.2	15.7	16.3	16.6	15.4	16.0	14.6	13.5	13.8	12.8	11.4	15.5	13.6	14.3	11.7	14.5	12.1	9.8	5.7								
1999	14.9	14.7	16.3	18.3	17.3	16.7	16.7	16.5	16.3	15.9	16.5	16.5	15.7	16.3	15.0	14.0	14.3	13.4	12.2	16.0	14.3	15.1	13.0	15.6	13.9	13.0	12.6	19.9							
2000	14.3	14.1	15.6	17.5	16.5	15.9	15.9	15.6	15.5	15.0	15.5	15.5	14.6	15.1	13.8	12.9	13.1	12.2	10.9	14.2	12.5	12.9	10.9	12.7	10.8	9.4	7.9	9.0	-0.9						
30-Yr 2001	13.8	13.6	15.0	16.8	15.8	15.3	15.2	14.9	14.7	14.3	14.7	14.7	13.8	14.2	13.0	12.0	12.1	11.3	10.1	12.9	11.3	11.5	9.6	10.9	9.1	7.6	6.0	6.1	-0.1	0.7					
2002	13.0	12.7	14.0	15.7	14.7	14.2	14.0	13.7	13.5	13.0	13.4	13.2	12.3	12.6	11.4	10.4	10.4	9.5	8.3	10.7	9.1	9.0	7.1	7.9	6.0	4.3	2.4	1.6	-3.8	-5.3	-10.9				
2003	13.8	13.6	14.9	16.6	15.7	15.2	15.1	14.8	14.7	14.2	14.6	14.9	13.8	14.2	13.0	12.2	12.3	11.6	10.6	13.0	11.7	11.9	10.4	11.5	10.2	9.3	8.5	9.1	6.6	9.2	13.7	45.1			
2004	14.1	13.8	15.1	16.8	15.9	15.4	15.3	15.1	14.9	14.5	14.9	14.9	14.1	14.5	13.5	12.7	12.8	12.2	11.3	13.6	12.4	12.7	11.4	12.5	11.4	10.8	10.3	11.1	9.4	12.2	16.3	32.9	21.7		
2005	14.0	13.8	15.0	16.6	15.7	15.3	15.2	14.9	14.8	14.4	14.8	14.7	14.0	14.4	13.4	12.6	12.8	12.1	11.3	13.4	12.3	12.6	11.4	12.4	11.4	10.8	10.5	11.1	9.8	12.0	15.1	25.3	16.4	11.3	
35-Yr 2006	14.2	14.0	15.2	16.8	16.0	15.5	15.4	15.2	15.1	14.7	15.1	15.1	14.4	14.7	13.8	13.1	13.3	12.7	11.9	14.0	13.0	13.3	12.2	13.2	12.4	12.0	11.8	12.6	11.6	13.8	16.6	24.7	18.5	17.0	23.0
	1972	1973	1974	1975	1976	1977	1978	1979	1980	1981	1982	1983	1984	1985	1986	1987	1988	1989	1990	1991	1992	1993	1994	1995	1996	1997	1998	1999	2000	2001	2002	2003	2004	2005	2006

How to read the Annualized Returns Matrix: You can locate the annualized compounded rate of return for this simulated Index Portfolio for a designated time period by following these easy instructions: Locate the column for the beginning year of the period. Years are labeled at the top and the bottom of each column. Then, locate the ending year of the period on the left-most vertical column. The annualized return can be found where the first year's column intersects with the ending year's row. IFA advisory fees of 0.9% per year and DFA mutual fund expense ratios have been deducted from these results. The 10-Yr diagonal (highlighted, starting from far left column) represents the estimated average holding period for investors who score 90 on the Risk Capacity Survey at ifa.com. Sources, Updates, and Disclosures: ifa.com/btp.

INDEX PORTFOLIO 90: GOLD

Growth of $1 Matrix ($)
35 years of Index Portfolio 100 (1972–2006)
Returns Net of IFA and DFA Fees

	1972	1973	1974	1975	1976	1977	1978	1979	1980	1981	1982	1983	1984	1985	1986	1987	1988	1989	1990	1991	1992	1993	1994	1995	1996	1997	1998	1999	2000	2001	2002	2003	2004	2005	2006
1-Yr 1972	1.22																																		
1973	0.98	0.80																																	
1974	0.73	0.60	0.75																																
1975	1.07	0.88	1.09	1.46																															
5-Yr 1976	1.40	1.14	1.43	1.90	1.31																														
1977	1.64	1.35	1.68	2.23	1.53	1.18																													
1978	2.00	1.64	2.05	2.72	1.87	1.43	1.22																												
1979	2.37	1.95	2.43	3.23	2.22	1.70	1.45	1.19																											
1980	2.97	2.43	3.04	4.04	2.78	2.13	1.81	1.48	1.25																										
10-Yr 1981	3.13	2.57	3.21	4.26	2.93	2.24	1.91	1.56	1.32	1.05																									
1982	3.63	2.98	3.72	4.95	3.40	2.60	2.21	1.82	1.53	1.22	1.16																								
1983	4.78	3.92	4.89	6.51	4.47	3.42	2.91	2.39	2.01	1.61	1.53	1.32																							
1984	5.10	4.19	5.23	6.95	4.77	3.66	3.11	2.55	2.15	1.72	1.63	1.40	1.07																						
1985	6.94	5.70	7.11	9.46	6.50	4.97	4.23	3.47	2.92	2.34	2.22	1.91	1.45	1.36																					
15-Yr 1986	8.92	7.32	9.14	12.15	8.34	6.39	5.44	4.46	3.76	3.01	2.85	2.46	1.87	1.75	1.28																				
1987	9.85	8.08	10.09	13.41	9.21	7.06	6.00	4.92	4.15	3.32	3.15	2.71	2.06	1.93	1.42	1.10																			
1988	12.22	10.03	12.52	16.65	11.44	8.76	7.45	6.11	5.15	4.12	3.90	3.37	2.56	2.40	1.76	1.37	1.24																		
1989	15.50	12.71	15.88	21.11	14.50	11.11	9.45	7.75	6.53	5.22	4.95	4.27	3.24	3.04	2.23	1.74	1.57	1.27																	
1990	12.93	10.61	13.24	17.61	12.10	9.26	7.88	6.46	5.44	4.36	4.13	3.56	2.71	2.53	1.86	1.45	1.31	1.06	0.83																
20-Yr 1991	16.81	13.79	17.22	22.90	15.73	12.05	10.25	8.40	7.08	5.66	5.37	4.63	3.52	3.30	2.42	1.89	1.71	1.38	1.08	1.30															
1992	18.37	15.07	18.82	25.02	17.19	13.16	11.20	9.18	7.73	6.19	5.87	5.06	3.84	3.62	2.65	2.06	1.87	1.50	1.19	1.42	1.09														
1993	23.56	19.33	24.14	32.09	22.05	16.89	14.37	11.78	9.92	7.94	7.53	6.49	4.93	4.62	3.37	2.64	2.39	1.93	1.52	1.82	1.40	1.28													
1994	23.78	19.51	24.36	32.39	22.25	17.04	14.50	11.89	10.01	8.01	7.60	6.55	4.98	4.66	3.43	2.67	2.42	1.95	1.53	1.84	1.41	1.29	1.01												
1995	29.09	23.86	29.80	39.62	27.22	20.84	17.74	14.54	12.25	9.80	9.29	8.01	6.09	5.70	4.19	3.26	2.95	2.38	1.88	2.25	1.73	1.58	1.23	1.22											
25-Yr 1996	33.97	27.87	34.79	46.26	31.78	24.34	20.71	16.98	14.30	11.45	10.85	9.35	7.11	6.66	4.89	3.81	3.45	2.78	2.19	2.63	2.02	1.85	1.44	1.43	1.17										
1997	38.70	31.75	39.64	52.71	36.21	27.73	23.60	19.35	16.30	13.04	12.36	10.66	8.10	7.59	5.57	4.34	3.93	3.17	2.50	2.99	2.30	2.11	1.63	1.63	1.33	1.14									
1998	40.92	33.57	41.92	55.73	38.29	29.32	24.95	20.46	17.23	13.79	13.07	11.27	8.56	8.02	5.89	4.59	4.16	3.35	2.64	3.17	2.43	2.23	1.72	1.72	1.41	1.20	1.06								
1999	49.06	40.25	50.26	66.82	45.91	35.16	29.92	24.53	20.66	16.53	15.67	13.51	10.27	9.62	7.07	5.50	4.98	4.01	3.17	3.80	2.92	2.67	2.08	2.06	1.69	1.44	1.27	1.20							
30-Yr 2000	48.60	39.87	49.79	66.20	45.48	34.83	29.63	24.30	20.47	16.38	15.53	13.39	10.17	9.53	7.00	5.45	4.94	3.98	3.14	3.76	2.89	2.65	2.06	2.04	1.67	1.43	1.26	1.19	0.99						
2001	48.94	40.15	50.13	66.65	45.79	35.07	29.84	24.47	20.51	16.49	15.63	13.48	12.01	9.59	7.05	5.49	4.97	4.00	3.16	3.79	2.91	2.66	2.08	2.06	1.68	1.44	1.26	1.20	1.00	1.01					
2002	43.61	35.78	44.68	59.40	40.81	31.25	26.59	21.80	18.36	14.70	13.93	12.01	9.13	8.55	6.28	4.89	4.43	3.57	2.81	3.37	2.59	2.37	1.83	1.83	1.50	1.28	1.13	1.07	0.90	0.90	0.89				
2003	63.30	51.93	64.84	86.22	59.23	45.36	38.60	31.65	26.65	21.33	20.22	17.43	13.25	12.41	9.12	7.10	6.43	5.18	4.08	4.90	3.77	3.45	2.66	2.66	2.18	1.86	1.64	1.55	1.30	1.29	1.45	1.45			
2004	77.04	63.20	78.91	104.92	72.08	55.21	46.97	38.51	32.44	25.96	24.61	21.22	16.12	15.10	11.10	8.64	7.82	6.30	4.97	5.96	4.58	4.19	3.27	3.24	2.65	2.27	1.99	1.88	1.57	1.57	1.77	1.22	1.22		
2005	85.76	70.36	87.85	116.80	80.24	61.46	52.29	42.87	36.11	28.90	27.40	23.62	17.95	16.81	12.35	9.62	8.71	7.02	5.53	6.63	5.10	4.67	3.61	3.61	2.95	2.52	2.22	2.10	1.75	1.75	1.97	1.35	1.37	1.11	
35-Yr 2006	105.45	86.51	108.02	143.62	98.67	75.57	64.30	52.72	44.40	35.53	33.69	29.04	22.07	20.67	15.19	11.82	10.71	8.63	6.80	8.16	6.27	5.74	4.43	4.48	3.63	3.10	2.72	2.58	2.15	2.15	2.42	1.67	1.67	1.37	1.23
	1972	1973	1974	1975	1976	1977	1978	1979	1980	1981	1982	1983	1984	1985	1986	1987	1988	1989	1990	1991	1992	1993	1994	1995	1996	1997	1998	1999	2000	2001	2002	2003	2004	2005	2006

How to read the Growth of $1 Matrix: You can locate the growth of a dollar invested in this simulated Index Portfolio for a designated time period by following these easy instructions: Locate the column for the beginning year of the period. Years are labeled at the top and the bottom of each column. Then, locate the ending year of the period on the left-most vertical column. The growth of a dollar over the time period can be found where the first year's column intersects with the ending year's row. IFA advisory fees of 0.9% per year and DFA mutual fund expense ratios have been deducted from these results. The 10-Yr diagonal (highlighted, starting from far left column) represents the estimated average holding period for investors who score 90 on the Risk Capacity Survey at ifa.com. Sources, Updates, and Disclosures: ifa.com/btp.

Index Portfolio 90: Gold

Monthly Rolling Period Analysis*
Based on 50 Years (600 months) of Monthly Data
Jan 1957 to Dec 2006

Examples of 10 Year Monthly Rolling Periods**

Periods

1	Jan 57 ◄— 10 Years —►	Dec 66
2	Feb 57 ◄— 10 Years —►	Jan 67
3	Mar 57 ◄— 10 Years —►	Feb 67
4	Apr 57 ◄— 10 Years —►	Mar 67

481

Year 1957   1958   1959   1960   1961   1962   1963   1964   1965   1966   1967   1968   1969

Per Period Number of: Yrs	Months	# of Rolling Periods	Average Ann'lzd Rtn. %*	Std. Dev. of Avg. Ann'lzd Rtn. %*	Lowest Rolling Period Date	Lowest Rolling Period Return	Growth of $1 in Lowest Period	Highest Rolling Period Date	Highest Rolling Period Return	Growth of $1 in Highest Period	Average Growth of $1
0.08	1	600	1.15*	4.08*	10/87-10/87	-20.22	$0.80	1/75-1/75	22.56	$1.23	$1.01
0.25	3	598	3.53*	7.95*	9/87-11/87	-23.17	$0.77	1/75-3/75	36.24	$1.36	$1.04
0.5	6	595	7.17*	11.76*	4/74-9/74	-27.78	$0.72	1/75-6/75	50.55	$1.51	$1.07
1	12	589	14.87	16.85	10/73-9/74	-34.51	$0.65	1/58-12/58	61.10	$1.61	$1.15
2	24	577	14.13	10.74	1/73-12/74	-22.39	$0.60	12/66-11/68	44.00	$2.07	$1.59
3	36	565	13.70	8.13	1/72-12/74	-9.79	$0.73	8/84-7/87	37.25	$2.59	$1.49
4	48	553	13.51	6.72	1/71-12/74	-2.12	$0.92	7/82-6/86	32.16	$3.05	$1.69
5	60	541	13.37	6.09	10/69-9/74	-2.47	$0.88	8/82-7/87	32.81	$4.13	$1.93
6	72	529	13.42	5.50	1/69-12/74	-5.59	$0.71	10/81-9/87	26.88	$4.17	$2.20
7	84	517	13.50	4.93	1/68-12/74	-0.76	$0.95	8/82-7/89	26.79	$5.27	$2.52
8	96	505	13.56	4.47	12/68-11/76	2.69	$1.24	8/82-7/90	23.85	$5.54	$2.89
9	108	493	13.63	4.27	1/66-12/74	2.98	$1.30	1/75-12/83	23.13	$6.51	$3.32
10**	**120**	**481**	**13.70**	**4.03**	**1/65-12/74**	**5.12**	**$1.65**	**9/77-8/87**	**23.05**	**$7.96**	**$3.82**
11	132	469	13.73	3.88	1/64-12/74	6.11	$1.92	1/75-12/85	22.66	$9.46	$4.40
12	144	457	13.71	3.70	1/63-12/74	7.29	$2.33	10/75-9/87	23.18	$12.20	$5.03
13	156	445	13.72	3.59	1/62-12/74	5.90	$2.11	10/74-9/87	23.81	$16.06	$5.76
14	168	433	13.80	3.40	1/61-12/74	7.18	$2.64	1/75-12/88	22.25	$16.65	$6.63
15	180	421	13.85	3.24	1/60-12/74	6.23	$2.48	1/75-12/89	22.54	$21.09	$7.62
20	240	361	14.34	2.00	1/57-12/76	10.59	$7.49	10/74-9/94	19.05	$32.70	$15.45
30	360	241	14.33	0.73	4/73-3/03	12.63	$35.45	1/75-12/04	16.78	$104.97	$56.57
40	480	121	13.63	0.44	4/63-3/03	12.75	$121.52	4/58-3/98	14.80	$249.85	$168.09
50	600	1	13.51	0.00	1/57-12/06	13.51	$564.55	1/57-12/06	13.51	$564.55	$564.55

10 Year Monthly Rolling Periods** - Jan 1957 to Dec 2006 - 481 Monthly Rolling Periods Over 50 Years

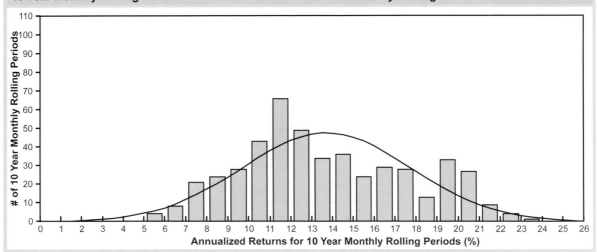

*Sources, Updates, and Disclosures: ifa.com/btp. Returns are net of IFA & DFA fees. The returns and standard deviation shown for 1, 3, and 6 month periods are not annualized. Past performance does not guarantee future results. **10 years represents the estimated average holding period for investors who score 90 on the Risk Capacity Survey at ifa.com.

RISK CAPACITY 85
ORANGE

Index Portfolio 85: Orange

⁸⁵

Index Allocations

General Asset Class		Specific Index	
38%	US Large	19%	IFA US Large Company Index
		19%	IFA US Large Cap Value Index
19%	US Small	9.5%	IFA US Micro Cap Index
		9.5%	IFA US Small Cap Value Index
9.5%	Real Estate	9.5%	IFA Real Estate Index
19%	International	9.5%	IFA International Value Index
		4.75%	IFA International Small Company Index
		4.75%	IFA International Small Cap Value Index
9.5%	Emerging Markets	2.85%	IFA Emerging Markets Index
		2.85%	IFA Emerging Markets Value Index
		3.80%	IFA Emerging Markets Small Cap Index
5%	Fixed Income	1.25%	IFA One-Year Fixed Income Index
		1.25%	IFA Two-Year Global Fixed Income Index
		1.25%	IFA Five-Year Gov't Income Index
		1.25%	IFA Five-Year Global Fixed Income Index

Index Portfolio - Simulated Returns and Volatility Data*

	1yr ending 2006	1yr ending 2005	1yr ending 2004	1yr ending 2003	3yrs 2004-2006	5yrs 2002-2006	10yrs 1996-2006	25yrs 1982-2006	35yrs 1972-2006	50yrs 1957-2006	80yrs 1927-2006
Growth of $1	1.22	1.11	1.21	1.43	1.63	2.10	3.01	30.93	95.39	491.76	8,016
Annualized Return %	21.99	10.79	20.66	42.95	17.70	15.98	11.64	14.71	13.91	13.20	11.89
Annualized Volatility (Standard Deviation %)	8.99	9.44	10.15	11.89	9.35	12.01	13.38	12.57	13.44	13.47	23.58

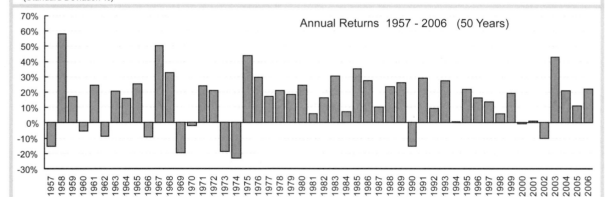

Annual Returns 1957 - 2006 (50 Years)

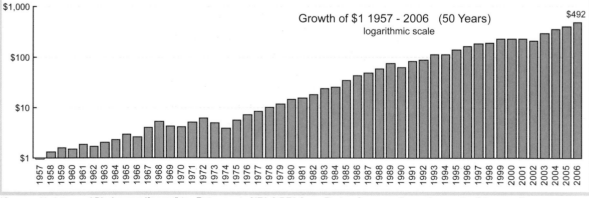

Growth of $1 1957 - 2006 (50 Years)
logarithmic scale

*Sources, Updates, and Disclosures: ifa.com/btp. Returns net of IFA & DFA fees. Past performance does not guarantee future results.

INDEX PORTFOLIO 85: ORANGE

Annualized Returns Matrix (%)
35 years of Index Portfolio 85 (1972-2006)
Returns Net of IFA and DFA Fees

The table below is a triangular "Annualized Returns Matrix." Columns are labeled by the **beginning year** (1972–2006, at top and bottom). Rows are labeled by **ending year** on the left together with the holding-period labels (1-Yr, 5-Yr, 10-Yr, 15-Yr, 20-Yr, 25-Yr, 30-Yr, 35-Yr). Each cell gives the annualized compounded return for the period from its column's beginning year through its row's ending year.

End / Period	1972	1973	1974	1975	1976	1977	1978	1979	1980	1981	1982	1983	1984	1985	1986	1987	1988	1989	1990	1991	1992	1993	1994	1995	1996	1997	1998	1999	2000	2001	2002	2003	2004	2005	2006
1972 (1-Yr)	21.0																																		
1973	-0.8	-18.7																																	
1974	-8.9	-21.0	-23.2																																
1975	2.1	-3.6	5.0	43.6																															
1976 (5-Yr)	7.0	3.8	12.6	29.4	29.4																														
1977	8.6	6.3	13.6	22.9	16.8	16.8																													
1978	10.3	8.6	15.1	21.3	18.9	21.0	21.0																												
1979	11.2	9.9	15.6	21.8	19.6	18.7	19.6	18.2																											
1980	12.6	11.6	16.8	22.3	20.0	20.0	21.1	24.2	24.2																										
1981 (10-Yr)	11.9	11.0	15.4	19.0	17.0	17.1	17.1	15.8	14.7	5.9																									
1982	12.3	11.5	15.4	18.6	16.9	16.9	16.9	15.9	15.2	10.9	16.2																								
1983	13.7	13.1	16.9	19.1	17.9	18.7	18.8	18.3	18.3	17.1	23.1	30.4																							
1984	13.2	12.6	15.9	18.5	17.2	17.3	17.3	16.6	16.3	14.5	18.8	18.1	7.0																						
1985	14.6	14.1	17.4	20.0	19.0	19.3	19.1	19.2	19.2	18.3	21.6	23.5	20.2	34.9																					
1986 (15-Yr)	15.4	15.0	18.2	20.7	19.9	20.2	20.1	20.4	20.4	19.8	22.8	24.5	22.6	31.2	27.5																				
1987	15.1	14.7	17.6	21.5	19.9	19.2	19.0	18.3	18.3	17.1	20.6	21.5	19.3	23.7	18.5	10.1																			
1988	15.6	15.2	18.3	21.6	19.3	19.5	19.2	19.5	19.0	18.3	20.9	21.8	20.1	23.6	20.1	16.5	23.2																		
1989	16.1	15.8	18.4	21.9	19.8	20.0	20.0	19.5	19.7	19.7	21.5	22.3	21.0	24.1	21.5	19.5	24.5	25.8																	
1990 (20-Yr)	14.2	13.8	16.1	19.1	17.7	17.7	16.9	16.4	16.4	15.6	16.7	16.8	15.0	16.4	13.0	9.6	9.5	3.2	-15.4																
1991	14.9	14.6	16.8	19.7	18.3	18.1	17.4	17.4	17.4	16.8	17.9	18.1	16.7	18.1	15.5	13.3	14.1	11.2	4.5	29.1															
1992	14.6	14.3	16.4	19.1	17.1	17.1	17.1	16.1	16.1	16.1	16.7	16.8	16.7	17.0	15.5	14.1	12.6	10.6	6.0	18.6	9.1														
1993	15.1	14.9	16.9	19.5	18.3	17.5	17.7	16.9	16.9	16.9	17.9	18.1	16.9	18.0	16.1	14.5	15.3	13.8	10.9	21.4	17.8	27.2													
1994	14.5	14.2	16.1	18.5	17.3	16.6	16.4	16.2	15.7	15.7	16.5	16.5	15.3	16.2	14.3	12.7	13.1	11.5	8.8	15.9	11.8	13.2	0.8												
1995	14.8	14.5	16.3	18.6	17.5	16.9	16.9	16.7	16.1	16.1	16.8	16.9	15.8	16.7	15.0	13.7	14.1	12.9	10.9	17.0	14.2	16.0	10.7	21.7											
1996 (25-Yr)	14.8	14.5	16.2	18.5	16.7	16.9	16.6	16.5	16.1	16.1	16.8	16.9	15.9	16.4	15.0	13.9	14.4	13.3	11.6	16.9	14.6	16.0	10.7	18.9	16.3										
1997	14.8	14.5	16.2	18.3	-7.3	16.7	16.5	16.4	15.9	15.9	16.6	16.6	15.7	16.4	15.0	13.9	14.3	13.3	11.9	16.4	14.4	15.5	12.5	18.9	17.1	13.5									
1998	14.4	14.2	15.7	17.7	16.7	16.2	16.2	15.9	15.3	15.3	15.9	15.5	15.0	15.6	14.2	13.2	13.5	12.5	11.2	15.0	13.1	13.8	11.3	14.1	11.7	9.6	5.7								
1999	14.6	14.4	15.9	17.8	16.8	16.3	16.3	16.0	15.5	15.5	16.1	16.1	15.8	15.8	14.6	13.6	13.9	13.1	11.9	15.5	13.9	14.6	12.6	15.1	13.5	12.6	12.2	19.1							
2000	14.0	13.8	15.2	17.0	16.1	15.5	15.5	15.1	14.7	14.7	15.2	15.1	14.7	14.7	13.5	12.6	12.7	11.9	10.7	13.7	12.2	12.3	10.6	12.3	10.6	9.2	7.8	8.8	-0.6						
2001	13.6	13.3	14.7	16.4	15.4	14.8	14.8	14.4	14.0	14.0	14.7	13.0	12.1	12.4	11.2	10.2	11.7	11.0	9.9	12.5	11.7	12.7	9.3	10.6	8.9	7.5	6.0	6.1	0.1	0.9					
2002	12.7	12.5	13.7	15.3	-4.4	13.8	13.7	13.2	12.8	12.8	13.1	13.0	12.1	12.4	11.2	10.2	10.2	9.4	8.2	10.4	8.9	6.0	7.0	7.8	6.0	4.3	2.6	1.8	-3.4	-4.7	-10.0				
2003	13.6	13.3	14.6	16.2	15.3	14.8	14.7	14.3	13.9	13.9	14.2	14.2	13.5	13.8	12.8	12.1	12.1	11.3	10.4	12.7	11.4	11.6	10.1	11.2	10.0	9.1	8.4	9.0	6.6	9.1	13.4	43.0			
2004	13.8	13.6	14.8	16.3	15.5	15.0	15.0	14.6	14.2	14.2	14.6	14.5	13.8	14.2	13.2	12.5	12.5	11.9	11.0	13.2	12.1	12.3	11.1	12.2	11.1	10.5	10.1	9.3	9.3	11.9	15.8	31.3	20.7		
2005	13.7	13.5	14.7	16.1	15.3	14.9	14.8	14.4	14.1	14.1	14.4	14.3	13.7	14.0	13.0	12.4	12.4	11.8	11.0	13.2	12.2	12.4	11.8	12.0	10.5	10.2	10.5	9.5	9.5	11.7	14.5	24.1	15.6	10.8	
2006 (35-Yr)	13.9	13.7	14.9	16.3	15.5	15.1	15.0	14.8	14.4	14.7	14.7	14.7	14.0	14.3	13.4	12.8	12.9	12.4	11.6	13.6	12.6	12.9	11.8	12.8	12.1	11.6	11.4	12.2	13.3	12.1	11.2	16.0	17.7	16.3	22.0
	1972	1973	1974	1975	1976	1977	1978	1979	1980	1981	1982	1983	1984	1985	1986	1987	1988	1989	1990	1991	1992	1993	1994	1995	1996	1997	1998	1999	2000	2001	2002	2003	2004	2005	2006

How to read the Annualized Returns Matrix: You can locate the annualized compounded rate of return for this simulated Index Portfolio for a designated time period by following these easy instructions: Locate the column for the beginning year of the period. Years are labeled at the top and the bottom of each column. Then, locate the ending year of the period on the left-most vertical column. The annualized return can be found where the first year's column intersects with the ending year's row. IFA advisory fees of 0.9% per year and DFA mutual fund expense ratios have been deducted from these results. The 10-Yr diagonal (highlighted, starting from far left column) represents the estimated average holding period for investors who score 85 on the Risk Capacity Survey at ifa.com. Sources, Updates, and Disclosures: ifa.com/btp.

INDEX PORTFOLIO 85: ORANGE

Growth of $1 Matrix ($)
35 years of Index Portfolio 85 (1972–2006)
Returns Net of IFA and DFA Fees

Period markers (rows, by ending year): **1-Yr** = 1972, **5-Yr** = 1976, **10-Yr** = 1981, **15-Yr** = 1986, **20-Yr** = 1991, **25-Yr** = 1996, **30-Yr** = 2001, **35-Yr** = 2006.

End	1972	1973	1974	1975	1976	1977	1978	1979	1980	1981	1982	1983	1984	1985	1986	1987	1988	1989	1990	1991	1992	1993	1994	1995	1996	1997	1998	1999	2000	2001	2002	2003	2004	2005	2006
1972	1.21																																		
1973	0.98	0.81																																	
1974	0.76	0.62	0.77																																
1975	1.09	0.90	1.10	1.44																															
1976	1.40	1.16	1.43	1.86	1.29																														
1977	1.64	1.36	1.67	2.17	1.51	1.17																													
1978	1.99	1.64	2.02	2.63	1.83	1.41	1.21																												
1979	2.35	1.94	2.39	3.11	2.16	1.67	1.43	1.18																											
1980	2.91	2.41	2.96	3.86	2.68	2.07	1.78	1.47	1.24																										
1981	3.08	2.55	3.14	4.08	2.84	2.20	1.88	1.55	1.31	1.06																									
1982	3.58	2.96	3.64	4.74	3.30	2.55	2.18	1.80	1.53	1.23	1.16																								
1983	4.67	3.86	4.75	6.18	4.31	3.33	2.85	2.35	1.99	1.60	1.51	1.30																							
1984	5.00	4.13	5.08	6.62	4.61	3.56	3.05	2.52	2.13	1.72	1.62	1.40	1.07																						
1985	6.74	5.58	6.86	8.93	6.22	4.80	4.11	3.40	2.88	2.32	2.19	1.88	1.44	1.35																					
1986	8.60	7.11	8.75	11.39	7.93	6.13	5.24	4.33	3.67	2.95	2.79	2.40	1.84	1.72	1.28																				
1987	9.47	7.83	9.63	12.54	8.73	6.75	5.78	4.77	4.04	3.25	3.07	2.64	2.03	1.89	1.40	1.10																			
1988	11.67	9.65	11.87	15.45	10.76	8.31	7.12	5.88	4.98	4.01	3.79	3.26	2.50	2.34	1.73	1.36	1.23																		
1989	14.69	12.14	14.93	19.44	13.54	10.46	8.96	7.40	6.26	5.04	4.76	4.10	3.14	2.94	2.18	1.71	1.55	1.26																	
1990	12.43	10.27	12.63	16.45	11.45	8.85	7.58	6.26	5.30	4.27	4.03	3.47	2.66	2.49	1.84	1.44	1.31	1.06	0.85																
1991	16.04	13.26	16.31	21.23	14.78	11.42	9.78	8.08	6.84	5.51	5.20	4.48	3.43	3.21	2.38	1.86	1.69	1.37	1.09	1.29															
1992	17.50	14.46	17.79	23.16	16.12	12.46	10.67	8.81	7.46	6.01	5.67	4.88	3.75	3.50	2.59	2.03	1.85	1.50	1.19	1.41	1.09														
1993	22.25	18.39	22.62	29.45	20.51	15.84	13.57	11.21	9.48	7.64	7.21	6.21	4.76	4.45	3.30	2.59	2.37	1.91	1.51	1.80	1.39	1.27													
1994	22.42	18.54	22.80	29.68	20.67	15.97	13.67	11.29	9.56	7.70	7.27	6.26	4.80	4.49	3.32	2.61	2.37	1.92	1.53	1.80	1.40	1.28	1.01												
1995	27.28	22.55	27.74	36.11	25.14	19.43	16.63	13.74	11.63	9.37	8.85	7.61	5.84	5.46	4.04	3.17	2.88	2.34	1.86	2.20	1.70	1.56	1.23	1.22											
1996	31.72	26.22	32.25	41.98	29.23	22.59	19.34	15.98	13.52	10.89	10.28	8.85	6.79	6.34	4.70	3.69	3.35	2.72	2.16	2.55	1.98	1.81	1.43	1.41	1.16										
1997	36.01	29.77	36.61	47.66	33.19	25.64	21.95	18.14	15.35	12.36	11.68	10.05	7.71	7.20	5.34	4.19	3.80	3.08	2.45	2.90	2.24	2.06	1.62	1.61	1.32	1.14									
1998	38.07	31.47	38.71	50.39	35.09	27.11	23.21	19.18	16.23	13.07	12.34	10.63	8.15	7.62	5.64	4.43	4.02	3.26	2.59	3.06	2.37	2.18	1.70	1.70	1.40	1.20	1.06								
1999	45.33	37.47	46.09	60.00	41.78	32.28	27.64	22.83	19.32	15.56	14.70	12.65	9.70	9.07	6.72	5.27	4.79	3.88	3.09	3.65	2.83	2.59	2.04	2.02	1.71	1.43	1.26	1.19							
2000	45.05	37.24	45.81	59.63	41.52	32.08	27.47	22.69	19.20	15.47	14.61	12.58	9.65	9.01	6.68	5.24	4.76	3.86	3.07	3.63	2.81	2.58	2.02	2.01	1.65	1.42	1.25	1.18	0.99						
2001	45.46	37.58	46.22	60.18	41.90	32.37	27.72	22.90	19.38	15.61	14.74	12.69	9.73	9.09	6.74	5.29	4.80	3.89	3.09	3.66	2.83	2.60	2.04	2.03	1.67	1.43	1.26	1.19	1.00	1.01					
2002	40.92	33.83	41.60	54.17	37.71	29.14	24.95	20.61	17.44	14.05	13.27	11.42	8.76	8.19	6.07	4.76	4.32	3.51	2.79	3.29	2.55	2.34	1.84	1.82	1.50	1.29	1.14	1.07	0.90	0.91	0.90				
2003	58.50	48.36	59.47	77.43	53.91	41.65	35.67	29.47	24.94	20.08	18.97	16.33	12.52	11.70	8.67	6.80	6.18	5.01	3.98	4.71	3.65	3.34	2.63	2.61	2.14	1.84	1.62	1.54	1.29	1.30	1.29	1.43			
2004	70.59	58.35	71.76	93.43	65.05	50.26	43.03	35.55	30.09	24.23	22.89	19.70	15.11	14.12	10.47	8.21	7.45	6.05	4.80	5.68	4.40	4.03	3.17	3.15	2.59	2.23	1.96	1.85	1.55	1.56	1.55	1.72	1.21		
2005	78.20	64.65	79.50	103.51	72.07	55.68	47.68	39.39	33.33	26.85	25.36	21.83	16.74	15.64	11.59	9.09	8.26	6.70	5.32	6.29	4.87	4.47	3.51	3.49	2.87	2.47	2.17	2.05	1.73	1.74	1.72	1.91	1.34	1.11	
2006	95.40	78.86	96.99	126.27	87.92	67.93	58.16	48.05	40.66	32.75	30.93	26.63	20.42	19.08	14.14	11.09	10.07	8.17	6.49	7.68	5.95	5.45	4.29	4.25	3.50	3.01	2.65	2.51	2.10	2.12	2.10	2.33	1.63	1.35	1.22

| Begin year → | 1972 | 1973 | 1974 | 1975 | 1976 | 1977 | 1978 | 1979 | 1980 | 1981 | 1982 | 1983 | 1984 | 1985 | 1986 | 1987 | 1988 | 1989 | 1990 | 1991 | 1992 | 1993 | 1994 | 1995 | 1996 | 1997 | 1998 | 1999 | 2000 | 2001 | 2002 | 2003 | 2004 | 2005 | 2006 |

How to read the Growth of $1 Matrix: You can locate the growth of a dollar invested in this simulated Index Portfolio for a designated time period by following these easy instructions: Locate the column for the beginning year of the period. Years are labeled at the top and the bottom of each column. Then, locate the ending year of the period on the left-most vertical column. The growth of a dollar over the time period can be found where the first year's column intersects with the ending year's row. IFA advisory fees of 0.9% per year and DFA mutual fund expense ratios have been deducted from these results. The 10-Yr diagonal (highlighted, starting from far left column) represents the estimated average holding period for investors who score 85 on the Risk Capacity Survey at ifa.com. Sources, Updates, and Disclosures: ifa.com/btp.

Index Portfolio 85: Orange

Monthly Rolling Period Analysis*
Based on 50 years (600 months) of Monthly Data
Jan 1957 to Dec 2006

Examples of 10 Year Monthly Rolling Periods**

Periods

1	Jan 57	← 10 Years →	Dec 66
2	Feb 57	← 10 Years →	Jan 67
3	Mar 57	← 10 Years →	Feb 67
4	Apr 57	← 10 Years →	Mar 67

481

Year 1957 1958 1959 1960 1961 1962 1963 1964 1965 1966 1967 1968 1969

Per Period Number of: Yrs	Months	# of Rolling Periods	Average Ann'lzd Rtn %*	Std. Dev. of Avg. Ann'lzd Rtn. %*	Lowest Rolling Period Date	Lowest Rolling Period Return	Growth of $1 in Lowest Period	Highest Rolling Period Date	Highest Rolling Period Return	Growth of $1 in Highest Period	Average Growth of $1
0.08	1	600	1.11*	3.89*	10/87-10/87	-19.35	$0.81	1/75-1/75	21.48	$1.21	$1.01
0.25	3	598	3.43*	7.57*	9/87-11/87	-22.20	$0.78	1/75-3/75	34.50	$1.35	$1.03
0.5	6	595	6.96*	11.18*	4/74-9/74	-26.28	$0.74	1/75-6/75	48.14	$1.48	$1.07
1	12	589	14.43	16.00	10/73-9/74	-32.65	$0.67	1/58-12/58	57.99	$1.58	$1.14
2	24	577	13.76	10.20	1/73-12/74	-20.98	$0.62	12/66-11/68	42.01	$2.02	$1.57
3	36	565	13.37	7.72	1/72-12/74	-8.93	$0.76	8/84-7/87	35.91	$2.51	$1.48
4	48	553	13.20	6.40	1/71-12/74	-1.61	$0.94	7/82-6/86	31.19	$2.96	$1.67
5	60	541	13.07	5.82	10/69-9/74	-1.92	$0.91	8/82-7/87	31.69	$3.96	$1.90
6	72	529	13.12	5.27	1/69-12/74	-4.91	$0.74	10/81-9/87	26.14	$4.03	$2.16
7	84	517	13.20	4.73	1/68-12/74	-0.31	$0.98	8/82-7/89	25.92	$5.02	$2.47
8	96	505	13.26	4.30	12/68-11/76	2.99	$1.27	8/82-7/90	23.12	$5.28	$2.82
9	108	493	13.33	4.11	1/66-12/74	3.24	$1.33	1/75-12/83	22.44	$6.18	$3.23
10**	**120**	**481**	**13.40**	**3.88**	**1/65-12/74**	**5.26**	**$1.67**	**9/77-8/87**	**22.41**	**$7.55**	**$3.71**
11	132	469	13.44	3.74	1/64-12/74	6.17	$1.93	1/75-12/85	22.02	$8.93	$4.26
12	144	457	13.42	3.57	1/63-12/74	7.28	$2.32	10/75-9/87	22.51	$11.43	$4.85
13	156	445	13.43	3.46	1/62-12/74	5.94	$2.12	10/74-9/87	23.10	$14.91	$5.55
14	168	433	13.51	3.28	1/61-12/74	7.15	$2.63	1/75-12/88	21.60	$15.46	$6.37
15	180	421	13.56	3.13	1/60-12/74	6.25	$2.48	1/75-12/89	21.88	$19.45	$7.30
20	240	361	14.04	1.93	1/57-12/76	10.40	$7.23	10/74-9/94	18.54	$30.01	$14.60
30	360	241	14.03	0.69	4/73-3/03	12.42	$33.52	1/75-12/04	16.33	$93.49	$52.16
40	480	121	13.34	0.41	4/63-3/03	12.51	$111.60	4/58-3/98	14.44	$220.35	$151.39
50	600	1	13.20	0.00	1/57-12/06	13.20	$492.40	1/57-12/06	13.20	$492.40	$492.40

10 Year Monthly Rolling Periods** - Jan 1957 to Dec 2006 - 481 Monthly Rolling Periods Over 50 Years

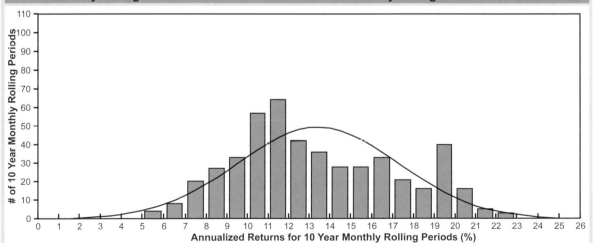

*Sources, Updates, and Disclosures: ifa.com/btp. Returns are net of IFA & DFA fees. The returns and standard deviation shown for 1, 3, and 6 month periods are not annualized. Past performance does not guarantee future results. **10 years represents the estimated average holding period for investors who score 85 on the Risk Capacity Survey at ifa.com.

Appendix A

263

RISK CAPACITY 80
PURPLE

Index Allocations

General Asset Class		Specific Index	
36%	US Large	18%	IFA US Large Company Index
		18%	IFA US Large Cap Value Index
18%	US Small	9%	IFA US Micro Cap Index
		9%	IFA US Small Cap Value Index
9%	Real Estate	9%	IFA Real Estate Index
18%	International	9%	IFA International Value Index
		4.5%	IFA International Small Company Index
		4.5%	IFA International Small Cap Value Index
9%	Emerging Markets	2.7%	IFA Emerging Markets Index
		2.7%	IFA Emerging Markets Value Index
		3.6%	IFA Emerging Markets Small Cap Index
10%	Fixed Income	2.5%	IFA One-Year Fixed Income Index
		2.5%	IFA Two-Year Global Fixed Income Index
		2.5%	IFA Five-Year Gov't Income Index
		2.5%	IFA Five-Year Global Fixed Income Index

Index Portfolio - Simulated Returns and Volatility Data*

	1yr ending 2006	1yr ending 2005	1yr ending 2004	1yr ending 2003	3yrs 2004-2006	5yrs 2002-2006	10yrs 1996-2006	25yrs 1982-2006	35yrs 1972-2006	50yrs 1957-2006	80yrs 1927-2006
Growth of $1	1.21	1.10	1.20	1.41	1.60	2.04	2.91	28.37	86.12	425.67	6,622
Annualized Return %	21.01	10.27	19.62	40.76	16.87	15.35	11.28	14.32	13.58	12.87	11.63
Annualized Volatility (Standard Deviation %)	8.54	8.93	9.69	11.28	8.89	11.35	12.66	11.94	12.77	12.79	22.32

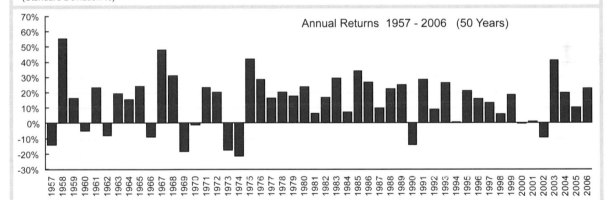

Annual Returns 1957 - 2006 (50 Years)

Growth of $1 1957 - 2006 (50 Years)
logarithmic scale
$426

*Sources, Updates, and Disclosures: ifa.com/btp. Returns net of IFA & DFA fees. Past performance does not guarantee future results.

Annualized Returns Matrix (%)
35 years of Index Portfolio 80 (1972-2006)
Returns Net of IFA and DFA Fees

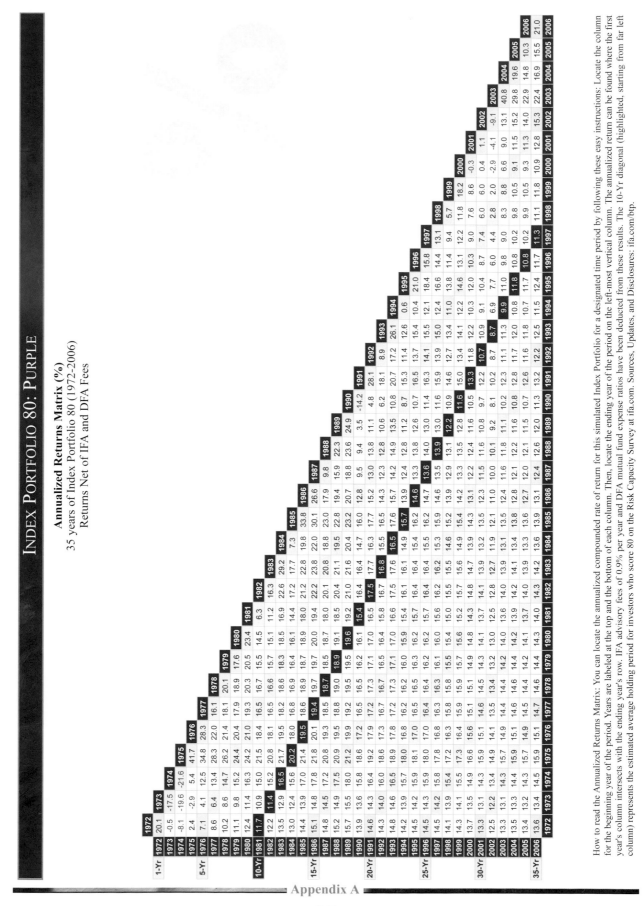

How to read the Annualized Returns Matrix: You can locate the annualized compounded rate of return for this simulated Index Portfolio for a designated time period by following these easy instructions: Locate the column for the beginning year of the period. Years are labeled at the top and the bottom of each column. Then, locate the ending year of the period on the left-most vertical column. The annualized return can be found where the first year's column intersects with the ending year's row. IFA advisory fees of 0.9% per year and DFA mutual fund expense ratios have been deducted from these results. The 10-Yr diagonal (highlighted, starting from far left column) represents the estimated average holding period for investors who score 80 on the Risk Capacity Survey at ifa.com. Sources, Updates, and Disclosures: ifa.com/btp.

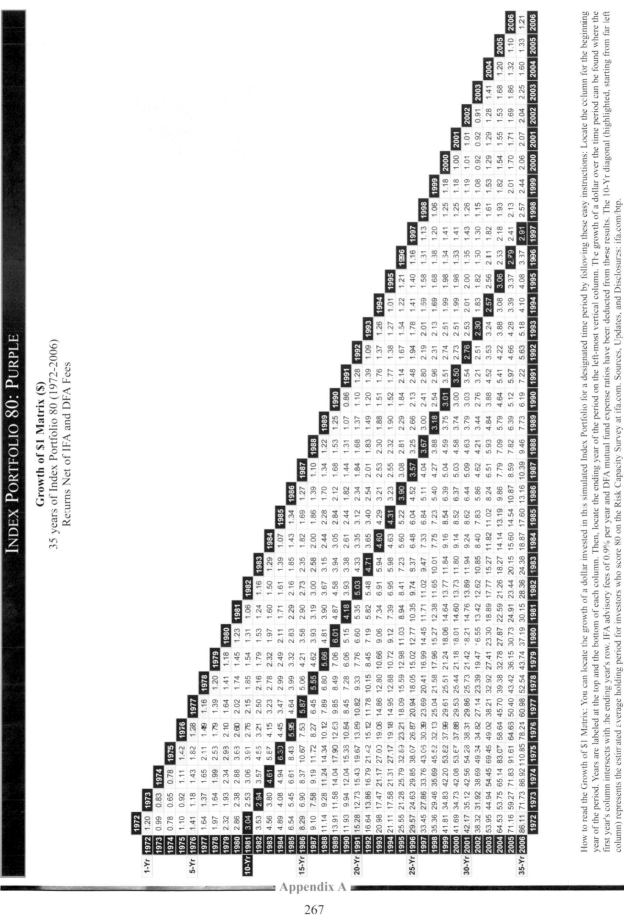

INDEX PORTFOLIO 80: PURPLE

Growth of $1 Matrix ($)
35 years of Index Portfolio 80 (1972-2006)
Returns Net of IFA and DFA Fees

How to read the Growth of $1 Matrix: You can locate the growth of a dollar invested in this simulated Index Portfolio for a designated time period by following these easy instructions: Locate the column for the beginning year of the period. Years are labeled at the top and the bottom of each column. Then, locate the ending year of the period on the left-most vertical column. The growth of a dollar over the time period can be found where the first year's column intersects with the ending year's row. IFA advisory fees of 0.9% per year and DFA mutual fund expense ratios have been deducted from these results. The 10-Yr diagonal (highlighted, starting from far left column) represents the estimated average holding period for investors who score 80 on the Risk Capacity Survey at ifa.com. Sources, Updates, and Disclosures: ifa.com/btp.

Index Portfolio 80: Purple
Monthly Rolling Period Analysis*
Based on 50 Years (600 months) of Monthly Data
Jan 1957 to Dec 2006

Examples of 10 Year Monthly Rolling Periods**

Periods

1	Jan 57	← 10 Years →	Dec 66
2	Feb 57	← 10 Years →	Jan 67
3	Mar 57	← 10 Years →	Feb 67
4	Apr 57	← 10 Years →	Mar 67
481			

Year 1957   1958   1959   1960   1961   1962   1963   1964   1965   1966   1967   1968   1969

Per Period Number of: Yrs	Months	# of Rolling Periods	Average Ann'lzd Rtn. %*	Std. Dev. of Avg. Ann'lzd Rtn. %*	Lowest Rolling Period Date	Lowest Rolling Period Return	Growth of $1 in Lowest Period	Highest Rolling Period Date	Highest Rolling Period Return	Growth of $1 in Highest Period	Average Growth of $1
0.08	1	600	1.08*	3.69*	10/87-10/87	-18.46	$0.82	1/75-1/75	20.39	$1.20	$1.01
0.25	3	598	3.33*	7.19*	9/87-11/87	-21.21	$0.79	1/75-3/75	32.77	$1.33	$1.03
0.5	6	595	6.75*	10.61*	4/74-9/74	-24.77	$0.75	1/75-6/75	45.74	$1.46	$1.07
1	12	589	13.98	15.16	10/73-9/74	-30.78	$0.69	7/82-6/83	55.07	$1.55	$1.14
2	24	577	13.39	9.67	1/73-12/74	-19.56	$0.65	12/66-11/68	40.03	$1.96	$1.54
3	36	565	13.03	7.33	1/72-12/74	-8.08	$0.78	8/84-7/87	34.57	$2.44	$1.46
4	48	553	12.88	6.09	1/71-12/74	-1.11	$0.96	7/82-6/86	30.21	$2.87	$1.65
5	60	541	12.76	5.56	10/69-9/74	-1.39	$0.93	8/82-7/87	30.57	$3.80	$1.87
6	72	529	12.81	5.04	1/69-12/74	-4.25	$0.77	10/81-9/87	25.40	$3.89	$2.12
7	84	517	12.89	4.54	1/68-12/74	0.12	$1.01	8/82-7/89	25.06	$4.78	$2.42
8	96	505	12.96	4.14	12/68-11/76	3.29	$1.30	8/82-7/90	22.38	$5.03	$2.75
9	108	493	13.02	3.96	1/66-12/74	3.49	$1.36	1/75-12/83	21.74	$5.87	$3.15
10**	120	481	13.09	3.74	1/65-12/74	5.37	$1.69	9/77-8/87	21.77	$7.17	$3.60
11	132	469	13.13	3.61	1/64-12/74	6.22	$1.94	1/75-12/85	21.38	$8.43	$4.11
12	144	457	13.12	3.45	1/63-12/74	7.25	$2.32	10/75-9/87	21.83	$10.69	$4.68
13	156	445	13.13	3.34	1/62-12/74	5.97	$2.13	10/74-9/87	22.40	$13.84	$5.33
14	168	433	13.21	3.17	1/61-12/74	7.10	$2.61	1/75-12/88	20.95	$14.34	$6.11
15	180	421	13.26	3.02	1/60-12/74	6.25	$2.48	1/75-12/89	21.21	$17.91	$6.98
20	240	361	13.73	1.87	1/57-12/76	10.20	$6.98	10/74-9/94	18.03	$27.53	$13.79
30	360	241	13.72	0.64	4/73-3/03	12.21	$31.69	1/75-12/04	15.87	$83.01	$47.99
40	480	121	13.04	0.39	4/63-3/03	12.25	$101.73	4/58-3/98	14.08	$194.26	$135.89
50	600	1	12.87	0.00	1/57-12/06	12.87	$425.53	1/57-12/06	12.87	$425.53	$425.53

10 Year Monthly Rolling Periods** - Jan 1957 to Dec 2006 - 481 Monthly Rolling Periods Over 50 Years

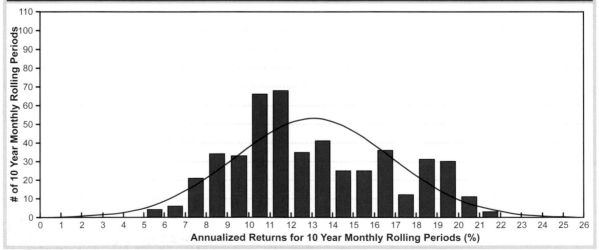

*Sources, Updates, and Disclosures: ifa.com/btp. Returns are net of IFA & DFA fees. The returns and standard deviation shown for 1, 3, and 6 month periods are not annualized. Past performance does not guarantee future results. **10 years represents the estimated average holding period for investors who score 80 on the Risk Capacity Survey at ifa.com.

RISK CAPACITY 75
DARK BLUE

Index Allocations

General Asset Class		Specific Index	
34%	US Large	17%	IFA US Large Company Index
		17%	IFA US Large Cap Value Index
17%	US Small	8.5%	IFA US Micro Cap Index
		8.5%	IFA US Small Cap Value Index
8.5%	Real Estate	8.5%	IFA Real Estate Index
17%	International	8.5%	IFA International Value Index
		4.25%	IFA International Small Company Index
		4.25%	IFA International Small Cap Value Index
8.5%	Emerging Markets	2.55%	IFA Emerging Markets Index
		2.55%	IFA Emerging Markets Value Index
		3.40%	IFA Emerging Markets Small Cap Index
15%	Fixed Income	3.75%	IFA One-Year Fixed Income Index
		3.75%	IFA Two-Year Global Fixed Income Index
		3.75%	IFA Five-Year Gov't Income Index
		3.75%	IFA Five-Year Global Fixed Income Index

Index Portfolio - Simulated Returns and Volatility Data*

	1yr ending 2006	1yr ending 2005	1yr ending 2004	1yr ending 2003	3yrs 2004-2006	5yrs 2002-2006	10yrs 1996-2006	25yrs 1982-2006	35yrs 1972-2006	50yrs 1957-2006	80yrs 1927-2006
Growth of $1	1.20	1.10	1.19	1.39	1.56	1.99	2.82	25.99	77.56	366.91	5,395
Annualized Return %	20.04	9.74	18.58	38.57	16.03	14.72	10.92	13.92	13.24	12.54	11.34
Annualized Volatility (Standard Deviation %)	8.09	8.42	9.22	10.68	8.42	10.68	11.94	11.32	12.10	12.11	21.08

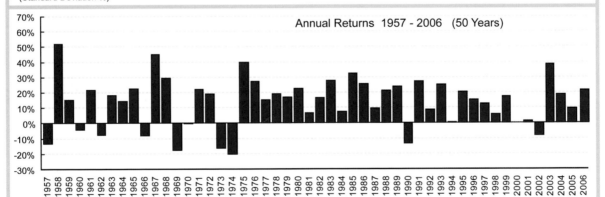

Annual Returns 1957 - 2006 (50 Years)

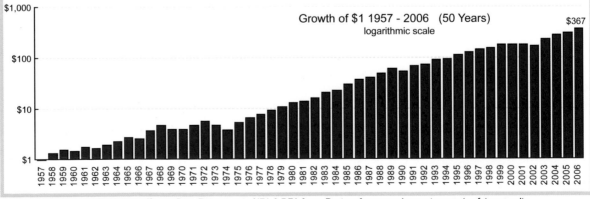

Growth of $1 1957 - 2006 (50 Years)
logarithmic scale

$367

*Sources, Updates, and Disclosures: ifa.com/btp. Returns net of IFA & DFA fees. Past performance does not guarantee future results.

INDEX PORTFOLIO 75: DARK BLUE

Annualized Returns Matrix (%)
35 years of Index Portfolio 75 (1972-2006)
Returns Net of IFA and DFA Fees

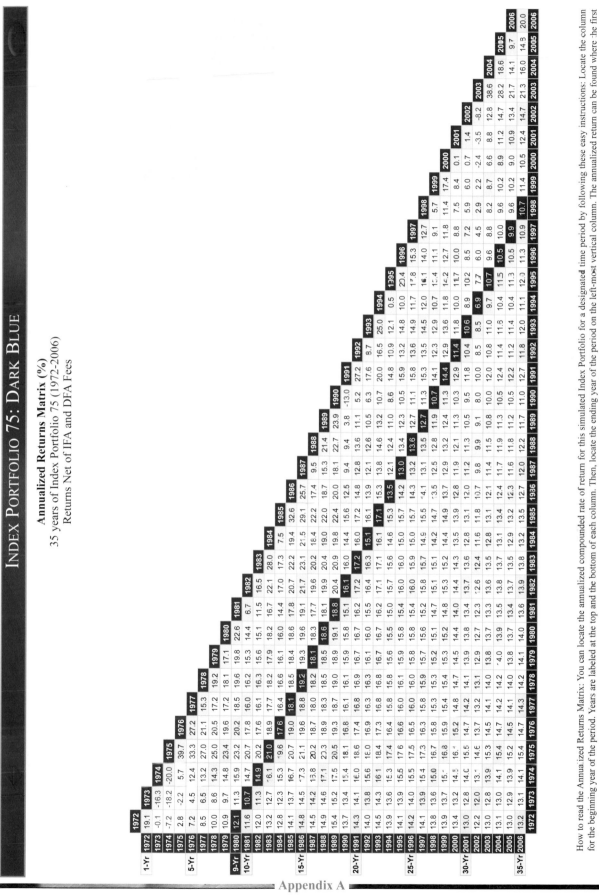

How to read the Annualized Returns Matrix: You can locate the annualized compounded rate of return for this simulated Index Portfolio for a designated time period by following these easy instructions: Locate the column for the beginning year of the period. Years are labeled at the top and the bottom of each column. Then, locate the ending year of the period on the left-most vertical column. The annualized return can be found where the first year's column intersects with the ending year's row. IFA advisory fees of 0.9% per year and DFA mutual fund expense ratios have been deducted from these results. The 9-Yr diagonal (highlighted, starting from far left column) represents the estimated average holding period for investors who score 75 on the Risk Capacity Survey at ifa.com. Sources, Updates, and Disclosures: ifa.com/btp.

Growth of $1 Matrix ($)
35 years of Index Portfolio 75 (1972-2006)
Returns Net of IFA and DFA Fees

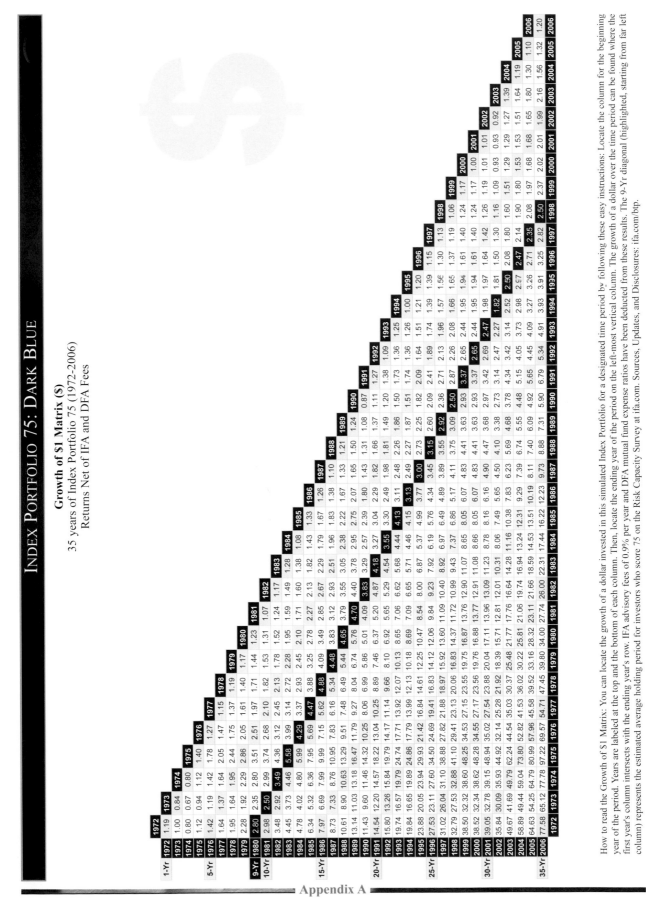

How to read the Growth of $1 Matrix: You can locate the growth of a dollar invested in this simulated Index Portfolio for a designated time period by following these easy instructions: Locate the column for the beginning year of the period. Years are labeled at the top and the bottom of each column. Then, locate the ending year of the period on the left-most vertical column. The growth of a dollar over the time period can be found where the first year's column intersects with the ending year's row. IFA advisory fees of 0.9% per year and DFA mutual fund expense ratios have been deducted from these results. The 9-Yr diagonal (highlighted, starting from far left column) represents the estimated average holding period for investors who score 75 on the Risk Capacity Survey at ifa.com. Sources, Updates, and Disclosures: ifa.com/btp.

Index Portfolio 75: Dark Blue

Monthly Rolling Period Analysis*
Based on 50 years (600 months) of Monthly Data
Jan 1957 to Dec 2006

Examples of 9 Year Monthly Rolling Periods**

Periods

1	Jan 57	←— 9 Years —→	Dec 65
2	Feb 57	←— 9 Years —→	Jan 66
3	Mar 57	←— 9 Years —→	Feb 66
4	Apr 57	←— 9 Years —→	Mar 66

493

Year 1957 1958 1959 1960 1961 1962 1963 1964 1965 1966 1967 1968 1969

Per Period Number of:		# of Rolling Periods	Average Ann'lzd Rtn. %*	Std. Dev. of Avg. Ann'lzd Rtn. %*	Lowest Rolling Period Date	Lowest Rolling Period Return	Growth of $1 in Lowest Period	Highest Rolling Period Date	Highest Rolling Period Return	Growth of $1 in Highest Period	Average Growth of $1
Yrs	Months										
0.08	1	600	1.05*	3.50*	10/87-10/87	-17.55	$0.82	1/75-1/75	19.31	$1.19	$1.01
0.25	3	598	3.23*	6.80*	9/87-11/87	-20.19	$0.80	1/75-3/75	31.04	$1.31	$1.03
0.5	6	595	6.54*	10.03*	4/74-9/74	-23.26	$0.77	1/75-6/75	43.33	$1.43	$1.07
1	12	589	13.53	14.31	10/73-9/74	-28.89	$0.71	7/82-6/83	52.75	$1.53	$1.14
2	24	577	13.01	9.14	1/73-12/74	-18.15	$0.67	12/66-11/68	38.04	$1.91	$1.52
3	36	565	12.68	6.94	1/72-12/74	-7.25	$0.80	8/84-7/87	33.23	$2.36	$1.45
4	48	553	12.55	5.78	1/71-12/74	-0.63	$0.98	7/82-6/86	29.24	$2.79	$1.63
5	60	541	12.44	5.30	10/69-9/74	-0.86	$0.96	8/82-7/87	29.46	$3.64	$1.84
6	72	529	12.49	4.82	1/69-12/74	-3.59	$0.80	10/81-9/87	24.66	$3.75	$2.08
7	84	517	12.57	4.35	1/68-12/74	0.55	$1.04	8/82-7/89	24.21	$4.56	$2.36
8	96	505	12.64	3.98	12/68-11/76	3.57	$1.32	8/82-7/90	21.65	$4.80	$2.68
9**	**108**	**493**	**12.70**	**3.81**	**1/66-12/74**	**3.71**	**$1.39**	**1/75-12/83**	**21.04**	**$5.58**	**$3.06**
10	120	481	12.78	3.60	1/65-12/74	5.47	$1.70	9/77-8/87	21.13	$6.80	$3.49
11	132	469	12.82	3.47	1/64-12/74	6.26	$1.95	1/75-12/85	20.74	$7.95	$3.98
12	144	457	12.81	3.33	1/63-12/74	7.21	$2.31	10/75-9/87	21.16	$10.01	$4.51
13	156	445	12.83	3.23	1/62-12/74	5.99	$2.13	10/74-9/87	21.69	$12.83	$5.13
14	168	433	12.91	3.06	1/61-12/74	7.04	$2.59	1/75-12/88	20.30	$13.30	$5.85
15	180	421	12.96	2.92	1/60-12/74	6.25	$2.48	1/75-12/89	20.53	$16.46	$6.67
20	240	361	13.41	1.82	1/57-12/76	9.98	$6.70	10/74-9/94	17.52	$25.25	$13.00
30	360	241	13.40	0.60	4/73-3/03	11.99	$29.88	1/75-12/04	15.42	$73.86	$44.06
40	480	121	12.73	0.37	4/63-3/03	11.99	$92.72	4/58-3/98	13.70	$169.99	$121.64
50	600	1	12.54	0.00	1/57-12/06	12.54	$367.57	1/57-12/06	12.54	$367.57	$367.57

9 Year Monthly Rolling Periods** - Jan 1957 to Dec 2006 - 493 Monthly Rolling Periods Over 50 Years

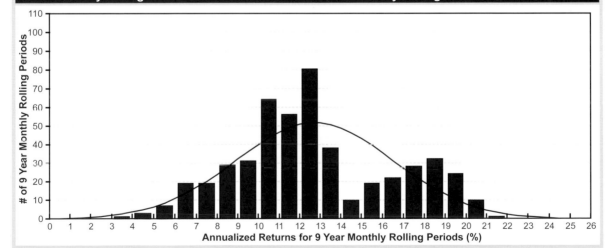

*Sources, Updates, and Disclosures: ifa.com/btp. Returns are net of IFA & DFA fees. The returns and standard deviation shown for 1, 3, and 6 month periods are not annualized. Past performance does not guarantee future results. **9 years represents the estimated average holding period for investors who score 75 on the Risk Capacity Survey at ifa.com.

RISK CAPACITY 70
DARK TEAL

Index Allocations

General Asset Class		Specific Index	
32%	US Large	16%	IFA US Large Company Index
		16%	IFA US Large Cap Value Index
16%	US Small	8%	IFA US Micro Cap Index
		8%	IFA US Small Cap Value Index
8%	Real Estate	8%	IFA Real Estate Index
16%	International	8%	IFA International Value Index
		4%	IFA International Small Company Index
		4%	IFA International Small Cap Value Index
8%	Emerging Markets	2.4%	IFA Emerging Markets Index
		2.4%	IFA Emerging Markets Value Index
		3.2%	IFA Emerging Markets Small Cap Index
20%	Fixed Income	5%	IFA One-Year Fixed Income Index
		5%	IFA Two-Year Global Fixed Income Index
		5%	IFA Five-Year Gov't Income Index
		5%	IFA Five-Year Global Fixed Income Index

Index Portfolio - Simulated Returns and Volatility Data*

	1yr ending 2006	1yr ending 2005	1yr ending 2004	1yr ending 2003	3yrs 2004-2006	5yrs 2002-2006	10yrs 1996-2006	25yrs 1982-2006	35yrs 1972-2006	50yrs 1957-2006	80yrs 1927-2006
Growth of $1	1.19	1.09	1.18	1.36	1.53	1.93	2.73	23.78	69.69	314.91	4337.00
Annualized Return %	19.06	9.21	17.54	36.39	15.19	14.07	10.55	13.51	12.89	12.19	11.04
Annualized Volatility (Standard Deviation %)	7.63	7.91	8.76	10.07	7.96	10.03	11.22	10.69	11.43	11.43	19.85

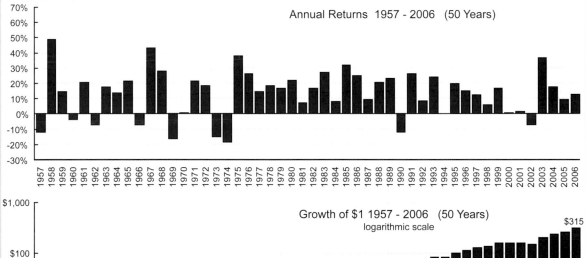

Annual Returns 1957 - 2006 (50 Years)

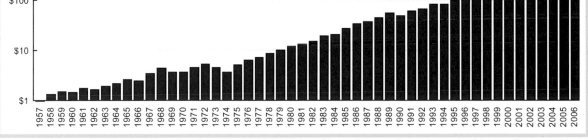

Growth of $1 1957 - 2006 (50 Years)
logarithmic scale

$315

*Sources, Updates, and Disclosures: ifa.com/btp. Returns net of IFA & DFA fees. Past performance does not guarantee future results.

INDEX PORTFOLIO 70: DARK TEAL

Annualized Returns Matrix (%)
35 years of Index Portfolio 70 (1972-2006)
Returns Net of IFA and DFA Fees

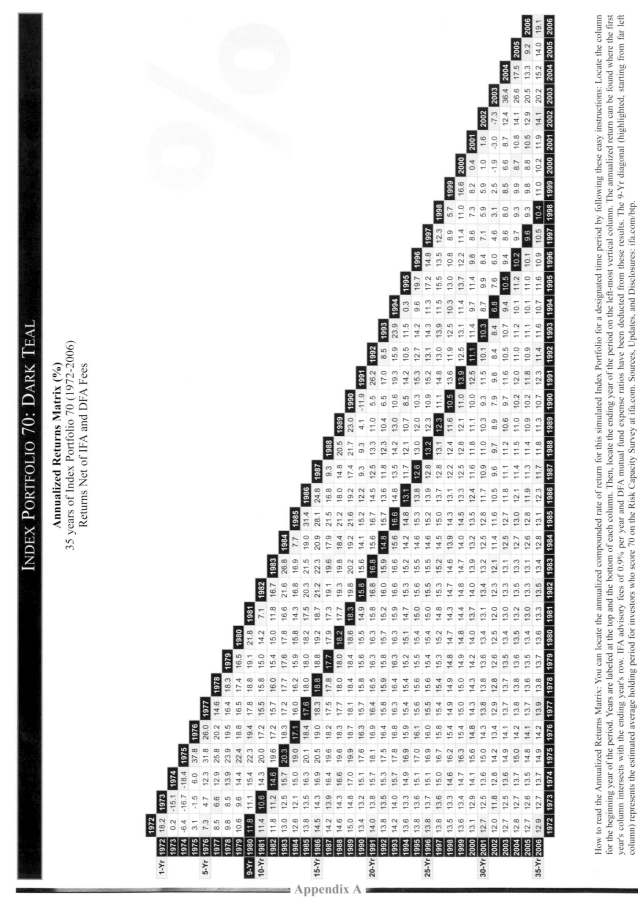

How to read the Annualized Returns Matrix: You can locate the annualized compounded rate of return for this simulated Index Portfolio for a designated time period by following these easy instructions: Locate the column for the beginning year of the period. Years are labeled at the top and the bottom of each column. Then, locate the ending year of the period on the left-most vertical column. The annualized return can be found where the first year's column intersects with the ending year's row. IFA advisory fees of 0.9% per year and DFA mutual fund expense ratios have been deducted from these results. The 9-Yr diagonal (highlighted, starting from far left column) represents the estimated average holding period for investors who score 70 on the Risk Capacity Survey at ifa.com. Sources, Updates, and Disclosures: ifa.com/btp.

Growth of $1 Matrix ($)
35 years of Index Portfolio 70 (1972-2006)
Returns Net of IFA and DFA Fees

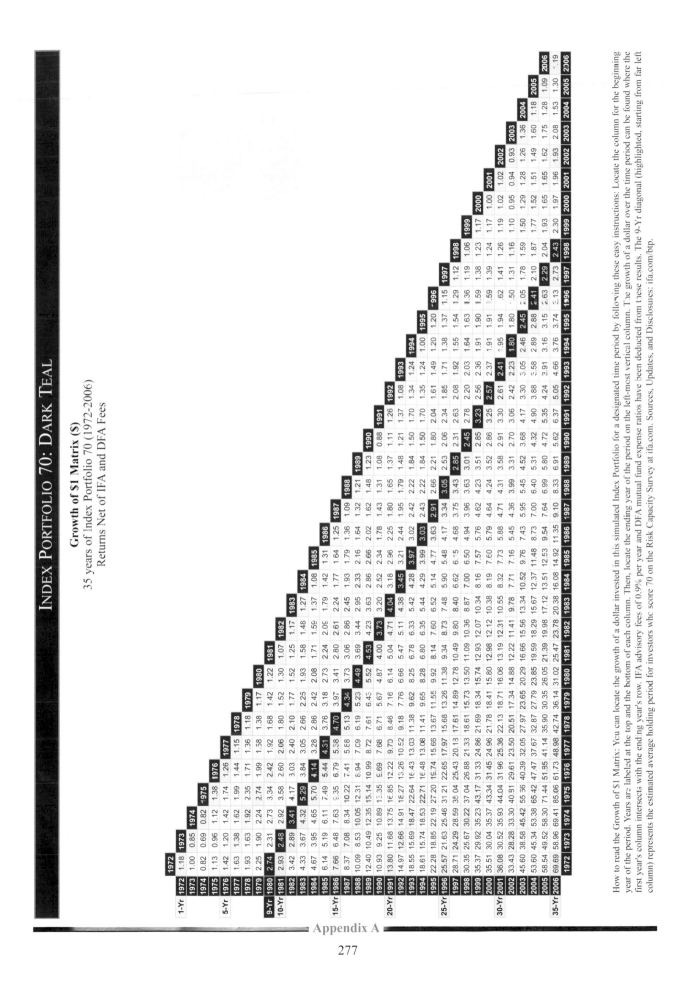

How to read the Growth of $1 Matrix: You can locate the growth of a dollar invested in this simulated Index Portfolio for a designated time period by following these easy instructions: Locate the column for the beginning year of the period. Years are labeled at the top and the bottom of each column. Then, locate the ending year of the time period on the left-most vertical column. The growth of a dollar over the time period can be found where the first year's column intersects with the ending year's row. IFA advisory fees of 0.9% per year and DFA mutual fund expense ratios have been deducted from these results. The 9-Yr diagonal (highlighted, starting from far left column) represents the estimated average holding period for investors who score 70 on the Risk Capacity Survey at ifa.com. Sources, Updates, and Disclosures: ifa.com/btp.

Index Portfolio 70: Dark Teal

Monthly Rolling Period Analysis*
Based on 50 Years (600 months) of Monthly Data
Jan 1957 to Dec 2006

Examples of 9 Year Monthly Rolling Periods**

Periods

1	Jan 57	← 9 Years →	Dec 65
2	Feb 57	← 9 Years →	Jan 66
3	Mar 57	← 9 Years →	Feb 66
4	Apr 57	← 9 Years →	Mar 66

493

Year 1957 1958 1959 1960 1961 1962 1963 1964 1965 1966 1967 1968 1969

Per Period Number of: Yrs	Months	# of Rolling Periods	Average Ann'lzd Rtn. %*	Std. Dev. of Avg. Ann'lzd Rtn. %*	Lowest Rolling Period Date	Lowest Rolling Period Return	Growth of $1 in Lowest Period	Highest Rolling Period Date	Highest Rolling Period Return	Growth of $1 in Highest Period	Average Growth of $1
0.08	1	600	1.02*	3.30*	10/87-10/87	-16.62	$0.83	1/75-1/75	18.23	$1.18	$1.01
0.25	3	598	3.12*	6.42*	9/87-11/87	-19.14	$0.81	1/75-3/75	29.31	$1.29	$1.03
0.5	6	595	6.33*	9.46*	4/74-9/74	-21.73	$0.78	1/75-6/75	40.92	$1.41	$1.06
1	12	589	13.09	13.48	10/73-9/74	-26.98	$0.73	7/82-6/83	50.45	$1.50	$1.13
2	24	577	12.62	8.62	1/73-12/74	-16.74	$0.69	12/66-11/68	36.05	$1.85	$1.50
3	36	565	12.33	6.55	1/72-12/74	-6.43	$0.82	8/84-7/87	31.90	$2.29	$1.43
4	48	553	12.21	5.48	1/71-12/74	-0.17	$0.99	7/82-6/86	28.27	$2.71	$1.61
5	60	541	12.12	5.05	11/69-10/74	-0.36	$0.98	8/82-7/87	28.35	$3.48	$1.81
6	72	529	12.17	4.61	1/69-12/74	-2.95	$0.84	10/81-9/87	23.91	$3.62	$2.04
7	84	517	12.25	4.17	1/68-12/74	0.95	$1.07	8/82-7/89	23.35	$4.34	$2.31
8	96	505	12.32	3.83	12/68-11/76	3.83	$1.35	10/81-9/89	21.02	$4.60	$2.62
9**	**108**	**493**	**12.38**	**3.67**	**1/66-12/74**	**3.92**	**$1.41**	**1/75-12/83**	**20.33**	**$5.29**	**$2.97**
10	120	481	12.45	3.47	1/65-12/74	5.56	$1.72	9/77-8/87	20.49	$6.45	$3.38
11	132	469	12.50	3.35	1/64-12/74	6.28	$1.95	1/75-12/85	20.09	$7.49	$3.84
12	144	457	12.50	3.21	1/63-12/74	7.15	$2.29	1/75-12/86	20.48	$9.35	$4.35
13	156	445	12.52	3.11	1/62-12/74	5.99	$2.13	10/74-9/87	20.97	$11.88	$4.93
14	168	433	12.59	2.95	1/61-12/74	6.97	$2.57	1/75-12/88	19.64	$12.31	$5.61
15	180	421	12.65	2.82	1/60-12/74	6.23	$2.48	1/75-12/89	19.86	$15.14	$6.37
20	240	361	13.08	1.76	1/57-12/76	9.75	$6.43	10/74-9/94	17.00	$23.11	$12.24
30	360	241	13.08	0.56	4/73-3/03	11.77	$28.17	1/75-12/04	14.95	$65.35	$40.37
40	480	121	12.41	0.34	4/63-3/03	11.73	$84.49	4/58-3/98	13.32	$148.68	$108.52
50	600	1	12.19	0.00	1/57-12/06	12.19	$314.56	1/57-12/06	12.19	$314.56	$314.56

9 Year Monthly Rolling Periods** - Jan 1957 to Dec 2006 - 493 Monthly Rolling Periods Over 50 Years

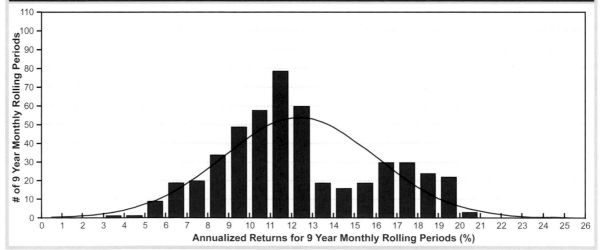

*Sources, Updates, and Disclosures: ifa.com/btp. Returns are net of IFA & DFA fees. The returns and standard deviation shown for 1, 3, and 6 month periods are not annualized. Past performance does not guarantee future results. **9 years represents the estimated average holding period for investors who score 70 on the Risk Capacity Survey at ifa.com.

RISK CAPACITY 65
DARK GREEN

Index Portfolio 65: Dark Green

Index Allocations

General Asset Class		Specific Index	
30%	US Large	15%	IFA US Large Company Index
		15%	IFA US Large Cap Value Index
15%	US Small	7.5%	IFA US Micro Cap Index
		7.5%	IFA US Small Cap Value Index
7.5%	Real Estate	7.5%	IFA Real Estate Index
15%	International	7.5%	IFA International Value Index
		3.75%	IFA International Small Company Index
		3.75%	IFA International Small Cap Value Index
7.5%	Emerging Markets	2.25%	IFA Emerging Markets Index
		2.25%	IFA Emerging Markets Value Index
		3.00%	IFA Emerging Markets Small Cap Index
25%	Fixed Income	6.25%	IFA One-Year Fixed Income Index
		6.25%	IFA Two-Year Global Fixed Income Index
		6.25%	IFA Five-Year Gov't Income Index
		6.25%	IFA Five-Year Global Fixed Income Index

Index Portfolio - Simulated Returns and Volatility Data*

	1yr ending 2006	1yr ending 2005	1yr ending 2004	1yr ending 2003	3yrs 2004-2006	5yrs 2002-2006	10yrs 1996-2006	25yrs 1982-2006	35yrs 1972-2006	50yrs 1957-2006	80yrs 1927-2006
Growth of $1	1.18	1.09	1.16	1.34	1.50	1.88	2.63	21.73	62.46	269.12	3,439
Annualized Return %	18.09	8.68	16.50	34.20	14.35	13.42	10.17	13.11	12.54	11.84	10.71
Annualized Volatility (Standard Deviation %)	7.17	7.40	8.29	9.47	7.49	9.37	10.50	10.06	10.77	10.76	18.63

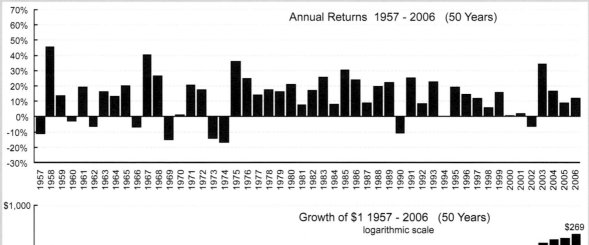

Annual Returns 1957 - 2006 (50 Years)

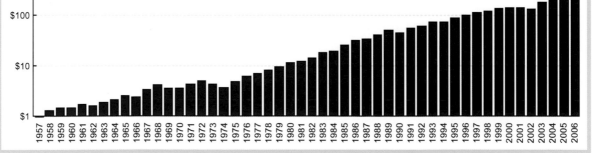

Growth of $1 1957 - 2006 (50 Years)
logarithmic scale

$269

*Sources, Updates, and Disclosures: ifa.com/btp. Returns net of IFA & DFA fees. Past performance does not guarantee future results.

Index Portfolio 65: Dark Green

Annualized Returns Matrix (%)
35 years of Index Portfolio 65 (1972-2006)
Returns Net of IFA and DFA Fees

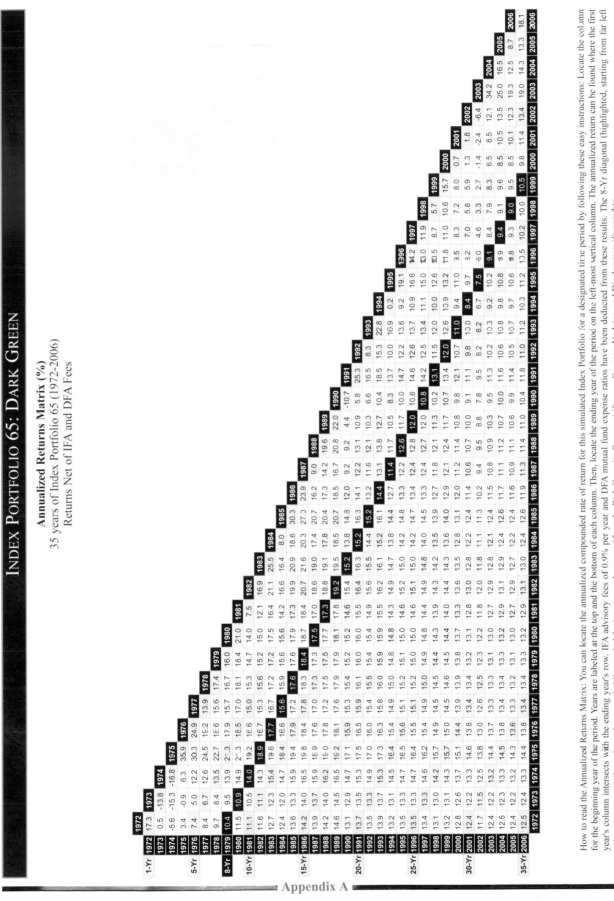

How to read the Annualized Returns Matrix: You can locate the annualized compounded rate of return for this simulated Index Portfolio for a designated time period by following these easy instructions: Locate the column for the beginning year of the period. Then, locate the ending year of the period on the left-most vertical column. The annualized return can be found where the first year's column intersects with the ending year's row. IFA advisory fees of 0.9% per year and DFA mutual fund expense ratios have been deducted from these results. The 8-Yr diagonal (highlighted, starting from far left column) represents the estimated average holding period for investors who score 65 on the Risk Capacity Survey at ifa.com. Sources, Updates, and Disclosures: ifa.com/btp.

INDEX PORTFOLIO 65: DARK GREEN

Growth of $1 Matrix ($)
35 years of Index Portfolio 65 (1972-2006)
Returns Net of IFA and DFA Fees

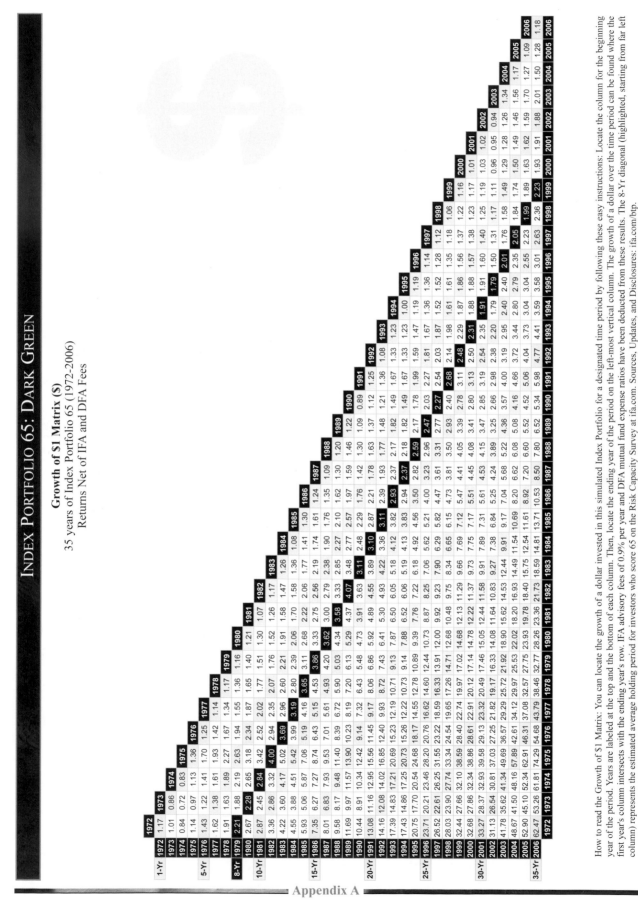

How to read the Growth of $1 Matrix: You can locate the growth of a dollar invested in this simulated Index Portfolio for a designated time period by following these easy instructions: Locate the column for the beginning year of the period. Years are labeled at the top and the bottom of each column. Then, locate the ending year of the period on the left-most vertical column. The growth of a dollar over the time period can be found where the first year's column intersects with the ending year's row. IFA advisory fees of 0.9% per year and DFA mutual fund expense ratios have been deducted from these results. The 8-Yr diagonal (highlighted, starting from far left column) represents the estimated average holding period for investors who score 65 on the Risk Capacity Survey at ifa.com. Sources, Updates, and Disclosures: ifa.com/btp.

Index Portfolio 65: Dark Green

Monthly Rolling Period Analysis*
Based on 50 years (600 months) of Monthly Data
Jan 1957 to Dec 2006

Examples of 8 Year Monthly Rolling Periods**

Periods

1	Jan 57	← 8 Years →	Dec 64
2	Feb 57	← 8 Years →	Jan 65
3	Mar 57	← 8 Years →	Feb 65
4	Apr 57	← 8 Years →	Mar 65
505			

Year 1957 1958 1959 1960 1961 1962 1963 1964 1965 1966 1967 1968 1969

Per Period Number of: Yrs	Months	# of Rolling Periods	Average Ann'lzd Rtn. %*	Std. Dev. of Avg. Ann'lzd Rtn. %*	Lowest Rolling Period Date	Lowest Rolling Period Return	Growth of $1 in Lowest Period	Highest Rolling Period Date	Highest Rolling Period Return	Growth of $1 in Highest Period	Average Growth of $1
0.00	1	000	0.99*	3.11⁺	10/87-10/87	-15.66	$0.84	1/75-1/75	17.15	$1.17	$1.01
0.25	3	598	3.02*	6.04*	9/87-11/87	-18.07	$0.82	1/75-3/75	27.57	$1.28	$1.03
0.5	6	595	6.11*	8.88*	4/74-9/74	-20.19	$0.80	1/75-6/75	38.51	$1.39	$1.06
1	12	589	12.64	12.65	10/73-9/74	-25.06	$0.75	7/82-6/83	48.18	$1.48	$1.13
2	24	577	12.23	8.11	1/73-12/74	-15.34	$0.72	12/66-11/68	34.06	$1.80	$1.48
3	36	565	11.97	6.18	1/72-12/74	-5.62	$0.84	8/84-7/87	30.57	$2.23	$1.42
4	48	553	11.87	5.19	1/71-12/74	0.28	$1.01	7/82-6/86	27.30	$2.63	$1.59
5	60	541	11.78	4.80	11/69-10/74	0.12	$1.01	8/82-7/87	27.24	$3.34	$1.78
6	72	529	11.84	4.40	1/69-12/74	-2.31	$0.87	10/81-9/87	23.16	$3.49	$2.00
7	84	517	11.92	4.00	1/68-12/74	1.35	$1.10	8/82-7/89	22.49	$4.14	$2.26
8**	**96**	**505**	**11.99**	**3.68**	**12/68-11/76**	**4.08**	**$1.38**	**10/81-9/89**	**20.38**	**$4.41**	**$2.55**
9	108	493	12.05	3.53	1/66-12/74	4.12	$1.44	1/75-12/83	19.62	$5.01	$2.89
10	120	481	12.13	3.34	10/64-9/74	5.61	$1.73	9/77-8/87	19.84	$6.11	$3.27
11	132	469	12.17	3.23	1/64-12/74	6.28	$1.95	1/75-12/85	19.44	$7.06	$3.71
12	144	457	12.17	3.10	1/63-12/74	7.07	$2.27	1/75-12/86	19.80	$8.74	$4.18
13	156	445	12.19	3.01	1/62-12/74	5.98	$2.13	10/74-9/87	20.25	$10.99	$4.73
14	168	433	12.27	2.85	1/61-12/74	6.88	$2.54	1/75-12/88	18.98	$11.39	$5.37
15	180	421	12.33	2.72	1/60-12/74	6.19	$2.46	1/75-12/89	19.18	$13.90	$6.08
20	240	361	12.75	1.71	1/57-12/76	9.50	$6.14	10/74-9/94	16.47	$21.10	$11.51
30	360	241	12.75	0.52	4/73-3/03	11.53	$26.41	1/75-12/04	14.49	$57.95	$36.90
40	480	121	12.08	0.32	4/63-3/03	11.45	$76.42	4/58-3/98	12.93	$129.53	$96.51
50	600	1	11.84	0.00	1/57-12/06	11.84	$269.07	1/57-12/06	11.84	$269.07	$269.07

8 Year Monthly Rolling Periods** - Jan 1957 to Dec 2006 - 505 Monthly Rolling Periods Over 50 Years

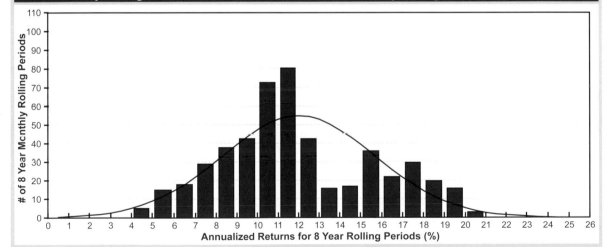

*Sources, Updates, and Disclosures: ifa.com/btp. Returns are net of IFA & DFA fees. The returns and standard deviation shown for 1, 3, and 6 month periods are not annualized. Past performance does not guarantee future results. **8 years represents the estimated average holding period for investors who score 65 on the Risk Capacity Survey at ifa.com.

Appendix A

283

RISK CAPACITY 60
GREEN

Index Allocations

General Asset Class		Specific Index	
28%	US Large	14%	IFA US Large Company Index
		14%	IFA US Large Cap Value Index
14%	US Small	7%	IFA US Micro Cap Index
		7%	IFA US Small Cap Value Index
7%	Real Estate	7%	IFA Real Estate Index
14%	International	7%	IFA International Value Index
		3.5%	IFA International Small Company Index
		3.5%	IFA International Small Cap Value Index
7%	Emerging Markets	2.1%	IFA Emerging Markets Index
		2.1%	IFA Emerging Markets Value Index
		2.8%	IFA Emerging Markets Small Cap Index
30%	Fixed Income	7.5%	IFA One-Year Fixed Income Index
		7.5%	IFA Two-Year Global Fixed Income Index
		7.5%	IFA Five-Year Gov't Income Index
		7.5%	IFA Five-Year Global Fixed Income Index

Index Portfolio - Simulated Returns and Volatility Data*

	1yr ending 2006	1yr ending 2005	1yr ending 2004	1yr ending 2003	3yrs 2004-2006	5yrs 2002-2006	10yrs 1996-2006	25yrs 1982-2006	35yrs 1972-2006	50yrs 1957-2006	80yrs 1927-2006
Growth of $1	1.17	1.08	1.15	1.32	1.46	1.82	2.54	19.83	55.84	229.00	2,692
Annualized Return %	17.12	8.16	15.46	32.01	13.51	12.77	9.79	12.69	12.18	11.48	10.38
Annualized Volatility (Standard Deviation %)	6.71	6.90	7.82	8.86	7.03	8.71	9.78	9.43	10.10	10.08	17.42

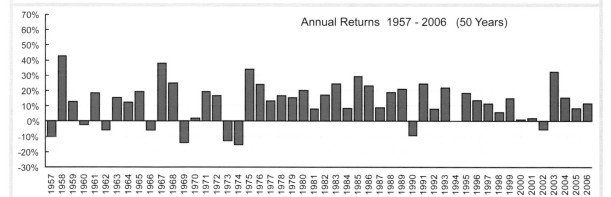

Annual Returns 1957 - 2006 (50 Years)

Growth of $1 1957 - 2006 (50 Years)
logarithmic scale
$229

*Sources, Updates, and Disclosures: ifa.com/btp. Returns net of IFA & DFA fees. Past performance does not guarantee future results.

Appendix A

INDEX PORTFOLIO 60: GREEN

Annualized Returns Matrix (%)
35 years of Index Portfolio 60 (1972-2006)
Returns Net of IFA and DFA Fees

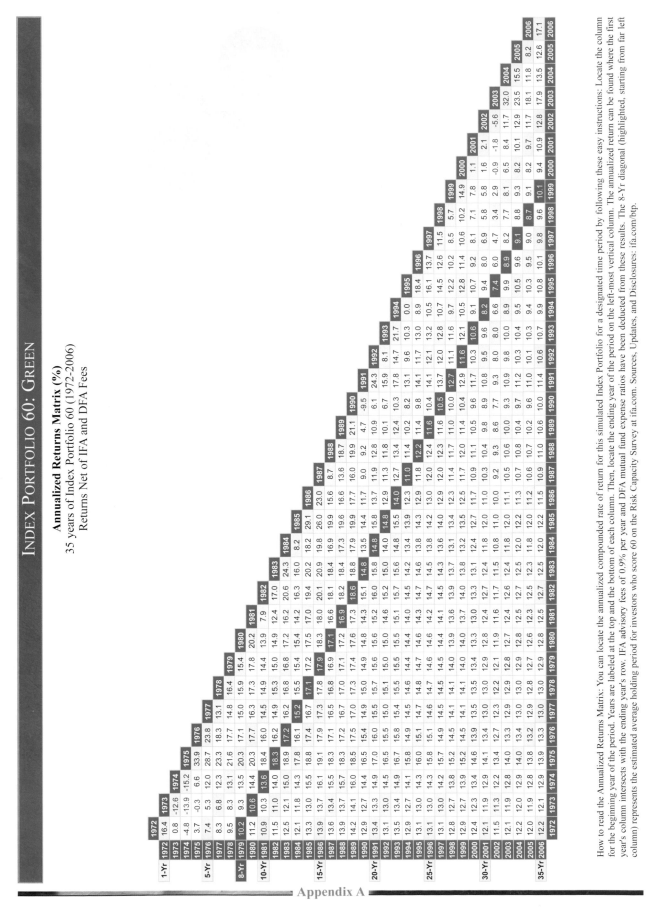

How to read the Annualized Returns Matrix: You can locate the annualized compounded rate of return for this simulated Index Portfolio for a designated time period by following these easy instructions: Locate the column for the beginning year of the period. Years are labeled at the top and the bottom of each column. Then, locate the ending year of the period on the left-most vertical column. The annualized return can be found where the first year's column intersects with the ending year's row. IFA advisory fees of 0.9% per year and DFA mutual fund expense ratios have been deducted from these results. The 8-Yr diagonal (highlighted, starting from far left column) represents the estimated average holding period for investors who score 60 on the Risk Capacity Survey at ifa.com. Sources, Updates, and Disclosures: ifa.com/btp.

INDEX PORTFOLIO 60: GREEN

Growth of $1 Matrix ($)
35 years of Index Portfolio 60 (1972-2006)
Returns Net of IFA and DFA Fees

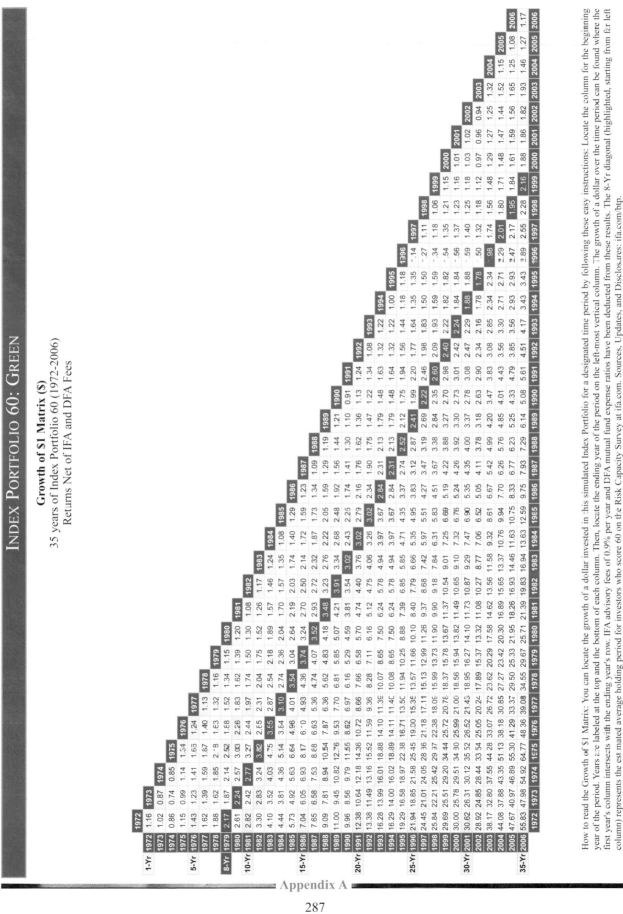

How to read the Growth of $1 Matrix: You can locate the growth of a dollar invested in this simulated Index Portfolio for a designated time period by following these easy instructions: Locate the column for the beginning year of the period. Years are labeled at the top and the bottom of each column. Then, locate the ending year of the period on the left-most vertical column. The growth of a dollar over the time period can be found where the first year's column intersects with the ending year's row. IFA advisory fees of 0.9% per year and DFA mutual fund expense ratios have been deducted from these results. The 8-Yr diagonal (highlighted, starting from far left column) represents the estimated average holding period for investors who score 60 on the Risk Capacity Survey at ifa.com. Sources, Updates, and Disclosures: ifa.com/btp.

Index Portfolio 60: Green
Monthly Rolling Period Analysis*
Based on 50 Years (600 months) of Monthly Data
Jan 1957 to Dec 2006

Examples of 8 Year Monthly Rolling Periods**

Periods

1	Jan 57	← 8 Years →	Dec 64
2	Feb 57	← 8 Years →	Jan 65
3	Mar 57	← 8 Years →	Feb 65
4	Apr 57	← 8 Years →	Mar 65

505

Year 1957   1958   1959   1960   1961   1962   1963   1964   1965   1966   1967   1968   1969

Per Period Number of:		# of Rolling Periods	Average Ann'lzd Rtn. %*	Std. Dev. of Avg. Ann'lzd Rtn. %*	Lowest Rolling Period Date	Lowest Rolling Period Return	Growth of $1 in Lowest Period	Highest Rolling Period Date	Highest Rolling Period Return	Growth of $1 in Highest Period	Average Growth of $1
Yrs	Months										
0.08	1	600	0.95*	2.91*	10/87-10/87	-14.67	$0.85	1/75-1/75	16.06	$1.16	$1.01
0.25	3	598	2.91*	5.66*	9/87-11/87	-16.96	$0.83	1/75-3/75	25.84	$1.26	$1.03
0.5	6	595	5.90*	8.31*	4/74-9/74	-18.65	$0.81	1/75-6/75	36.11	$1.36	$1.06
1	12	589	12.18	11.82	10/73-9/74	-23.12	$0.77	7/82-6/83	45.94	$1.46	$1.12
2	24	577	11.83	7.60	1/73-12/74	-13.93	$0.74	12/66-11/68	32.06	$1.74	$1.45
3	36	565	11.61	5.81	1/72-12/74	-4.83	$0.86	8/84-7/87	29.24	$2.16	$1.40
4	48	553	11.52	4.91	1/71-12/74	0.71	$1.03	7/82-6/86	26.34	$2.55	$1.56
5	60	541	11.44	4.56	11/69-10/74	0.59	$1.03	8/82-7/87	26.13	$3.19	$1.75
6	72	529	11.50	4.20	1/69-12/74	-1.69	$0.90	10/81-9/87	22.40	$3.36	$1.96
7	84	517	11.58	3.83	1/68-12/74	1.73	$1.13	8/82-7/89	21.64	$3.94	$2.21
8**	96	505	11.65	3.54	12/68-11/76	4.32	$1.40	10/81-9/89	19.74	$4.23	$2.48
9	108	493	11.71	3.40	1/66-12/74	4.29	$1.46	3/78-2/87	19.04	$4.80	$2.80
10	120	481	11.79	3.22	10/64-9/74	5.64	$1.73	9/77-8/87	19.19	$5.79	$3.17
11	132	469	11.84	3.11	1/64-12/74	6.27	$1.95	1/75-12/85	18.78	$6.64	$3.58
12	144	457	11.84	2.99	1/63-12/74	6.99	$2.25	1/75-12/86	19.13	$8.17	$4.02
13	156	445	11.87	2.90	1/62-12/74	5.95	$2.12	10/74-9/87	19.53	$10.17	$4.53
14	168	433	11.94	2.75	1/61-12/74	6.78	$2.51	1/75-12/88	18.32	$10.54	$5.13
15	180	421	12.00	2.63	1/60-12/74	6.15	$2.45	10/74-9/89	18.51	$12.77	$5.80
20	240	361	12.41	1.67	1/57-12/76	9.24	$5.86	10/74-9/94	15.94	$19.26	$10.81
30	360	241	12.40	0.48	4/73-3/03	11.29	$24.76	1/75-12/04	14.01	$51.08	$33.65
40	480	121	11.75	0.29	4/63-3/03	11.17	$69.10	4/58-3/98	12.52	$111.99	$85.54
50	600	1	11.48	0.00	1/57-12/06	11.48	$229.01	1/57-12/06	11.48	$229.01	$229.01

8 Year Monthly Rolling Periods** - Jan 1957 to Dec 2006 - 505 Monthly Rolling Periods Over 50 Years

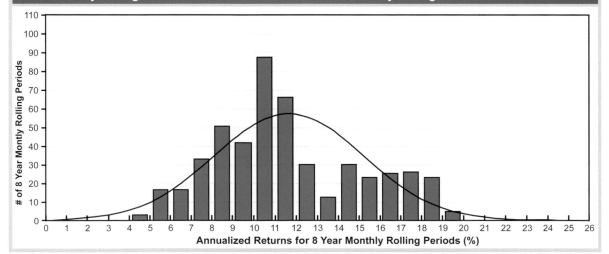

Annualized Returns for 8 Year Monthly Rolling Periods (%)

*Sources, Updates, and Disclosures: ifa.com/btp. Returns are net of IFA & DFA fees. The returns and standard deviation shown for 1, 3, and 6 month periods are not annualized. Past performance does not guarantee future results. **8 years represents the estimated average holding period for investors who score 60 on the Risk Capacity Survey at ifa.com.

Appendix A

RISK CAPACITY 55
OLIVE

Index Allocations

General Asset Class		Specific Index	
26%	US Large	13%	IFA US Large Company Index
		13%	IFA US Large Cap Value Index
13%	US Small	6.5%	IFA US Micro Cap Index
		6.5%	IFA US Small Cap Value Index
6.5%	Real Estate	6.5%	IFA Real Estate Index
13%	International	6.5%	IFA International Value Index
		3.25%	IFA International Small Company Index
		3.25%	IFA International Small Cap Value Index
6.5%	Emerging Markets	1.95%	IFA Emerging Markets Index
		1.95%	IFA Emerging Markets Value Index
		2.60%	IFA Emerging Markets Small Cap Index
35%	Fixed Income	8.75%	IFA One-Year Fixed Income Index
		8.75%	IFA Two-Year Global Fixed Income Index
		8.75%	IFA Five-Year Gov't Income Index
		8.75%	IFA Five-Year Global Fixed Income Index

Index Portfolio - Simulated Returns and Volatility Data*

	1yr ending 2006	1yr ending 2005	1yr ending 2004	1yr ending 2003	3yrs 2004-2006	5yrs 2002-2006	10yrs 1996-2006	25yrs 1982-2006	35yrs 1972-2006	50yrs 1957-2006	80yrs 1927-2006
Growth of $1	1.16	1.08	1.14	1.30	1.43	1.77	2.46	18.07	49.81	194.00	2,079
Annualized Return %	16.14	7.63	14.42	29.82	12.67	12.10	9.41	12.27	11.81	11.11	10.02
Annualized Volatility (Standard Deviation %)	6.24	6.39	7.36	8.26	6.56	8.06	9.07	8.81	9.43	9.41	16.21

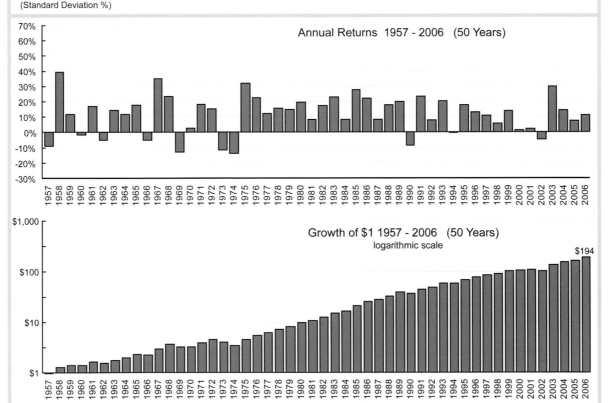

Annual Returns 1957 - 2006 (50 Years)

Growth of $1 1957 - 2006 (50 Years)
logarithmic scale

$194

*Sources, Updates, and Disclosures: ifa.com/btp. Returns net of IFA & DFA fees. Past performance does not guarantee future results.

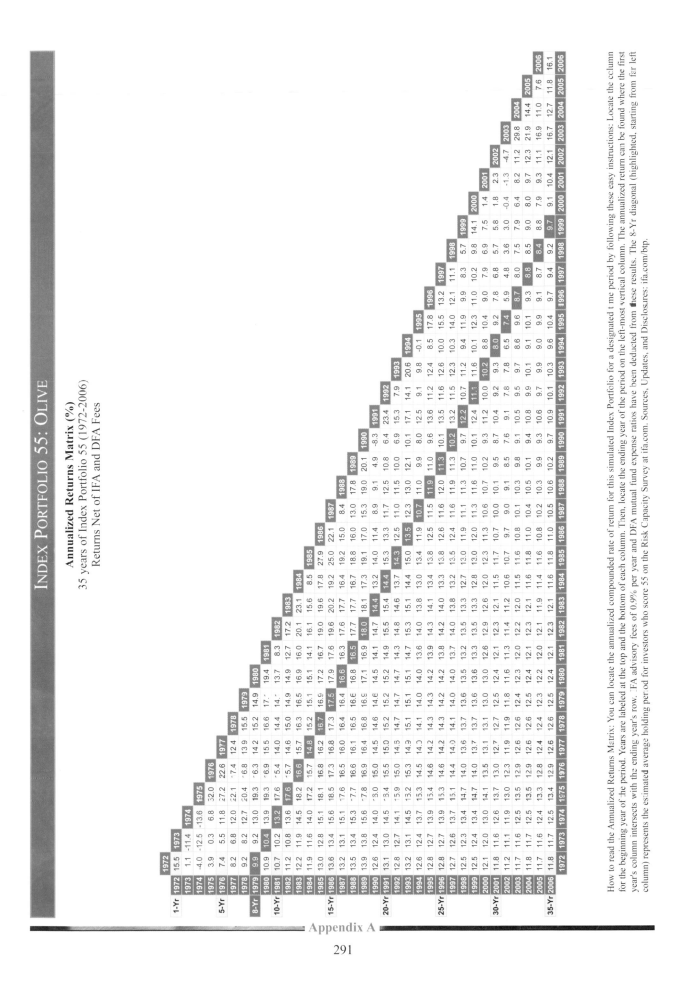

INDEX PORTFOLIO 55: OLIVE

Annualized Returns Matrix (%)
35 years of Index Portfolio 55 (1972–2006)
Returns Net of IFA and DFA Fees

How to read the Annualized Returns Matrix: You can locate the annualized compounded rate of return for this simulated Index Portfolio for a designated time period by following these easy instructions: Locate the column for the beginning year of the period. Years are labeled at the top and the bottom of each column. Then, locate the ending year of the period on the left-most vertical column. The annualized return can be found where the first year's column intersects with the ending year's row. IFA advisory fees of 0.9% per year and DFA mutual fund expense ratios have been deducted from these results. The 8-Yr diagonal (highlighted, starting from far left column) represents the estimated average holding period for investors who score 55 on the Risk Capacity Survey at ifa.com. Sources, Updates, and Disclosures: ifa.com/btp.

Growth of $1 Matrix ($)
35 years of Index Portfolio 55 (1972-2006)
Returns Net of IFA and DFA Fees

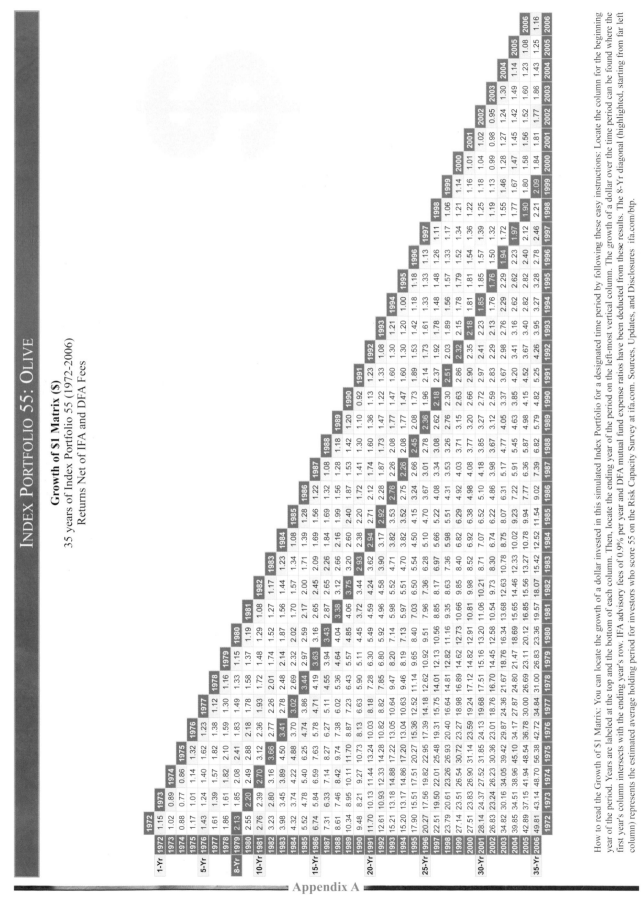

How to read the Growth of $1 Matrix: You can locate the growth of a dollar invested in this simulated Index Portfolio for a designated time period by following these easy instructions: Locate the column for the beginning year of the period. Years are labeled at the top and the bottom of each column. Then, locate the ending year of the period on the left-most vertical column. The growth of a dollar over the time period can be found where the first year's column intersects with the ending year's row. IFA advisory fees of 0.9% per year and DFA mutual fund expense ratios have been deducted from these results. The 8-Yr diagonal (highlighted, starting from far left column) represents the estimated average holding period for investors who score 55 on the Risk Capacity Survey at ifa.com. Sources, Updates, and Disclosures ifa.com/btp.

Index Portfolio 55: Olive

Monthly Rolling Period Analysis[*]
Based on 50 years (600 months) of Monthly Data
Jan 1957 to Dec 2006

Examples of 8 Year Monthly Rolling Periods**

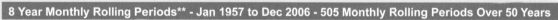

Periods

1	Jan 57	← 8 Years →	Dec 64
2	Feb 57	← 8 Years →	Jan 65
3	Mar 57	← 8 Years →	Feb 65
4	Apr 57	← 8 Years →	Mar 65

505

Year 1957 1958 1959 1960 1961 1962 1963 1964 1965 1966 1967 1968 1969

Per Period Number of: Yrs	Months	# of Rolling Periods	Average Ann'lzd Rtn. %*	Std. Dev. of Avg. Ann'lzd Rtn. %*	Lowest Rolling Period Date	Lowest Rolling Period Return	Growth of $1 in Lowest Period	Highest Rolling Period Date	Highest Rolling Period Return	Growth of $1 in Highest Period	Average Growth of $1
0.08	1	600	0.92*	2.72*	10/87-10/87	-13.65	$0.86	1/75-1/75	14.98	$1.16	$1.01
0.25	3	598	2.81*	5.28*	9/07-11/87	-15.83	$0.84	1/75-3/75	24.11	$1.24	$1.03
0.5	6	595	5.68*	7.74*	4/74-9/74	-17.10	$0.83	1/75-6/75	33.70	$1.34	$1.06
1	12	589	11.73	11.01	10/73-9/74	-21.17	$0.79	7/82-6/83	43.73	$1.44	$1.12
2	24	577	11.43	7.11	1/73-12/74	12.52	$0.77	12/66-11/68	30.06	$1.69	$1.43
3	36	565	11.23	5.45	1/72-12/74	-4.04	$0.88	8/84-7/87	27.91	$2.09	$1.39
4	48	553	11.16	4.64	1/71-12/74	1.13	$1.05	7/82-6/86	25.37	$2.47	$1.54
5	60	541	11.10	4.33	11/69-10/74	1.04	$1.05	8/82-7/87	25.03	$3.06	$1.72
6	72	529	11.15	4.00	1/69-12/74	-1.08	$0.94	10/81-9/87	21.64	$3.24	$1.92
7	84	517	11.23	3.67	1/68-12/74	2.10	$1.16	8/82-7/89	20.79	$3.75	$2.16
8**	96	505	11.30	3.40	12/68-11/76	4.54	$1.43	10/81-9/89	19.10	$4.05	$2.42
9	108	493	11.37	3.27	1/66-12/74	4.45	$1.48	3/78-2/87	18.45	$4.59	$2.72
10	120	481	11.44	3.11	10/64-9/74	5.65	$1.73	9/77-8/87	18.53	$5.47	$3.06
11	132	469	11.49	3.00	1/64-12/74	6.24	$1.95	1/75-12/85	18.13	$6.25	$3.45
12	144	457	11.50	2.89	1/63-12/74	6.88	$2.22	1/75-12/86	18.45	$7.63	$3.87
13	156	445	11.53	2.81	1/62-12/74	5.91	$2.11	10/74-9/87	18.80	$9.39	$4.35
14	168	433	11.61	2.66	1/61-12/74	6.66	$2.47	1/75-12/88	17.66	$9.75	$4.90
15	180	421	11.66	2.54	1/60-12/74	6.09	$2.43	10/74-9/89	17.84	$11.73	$5.52
20	240	361	12.06	1.63	1/57-12/76	8.97	$5.57	10/74-9/94	15.40	$17.54	$10.14
30	360	241	12.06	0.44	4/73-3/03	11.05	$23.20	1/75-12/04	13.54	$45.13	$30.62
40	480	121	11.41	0.27	4/63-3/03	10.88	$62.25	4/58-3/98	12.11	$96.78	$75.61
50	600	1	11.11	0.00	1/57-12/06	11.11	$193.94	1/57-12/06	11.11	$193.94	$193.94

8 Year Monthly Rolling Periods** - Jan 1957 to Dec 2006 - 505 Monthly Rolling Periods Over 50 Years

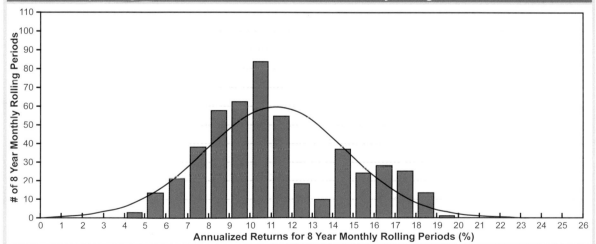

*Sources, Updates, and Disclosures: ifa.com/btp. Returns are net of IFA & DFA fees. The returns and standard deviation shown for 1, 3, and 6 month periods are not annualized. Past performance does not guarantee future results. **8 years represents the estimated average holding period for investors who score 55 on the Risk Capacity Survey at ifa.com.

RISK CAPACITY 50
SEA GREEN

Index Allocations

General Asset Class		Specific Index	
24%	US Large	12%	IFA US Large Company Index
		12%	IFA US Large Cap Value Index
12%	US Small	6%	IFA US Micro Cap Index
		6%	IFA US Small Cap Value Index
6%	Real Estate	6%	IFA Real Estate Index
12%	International	6%	IFA International Value Index
		3%	IFA International Small Company Index
		3%	IFA International Small Cap Value Index
6%	Emerging Markets	1.8%	IFA Emerging Markets Index
		1.8%	IFA Emerging Markets Value Index
		2.4%	IFA Emerging Markets Small Cap Index
40%	Fixed Income	10%	IFA One-Year Fixed Income Index
		10%	IFA Two-Year Global Fixed Income Index
		10%	IFA Five-Year Gov't Income Index
		10%	IFA Five-Year Global Fixed Income Index

Index Portfolio - Simulated Returns and Volatility Data*

	1yr ending 2006	1yr ending 2005	1yr ending 2004	1yr ending 2003	3yrs 2004-2006	5yrs 2002-2006	10yrs 1996-2006	25yrs 1982-2006	35yrs 1972-2006	50yrs 1957-2006	80yrs 1927-2006
Growth of $1	1.15	1.07	1.13	1.28	1.40	1.72	2.37	16.44	44.32	163.63	1,585
Annualized Return %	15.17	7.10	13.38	27.63	11.83	11.42	9.01	11.85	11.44	10.73	9.65
Annualized Volatility (Standard Deviation %)	5.77	5.89	6.89	7.66	6.09	7.41	8.35	8.18	8.77	8.74	15.01

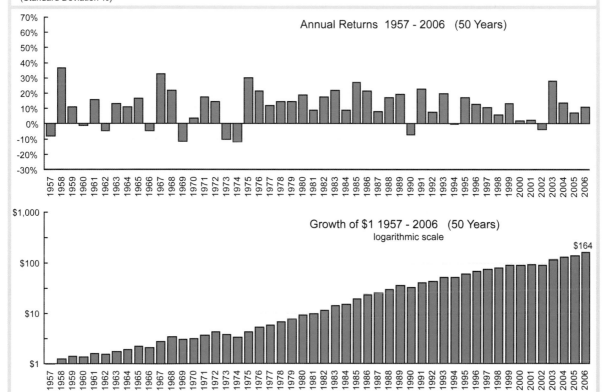

Annual Returns 1957 - 2006 (50 Years)

Growth of $1 1957 - 2006 (50 Years)
logarithmic scale
$164

*Sources, Updates, and Disclosures: ifa.com/btp. Returns net of IFA & DFA fees. Past performance does not guarantee future results.

Annualized Returns Matrix (%)
35 years of Index Portfolio 50 (1972-2006)
Returns Net of IFA and DFA Fees

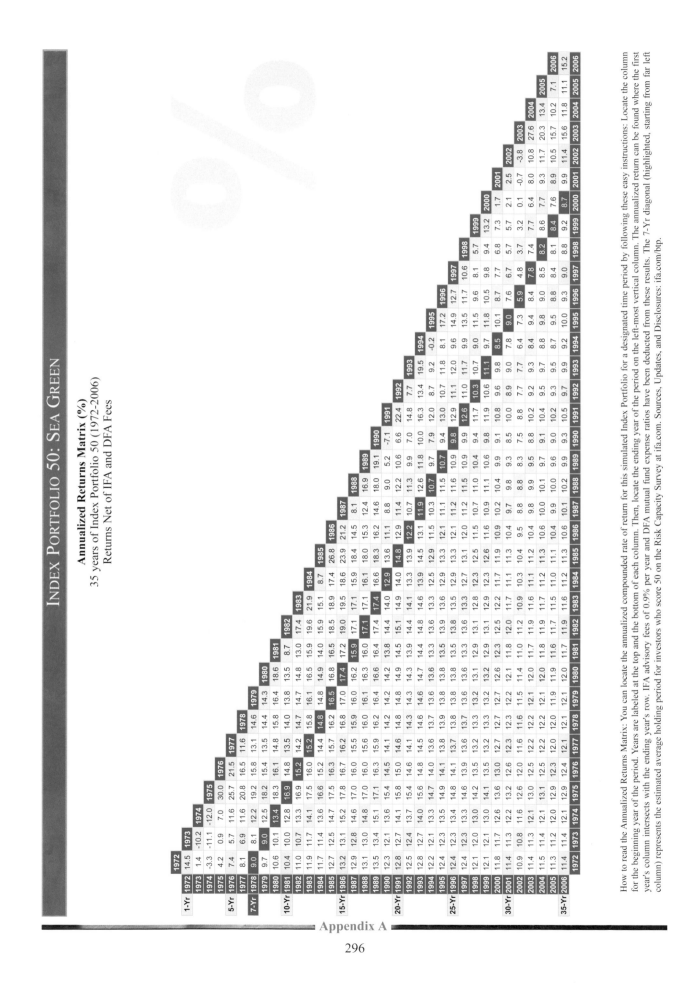

How to read the Annualized Returns Matrix: You can locate the annualized compounded rate of return for this simulated Index Portfolio for a designated time period by following these easy instructions: Locate the column for the beginning year of the period. Years are labeled at the top and the bottom of each column. Then, locate the ending year of the period on the left-most vertical column. The annualized return can be found where the first year's column intersects with the ending year's row. IFA advisory fees of 0.9% per year and DFA mutual fund expense ratios have been deducted from these results. The 7-Yr diagonal (highlighted, starting from far left column) represents the estimated average holding period for investors who score 50 on the Risk Capacity Survey at ifa.com. Sources, Updates, and Disclosures: ifa.com/bfp.

Growth of $1 Matrix ($)
35 years of Index Portfolio 50 (1972-2006)
Returns Net of IFA and DFA Fees

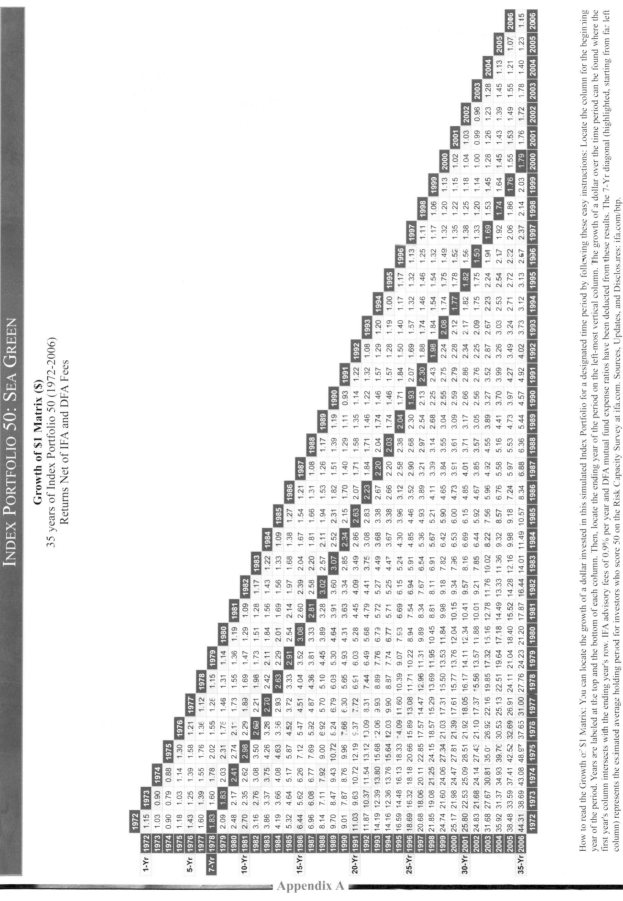

How to read the Growth of $1 Matrix: You can locate the growth of a dollar invested in this simulated Index Portfolio for a designated time period by following these easy instructions: Locate the column for the beginning year of the period. Years are labeled at the top and the bottom of each column. Then, locate the ending year of the period on the left-most vertical column. The growth of a dollar over the time period can be found where the first year's column intersects with the ending year's row. IFA advisory fees of 0.9% per year and DFA mutual fund expense ratios have been deducted from these results. The 7-Yr diagonal (highlighted, starting from far left column) represents the estimated average holding period for investors who score 50 on the Risk Capacity Survey at ifa.com. Sources, Updates, and Disclosures: ifa.com/btp.

Index Portfolio 50: Sea Green
Monthly Rolling Period Analysis*
Based on 50 Years (600 months) of Monthly Data
Jan 1957 to Dec 2006

Examples of 7 Year Monthly Rolling Periods**

Periods

1	Jan 57	← 7 Years →	Dec 63
2	Feb 57	← 7 Years →	Jan 64
3	Mar 57	← 7 Years →	Feb 64
4	Apr 57	← 7 Years →	Mar 64

517

Year 1957   1958   1959   1960   1961   1962   1963   1964   1965   1966   1967   1968   1969

Per Period Number of: Yrs	Months	# of Rolling Periods	Average Ann'lzd Rtn. %*	Std. Dev. of Avg. Ann'lzd Rtn. %*	Lowest Rolling Period Date	Lowest Rolling Period Return	Growth of $1 in Lowest Period	Highest Rolling Period Date	Highest Rolling Period Return	Growth of $1 in Highest Period	Average Growth of $1
0.08	1	600	0.88*	2.52*	10/87-10/87	-12.61	$0.87	1/75-1/75	13.90	$1.14	$1.01
0.25	3	598	2.70*	4.90*	9/87-11/87	-14.66	$0.85	1/75-3/75	22.38	$1.22	$1.03
0.5	6	595	5.46*	7.18*	4/74-9/74	-15.53	$0.84	1/75-6/75	31.29	$1.31	$1.05
1	12	589	11.27	10.20	10/73-9/74	-19.19	$0.81	7/82-6/83	41.55	$1.42	$1.11
2	24	577	11.02	6.62	1/73-12/74	-11.11	$0.79	12/66-11/68	28.07	$1.64	$1.41
3	36	565	10.86	5.11	1/72-12/74	-3.28	$0.90	8/84-7/87	26.59	$2.03	$1.37
4	48	553	10.80	4.38	1/71-12/74	1.53	$1.06	7/82-6/86	24.41	$2.40	$1.52
5	60	541	10.74	4.11	11/69-10/74	1.49	$1.08	8/82-7/87	23.93	$2.92	$1.69
6	72	529	10.80	3.82	1/69-12/74	-0.48	$0.97	10/81-9/87	20.88	$3.12	$1.88
7**	84	517	10.88	3.51	1/68-12/74	2.45	$1.18	4/80-3/87	19.99	$3.58	$2.11
8	96	505	10.95	3.28	12/68-11/76	4.74	$1.45	10/81-9/89	18.46	$3.88	$2.35
9	108	493	11.02	3.16	1/66-12/74	4.60	$1.50	3/78-2/87	17.87	$4.39	$2.64
10	120	481	11.09	3.00	10/64-9/74	5.65	$1.73	9/77-8/87	17.88	$5.18	$2.96
11	132	469	11.14	2.90	1/64-12/74	6.19	$1.94	1/75-12/85	17.47	$5.88	$3.32
12	144	457	11.16	2.79	1/63-12/74	6.77	$2.19	1/75-12/86	17.77	$7.12	$3.72
13	156	445	11.19	2.71	1/62-12/74	5.86	$2.10	10/74-9/87	18.06	$8.66	$4.16
14	168	433	11.26	2.57	1/61-12/74	6.53	$2.42	1/75-12/88	16.99	$9.00	$4.68
15	180	421	11.32	2.46	1/60-12/74	6.01	$2.40	10/74-9/89	17.16	$10.76	$5.26
20	240	361	11.70	1.59	2/57-1/77	8.67	$5.27	10/74-9/94	14.86	$15.97	$9.50
30	360	241	11.70	0.41	4/73-3/03	10.79	$21.63	1/75-12/04	13.06	$39.74	$27.81
40	480	121	11.06	0.24	4/63-3/03	10.58	$55.86	4/58-3/98	11.69	$83.29	$66.62
50	600	1	10.73	0.00	1/57-12/06	10.73	$163.40	1/57-12/06	10.73	$163.40	$163.40

7 Year Monthly Rolling Periods** - Jan 1957 to Dec 2006 - 517 Monthly Rolling Periods Over 50 Years

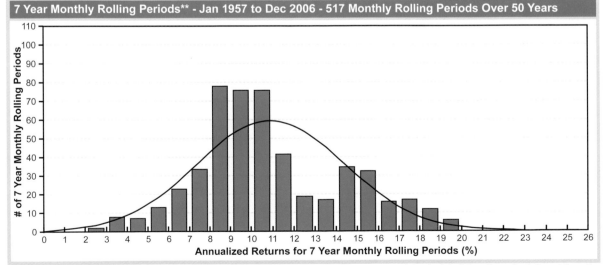

*Sources, Updates, and Disclosures: ifa.com/btp. Returns are net of IFA & DFA fees. The returns and standard deviation shown for 1, 3, and 6 month periods are not annualized. Past performance does not guarantee future results. **7 years represents the estimated average holding period for investors who score 50 on the Risk Capacity Survey at ifa.com.

Appendix A

298

RISK CAPACITY 45
TEAL

Index Portfolio 45: Teal

Index Allocations

General Asset Class		Specific Index	
22%	US Large	11%	IFA US Large Company Index
		11%	IFA US Large Cap Value Index
11%	US Small	5.5%	IFA US Micro Cap Index
		5.5%	IFA US Small Cap Value Index
5.5%	Real Estate	5.5%	IFA Real Estate Index
11%	International	5.5%	IFA International Value Index
		2.75%	IFA International Small Company Index
		2.75%	IFA International Small Cap Value Index
5.5%	Emerging Markets	1.65%	IFA Emerging Markets Index
		1.65%	IFA Emerging Markets Value Index
		2.20%	IFA Emerging Markets Small Cap Index
45%	Fixed Income	11.25%	IFA One-Year Fixed Income Index
		11.25%	IFA Two-Year Global Fixed Income Index
		11.25%	IFA Five-Year Gov't Income Index
		11.25%	IFA Five-Year Global Fixed Income Index

Index Portfolio - Simulated Returns and Volatility Data*

	1yr ending 2006	1yr ending 2005	1yr ending 2004	1yr ending 2003	3yrs 2004-2006	5yrs 2002-2006	10yrs 1996-2006	25yrs 1982-2006	35yrs 1972-2006	50yrs 1957-2006	80yrs 1927-2006
Growth of $1	1.14	1.07	1.12	1.25	1.37	1.67	2.29	14.94	39.33	137.40	1,193
Annualized Return %	14.19	6.57	12.34	25.45	10.99	10.74	8.62	11.42	11.06	10.35	9.26
Annualized Volatility (Standard Deviation %)	5.30	5.38	6.43	7.07	5.63	6.77	7.64	7.56	8.11	8.07	13.82

Annual Returns 1957 - 2006 (50 Years)

Growth of $1 1957 - 2006 (50 Years)
logarithmic scale

$137

*Sources, Updates, and Disclosures: ifa.com/btp. Returns net of IFA & DFA fees. Past performance does not guarantee future results.

Annualized Returns Matrix (%)
35 years of Index Portfolio 45 (1972–2006)
Returns Net of IFA and DFA Fees

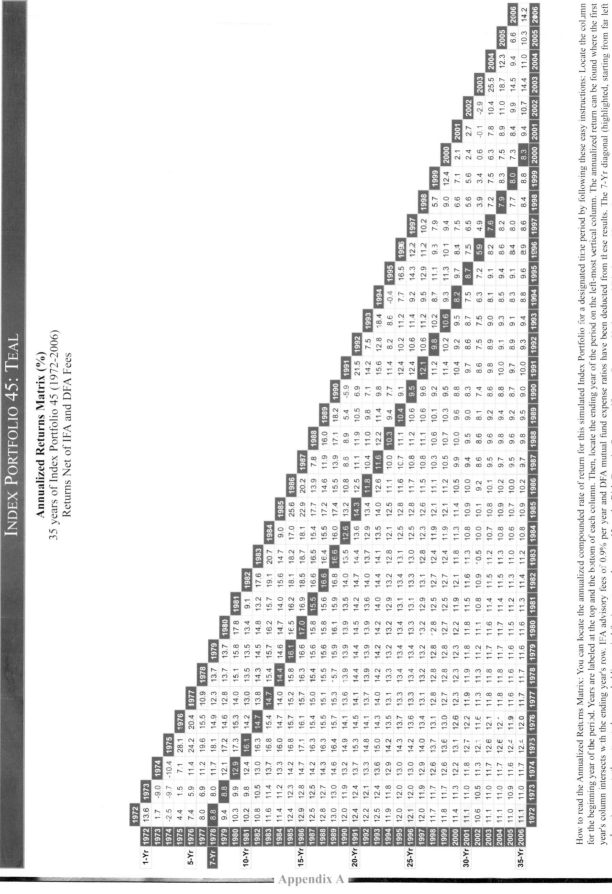

How to read the Annualized Returns Matrix: You can locate the annualized compounded rate of return for this simulated Index Portfolio for a designated time period by following these easy instructions: Locate the column for the beginning year of the period. Years are labeled at the top and the bottom of each column. Then, locate the ending year of the period on the left-most vertical column. The annualized return can be found where the first year's column intersects with the ending year's row. IFA advisory fees of 0.9% per year and DFA mutual fund expense ratios have been deducted from these results. The 7-Yr diagonal (highlighted, starting from far left column) represents the estimated average holding period for investors who score 45 on the Risk Capacity Survey at ifa.com. Sources, Updates, and Disclosures: ifa.com/btp.

Growth of $1 Matrix ($)
35 years of Index Portfolio 45 (1972-2006)
Returns Net of IFA and DFA Fees

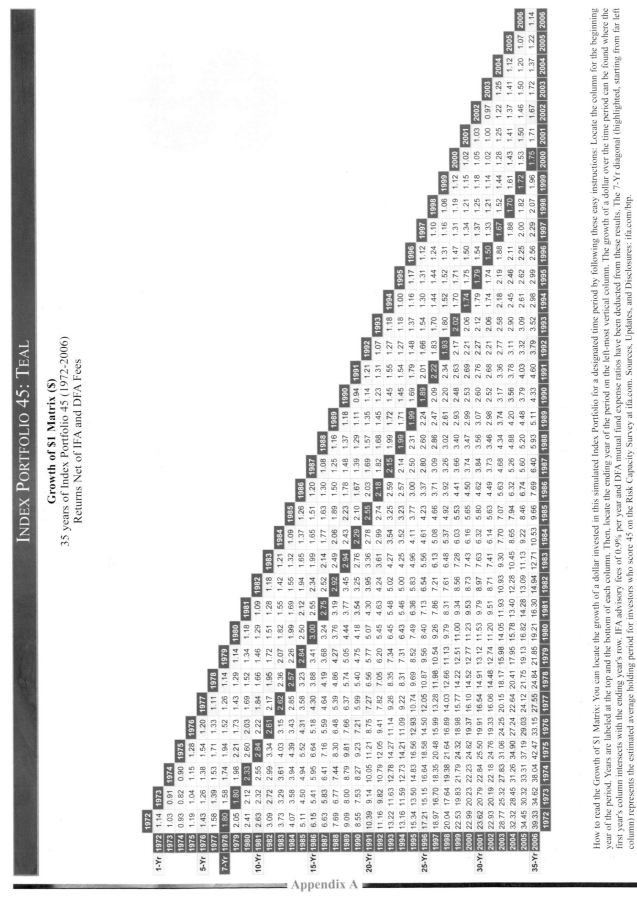

How to read the Growth of $1 Matrix: You can locate the growth of a dollar invested in this simulated Index Portfolio for a designated time period by following these easy instructions: Locate the column for the beginning year of the period. Years are labeled at the top and the bottom of each column. Then, locate the ending year of the period on the left-most vertical column. The growth of a dollar over the time period can be found where the first year's column intersects with the ending year's row. IFA advisory fees of 0.9% per year and DFA mutual fund expense ratios have been deducted from these results. The 7-Yr diagonal (highlighted, starting from far left column) represents the estimated average holding period for investors who score 45 on the Risk Capacity Survey at ifa.com. Sources, Updates, and Disclosures: ifa.com/btp.

Index Portfolio 45: Teal

Monthly Rolling Period Analysis*
Based on 50 years (600 months) of Monthly Data
Jan 1957 to Dec 2006

Examples of 7 Year Monthly Rolling Periods**

Periods

1	Jan 57	← 7 Years →	Dec 63
2	Feb 57	← 7 Years →	Jan 64
3	Mar 57	← 7 Years →	Feb 64
4	Apr 57	← 7 Years →	Mar 64

517

Year 1957   1958   1959   1960   1961   1962   1963   1964   1965   1966   1967   1968   1969

Per Period Number of: Yrs	Months	# of Rolling Periods	Average Ann'lzd Rtn. %*	Std. Dev. of Avg. Ann'lzd Rtn %*	Lowest Rolling Period Date	Lowest Rolling Period Return	Growth of $1 in Lowest Period	Highest Rolling Period Date	Highest Rolling Period Return	Growth of $1 in Highest Period	Average Growth of $1
0.08	1	600	0.85*	2.33*	10/87-10/87	-11.53	$0.88	1/75-1/75	12.82	$1.13	$1.01
0.25	3	598	2.59*	4.52*	9/87-11/87	-13.47	$0.87	1/75-3/75	20.65	$1.21	$1.03
0.5	6	595	5.24*	6.62*	4/74-9/74	-13.96	$0.86	1/75-6/75	28.88	$1.29	$1.05
1	12	589	10.82	9.41	10/73-9/74	-17.21	$0.83	7/82-6/83	39.40	$1.39	$1.11
2	24	577	10.61	6.15	1/73-12/74	-9.71	$0.82	7/84-6/86	26.66	$1.60	$1.39
3	36	565	10.47	4.78	1/72-12/74	-2.52	$0.93	8/84-7/87	25.26	$1.97	$1.36
4	48	553	10.43	4.13	1/71-12/74	1.92	$1.08	7/82-6/86	23.44	$2.32	$1.50
5	60	541	10.38	3.90	11/69-10/74	1.93	$1.10	8/82-7/87	22.83	$2.80	$1.66
6	72	529	10.44	3.64	1/69-12/74	0.11	$1.01	10/81-9/87	20.11	$3.00	$1.84
7**	**84**	**517**	**10.52**	**3.37**	**1/68-12/74**	**2.79**	**$1.21**	**4/80-3/87**	**19.37**	**$3.45**	**$2.05**
8	96	505	10.59	3.16	12/68-11/76	4.93	$1.47	10/81-9/89	17.82	$3.71	$2.29
9	108	493	10.66	3.04	1/66-12/74	4.72	$1.51	3/78-2/87	17.28	$4.20	$2.56
10	120	481	10.73	2.89	10/64-9/74	5.63	$1.73	9/77-8/87	17.21	$4.89	$2.86
11	132	469	10.78	2.80	1/64-12/74	6.13	$1.92	1/75-12/85	16.80	$5.52	$3.20
12	144	457	10.80	2.70	1/63-12/74	6.63	$2.16	1/75-12/86	17.08	$6.63	$3.57
13	156	445	10.83	2.62	1/62-12/74	5.79	$2.08	10/74-9/87	17.32	$7.98	$3.98
14	168	433	10.91	2.49	1/61-12/74	6.38	$2.38	1/75-12/88	16.32	$8.30	$4.46
15	180	421	10.96	2.38	1/60-12/74	5.93	$2.37	10/74-9/89	16.48	$9.86	$5.00
20	240	361	11.34	1.55	2/57-1/77	8.35	$4.97	10/74-9/94	14.32	$14.54	$8.88
30	360	241	11.34	0.38	2/73-1/03	10.53	$20.16	1/75-12/04	12.57	$34.89	$25.19
40	480	121	10.70	0.22	4/63-3/03	10.27	$49.92	4/58-3/98	11.27	$71.63	$58.49
50	600	1	10.35	0.00	1/57-12/06	10.35	$137.60	1/57-12/06	10.35	$137.60	$137.60

7 Year Monthly Rolling Periods - Jan 1957 to Dec 2006 - 517 Monthly Rolling Periods Over 50 Years**

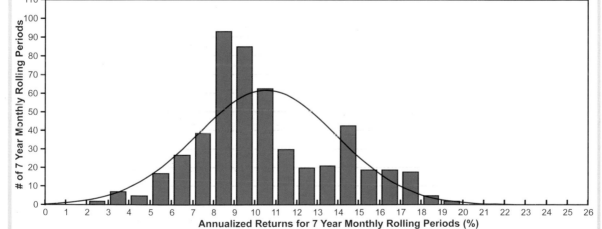

*Sources, Updates, and Disclosures: ifa.com/btp. Returns are net of IFA & DFA fees. The returns and standard deviation shown for 1, 3, and 6 month periods are not annualized. Past performance does not guarantee future results. **7 years represents the estimated average holding period for investors who score 45 on the Risk Capacity Survey at ifa.com.

Appendix A

303

RISK CAPACITY 40
AQUA

Index Portfolio 40: Aqua

Index Allocations

General Asset Class		Specific Index	
20%	US Large	10%	IFA US Large Company Index
		10%	IFA US Large Cap Value Index
10%	US Small	5%	IFA US Micro Cap Index
		5%	IFA US Small Cap Value Index
5%	Real Estate	5%	IFA Real Estate Index
10%	International	5%	IFA International Value Index
		2.5%	IFA International Small Company Index
		2.5%	IFA International Small Cap Value Index
5%	Emerging Markets	1.5%	IFA Emerging Markets Index
		1.5%	IFA Emerging Markets Value Index
		2.0%	IFA Emerging Markets Small Cap Index
50%	Fixed Income	12.5%	IFA One-Year Fixed Income Index
		12.5%	IFA Two-Year Global Fixed Income Index
		12.5%	IFA Five-Year Gov't Income Index
		12.5%	IFA Five-Year Global Fixed Income Index

Index Portfolio - Simulated Returns and Volatility Data*

	1yr ending 2006	1yr ending 2005	1yr ending 2004	1yr ending 2003	3yrs 2004-2006	5yrs 2002-2006	10yrs 1996-2006	25yrs 1982-2006	35yrs 1972-2006	50yrs 1957-2006	80yrs 1927-2006
Growth of $1	1.13	1.06	1.11	1.23	1.34	1.61	2.20	13.56	34.82	114.85	885.98
Annualized Return %	13.22	6.04	11.30	23.26	10.15	10.05	8.21	10.99	10.68	9.95	8.85
Annualized Volatility (Standard Deviation %)	4.83	4.88	5.97	6.48	5.17	6.13	6.93	6.94	7.45	7.41	12.63

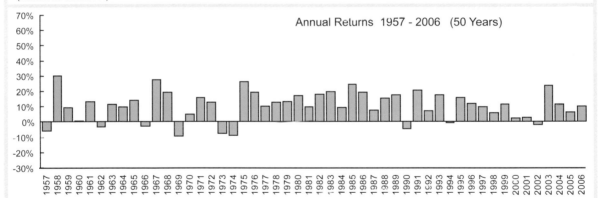

Annual Returns 1957 - 2006 (50 Years)

Growth of $1 1957 - 2006 (50 Years)
logarithmic scale

$115

*Sources, Updates, and Disclosures: ifa.com/btp. Returns net of IFA & DFA fees. Past performance does not guarantee future results.

Annualized Returns Matrix (%)
35 years of Index Portfolio 40 (1972–2006)
Returns Net of IFA and DFA Fees

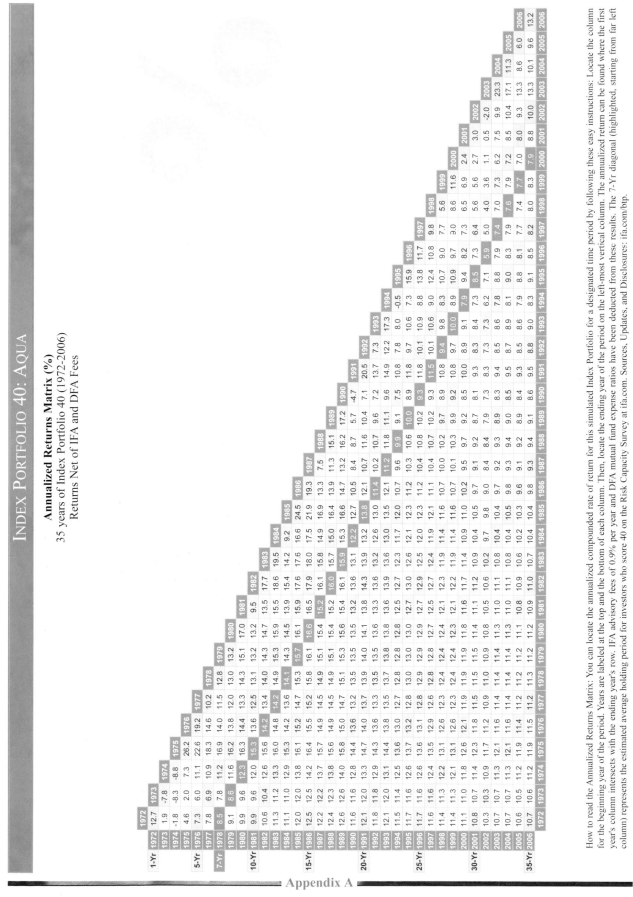

How to read the Annualized Returns Matrix: You can locate the annualized compounded rate of return for this simulated Index Portfolio for a designated time period by following these easy instructions: Locate the column for the beginning year of the period. Then, locate the ending year of the period on the left-most vertical column. The annualized return can be found where the first year's column intersects with the ending year's row. IFA advisory fees of 0.9% per year and DFA mutual fund expense ratios have been deducted from these results. The 7-Yr diagonal (highlighted, starting from far left column) represents the estimated average holding period for investors who score 40 on the Risk Capacity Survey at ifa.com. Sources, Updates, and Disclosures: ifa.com/btp.

Growth of $1 Matrix ($)
35 years of Index Portfolio 40 (1972-2006)
Returns Net of IFA and DFA Fees

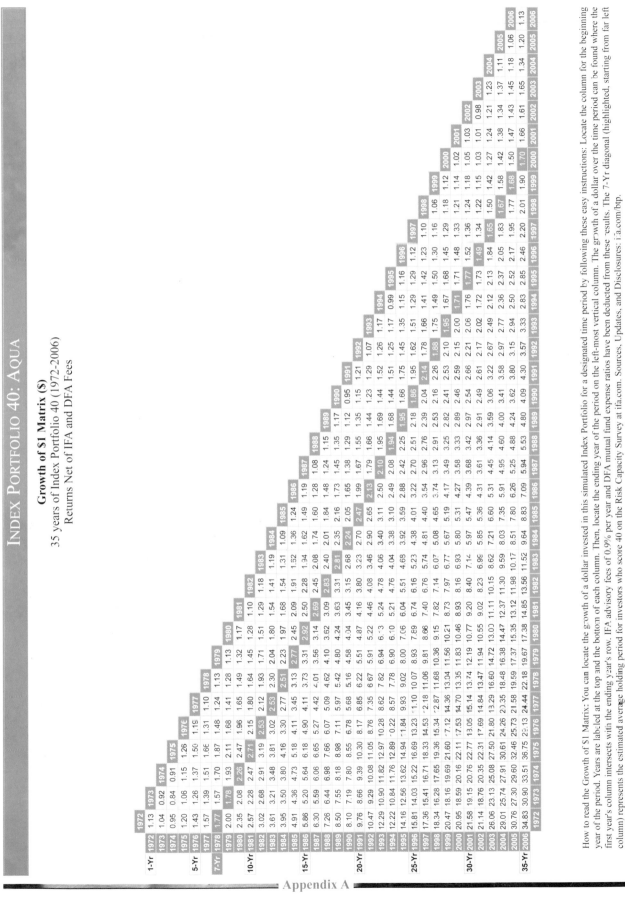

How to read the Growth of $1 Matrix: You can locate the growth of a dollar invested in this simulated Index Portfolio for a designated time period by following these easy instructions: Locate the column for the beginning year of the period. Years are labeled at the top and the bottom of each column. Then, locate the ending year of the period on the left-most vertical column. The growth of a dollar over the time period can be found where the first year's column intersects with the ending year's row. IFA advisory fees of 0.9% per year and DFA mutual fund expense ratios have been deducted from these results. The 7-Yr diagonal (highlighted, starting from far left column) represents the estimated average holding period for investors who score 40 on the Risk Capacity Survey at ifa.com. Sources, Updates, and Disclosures: ifa.com/btp.

Index Portfolio 40: Aqua
Monthly Rolling Period Analysis*
Based on 50 Years (600 months) of Monthly Data
Jan 1957 to Dec 2006

Examples of 7 Year Monthly Rolling Periods**

Periods

1	Jan 57	← 7 Years →	Dec 63
2	Feb 57	← 7 Years →	Jan 64
3	Mar 57	← 7 Years →	Feb 64
4	Apr 57	← 7 Years →	Mar 64

517

Year 1957   1958   1959   1960   1961   1962   1963   1964   1965   1966   1967   1968   1969

Per Period Number of: Yrs	Months	# of Rolling Periods	Average Ann'lzd Rtn. %*	Std. Dev. of Avg. Ann'lzd Rtn. %*	Lowest Rolling Period Date	Lowest Rolling Period Return	Growth of $1 in Lowest Period	Highest Rolling Period Date	Highest Rolling Period Return	Growth of $1 in Highest Period	Average Growth of $1
0.08	1	600	0.82*	2.14*	10/87-10/87	-10.43	$0.90	1/75-1/75	11.73	$1.12	$1.01
0.25	3	598	2.48*	4.15*	9/87-11/87	-12.23	$0.88	1/75-3/75	18.91	$1.19	$1.02
0.5	6	595	5.02*	6.06*	4/74-9/74	-12.38	$0.88	1/75-6/75	26.47	$1.26	$1.05
1	12	589	10.36	8.63	10/73-9/74	-15.20	$0.85	7/82-6/83	37.27	$1.37	$1.10
2	24	577	10.19	5.69	1/73-12/74	-8.30	$0.84	7/84-6/86	25.56	$1.58	$1.36
3	36	565	10.08	4.46	1/72-12/74	-1.78	$0.95	8/84-7/87	23.94	$1.90	$1.34
4	48	553	10.05	3.89	1/71-12/74	2.30	$1.10	7/82-6/86	22.48	$2.25	$1.48
5	60	541	10.01	3.70	4/98-3/03	2.27	$1.12	8/82-7/87	21.73	$2.67	$1.63
6	72	529	10.07	3.47	1/69-12/74	0.69	$1.04	10/81-9/87	19.34	$2.89	$1.81
7**	84	517	10.15	3.23	1/68-12/74	3.11	$1.24	4/80-3/87	18.76	$3.33	$2.00
8	96	505	10.22	3.04	12/68-11/76	5.11	$1.49	10/81-9/89	17.17	$3.55	$2.23
9	108	493	10.29	2.94	1/66-12/74	4.83	$1.53	3/78-2/87	16.69	$4.01	$2.48
10	120	481	10.36	2.80	10/64-9/74	5.60	$1.72	9/77-8/87	16.55	$4.63	$2.76
11	132	469	10.41	2.70	1/64-12/74	6.06	$1.91	1/75-12/85	16.13	$5.18	$3.08
12	144	457	10.44	2.62	1/63-12/74	6.48	$2.12	1/75-12/86	16.40	$6.19	$3.42
13	156	445	10.47	2.54	1/62-12/74	5.71	$2.06	10/74-9/87	16.58	$7.35	$3.81
14	168	433	10.55	2.41	1/61-12/74	6.23	$2.33	1/75-12/88	15.65	$7.66	$4.25
15	180	421	10.60	2.30	1/60-12/74	5.83	$2.34	10/74-9/89	15.80	$9.03	$4.75
20	240	361	10.97	1.52	2/57-1/77	8.02	$4.68	10/74-9/94	13.77	$13.20	$8.30
30	360	241	10.96	0.35	2/73-1/03	10.26	$18.73	1/75-12/04	12.08	$30.61	$22.77
40	480	121	10.33	0.19	4/63-3/03	9.96	$44.61	4/58-3/98	10.83	$61.14	$51.20
50	600	1	9.95	0.00	1/57-12/06	9.95	$114.75	1/57-12/06	9.95	$114.75	$114.75

7 Year Monthly Rolling Periods** - Jan 1957 to Dec 2006 - 517 Monthly Rolling Periods Over 50 Years

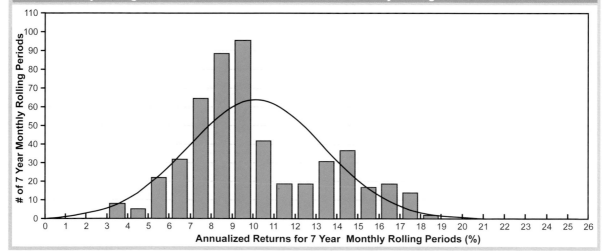

*Sources, Updates, and Disclosures: ifa.com/btp. Returns are net of IFA & DFA fees. The returns and standard deviation shown for 1, 3, and 6 month periods are not annualized. Past performance does not guarantee future results. **7 years represents the estimated average holding period for investors who score 40 on the Risk Capacity Survey at ifa.com.

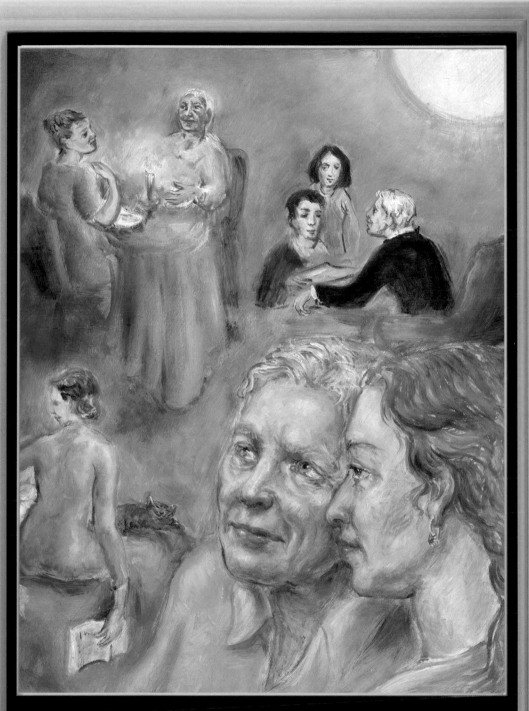

RISK CAPACITY 35
SKY BLUE

Index Portfolio 35: Sky Blue

Index Allocations

General Asset Class		Specific Index	
18%	US Large	9%	IFA US Large Company Index
		9%	IFA US Large Cap Value Index
9%	US Small	4.5%	IFA US Micro Cap Index
		4.5%	IFA US Small Cap Value Index
4.5%	Real Estate	4.5%	IFA Real Estate Index
9%	International	4.5%	IFA International Value Index
		2.25%	IFA International Small Company Index
		2.25%	IFA International Small Cap Value Index
4.5%	Emerging Markets	1.35%	IFA Emerging Markets Index
		1.35%	IFA Emerging Markets Value Index
		1.80%	IFA Emerging Markets Small Cap Index
55%	Fixed Income	13.75%	IFA One-Year Fixed Income Index
		13.75%	IFA Two-Year Global Fixed Income Index
		13.75%	IFA Five-Year Gov't Income Index
		13.75%	IFA Five-Year Global Fixed Income Index

Index Portfolio - Simulated Returns and Volatility Data*

	1yr ending 2006	1yr ending 2005	1yr ending 2004	1yr ending 2003	3yrs 2004-2006	5yrs 2002-2006	10yrs 1996-2006	25yrs 1982-2006	35yrs 1972-2006	50yrs 1957-2006	80yrs 1927-2006
Growth of $1	1.12	1.06	1.10	1.21	1.31	1.56	2.12	12.29	30.75	95.57	649.35
Annualized Return %	12.25	5.52	10.26	21.07	9.30	9.35	7.81	10.56	10.28	9.55	8.43
Annualized Volatility (Standard Deviation %)	4.35	4.39	5.52	5.91	4.71	5.50	6.23	6.32	6.80	6.76	11.44

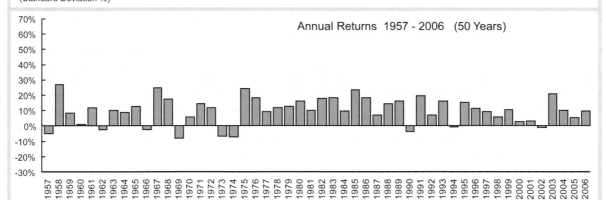

Annual Returns 1957 - 2006   (50 Years)

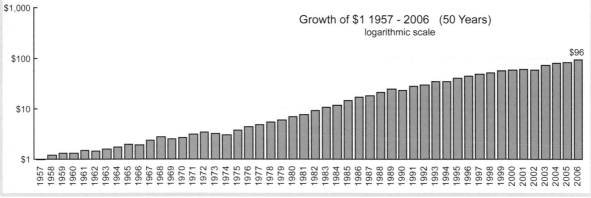

Growth of $1 1957 - 2006   (50 Years)
logarithmic scale

$96

*Sources, Updates, and Disclosures: ifa.com/btp. Returns net of IFA & DFA fees. Past performance does not guarantee future results.

INDEX PORTFOLIO 35: SKY BLUE

Annualized Returns Matrix (%)
35 years of Index Portfolio 35 (1972-2006)
Returns Net of IFA and DFA Fees

Period	End\Start	1972	1973	1974	1975	1976	1977	1978	1979	1980	1981	1982	1983	1984	1985	1986	1987	1988	1989	1990	1991	1992	1993	1994	1995	1996	1997	1998	1999	2000	2001	2002	2003	2004	2005	2006
1-Yr	1972	11.8																																		
	1973	2.2	-6.6																																	
	1974	-1.0	-6.9	-7.2																																
	1975	4.7	2.5	7.4	24.2																															
5-Yr	1976	7.3	6.2	10.8	21.1	18.1																														
6-Yr	1977	7.6	6.8	10.5	17.1	13.7	9.4																													
	1978	8.2	7.7	10.7	15.8	13.1	10.6	11.9																												
	1979	8.8	8.4	11.1	15.1	13.0	11.3	12.2	12.6																											
	1980	9.6	9.3	11.8	15.3	13.6	12.5	13.6	14.4	16.2																										
	1981	9.6	9.4	11.5	14.5	13.0	12.0	12.9	12.9	13.0	9.9																									
10-Yr	1982	10.3	10.2	12.2	14.9	13.7	12.9	13.7	14.1	14.6	13.8	17.9																								
	1983	11.0	10.9	12.8	15.3	14.2	13.7	14.4	14.9	15.5	15.3	18.1	18.3																							
	1984	10.9	10.8	12.5	14.7	13.7	13.2	13.7	14.0	14.3	13.8	15.1	13.8	9.5																						
	1985	11.7	11.7	13.4	15.5	14.5	14.2	14.9	15.3	15.7	15.6	16.9	16.9	16.2	23.3																					
15-Yr	1986	12.1	12.2	13.8	15.7	14.7	14.5	15.2	15.7	16.1	16.1	17.1	17.3	16.9	20.8	18.4																				
	1987	11.8	11.8	13.3	15.0	14.0	13.7	14.4	14.8	15.2	14.8	15.6	15.2	14.4	16.1	12.7	7.3																			
	1988	12.0	12.0	13.3	15.0	14.0	14.0	14.4	14.7	15.0	14.7	15.4	15.0	14.4	15.6	13.2	10.7	14.2																		
	1989	12.2	12.2	13.5	15.1	14.2	14.2	14.6	14.8	15.0	14.9	15.5	15.2	14.7	15.8	14.0	12.5	14.2	16.3																	
	1990	11.7	11.7	12.8	14.1	13.1	12.8	13.1	13.5	13.7	13.2	13.6	13.1	12.5	13.3	11.7	10.4	11.2	5.9	-3.6																
20-Yr	1991	11.7	11.5	12.7	13.9	13.3	13.0	13.4	13.5	13.7	13.1	13.9	13.4	12.8	13.3	12.2	10.4	11.2	10.3	7.4	19.6															
	1992	11.5	11.5	12.5	13.7	12.8	12.5	13.1	13.2	13.5	12.9	13.9	13.4	12.8	13.3	11.7	11.2	10.2	9.7	7.3	13.1	7.0														
	1993	11.7	11.7	12.7	13.9	13.0	13.1	13.4	13.6	13.7	13.2	13.5	13.1	12.6	13.1	11.7	10.3	10.3	9.9	7.3	14.2	11.5	16.2													
	1994	11.1	11.1	12.0	13.1	12.2	12.4	12.4	12.4	12.4	12.1	12.3	11.9	11.3	11.5	10.2	9.2	9.9	8.6	7.3	10.2	7.4	7.4	-0.7												
	1995	11.3	11.3	12.2	13.2	12.5	12.6	12.6	12.5	12.6	12.3	12.5	12.1	11.6	11.8	10.7	9.9	10.2	8.8	7.3	11.2	9.2	10.0	7.0	15.2											
25-Yr	1996	11.3	11.3	12.1	13.1	12.7	12.6	12.5	12.5	12.6	12.3	12.4	12.0	11.8	11.8	10.7	10.2	10.3	9.7	8.6	11.2	9.6	10.3	6.4	13.2	11.2										
	1997	11.2	11.2	12.0	13.1	12.4	12.3	12.5	12.3	12.5	12.1	12.4	12.0	11.4	11.8	10.7	10.0	10.3	9.9	9.0	11.2	10.1	10.1	8.6	11.9	10.3	9.4									
	1998	11.0	11.0	11.7	12.6	12.1	12.2	12.3	12.0	12.0	11.7	11.8	11.5	11.0	11.1	10.3	9.8	10.2	9.4	8.6	10.3	9.0	10.1	8.0	10.3	8.7	8.5	5.6								
	1999	11.0	11.0	11.7	12.5	12.1	12.1	11.9	11.9	11.9	11.7	11.8	11.4	11.0	11.1	10.3	9.9	9.5	9.5	8.9	10.3	9.2	9.5	8.5	10.4	9.2	8.1	6.3	10.7							
	2000	10.7	10.7	11.4	12.1	11.7	11.7	11.5	11.5	11.4	11.2	11.3	10.9	10.5	10.6	9.8	9.2	9.3	8.9	8.3	9.5	8.5	8.7	7.6	9.1	7.9	7.1	6.3	6.6	2.7						
30-Yr	2001	10.4	10.4	11.1	11.8	11.2	11.1	11.2	11.1	11.1	10.8	10.9	10.5	10.1	10.1	9.3	8.8	8.9	8.5	7.8	8.9	8.2	8.0	7.1	8.2	7.1	5.3	3.6	6.3	5.5	3.2					
	2002	10.0	10.0	10.6	11.3	10.9	10.9	10.6	10.6	10.5	10.2	10.9	10.5	10.0	10.0	9.4	8.1	8.2	7.8	7.1	8.2	7.1	7.1	6.1	7.0	5.9	3.3	5.0	3.8	1.6	1.0	-1.1				
	2003	10.4	10.3	10.9	11.6	11.2	11.0	11.0	11.0	10.9	10.7	10.4	10.4	10.0	10.1	9.4	8.8	8.9	8.6	8.1	9.0	8.3	8.3	7.5	7.7	7.0	5.0	7.2	7.0	6.1	7.3	9.4	21.1			
	2004	10.4	10.3	10.9	11.6	11.2	11.0	11.0	11.0	10.9	10.7	10.7	10.4	10.0	10.1	9.4	8.9	9.0	8.7	8.2	9.1	8.5	8.0	7.8	8.0	7.6	7.6	7.3	7.6	6.9	8.0	9.7	15.5	10.3		
	2005	10.2	10.2	10.7	11.4	11.0	10.9	10.7	10.8	10.7	10.5	10.2	10.2	9.8	9.8	9.2	8.5	9.0	8.4	8.0	8.1	8.1	7.6	7.6	7.7	7.1	7.3	7.1	7.3	7.5	8.6	9.7	12.1	7.9	5.5	
35-Yr	2006	10.3	10.2	11.0	11.4	11.0	10.7	10.8	10.8	10.7	10.5	10.6	10.3	9.9	9.3	8.9	8.7	9.0	8.7	8.3	9.1	8.4	8.5	7.9	8.1	8.1	7.8	7.6	7.9	7.5	8.3	9.3	12.1	9.3	8.8	12.3

How to read the Annualized Returns Matrix: You can locate the annualized compounded rate of return for this simulated Index Portfolio for a designated time period by following these easy instructions: Locate the column for the beginning year of the period. Years are labeled at the top and the bottom of each column. Then, locate the ending year of the period on the left-most vertical column. The annualized return can be found where the first year's column intersects with the ending year's row. IFA advisory fees of 0.9% per year and DFA mutual fund expense ratios have been deducted from these results. The 6-Yr diagonal (highlighted, starting from far left column) represents the estimated average holding period for investors who score 35 on the Risk Capacity Survey at ifa.com. Sources, Updates, and Disclosures: ifa.com/btp.

INDEX PORTFOLIO 35: SKY BLUE

Growth of $1 Matrix ($)
35 years of Index Portfolio 35 (1972–2006)
Returns Net of IFA and DFA Fees

Period	End Yr	1972	1973	1974	1975	1976	1977	1978	1979	1980	1981	1982	1983	1984	1985	1986	1987	1988	1989	1990	1991	1992	1993	1994	1995	1996	1997	1998	1999	2000	2001	2002	2003	2004	2005	2006
1-Yr	1972	1.12																																		
	1973	1.04	0.93																																	
	1974	0.97	0.87	0.93																																
	1975	1.20	1.08	1.15	1.24																															
5-Yr	1976	1.42	1.27	1.36	1.47	1.18																														
6-Yr	1977	1.56	1.39	1.49	1.61	1.29	1.09																													
	1978	1.74	1.56	1.67	1.80	1.45	1.22	1.12																												
	1979	1.96	1.75	1.88	2.02	1.63	1.38	1.26	1.13																											
	1980	2.28	2.04	2.18	2.45	1.90	1.60	1.46	1.31	1.16																										
10-Yr	1981	2.50	2.24	2.40	2.58	2.08	1.76	1.61	1.44	1.28	1.10																									
	1982	2.95	2.64	2.83	3.05	2.45	2.08	1.90	1.70	1.51	1.30	1.18																								
	1983	3.49	3.12	3.34	3.60	2.90	2.46	2.24	2.01	1.78	1.53	1.39	1.18																							
	1984	3.82	3.42	3.66	3.94	3.17	2.69	2.46	2.20	1.95	1.68	1.53	1.29	1.09																						
	1985	4.71	4.21	4.51	4.86	3.91	3.31	3.03	2.71	2.40	2.07	1.88	1.60	1.35	1.23																					
15-Yr	1986	5.58	4.99	5.34	5.76	4.63	3.92	3.59	3.21	2.85	2.45	2.23	1.89	1.60	1.46	1.18																				
	1987	5.98	5.35	5.73	6.17	4.97	4.21	3.85	3.44	3.05	2.63	2.39	2.03	1.71	1.57	1.27	1.07																			
	1988	6.83	6.11	6.54	7.05	5.68	4.81	4.39	3.93	3.49	3.00	2.73	2.32	1.96	1.79	1.45	1.23	1.14																		
	1989	7.95	7.11	7.61	8.20	6.60	5.59	5.11	4.57	4.05	3.49	3.17	2.69	2.28	2.08	1.69	1.42	1.33	1.16																	
	1990	7.66	6.86	7.34	7.91	6.37	5.39	4.93	4.41	3.91	3.36	3.06	2.60	2.20	2.01	1.63	1.37	1.28	1.12	0.96																
20-Yr	1991	9.16	8.20	8.77	9.46	7.61	6.45	5.89	5.27	4.68	4.02	3.66	3.10	2.62	2.40	1.95	1.64	1.53	1.34	1.15	1.20															
	1992	9.81	8.77	9.39	10.12	8.15	6.90	6.31	5.64	5.00	4.31	3.92	3.32	2.81	2.57	2.08	1.76	1.64	1.44	1.23	1.28	1.07														
	1993	11.40	10.20	10.92	11.76	9.47	8.02	7.33	6.55	5.82	5.01	4.55	3.86	3.27	2.98	2.42	2.04	1.91	1.67	1.43	1.49	1.24	1.16													
	1994	11.32	10.13	10.84	11.68	9.40	7.96	7.28	6.51	5.78	4.97	4.52	3.84	3.24	2.96	2.40	2.04	1.89	1.66	1.43	1.48	1.24	1.15	0.99												
	1995	13.04	11.67	12.49	13.46	10.84	9.18	8.39	7.50	6.66	5.73	5.21	4.42	3.74	3.41	2.77	2.34	2.18	1.91	1.64	1.70	1.42	1.33	1.14	1.15											
25-Yr	1996	14.50	12.98	13.89	14.97	12.05	10.20	9.33	8.34	7.40	6.37	5.79	4.91	4.16	3.80	3.08	2.60	2.42	2.12	1.83	1.89	1.58	1.48	1.27	1.28	1.11										
	1997	15.87	14.20	15.19	16.38	13.18	11.16	10.20	9.12	8.10	6.97	6.34	5.38	4.55	4.15	3.37	2.84	2.65	2.32	2.00	2.07	1.73	1.62	1.39	1.40	1.22	1.09									
	1998	16.76	15.00	16.05	17.30	13.92	11.79	10.78	9.63	8.55	7.36	6.70	5.68	4.80	4.39	3.56	3.00	2.80	2.45	2.11	2.19	1.83	1.71	1.47	1.48	1.29	1.16	1.06								
	1999	18.56	16.60	17.77	19.15	15.42	13.06	11.93	10.67	9.47	8.15	7.41	6.29	5.32	4.86	3.94	3.33	3.10	2.72	2.34	2.42	2.03	1.89	1.64	1.64	1.42	1.28	1.17	1.11							
	2000	19.06	17.05	18.25	19.67	15.84	13.41	12.26	10.96	9.73	8.37	7.62	6.46	5.46	4.99	4.05	3.42	3.19	2.79	2.40	2.49	2.08	1.94	1.67	1.68	1.46	1.31	1.20	1.14	1.03						
30-Yr	2001	19.67	17.60	18.84	20.30	16.34	13.84	12.65	11.31	10.04	8.64	7.86	6.67	5.64	5.15	4.18	3.53	3.29	2.88	2.49	2.57	2.15	2.01	1.73	1.74	1.51	1.36	1.24	1.17	1.06	1.03					
	2002	19.45	17.40	18.62	20.07	16.16	13.69	12.51	11.18	9.93	8.54	7.77	6.59	5.57	5.09	4.13	3.49	3.25	2.85	2.45	2.54	2.12	1.98	1.71	1.72	1.49	1.34	1.23	1.16	1.05	1.02	0.99				
	2003	23.55	21.07	22.55	24.30	19.57	16.57	15.14	13.54	12.02	10.34	9.41	7.98	6.75	6.16	5.00	4.22	3.94	3.45	2.96	3.07	2.57	2.40	2.07	2.08	1.81	1.62	1.48	1.40	1.27	1.24	1.20	1.21			
	2004	25.97	23.23	24.86	26.80	21.57	18.27	16.70	14.93	13.25	11.40	10.37	8.80	7.44	6.80	5.51	4.65	4.34	3.80	3.27	3.39	2.83	2.65	2.28	2.29	1.99	1.79	1.64	1.55	1.40	1.36	1.32	1.33	1.10		
	2005	27.40	24.51	26.24	28.28	22.76	19.28	17.62	15.75	13.98	12.03	10.95	9.28	7.85	7.17	5.82	4.91	4.58	4.01	3.45	3.58	2.99	2.79	2.40	2.42	2.10	1.89	1.73	1.63	1.44	1.39	1.41	1.41	1.16	1.06	
35-Yr	2006	30.76	27.52	29.45	31.74	25.55	21.64	19.77	17.68	15.70	13.50	12.29	10.42	8.81	8.05	6.53	5.51	5.14	4.50	3.87	4.01	3.36	3.14	2.70	2.72	2.36	2.12	1.94	1.84	1.66	1.61	1.56	1.58	1.31	1.18	1.12

How to read the Growth of $1 Matrix: You can locate the growth of a dollar invested in this simulated Index Portfolio for a designated time period by following these easy instructions: Locate the column for the beginning year of the period. Years are labeled at the top and the bottom of each column. Then, locate the ending year of the period on the left-most vertical column. The growth of a dollar over the time period can be found where the first year's column intersects with the ending year's row. IFA advisory fees of 0.9% per year and DFA mutual fund expense ratios have been deducted from these results. The 6-Yr diagonal (highlighted, starting from far left column) represents the estimated average holding period for investors who score 35 on the Risk Capacity Survey at ifa.com. Sources, Updates, and Disclosures: ifa.com/btp.

Index Portfolio 35: Sky Blue

Monthly Rolling Period Analysis*
Based on 50 years (600 months) of Monthly Data
Jan 1957 to Dec 2006

Examples of 6 Year Monthly Rolling Periods**

Periods

1	Jan 57	◄— 6 Years —►	Dec 62
2	Feb 57	◄— 6 Years —►	Jan 63
3	Mar 57	◄— 6 Years —►	Feb 63
4	Apr 57	◄— 6 Years —►	Mar 63

529

Year 1957 1958 1959 1960 1961 1962 1963 1964 1965 1966 1967 1968 1969

Per Period Number of: Yrs	Months	# of Rolling Periods	Average Ann'lzd Rtn. %*	Std. Dev. of Avg. Ann'lzd Rtn. %*	Lowest Rolling Period Date	Lowest Rolling Period Return	Growth of $1 in Lowest Period	Highest Rolling Period Date	Highest Rolling Period Return	Growth of $1 in Highest Period	Average Growth of $1
0.08	1	600	0.78*	1.95*	10/87-10/87	-9.29	$0.91	1/75-1/75	10.65	$1.11	$1.01
0.25	3	598	2.38*	3.77*	9/87-11/87	-10.97	$0.89	1/75-3/75	17.18	$1.17	$1.02
0.5	6	595	4.80*	5.51*	4/74-9/74	-10.79	$0.89	1/75-6/75	24.07	$1.24	$1.05
1	12	589	9.89	7.87	10/73-9/74	-13.18	$0.87	7/82-6/83	35.16	$1.35	$1.10
2	24	577	9.77	5.25	1/73-12/74	-6.89	$0.87	7/84-6/86	24.46	$1.55	$1.34
3	36	565	9.68	4.16	1/72-12/74	-1.05	$0.97	8/84-7/87	22.63	$1.84	$1.33
4	48	553	9.66	3.67	1/71-12/74	2.66	$1.11	7/82-6/86	21.51	$2.18	$1.46
5	60	541	9.64	3.52	4/98-3/03	2.57	$1.14	8/82-7/87	20.63	$2.55	$1.60
6**	**72**	**529**	**9.70**	**3.32**	**1/69-12/74**	**1.26**	**$1.08**	**10/81-9/87**	**18.56**	**$2.78**	**$1.77**
7	84	517	9.77	3.11	1/68-12/74	3.43	$1.27	4/80-3/87	18.14	$3.21	$1.95
8	96	505	9.84	2.94	10/67-9/75	5.26	$1.51	10/81-9/89	16.52	$3.40	$2.16
9	108	493	9.91	2.84	1/66-12/74	4.93	$1.54	3/78-2/87	16.10	$3.83	$2.40
10	120	481	9.98	2.71	10/64-9/74	5.55	$1.72	9/77-8/87	15.88	$4.37	$2.66
11	132	469	10.04	2.62	7/59-6/70	5.95	$1.89	1/75-12/85	15.46	$4.80	$2.96
12	144	457	10.07	2.54	1/63-12/74	6.32	$2.09	1/75-12/86	15.70	$5.75	$3.28
13	156	445	10.10	2.46	1/62-12/74	5.61	$2.03	10/74-9/87	15.83	$6.76	$3.64
14	168	433	10.18	2.34	1/61-12/74	6.06	$2.28	1/75-12/88	14.97	$7.05	$4.05
15	180	421	10.24	2.23	1/60-12/74	5.72	$2.30	10/74-9/89	15.12	$8.27	$4.50
20	240	361	10.59	1.49	2/57-1/77	7.68	$4.39	10/74-9/94	13.21	$11.96	$7.74
30	360	241	10.58	0.33	1/57-12/86	9.98	$17.35	1/75-12/04	11.58	$26.77	$20.53
40	480	121	9.96	0.17	4/63-3/03	9.64	$39.70	4/58-3/98	10.39	$52.14	$44.67
50	600	1	9.55	0.00	1/57-12/06	9.55	$95.64	1/57-12/06	9.55	$95.64	$95.64

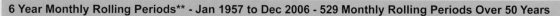

6 Year Monthly Rolling Periods** - Jan 1957 to Dec 2006 - 529 Monthly Rolling Periods Over 50 Years

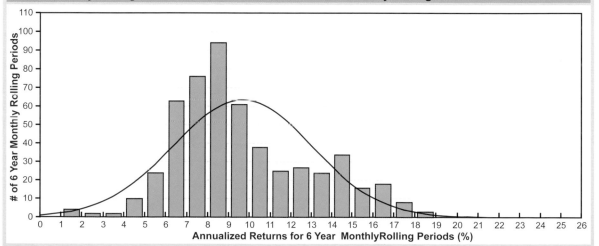

*Sources, Updates, and Disclosures: ifa.com/btp. Returns are net of IFA & DFA fees. The returns and standard deviation shown for 1, 3, and 6 month periods are not annualized. Past performance does not guarantee future results. **6 years represents the estimated average holding period for investors who score 35 on the Risk Capacity Survey at ifa.com.

Risk Capacity 30
Pale Blue

Index Allocations

General Asset Class		Specific Index	
16%	US Large	8%	IFA US Large Company Index
		8%	IFA US Large Cap Value Index
8%	US Small	4%	IFA US Micro Cap Index
		4%	IFA US Small Cap Value Index
4%	Real Estate	4%	IFA Real Estate Index
8%	International	4%	IFA International Value Index
		2%	IFA International Small Company Index
		2%	IFA International Small Cap Value Index
4%	Emerging Markets	1.2%	IFA Emerging Markets Index
		1.2%	IFA Emerging Markets Value Index
		1.6%	IFA Emerging Markets Small Cap Index
60%	Fixed Income	15%	IFA One-Year Fixed Income Index
		15%	IFA Two-Year Global Fixed Income Index
		15%	IFA Five-Year Gov't Income Index
		15%	IFA Five-Year Global Fixed Income Index

Index Portfolio - Simulated Returns and Volatility Data*

	1yr ending 2006	1yr ending 2005	1yr ending 2004	1yr ending 2003	3yrs 2004-2006	5yrs 2002-2006	10yrs 1996-2006	25yrs 1982-2006	35yrs 1972-2006	50yrs 1957-2006	80yrs 1927-2006
Growth of $1	1.11	1.05	1.09	1.19	1.28	1.51	2.04	11.12	27.09	79.15	469.57
Annualized Return %	11.27	4.99	9.22	18.88	8.46	8.64	7.39	10.11	9.89	9.14	7.99
Annualized Volatility (Standard Deviation %)	3.87	3.90	5.08	5.35	4.26	4.89	5.53	5.71	6.16	6.11	10.26

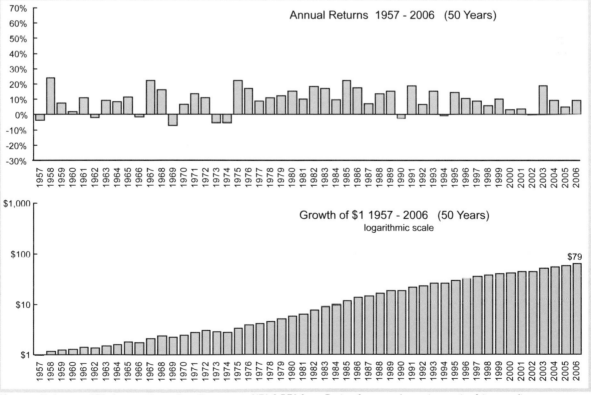

Annual Returns 1957 - 2006 (50 Years)

Growth of $1 1957 - 2006 (50 Years)
logarithmic scale

$79

*Sources, Updates, and Disclosures: ifa.com/btp. Returns net of IFA & DFA fees. Past performance does not guarantee future results.

INDEX PORTFOLIO 30: PALE BLUE

Annualized Returns Matrix (%)
35 years of Index Portfolio 30 (1972–2006)
Returns Net of IFA and DFA Fees

	1972	1973	1974	1975	1976	1977	1978	1979	1980	1981	1982	1983	1984	1985	1986	1987	1988	1989	1990	1991	1992	1993	1994	1995	1996	1997	1998	1999	2000	2001	2002	2003	2004	2005	2006
1-Yr 1972	10.9																																		
1973	2.4	-5.4																																	
1974	-0.3	-5.5	-5.6																																
1975	4.9	3.0	7.4	22.3																															
5-Yr 1976	7.2	6.3	10.5	16.9	16.9																														
1977	7.4	6.8	10.1	15.8	12.7	8.7																													
1978	7.9	7.5	10.2	14.6	12.1	9.8	10.9																												
1979	8.4	8.1	10.5	14.1	12.1	10.6	11.5	12.1																											
1980	9.2	9.0	11.2	14.3	12.8	11.8	12.8	13.7	15.4																										
10-Yr 1981	9.3	9.1	11.1	13.7	12.4	11.5	12.2	12.6	12.8	10.3																									
1982	10.1	10.0	11.9	14.3	13.2	12.5	13.3	13.9	14.6	14.1	18.1																								
1983	10.6	10.6	12.4	14.6	13.6	13.2	13.9	14.6	15.2	15.1	17.6	17.1																							
1984	10.6	10.6	12.1	14.1	13.2	12.7	13.3	13.7	14.1	13.7	14.9	13.3	9.7																						
1985	11.4	11.4	12.9	14.8	14.1	13.7	14.4	14.9	15.4	15.4	16.7	15.8	13.3	22.1																					
15-Yr 1986	11.8	11.8	13.3	15.0	14.4	14.1	14.7	15.2	15.7	15.7	16.8	16.5	16.2	19.8	17.5																				
1987	11.5	11.5	12.8	14.4	13.7	13.4	13.9	14.3	14.5	14.4	15.1	14.5	13.9	15.4	12.1	7.0																			
1988	11.6	11.6	13.0	14.4	13.8	13.6	14.0	14.3	14.5	14.4	15.0	14.8	14.3	15.3	13.2	10.9	13.3																		
1989	11.8	11.8	13.0	14.4	13.8	13.6	14.0	14.3	14.5	14.5	14.9	14.5	14.1	14.9	13.2	11.8	14.3	15.3																	
1990	11.0	11.0	12.0	13.2	12.7	12.4	12.6	12.8	12.9	12.6	12.9	12.2	11.4	11.9	9.9	8.1	8.5	6.1	-2.4																
20-Yr 1991	11.3	11.4	12.4	13.5	13.1	12.8	13.1	13.2	13.3	13.1	13.4	12.9	12.4	12.8	11.3	10.1	10.9	10.1	7.6	18.6															
1992	11.1	11.1	12.1	13.2	12.8	12.4	12.6	12.8	12.8	12.6	12.9	12.3	11.8	12.0	10.7	9.6	10.1	9.3	7.3	12.6	6.8														
1993	11.3	11.3	12.2	13.3	12.8	12.6	12.8	12.9	13.0	12.8	13.0	12.5	12.1	12.4	11.2	10.6	10.9	10.4	9.4	13.4	10.9	15.2													
1994	10.8	10.7	11.6	12.5	12.0	11.8	11.9	12.0	12.0	11.8	11.9	11.4	10.9	11.0	9.8	8.9	9.2	8.5	7.2	10.3	8.4	9.2	-0.8												
25-Yr 1995	10.9	10.9	11.7	12.6	12.1	11.9	12.1	12.2	12.2	11.9	12.1	11.6	11.2	11.3	10.3	9.5	9.8	9.3	8.4	10.6	8.7	9.4	6.6	14.6											
1996	10.9	10.9	11.7	12.6	12.1	11.9	12.1	12.1	12.1	12.0	12.1	11.6	11.3	11.3	10.3	9.6	9.9	9.5	8.7	10.6	9.1	9.7	7.9	12.6	10.7										
1997	10.8	10.8	11.6	12.5	12.1	11.8	12.0	12.1	12.1	11.9	12.0	11.5	11.1	11.2	10.3	9.6	9.9	9.4	8.7	10.4	9.1	9.6	8.2	11.4	9.8	9.0									
1998	10.6	10.6	11.3	12.1	11.7	11.4	11.6	11.6	11.6	11.4	11.4	11.0	10.6	10.7	9.8	9.0	9.4	9.0	8.4	9.8	8.6	8.9	7.7	9.9	8.4	7.3	5.6								
1999	10.6	10.6	11.3	12.0	11.6	11.5	11.5	11.5	11.6	11.3	11.3	10.9	10.6	10.6	9.8	9.3	9.5	9.1	8.5	9.8	8.8	9.0	8.0	9.9	8.8	8.2	7.7	9.9							
2000	10.3	10.3	10.9	11.6	11.2	11.0	11.1	11.1	11.1	10.9	10.9	10.5	10.1	10.1	9.4	8.8	9.0	8.6	8.0	9.1	8.1	8.3	7.3	8.7	7.6	6.9	6.1	7.7	3.0						
30-Yr 2001	10.1	10.1	10.7	11.3	10.9	10.7	10.8	10.8	10.7	10.5	10.5	10.1	9.7	9.7	9.0	8.4	8.6	8.2	7.6	8.6	7.6	7.8	6.8	8.0	6.9	6.2	5.5	6.4	3.2	3.4					
2002	9.7	9.7	10.3	10.9	10.5	10.2	10.3	10.3	10.1	10.0	10.0	9.6	9.2	9.1	8.4	7.9	8.2	7.6	6.9	7.9	6.9	6.9	5.9	6.9	5.9	5.1	4.3	5.4	3.2	1.6	-0.2				
2003	10.0	10.0	10.5	11.1	10.8	10.5	10.6	10.6	10.5	10.3	10.3	10.0	9.6	9.6	9.0	8.4	8.6	8.3	7.8	8.6	7.8	7.9	7.0	8.2	7.4	6.8	6.0	7.0	6.0	7.0	8.9	18.9			
2004	10.0	10.0	10.5	11.1	10.7	10.5	10.6	10.5	10.3	10.1	10.3	10.0	9.6	9.6	9.0	8.5	8.6	8.4	7.9	8.7	7.9	8.0	7.2	8.3	7.6	7.0	6.6	7.2	6.7	7.6	9.0	13.9	9.2		
2005	9.8	9.8	10.3	10.9	10.5	10.3	10.4	10.3	10.1	10.0	10.1	9.7	9.4	9.4	8.8	8.4	8.4	8.1	7.7	8.4	7.7	7.8	7.0	8.0	7.3	6.7	6.4	6.9	6.4	7.1	8.0	10.9	7.1	5.0	
35-Yr 2006	9.9	9.9	10.4	10.9	10.5	10.3	10.4	10.3	10.1	10.1	10.1	9.8	9.5	9.5	8.9	8.5	8.6	8.3	7.9	8.6	8.0	8.0	7.5	8.2	7.7	7.2	7.0	7.4	7.1	7.8	8.6	11.0	8.5	8.1	11.3
	1972	1973	1974	1975	1976	1977	1978	1979	1980	1981	1982	1983	1984	1985	1986	1987	1988	1989	1990	1991	1992	1993	1994	1995	1996	1997	1998	1999	2000	2001	2002	2003	2004	2005	2006

How to read the Annualized Returns Matrix: You can locate the annualized compounded rate of return for this simulated Index Portfolio for a designated time period by following these easy instructions: Locate the column for the beginning year of the period. Years are labeled at the top and the bottom of each column. Then, locate the ending year of the period on the left-most vertical column. The annualized return can be found where the first year's column intersects with the ending year's row. IFA advisory fees of 0.9% per year and DFA mutual fund expense ratios have been deducted from these results. The 5-Yr diagonal (highlighted, starting from far left column) represents the estimated average holding period for investors who score 30 on the Risk Capacity Survey at ifa.com. Sources, Updates, and Disclosures: ifa.com/btp.

INDEX PORTFOLIO 30: PALE BLUE

Growth of $1 Matrix ($)
35 years of Index Portfolio 30 (1972–2006)
Returns Net of IFA and DFA Fees

Period	End	1972	1973	1974	1975	1976	1977	1978	1979	1980	1981	1982	1983	1984	1985	1986	1987	1988	1989	1990	1991	1992	1993	1994	1995	1996	1997	1998	1999	2000	2001	2002	2003	2004	2005	2006
1-Yr	1972	1.11																																		
	1973	1.05	1.11																																	
	1974	0.99	0.89	0.95																																
	1975	1.21	1.09	1.15	1.22																															
5-Yr	1976	1.42	1.28	1.35	1.45	1.17																														
	1977	1.54	1.39	1.47	1.55	1.27	1.09																													
	1978	1.71	1.54	1.63	1.72	1.41	1.21	1.11																												
	1979	1.91	1.73	1.82	1.93	1.58	1.35	1.24	1.12																											
	1980	2.21	1.99	2.11	2.23	1.82	1.56	1.44	1.29	1.15																										
10-Yr	1981	2.44	2.20	2.32	2.46	2.01	1.72	1.58	1.43	1.27	1.10																									
	1982	2.88	2.60	2.74	2.91	2.38	2.03	1.87	1.68	1.50	1.30	1.18																								
	1983	3.37	3.04	3.21	3.40	2.78	2.38	2.19	1.97	1.76	1.52	1.38	1.17																							
	1984	3.70	3.33	3.52	3.73	3.05	2.61	2.40	2.16	1.93	1.67	1.52	1.28	1.10																						
	1985	4.51	4.07	4.30	4.56	3.73	3.19	2.93	2.64	2.36	2.04	1.85	1.57	1.34	1.22																					
15-Yr	1986	5.30	4.78	5.05	5.36	4.38	3.75	3.45	3.11	2.77	2.40	2.18	1.84	1.57	1.44	1.18																				
	1987	5.67	5.12	5.41	5.73	4.68	4.01	3.69	3.32	2.96	2.57	2.33	1.97	1.68	1.54	1.26	1.07																			
	1988	6.43	5.80	6.13	6.49	5.31	4.54	4.18	3.76	3.36	2.91	2.64	2.23	1.91	1.74	1.42	1.21	1.13																		
	1989	7.41	6.69	7.06	7.49	6.12	5.23	4.82	4.34	3.87	3.36	3.04	2.58	2.20	2.01	1.64	1.40	1.31	1.13																	
	1990	7.24	6.53	6.90	7.31	5.98	5.11	4.70	4.24	3.78	3.28	2.97	2.52	2.15	1.96	1.60	1.36	1.28	1.15	0.98																
20-Yr	1991	8.58	7.74	8.18	8.67	7.09	6.06	5.58	5.03	4.49	3.89	3.52	2.98	2.55	2.32	1.90	1.62	1.51	1.36	1.16	1.19															
	1992	9.17	8.27	8.74	9.26	7.57	6.48	5.96	5.37	4.79	4.15	3.76	3.19	2.72	2.48	2.03	1.73	1.62	1.43	1.24	1.27	1.07														
	1993	10.56	9.52	10.06	10.66	8.72	7.46	6.86	6.18	5.52	4.78	4.33	3.67	3.14	2.86	2.34	1.99	1.86	1.64	1.42	1.46	1.23	1.15													
	1994	10.47	9.44	9.98	10.57	8.65	7.39	6.80	6.13	5.47	4.74	4.30	3.64	3.11	2.83	2.32	1.97	1.85	1.63	1.41	1.45	1.22	1.14	0.99												
	1995	12.00	10.82	11.43	12.12	9.91	8.47	7.79	7.03	6.27	5.43	4.92	4.17	3.56	3.25	2.66	2.26	2.11	1.87	1.62	1.66	1.40	1.31	1.14	1.15											
25-Yr	1996	13.28	11.98	12.66	13.41	10.97	9.38	8.63	7.78	6.94	6.01	5.45	4.62	3.94	3.59	2.94	2.50	2.34	2.07	1.79	1.84	1.55	1.45	1.26	1.27	1.11										
	1997	14.47	13.06	13.41	14.62	11.95	10.22	9.40	8.43	7.56	6.55	5.94	5.03	4.30	3.92	3.21	2.73	2.55	2.25	1.95	2.00	1.69	1.58	1.38	1.37	1.21	1.09									
	1998	15.29	13.79	14.57	15.44	12.62	10.80	9.93	8.95	7.99	6.92	6.27	5.31	4.54	4.14	3.39	2.88	2.69	2.38	2.06	2.11	1.78	1.67	1.46	1.45	1.27	1.15	1.06								
	1999	16.80	15.15	16.01	16.97	13.87	11.86	10.92	9.84	8.78	7.60	6.89	5.84	4.99	4.55	3.72	3.17	2.96	2.61	2.32	2.27	1.96	1.83	1.59	1.59	1.40	1.27	1.16	1.10							
	2000	17.31	15.61	16.50	17.48	14.30	12.23	11.25	10.14	9.05	7.84	7.10	6.02	5.14	4.68	3.84	3.26	3.05	2.69	2.39	2.34	2.02	1.89	1.64	1.65	1.44	1.30	1.20	1.13	1.03						
30-Yr	2001	17.90	16.15	17.06	18.04	14.79	12.64	11.63	10.43	9.36	8.10	7.35	6.22	5.32	4.85	3.97	3.38	3.16	2.79	2.47	2.42	2.09	1.95	1.70	1.71	1.49	1.35	1.24	1.17	1.07	1.03					
	2002	17.86	16.11	17.02	18.00	14.75	12.62	11.61	10.46	9.33	8.09	7.33	6.21	5.30	4.83	3.96	3.37	3.15	2.78	2.47	2.41	2.08	1.95	1.69	1.71	1.49	1.35	1.23	1.17	1.06	1.03	1.00				
	2003	21.23	19.16	20.24	21.45	17.54	15.00	13.80	12.44	11.10	9.61	8.72	7.38	6.31	5.75	4.71	4.00	3.74	3.30	2.93	2.86	2.47	2.32	2.03	2.01	1.77	1.60	1.47	1.39	1.26	1.23	1.19	1.19			
	2004	23.19	20.92	22.10	23.42	19.16	16.38	15.07	13.58	12.12	10.50	9.52	8.06	6.89	6.28	5.14	4.37	4.09	3.61	3.21	3.13	2.70	2.53	2.22	2.20	1.93	1.75	1.60	1.52	1.38	1.34	1.30	1.30	1.09		
	2005	24.35	21.97	23.21	24.59	20.11	17.20	15.82	14.26	12.73	11.02	9.99	8.46	7.23	6.59	5.40	4.59	4.29	3.79	3.36	3.29	2.84	2.66	2.33	2.31	2.03	1.83	1.68	1.59	1.45	1.41	1.36	1.36	1.15	1.05	
35-Yr	2006	27.09	24.44	25.82	27.36	22.38	19.14	17.60	15.87	14.16	12.27	11.12	9.42	8.04	7.33	6.00	5.11	4.78	4.22	3.66	3.74	3.16	2.95	2.57	2.59	2.26	2.04	1.87	1.77	1.61	1.57	1.51	1.52	1.28	1.17	1.11
		1972	1973	1974	1975	1976	1977	1978	1979	1980	1981	1982	1983	1984	1985	1986	1987	1988	1989	1990	1991	1992	1993	1994	1995	1996	1997	1998	1999	2000	2001	2002	2003	2004	2005	2006

How to read the Growth of $1 Matrix: You can locate the growth of a dollar invested in this simulated Index Portfolio for a designated time period by following these easy instructions: Locate the column for the beginning year of the period. Years are labeled at the top and the bottom of each column. Then, locate the ending year of the period on the left-most vertical column. The growth of a dollar over the time period can be found where the first year's column intersects with the ending year's row. IFA advisory fees of 0.9% per year and DFA mutual fund expense ratios have been deducted from these results. The 5-Yr diagonal (highlighted, starting from far left column) represents the estimated average holding period for investors who score 30 on the Risk Capacity Survey at ifa.com. Sources, Updates, and Disclosures: ifa.com/btp.

Index Portfolio 30: Pale Blue

Monthly Rolling Period Analysis*
Based on 50 Years (600 months) of Monthly Data
Jan 1957 to Dec 2006

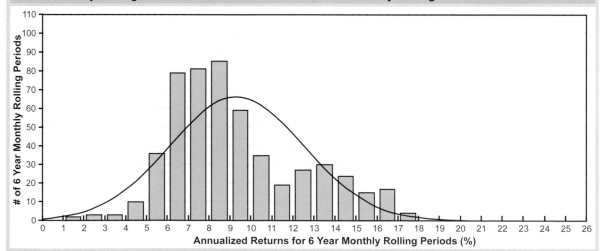

Examples of 6 Year Monthly Rolling Periods**

Periods

1	Jan 57	← 6 Years →	Dec 62
2	Feb 57	← 6 Years →	Jan 62
3	Mar 57	← 6 Years →	Feb 63
4	Apr 57	← 6 Years →	Mar 63

529

Year 1957   1958   1959   1960   1961   1962   1963   1964   1965   1966   1967   1968   1969

Per Period Number of: Yrs	Months	# of Rolling Periods	Average Ann'lzd Rtn. %*	Std. Dev. of Avg. Ann'lzd Rtn. %*	Lowest Rolling Period Date	Lowest Rolling Period Return	Growth of $1 in Lowest Period	Highest Rolling Period Date	Highest Rolling Period Return	Growth of $1 in Highest Period	Average Growth of $1
0.08	1	600	0.75*	1.76*	10/87-10/87	-8.12	$0.92	1/75-1/75	9.57	$1.10	$1.01
0.25	3	598	2.27*	3.41*	9/87-11/87	-9.66	$0.90	1/75-3/75	15.45	$1.15	$1.02
0.5	6	595	4.58*	4.98*	4/74-9/74	-9.18	$0.91	1/75-6/75	21.66	$1.22	$1.05
1	12	589	9.43	7.13	10/73-9/74	-11.15	$0.89	7/82-6/83	33.09	$1.33	$1.09
2	24	577	9.34	4.83	1/73-12/74	-5.49	$0.89	7/84-6/86	23.36	$1.52	$1.32
3	36	565	9.27	3.88	1/72-12/74	-0.33	$0.99	8/84-7/87	21.31	$1.79	$1.31
4	48	553	9.27	3.47	1/71-12/74	3.00	$1.13	7/82-6/86	20.55	$2.11	$1.43
5	60	541	9.26	3.35	4/98-3/03	2.86	$1.15	8/82-7/87	19.54	$2.44	$1.57
6*	**72**	**529**	**9.32**	**3.18**	**1/69-12/74**	**1.81**	**$1.11**	**10/81-9/87**	**17.79**	**$2.67**	**$1.73**
7	84	517	9.39	2.99	1/68-12/74	3.72	$1.29	4/80-3/87	17.51	$3.09	$1.91
8	96	505	9.46	2.85	10/67-9/75	5.33	$1.52	4/80-3/88	15.92	$3.26	$2.10
9	108	493	9.53	2.75	1/66-12/74	5.00	$1.55	3/78-2/87	15.50	$3.66	$2.32
10	120	481	9.60	2.63	10/64-9/74	5.48	$1.70	9/77-8/87	15.21	$4.12	$2.57
11	132	469	9.66	2.54	7/59-6/70	5.68	$1.84	9/75-8/86	14.79	$4.56	$2.84
12	144	457	9.69	2.46	1/63-12/74	6.15	$2.05	1/75-12/86	15.01	$5.36	$3.14
13	156	445	9.73	2.39	1/62-12/74	5.50	$2.01	10/74-9/87	15.07	$6.20	$3.47
14	168	433	9.80	2.27	1/61-12/74	5.87	$2.22	1/75-12/88	14.29	$6.49	$3.85
15	180	421	9.86	2.17	1/60-12/74	5.59	$2.26	10/74-9/89	14.43	$7.55	$4.27
20	240	361	10.20	1.47	2/57-1/77	7.32	$4.11	10/74-9/94	12.66	$10.85	$7.21
30	360	241	10.20	0.31	1/57-12/86	9.56	$15.47	1/75-12/04	11.08	$23.39	$18.47
40	480	121	9.58	0.14	4/63-3/03	9.31	$35.19	4/58-3/98	9.93	$44.12	$38.84
50	600	1	9.14	0.00	1/57-12/06	9.14	$79.29	1/57-12/06	9.14	$79.29	$79.29

6 Year Monthly Rolling Periods** - Jan 1957 to Dec 2006 - 529 Monthly Rolling Periods Over 50 Years

X-axis: Annualized Returns for 6 Year Monthly Rolling Periods (%)
Y-axis: # of 6 Year Monthly Rolling Periods

*Sources, Updates, and Disclosures: ifa.com/btp. Returns are net of IFA & DFA fees. The returns and standard deviation shown for 1, 3, and 6 month periods are not annualized. Past performance does not guarantee future results. **6 years represents the estimated average holding period for investors who score 30 on the Risk Capacity Survey at ifa.com.

Appendix A

318

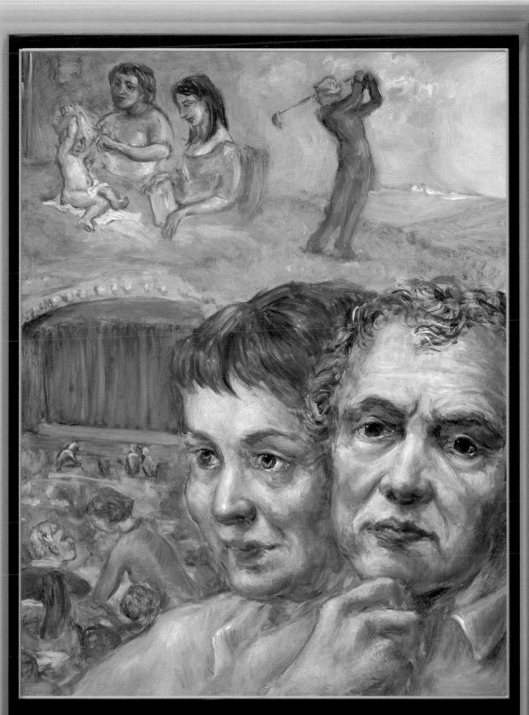

RISK CAPACITY 25
ICE BLUE

Index Portfolio 25: Ice Blue

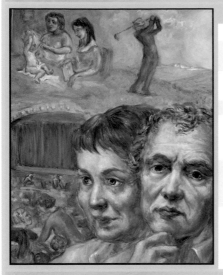

Index Allocations

General Asset Class		Specific Index	
14%	US Large	7%	IFA US Large Company Index
		7%	IFA US Large Cap Value Index
7%	US Small	3.5%	IFA US Micro Cap Index
		3.5%	IFA US Small Cap Value Index
3.5%	Real Estate	3.5%	IFA Real Estate Index
7%	International	3.5%	IFA International Value Index
		1.75%	IFA International Small Company Index
		1.75%	IFA International Small Cap Value Index
3.5%	Emerging Markets	1.05%	IFA Emerging Markets Index
		1.05%	IFA Emerging Markets Value Index
		1.40%	IFA Emerging Markets Small Cap Index
65%	Fixed Income	16.25%	IFA One-Year Fixed Income Index
		16.25%	IFA Two-Year Global Fixed Income Index
		16.25%	IFA Five-Year Gov't Income Index
		16.25%	IFA Five-Year Global Fixed Income Index

Index Portfolio - Simulated Returns and Volatility Data*

	1yr ending 2006	1yr ending 2005	1yr ending 2004	1yr ending 2003	3yrs 2004-2006	5yrs 2002-2006	10yrs 1996-2006	25yrs 1982-2006	35yrs 1972-2006	50yrs 1957-2006	80yrs 1927-2006
Growth of $1	1.10	1.04	1.08	1.17	1.25	1.46	1.96	10.05	23.81	65.24	335.01
Annualized Return %	10.30	4.46	8.18	16.70	7.62	7.92	6.97	9.67	9.48	8.72	7.54
Annualized Volatility (Standard Deviation %)	3.39	3.42	4.65	4.82	3.81	4.29	4.84	5.11	5.53	5.47	9.08

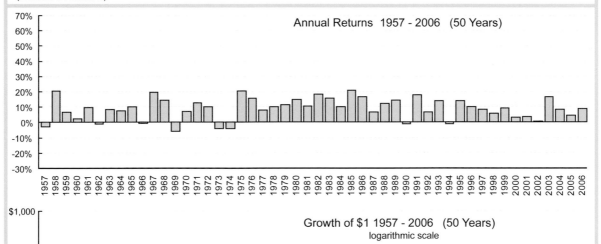

Annual Returns 1957 - 2006 (50 Years)

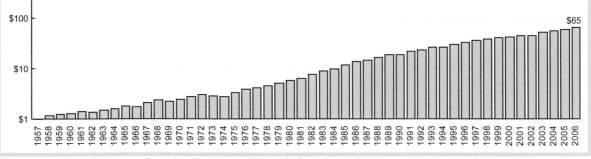

Growth of $1 1957 - 2006 (50 Years)
logarithmic scale

$65

INDEX PORTFOLIO 25: ICE BLUE

Annualized Returns Matrix (%)
35 years of Index Portfolio 25 (1972-2006)
Returns Net of IFA and DFA Fees

	1972	1973	1974	1975	1976	1977	1978	1979	1980	1981	1982	1983	1984	1985	1986	1987	1988	1989	1990	1991	1992	1993	1994	1995	1996	1997	1998	1999	2000	2001	2002	2003	2004	2005	2006
1-Yr 1972	9.9																																		
1973	2.7	-4.1																																	
1974	0.4	-4.1	-4.0																																
1975	5.0	3.4	7.5	20.3																															
5-Yr 1976	7.1	6.4	10.2	18.1	15.8																														
1977	7.2	6.7	9.6	14.6	11.8	8.0																													
1978	7.6	7.3	9.7	13.4	11.2	9.0	10.0																												
1979	8.1	7.9	10.0	13.0	11.3	9.8	10.8	11.5																											
1980	8.8	8.7	10.7	13.3	12.0	11.0	12.0	13.1	14.6																										
10-Yr 1981	9.0	8.9	10.7	13.6	11.7	10.9	11.7	12.3	12.7	10.7																									
1982	9.8	9.8	11.5	12.7	12.1	12.1	13.0	13.7	14.5	14.4	18.3																								
1983	10.3	10.3	11.9	13.5	12.3	12.7	13.5	14.2	14.8	14.9	17.0	15.9																							
1984	10.3	10.3	11.7	13.4	12.7	12.3	13.0	13.5	13.8	13.6	14.6	12.9	10.0																						
1985	11.0	11.1	12.5	14.1	13.5	13.2	13.9	14.5	15.0	15.1	15.5	15.5	15.3	21.0																					
15-Yr 1986	11.4	11.5	12.8	14.3	13.8	13.6	14.2	14.8	15.2	15.3	15.8	15.8	15.7	18.8	16.6																				
1987	11.1	11.2	12.5	13.7	13.2	12.9	13.4	13.8	14.1	14.0	14.3	13.9	13.4	14.6	11.5	6.7																			
1988	11.2	11.2	12.3	13.6	13.1	12.9	13.3	13.7	13.9	13.8	14.3	13.6	13.2	14.0	12.4	9.5	12.4																		
1989	11.3	11.4	12.5	13.7	13.2	13.0	13.4	13.7	14.0	13.9	14.3	13.7	13.7	14.1	13.4	11.1	13.4	14.4																	
1990	10.6	10.7	11.6	12.7	12.2	11.9	12.4	12.5	12.5	12.3	12.5	11.8	11.2	11.4	9.6	7.9	8.3	6.3	-1.2																
20-Yr 1991	11.0	11.0	11.9	13.0	12.6	12.3	12.6	12.9	12.9	12.8	12.9	12.4	12.0	12.3	10.9	9.8	10.6	10.0	7.8	17.7															
1992	10.8	10.8	11.7	12.6	12.2	11.9	12.2	12.4	12.4	12.2	12.4	11.8	11.4	11.6	10.3	9.2	9.8	9.1	7.4	12.0	6.6														
1993	10.9	11.0	11.8	12.7	12.3	12.1	12.5	12.5	12.5	12.4	12.5	12.0	11.6	11.8	10.7	9.9	10.5	10.1	9.0	12.7	10.3	14.1													
1994	10.4	10.4	11.1	11.9	11.5	11.3	11.6	11.6	11.6	11.4	11.4	10.9	10.4	10.5	9.4	8.5	8.8	8.2	7.0	9.1	6.4	6.3	-1.0												
25-Yr 1995	10.5	10.5	11.3	12.0	11.6	11.4	11.7	11.7	11.6	11.5	11.6	11.1	10.7	10.7	9.8	9.1	9.4	9.0	8.1	10.1	8.2	8.8	6.2	13.9											
1996	10.5	10.5	11.2	12.0	11.6	11.4	11.6	11.6	11.5	11.5	11.5	11.1	10.7	10.7	9.8	9.2	9.5	9.2	8.4	10.1	8.6	9.1	7.5	12.0	10.2										
1997	10.4	10.4	11.1	11.8	11.4	11.2	11.4	11.5	11.3	11.3	11.3	10.9	10.5	10.6	9.7	9.1	9.4	9.1	8.4	9.9	8.6	9.0	7.8	10.9	9.4	8.6									
1998	10.2	10.3	10.9	11.5	11.2	11.0	11.1	11.1	11.0	11.0	11.0	10.5	10.2	10.2	9.4	8.8	9.0	8.7	8.1	9.3	8.2	8.4	7.3	9.5	8.1	7.1	5.6								
1999	10.2	10.2	10.8	11.4	11.1	10.9	11.0	11.0	10.9	10.9	10.9	10.4	10.1	10.1	9.4	8.9	9.0	8.7	8.2	9.3	8.3	8.5	7.6	9.4	8.3	7.7	7.3	9.1							
30-Yr 2000	10.0	10.0	10.5	11.1	10.8	10.6	10.7	10.7	10.5	10.5	10.0	10.0	9.7	9.7	9.2	8.5	8.6	8.3	7.7	8.7	7.7	7.9	7.0	8.4	7.3	6.6	5.4	5.3	3.4						
2001	9.7	9.7	10.3	10.8	10.5	10.3	10.4	10.4	10.3	10.1	10.1	9.7	9.4	9.3	8.6	8.1	8.2	7.9	7.4	8.2	7.3	7.4	6.6	7.7	6.7	6.0	4.4	4.1	2.6	0.7					
2002	9.4	9.4	9.9	10.5	10.1	9.9	10.0	9.9	9.7	9.7	9.6	9.2	8.9	8.8	8.2	7.6	7.7	7.4	6.9	7.6	6.7	6.7	5.9	6.8	5.8	5.1	4.4	4.1	2.6	2.1	0.7				
2003	9.7	9.6	10.1	10.7	10.3	10.1	10.2	10.2	10.0	10.0	10.0	9.6	9.3	9.2	8.6	8.2	8.3	8.0	7.5	8.2	7.5	7.6	6.9	7.9	7.1	6.7	6.4	6.5	5.9	6.8	8.4	16.7			
2004	9.6	9.6	10.1	10.6	10.3	10.1	10.2	10.1	9.9	9.9	9.9	9.5	9.2	9.2	8.6	8.2	8.2	8.0	7.6	8.2	7.5	7.6	7.1	7.9	7.2	6.9	6.6	6.8	6.4	7.1	8.3	12.4	8.2		
2005	9.5	9.4	9.9	10.4	10.1	9.9	9.9	9.9	9.7	9.7	9.6	9.3	9.0	8.9	8.4	8.0	8.0	7.8	7.4	8.0	7.3	7.4	6.8	7.6	7.0	6.6	6.4	6.5	6.0	6.6	7.3	9.7	6.3	4.5	
35-Yr 2006	9.5	9.5	9.9	10.4	10.1	9.9	9.9	9.9	9.9	9.7	9.7	9.3	9.0	9.0	8.5	8.1	8.2	7.9	7.6	8.1	7.5	7.6	7.1	7.8	7.3	7.0	6.8	6.9	6.6	7.2	7.9	9.8	7.6	7.3	10.3
	1972	1973	1974	1975	1976	1977	1978	1979	1980	1981	1982	1983	1984	1985	1986	1987	1988	1989	1990	1991	1992	1993	1994	1995	1996	1997	1998	1999	2000	2001	2002	2003	2004	2005	2006

How to read the Annualized Returns Matrix: You can locate the annualized compounded rate of return for this simulated Index Portfolio for a designated time period by following these easy instructions: Locate the column for the beginning year of the period. Years are labeled at the top and the bottom of each column. Then, locate the ending year of the period on the left-most vertical column. The annualized return can be found where the first year's column intersects with the ending year's row. IFA advisory fees of 0.9% per year and DFA mutual fund expense ratios have been deducted from these results. The 5-Yr diagonal (highlighted, starting from far left column) represents the estimated average holding period for investors who score 25 on the Risk Capacity Survey at ifa.com. Sources, Updates, and Disclosures: ifa.com/btp.

INDEX PORTFOLIO 25: ICE BLUE

Growth of $1 Matrix ($)
35 years of Index Portfolio 25 (1972-2006)
Returns Net of IFA and DFA Fees

Period	End	1972	1973	1974	1975	1976	1977	1978	1979	1980	1981	1982	1983	1984	1985	1986	1987	1988	1989	1990	1991	1992	1993	1994	1995	1996	1997	1998	1999	2000	2001	2002	2003	2004	2005	2006
1-Yr	1972	1.10																																		
	1973	1.05	0.96																																	
	1974	1.01	0.92	0.96																																
	1975	1.22	1.11	1.15	1.20																															
5-Yr	1976	1.41	1.28	1.34	1.39	1.16																														
	1977	1.52	1.38	1.44	1.50	1.25	1.08																													
	1978	1.67	1.52	1.59	1.66	1.38	1.19	1.10																												
	1979	1.87	1.70	1.77	1.85	1.53	1.32	1.23	1.12																											
	1980	2.14	1.95	2.03	2.12	1.76	1.52	1.41	1.28	1.15																										
10-Yr	1981	2.37	2.16	2.25	2.34	1.95	1.68	1.56	1.42	1.27	1.11																									
	1982	2.80	2.55	2.66	2.77	2.30	1.99	1.84	1.67	1.50	1.31	1.18																								
	1983	3.25	2.95	3.08	3.21	2.67	2.30	2.13	1.94	1.74	1.52	1.37	1.16																							
	1984	3.57	3.25	3.39	3.53	2.93	2.53	2.35	2.13	1.91	1.67	1.51	1.27	1.10																						
	1985	4.32	3.93	4.10	4.27	3.55	3.06	2.84	2.58	2.31	2.02	1.82	1.54	1.33	1.21																					
15-Yr	1986	5.03	4.58	4.78	4.98	4.14	3.57	3.31	3.01	2.70	2.35	2.12	1.80	1.55	1.41	1.17																				
	1987	5.37	4.89	5.10	5.31	4.41	3.81	3.53	3.21	2.88	2.51	2.27	1.92	1.65	1.50	1.24	1.07																			
	1988	6.04	5.49	5.73	5.97	4.96	4.28	3.97	3.61	3.23	2.82	2.55	2.15	1.86	1.69	1.40	1.20	1.12																		
	1989	6.90	6.28	6.55	6.83	5.67	4.90	4.54	4.12	3.70	3.23	2.91	2.46	2.13	1.93	1.60	1.37	1.29	1.14																	
	1990	6.82	6.21	6.47	6.75	5.61	4.84	4.48	4.08	3.65	3.19	2.88	2.43	2.10	1.91	1.58	1.36	1.27	1.13	0.99																
20-Yr	1991	8.03	7.30	7.62	7.94	6.59	5.69	5.27	4.79	4.30	3.75	3.39	2.86	2.47	2.25	1.86	1.59	1.49	1.33	1.16	1.18															
	1992	8.56	7.79	8.12	8.46	7.03	6.07	5.62	5.11	4.58	4.00	3.61	3.05	2.64	2.40	1.98	1.70	1.59	1.42	1.24	1.25	1.07														
	1993	9.76	8.88	9.26	9.65	8.02	6.93	6.41	5.83	5.23	4.56	4.12	3.48	3.01	2.73	2.26	1.94	1.82	1.62	1.41	1.43	1.22	1.14													
	1994	9.66	8.79	9.17	9.56	7.94	6.86	6.35	5.77	5.18	4.52	4.08	3.45	2.98	2.71	2.24	1.92	1.80	1.60	1.40	1.42	1.20	1.13	0.99												
	1995	11.01	10.02	10.45	10.89	9.05	7.81	7.24	6.58	5.90	5.15	4.65	3.93	3.39	3.08	2.55	2.19	2.05	1.82	1.60	1.61	1.37	1.29	1.13	1.14											
25-Yr	1996	12.13	11.04	11.51	12.00	9.97	8.61	7.97	7.25	6.50	5.67	5.12	4.33	3.74	3.40	2.81	2.41	2.26	2.01	1.78	1.76	1.51	1.42	1.24	1.26	1.10										
	1997	13.17	11.98	12.50	13.02	10.82	9.35	8.66	7.87	7.06	6.15	5.56	4.70	4.06	3.69	3.05	2.62	2.45	2.18	1.93	1.91	1.64	1.54	1.35	1.36	1.20	1.20									
	1998	13.91	12.65	13.20	13.76	11.43	9.87	9.14	8.31	7.45	6.50	5.87	4.96	4.29	3.90	3.22	2.76	2.59	2.30	2.04	2.02	1.73	1.63	1.43	1.44	1.26	1.15	1.06								
	1999	15.17	13.80	14.40	15.00	12.47	10.77	9.97	9.06	8.13	7.09	6.40	5.42	4.67	4.25	3.51	3.01	2.83	2.51	2.22	2.20	1.89	1.77	1.55	1.57	1.38	1.25	1.15	1.09							
	2000	15.69	14.27	14.89	15.51	12.89	11.13	10.31	9.37	8.40	7.33	6.62	5.60	4.83	4.39	3.63	3.12	2.92	2.60	2.30	2.27	1.95	1.83	1.61	1.62	1.42	1.29	1.19	1.13	1.03						
30-Yr	2001	16.26	14.79	15.43	16.08	13.36	11.54	10.68	9.71	8.71	7.60	6.86	5.80	5.01	4.55	3.77	3.23	3.03	2.69	2.38	2.36	2.03	1.90	1.68	1.68	1.48	1.34	1.23	1.17	1.07	1.04					
	2002	16.37	14.89	15.53	16.18	13.45	11.61	10.76	9.78	8.77	7.65	6.91	5.84	5.04	4.58	3.79	3.25	3.05	2.71	2.40	2.37	2.04	1.91	1.69	1.69	1.49	1.35	1.24	1.18	1.08	1.04	1.04				
	2003	19.10	17.37	18.12	18.89	15.69	13.55	12.55	11.41	10.23	8.92	8.06	6.82	5.88	5.35	4.42	3.79	3.56	3.16	2.80	2.77	2.38	2.23	1.98	1.98	1.73	1.57	1.45	1.37	1.26	1.22	1.17	1.17			
	2004	20.66	18.79	19.61	20.43	16.98	14.66	13.58	12.34	11.07	9.65	8.72	7.37	6.36	5.79	4.79	4.10	3.85	3.42	3.03	2.99	2.57	2.41	2.14	2.14	1.88	1.70	1.57	1.49	1.36	1.32	1.27	1.26	1.08		
	2005	21.58	19.63	20.48	21.34	17.73	15.31	14.18	12.89	11.56	10.08	9.11	7.70	6.65	6.05	5.00	4.29	4.02	3.57	3.16	3.13	2.69	2.52	2.23	2.23	1.96	1.78	1.64	1.55	1.42	1.38	1.33	1.32	1.13	1.04	
35-Yr	2006	23.81	21.66	22.59	23.54	19.56	16.89	15.64	14.22	12.75	11.12	10.05	8.50	7.33	6.67	5.51	4.73	4.43	3.94	3.49	3.45	2.97	2.78	2.46	2.46	2.16	1.96	1.81	1.71	1.57	1.52	1.46	1.45	1.25	1.15	1.10
		1972	1973	1974	1975	1976	1977	1978	1979	1980	1981	1982	1983	1984	1985	1986	1987	1988	1989	1990	1991	1992	1993	1994	1995	1996	1997	1998	1999	2000	2001	2002	2003	2004	2005	2006

How to read the Growth of $1 Matrix: You can locate the growth of a dollar invested in this simulated Index Portfolio for a designated time period by following these easy instructions: Locate the column for the beginning year of the period. Years are labeled at the top and the bottom of each column. Then, locate the ending year of the period on the left-most vertical column. The growth of a dollar over the time period can be found where the first year's column intersects with the ending year's row. IFA advisory fees of 0.9% per year and DFA mutual fund expense ratios have been deducted from these results. The 5-Yr diagonal (highlighted, starting from far left column) represents the estimated average holding period for investors who score 25 on the Risk Capacity Survey at ifa.com. Sources, Updates, and Disclosures: ifa.com/btp.

Index Portfolio 25: Ice Blue

Monthly Rolling Period Analysis
Based on 50 years (600 months) of Monthly Data
Jan 1957 to Dec 2006

Examples of 5 Year Monthly Rolling Periods**

Periods

1	Jan 57	← 5 Years →	Dec 61
2	Feb 57	← 5 Years →	Jan 62
3	Mar 57	← 5 Years →	Feb 62
4	Apr 57	← 5 Years →	Mar 62

541

Year 1957 1958 1959 1960 1961 1962 1963 1964 1965 1966 1967 1968 1969

Per Period Number of: Yrs	Months	# of Rolling Periods	Average Ann'lzd Rtn. %*	Std. Dev. of Avg. Ann'lzd Rtn. %*	Lowest Rolling Period Date	Lowest Rolling Period Return	Growth of $1 in Lowest Period	Highest Rolling Period Date	Highest Rolling Period Return	Growth of $1 in Highest Period	Average Growth of $1
0.08	1	600	0.71*	1.58*	10/87-10/87	-6.91	$0.93	1/75-1/75	8.49	$1.08	$1.01
0.25	3	598	2.16*	3.05*	9/87-11/87	-8.32	$0.92	1/75-3/75	13.72	$1.14	$1.02
0.5	6	595	4.36*	4.15*	4/74-9/74	-7.57	$0.92	1/75-6/75	19.25	$1.19	$1.04
1	12	589	8.00	6.43	10/73-9/74	-9.10	$0.91	7/82-6/83	31.03	$1.31	$1.09
2	24	577	8.90	4.44	1/73-12/74	-4.08	$0.92	7/84-6/86	22.25	$1.49	$1.30
3	36	565	8.86	3.63	1/72-12/74	0.38	$1.01	8/84-7/87	20.00	$1.73	$1.29
4	48	553	8.87	3.29	1/71-12/74	3.33	$1.14	7/82-6/86	19.59	$2.05	$1.41
5**	**60**	**541**	**8.87**	**3.19**	**4/98-3/03**	**3.16**	**$1.17**	**8/82-7/87**	**18.45**	**$2.33**	**$1.54**
6	72	529	8.93	3.05	12/68-11/74	2.36	$1.15	4/80-3/86	17.15	$2.58	$1.69
7	84	517	9.00	2.89	10/67-9/74	3.98	$1.31	4/80-3/87	16.89	$2.98	$1.86
8	96	505	9.07	2.76	1/59-12/66	5.20	$1.50	4/80-3/88	15.38	$3.14	$2.04
9	108	493	9.14	2.67	1/66-12/74	5.06	$1.56	3/78-2/87	14.90	$3.49	$2.25
10	120	481	9.21	2.55	10/64-9/74	5.40	$1.69	9/77-8/87	14.53	$3.88	$2.48
11	132	469	9.27	2.47	7/59-6/70	5.39	$1.78	9/75-8/86	14.18	$4.30	$2.73
12	144	457	9.30	2.40	1/63-12/74	5.95	$2.00	9/74-8/86	14.32	$4.98	$3.00
13	156	445	9.35	2.32	1/62-12/74	5.38	$1.98	10/74-9/87	14.31	$5.69	$3.31
14	168	433	9.42	2.20	9/60-8/74	5.65	$2.16	1/75-12/88	13.61	$5.97	$3.66
15	180	421	9.48	2.11	1/60-12/74	5.45	$2.22	10/74-9/89	13.73	$6.89	$4.04
20	240	361	9.81	1.45	2/57-1/77	6.94	$3.83	10/74-9/94	12.09	$9.80	$6.70
30	360	241	9.80	0.30	1/57-12/86	9.14	$13.79	1/75-12/04	10.58	$20.43	$16.59
40	480	121	9.19	0.12	4/63-3/03	8.97	$31.07	11/57-10/97	9.47	$37.31	$33.67
50	600	1	8.72	0.00	1/57-12/06	8.72	$65.38	1/57-12/06	8.72	$65.38	$65.38

5 Year Monthly Rolling Periods** - Jan 1957 to Dec 2006 - 541 Monthly Rolling Periods Over 50 Years

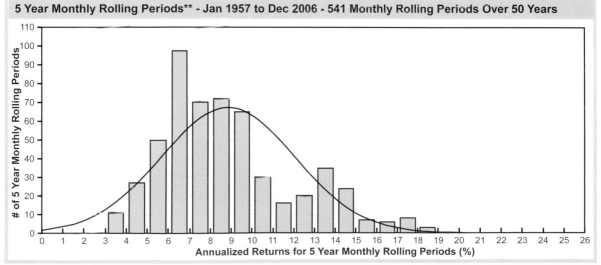

*Sources, Updates, and Disclosures: ifa.com/btp. Returns are net of IFA & DFA fees. The returns and standard deviation shown for 1, 3, and 6 month periods are not annualized. Past performance does not guarantee future results. **5 years represents the estimated average holding period for investors who score 25 on the Risk Capacity Survey at ifa.com.

RISK CAPACITY 20
LIGHT TURQUOISE

Index Portfolio 20: Light Turquoise

Index Allocations

General Asset Class		Specific Index	
12%	US Large	6%	IFA US Large Company Index
		6%	IFA US Large Cap Value Index
6%	US Small	3%	IFA US Micro Cap Index
		3%	IFA US Small Cap Value Index
3%	Real Estate	3%	IFA Real Estate Index
6%	International	3%	IFA International Value Index
		1.5%	IFA International Small Company Index
		1.5%	IFA International Small Cap Value Index
3%	Emerging Markets	0.9%	IFA Emerging Markets Index
		0.9%	IFA Emerging Markets Value Index
		1.2%	IFA Emerging Markets Small Cap Index
70%	Fixed Income	17.5%	IFA One-Year Fixed Income Index
		17.5%	IFA Two-Year Global Fixed Income Index
		17.5%	IFA Five-Year Gov't Income Index
		17.5%	IFA Five-Year Global Fixed Income Index

Index Portfolio - Simulated Returns and Volatility Data*

	1yr ending 2006	1yr ending 2005	1yr ending 2004	1yr ending 2003	3yrs 2004-2006	5yrs 2002-2006	10yrs 1996-2006	25yrs 1982-2006	35yrs 1972-2006	50yrs 1957-2006	80yrs 1927-2006
Growth of $1	1.09	1.04	1.07	1.15	1.22	1.42	1.89	9.06	20.87	53.52	235.73
Annualized Return %	9.32	3.93	7.14	14.51	6.78	7.20	6.55	9.22	9.07	8.29	7.07
Annualized Volatility (Standard Deviation %)	2.91	2.95	4.24	4.32	3.38	3.71	4.17	4.53	4.92	4.86	7.91

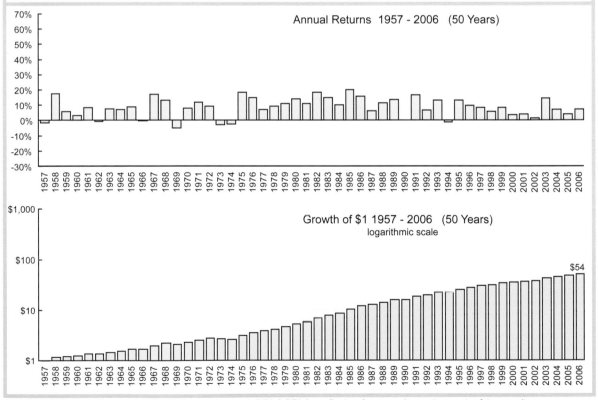

Annual Returns 1957 - 2006 (50 Years)

Growth of $1 1957 - 2006 (50 Years)
logarithmic scale

$54

*Sources, Updates, and Disclosures: ifa.com/btp. Returns net of IFA & DFA fees. Past performance does not guarantee future results.

Annualized Returns Matrix (%)
35 years of Index Portfolio 20 (1972–2006)
Returns Net of IFA and DFA Fees

The matrix below shows annualized compounded rates of return. Rows (left-most column) are the **ending year** of the period; columns (labeled at top and bottom) are the **beginning year** of the period. Period-length labels (1-Yr, 5-Yr, 10-Yr, 15-Yr, 20-Yr, 25-Yr, 30-Yr, 35-Yr) are shown in the far-left column.

Period	End \ Begin	1972	1973	1974	1975	1976	1977	1978	1979	1980	1981	1982	1983	1984	1985	1986	1987	1988	1989	1990	1991	1992	1993	1994	1995	1996	1997	1998	1999	2000	2001	2002	2003	2004	2005	2006
1-Yr	1972	9.0																																		
	1973	2.9	-2.9																																	
	1974	1.1	-2.7	-2.4																																
	1975	5.2	3.9	7.5	18.4																															
5-Yr	1976	7.0	6.5	9.8	16.5	14.7																														
	1977	7.0	6.6	9.2	13.3	10.9	7.2																													
	1978	7.3	7.0	9.2	12.3	10.3	8.2	9.1																												
	1979	7.8	7.6	9.5	12.0	10.5	9.1	10.0	11.0																											
	1980	8.4	8.4	10.1	12.3	11.1	10.3	11.3	12.4	13.9																										
10-Yr	1981	8.7	8.7	10.2	12.1	11.1	10.4	11.2	12.0	12.5	11.1																									
	1982	9.5	9.6	11.1	12.9	12.1	11.7	12.6	13.6	14.4	14.7	18.4																								
	1983	10.0	10.0	11.4	13.1	12.4	12.1	13.0	13.8	14.5	14.7	16.5	14.7																							
	1984	10.0	10.1	11.3	12.8	12.2	11.9	12.6	13.2	13.6	13.6	14.4	12.4	10.2																						
15-Yr	1985	10.7	10.8	12.0	13.4	12.9	12.7	13.5	14.1	14.6	14.8	15.7	14.8	14.9	19.8																					
	1986	11.0	11.1	12.3	13.6	13.2	13.0	13.7	14.3	14.8	15.0	15.7	15.2	15.7	17.7	15.7																				
	1987	10.7	10.8	11.9	13.0	12.6	12.4	13.0	13.4	13.7	13.7	14.1	13.3	13.8	14.9	10.9	6.4																			
	1988	10.7	10.8	11.8	13.0	12.5	12.3	12.8	13.2	13.4	13.4	13.7	13.0	13.2	13.8	11.1	8.9	11.5																		
	1989	10.9	11.0	11.9	13.0	12.6	12.4	12.9	13.2	13.4	13.3	13.7	13.0	13.2	13.7	11.7	11.1	13.2	13.4																	
20-Yr	1990	10.3	10.4	11.2	12.1	11.7	11.5	11.8	12.0	12.1	12.1	12.1	11.3	11.3	11.3	9.3	7.7	8.1	6.5	0.0																
	1991	10.6	10.7	11.5	12.4	12.0	11.8	12.2	12.4	12.5	12.4	12.5	11.9	11.7	11.7	10.5	9.4	10.2	9.8	8.0	16.7															
	1992	10.4	10.5	11.2	12.1	11.7	11.5	11.8	12.0	12.0	12.0	12.0	11.3	11.1	11.0	9.9	9.5	9.9	8.9	7.5	11.5	6.4														
	1993	10.5	10.6	11.3	12.1	11.8	11.6	11.8	12.0	12.0	11.9	12.0	11.3	11.2	11.3	10.3	9.9	10.3	9.5	8.9	12.0	9.7	13.0													
	1994	10.0	10.0	10.7	11.4	11.0	10.8	11.0	11.1	11.0	11.0	11.0	10.4	10.2	10.3	9.2	8.5	8.8	7.8	6.8	8.5	5.9	5.7	-1.1												
25-Yr	1995	10.1	10.2	10.8	11.5	11.1	10.9	11.2	11.3	11.1	11.1	11.1	10.6	10.3	10.3	9.4	8.7	9.0	8.2	7.2	8.9	6.4	7.1	5.8	13.3											
	1996	10.1	10.1	10.7	11.4	11.1	10.9	11.1	11.2	11.0	11.0	11.0	10.5	10.2	10.2	9.4	8.7	9.0	8.5	7.9	9.5	8.1	8.5	7.4	11.5	9.7										
	1997	10.1	10.1	10.7	11.2	10.9	10.7	10.9	11.0	10.9	10.9	11.0	10.4	10.1	10.1	9.3	8.7	9.0	8.7	8.1	9.3	8.1	8.5	7.4	10.4	9.7	9.7									
	1998	9.9	9.9	10.4	11.0	10.7	10.5	10.7	10.8	10.6	10.6	10.7	10.1	9.8	9.8	9.0	8.4	8.6	8.4	7.8	8.8	7.8	8.0	7.0	9.1	7.8	6.9	5.6								
	1999	9.8	9.8	10.3	10.9	10.6	10.4	10.6	10.6	10.4	10.4	10.5	10.0	9.7	9.7	8.8	8.3	8.6	8.3	7.9	8.8	7.7	8.0	7.2	9.0	7.8	7.3	6.9	8.2							
30-Yr	2000	9.6	9.6	10.1	10.6	10.3	10.1	10.3	10.4	10.1	10.1	10.0	9.6	9.3	9.3	8.5	8.0	8.2	8.1	7.5	8.3	7.4	7.5	6.7	8.1	7.1	6.4	5.8	5.9	3.7						
	2001	9.4	9.4	9.9	10.3	10.0	9.8	10.0	10.0	9.8	9.7	9.7	9.3	9.0	9.0	8.3	7.8	7.9	7.8	7.3	8.0	7.1	7.1	6.3	7.5	6.5	5.9	5.3	5.3	3.8	3.9					
	2002	9.1	9.1	9.6	10.0	9.6	9.4	9.6	9.6	9.3	9.3	9.2	8.9	8.6	8.5	7.9	7.3	7.5	7.4	6.9	7.5	6.5	6.5	5.8	6.7	5.8	5.2	4.6	4.3	3.0	2.7	1.6				
	2003	9.3	9.3	9.7	10.2	9.9	9.7	9.8	9.8	9.6	9.6	9.4	9.1	8.9	8.8	8.2	7.8	7.9	7.8	7.3	7.8	7.2	7.2	6.6	7.5	6.8	6.2	5.8	5.8	4.3	5.2	7.8	14.5			
	2004	9.2	9.2	9.6	10.1	9.8	9.6	9.7	9.7	9.5	9.4	9.3	9.0	8.7	8.7	8.1	7.6	7.8	7.6	7.2	7.6	7.0	7.2	6.5	7.5	6.7	6.3	6.0	6.1	5.7	6.1	6.5	7.8	10.8		
35-Yr	2005	9.1	9.1	9.5	9.9	9.6	9.4	9.5	9.6	9.3	9.3	9.2	8.9	8.6	8.6	8.0	7.6	7.7	7.6	7.2	7.7	7.1	7.2	6.6	7.5	6.8	6.5	6.2	6.2	5.7	6.1	6.7	8.4	5.5	3.9	
	2006	9.1	9.1	9.5	9.8	9.6	9.4	9.5	9.5	9.2	9.2	9.2	8.9	8.6	8.5	8.0	7.6	7.7	7.6	7.1	7.6	6.9	7.1	6.5	7.4	6.8	6.4	6.2	6.2	5.6	6.1	6.6	7.2	6.8	6.6	9.3

How to read the Annualized Returns Matrix: You can locate the annualized compounded rate of return for this simulated Index Portfolio for a designated time period by following these easy instructions: Locate the column for the beginning year of the period. Then, locate the ending year of the period on the left-most vertical column. The annualized return can be found where the first year's column intersects with the ending year's row. IFA advisory fees of 0.9% per year and DFA mutual fund expense ratios have been deducted from these results. The 5-Yr diagonal (highlighted, starting from far left column) represents the estimated average holding period for investors who score 20 on the Risk Capacity Survey at ifa.com. Sources, Updates, and Disclosures: ifa.com/btp.

INDEX PORTFOLIO 20: LIGHT TURQUOISE

Growth of $1 Matrix ($)

35 years of Index Portfolio 20 (1972-2006)

Returns Net of IFA and DFA Fees

Period	Year	1972	1973	1974	1975	1976	1977	1978	1979	1980	1981	1982	1983	1984	1985	1986	1987	1988	1989	1990	1991	1992	1993	1994	1995	1996	1997	1998	1999	2000	2001	2002	2003	2004	2005	2006
1-Yr	1972	1.09																																		
	1973	1.06	0.97																																	
	1974	1.03	0.95	0.98																																
	1975	1.22	1.12	1.16	1.18																															
5-Yr	1976	1.40	1.29	1.32	1.36	1.15																														
	1977	1.50	1.38	1.42	1.46	1.23	1.07																													
	1978	1.64	1.50	1.55	1.59	1.34	1.17	1.09																												
	1979	1.82	1.67	1.72	1.76	1.49	1.30	1.21	1.11																											
	1980	2.07	1.90	1.96	2.01	1.69	1.48	1.38	1.26	1.14																										
10-Yr	1981	2.30	2.11	2.18	2.23	1.88	1.64	1.53	1.40	1.26	1.11																									
	1982	2.73	2.50	2.58	2.64	2.23	1.94	1.81	1.66	1.50	1.32	1.18																								
	1983	3.13	2.87	2.95	3.03	2.56	2.23	2.08	1.91	1.72	1.51	1.36	1.15																							
	1984	3.44	3.16	3.26	3.34	2.82	2.46	2.29	2.10	1.89	1.66	1.50	1.26	1.10																						
	1985	4.13	3.79	3.90	4.00	3.38	2.94	2.75	2.52	2.27	1.99	1.79	1.51	1.32	1.20																					
15-Yr	1986	4.77	4.38	4.51	4.62	3.90	3.40	3.18	2.91	2.62	2.30	2.07	1.75	1.53	1.39	1.16																				
	1987	5.08	4.66	4.80	4.92	4.15	3.62	3.38	3.10	2.79	2.45	2.21	1.86	1.62	1.47	1.23	1.06																			
	1988	5.66	5.20	5.35	5.49	4.63	4.04	3.77	3.45	3.11	2.73	2.46	2.08	1.81	1.64	1.37	1.19	1.12																		
	1989	6.42	5.89	6.07	6.22	5.25	4.58	4.27	3.92	3.53	3.10	2.79	2.36	2.05	1.86	1.56	1.35	1.26	1.13																	
	1990	6.42	5.89	6.07	6.22	5.25	4.58	4.27	3.92	3.53	3.10	2.79	2.36	2.05	1.86	1.56	1.35	1.26	1.13	1.00																
20-Yr	1991	7.50	6.88	7.08	7.26	6.13	5.35	4.99	4.57	4.12	3.62	3.26	2.75	2.40	2.18	1.82	1.57	1.48	1.32	1.17	1.17															
	1992	7.98	7.32	7.54	7.73	6.53	5.69	5.31	4.86	4.38	3.85	3.47	2.93	2.55	2.32	1.95	1.67	1.57	1.40	1.24	1.24	1.06														
	1993	9.01	8.27	8.52	8.73	7.37	6.43	5.99	5.50	4.95	4.35	3.91	3.31	2.88	2.62	2.16	1.89	1.77	1.59	1.40	1.40	1.20	1.13													
	1994	8.91	8.17	8.42	8.63	7.29	6.35	5.93	5.43	4.90	4.30	3.87	3.27	2.85	2.59	2.16	1.87	1.75	1.57	1.39	1.39	1.19	1.12	0.99												
	1995	10.09	9.26	9.54	9.77	8.26	7.20	6.71	6.15	5.55	4.87	4.33	3.70	3.23	2.93	2.45	2.11	1.99	1.78	1.57	1.57	1.35	1.27	1.12	1.13											
25-Yr	1996	11.07	10.15	10.46	10.72	9.05	7.90	7.36	6.75	6.08	5.34	4.81	4.06	3.54	3.21	2.68	2.32	2.18	1.95	1.72	1.72	1.48	1.39	1.24	1.24	1.10										
	1997	11.97	10.98	11.31	11.59	9.79	8.54	7.96	7.30	6.58	5.78	5.20	4.39	3.83	3.48	2.90	2.51	2.36	2.11	1.86	1.86	1.60	1.50	1.34	1.34	1.19	1.08									
	1998	12.64	11.60	11.95	12.24	10.34	9.02	8.41	7.71	6.95	6.10	5.49	4.64	4.04	3.67	3.06	2.65	2.49	2.23	1.97	1.97	1.69	1.58	1.40	1.42	1.25	1.14	1.06								
	1999	14.19	13.02	13.41	13.73	11.19	9.76	9.10	8.34	7.52	6.60	5.94	5.02	4.38	3.97	3.32	2.87	2.69	2.42	2.13	2.13	1.83	1.72	1.52	1.54	1.36	1.24	1.14	1.08							
	2000	14.74	13.52	13.93	14.15	12.06	10.51	9.81	8.99	8.10	7.11	6.40	5.41	4.72	4.28	3.57	3.09	2.90	2.60	2.30	2.30	1.97	1.85	1.64	1.65	1.46	1.33	1.23	1.12	1.04						
30-Yr	2001	14.97	13.73	14.15	14.50	12.24	10.68	9.96	9.13	8.23	7.22	6.50	5.49	4.79	4.35	3.63	3.14	2.95	2.64	2.33	2.33	2.00	1.88	1.66	1.68	1.48	1.35	1.25	1.18	1.05	1.04					
	2002	14.97	13.73	14.15	14.50	12.23	10.68	9.96	9.13	8.23	7.22	6.50	5.49	4.79	4.35	3.63	3.14	2.95	2.64	2.33	2.33	2.00	1.88	1.66	1.68	1.48	1.36	1.25	1.18	1.05	1.04	1.02				
	2003	17.14	15.73	16.20	16.85	14.02	12.23	11.40	10.45	9.42	8.27	7.45	6.29	5.48	4.98	4.15	3.59	3.38	3.03	2.67	2.67	2.29	2.15	1.90	1.92	1.70	1.55	1.43	1.36	1.25	1.21	1.15	1.15			
	2004	18.37	16.85	17.35	18.04	15.02	13.10	12.22	11.20	10.09	8.86	7.98	6.74	5.88	5.33	4.45	3.85	3.62	3.24	2.86	2.86	2.45	2.30	2.04	2.06	1.82	1.66	1.53	1.45	1.34	1.29	1.23	1.25	1.07		
	2005	19.09	17.51	18.04	18.49	15.61	13.61	12.70	11.64	10.49	9.21	8.29	7.00	6.11	5.54	4.63	4.00	3.76	3.37	2.97	2.97	2.55	2.39	2.12	2.14	1.89	1.72	1.59	1.51	1.39	1.35	1.29	1.28	1.22	1.04	
35-Yr	2006	20.87	19.14	19.72	20.21	17.07	14.88	13.88	12.72	11.47	10.07	9.06	7.65	6.68	6.06	5.06	4.37	4.11	3.68	3.25	3.25	2.78	2.62	2.34	2.07	1.89	1.74	1.65	1.52	1.47	1.42	1.39	1.28	1.22	1.14	1.09
		1972	1973	1974	1975	1976	1977	1978	1979	1980	1981	1982	1983	1984	1985	1986	1987	1988	1989	1990	1991	1992	1993	1994	1995	1996	1997	1998	1999	2000	2001	2002	2003	2004	2005	2006

How to read the Growth of $1 Matrix: You can locate the growth of a dollar invested in this simulated Index Portfolio for a designated time period by following these easy instructions: Locate the column for the beginning year of the period. Years are labeled at the top and the bottom of each column. Then, locate the ending year of the period on the left-most vertical column. The growth of a dollar over the time period can be found where the first year's column intersects with the ending year's row. IFA advisory fees of 0.9% per year and DFA mutual fund expense ratios have been deducted from these results. The 5-Yr diagonal (highlighted, starting from far left column) represents the estimated average holding period for investors who score 20 on the Risk Capacity Survey at ifa.com. Sources, Updates, and Disclosures: ifa.com/btp.

Index Portfolio 20: Light Turquoise

Monthly Rolling Period Analysis*
Based on 50 Years (600 months) of Monthly Data
Jan 1957 to Dec 2006

Examples of 5 Year Monthly Rolling Periods**

Periods

1	Jan 57 ← 5 Years → Dec 61
2	Feb 57 ← 5 Years → Jan 62
3	Mar 57 ← 5 Years → Feb 62
4	Apr 57 ← 5 Years → Mar 62
⋮ 541	

Year 1957 1958 1959 1960 1961 1962 1963 1964 1965 1966 1967 1968 1969

Per Period Number of: Yrs	Months	# of Rolling Periods	Average Ann'lzd Rtn. %*	Std. Dev. of Avg. Ann'lzd Rtn. %*	Lowest Rolling Period Date	Lowest Rolling Period Return	Growth of $1 in Lowest Period	Highest Rolling Period Date	Highest Rolling Period Return	Growth of $1 in Highest Period	Average Growth of $1
0.08	1	600	0.68*	1.40*	10/87-10/87	-5.66	$0.94	1/75-1/75	7.40	$1.07	$1.01
0.25	3	598	2.05*	2.71*	9/87-11/87	-6.93	$0.93	1/75-3/75	11.98	$1.12	$1.02
0.5	6	595	4.13*	3.95*	4/74-9/74	-5.95	$0.94	7/82-12/82	16.95	$1.17	$1.04
1	12	589	8.49	5.76	6/69-5/70	-7.14	$0.93	7/82-6/83	29.00	$1.29	$1.08
2	24	577	8.46	4.10	1/73-12/74	-2.68	$0.95	7/84-6/86	21.15	$1.47	$1.27
3	36	565	8.44	3.42	1/72-12/74	1.07	$1.03	8/84-7/87	18.69	$1.67	$1.28
4	48	553	8.46	3.14	1/71-12/74	3.65	$1.15	7/82-6/86	18.63	$1.98	$1.39
5**	60	541	8.47	3.06	4/98-3/03	3.45	$1.18	7/82-6/87	17.45	$2.23	$1.51
6	72	529	8.53	2.93	12/68-11/74	2.85	$1.18	4/80-3/86	16.59	$2.51	$1.65
7	84	517	8.60	2.80	10/67-9/74	4.20	$1.33	4/80-3/87	16.26	$2.87	$1.81
8	96	505	8.67	2.69	1/59-12/66	4.85	$1.46	4/80-3/88	14.84	$3.03	$1.98
9	108	493	8.74	2.60	6/61-5/70	4.86	$1.53	3/78-2/87	14.30	$3.33	$2.17
10	120	481	8.81	2.49	7/60-6/70	5.29	$1.67	9/77-8/87	13.85	$3.66	$2.38
11	132	469	8.87	2.40	7/59-6/70	5.09	$1.73	9/75-8/86	13.57	$4.05	$2.62
12	144	457	8.91	2.34	7/58-6/70	5.69	$1.94	9/74-8/86	13.66	$4.65	$2.87
13	156	445	8.95	2.26	1/62-12/74	5.24	$1.94	10/74-9/87	13.55	$5.22	$3.15
14	168	433	9.03	2.15	9/60-8/74	5.40	$2.09	1/75-12/88	12.93	$5.49	$3.47
15	180	421	9.08	2.05	1/60-12/74	5.30	$2.17	10/74-9/89	13.03	$6.28	$3.82
20	240	361	9.40	1.44	2/57-1/77	6.55	$3.56	10/74-9/94	11.52	$8.85	$6.22
30	360	241	9.40	0.30	1/57-12/86	8.71	$12.25	1/75-12/04	10.07	$17.79	$14.85
40	480	121	8.79	0.10	4/61-3/01	8.62	$27.31	12/66-11/06	9.04	$31.87	$29.08
50	600	1	8.29	0.00	1/57-12/06	8.29	$53.63	1/57-12/06	8.29	$53.63	$53.63

5 Year Monthly Rolling Periods** - Jan 1957 to Dec 2006 - 541 Monthly Rolling Periods Over 50 Years

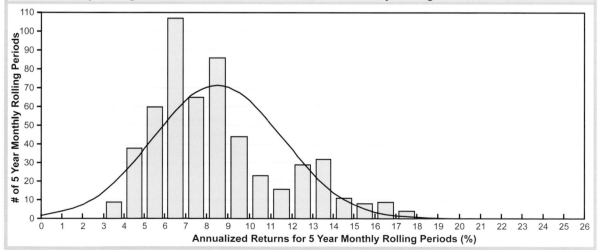

*Sources, Updates, and Disclosures: ifa.com/btp. Returns are net of IFA & DFA fees. The returns and standard deviation shown for 1, 3, and 6 month periods are not annualized. Past performance does not guarantee future results. **5 years represents the estimated average holding period for investors who score 20 on the Risk Capacity Survey at ifa.com.

RISK CAPACITY 15
LIGHT GREEN

Index Portfolio 15: Light Green

Index Allocations

General Asset Class		Specific Index	
10%	US Large	5%	IFA US Large Company Index
		5%	IFA US Large Cap Value Index
5%	US Small	2.5%	IFA US Micro Cap Index
		2.5%	IFA US Small Cap Value Index
2.5%	Real Estate	2.5%	IFA Real Estate Index
5%	International	2.5%	IFA International Value Index
		1.25%	IFA International Small Company Index
		1.25%	IFA International Small Cap Value Index
2.5%	Emerging Markets	0.75%	IFA Emerging Markets Index
		0.75%	IFA Emerging Markets Value Index
		1.0%	IFA Emerging Markets Small Cap Index
75%	Fixed Income	18.75%	IFA One-Year Fixed Income Index
		18.75%	IFA Two-Year Global Fixed Income Index
		18.75%	IFA Five-Year Gov't Income Index
		18.75%	IFA Five-Year Global Fixed Income Index

Index Portfolio - Simulated Returns and Volatility Data*

	1yr ending 2006	1yr ending 2005	1yr ending 2004	1yr ending 2003	3yrs 2004-2006	5yrs 2002-2006	10yrs 1996-2006	25yrs 1982-2006	35yrs 1972-2006	50yrs 1957-2006	80yrs 1927-2006
Growth of $1	1.08	1.03	1.06	1.12	1.19	1.37	1.81	8.17	18.24	43.69	163.56
Annualized Return %	8.35	3.41	6.10	12.32	5.93	6.46	6.11	8.76	8.65	7.85	6.58
Annualized Volatility (Standard Deviation %)	2.42	2.51	3.85	3.87	2.97	3.18	3.52	3.97	4.33	4.27	6.74

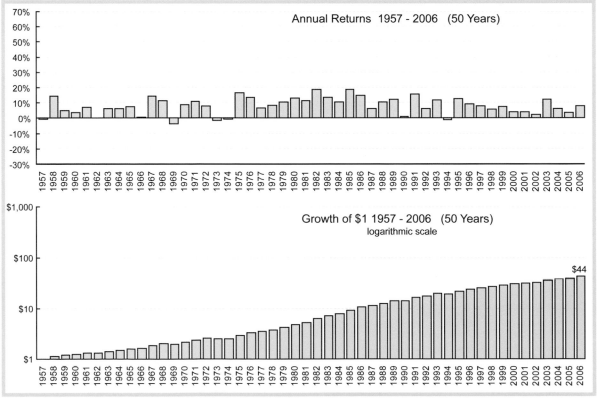

*Sources, Updates, and Disclosures: ifa.com/btp. Returns net of IFA & DFA fees. Past performance does not guarantee future results.

INDEX PORTFOLIO 15: LIGHT GREEN

Annualized Returns Matrix (%)
35 years of Index Portfolio 15 (1972–2006)
Returns Net of IFA and DFA Fees

Period	'72	'73	'74	'75	'76	'77	'78	'79	'80	'81	'82	'83	'84	'85	'86	'87	'88	'89	'90	'91	'92	'93	'94	'95	'96	'97	'98	'99	'00	'01	'02	'03	'04	'05	'06
1-Yr 1972	8.1																																		
1973	3.1	-1.7																																	
1974	1.8	-1.3	-0.5																																
1975	5.2	4.3	7.5	16.5																															
5-Yr 1976	6.9	6.5	9.5	15.0	13.5																														
1977	6.8	6.5	8.7	12.1	10.0	6.5																													
1978	7.0	6.8	8.5	11.1	9.4	7.3	8.2																												
1979	7.4	7.3	8.3	11.0	9.6	8.3	9.3	10.4																											
1980	8.0	8.0	9.5	11.3	10.3	9.5	10.5	11.7	13.1																										
10-Yr 1981	8.4	8.4	9.7	11.3	10.5	9.9	10.8	11.7	12.3	11.5																									
1982	9.3	9.4	10.7	12.2	11.6	11.3	12.3	13.4	15.0	16.0	18.6																								
1983	9.6	9.7	11.0	12.4	11.8	11.6	12.5	13.7	14.3	14.5	16.0	13.4																							
1984	9.7	9.8	11.0	12.4	11.7	11.5	12.2	12.9	13.4	13.5	14.1	11.9	10.5																						
1985	10.3	10.5	11.5	12.7	12.4	12.2	13.0	13.7	14.2	14.5	15.2	14.1	14.5	18.6																					
15-Yr 1986	10.6	10.8	11.8	12.9	12.6	12.5	13.2	13.8	14.3	14.5	15.1	14.3	14.6	16.7	14.8																				
1987	10.3	10.4	11.4	12.4	12.0	11.9	12.4	12.9	13.3	13.3	13.6	12.6	13.0	13.0	9.1	6.1																			
1988	10.3	10.5	11.3	12.2	11.9	11.8	12.3	12.7	13.0	12.9	13.2	12.3	12.4	12.0	10.6	8.3	10.6																		
1989	10.4	10.6	11.4	12.3	12.0	11.8	12.3	12.7	12.9	12.9	13.1	12.3	12.4	12.1	11.5	10.9	11.5	12.4																	
1990	9.9	10.0	10.8	11.5	11.0	11.0	11.4	11.7	11.8	11.7	11.7	10.8	10.8	10.5	9.4	8.6	8.0	7.5	1.2																
20-Yr 1991	10.2	10.3	11.0	11.8	11.5	11.3	11.7	12.0	12.1	12.0	12.1	11.4	11.6	11.2	10.9	10.4	10.0	9.6	8.2	15.8															
1992	10.0	10.1	10.8	11.5	11.2	11.0	11.3	11.6	11.6	12.1	12.1	10.9	10.9	10.6	9.5	9.1	8.6	8.2	7.6	8.2	6.2														
1993	10.1	10.2	10.8	11.5	11.2	11.1	11.4	11.6	11.7	12.1	11.5	10.9	10.7	10.7	9.8	9.6	9.1	8.8	8.6	9.0	11.9	11.9													
1994	9.6	9.6	10.2	10.8	10.5	10.3	10.6	10.7	10.7	11.5	11.6	9.9	9.5	9.5	8.5	7.7	7.0	6.6	6.6	6.9	7.9	5.1	-1.3												
1995	9.7	9.8	10.4	10.9	10.7	10.5	10.7	10.8	10.8	11.2	10.5	10.0	9.8	9.7	8.9	8.0	8.5	7.6	7.7	7.9	8.9	7.5	5.4	-2.7											
25-Yr 1996	9.7	9.7	10.3	10.8	10.5	10.4	10.6	10.7	10.6	11.2	10.6	9.9	9.7	9.5	8.9	8.3	8.4	7.6	7.6	7.9	8.8	7.9	6.7	7.2	0.9										
1997	9.6	9.7	10.3	10.8	10.5	10.3	10.6	10.6	10.5	11.1	10.4	9.8	9.7	9.3	8.8	8.3	8.2	7.7	7.8	8.2	8.8	7.5	6.7	7.9	8.5	7.7									
1998	9.5	9.5	10.1	10.5	10.2	10.1	10.3	10.3	10.2	10.9	10.1	9.6	9.5	9.1	8.5	8.0	8.2	7.6	7.3	7.3	8.4	7.5	6.7	8.8	7.5	6.7	5.6								
1999	9.4	9.4	9.9	10.3	10.1	9.9	10.1	10.2	10.2	10.9	9.9	9.5	9.1	9.1	8.5	7.7	8.2	7.5	7.2	7.0	8.2	7.5	6.7	8.5	7.5	6.9	6.5	7.4							
2000	9.2	9.2	9.7	10.1	9.8	9.7	9.9	10.0	10.0	10.2	9.6	9.2	8.9	8.8	8.2	7.5	7.9	7.2	6.9	6.7	7.8	7.1	6.3	7.7	7.5	6.5	6.5	7.4	4.0						
30-Yr 2001	9.0	9.1	9.5	9.9	9.6	9.5	9.6	9.9	9.7	10.0	9.3	9.0	8.6	8.5	7.9	7.5	7.6	7.0	6.6	6.7	7.2	6.4	5.7	7.2	6.3	5.8	5.3	5.7	4.1	4.1					
2002	8.8	8.8	9.2	9.6	9.3	9.2	9.3	9.5	9.4	9.1	9.0	8.5	8.3	8.2	7.6	7.2	7.2	6.6	6.3	6.3	6.8	6.1	5.7	6.6	5.8	5.2	4.7	4.5	3.5	3.3	2.4				
2003	8.9	8.9	9.3	9.7	9.4	9.3	9.4	9.5	9.4	9.3	9.2	8.7	8.5	8.4	7.8	7.5	7.5	7.0	7.0	6.8	7.4	6.8	6.3	7.2	6.2	6.2	5.9	6.0	5.7	6.2	7.3	12.3			
2004	8.8	8.8	9.2	9.4	9.3	9.2	9.3	9.3	9.3	9.1	9.0	8.6	8.4	8.3	7.4	7.2	7.5	6.7	6.9	6.7	7.3	6.7	6.3	7.1	6.5	6.2	6.0	6.0	5.7	6.2	6.9	9.2	6.1		
2005	8.7	8.7	9.1	9.3	9.2	9.0	9.1	9.1	9.0	8.9	8.8	8.4	8.1	8.0	7.5	7.2	7.2	6.7	6.7	6.5	7.1	6.5	6.1	6.8	6.2	5.9	5.6	5.6	5.4	5.6	6.0	7.2	4.7	3.4	
35-Yr 2006	8.6	8.7	9.0	9.1	9.1	9.0	9.0	9.1	9.0	8.9	8.8	8.4	8.2	8.1	7.6	7.3	7.3	7.1	6.8	6.6	7.2	6.6	6.2	6.9	6.4	6.1	5.9	6.0	5.8	6.1	6.5	7.5	5.9	5.9	8.3
	1972	1973	1974	1975	1976	1977	1978	1979	1980	1981	1982	1983	1984	1985	1986	1987	1988	1989	1990	1991	1992	1993	1994	1995	1996	1997	1998	1999	2000	2001	2002	2003	2004	2005	2006

How to read the Annualized Returns Matrix: You can locate the annualized compounded rate of return for this simulated Index Portfolio for a designated time period by following these easy instructions: Locate the column for the beginning year of the period. Years are labeled at the top and the bottom of each column. Then, locate the ending year of the period on the left-most vertical column. The annualized return can be found where the first year's column intersects with the ending year's row. IFA advisory fees of 0.9% per year and DFA mutual fund expense ratios have been deducted from these results. The 5-Yr diagonal (highlighted, starting from far left column) represents the estimated average holding period for investors who score 15 on the Risk Capacity Survey at ifa.com. Sources, Updates, and Disclosures: ifa.com/btp.

INDEX PORTFOLIO 15: LIGHT GREEN

Growth of $1 Matrix ($)
35 years of Index Portfolio 15 (1972–2006)
Returns Net of IFA and DFA Fees

	1972	1973	1974	1975	1976	1977	1978	1979	1980	1981	1982	1983	1984	1985	1986	1987	1988	1989	1990	1991	1992	1993	1994	1995	1996	1997	1998	1999	2000	2001	2002	2003	2004	2005	2006
1-Yr 1972	1.08																																		
1973	1.06	0.98																																	
1974	1.05	0.97	0.99																																
1975	1.23	1.14	1.15	1.16																															
5-Yr 1976	1.39	1.29	1.31	1.32	1.14																														
1977	1.48	1.37	1.40	1.41	1.21	1.06																													
1978	1.60	1.48	1.51	1.52	1.31	1.15	1.08																												
1979	1.77	1.64	1.67	1.68	1.44	1.27	1.19	1.10																											
1980	2.00	1.85	1.89	1.90	1.63	1.44	1.35	1.25	1.13																										
10-Yr 1981	2.23	2.07	2.10	2.12	1.82	1.60	1.51	1.39	1.26	1.12																									
1982	2.65	2.45	2.49	2.51	2.16	1.90	1.79	1.65	1.50	1.32	1.19																								
1983	3.01	2.78	2.83	2.85	2.45	2.16	2.03	1.87	1.70	1.50	1.35	1.13																							
1984	3.32	3.07	3.12	3.15	2.71	2.38	2.24	2.07	1.87	1.66	1.49	1.25	1.10																						
1985	3.94	3.64	3.71	3.74	3.21	2.83	2.65	2.45	2.22	1.97	1.76	1.49	1.31	1.19																					
15-Yr 1986	4.52	4.18	4.25	4.29	3.68	3.24	3.05	2.82	2.55	2.26	2.02	1.71	1.50	1.36	1.15																				
1987	4.80	4.44	4.51	4.55	3.91	3.44	3.23	2.99	2.71	2.39	2.15	1.81	1.60	1.44	1.22	1.06																			
1988	5.30	4.91	4.99	5.04	4.32	3.81	3.58	3.31	2.99	2.65	2.37	2.00	1.77	1.60	1.35	1.17	1.11																		
1989	5.96	5.52	5.61	5.66	4.86	4.28	4.02	3.72	3.37	2.98	2.67	2.25	1.98	1.80	1.51	1.32	1.24	1.12																	
1990	6.03	5.58	5.68	5.73	4.92	4.33	4.07	3.76	3.41	3.01	2.70	2.28	2.01	1.82	1.53	1.34	1.26	1.14	1.01																
20-Yr 1991	6.99	6.46	6.57	6.63	5.69	5.01	4.71	4.35	3.94	3.49	3.13	2.64	2.32	2.10	1.77	1.55	1.46	1.32	1.17	1.16															
1992	7.42	6.87	6.98	7.04	6.05	5.33	5.00	4.62	4.19	3.70	3.32	2.80	2.47	2.24	1.88	1.64	1.55	1.40	1.24	1.23	1.06														
1993	8.30	7.68	7.81	7.88	6.77	5.96	5.60	5.17	4.69	4.14	3.72	3.13	2.76	2.50	2.11	1.84	1.73	1.56	1.39	1.38	1.19	1.12													
1994	8.19	7.58	7.71	7.78	6.68	5.88	5.52	5.11	4.62	4.09	3.67	3.09	2.73	2.47	2.08	1.81	1.71	1.54	1.37	1.36	1.17	1.10	0.99												
1995	9.23	8.54	8.69	8.76	7.52	6.63	6.22	5.75	5.21	4.61	4.13	3.48	3.07	2.78	2.34	2.04	1.92	1.74	1.55	1.53	1.32	1.24	1.11	1.13											
25-Yr 1996	10.08	9.32	9.48	9.56	8.21	7.23	6.79	6.28	5.69	5.03	4.51	3.80	3.35	3.04	2.56	2.23	2.10	1.90	1.69	1.67	1.44	1.36	1.21	1.23	1.09										
1997	10.86	10.04	10.22	10.31	8.85	7.79	7.32	6.77	6.13	5.42	4.86	4.10	3.61	3.27	2.76	2.40	2.26	2.05	1.82	1.80	1.55	1.46	1.31	1.32	1.18	1.08									
1998	11.46	10.61	10.79	10.88	9.34	8.23	7.73	7.14	6.47	5.72	5.13	4.33	3.81	3.45	2.91	2.54	2.39	2.16	1.92	1.90	1.64	1.54	1.38	1.40	1.24	1.14	1.06								
1999	12.31	11.39	11.59	11.69	10.03	8.84	8.30	7.67	6.95	6.15	5.51	4.65	4.10	3.71	3.13	2.72	2.57	2.32	2.06	2.04	1.76	1.66	1.48	1.50	1.33	1.22	1.13	1.07							
2000	12.81	11.85	12.06	12.16	10.44	9.20	8.64	7.98	7.23	6.39	5.73	4.84	4.26	3.86	3.25	2.83	2.67	2.41	2.15	2.12	1.83	1.73	1.54	1.56	1.39	1.27	1.18	1.12	1.04						
30-Yr 2001	13.34	12.34	12.55	12.66	10.87	9.57	8.99	8.31	7.53	6.66	5.97	5.03	4.44	4.02	3.39	2.95	2.78	2.51	2.24	2.21	1.91	1.80	1.61	1.63	1.44	1.32	1.23	1.16	1.08	1.04					
2002	13.66	12.64	12.86	12.97	11.13	9.81	9.21	8.51	7.71	6.82	6.12	5.16	4.55	4.12	3.47	3.02	2.85	2.58	2.29	2.26	1.96	1.84	1.65	1.67	1.48	1.36	1.26	1.20	1.11	1.07	1.02				
2003	15.34	14.19	14.44	14.56	12.50	11.01	10.34	9.56	8.66	7.66	6.87	5.79	5.11	4.62	3.90	3.40	3.20	2.89	2.57	2.54	2.20	2.07	1.85	1.87	1.66	1.52	1.41	1.34	1.25	1.20	1.15	1.12			
2004	16.28	15.06	15.32	15.45	13.27	11.69	10.97	10.15	9.19	8.13	7.29	6.15	5.42	4.90	4.13	3.60	3.39	3.07	2.73	2.70	2.33	2.19	1.96	1.99	1.76	1.62	1.50	1.42	1.32	1.27	1.22	1.19	1.06		
2005	16.83	15.57	15.85	15.98	13.72	12.08	11.35	10.49	9.50	8.40	7.54	6.35	5.60	5.07	4.28	3.73	3.51	3.17	2.82	2.79	2.41	2.27	2.03	2.05	1.82	1.67	1.55	1.47	1.37	1.31	1.26	1.23	1.10	1.03	
35-Yr 2006	18.24	16.87	17.17	17.31	14.87	13.09	12.30	11.37	10.29	9.11	8.17	6.89	6.07	5.50	4.63	4.04	3.80	3.44	3.06	3.02	2.61	2.46	2.20	2.23	1.98	1.81	1.68	1.59	1.48	1.42	1.37	1.34	1.19	1.12	1.08
	1972	1973	1974	1975	1976	1977	1978	1979	1980	1981	1982	1983	1984	1985	1986	1987	1988	1989	1990	1991	1992	1993	1994	1995	1996	1997	1998	1999	2000	2001	2002	2003	2004	2005	2006

How to read the Growth of $1 Matrix: You can locate the growth of a dollar invested in this simulated Index Portfolio for a designated time period by following these easy instructions: Locate the column for the beginning year of the period. Years are labeled at the top and the bottom of each column. Then, locate the ending year of the period on the left-most vertical column. The growth of a dollar over the time period can be found where the first year's column intersects with the ending year's row. IFA advisory fees of 0.9% per year and DFA mutual fund expense ratios have been deducted from these results. The 5-Yr diagonal (highlighted, starting from far left column) represents the estimated average holding period for investors who score 15 on the Risk Capacity Survey at ifa.com. Sources, Updates, and Disclosures: ifa.com/btp.

Index Portfolio 15: Light Green

Monthly Rolling Period Analysis*
Based on 50 years (600 months) of Monthly Data
Jan 1957 to Dec 2006

Examples of 5 Year Monthly Rolling Periods**

Periods

1	Jan 57	← 5 Years →	Dec 61
2	Feb 57	← 5 Years →	Jan 62
3	Mar 57	← 5 Years →	Feb 62
4	Apr 57	← 5 Years →	Mar 62
:			
541			

Year 1957　1958　1959　1960　1961　1962　1963　1964　1965　1966　1967　1968　1969

Per Period Number of: Yrs	Months	# of Rolling Periods	Average Ann'lzd Rtn. %*	Std. Dev. of Avg. Ann'lzd Rtn. %*	Lowest Rolling Period Date	Lowest Rolling Period Return	Growth of $1 in Lowest Period	Highest Rolling Period Date	Highest Rolling Period Return	Growth of $1 in Highest Period	Average Growth of $1
0.08	1	600	0.64*	1.23*	10/87-10/87	-4.38	$0.96	1/75-1/75	6.32	$1.06	$1.01
0.25	3	598	1.93*	2.38*	9/87-11/87	-5.50	$0.95	4/80-6/80	11.47	$1.11	$1.02
0.5	6	595	3.90*	3.48*	3/74-8/74	-4.64	$0.06	7/02-12/02	16.32	$1.16	$1.04
1	12	589	8.02	5.16	6/69-5/70	-5.37	$0.95	7/82-6/83	27.00	$1.27	$1.08
2	24	577	8.01	3.79	1/73-12/74	-1.27	$0.97	7/84-6/86	20.04	$1.44	$1.25
3	36	565	8.01	3.24	1/72-12/74	1.75	$1.05	8/84-7/87	17.38	$1.62	$1.26
4	48	553	8.05	3.01	3/59-2/63	3.82	$1.16	7/82-6/86	17.67	$1.92	$1.37
5**	**60**	**541**	**8.06**	**2.94**	**9/61-8/66**	**3.65**	**$1.20**	**9/81-8/86**	**16.55**	**$2.15**	**$1.48**
6	72	529	8.13	2.83	10/68-9/74	3.31	$1.22	4/80-3/86	16.03	$2.44	$1.61
7	84	517	8.19	2.72	9/59-8/66	4.12	$1.33	4/80-3/87	15.63	$2.76	$1.76
8	96	505	8.26	2.62	12/58-11/66	4.49	$1.42	4/80-3/88	14.29	$2.91	$1.92
9	108	493	8.33	2.54	6/61-5/70	4.53	$1.49	3/78-2/87	13.70	$3.18	$2.10
10	120	481	8.40	2.43	7/60-6/70	4.91	$1.61	9/77-8/87	13.16	$3.44	$2.29
11	132	469	8.46	2.35	7/59-6/70	4.78	$1.67	9/75-8/86	12.95	$3.82	$2.51
12	144	457	8.50	2.28	7/58-6/70	5.20	$1.84	9/74-8/86	13.01	$4.34	$2.74
13	156	445	8.55	2.21	9/61-8/74	5.07	$1.90	9/74-8/87	12.81	$4.79	$3.00
14	168	433	8.63	2.10	9/60-8/74	5.13	$2.01	10/75-9/89	12.27	$5.05	$3.30
15	180	421	8.69	2.01	9/59-8/74	5.10	$2.11	10/74-9/89	12.33	$5.72	$3.61
20	240	361	8.99	1.42	2/57-1/77	6.15	$3.30	9/74-8/94	10.97	$8.02	$5.77
30	360	241	8.99	0.31	1/57-12/86	8.26	$10.82	1/75-12/04	9.56	$15.47	$13.27
40	480	121	8.38	0.09	3/59-2/99	8.23	$23.65	12/66-11/06	8.61	$27.21	$25.03
50	600	1	7.85	0.00	1/57-12/06	7.85	$43.75	1/57-12/06	7.85	$43.75	$43.75

5 Year Monthly Rolling Periods** - Jan 1957 to Dec 2006 - 541 Monthly Rolling Periods Over 50 Years

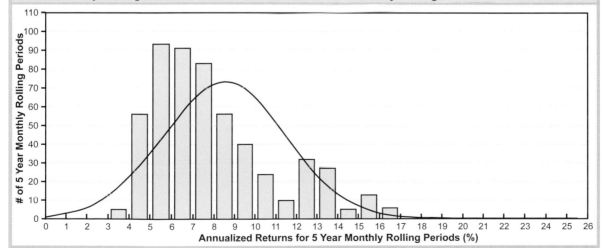

*Sources, Updates, and Disclosures: ifa.com/btp. Returns are net of IFA & DFA fees. The returns and standard deviation shown for 1, 3, and 6 month periods are not annualized. Past performance does not guarantee future results. **5 years represents the estimated average holding period for investors who score 15 on the Risk Capacity Survey at ifa.com.

RISK CAPACITY 10
LIGHT YELLOW

Index Portfolio 10: Light Yellow

Index Allocations

General Asset Class		Specific Index	
8%	US Large	4%	IFA US Large Company Index
		4%	IFA US Large Cap Value Index
4%	US Small	2%	IFA US Micro Cap Index
		2%	IFA US Small Cap Value Index
2%	Real Estate	2%	IFA Real Estate Index
4%	International	2%	IFA International Value Index
		1%	IFA International Small Company Index
		1%	IFA International Small Cap Value Index
2%	Emerging Markets	0.6%	IFA Emerging Markets Index
		0.6%	IFA Emerging Markets Value Index
		0.8%	IFA Emerging Markets Small Cap Index
80%	Fixed Income	20%	IFA One-Year Fixed Income Index
		20%	IFA Two-Year Global Fixed Income Index
		20%	IFA Five-Year Gov't Income Index
		20%	IFA Five-Year Global Fixed Income Index

Index Portfolio - Simulated Returns and Volatility Data*

	1yr ending 2006	1yr ending 2005	1yr ending 2004	1yr ending 2003	3yrs 2004-2006	5yrs 2002-2006	10yrs 1996-2006	25yrs 1982-2006	35yrs 1972-2006	50yrs 1957-2006	80yrs 1927-2006
Growth of $1	1.07	1.03	1.05	1.10	1.16	1.32	1.74	7.35	15.91	35.49	111.86
Annualized Return %	7.38	2.88	5.06	10.13	5.09	5.72	5.68	8.30	8.23	7.40	6.07
Annualized Volatility (Standard Deviation %)	1.93	2.10	3.50	3.50	2.59	2.71	2.90	3.45	3.79	3.72	5.60

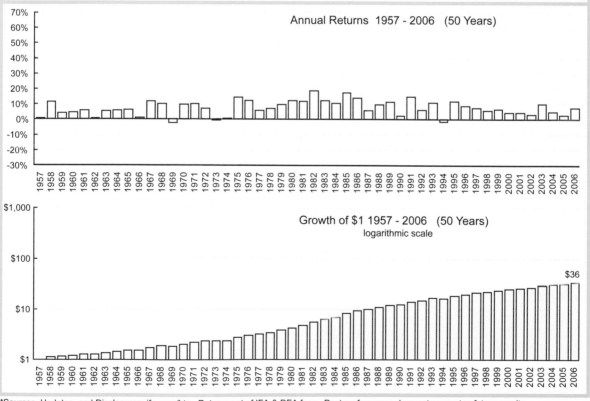

Annual Returns 1957 - 2006 (50 Years)

Growth of $1 1957 - 2006 (50 Years)
logarithmic scale

$36

*Sources, Updates, and Disclosures: ifa.com/btp. Returns net of IFA & DFA fees. Past performance does not guarantee future results.

INDEX PORTFOLIO 10: LIGHT YELLOW

Annualized Returns Matrix (%)
35 years of Index Portfolio 10 (1972–2006)
Returns Net of IFA and DFA Fees

Period / End \ Start	1972	1973	1974	1975	1976	1977	1978	1979	1980	1981	1982	1983	1984	1985	1986	1987	1988	1989	1990	1991	1992	1993	1994	1995	1996	1997	1998	1999	2000	2001	2002	2003	2004	2005	2006
1-Yr 1972	7.2																																		
1973	3.3	-0.5																																	
1974	2.4	0.1	0.8																																
4-Yr 1975	5.3	4.7	7.4	14.5																															
5-Yr 1976	6.7	6.6	9.1	13.5	12.4																														
1977	6.5	6.4	8.2	10.8	9.0	5.8																													
1978	6.6	6.6	8.0	9.9	8.4	6.5	7.3																												
1979	7.0	7.0	8.3	9.9	8.8	7.6	8.6	9.9																											
1980	7.6	7.7	8.9	10.3	9.5	8.8	9.8	11.1	12.3																										
10-Yr 1981	8.0	8.1	9.3	10.5	9.9	9.4	10.3	11.3	12.1	11.9																									
1982	9.0	9.1	10.3	11.5	11.1	10.9	11.9	13.2	14.3	15.3	18.8																								
1983	9.2	9.4	10.5	11.6	11.2	11.1	12.0	13.0	13.8	14.3	15.4	12.2																							
1984	9.3	9.5	10.5	11.5	11.2	11.0	11.8	12.6	13.1	13.8	13.4	11.5	10.7																						
1985	9.9	10.1	11.1	12.0	11.8	11.7	12.5	13.3	13.8	14.2	14.7	13.4	13.8	17.5																					
15-Yr 1986	10.2	10.4	11.3	12.2	12.0	11.9	12.7	13.3	13.8	14.1	14.0	14.0	14.0	15.7	13.9																				
1987	9.9	10.1	10.9	11.7	11.4	11.2	11.9	12.5	12.9	13.1	12.9	12.3	12.0	12.3	9.8	5.8																			
1988	9.9	10.1	10.8	11.5	11.3	11.2	11.7	12.2	12.6	12.7	12.4	11.8	11.5	11.6	9.6	7.7	9.7																		
1989	9.6	9.7	10.1	10.9	10.7	10.6	11.0	11.4	11.6	11.6	11.3	10.8	10.5	10.6	9.0	7.8	8.6	11.5																	
1990	9.6	9.7	10.0	10.7	10.6	10.4	10.7	11.0	11.1	11.1	10.9	10.4	10.2	10.2	8.6	7.5	8.0	7.9	2.4																
20-Yr 1991	9.8	10.0	10.6	11.2	11.0	10.9	11.2	11.6	11.7	11.6	11.6	11.1	11.1	11.4	10.5	9.0	9.5	9.4	7.9	14.8															
1992	9.6	9.8	10.3	10.9	10.7	10.6	10.9	11.2	11.3	11.2	11.1	10.4	10.1	10.2	9.1	7.8	8.1	8.0	6.9	8.4	6.0														
1993	9.7	10.0	10.3	10.9	10.8	10.6	10.9	11.1	11.3	11.3	11.4	10.9	10.4	10.8	9.3	8.3	8.2	8.3	7.7	10.3	7.4	10.8													
1994	9.2	9.4	9.8	10.3	10.2	10.1	10.4	10.4	10.4	10.2	10.1	9.6	9.1	8.9	8.0	7.3	7.3	7.5	6.4	7.4	5.0	6.9	-1.4												
1995	9.3	9.4	9.9	10.3	10.1	10.0	10.2	10.4	10.4	10.3	10.2	9.6	9.3	9.2	8.4	7.8	8.1	7.9	7.3	8.3	6.3	6.9	5.1	12.0											
25-Yr 1996	9.3	9.4	9.8	10.2	10.0	9.9	10.1	10.3	10.2	10.1	10.2	9.5	9.2	9.1	8.1	7.8	8.2	8.0	7.5	8.3	6.7	7.4	6.3	10.3	8.7										
1997	9.2	9.3	9.7	10.1	9.9	9.8	10.0	10.1	10.1	9.9	9.9	9.4	9.0	8.8	7.9	7.7	7.9	7.7	7.2	8.2	6.9	7.4	6.5	9.3	8.0	7.3									
1998	9.1	9.1	9.5	9.9	9.8	9.6	9.8	9.9	9.8	9.7	9.7	9.1	8.8	8.6	7.8	7.7	7.8	7.6	7.1	7.9	6.9	7.4	6.3	8.4	7.2	6.5	5.6								
1999	9.0	9.0	9.4	9.8	9.7	9.5	9.7	9.7	9.6	9.5	9.5	9.0	8.6	8.0	7.7	7.6	7.7	7.6	7.2	7.7	6.9	7.0	6.4	8.0	7.0	6.5	6.1	6.6							
2000	8.8	8.9	9.2	9.6	9.4	9.2	9.4	9.5	9.3	9.3	9.2	8.7	8.4	7.8	7.4	7.5	7.3	6.9	6.9	7.4	6.6	6.7	6.1	7.4	6.6	6.0	5.5	5.5	4.4						
30-Yr 2001	8.6	8.7	9.0	9.4	9.2	9.0	9.2	9.3	9.1	9.0	9.0	8.5	8.3	8.1	7.6	7.2	7.2	7.1	6.7	7.1	6.4	6.4	5.9	7.0	6.1	5.6	5.2	5.1	4.4	4.3					
2002	8.5	8.5	8.8	9.2	9.1	8.8	8.9	9.0	8.8	8.7	8.7	8.2	8.0	7.8	7.3	6.9	7.0	6.8	6.4	6.8	6.1	6.1	5.6	6.5	5.7	5.2	4.8	4.6	4.0	3.8	3.3				
2003	8.5	8.6	8.9	9.2	9.2	8.9	9.1	9.1	8.9	8.8	8.8	8.3	8.1	8.0	7.5	7.2	7.2	7.0	6.7	7.0	6.4	6.4	6.0	6.9	6.3	5.9	5.7	5.7	5.5	5.9	6.7	10.1			
2004	8.4	8.5	8.6	8.9	9.0	8.7	8.8	8.9	8.7	8.6	8.6	8.1	8.0	7.8	7.3	7.1	7.1	6.9	6.6	6.9	6.3	6.3	5.9	6.7	6.1	5.8	5.6	5.6	5.4	5.7	6.1	7.6	5.1		
2005	8.3	8.3	8.6	8.8	8.8	8.5	8.6	8.7	8.6	8.3	8.3	7.9	7.7	7.6	7.1	7.1	6.8	6.7	6.4	6.6	6.1	6.2	5.7	6.4	5.9	5.8	5.3	5.2	5.5	5.0	5.7	6.0	4.0	2.9	
35-Yr 2006	8.2	8.3	8.5	8.8	8.8	8.5	8.6	8.7	8.6	8.4	8.3	7.9	7.7	7.6	7.1	7.1	6.8	6.7	6.4	6.7	6.1	6.2	5.8	6.4	5.9	5.7	5.5	5.3	5.5	5.1	5.7	6.3	5.1	5.1	7.4

How to read the Annualized Returns Matrix: You can locate the annualized compounded rate of return for this simulated Index Portfolio for a designated time period by following these easy instructions: Locate the column for the beginning year of the period. Years are labeled at the top and the bottom of each column. Then, locate the ending year of the period on the left-most vertical column. The annualized return can be found where the first year's column intersects with the ending year's row. IFA advisory fees of 0.9% per year and DFA mutual fund expense ratios have been deducted from these results. The 4-Yr diagonal (highlighted, starting from far left column) represents the estimated average holding period for investors who score 10 on the Risk Capacity Survey at ifa.com. Sources, Updates, and Disclosures: ifa.com/btp.

INDEX PORTFOLIO 10: LIGHT YELLOW

Growth of $1 Matrix ($)
35 years of Index Portfolio 10 (1972–2006)
Returns Net of IFA and DFA Fees

Period	Year	1972	1973	1974	1975	1976	1977	1978	1979	1980	1981	1982	1983	1984	1985	1986	1987	1988	1989	1990	1991	1992	1993	1994	1995	1996	1997	1998	1999	2000	2001	2002	2003	2004	2005	2006
1-Yr	1972	1.07																																		
	1973	1.07	1.00																																	
	1974	1.07	1.00	1.01																																
4-Yr	1975	1.23	1.15	1.15	1.12																															
5-Yr	1976	1.38	1.29	1.30	1.29	1.12																														
	1977	1.46	1.36	1.37	1.36	1.19	1.06																													
	1978	1.57	1.46	1.47	1.46	1.27	1.13	1.07																												
	1979	1.72	1.61	1.62	1.60	1.40	1.25	1.18	1.10																											
	1980	1.93	1.81	1.81	1.80	1.57	1.40	1.32	1.23	1.12																										
10-Yr	1981	2.17	2.02	2.03	2.02	1.76	1.57	1.48	1.38	1.26	1.12																									
	1982	2.57	2.40	2.41	2.39	2.09	1.86	1.76	1.64	1.49	1.33	1.19																								
	1983	2.89	2.69	2.71	2.69	2.35	2.09	1.97	1.84	1.67	1.49	1.33	1.12																							
	1984	3.19	2.98	3.00	2.97	2.60	2.31	2.18	2.04	1.85	1.65	1.48	1.24	1.11																						
	1985	3.75	3.50	3.52	3.49	3.05	2.71	2.57	2.39	2.18	1.94	1.73	1.46	1.30	1.17																					
15-Yr	1986	4.27	3.99	4.01	3.98	3.47	3.09	2.92	2.72	2.48	2.21	1.97	1.66	1.48	1.34	1.14																				
	1987	4.52	4.22	4.24	4.21	3.67	3.27	3.09	2.88	2.62	2.34	2.09	1.76	1.57	1.42	1.20	1.06																			
	1988	4.96	4.63	4.65	4.62	4.03	3.59	3.39	3.16	2.88	2.56	2.29	1.93	1.72	1.55	1.32	1.16	1.10																		
	1989	5.53	5.16	5.19	5.15	4.50	4.00	3.78	3.53	3.21	2.86	2.55	2.15	1.92	1.73	1.47	1.29	1.22	1.11																	
	1990	5.66	5.28	5.31	5.27	4.60	4.09	3.87	3.61	3.29	2.93	2.62	2.20	1.96	1.77	1.51	1.33	1.25	1.14	1.02																
20-Yr	1991	6.50	6.07	6.10	6.05	5.28	4.70	4.44	4.14	3.77	3.36	3.00	2.53	2.25	2.03	1.73	1.52	1.44	1.31	1.18	1.15															
	1992	6.89	6.43	6.46	6.41	5.60	4.98	4.71	4.39	4.00	3.56	3.18	2.68	2.39	2.16	1.84	1.61	1.52	1.39	1.25	1.22	1.06														
	1993	7.63	7.12	7.16	7.11	6.20	5.52	5.22	4.87	4.43	3.95	3.53	2.97	2.65	2.39	2.03	1.79	1.69	1.54	1.38	1.35	1.17	1.11													
	1994	7.53	7.02	7.06	7.00	6.12	5.44	5.15	4.80	4.37	3.89	3.48	2.93	2.61	2.36	2.01	1.76	1.66	1.52	1.36	1.33	1.16	1.09	0.99												
	1995	8.43	7.87	7.91	7.85	6.85	6.09	5.76	5.37	4.89	4.36	3.89	3.28	2.92	2.64	2.24	1.97	1.86	1.70	1.52	1.49	1.30	1.22	1.10	1.12											
25-Yr	1996	9.16	8.55	8.59	8.52	7.44	6.62	6.26	5.84	5.31	4.73	4.23	3.56	3.17	2.87	2.44	2.14	2.03	1.85	1.66	1.62	1.41	1.33	1.20	1.22	1.09										
	1997	9.83	9.17	9.22	9.15	7.99	7.11	6.72	6.27	5.70	5.08	4.54	3.82	3.41	3.08	2.62	2.30	2.17	1.98	1.78	1.74	1.51	1.43	1.29	1.31	1.17	1.07									
	1998	10.38	9.69	9.73	9.66	8.44	7.50	7.10	6.62	6.02	5.36	4.79	4.04	3.60	3.25	2.77	2.43	2.30	2.09	1.88	1.83	1.60	1.51	1.36	1.33	1.23	1.13	1.06								
	1999	11.06	10.32	10.37	10.30	8.99	8.00	7.56	7.05	6.42	5.72	5.11	4.30	3.83	3.46	2.95	2.59	2.45	2.23	2.00	1.95	1.70	1.60	1.45	1.47	1.31	1.21	1.13	1.07							
	2000	11.55	10.77	10.83	10.75	9.38	8.35	7.89	7.36	6.70	5.97	5.33	4.49	4.00	3.61	3.08	2.70	2.55	2.33	2.09	2.04	1.78	1.68	1.51	1.53	1.37	1.26	1.17	1.11	1.04						
30-Yr	2001	12.05	11.24	11.30	11.21	9.79	8.71	8.24	7.68	6.99	6.23	5.56	4.68	4.17	3.77	3.21	2.82	2.66	2.43	2.18	2.13	1.85	1.75	1.58	1.60	1.43	1.32	1.23	1.16	1.09	1.04					
	2002	12.45	11.61	11.67	11.58	10.11	9.00	8.51	7.93	7.22	6.43	5.75	4.84	4.31	3.90	3.32	2.91	2.75	2.51	2.25	2.20	1.91	1.81	1.63	1.65	1.48	1.36	1.27	1.20	1.13	1.08	1.03				
	2003	13.71	12.79	12.86	12.76	11.14	9.91	9.37	8.74	7.95	7.08	6.33	5.33	4.75	4.29	3.65	3.21	3.03	2.76	2.48	2.42	2.11	1.99	1.80	1.82	1.63	1.50	1.39	1.32	1.24	1.19	1.14	1.10			
	2004	14.40	13.44	13.51	13.40	11.70	10.41	9.85	9.18	8.36	7.44	6.65	5.60	4.99	4.51	3.84	3.37	3.18	2.90	2.60	2.54	2.22	2.09	1.89	1.91	1.71	1.57	1.46	1.39	1.30	1.25	1.20	1.16	1.05		
	2005	14.82	13.82	13.89	13.79	12.04	10.71	10.13	9.44	8.60	7.66	6.84	5.76	5.13	4.64	3.95	3.47	3.28	2.99	2.68	2.62	2.28	2.15	1.94	1.97	1.76	1.62	1.51	1.43	1.34	1.28	1.23	1.19	1.08	1.03	
35-Yr	2006	15.91	14.85	14.92	14.81	12.93	11.50	10.88	10.14	9.23	8.22	7.35	6.19	5.51	4.98	4.24	3.72	3.52	3.21	2.88	2.81	2.45	2.31	2.08	2.11	1.89	1.74	1.62	1.53	1.44	1.38	1.32	1.28	1.16	1.10	1.07
		1972	1973	1974	1975	1976	1977	1978	1979	1980	1981	1982	1983	1984	1985	1986	1987	1988	1989	1990	1991	1992	1993	1994	1995	1996	1997	1998	1999	2000	2001	2002	2003	2004	2005	2006

How to read the Growth of $1 Matrix: You can locate the growth of a dollar invested in this simulated Index Portfolio for a designated time period by following these easy instructions: Locate the column for the beginning year of the period. Years are labeled at the top and the bottom of each column. Then, locate the ending year of the period on the left-most vertical column. The growth of a dollar over the time period can be found where the first year's column intersects with the ending year's row. IFA advisory fees of 0.9% per year and DFA mutual fund expense ratios have been deducted from these results. The 4-Yr diagonal (highlighted, starting from far left column) represents the estimated average holding period for investors who score 10 on the Risk Capacity Survey at ifa.com. Sources, Updates, and Disclosures: ifa.com/btp.

Index Portfolio 10: Light Yellow

Monthly Rolling Period Analysis*
Based on 50 Years (600 months) of Monthly Data
Jan 1957 to Dec 2006

Examples of 4 Year Monthly Rolling Periods**

Periods

1 | Jan 57 ← 4 Years → Dec 60 |
2 | Feb 57 ← 4 Years → Jan 61 |
3 | Mar 57 ← 4 Years → Feb 61 |
4 | Apr 57 ← 4 Years → Mar 61 |
:
553

Year 1957 | 1958 | 1959 | 1960 | 1961 | 1962 | 1963 | 1964 | 1965 | 1966 | 1967 | 1968 | 1969

Per Period Number of: Yrs	Months	# of Rolling Periods	Average Ann'lzd Rtn. %*	Std. Dev. of Avg. Ann'lzd Rtn. %*	Lowest Rolling Period Date	Lowest Rolling Period Return	Growth of $1 in Lowest Period	Highest Rolling Period Date	Highest Rolling Period Return	Growth of $1 in Highest Period	Average Growth of $1
0.08	1	600	0.60*	1.07*	10/79-10/79	-3.17	$0.97	4/80-4/80	5.57	$1.06	$1.01
0.25	3	598	1.82*	2.08*	9/87-11/87	-4.03	$0.96	4/80-6/80	11.17	$1.11	$1.02
0.5	6	595	3.68*	3.06*	3/74-8/74	-3.39	$0.97	7/82-12/82	15.70	$1.16	$1.04
1	12	589	7.55	4.64	6/69-5/70	-3.58	$0.96	7/82-6/83	25.02	$1.25	$1.08
2	24	577	7.55	3.55	1/73-12/74	0.13	$1.00	7/84-6/86	18.94	$1.41	$1.23
3	36	565	7.58	3.10	1/72-12/74	2.42	$1.07	4/80-3/83	16.59	$1.58	$1.25
4**	48	553	7.63	2.91	3/59-2/63	3.61	$1.15	7/82-6/86	16.71	$1.86	$1.35
5	60	541	7.65	2.85	9/61-8/66	3.31	$1.18	9/81-8/86	15.99	$2.10	$1.46
6	72	529	7.71	2.76	9/60-8/66	3.59	$1.24	4/80-3/86	15.46	$2.37	$1.58
7	84	517	7.78	2.66	9/59-8/66	3.81	$1.30	4/80-3/87	14.99	$2.66	$1.71
8	96	505	7.85	2.57	12/58-11/66	4.09	$1.38	4/80-3/88	13.74	$2.80	$1.86
9	108	493	7.92	2.49	6/61-5/70	4.19	$1.45	3/78-2/87	13.09	$3.03	$2.02
10	120	481	7.99	2.38	1/57-12/66	4.45	$1.55	11/79-10/89	12.61	$3.28	$2.21
11	132	469	8.05	2.30	6/59-5/70	4.43	$1.61	9/75-8/86	12.33	$3.59	$2.40
12	144	457	8.09	2.24	7/58-6/70	4.69	$1.73	9/74-8/86	12.34	$4.04	$2.62
13	156	445	8.15	2.16	6/57-5/70	4.71	$1.82	9/74-8/87	12.08	$4.40	$2.86
14	168	433	8.22	2.05	9/60-8/74	4.85	$1.94	10/75-9/89	11.61	$4.65	$3.12
15	180	421	8.28	1.96	9/59-8/74	4.87	$2.04	10/74-9/89	11.63	$5.21	$3.41
20	240	361	8.57	1.42	2/57-1/77	5.73	$3.05	9/74-8/94	10.41	$7.25	$5.34
30	360	241	8.57	0.32	1/57-12/86	7.81	$9.54	7/70-6/00	9.09	$13.60	$11.83
40	480	121	7.97	0.08	4/57-3/97	7.82	$20.32	12/66-11/06	8.17	$23.14	$21.48
50	600	1	7.40	0.00	1/57-12/06	7.40	$35.50	1/57-12/06	7.40	$35.50	$35.50

4 Year Monthly Rolling Periods** - Jan 1957 to Dec 2006 - 553 Monthly Rolling Periods Over 50 Years

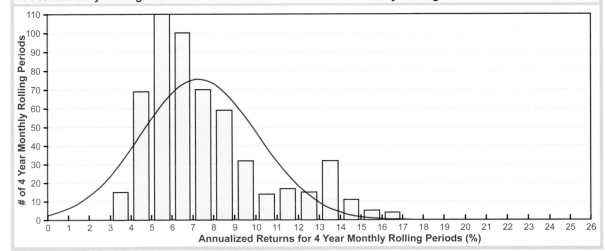

*Sources, Updates, and Disclosures: ifa.com/btp. Returns are net of IFA & DFA fees. The returns and standard deviation shown for 1, 3, and 6 month periods are not annualized. Past performance does not guarantee future results. **4 years represents the estimated average holding period for investors who score 10 on the Risk Capacity Survey at ifa.com.

RISK CAPACITY 5
IVORY

Index Portfolio 5: Ivory

Index Allocations

General Asset Class		Specific Index	
6%	US Large	3%	IFA US Large Company Index
		3%	IFA US Large Cap Value Index
3%	US Small	1.5%	IFA US Micro Cap Index
		1.5%	IFA US Small Cap Value Index
1.5%	Real Estate	1.5%	IFA Real Estate Index
3%	International	1.5%	IFA International Value Index
		0.75%	IFA International Small Company Index
		0.75%	IFA International Small Cap Value Index
1.5%	Emerging Markets	0.45%	IFA Emerging Markets Index
		0.45%	IFA Emerging Markets Value Index
		0.60%	IFA Emerging Markets Small Cap Index
85%	Fixed Income	21.25%	IFA One-Year Fixed Income Index
		21.25%	IFA Two-Year Global Fixed Income Index
		21.25%	IFA Five-Year Gov't Income Index
		21.25%	IFA Five-Year Global Fixed Income Index

Index Portfolio - Simulated Returns and Volatility Data*

	1yr ending 2006	1yr ending 2005	1yr ending 2004	1yr ending 2003	3yrs 2004-2006	5yrs 2002-2006	10yrs 1996-2006	25yrs 1982-2006	35yrs 1972-2006	50yrs 1957-2006	80yrs 1927-2006
Growth of $1	1.06	1.02	1.04	1.08	1.13	1.27	1.67	6.60	13.83	28.68	75.38
Annualized Return %	6.40	2.35	4.03	7.94	4.25	4.97	5.23	7.84	7.79	6.94	5.55
Annualized Volatility (Standard Deviation %)	1.45	1.75	3.20	3.23	2.25	2.36	2.36	2.99	3.31	3.24	4.49

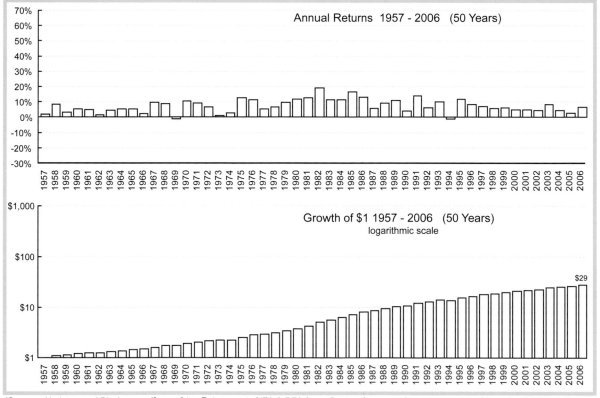

Annual Returns 1957 - 2006 (50 Years)

Growth of $1 1957 - 2006 (50 Years)
logarithmic scale

$29

*Sources, Updates, and Disclosures: ifa.com/btp. Returns net of IFA & DFA fees. Past performance does not guarantee future results.

INDEX PORTFOLIO 5: IVORY

Annualized Returns Matrix (%)
35 years of Index Portfolio 5 (1972–2006)
Returns Net of IFA and DFA Fees

Period / End	1972	1973	1974	1975	1976	1977	1978	1979	1980	1981	1982	1983	1984	1985	1986	1987	1988	1989	1990	1991	1992	1993	1994	1995	1996	1997	1998	1999	2000	2001	2002	2003	2004	2005	2006
1-Yr 1972	6.3																																		
1973	3.4	0.7																																	
1974	3.1	1.5	2.4																																
4-Yr 1975	5.4	5.1	7.4	12.6																															
5-Yr 1976	6.5	6.6	8.6	11.9	11.3																														
1977	6.3	6.3	7.7	9.6	8.1	5.0																													
1978	6.3	6.3	7.4	8.8	7.5	5.7	6.3																												
1979	6.7	6.7	7.8	8.9	8.0	6.9	7.8	9.3																											
1980	7.2	7.3	8.3	9.3	8.6	8.0	9.0	10.4	11.5																										
10-Yr 1981	7.7	7.8	8.8	9.7	9.2	8.8	9.8	11.0	11.9	12.3																									
1982	8.7	8.9	9.9	10.8	10.6	10.6	11.6	13.0	14.2	15.6	18.9																								
1983	8.9	9.1	10.0	10.9	10.6	10.5	11.5	12.6	13.4	14.0	14.9	11.0																							
1984	9.0	9.2	10.1	10.9	10.7	10.6	11.4	12.3	12.9	13.2	13.5	11.0	10.9																						
1985	9.5	9.8	10.6	11.3	11.2	11.2	12.0	12.8	13.4	13.8	14.2	12.7	13.6	16.3																					
15-Yr 1986	9.7	10.0	10.7	11.5	11.4	11.4	12.1	12.8	13.4	13.7	14.0	12.8	13.3	14.6	12.9																				
1987	9.5	9.7	10.4	11.0	10.9	10.8	11.4	12.0	12.3	12.5	12.5	11.3	11.3	11.5	9.1	5.5																			
1988	9.4	9.6	10.3	10.9	10.7	10.7	11.2	11.7	11.9	12.0	12.0	10.8	10.8	10.8	9.0	7.1	8.8																		
1989	9.5	9.7	10.3	10.8	10.7	10.6	11.1	11.6	11.8	11.8	11.8	10.8	10.8	10.7	8.8	8.2	9.6	10.5																	
1990	9.2	9.3	9.9	10.4	10.2	10.1	10.5	11.0	11.0	11.0	10.8	9.9	9.7	9.5	8.2	7.1	7.6	7.0	3.6																
20-Yr 1991	9.4	9.6	10.1	10.6	10.4	10.4	10.8	11.1	11.3	11.2	11.1	10.3	10.2	10.1	9.1	8.4	9.1	9.2	8.6	13.8															
1992	9.2	9.4	9.9	10.3	10.1	10.1	10.4	10.7	10.8	10.8	10.6	9.8	9.7	9.6	8.6	7.9	8.4	8.4	7.6	9.7	5.8														
1993	9.3	9.4	9.9	10.3	10.1	10.1	10.4	10.7	10.7	10.7	10.6	9.8	9.7	9.6	8.8	8.2	8.6	8.6	8.2	9.7	7.7	9.7													
1994	8.8	8.9	9.3	9.6	9.5	9.4	9.6	9.8	9.9	9.8	9.6	8.8	8.6	8.4	7.6	6.9	7.1	6.8	6.1	6.8	4.5	3.9	-1.6												
1995	8.9	9.0	9.5	9.7	9.6	9.5	9.7	9.9	10.0	9.9	9.7	9.0	8.9	8.7	7.9	7.4	7.6	7.5	7.0	7.7	6.2	6.3	4.7	11.4											
25-Yr 1996	8.8	8.9	9.3	9.5	9.5	9.4	9.6	9.8	9.9	9.8	9.6	9.0	8.8	8.6	8.0	7.5	7.7	7.6	7.1	7.8	6.6	6.8	5.8	9.7	8.1										
1997	8.8	8.9	9.3	9.4	9.4	9.3	9.5	9.7	9.7	9.6	9.4	8.8	8.7	8.5	7.9	7.4	7.6	7.5	7.1	7.6	6.6	6.8	6.1	8.8	7.5	6.9									
1998	8.6	8.7	9.1	9.2	9.2	9.1	9.3	9.5	9.5	9.4	9.2	8.6	8.5	8.3	7.7	7.3	7.4	7.3	6.9	7.4	6.5	6.6	6.0	8.0	6.9	6.2	5.6								
1999	8.5	8.6	8.9	9.0	9.1	9.0	9.1	9.3	9.3	9.2	9.0	8.4	8.3	8.1	7.6	7.1	7.3	7.2	6.8	7.2	6.4	6.5	5.9	7.5	6.6	6.1	5.7	5.7							
2000	8.4	8.5	8.9	9.0	8.9	8.8	9.0	9.1	9.1	8.9	8.8	8.2	8.1	7.9	7.4	7.0	7.1	6.9	6.6	6.9	6.2	6.2	5.8	7.0	6.2	5.7	5.3	5.2	4.7						
30-Yr 2001	8.3	8.3	8.6	8.7	8.7	8.6	8.8	8.9	8.9	8.7	8.6	8.0	7.9	7.7	7.2	6.8	6.9	6.8	6.5	6.7	6.0	6.1	5.6	6.7	5.9	5.5	5.1	5.0	4.6	4.6					
2002	8.1	8.2	8.5	8.7	8.5	8.4	8.6	8.7	8.6	8.5	8.3	7.8	7.7	7.5	7.0	6.6	6.7	6.6	6.3	6.5	5.9	5.9	5.5	6.4	5.7	5.3	5.0	4.8	4.5	4.4	4.2				
2003	8.1	8.2	8.5	8.7	8.5	8.4	8.6	8.6	8.6	8.5	8.3	7.8	7.7	7.5	7.1	6.7	6.8	6.7	6.4	6.6	6.0	6.1	5.7	6.5	6.0	5.7	5.4	5.4	5.3	5.6	6.0	7.9			
2004	8.0	8.1	8.3	8.5	8.4	8.3	8.4	8.5	8.4	8.3	8.1	7.7	7.5	7.3	6.9	6.6	6.6	6.5	6.2	6.4	5.9	5.9	5.5	6.3	5.7	5.4	5.2	5.2	5.1	5.2	5.4	5.9	4.0		
2005	7.8	7.9	8.1	8.3	8.2	8.1	8.2	8.2	8.2	8.1	7.9	7.4	7.3	7.1	6.7	6.3	6.4	6.3	6.0	6.2	5.6	5.6	5.3	5.9	5.4	5.1	4.9	4.8	4.6	4.6	4.6	4.7	3.2	2.4	
35-Yr 2006	7.8	7.8	8.1	8.2	8.1	8.0	8.1	8.2	8.1	8.0	7.8	7.4	7.2	7.1	6.7	6.3	6.4	6.3	6.0	6.2	5.7	5.7	5.4	6.0	5.5	5.2	5.0	5.0	4.9	4.9	5.0	5.2	4.2	4.4	6.4
	1972	**1973**	**1974**	**1975**	**1976**	**1977**	**1978**	**1979**	**1980**	**1981**	**1982**	**1983**	**1984**	**1985**	**1986**	**1987**	**1988**	**1989**	**1990**	**1991**	**1992**	**1993**	**1994**	**1995**	**1996**	**1997**	**1998**	**1999**	**2000**	**2001**	**2002**	**2003**	**2004**	**2005**	**2006**

How to read the Annualized Returns Matrix: You can locate the annualized compounded rate of return for this simulated Index Portfolio for a designated time period by following these easy instructions: Locate the column for the beginning year of the period. Then, locate the ending year of the period on the left-most vertical column. The annualized return can be found where the first year's column intersects with the ending year's row. IFA advisory fees of 0.9% per year and DFA mutual fund expense ratios have been deducted from these results. The 4-Yr diagonal (highlighted, starting from far left column) represents the estimated average holding period for investors who score 5 on the Risk Capacity Survey at ifa.com. Sources, Updates, and Disclosures: ifa.com/btp.

Appendix A

INDEX PORTFOLIO 5: IVORY

Growth of $1 Matrix ($)
35 years of Index Portfolio 5 (1972–2006)
Returns Net of IFA and DFA Fees

Period	End Yr	1972	1973	1974	1975	1976	1977	1978	1979	1980	1981	1982	1983	1984	1985	1986	1987	1988	1989	1990	1991	1992	1993	1994	1995	1996	1997	1998	1999	2000	2001	2002	2003	2004	2005	2006
1-Yr	1972	1.06																																		
	1973	1.07	1.01																																	
	1974	1.10	1.03	1.02																																
4-Yr	1975	1.23	1.16	1.15	1.13																															
5-Yr	1976	1.37	1.29	1.28	1.25	1.11																														
	1977	1.44	1.36	1.35	1.32	1.17	1.05																													
	1978	1.53	1.44	1.43	1.40	1.24	1.12	1.06																												
	1979	1.67	1.58	1.57	1.53	1.36	1.22	1.16	1.09																											
	1980	1.87	1.76	1.74	1.70	1.51	1.36	1.30	1.22	1.11																										
10-Yr	1981	2.10	1.97	1.96	1.91	1.70	1.53	1.46	1.37	1.25	1.11																									
	1982	2.49	2.35	2.33	2.28	2.02	1.82	1.73	1.63	1.49	1.34	1.19																								
	1983	2.77	2.61	2.59	2.53	2.24	2.02	1.92	1.81	1.65	1.48	1.32	1.11																							
	1984	3.07	2.89	2.87	2.80	2.49	2.24	2.13	2.00	1.83	1.65	1.46	1.23	1.11																						
	1985	3.57	3.36	3.34	3.26	2.90	2.60	2.48	2.33	2.13	1.91	1.70	1.43	1.29	1.16																					
15-Yr	1986	4.03	3.80	3.77	3.68	3.27	2.94	2.80	2.63	2.41	2.16	1.92	1.62	1.46	1.31	1.13																				
	1987	4.26	4.01	3.98	3.89	3.45	3.10	2.95	2.78	2.54	2.28	2.03	1.71	1.54	1.39	1.19	1.06																			
	1988	4.63	4.36	4.33	4.23	3.76	3.38	3.22	3.02	2.77	2.48	2.21	1.86	1.67	1.51	1.30	1.15	1.09																		
	1989	5.12	4.82	4.79	4.67	4.15	3.73	3.55	3.34	3.06	2.74	2.44	2.05	1.85	1.67	1.43	1.27	1.20	1.11																	
20-Yr	1990	5.30	4.99	4.96	4.84	4.30	3.86	3.68	3.46	3.17	2.84	2.53	2.13	1.92	1.73	1.48	1.31	1.25	1.14	1.04																
	1991	6.04	5.68	5.64	5.51	4.89	4.40	4.19	3.94	3.60	3.23	2.88	2.42	2.18	1.97	1.69	1.50	1.42	1.30	1.18	1.14															
	1992	6.39	6.01	5.97	5.83	5.18	4.66	4.43	4.17	3.81	3.42	3.05	2.56	2.31	2.08	1.79	1.58	1.50	1.38	1.25	1.20	1.06														
	1993	7.01	6.59	6.55	6.40	5.68	5.11	4.86	4.57	4.18	3.75	3.34	2.81	2.53	2.28	1.96	1.74	1.65	1.51	1.37	1.32	1.16	1.10													
	1994	6.90	6.49	6.44	6.30	5.59	5.03	4.79	4.50	4.12	3.69	3.29	2.77	2.49	2.25	1.93	1.71	1.62	1.49	1.35	1.30	1.14	1.08	0.98												
25-Yr	1995	7.68	7.23	7.18	7.01	6.23	5.60	5.33	5.01	4.59	4.11	3.66	3.08	2.77	2.50	2.15	1.90	1.80	1.66	1.50	1.45	1.27	1.20	1.10	1.11											
	1996	8.31	7.82	7.76	7.58	6.73	6.05	5.76	5.42	4.96	4.45	3.96	3.33	3.00	2.70	2.33	2.06	1.95	1.79	1.62	1.57	1.38	1.30	1.19	1.20	1.08										
	1997	8.88	8.36	8.30	8.11	7.20	6.47	6.16	5.80	5.30	4.76	4.24	3.56	3.21	2.89	2.49	2.20	2.09	1.92	1.73	1.67	1.47	1.39	1.27	1.29	1.16	1.07									
	1998	9.38	8.82	8.76	8.56	7.60	6.83	6.51	6.12	5.60	5.02	4.47	3.76	3.39	3.05	2.62	2.32	2.20	2.02	1.83	1.77	1.55	1.47	1.34	1.36	1.22	1.13	1.06								
	1999	9.91	9.33	9.26	9.05	8.04	7.22	6.88	6.47	5.92	5.31	4.73	3.98	3.58	3.23	2.78	2.46	2.33	2.14	1.94	1.87	1.64	1.55	1.41	1.44	1.29	1.19	1.12	1.06							
	2000	10.38	9.77	9.70	9.47	8.42	7.56	7.20	6.77	6.20	5.56	4.95	4.16	3.75	3.38	2.91	2.57	2.44	2.24	2.03	1.96	1.72	1.62	1.48	1.51	1.35	1.25	1.17	1.11	1.05						
30-Yr	2001	10.85	10.21	10.14	9.91	8.80	7.91	7.53	7.08	6.48	5.81	5.18	4.35	3.92	3.53	3.04	2.69	2.55	2.34	2.12	2.05	1.80	1.70	1.55	1.57	1.41	1.31	1.22	1.16	1.09	1.05					
	2002	11.31	10.64	10.57	10.33	9.17	8.24	7.85	7.38	6.75	6.06	5.39	4.54	4.09	3.68	3.17	2.80	2.66	2.44	2.21	2.13	1.87	1.77	1.61	1.64	1.47	1.36	1.27	1.21	1.14	1.09	1.04				
	2003	12.21	11.49	11.41	11.14	9.90	8.90	8.47	7.97	7.29	6.54	5.82	4.90	4.41	3.97	3.42	3.03	2.87	2.63	2.38	2.30	2.02	1.91	1.74	1.77	1.59	1.47	1.37	1.30	1.23	1.18	1.12	1.08			
	2004	12.70	11.95	11.87	11.59	10.30	9.26	8.81	8.29	7.58	6.80	6.06	5.09	4.59	4.13	3.56	3.15	2.98	2.74	2.48	2.40	2.10	1.99	1.81	1.84	1.65	1.53	1.43	1.35	1.28	1.23	1.17	1.12	1.04		
	2005	13.00	12.23	12.15	11.87	10.54	9.47	9.02	8.48	7.76	6.96	6.20	5.21	4.69	4.23	3.64	3.22	3.05	2.81	2.54	2.45	2.15	2.03	1.86	1.88	1.69	1.57	1.46	1.39	1.31	1.25	1.20	1.15	1.06	1.02	
35-Yr	2006	13.83	13.02	12.92	12.63	11.21	10.08	9.60	9.03	8.26	7.41	6.60	5.55	5.00	4.50	3.87	3.43	3.25	2.98	2.70	2.61	2.29	2.16	1.97	2.01	1.80	1.67	1.56	1.48	1.40	1.33	1.27	1.22	1.13	1.09	1.06
		1972	1973	1974	1975	1976	1977	1978	1979	1980	1981	1982	1983	1984	1985	1986	1987	1988	1989	1990	1991	1992	1993	1994	1995	1996	1997	1998	1999	2000	2001	2002	2003	2004	2005	2006

How to read the Growth of $1 Matrix: You can locate the growth of a dollar invested in this simulated Index Portfolio for a designated time period by following these easy instructions: Locate the column for the beginning year of the period. Years are labeled at the top and the bottom of each column. Then, locate the ending year of the period on the left-most vertical column. The growth of a dollar over the time period can be found where the first year's column intersects with the ending year's row. IFA advisory fees of 0.9% per year and DFA mutual fund expense ratios have been deducted from these results. The 4-Yr diagonal (highlighted, starting from far left column) represents the estimated average holding period for investors who score 5 on the Risk Capacity Survey at ifa.com. Sources, Updates, and Disclosures: ifa.com/btp.

Examples of 4 Year Monthly Rolling Periods**

Periods

1	Jan 57 ← 4 Years → Dec 60
2	Feb 57 ← 4 Years → Jan 61
3	Mar 57 ← 4 Years → Feb 61
4	Apr 57 ← 4 Years → Mar 61
553	

Year 1957 1958 1959 1960 1961 1962 1963 1964 1965 1966 1967 1968 1969

Per Period Number of: Yrs	Months	# of Rolling Periods	Average Ann'lzd Rtn. %*	Std. Dev. of Avg. Ann'lzd Rtn. %*	Lowest Rolling Period Date	Lowest Rolling Period Return	Growth of $1 in Lowest Period	Highest Rolling Period Date	Highest Rolling Period Return	Growth of $1 in Highest Period	Average Growth of $1
0.08	1	600	0.57*	0.94*	10/79-10/79	-2.71	$0.97	4/80-4/80	5.56	$1.06	$1.01
0.25	3	598	1.71*	1.83*	2/94-4/94	3.27	$0.97	4/00-6/00	10.87	$1.11	$1.02
0.5	6	595	3.45*	2.71*	2/94-7/94	-2.63	$0.97	7/82-12/82	15.09	$1.15	$1.03
1	12	589	7.08	4.23	2/94-1/95	-2.27	$0.98	7/82-6/83	23.06	$1.23	$1.07
2	24	577	7.09	3.39	9/72-8/74	1.25	$1.03	7/84-6/86	17.83	$1.39	$1.21
3	36	565	7.14	3.01	5/61-4/64	2.82	$1.09	4/80-3/83	16.19	$1.57	$1.23
4**	**48**	**553**	**7.20**	**2.85**	**3/59-2/63**	**3.40**	**$1.14**	**7/82-6/86**	**15.75**	**$1.80**	**$1.33**
5	60	541	7.23	2.79	9/61-8/66	2.96	$1.16	9/81-8/86	15.43	$2.05	$1.43
6	72	529	7.29	2.70	9/60-8/66	3.16	$1.21	4/80-3/86	14.89	$2.30	$1.54
7	84	517	7.36	2.61	9/59-8/66	3.50	$1.27	4/80-3/87	14.36	$2.56	$1.67
8	96	505	7.43	2.53	12/58-11/66	3.68	$1.34	4/80-3/88	13.19	$2.69	$1.80
9	108	493	7.49	2.45	6/61-5/70	3.83	$1.40	3/78-2/87	12.48	$2.88	$1.95
10	120	481	7.56	2.35	1/57-12/66	3.97	$1.48	11/79-10/89	12.06	$3.12	$2.12
11	132	469	7.63	2.27	6/59-5/70	4.07	$1.55	9/75-8/86	11.71	$3.38	$2.30
12	144	457	7.68	2.20	6/58-5/70	4.17	$1.63	9/74-8/86	11.67	$3.76	$2.50
13	156	445	7.73	2.13	2/57-1/70	4.21	$1.71	9/74-8/87	11.34	$4.04	$2.71
14	168	433	7.80	2.02	9/60-8/74	4.56	$1.87	11/79-10/93	10.96	$4.29	$2.96
15	180	421	7.86	1.93	9/59-8/74	4.63	$1.97	10/74-9/89	10.92	$4.73	$3.22
20	240	361	8.15	1.41	2/57-1/77	5.29	$2.80	2/74-1/94	9.85	$6.55	$4.94
30	360	241	8.14	0.34	1/57-12/86	7.34	$8.37	7/70-6/00	8.65	$12.05	$10.52
40	480	121	7.55	0.08	4/57-3/97	7.36	$17.13	12/66-11/06	7.72	$19.58	$18.36
50	600	1	6.94	0.00	1/57-12/06	6.94	$28.64	1/57-12/06	6.94	$28.64	$28.64

4 Year Monthly Rolling Periods** - Jan 1957 to Dec 2006 - 553 Monthly Rolling Periods Over 50 Years

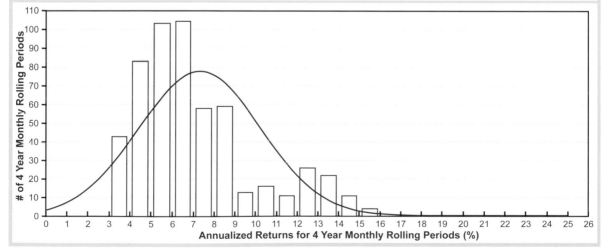

*Sources, Updates, and Disclosures: ifa.com/btp. Returns are net of IFA & DFA fees. The returns and standard deviation shown for 1, 3, and 6 month periods are not annualized. Past performance does not guarantee future results. **4 years represents the estimated average holding period for investors who score 5 on the Risk Capacity Survey at ifa.com.

Appendix A

IFA US LARGE COMPANY INDEX (TRACKS THE S&P 500)

Annualized Returns Matrix (%)
35 years (1972–2006)

Period	End	1972	1973	1974	1975	1976	1977	1978	1979	1980	1981	1982	1983	1984	1985	1986	1987	1988	1989	1990	1991	1992	1993	1994	1995	1996	1997	1998	1999	2000	2001	2002	2003	2004	2005	2006
1-Yr	1972	18.8																																		
	1973	0.6	-14.8																																	
	1974	-9.4	-20.9	-26.6																																
	1975	0.5	-5.0	0.3	37.1																															
5-Yr	1976	4.8	1.5	7.6	30.2	23.7																														
	1977	2.6	-0.3	3.7	16.3	7.1	-7.3																													
	1978	3.2	0.8	4.2	13.7	6.9	-0.7	6.5																												
	1979	5.0	3.1	6.4	14.6	9.6	5.3	12.2	18.3																											
	1980	7.7	6.4	9.8	17.4	13.8	11.5	18.5	25.1	32.3																										
10-Yr	1981	6.3	5.0	7.8	13.9	10.4	8.0	12.1	14.1	12.1	-5.0																									
	1982	7.6	6.6	9.2	14.8	11.9	10.1	13.9	15.9	15.1	7.3	21.3																								
	1983	8.8	7.9	10.5	15.6	13.2	11.7	15.3	17.1	16.8	12.1	21.8	22.4																							
	1984	8.6	7.8	10.1	14.6	12.4	11.0	13.9	15.2	14.6	10.6	16.4	14.0	6.1																						
15-Yr	1985	10.1	9.5	11.8	16.1	14.2	13.2	16.0	17.5	17.4	14.6	20.1	19.7	18.4	32.0																					
	1986	10.6	10.1	12.3	16.3	14.6	13.7	16.3	17.6	17.5	15.2	19.7	19.3	18.3	25.0	18.3																				
	1987	10.3	9.7	11.7	15.4	13.7	12.9	15.1	16.1	15.9	13.7	17.2	16.4	14.9	18.0	11.5	5.1																			
	1988	10.6	10.1	12.0	15.5	14.0	13.2	15.4	16.5	16.0	14.1	17.6	17.1	16.0	18.8	13.2	13.2	16.7																		
	1989	11.7	11.3	13.2	16.5	15.1	14.5	16.5	17.5	17.4	15.9	18.8	18.4	17.8	20.3	17.5	17.6	23.8	31.3																	
	1990	10.9	10.4	12.1	15.1	13.8	13.1	14.9	15.6	15.4	13.8	16.1	15.5	14.5	16.0	13.0	11.7	14.0	12.7	-3.2																
20-Yr	1991	11.8	11.4	13.1	16.0	14.8	14.2	15.9	16.7	16.5	15.2	17.4	17.0	16.4	17.9	15.7	15.2	17.9	18.3	12.2	30.1															
	1992	11.5	11.2	12.8	15.5	14.3	13.7	15.2	16.0	15.8	14.5	16.5	16.0	15.3	16.5	14.5	13.9	15.7	15.4	10.6	18.2	7.3														
	1993	11.4	11.1	12.6	15.2	14.0	13.5	14.9	15.5	15.3	14.1	15.9	15.4	14.7	15.7	13.9	13.2	14.6	14.2	10.3	16.3	10.6	9.6													
	1994	11.0	10.6	12.0	14.4	13.3	12.8	14.1	14.6	14.3	13.2	14.7	14.2	13.4	14.2	12.4	11.7	12.6	12.0	8.5	11.6	6.0	5.4	1.3												
25-Yr	1995	12.0	11.7	13.1	15.4	14.4	13.9	15.3	15.8	15.6	14.6	16.2	15.8	15.3	16.1	14.6	14.2	15.4	15.3	12.8	16.3	13.0	15.0	17.8	37.1											
	1996	12.4	12.1	13.5	15.7	14.8	14.4	15.6	16.2	16.0	15.1	16.6	16.3	15.8	16.6	15.3	15.0	16.2	16.1	14.1	17.3	14.9	16.9	19.4	29.6	22.6										
	1997	13.1	12.9	14.2	16.4	15.6	15.2	16.5	17.0	16.9	16.1	17.6	17.3	17.0	17.8	16.7	16.6	17.8	17.9	16.3	19.4	17.7	20.0	22.7	30.8	27.7	33.1									
	1998	13.6	13.5	14.8	16.9	16.1	15.8	17.0	17.6	17.5	16.8	18.2	18.0	17.7	18.6	17.5	17.5	18.7	19.0	17.6	20.6	19.2	21.4	23.9	30.2	28.0	30.9	28.7								
	1999	13.9	13.7	15.0	17.1	16.3	16.0	17.2	17.7	17.7	17.0	18.3	18.2	17.9	18.7	17.8	17.8	18.9	19.1	18.0	20.6	19.4	21.3	23.3	28.3	26.2	27.4	24.7	20.8							
30-Yr	2000	13.0	12.8	14.0	15.9	15.2	14.8	15.9	16.3	16.2	15.5	16.7	16.4	16.1	16.7	15.8	15.6	16.5	16.4	15.2	17.2	15.8	17.0	18.1	21.1	18.1	17.0	12.1	4.7	-9.3						
	2001	12.1	11.8	12.9	14.7	14.0	13.6	14.6	14.9	14.8	14.0	15.0	14.7	14.3	14.8	13.8	13.5	14.1	14.0	12.6	14.2	12.7	13.3	13.8	15.7	12.5	10.5	5.5	-1.2	-10.7	-12.1					
	2002	10.8	10.5	11.5	13.2	12.4	11.9	12.8	13.1	12.9	12.0	12.9	12.5	12.0	12.4	11.3	10.9	11.3	10.9	9.5	10.6	9.0	9.1	9.1	10.1	6.7	4.2	-0.7	-7.0	-14.7	-17.3	-22.2				
	2003	11.3	11.0	12.0	13.7	12.9	12.5	13.4	13.6	13.5	12.7	13.6	13.2	12.8	13.2	12.2	11.8	12.3	12.0	10.9	12.0	10.5	10.8	10.9	12.0	9.2	7.4	3.6	-0.7	-5.5	-4.2	0.0	28.5			
	2004	11.3	11.0	12.0	13.6	12.8	12.5	13.3	13.5	13.3	12.6	13.5	13.1	12.7	13.0	12.1	11.8	12.2	11.9	10.7	11.8	10.5	10.8	10.9	11.9	9.4	7.8	4.6	1.1	-2.5	-0.7	3.4	19.3	10.7		
	2005	11.1	10.8	11.7	13.3	12.5	12.2	13.0	13.2	13.0	12.3	13.1	12.7	12.3	12.6	11.7	11.4	11.8	11.5	10.3	11.3	10.1	10.3	10.3	11.2	8.9	7.5	4.7	1.6	-1.3	0.4	3.8	14.3	7.7	4.9	
35-Yr	2006	11.2	11.0	11.9	13.3	12.7	13.0	13.3	13.2	13.1	12.4	13.2	12.9	12.8	12.8	11.9	11.6	12.0	11.7	10.7	11.6	10.4	10.7	10.8	11.6	9.5	8.3	5.8	3.3	1.0	2.8	6.1	14.6	10.3	10.2	15.7
		1972	1973	1974	1975	1976	1977	1978	1979	1980	1981	1982	1983	1984	1985	1986	1987	1988	1989	1990	1991	1992	1993	1994	1995	1996	1997	1998	1999	2000	2001	2002	2003	2004	2005	2006

How to read the Annualized Returns Matrix: You can locate the annualized compounded rate of return for this simulated Index Portfolio for a designated time period by following these easy instructions: Locate the column for the beginning year of the period. Years are labeled at the top and the bottom of each column. Then, locate the ending year of the period on the left-most vertical column. The annualized return can be found where the first year's column intersects with the ending year's row. Sources, Updates, and Disclosures: ifa.com/btp.

IFA US Large Company Index (Tracks the S&P 500)

Growth of $1 Matrix ($)
35 years (1972-2006)

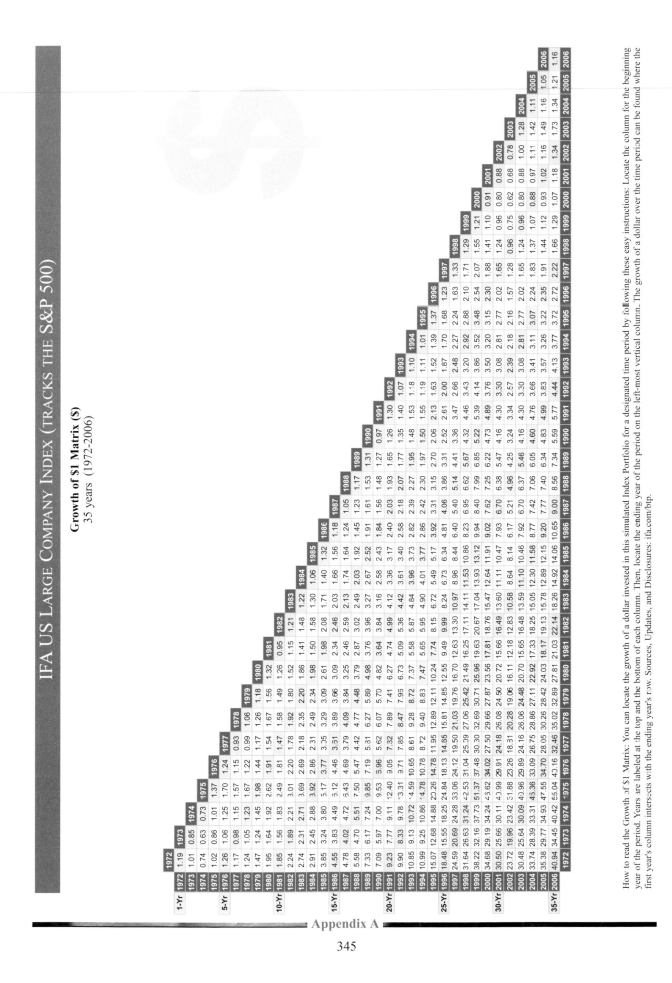

How to read the Growth of $1 Matrix: You can locate the growth of a dollar invested in this simulated Index Portfolio for a designated time period by following these easy instructions: Locate the column for the beginning year of the period. Years are labeled at the top and the bottom of each column. Then, locate the ending year of the period on the left-most vertical column. The growth of a dollar over the time period can be found where the first year's column intersects with the ending year's row. Sources, Updates, and Disclosures: ifa.com/btp.

IFA US Large Company Index (Tracks the S&P 500)
Monthly Rolling Period Analysis*
Based on 50 Years (600 months) of Monthly Data
Jan 1957 to Dec 2006

Examples of 10 Year Monthly Rolling Periods**

Periods

1	Jan 57	← 10 Years →	Dec 66
2	Feb 57	← 10 Years →	Jan 67
3	Mar 57	← 10 Years →	Feb 67
4	Apr 57	← 10 Years →	Mar 67

481

Year 1957   1958   1959   1960   1961   1962   1963   1964   1965   1966   1967   1968   1969

Per Period Number of: Yrs	Months	# of Rolling Periods	Average Ann'lzd Rtn. %*	Std. Dev. of Avg. Ann'lzd Rtn. %*	Lowest Rolling Period Date	Lowest Rolling Period Return	Growth of $1 in Lowest Period	Highest Rolling Period Date	Highest Rolling Period Return	Growth of $1 in Highest Period	Average Growth of $1
0.08	1	600	0.92*	4.15*	10/87-10/87	-21.53	$0.78	10/74-10/74	16.56	$1.17	$1.01
0.25	3	598	2.81*	7.30*	9/87-11/87	-29.56	$0.70	8/82-10/82	26.70	$1.27	$1.03
0.5	6	595	5.68*	10.83*	4/74-9/74	-30.86	$0.69	1/75-6/75	41.75	$1.42	$1.06
1	12	589	11.75	16.08	10/73-9/74	-39.00	$0.61	7/82-6/83	60.82	$1.61	$1.12
2	24	577	11.16	10.95	10/00-9/02	-23.74	$0.58	10/85-9/87	37.25	$1.88	$1.40
3	36	565	10.86	8.92	4/00-3/03	-16.23	$0.59	8/84-7/87	33.25	$2.37	$1.39
4	48	553	10.77	7.76	4/99-3/03	-8.79	$0.69	7/82-6/86	30.73	$2.92	$1.55
5	60	541	10.67	7.16	10/69-9/74	-4.26	$0.80	2/95-1/00	29.57	$3.65	$1.73
6	72	529	10.77	6.45	10/68-9/74	-4.64	$0.75	4/94-3/00	24.62	$3.75	$1.94
7	84	517	10.93	5.74	10/67-9/74	-2.74	$0.82	8/82-7/89	22.94	$4.24	$2.19
8	96	505	11.04	5.19	10/66-9/74	0.89	$1.07	4/80-3/88	20.73	$4.51	$2.45
9	108	493	11.11	4.91	10/65-9/74	-0.64	$0.94	11/90-10/99	20.75	$5.46	$2.76
10**	120	481	11.15	4.66	10/64-9/74	0.38	$1.04	9/90-8/00	19.22	$5.80	$3.11
11	132	469	11.15	4.48	10/63-9/74	2.10	$1.26	1/89-12/99	19.12	$6.85	$3.49
12	144	457	11.12	4.32	3/66-2/78	3.19	$1.46	12/87-11/99	19.04	$8.10	$3.90
13	156	445	11.09	4.23	10/61-9/74	2.83	$1.44	8/84-7/97	18.75	$9.34	$4.37
14	168	433	11.12	4.10	11/64-10/78	4.30	$1.80	8/84-7/98	18.78	$11.13	$4.94
15	180	421	11.14	4.02	10/59-9/74	3.98	$1.80	8/82-7/97	19.47	$14.42	$5.58
20	240	361	11.35	3.23	6/59-5/79	6.30	$3.39	4/80-3/00	18.06	$27.67	$10.08
30	360	241	11.31	1.19	1/59-12/88	9.57	$15.51	7/70-6/00	14.35	$55.86	$26.23
40	480	121	11.06	0.77	5/65-4/05	10.04	$45.92	4/58-3/98	12.34	$105.05	$68.98
50	600	1	10.47	1.00	1/57-12/06	10.47	$145.28	1/57-12/06	10.47	$145.28	$145.28

10 Year Monthly Rolling Periods** - Jan 1957 to Dec 2006 - 481 Monthly Rolling Periods Over 50 Years

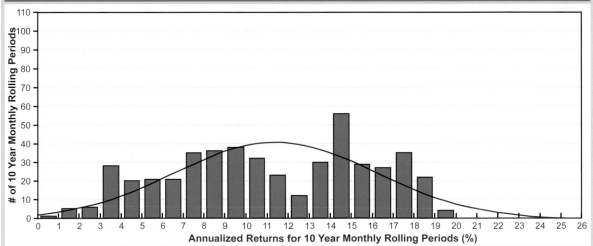

*Sources, Updates, and Disclosures: ifa.com/btp. Returns are net of DFA fees. The returns and standard deviation shown for 1, 3, and 6 month periods are not annualized. Past performance does not guarantee future results. **The 10-year holding period was chosen because the one-year standard deviation of the S&P 500 approximates that of Index Portfolio 90, which has a recommended holding period of 10 years.

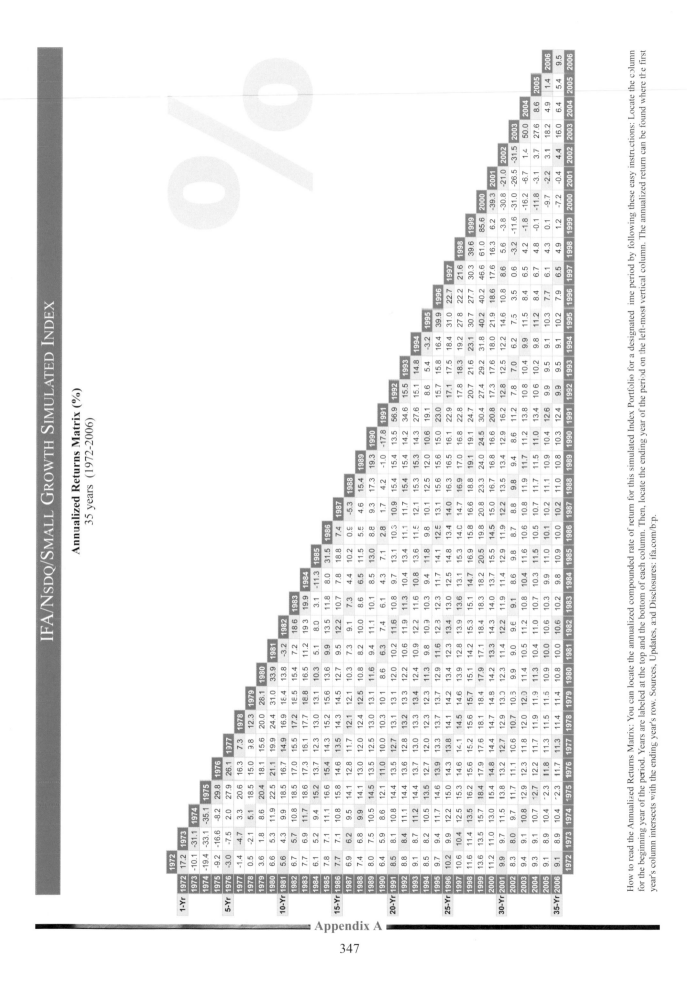

IFA/NSDQ/SMALL GROWTH SIMULATED INDEX

Annualized Returns Matrix (%)
35 years (1972-2006)

How to read the Annualized Returns Matrix: You can locate the annualized compounded rate of return for this simulated Index Portfolio for a designated time period by following these easy instructions: Locate the column for the beginning year of the period. Years are labeled at the top and the bottom of each column. Then, locate the ending year of the period on the left-most vertical column. The annualized return can be found where the first year's column intersects with the ending year's row. Sources, Updates, and Disclosures: ifa.com/b/p.

IFA/Nsdq/Small Growth Simulated Index

Growth of $1 Matrix ($)
35 years (1972–2006)

	Year	1972	1973	1974	1975	1976	1977	1978	1979	1980	1981	1982	1983	1984	1985	1986	1987	1988	1989	1990	1991	1992	1993	1994	1995	1996	1997	1998	1999	2000	2001	2002	2003	2004	2005	2006
1-Yr	1972	1.17																																		
	1973	0.81	0.69																																	
	1974	0.52	0.45	0.65																																
	1975	0.68	0.58	0.84	1.30																															
5-Yr	1976	0.86	0.73	1.06	1.64	1.26																														
	1977	0.92	0.79	1.14	1.76	1.35	1.07																													
	1978	1.03	0.88	1.28	1.97	1.52	1.21	1.12																												
	1979	1.32	1.13	1.64	2.53	1.95	1.54	1.44	1.28																											
	1980	1.77	1.51	2.19	3.38	2.61	2.07	1.93	1.72	1.34																										
10-Yr	1981	1.72	1.46	2.12	3.27	2.52	2.00	1.86	1.66	1.30	0.97																									
	1982	2.04	1.74	2.52	3.88	2.99	2.37	2.21	1.97	1.54	1.15	1.19																								
	1983	2.44	2.08	3.02	4.66	3.59	2.85	2.65	2.36	1.84	1.38	1.42	1.20																							
	1984	2.16	1.85	2.68	4.13	3.18	2.52	2.35	2.09	1.63	1.22	1.26	1.06	0.89																						
	1985	2.85	2.43	3.52	5.43	4.19	3.32	3.09	2.75	2.15	1.61	1.66	1.40	1.17	1.32																					
15-Yr	1986	3.06	2.61	3.78	5.83	4.49	3.56	3.32	2.96	2.31	1.72	1.78	1.50	1.25	1.41	1.07																				
	1987	2.90	2.47	3.58	5.52	4.26	3.38	3.15	2.80	2.19	1.63	1.69	1.42	1.19	1.34	1.02	0.95																			
	1988	3.34	2.85	4.14	6.38	4.91	3.90	3.63	3.23	2.52	1.89	1.95	1.64	1.37	1.54	1.17	1.09	1.15																		
	1989	3.99	3.40	4.93	7.60	5.86	4.65	4.33	3.86	3.01	2.25	2.32	1.96	1.64	1.84	1.40	1.30	1.38	1.19																	
	1990	3.28	2.79	4.05	6.25	4.82	3.82	3.56	3.17	2.47	1.85	1.91	1.61	1.34	1.51	1.15	1.07	1.13	0.98	0.82																
20-Yr	1991	5.14	4.38	6.36	9.80	7.55	5.99	5.58	4.97	3.88	2.90	2.99	2.52	2.10	2.37	1.80	1.68	1.77	1.54	1.29	1.57															
	1992	5.93	5.06	7.34	11.32	8.72	6.92	6.44	5.74	4.48	3.35	3.46	2.91	2.43	2.74	2.08	1.94	2.05	1.77	1.49	1.81	1.15														
	1993	6.81	5.81	8.43	12.99	10.01	7.94	7.40	6.59	5.14	3.84	3.97	3.34	2.79	3.14	2.39	2.23	2.35	2.04	1.71	2.08	1.32	1.15													
	1994	6.59	5.62	8.16	12.57	9.69	7.68	7.16	6.37	4.98	3.72	3.84	3.24	2.70	3.04	2.31	2.16	2.28	1.97	1.65	2.01	1.28	1.11	0.97												
	1995	9.22	7.87	11.41	17.59	13.55	10.75	10.02	8.92	6.96	5.20	5.37	4.53	3.78	4.26	3.24	3.02	3.18	2.76	2.31	2.81	1.79	1.55	1.35	1.40											
25-Yr	1996	11.31	9.65	14.00	21.58	16.63	13.19	12.29	10.94	8.54	6.38	6.59	5.56	4.63	5.23	3.97	3.70	3.91	3.38	2.84	3.45	2.20	1.91	1.66	1.72	1.23										
	1997	13.76	11.74	17.03	26.25	20.23	16.04	14.95	13.31	10.39	7.76	8.02	6.76	5.64	6.36	4.83	4.50	4.75	4.12	3.45	4.20	2.68	2.32	2.02	2.09	1.49	1.22									
	1998	19.21	16.39	23.78	36.65	28.24	22.40	20.87	18.59	14.51	10.84	11.19	9.44	7.87	8.87	6.75	6.29	6.63	5.75	4.82	5.87	3.74	3.24	2.82	2.92	2.08	1.70	1.40								
	1999	35.66	30.43	44.14	68.03	52.42	41.57	38.74	34.50	26.92	20.11	20.78	17.51	14.61	16.47	12.53	11.67	12.31	10.67	8.95	10.89	6.94	6.01	5.24	5.41	3.87	3.15	2.59	1.86							
	2000	21.65	18.48	26.80	41.31	31.83	25.24	23.52	20.95	16.35	12.21	12.62	10.63	8.87	10.00	7.61	7.08	7.48	6.48	5.43	6.61	4.21	3.65	3.18	3.29	2.35	1.91	1.57	1.13	0.61						
30-Yr	2001	17.10	14.59	21.16	32.62	25.13	19.93	18.57	16.54	12.91	9.64	9.96	8.40	7.00	7.90	6.01	5.59	5.90	5.12	4.29	5.22	3.33	2.88	2.51	2.59	1.85	1.51	1.24	0.89	0.48	0.79					
	2002	11.71	9.99	14.49	22.34	17.21	13.65	12.72	11.33	8.84	6.60	6.82	5.75	4.80	5.41	4.11	3.83	4.04	3.50	2.94	3.57	2.28	1.97	1.72	1.78	1.27	1.03	0.85	0.61	0.33	0.54	0.68				
	2003	17.56	14.99	21.74	33.51	25.82	20.48	19.08	16.99	13.26	9.91	10.23	8.63	7.20	8.11	6.17	5.75	6.06	5.25	4.41	5.36	3.42	2.96	2.58	2.67	1.90	1.55	1.28	0.91	0.49	0.81	1.03	1.50			
	2004	19.07	16.28	23.61	36.39	28.04	22.24	20.72	18.45	14.40	10.76	11.11	9.37	7.81	8.81	6.70	6.24	6.59	5.71	4.79	5.82	3.71	3.22	2.80	2.89	2.07	1.69	1.39	0.99	0.53	0.88	1.12	1.63	1.09		
	2005	19.34	16.50	23.93	36.89	28.43	22.54	21.01	18.71	14.60	10.91	11.27	9.50	7.92	8.93	6.79	6.33	6.68	5.79	4.85	5.90	3.76	3.26	2.84	2.93	2.10	1.71	1.41	1.01	0.54	0.89	1.13	1.65	1.10	1.01	
35-Yr	2006	21.18	18.07	26.21	40.40	31.13	24.69	23.01	20.49	15.99	11.94	12.34	10.40	8.68	9.78	7.44	6.93	7.31	6.34	5.31	6.47	4.12	3.57	3.11	3.21	2.30	1.87	1.54	1.10	0.59	0.98	1.24	1.81	1.21	1.11	1.10
		1972	1973	1974	1975	1976	1977	1978	1979	1980	1981	1982	1983	1984	1985	1986	1987	1988	1989	1990	1991	1992	1993	1994	1995	1996	1997	1998	1999	2000	2001	2002	2003	2004	2005	2006

How to read the Growth of $1 Matrix: You can locate the growth of a dollar invested in this simulated Index Portfolio for a designated time period by following these easy instructions: Locate the column for the beginning year of the period. Years are labeled at the top and the bottom of each column. Then, locate the ending year of the period on the left-most vertical column. The growth of a dollar over the time period can be found where the first year's column intersects with the ending year's row. Sources, Updates, and Disclosures: ifa.com/btp.

Appendix B

IFA INDEXES
Sources and Descriptions of Data

The following descriptions of IFA Indexes indicate how indexes are strung together to simulate similar risk and return characteristics back to 1927. This reduces the standard error of the mean which is unacceptably high for periods less than 20 or 30 years. When IFA Indexes are shown in Index Portfolios, all returns data reflects a deduction of 0.9% annual investment advisory fee, which is the maximum Index Funds Advisors (IFA) fee. Fees are based on assets under management at IFA. Unless indicated otherwise, data shown for each individual IFA Index is shown without a deduction of the IFA advisory fee. This method is used because the creation, choice, monitoring and rebalancing of diversified index portfolios are the services of the independent investment advisor. Therefore, fees are deducted from the whole portfolio data.

Live Dimensional Fund Advisors' (DFA) fund data reflects the deduction of mutual fund advisory fees, mutual fund company brokerage fees, other expenses incurred by the mutual funds and incorporates actual trading results. Simulated index data also reflects DFA's current mutual fund expense ratios for the entire period. Both simulated and live data reflect total returns, including dividends, except for IFA/NSDQ. For a graphic representation of the IFA Indexes labeled below, see Figure B-1, a Time Series Construction of the IFA Indexes spanning the last 80 years. Additionally, descriptions regarding the construction of the individual IFA Indexes can be found on the following pages.

IFA Indexes Legend

LC IFA U.S. Large Company Index	**EM** IFA Emerging Markets Index
LV IFA U.S. Large Value Index	**EV** IFA Emerging Market Value Index
MC IFA U.S. Micro Cap Index	**ES** IFA Emerging Small Cap Index
SV IFA U.S. Small Cap Value Index	**1F** IFA One-Year Fixed Income Index
RE IFA Real Estate Securities Index	**2F** IFA Two-Year Global Fixed Income Index
IV IFA International Value Index	**5G** IFA Five-Year Government Index
IS IFA International Small Company Index	**5F** IFA Five-Year Global Fixed Income Index
ISV IFA International Small Cap Value Index	**N** IFA/NSDQ/Small Growth Strategy

IFA Indexes Time Series Construction
80 Years (1927 - 2006)

| 1927 | ← 40 years → | 1967 | 1968 | 1969 | 1970 | 1971 | 1972 | 1973 | 1974 | 1975 | 1976 | 1977 | 1978 | 1979 | 1980 | 1981 | 1982 | 1983 | 1984 | 1985 | 1986 | 1987 | 1988 | 1989 | 1990 | 1991 | 1992 | 1993 | 1994 | 1995 | 1996 | 1997 | 1998 | 1999 | 2000 | 2001 | 2002 | 2003 | 2004 | 2005 | 2006 |

Simulated Index ┊ Live Mutual Fund

IFA U.S. Large Company Index (LC)
LC — S&P 500 Index Simulation (Sim.) Returns less fees for DFLCX | DFA US Large Company (DFLCX)

IFA U.S. Large Cap Value Index (LV)
LV — Fama/French (F/F) Large Cap Value Simulation excluding Utilities, less fees for DFLVX | DFA US Large Cap Value (DFLVX)

IFA U.S. Micro Cap Index (MC)
MC — CRSP 9-10, NYSE, AMEX, and OTC less fees for DFSCX | DFA US Micro Cap (DFSCX)

IFA U.S. Small Cap Value Index (SV)
SV — Fama/French Small Cap Value Strategy less fees for DFSVX | DFA US Small Cap Value (DFSVX)

IFA Real Estate Index (RE)
RE — Allocated 50% (SV) and 50% (MC) | Don Keim Equity REITS Index, less fees for DFREX | DFA Real Estate Securities (DFREX)

IFA int'l Value Index (IV)
IV — (LV) | 6a | 6b | F/F Int'l Value Simulation less fees for DFIVX | 6c | DFA int'l Value Portfolio (DFIVX)

6a: FTSE All-Shares Index in $US   6b: MSCI EAFE Gross Dividends   6c: DFA Int'l High BtM Portfolio (6a, b, and c are less fees for DFIVX)

IFA Int'l Small Company Index (IS)
IS — F/F US Small Neutral Index Portfolio | DFA Int'l Small Company Simulation less fees for DFISX | DFA Int'l Small Company Portfolio (DFISX)

IFA International Small Cap Value Index (ISV)
ISV — (SV) | (IS) | DFA Int'l Small Cap Value Simulation less fees for DISVX | DFA Int'l Small Cap Value Portfolio (DISVX)

IFA Emerging (Emg) Markets Index (EM)
EM — Allocated 50% (LV) & 50% (MC) | Allocated 50% (IV) and 50% (IS) | DFA Emerging Markets Simulation | DFA Emerging Markets Port. (DFEMX)

IFA Emerging Markets Value Index (EV)
EV — IFA US Small Cap Value Index | Allocated 50% (IV) and 50% (IS) | (EM) F/F Emerging Markets Value Simulation | DFA Emg. Markets Value Port. (DFEVX)

IFA Emerging Markets Small Cap Index (ES)
ES — IFA U.S. Micro Cap Index | Allocated 50% (IV) and 50% (IS) | (EM) F/F Emerging Markets Small Simulation | DFA Emg. Markets SmallCap Port. (DEMSX)

IFA One-Year Fixed Income Index (1F)
1F — 1-Mo. US T-Bills | 1-Year T-Note Index less fees for DFIHX | DFA 1-Year Fixed Income Fund (DFIHX)

IFA 2-Year Global Fixed Income Index (2F)
2F — 5-Yr US T-Notes, less fees for DFFGX | DFA 2 Year T-Note Simulation, less fees for DFGFX | DFA 2-Year Global Fixed Income Fund (DFGFX)

IFA 5-Yr Government Fixed Income Index (5F)
5G — 5-Yr US T-Notes, less fees for DFFGX | Lehman Inter. Gov't Bond Index, less fees for DFFGX | DFA 5-Year Gov't Income Fund (DFFGX)

IFA 5-Yr Global Fixed Income Index (5F)
5F — IFA 5-Year Government Index | 33% (1F) + 33% (2F) + 33% (5G) | 15a | DFA 5-Year Global Fixed Income Fund (DFGBX)

15a: Lehman Hedged Global Fix Income Index, less fees for DFGBX

For further detail on the IFA Indexes, see Appendix B   Sources, Updates, and Disclosures: ifa.com/btp

LC | IFA U.S. Large Company Index

Jan 1991 - Present: DFA US Large Company | DFLCX
Jan 1927 - Dec 1990: S&P 500 Returns less fees for DFA US Large Company. Data courtesy of Ibbotson Associates via DFA Returns Program

DFA US Large Company Portfolio   SYMBOL: DFLCX

Investment Objective

The DFA US Large Company Portfolio is a no-load mutual fund designed to approximate the investment performance of the S&P 500 Index, both in terms of the price of the Portfolio's shares and its total investment return. The Portfolio intends to invest in all of the stocks that comprise the S&P 500 Index in approximately the same proportions as they are represented in the Index. The S&P 500 Index is comprised of a broad and diverse group of stocks, most of which are traded on the NYSE. Generally, these are the US stocks with the largest market capitalizations and, as a group, represent approximately 70% of the total market capitalization of all publicly traded US stocks.

Average Annual Total Returns

All Data as of Dec. 31, 2006, unless otherwise indicated.

	One Year	Three Years	Five Years	Ten Years
US Large Company Index Portfolio	15.71%	10.33%	6.06%	8.28%
S&P 500 Index	15.80%	10.44%	6.19%	8.42%

Portfolio Characteristics

Number of Holdings	500	Price / Earnings (excludes negatives)	16.31
Weighted Average Market Cap	$101,287M	Dividend Yield	1.79%
Weighted Average Book-to-Market	0.39	Expense Ratio (as of 11/30/05)	0.15%

LV | IFA U.S. Large Cap Value Index

Mar 1993 - Present: DFA US Large Cap Value | DFLVX
Jan 1927 - Feb 1993: Fama/French Large Cap Value Simulation excluding Utilities, less fees for DFA US Large Cap Value

DFA US Large Cap Value Portfolio   SYMBOL: DFLVX

Investment Objective

The DFA US Large Cap Value Portfolio is a no-load mutual fund designed to capture the returns and diversification benefits of a broad cross-section of US value companies, on a market cap-weighted basis. The Portfolio invests in securities of US companies whose size (based primarily on market capitalization) falls within the largest 90% of the market universe. The market universe is comprised of companies listed on the New York Stock Exchange, American Stock Exchange, and NASDAQ National Market System. After identifying the 90% of aggregate market capitalization, a value screen is applied to the universe. Securities are considered value stocks primarily because a company's shares have a high book value in relation to their market value (BtM). This BtM sort excludes firms with negative or zero book values. In assessing value, additional factors such as price to cash flow or price to earning ratios may be considered, as well as economic conditions and developments in the issuer's industry. The criteria for assessing value are subject to change from time to time.

Average Annual Total Returns

All Data as of Dec. 31, 2006, unless otherwise indicated.

	One Year	Three Years	Five Years	Ten Years
US Large Cap Value Index Portfolio	20.18%	16.14%	12.37%	11.92%
Russell 1000 Value Index	22.24%	15.08%	10.85%	11.00%

Portfolio Characteristics

Number of Holdings	213	Price / Earnings (excludes negatives)	14.03
Weighted Average Market Cap	$32,310M	Dividend Yield	1.42%
Weighted Average Book-to-Market	0.76	Expense Ratio (as of 11/30/05)	0.30%

MC IFA U.S. Micro Cap Index

Jan 1982 - Present: DFA US Micro Cap | DFSCX
Jan 1927 - Dec 1981: CRSP 9-10 Database, NYSE & AMEX & OTC, in different time periods - rebalanced quarterly and semi-annually
less fees for DFA US Micro Cap

DFA US Micro Cap Portfolio   SYMBOL: DFSCX

Investment Objective

The DFA US Micro Cap Portfolio is a no-load mutual fund designed to capture the returns and diversification benefits of a broad cross-section of US small cap companies, on a market cap-weighted basis. The portfolio generally invests in securities of US companies whose size (based primarily on market capitalization) falls within the smallest 5% of the market universe. The market universe is comprised of companies listed on the New York Stock Exchange, American Stock Exchange, and the NASDAQ Market System.

Average Annual Total Returns   All Data as of Dec. 31, 2006, unless otherwise indicated.

	One Year	Three Years	Five Years	Ten Years
US Micro Cap Index Portfolio	16.16%	13.27%	15.16%	13.48%
Russell 2000 Index	18.37%	13.56%	11.39%	9.44%

Portfolio Characteristics

Number of Holdings	2,442	Price / Earnings (excludes negatives)	20.20
Weighted Average Market Cap	$509M	Dividend Yield	0.76%
Weighted Average Book-to-Market	0.48	Expense Ratio (as of 11/30/05)	0.55%

SV IFA U.S. Small Cap Value Index

Apr 1993 - Present: DFA US Small Cap Value | DFSVX
Jan 1927 - Mar 1993: Fama/French Small Cap Value Strategy less fees for DFA US Small Cap Value Simulates Dimensional's Hold
Range and estimated trading costs less fees for DFA US Small Cap Value Courtesy Fama-French and CRSP: 6-10 Size,
(0.70 percentile and above) Book to Market excluding Utilities

DFA US Small Cap Value Portfolio   SYMBOL: DFSVX

Investment Objective

The DFA US Small Cap Value Portfolio is a no-load mutual fund designed to capture the returns and diversification benefits of a broad cross-section of US small value companies, on a market cap-weighted basis. The Portfolio invests in securities of US companies whose size (market capitalization) falls within the smallest 10% of the market universe. The market universe is comprised of companies listed on the New York Stock Exchange, American Stock Exchange, and NASDAQ National Market System. After identifying the 10% of aggregate market capitalization, a value screen is applied to the universe. Securities are considered value stocks primarily because a company's shares have a high book value in relation to their market value (BtM). This BtM sort excludes firms with negative or zero book values. In assessing value, additional factors such as price to cash flow or price to earning ratios may be considered, as well as economic conditions and developments in the issuer's industry. The criteria for assessing value are subject to change from time to time.

Average Annual Total Returns   All Data as of Dec. 31, 2006, unless otherwise indicated.

	One Year	Three Years	Five Years	Ten Years
US Small Cap Value Index Portfolio	21.55%	18.00%	18.90%	15.84%
Russell 2000 Value Index	23.48%	16.49%	15.38%	13.27%

Portfolio Characteristics

Number of Holdings	1,313	Price / Earnings (excludes negatives)	16.54
Weighted Average Market Cap	$1,035M	Dividend Yield	0.95%
Weighted Average Book-to-Market	0.71	Expense Ratio (as of 11/30/05)	0.55%

RE | IFA Real Estate Index
/ IFA U.S. Small Cap Value Index / IFA U.S. Microcap Index

Jan 1993 - Present: DFA Real Estate Securities | DFREX
Jan 1975 - Dec 1992: Simulated REIT from Don Keim Equity Reits Index, less fees for DFA Real Estate Securities. Source: Professor Donald B. Keim, Wharton School of Business, University of Pennsylvania. The index includes residential construction, commerce property development securities & REITs until Dec 1994. Jan 1995 to the present the index includes REITs only
Jan 1927 - Dec 1974: Allocated 50% IFA U.S. Small Cap Value Index and 50% IFA U.S. Micro Cap Index

DFA Real Estate Securities Portfolio | SYMBOL: DFREX

Investment Objective

The DFA Real Estate Securities Portfolio is a no-load mutual fund designed to achieve long-term capital appreciation. The Portfolio consists of shares of equity and hybrid Real Estate Investment Trusts (to the extent that at least 75% of REIT assets are equity investments). The Portfolio invests in all eligible securities traded on the New York Stock Exchange, the American Stock Exchange, and the NASDAQ National Market System. The Portfolio does not currently purchase shares of health care REITs. The Portfolio is well diversified with respect to both geography and property type.

Average Annual Total Returns
All Data as of Dec. 31, 2006, unless otherwise indicated.

	One Year	Three Years	Five Years	Ten Years
US Real Estate Securities Index Portfolio	35.26%	26.44%	23.35%	15.17%
Dow Jones Wilshire REIT Index	36.14%	27.38%	23.87%	15.30%

Portfolio Characteristics

Number of Holdings	113	Price / Earnings (excludes negatives)	41.18
Weighted Average Market Cap	$9,358M	Dividend Yield	3.44%
Weighted Average Book-to-Market	0.33	Expense Ratio (as of 11/30/05)	0.37%

EM | IFA Emerging Markets Index
/ IFA U.S. Micro Cap Index / IFA U.S. Small Cap Value Index

May 1994 to Present: DFA Emerging Markets Portfolio | DFEMX
Jan 1988 to Apr 1994: DFA Emerging Markets Simulation Minus 6 bp/month
Jan 1970 to Dec 1987: Allocated 50% IFA International Value Index and 50% IFA International Small Company Index
Jan 1927 to Dec 1969: Allocated 50% IFA U.S. Large Value Index and 50% IFA U.S. Micro Cap Index

DFA Emerging Markets Portfolio | SYMBOL: DFEMX

Investment Objective

The DFA Emerging Markets Portfolio is a no-load mutual fund designed to achieve long-term capital appreciation. The Portfolio pursues its objective by investing in emerging markets equity securities that Dimensional deems to be large company stocks at the time of purchase. Dimensional will consider, among other things, information disseminated by the International Finance Corporation in determining and approving countries that have emerging markets. The Portfolio currently invests in companies in Brazil, Chile, Czech Republic, Hungary, India, Indonesia, Israel, Malaysia, Mexico, Philippines, Poland, South Africa, South Korea, Taiwan, Thailand, and Turkey. Due to repatriation restrictions, the Portfolio currently holds but does not purchase securities in Argentina.

Average Annual Total Returns
All Data as of Dec. 31, 2006, unless otherwise indicated.

	One Year	Three Years	Five Years	Ten Years
Emerging Markets Index Portfolio	29.17%	29.65%	25.76%	10.11%
MSCI Emerging Markets Index (gross dividends)	32.59%	30.97%	26.97%	9.40%

Portfolio Characteristics

Number of Holdings	591	Price / Earnings (excludes negatives)	14.93
Weighted Average Market Cap	$19,171M	Dividend Yield	2.41%
Weighted Average Book-to-Market	0.36	Expense Ratio (as of 11/30/ 04)	0.69%

IFA Emerging Markets Value Index
/ IFA Emerging Markets Index / IFA US Small Cap Value

April 1998 - Present: DFA Emerging Markets Value Portfolio | DFEVX
Jan 1989 - Mar 1998: Fama/French Emerging Markets Value Simulation, less fees for DFA Emerging Markets Value Portfolio
Jan 1988 - Dec 1988: IFA Emerging Markets Index
Jan 1970 - Dec 1987: Allocated 50% IFA International Value and 50% IFA International Small Company Index
Jan 1927 - Dec 1969: IFA US Small Cap Value Index

DFA Emerging Value Markets Portfolio   SYMBOL: DFEVX

Investment Objective

The DFA Emerging Markets Value Portfolio is a no-load mutual fund designed to achieve long-term capital appreciation. The Portfolio pursues its objective by investing in emerging markets equity securities that are deemed by the Advisor to be value company stocks at the time of purchase. The Advisor will consider among other things the information disseminated by the International Finance Corporation in determining and approving countries that have emerging markets. Securities are considered value stocks primarily because a company's shares have a high book value in relation to their market value (BtM). This BtM sort excludes firms with negative or zero book values. In assessing value, additional factors such as price to cash flow or price to earning ratios may be considered, as well as economic conditions and development in the issuer's industry. The criteria for assessing value are subject to change from time to time. The Portfolio currently invests in companies in Brazil, Chile, Czech Republic, Hungary, India, Indonesia, Israel, Malaysia, Mexico, Philippines, Poland, South Africa, South Korea, Taiwan, Thailand, and Turkey. Due to repatriation restrictions, the Portfolio currently holds but does not purchase securitites in Argentina.

Average Annual Total Returns   All Data as of Dec. 31, 2006, unless otherwise indicated.

	One Year	Three Years	Five Years	Since 4/1/98 Inception
Emerging Markets Value Index Portfolio	37.93%	36.04%	34.12%	18.79%
MSCI Emerging Markets Index (gross dividends)	32.59%	30.97%	26.97%	11.88%

Portfolio Characteristics

Number of Holdings	1,797	Price / Earnings (excludes negatives)	12.26
Weighted Average Market Cap	$6,975M	Dividend Yield	2.78%
Weighted Average Book-to-Market	0.62	Expense Ratio (as of 11/30/05)	0.70%

IFA Emerging Markets Small Cap Index
/ IFA Emerging Markets Index / IFA US Microcap Index

March 1998 - Present: DFA Emerging Markets Small Cap Portfolio | DEMSX
Jan 1989 - Feb 1998: Fama/French Emgerging Markets Small Simulation, less fees for DFA Emerging Markets Small Cap
Jan 1988 - Dec 1988: IFA Emerging Markets Index
Jan 1970 - Dec 1987: Allocated 50% IFA International Value and 50% IFA International Small Company
Jan 1927 - Dec 1969: IFA U.S. Micro Cap Index

DFA Emerging Markets Small Cap Portfolio   SYMBOL: DEMSX

Investment Objective

The DFA Emerging Markets Small Cap Portfolio is a no-load mutual fund designed to achieve long-term capital appreciation. The Portfolio pursues its objective by investing in emerging markets equity securities that are deemed by Dimensional to be small company stocks at the time of purchase. Dimensional will consider, among other things, the information disseminated by the International Finance Corporation in determining and approving countries that have emerging markets. The Portfolio will invest in companies whose market capitalization is less than $2.3 billion. The Portfolio currently invests in companies in Brazil, Hungary, India, Indonesia, Israel, Malaysia, Mexico, Philippines, Poland, South Africa, South Korea, Taiwan, Thailand, and Turkey. Due to repatriation restrictions, the Portfolio currently holds but does not purchase securities in Argentina.

Average Annual Total Returns   All Data as of Dec. 31, 2006, unless otherwise indicated.

	One Year	Three Years	Five Years	Since 3/5/98 Inception
Emerging Markets Small Cap Portfolio	37.31%	30.56%	30.60%	18.26%
MSCI Emerging Markets Index (gross dividends)	32.59%	30.97%	26.97%	11.62%

Portfolio Characteristics

Number of Holdings	2,007	Price / Earnings (excludes negatives)	14.24
Weighted Average Market Cap	$1,129M	Dividend Yield	2.61%
Weighted Average Book-to-Market	0.58	Expense Ratio (as of 11/30/05)	0.97%

IFA International Value Index
/ IFA U.S. Large Cap Value Index

Mar 1994 - Present: DFA International Value Portfolio | DFIVX
July 1993 - Feb 1994: LWAS/DFA Int'l High Book to Market Portfolio
Jan 1975 - June 1993: Fama/French International Value Simulation less fees for DFA International Value Portfolio
Jan 1969 - Dec 1974: MSCI EAFE Gross Dividends less fees for DFA International Value Portfolio
Feb 1955 - Dec 1968: FTSE All-Shares Index in $US less fees for DFA International Value Portfolio
Jan 1927 - Jan 1955: IFA U.S. Large Cap Value Index

DFA International Value Portfolio   SYMBOL: DFIVX

Investment Objective

The DFA International Value Portfolio is a no-load mutual fund designed to achieve long-term capital appreciation. The Portfolio pursues its objective by investing in the stocks of large non-US companies which the Advisor believes to be value stocks at the time of purchase. Securities are considered value stocks primarily because a company's shares have a high book value in relation to their market value (BtM). This BtM sort excludes firms with negative or zero book values. In assessing value, additional factors such as price to cash flow or price to earning ratios may be considered, as well as economic conditions and development in the issuer's industry. The criteria for assessing value are subject to change from time to time. The Portfolio currently invests in companies in Australia, Austria, Belgium, Canada, Denmark, Finland, France, Germany, Greece, Hong Kong, Ireland, Italy, Japan, Netherlands, New Zealand, Norway, Portugal, Singapore, Spain, Sweden, Switzerland, and United Kingdom.

Average Annual Total Returns   All Data as of Dec. 31, 2006, unless otherwise indicated.

	One Year	Three Years	Five Years	Ten Years
International Value Index Portfolio	34.15%	25.82%	22.26%	11.58%
MSCI EAFE Index (net dividends)	26.34%	19.93%	14.98%	7.71%

Portfolio Characteristics

Number of Holdings	673	Price / Earnings (excludes negatives)	14.46
Weighted Average Market Cap	$46,054M	Dividend Yield	2.62%
Weighted Average Book-to-Market	0.58	Expense Ratio (as of 11/30/05)	0.48%

IFA International Small Company Index
/ Fama/French US Small Neutral Index Portfolio

Oct 1996 - Present: DFA International Small Company Portfolio | DFISX
Jan 1970 - Sept 1996: DFA Int'l Small Co. Simulation less fees for DFA International Small Company
Jan 1927 - Dec 1969: Fama/French US Small Neutral Index Portfolio, less fees for DFA International Small Company

DFA International Small Company Portfolio   SYMBOL: DFISX

Investment Objective

The DFA International Small Company Portfolio is a no-load mutual fund designed to achieve long-term capital appreciation. The Portfolio pursues its objective by investing in the small companies of Europe (25-50%), Japan (15-40%), Pacific Rim (0-25%), and United Kingdom (15-35%). The Portfolio currently invests in companies in Australia, Austria, Belgium, Denmark, Finland, France, Germany, Greece, Hong Kong, Ireland, Italy, Japan, Netherlands, New Zealand, Norway, Portugal, Singapore, Spain, Sweden, Switzerland, and United Kingdom.

Average Annual Total Returns   All Data as of Dec. 31, 2006, unless otherwise indicated.

	One Year	Three Years	Five Years	Ten Years
International Small Company Index Portfolio	24.88%	25.86%	26.23%	10.99%
MSCI EAFE Small Cap Index (price only)	17.35%	23.05%	21.59%	6.81%

Portfolio Characteristics

Number of Holdings	4,353	Price / Earnings (excludes negatives)	18.23
Weighted Average Market Cap	$1,292M	Dividend Yield	1.91%
Weighted Average Book-to-Market	0.50	Expense Ratio (as of 11/30/05)	0.64%

IFA International Small Cap Value Index

ISV / IFA International Small Company Index / IFA US Small Cap Value Index

Jan 1995 - Present: DFA International Small Cap Value Portfolio | DISVX
July 1981 - Dec 1994: DFA Int'l Small Cap Value Simulation less fees for DFA International Small Cap Value Portfolio
Jan 1970 - June 1981: IFA Internactional Small Company Index
Jan 1927 - Dec 1969: IFA U.S. Small Cap Value Index

DFA International Small Cap Value Portfolio · SYMBOL: DISVX

Investment Objective

The DFA International Small Cap Value Portfolio is a no-load mutual fund designed to achieve long-term capital appreciation. The Portfolio pursues its objective by investing in the stocks of small non-US companies which the Advisor believes to be value stocks at the time of purchase. Securities are considered value stocks primarily because a company's shares have a high book value in relation to their market value (BtM). This BtM sort excludes firms with negative or zero book values. In assessing value, additional factors such as price to cash flow or price to earning ratios may be considered, as well as economic conditions and developments in the issuer's industry. The criteria for assessing value are subject to change from time to time. The Portfolio currently invests in companies in Australia, Austria, Belgium, Canada, Denmark, Finland, France, Germany, Greece, Hong Kong, Ireland, Italy, Japan, Netherlands, New Zealand, Norway, Portugal, Singapore, Spain, Sweden, Switzerland, and United Kingdom.

Average Annual Total Returns

All Data as of Dec. 31, 2006, unless otherwise indicated.

	One Year	Three Years	Five Years	Ten Years
International Small Cap Value Index Portfolio	28.39%	28.72%	30.13%	12.82%
MSCI EAFE Small Cap Index (price only)	17.35%	23.05%	21.59%	6.81%

Portfolio Characteristics

Number of Holdings	2,418	Price / Earnings (excludes negatives)	16.05
Weighted Average Market Cap	$1,321M	Dividend Yield	2.44%
Weighted Average Book-to-Market	0.75	Expense Ratio (as of 11/30/05)	0.75%

IFA One-Year Fixed Income Index

1F / Eugene Fama Certificate of Deposit Simulation / Merrill Lynch 1 Year US Treasury Note Index
/ 1 Month US Treasury Bills

Aug 1983 - Present: DFA One-Year Fixed Income Fund | DFIHX
Jul 1963 - Jul 1983: One-Year T-Note Index less fees for DFA One-Year Fixed Income
Jan 1927 - Jun 1963: One-Month US Treasury Bills less fees for DFA One-Year Fixed Income

---

DFA One-Year Fixed Income Portfolio · SYMBOL: DFIHX

Investment Objective

The investment objective of the DFA One-Year Fixed Income Portfolio is to achieve stable real returns in excess of the rate of inflation with a minimum of risk. Generally, the Portfolio will acquire high quality obligations which mature within one year from the date of settlement. However, when greater returns are available, substantial investments may be made in securities maturing within two years from the date of settlement as well. In addition, the Portfolio intends to concentrate investments in the banking industry under certain circumstances. The Portfolio is diversified, and with respect to corporate debt obligations and commercial paper, the Portfolio generally invests in securities rated A1/P1 or better.

Average Annual Total Returns

All Data as of Dec. 31, 2006, unless otherwise indicated.

	One Year	Three Years	Five Years	Ten Years
One-Year Fixed Income Index Portfolio	4.78%	2.64%	2.69%	4.21%
Merrill Lynch One-Yr US Treasury Note Index	4.32%	2.49%	2.46%	4.26%
Merrill Lynch Six-Month US T-Bill Index	4.81%	3.03%	2.52%	4.00%

Portfolio Characteristics

Security Maturity Range	0-2 years
Average Portfolio Maturity Range	0-1 year
Expense Ratio (as of 11/30/05)	0.19%

IFA Two-Year Global Fixed Income Index
2F / DFA Two Year Global Fixed Income / 5-Year US Treasury Notes

Mar 1996 - Present: DFA Two-Year Global Fixed Income Fund | DFGFX
Jul 1952 - Feb 1996: DFA Two Year T-Note Simulation, less fees for DFA Two-Year Global Fixed Income
Jan 1927 - Jun 1952: Five-Year US Treasury Notes, less fees for DFA Two-Year Global Fixed Income

Two-Year Global Fixed Income Portfolio   **SYMBOL: DFGFX**

Investment Objective
The investment objective of the Two-Year Global Fixed Income Portfolio is to maximize total returns consistent with preservation of capital. Generally, the Portfolio will acquire high quality obligations which mature within two years from the date of settlement. The Portfolio expects to invest in obligations issued or guaranteed by countries that are members of the Organization of Economic Cooperation and Development ,but may invest in other countries as well. Investments in corporate debt obligations, bank obligations, commercial paper, repurchase agreements, and obligations of other domestic and foreign issuers with high quality ratings may also be included. The Portfolio will also enter into forward foreign currency contracts solely for the purpose of hedging against fluctuations in currency exchange rates. The Portfolio is diversified, and with respect to corporate debt obligations and commercial paper, the Portfolio generally invests in US securities rated A1/P1 or better and non-US securities rated AA/As2 or better.

Average Annual Total Returns
All Data as of Dec. 31, 2006, unless otherwise indicated.

	One Year	Three Years	Five Years	Ten Years
Two-Year Global Fixed Income Index Portfolio	4.46%	2.36%	2.85%	4.36%
Merrill Lynch 1-3 Year US Govt./Corp Index	4.25%	2.39%	3.20%	4.94%

Portfolio Characteristics

Security Maturity Range	0-2 years
Average Portfolio Maturity Range	0-2 years
Expense Ratio (as of 11/30/05)	0.21%

IFA Five Year Government Index
5G / DFA U.S. Government Instruments Simulation / 5-Year US Treasury Notes

Jun 1987- Present: DFA Five-Year Gov't Income Fund| DFFGX
Jan 1973 - May 1987: Lehman Inter. Gov't Bond Index, less fees for DFA Five-Year Gov't Income Index
Jan 1927 - Dec 1972: Five-Year US Treasury Notes, less fees for DFA Five-Year Gov't Income Index

DFA Five-Year Government Portfolio   **SYMBOL: DFFGX**

Investment Objective
The investment objective of the DFA Five-Year Government Portfolio is to maximize total returns available from the universe of debt obligations of the US government and US government agencies. Ordinarily, the Portfolio will invest at least 80% of its assets in US government obligations and US government agency obligations that mature within five years from the date of settlement. The Portfolio may also acquire repurchase agreements

Average Annual Total Returns
All Data as of Dec. 31, 2006, unless otherwise indicated.

	One Year	Three Years	Five Years	Ten Years
Five-Year Fixed Income Index Portfolio	4.51%	2.66%	4.43%	5.15%
Lehman Intermediate Govt Index 1-10 Years	3.84%	2.61%	3.92%	5.48%

Portfolio Characteristics

Security Maturity Range	0-5 years
Average Portfolio Maturity Range	0-5 years
Expense Ratio (as of 11/30/05)	0.25%

5F IFA Five-Year Global Fixed Income Index

/ Hedged Global Fixed Income Composite (Lehman Brothers) / IFA One-Yr Fixed Income Index / IFA Two-Yr Global Fixed Income Index / IFA Five-Yr Gov't Index / Eugene Fama U.S. T-Bond Index 5-10 Yrs / 5-Yr US Treasury Notes

Dec 1990 - Present: DFA Five-Year Global Fixed Income Fund | DFGBX
Jan 1987 - Nov 1990: Lehman Hedged Global FI Index, less fees for DFA Five-Year Global Fixed Income Index
Jan 1973 - Dec 1986: (One-Year Fixed + Two-Year Global + Five-Year Gov't)/3
Jan 1927 - Dec 1972: IFA Five-Year Government Index

DFA Five-Year Global Fixed Income Portfolio   SYMBOL: DFGBX

Investment Objective

The investment objective of the DFA Five-Year Global Fixed Income Portfolio is to provide a market rate of return for a fixed income portfolio with low relative volatility of returns. Generally, the Portfolio will invest in high quality obligations which mature within five years from the date of settlement. The Portfolio expects to invest primarily in obligations issued or guaranteed by any of the following countries (but may invest in other countries as well): US, Australia, Canada, Denmark, EMU countries, France, Japan, Sweden, Switzerland and United Kingdom. Investments in obligations of other foreign issuers rated AA or better, corporate debt obligations, bank obligations and commercial paper may also be included. The Portfolio will also enter into forward foreign currency contracts solely for the purpose of hedging against fluctuations in currency exchange rates.

Average Annual Total Returns   All Data as of Dec. 31, 2006, unless otherwise indicated.

	One Year	Three Years	Five Years	Ten Years
Five-Year Global Fixed Income Index Portfolio	3.89%	2.83%	4.33%	5.45%
Lehman Aggregate Index 1-30 Years	4.33%	3.70%	5.06%	6.24%

Portfolio Characteristics

Security Maturity Range	0-5 years
Average Portfolio Maturity Range	0-5 years
Expense Ratio (as of 11/30/05)	0.33%

N IFA NSDQ Index
IFA NASDAQ/ Small Growth Index

Mar 1971 to May 2006: NASDAQ % Change (Source: Yahoo! Finance)
Jan 1927 to Feb 1971: Fama/French Small Growth Simulation

Fama/French US Small Growth ex Utilities Simulated Portfolio

Investment Objective

US operating companies trading on the NYSE, AMEX or Nasdaq NMS with a maximum weight of any security in a portfolio is 4%. Exclusions are ADRs, Investment Companies, Tracking Stocks before 1993, non-US incorporated companies, Closed-end funds, Certificates, Shares of Beneficial Interests, Berkshire Hathaway Inc (Permco 540), negative book values, and Utilities.

Before March 1971, the small portfolios contain firms with market capitalization below the 55th percentile of all eligible NYSE firms and the large portfolios contain firms with market caps above the 50th percentile. From June 1996 to December 2000, the size breakpoint for all portfolios is the market cap of the median eligible NYSE firm. The BtM breakpoints for 1927 to February 1971 split the eligible NYSE firms with positive book equity into three categories: the top 30% are in value and the bottom 30% is in growth.

Average Annual Total Returns   All Data as of Dec. 31, 2006, unless otherwise indicated.

	One Year	Three Years	Five Years	Ten Years
IFA NSDQ Index	9.51%	6.43%	4.37%	6.47%

ARTICLES

Name	Article	Source

Step 1: Active Investors

Name	Article	Source
Tversky, Amos	The Psychology of Decision Making	ICFA Continuing Education, pg 7
Lewellen, W. G., R. C. Lease and G. G. Schlarbaum	Investment performance and Investor Behavior	Journal of Financial and Quantitative Analysis 14 (1), 1979, pg 29-58
Zweig, Jason	Is Your Brain Wired for Wealth, An Owner's Manual for the Investor's Brain: From Hunting Sloths to Picking Stocks.	Money Magazine, September 27, 2002

Step 2: Nobel Laureates

Name	Article	Source
Alfred Cowles	Liquidity Preference as Behavior Towards Risk	Reprinted from The Review of Economic Studies, No. 67, Feb. 1958
Harry Markowitz, Nobel Laureate	Portfolio Selection Nobel Prize Winning Research	The Journal of Finance: Volume VII, Number 1, March 1952
Wan, Dr. Siaw-Peng	Modern Portfolio Theory (Textbook Version of above)	Business 442: Investments, Chapter 5-5, 2000
Sharpe, William F. Nobel Laureate	The Arithmetic of Active Management	The Financial Analysts' Journal Vol 47, No 1, Jan/Feb 1991. pg 7-9
Sharpe, William F. Nobel Laureate	Mutual Fund Performance	Journal of Business 39(1), 1966, pg 119-138
Sharpe, William F. Nobel Laureate	Mutual Fund Performance and the Theory of Capital Asset Pricing: Reply.	Journal of Business 41(2), 1968, pg 235-236
Davis, Jim L.	Explaining Stock Market Returns	Dimensional Fund Advisor's Library, 2001
Elroy Dimson, London Business School, Massoud Mussavian, London Business School	Three Centuries of Asset Pricing	London Business School Accounting Subject Area, January, 2000
Elroy Dimson, London Business School, Massoud Mussavian, London Business School	A Brief History of Market Efficiency	European Financial Management, Volume 4, Number 1, March 1998, pg 91-193
Fama, Eugene	Efficient Capital Markets: A Review of the Theory and Empirical Work.	Journal of Finance, 25 (1970)(2), pg 383-417 (also see review of Part II)
Fama, Eugene	The Behavior of Stock Market Prices - LANDMARK PAPER	Journal of Business, Vol 38, Issue 1, Jan 1965, pg 34-105
Courtault, Jean-Michel	LOUIS BACHELIER ON THE CENTENARY OF THEORIE DE LA SPECULATION (english)	Mathematical Finance, Vol.10, No.3 (July 2000), pg 341–353, Copyright Blackwell Publishers, Inc.
Taqqu, Murad S., Boston University	Bachelier and His Times: A Conversation with Bernard Bru	Mathematical Finance - Bachelier Congress 2000, H. Geman, D. Madan, S.R. Pliska, T. Vorst (Eds.), Springer (July 9, 2001)) Copyright Springer-Verlag (also see Bachelier) (BFS#1,2000) (BFS#2, 2002)
Dr. Edward E. Yardeni and David A. Moss	The Triumph of Adam Smith	Prudential-Bache, Economics, July 17, 1990
Welch, Ivo	The Top Achievements, Challenges, and Failures of Finance	Yale School of Management Updated June 2001

Step 3: Stock Pickers

Brad M. Barber and Terrance Odean	All That Glitters	October 2003
Fama, Eugene	Random Walks in Stock Market Prices	The Financial Analysts Journal; Sep/Oct 1965: pg 55-59(1)
Odean & Barber	Trading Is Hazardous to Your Wealth: The Common Stock Performance of Individual Investors	Journal of Finance 55(2) April 2000
Sharpe, William F.	The Arithmetic of Active Management	The Financial Analysts' Journal Vol 47, No 1, Jan/Feb 1991. pg 7-9
Cowles, Alfred	Can Stock Market Forcasters Forcast?	Econometrica, 1, July 1933, pg 309-324
Cowles, Alfred	Stock Market Forcasting	Econometrica, 12, 1944
Cowles, Alfred	A Revision of Previous Conclusions Regarding Stock Price Behavior	Econometrica, 28(4), 1960
Barber, Lehavy	Prophets and Losses: Reassessing the Returns to Analysts' Stock Recommendations	Working Paper as of July 2001
Barber, Lehavy	Can Investors Profit from the Prophets? Security Analyst Recommendations and Stock Returns	The Journal of Finance: Volume LVI, Number 2, April 2001
Kritzman, M.	How to Detect Skill in Management Performance	Journal of Portfolio Mgmt. 12(2), 1986, pg 16-20
Grinblatt, Mark, Sheridan Titman and Russ Wermers	Momentum Investment strategies, Portfolio Performance, and Herding: A study of Mutual Fund Behavior	American Economic Review 85, 1995, pg 1088-1105
Johnson, Melissa	Overview: Small Cap Alpha Myth	Index Funds Advisors, 2002
Ennis, Richard M. Sebastian, Michael D.	The Small Cap Alpha Myth	Ennis Knupp & Associates, Inc., 2001
Horst, Jenke, et al	Eliminating Biases in Evaluating Mutual Fund Performance from a Survivorship Free Sample	October 23, 1998
Good, W. R.	Accountability for Pension Fund Performance	Financial Analysts Journal 40(1), 1984, pg 39-45
Carhart, Mark M.	Mutual Fund Survivorship	May 15, 1997
Liang, Bing	Hedge Funds: The Living and the Dead	Journal of Financial and Quantitative Analysis, Vol. 35, No 3, September 2000 (more)
Quigley, Garret, Sinquefield	Performance of UK Equity Unit Trusts	Journal of Asset Management, Vol 1,1, 2000
Levy, H.	Measuring Risk and Performance Over Alternative Investment Horizons	Financial Analysts Journal 40(2), 1984, pg 61-68
Granatelli, A., and J. D. Martin	Management Quality and Investment Performance	Financial Analysts Journal 40(6), 1984, pg 72-74
Brinson, G. P., J. J. Diermeier, and G. G. Schlarbaum	A Composite Portfolio Benchmark for Pension Plans	Financial Analysts Journal 42(2), 1986, pg 15-24
Dietz, Peter	Pension Fund Performance	Financial Analysts Journal 24(5), 1968 pg131-138
Schneider, T. H.	A Worksheet Technique for Measuring Performance	Financial Analysts Journal 25(3), 1969, pg 105-111
Gumperz, J., and E. Page	Misconceptions of Pension Fund Performance	Financial Analysts Journal 26(3), 1970, pg 30-34

Name	Article	Source
Bogle, J. C.	Mutual Fund Performance Evaluation.	Financial Analysts Journal 26(6), 1970, pg 25-34
Levy, H., and M. Sarnat	Investment Performance in an Imperfect Securites Marke and the Case for Mutual Funds	Financial Analysts Journal 28(2), 1972, pg 77
Spigelman, J. H.	What Basis for Superior Performance?	Financial Analysts Journal 30(3), 1974, pg 32-45
Beebower, G. L., and G. L. Bergstonn	A Performance Analysis of Pension and Profit-Sharing Portfolios: 1966-1975	Financial Analysts Journal 33(3), 1977, pg 31-42
Ferguson, R.	Performance Measurement Doesn't Make Sense	Financial Analysts Journal 36(3), 1980, pg 59-70
Good, W. R.	Measuring Performance	Financial Analysts Journal 39(3), 1983, pg 19-24
Odean, T. & Barber, B. M.	Too Many Cooks Spoil the Profits: Investment Club Performance	Financial Analysts' Journal January/February 2000
Grinblatt, Mark and Sheridan Titman	How to Evaluate a Portfolio Manager	Financial Markets and Portfolio Management 1 (2), 1989, pg 9-20
Grinblatt, Mark and Sheridan Titman	Performance Evaluation	Handbook in Operations Research and Management Science, Vol. 9: Finance Jarrow, R., Maksimovic, V., and Ziemba, W. (Eds.) (Elsevier Science), 1971, pg 581-609
Treynor, Jack and K. Mazuy	Can Mutual Funds Outguess the Market	Harvard Business Review 44, 1966, pg 131-36
Treynor, Jack	How to Rate Management of Investment Funds	Harvard Business Review 43, 1965, pg 63-75
Grinblatt, Mark and Sheridan Titman,	How to Avoid Games Portfolio Managers Play	Institutional Investor 23(Nov. 14),1989, pg 35-36
Fisher, L., and R. Weil	Coping with the Risk of Interest-Rate Fluctuations: Returns to Bondholders From Naive and Optimal Strategies	Journal of Business 44(4), 1971, pg 408-431
Cohen, K., and J. Pogue	Some Comments Concerning Mutual Fund Versus Random Portfolio Performance	Journal of Business 41(2), 1968, pg 180-190
Sharpe, William F.	Mutual Fund Performance and the Theory of Capital Asset Pricing: Reply.	Journal of Business 41(2), 1968, pg 235-236
Treynor, J. L., and F. Black	How to Use Security Analysis to Improve Portfolio Selection	Journal of Business 46(1), 1973, pg 66-86
Horowitz, I.	The "Reward to Variability" Ratio and Investment Performance	Journal of Business 39(4), 1966, pg 485-488
Sharpe, William F.	Mutual Fund Performance	Journal of Business 39(1), 1966, pg 119-138
Crenshaw, T. E.	Evaluation of Investment Performance	Journal of Business 50(4), 1977, pg 462-485
Mains, N.	Risk, the Pricing of Capital Assets, and the Evaluation of Investment Portfolios: Comment.	Journal of Business 50(3), 1997, pg 371-384
Henriksson, R. D., and R. C. Merton	On Market Timing and Investment Performance. II. Statistical Procedures for Evaluationg Forecasting Skills	Journal of Business 54(4), 1981, pg 513-533
Kon, S. J.	The Market-Timing Performance of Mutual Fund Managers	Journal of Business 56(3), 1983, pg 323-347
Admati, Anat R., and Stephen A. Ross	Measuring Investment Performance in a Rational Expectations Equilibrium Model	Journal of Business 58(11), 1985, pg 11-26
Grinblatt, Mark and Sheridan Titman,	Mutual Fund Performance: An Analysis of Quarterly Portfolio Holdings	Journal of Business 62(3), 1989, pg 393-416
Lee, C., and S. Rahman	Market Timing, Selectivity, and Mutual Fund Performance: An Empirical Investigation	Journal of Business 63(2), 1990, pg 261-278

Name	Article	Source
Grinblatt, Mark and Sheridan Titman	Performance Measurement Without Benchmarks: An Examination Of Mutual Fund Returns	Journal of Business 66(1), 1993, pg 47-68
Blake, Christopher R., Edwin J. Elton and Martin J. Gruber	The Performance Of Bond Mutual Funds	Journal of Business 66(3), 1993, pg 371-403
Elton, Edwin J., Martin J. Gruber and Christopher R. Blake	The Persistence Of Risk-Adjusted Mutual Fund Performance	Journal of Business 69(April 2), 1996, pg 133-157
Woodward, R. S.	The Peformance of UK Closed-End Funds: A Comparison of the Various Ranking Criteria	Journal of Business Finance and Accounting 10 (3), 1983, pg 419-427
Okunev, J.	An Alternative Measure of Mutual Fund Performance	Journal of Business Finance and Accounting 17(2), 1990, pg 247-264
Ashton, D. J.	A Problem in the Detection of Superior Investment Performance	Journal of Business Finance and Accounting 17(3), 1990, pg 337-350
Matulich, S.	Portfolio Performance with Lending or Borrowing	Journal of Business Finance and Accounting 2(3), 1975, pg 341-348
Peasnell, K. V., L. C. Skerratt and P. A. Taylor	An Arbitrage Rationale for Tests of Mutual Fund Performance	Journal of Business Finance and Accounting 6(3), 1979, pg 373-400
Morris, R. C., and, P. F. Pope	The Jensen Measure of Portfolio Performance in an Arbitrage Pricing Theory Context	Journal of Business Finance and Accounting 8(2), 1981, pg 203-220
Calvett, A. L., and J. Lefoll	Performance and Systematic Risk Stability of Canadian Mutual Funds Under Inflation	Journal of Business Finance and Accounting 8(2), 1981, pg 279-290
Belkaoui, A.	Judgement Related Issues in Performance Evaluation	Journal of Business Finance and Accounting 9(4), 1982, pg 489-500
Appleyard, A. R., N. Strong, and M. Walker	Mutual Fund Performance in the Context of Models of Equilibrium Capital Asset Pricing	Journal of Business Finance and Accounting 9(3), 1982, pg 289-296
Barnea, A., and D. E. Logue	Stock Trading and Portfolio Performance	Journal of Business Research 7, 76, pg 150-157
West, R.	Mutual Fund Performance and the Theory of Capital Asset Pricing: Some comments.	Journal of Business 41(2), 1968, pg 230-234
Francis, J., and F. Fabozzi	Stability of Mutual Fund Systematic Risk Statistics	Journal of BusinessResearch, 1980, pg 263-275
Bhattacharya, S., and P. Pfleiderer	Delegated Portfolio Management	Journal of Economic Theory 36, pg 1-25
Alexander, Gordon J., and Roger D. Stover	Consistency of Mutual Fund Performance During Varying Market Conditions	Journal of Economics and Business, 1980, pg219-226
Dybvig, P. H., and S. A. Ross	The Analytics of Performance Measurement Using a Security Market Line	Journal of Finance 40(2), 1985, pg 401-416
Dybvig, P. H., and S. A. Ross	Differential Information and Performance Measurement Using a Security Market Line	Journal of Finance 40(2), 1985, pg 383-400
Green, R.	Benchmark Portfolio Inefficiency and Deviations From the Security Market Line	Journal of Finance 41(3), 1986, pg 295-312
Elton, E. J., M. J. Gruber, and S. Grossman	Discrete Expectational Data and Portfolio Performance	Journal of Finance 41(3), 1986, pg 699-712
Cadsby, C. B.	Performance Hypothesis Testing with the Sharpe and Treynor Measures	Journal of Finance 41(5), 1986, pg 1175-1176
Lehmann, B., and D. Modest	Mutual Fund Performance Evaluation: A Comparison of Benchmarks and Benchmark Comparisons	Journal of Finance 42(2), 1987, pg 233-265
Cumby, R. E., and J. D. Glen	Evaluating the Performance of International Mutual Funds	Journal of Finance 45(2), 1990, pg 497-521

Name	Article	Source
Grinblatt, Mark and Sheridan Titman	The Persistence of Mutual Fund Performance	Journal of Finance 47, 1992, pg 1977-1984
Chopra, Navin, Charles M. C. Lee, Andrei Shleifer and Richard H. Thaler	Yes, Discounts On Closed-End Funds Are A Sentiment Index	Journal of Finance 48(2), 1993, pg 801-808
Daniel, Kent, Mark Grinblatt, Sheridan Titman and Russ Wermers	Measuring Mutual Fund Performance with Characteristic-Based Benchmarks	Journal of Finance (52) , 1997, pg 1035-1058
Dietz, Peter	Components of a Measurement Model: Rate of Return, Risk and Timing	Journal of Finance 23(2), 1968, pg 267-275
Bauman, W. S.	Evaluation of Prospective Investment Performance	Journal of Finance 23(2), 1968, pg 276-295
Robinson, R. S.	Measuring the Risk Dimension of Investment Performance	Journal of Finance 25(2), 1970, pg 455-468
Gaumintz, J.	Appraising Performance of Investment Portfolios	Journal of Finance 25(3), 1970, pg 555-560
Mills, H. D.	On the Measurement of Fund Performance	Journal of Finance 25(5), 1970, pg 1125-1132
Sarnat, M.	A Note on the Prediction of Portfolio Performance from Ex-Post Data	Journal of Finance 27(4), 1972, pg 903-906
Fama, E. F.	Components of Investment Performance	Journal of Finance 27(3), 1972, pg 551-567
McDonald, J.	French Mutual Fund Performance: Evaluation of Internationally-Diversified Portfolios	Journal of Finance 28(5), 1973, pg 1161-1180
Shashua, L., and Y. Goldschmidt	An Index for Evaluating Financial Performance	Journal of Finance 29(3), 1974, pg 797-814
Fabozzi, F., and J. Francis	Mutual Fund Systematic Risk for Bull and Bear Markets: An Empirical Examination	Journal of Finance 34(5), 1979, pg 1243-1250
Roll, R.	Ambiguity When Performance is Measured by the Securities Market Line	Journal of Finance 33(4), 1978, pg 1051-1069
Guy, J. R.	The Performance of the British Investment Trust Industry	Journal of Finance 33(2), 1978, pg 443-455
Kon, Stanley J., and Frank C. Jen	Estimation of Time-Varying Systematic Risk and Performance for Mutual Fund Portfolios: An Application of Switching Regression	Journal of Finance 33(2), 1978, pg 457-475
Tehranian, H.	Empirical Studies in Portfolio Performance Using Higher Degrees of Stochastic Dominance	Journal of Finance 35(1), 1980, pg 159-220
Peterson, D., and M. L. Rice	A Note on Ambiguity in Portfolio Performance Measures	Journal of Finance 35(5), 1980, pg 1251-1256
Jobson, J. D., and B. M. Korkie	Performance Hypothesis Testing with the Sharpe and Treynor Measures	Journal of Finance 36(4), 1981, pg 889-908
Nagorniak, J. J.	Risk Adjusted Equity Performance Measurement	Journal of Finance 37(2), 1982, pg 555-561
Chua, J. H., and R. S. Woodward	J.M. Keynes's Investment Performance: A note.	Journal of Finance 38(1), 1983, pg 232-236
Jobson, J. D., and B. Korkie	On the Jensen Measure and Marginal Improvements in Portfolio Performance	Journal of Finance 39(1), 1984, pg 245-252
Friend, I., and D. Vickers	Portfolio Selection and Investment Performance	Journal of Finance 39(1), 1965, pg 391-415
Malkiel, Burton G	Returns From Investing In Equity Mutual Funds 1971 To 1991	Journal of Finance 50(2), 1995, pg 549-572
Brown, Stephen J., William N. Goetzmann and Stephen A. Ross	Survival	Journal of Finance 50(3), 1995, pg 853-873

Name	Article	Source
Chevalier, Judith and Glenn Ellison	Are Some Mutual Fund Managers Better than Others? Cross-Sectional Patterns in Behavior and Performance	Journal of Finance 54, 1999, pg 875-899
Falkenstein, Eric G.	Preferences For Stock Characteristics As Revealed By Mutual Fund Portfolio Holdings	Journal of Finance 51(1,Mar), 1996, pg 111-135
Brown, Keith C., W. V. Harlow and Laura T. Starks	Of Tournaments And Temptations: An Analysis Of Managerial Incentives In The Mutual Fund Industry	Journal of Finance 51(1,Mar),1996, pg 85-110
Ferson, Wayne E. and Rudi W. Schadt	Measuring Fund Strategy And Performance In Changing Economic Conditions	Journal of Finance 51(2,Jun), 1996, pg 425-461
Gruber, Martin J.	Presidential Address: Another Puzzle: The Growth In Actively Managed Mutual Funds	Journal of Finance 51(3,Jul), 1996, 783-810
Smith, K., and D. Tito	Risk-Return Measures of Ex-Post Portfolio Performance	Journal of Financial and Quantitative Analysis 4(4), 1969, pg 449-471
Young, W. E., and R. H. Trent	Geometric Mean Approximations of Individual Security and Portfolio Performance	Journal of Financial and Quantitative Analysis 4(2), 1969, pg 179-200
Ang, James S., and Jess H. Chua	Composite Measures for the Evaluation of Investment Performance	Journal of Financial and Quantitative Analysis 14(2), 1979, pg 361-384
Shick, R., and J. Trieschmann	Some Further Evidence on the Performance of Property-Liability Insurance Companies' Stock Portfolios	Journal of Financial and Quantitative Analysis 13(1), 1978, pg 157-166
Lee, C., and F. Jen	Effects of Measurement Error on Systematic Risk and Performance Measurement	Journal of Financial and Quantitative Analysis 13(2), 1978, pg 299-312
Kim, T.	An Assessment of the Performance of Mutual Fund Management: 1969-1975	Journal of Financial and Quantitative Analysis 13(3), 1978, pg 385-406
Ang, James S.	A Note on the Leverage Effects on Portfolio Performance Measures	Journal of Financial and Quantitative Analysis 13(3), 1978, pg 567-572
Miller, R. E., and A. K. Gehr	Sample Size Bias and Sharpe's Performance Measure: A note.	Journal of Financial and Quantitative Analysis 13(5), 1978, pg 943-946
Saunders, A., C. Ward, and R. Woodward	Stochastic Dominance and the Performance of U.K. Unit Trusts	Journal of Financial and Quantitative Analysis 15(2), 1980, pg 323-330
Miller, T. W., and N. Gressis	Nonstationarity and Evaluation of Mutual Fund Returns	Journal of Financial and Quantitative Analysis 15(3),1980, pg 639-654
Fabozzi, F., J. Francis, and C. Lee.	Generalized Functional Form for Mutual Fund Returns	Journal of Financial and Quantitative Analysis 15(5), 1980, pg 1107-1120
Grinblatt, Mark and Sheridan Titman	A Study Of Monthly Mutual Fund Returns And Performance Evaluation Techniques	Journal of Financial and Quantitative Analysis 29(3), 1994, pg 419-444
Levy, R. A.	Measurement of Investment Performance	Journal of Financial and Quantitative Analysis 3(1), 1968, pg 35-58
Carlson, R.	Aggregate Performance of Mutual Funds, 1948-1967	Journal of Financial and Quantitative Analysis 5(1), 1970, pg 1-32
Arditti, F.	Another Look at Mutual Fund Performance	Journal of Financial and Quantitative Analysis 6(3), 1971, pg 909-912
Rothstein, M.	On Geometric and Arithmetic Portfolio Performance Indices	Journal of Financial and Quantitative Analysis 7(4), 1972, pg 1983-1992
Monroe, R., and, J. Trieschmann	Portfolio Performance of Property-Liability Insurance Companies	Journal of Financial and Quantitative Analysis 7(2), 1972, 1595-1611

Name	Article	Source
Swadener, P.	Portfolio Performance of Property Liability Insurance Companies: Comment	Journal of Financial and Quantitative Analysis 7(2), 1973, pg 1619-1623
Klemkosky, R.	The Bias in Composite Performance Measures	Journal of Financial and Quantitative Analysis 8(3), 1973, pg 505-514
Joy, M., and B. Porter	Stochastic Dominance and Mutual Fund Performance	Journal of Financial and Quantitative Analysis 9(1), 1974, pg 25-31
Schlarbaum, G.	The Investment Performance of the Common Stock Portfolios of Property-Liability Insurance Companies	Journal of Financial and Quantitative Analysis 9(1), 1974, pg 89-106
McDonald, J.	Objectives and Performance of Mutual Funds, 1960-1969	Journal of Financial and Quantitative Analysis 9(3), 1974, pg 311-333
Chordia, Tarun	The Structure Of Mutual Fund Charges	Journal of Financial Economics 41(1,May),pg3-39
Jobson, J. D., and B. Korkie	Potential Performance and Tests of Portfolio Efficiency	Journal of Financial Economics 10(4), 1982, pg 433-466
Copeland, T. E., and D. Mayers	The Value Line Enigma (1965-1978): A Case Study of Performance Measurement Issues	Journal of Financial Economics 10(3), 1982, pg 289-322
Connor, G., and R. A. Korajczyk	Performance Measurement with the Arbitrage Pricing Theory: A New Framework for Analysis	Journal of Financial Economics 15(3), 1986, pg 373-394
Pontiff, Jeffrey	Closed-End Fund Premia And Returns: Implications For Financial Market Equilibrium	Journal of Financial Economics 37(3), 1994, pg 341-370
Warther, Vincent A.	Aggregate Mutual Fund Flows And Security Returns	Journal of Financial Economics 39(2/3), 1995, pg 209-235
Cornell, B.	Asymmetric Information and Portfolio Performance Measurement	Journal of Financial Economics 7(4), 1979, pg 381-390
Roll, R.	Measuring Portfolio Performance and the Empirical Content of Asset Pricing Models: A Reply	Journal of Financial Economics 7(4), 1978, pg 391-400
Mayers, D., and E. M. Rice	Measureing Portfolio Performance and the Empirical Content of Asset Pricing Models	Journal of Financial Economics 7(1), 1979, pg 3-28
Verrecchia, R. E.	The Meyers-Rice Conjecture: A Counterexample	Journal of Financial Economics 8(1),80,pg 87-100
Chang, E., and W. Lewellen	An Arbitrage Pricing Approach to Evaluating Mutual Fund Performance	Journal of Financial Research 8(1), 1985, pg 15-30
Chevalier, Judith and Glenn Ellison	Risk Taking by Mutual Funds as a Response to Incentives	Journal of Political Economy 114, 1997, pg 389-432
Grinblatt, Mark and Sheridan Titman	How Clients Can Win the Gaming Game	Journal of Portfolio Management (Summer), 1987, pg 14-23
Smidt, S.	Investment Horizons and Performance Measurement	Journal of Portfolio Management 4(2), 1978, pg 18-22
Litzenberger, R., and H. B. Sosin	The Performance and Potential of Dual Purpose Funds	Journal of Portfolio Management 4(3), 1978, pg 56-68
Pohlman, R., J. Ang, and R. Hollinger	Performance and Timing: A Test of Hedge Funds	Journal of Portfolio Management 4(3), 78, 69-72
French D. W., and G. V. Henderson	How Well Does Performance Evaluation Perform?	Journal of Portfolio Management 1 1(2), 85,15-18
Brinson, G. P., and N. Fachler	Measuring Non-U.S. Equity Portfolio Performance	Journal of Portfolio Management 1 1(3), 85,73-76
Sharpe, William F.	Adjusting for Risk in Performance Measurement	Journal of Portfolio Management 1(2), 75, 29-34
Ferguson, R.	The Trouble with Performance Measurement	Journal of Portfolio Management 12(3), 86, 4-9

Name	Article	Source
Moses, E. A., J. M. Cheney, and E. T. Viet	A New and More Complete Performance Measure	Journal of Portfolio Management 13(4), 87, 24-33
Hagigi, M., and B. Kluger	Safety First: An Alternative Performance Measure	Journal of Portfolio Management 13(4), 87, 34-40
Zbesko, J.	Determinants of Performance in the Bull market	Journal of Portfolio Management 15(2), 89, 38-44
Tsetsekos, G. P., and R. Defusco	Portfolio Performance, Managerial Ownership, and the Size Effect	Journal of Portfolio Management 16(3), 90, 3-39
Bogle, J.	Selecting Equity Mutual Funds	Journal of Portfolio Management 18, 92, 94-100
Jeffrey, Robert H. and Robert D. Arnott	Is Your Alpha Big Enough To Cover Its Taxes?	Journal of Portfolio Management 19(3), 93, 15-26
Garcia, C. B. and F. J. Gould	Survivorship Bias	Journal of Portfolio Management 19(3), 93, 52-56
Armstrong, D.	Were Mutual Funds Worth the Candle?	Journal of Portfolio Management 2(4), 76, 46-51
Jeffrey, Robert H. and Robert D. Arnott	Is Your Alpha Big Enough To Cover Its Taxes?: Reply.	Journal of Portfolio Management 20(4), 1994, pg 96-97
Fung, William and David A. Hsieh	Survivorship Bias and Investment Style in the Rreturns of CTAs: The Information Content of Performance Track Records	Journal of Portfolio Management 24, 1997, pg 30-41
Fisher, Kenneth L. and Meir Statman	Investment Advice From Mutual Fund Companies	Journal of Portfolio Management 24(1,Fall), 9-25
Garcia, C. B., F. J. Gould and Christopher K. Ma	Survivorship Bias: Reply.	Journal of Portfolio Management 21(2), 105-107
Beckers, Stan	Manager Skills And Investment Performance: How Strong Is The Link?	Journal of Portfolio Management 23(4,Summer), 1997, pg 9-23
Fielitz, B. D., and M. T. Greene	Shortcomings in Portfolio Evaluation via MPT.	Journal of Portfolio Management 6(4), 80, 13-19
Roll, R.	Performance Evaluation and Benchmark Errors(I)	Journal of Portfolio Management 6(4), 80, 5-12
Roll, R.	Performance Evaluation and Benchmark Errors (II)	Journal of Portfolio Management 7(2), 81, 17-22
Ferri, M. G., and H. D. Oberhelman	How Well Do Money Market Funds Perform?	Journal of Portfolio Management 7(3), 81, 18-26
Shawky, H. A.	An Update on Mutual Funds: Better Grades	Journal of Portfolio Management 8(2), 82, 29-34
Burns, W. L., and D. R. Epley	The Performance of Portfolios of REITS + Stocks	Journal of Portfolio Management 8(3), 82, 37-42
Dunn, P. C., and R. D. Theisen	How Consistently Do Active Managers Win?	Journal of Portfolio Management 9(4), 83, 47-53
Kritzman, M.	Can Bond Managers Perform Consistently?	Journal of Portfolio Management 9(4), 83, 54-56
Christopherson, J. A., W. E. Ferson and A. L. Turner	Performance Evaluations Using Conditional Alphas and Betas	Journal of Portfolio Management, Fall 1999
Stewart, Scott D.	Is Consistency of Performance a Good Measure of Manager Skill?	Journal of Portfolio Management, Spring 1998
Levy, H.	Portfolio Performance and the Investment Horizon	Management Science 18(12), 1972, B645-B652
Grinblatt, Mark and Sheridan Titman	Adverse Risk Incentives and the Design of Performance-Based Contracts	Management Science 35, 1989, pg 807-822
Jensen, Michael, G.P. Szego and K. Shell (eds.),.	Optimal Utilization of Market Forecasts and the Evaluation of Investment Performance	Mathematical Methods in Investment and Finance (Elsevier, Amsterdam), 1972
Ippolito, R. A.	Efficiency with Costly Information: A Study of Mutual Fund Performance	Quarterly Journal of Economics 104, 89, 1-23
Chevalier, Judith and Glenn Ellison	Career Concerns of Mutual Fund Managers	Quarterly Journal of Economics 105(6), 1999, pg 1167-1200

Name	Article	Source
Brown, Stephen J., William N. Goetzmann Roger Ibbotson and Stephen A. Ross	Rejoinder: The J-Shape of Performance Persistence Given Survivorship Bias	Review of Economics and Statistics 79, 1997, pg 167-170
Fung, William and David A. Hsieh	Empirical Characteristics of Dynamic Trading Strategies: The Case of Hedge Funds	Review of Financial Studies 10, 1997, pg 275-302
Christopherson, J. A., W. E. Ferson and D. A. Glassman	Conditioning Manager Alphers on Economic Information: Another Look at Persistence of Performance	Review of Financial Studies 11, 1998, pg 111-142
Grinblatt, Mark and Sheridan Titman	Portfolio Performance Evaluation: Old Issues and New Insights	Review of Financial Studies 2, 1989, pg 393-421
Brown, Stephen J., William N. Goetzmann Roger Ibbotson and Stephen A. Ross	Survivorship Bias in Performance Studies	Review of Financial Studies 5(4),1997,pg 553-580
Elton, Edwin J., Martin J. Gruber, Sanjiv Das and Matthew Hlavka	Efficiency With Costly Information: A Reinterpretation Of Evidence From Managed Portfolios	Review of Financial Studies 6(1), 1996, pg 1-22
Chen, Z. and P. Knez	Portfolio Performance Measurement: Theory and Evidence	Review of Financial Studies 9, 1996, pg 551-556
Elton, Edwin J., Martin J. Gruber and Christopher R. Blake	Survivorship Bias And Mutual Fund Performance	Review of Financial Studies 9(4,Winter), 1996, pg 1097-1120
Connor, G., and R. A. Korajczyk	The Attributes, Behavior and Performance of US Mutual Funds	Review of Quantitative Finance and Accounting 1(), 1991, pg 5-26
Vos, Ed, Padrig Brown and Sean Christie, New Zealand	A Test of Persistence in the Performance of New Zealand and Australian Equity Mutual Funds	Accounting Research Journal 2(1995), pg 19-34
Grinblatt, Mark and Sheridan Titman	Performance Evaluation	The New Palgrave Dictionary of Money and Finance Newman, P., Milgate, M., and Eatwell, J. (Eds.)(Stockton Press, Volume 3 (N-Z)), 133-135
Simonson, D.	The Speculative Behavior of Mutual Funds	Journal of Finance 27(2), 1972, pg 381-391
Simon, J.	Does "Good Portfolio Management" Exist?	Management Science 15(6), 1969, B308-B324
Jensen, Michael	The Performance of Mutual Funds in the Period 1945-1964	Journal of Finance 23(2), 1968, pg 389-416
Kon, Stanley J., and Frank C. Jen	The Investment Performance of Mutual Funds: An Empirical Investigation of Timing, Selectivity, and Market Efficiency	Journal of Business 52(2), 1979, pg 263-289
Carhart, Mark	Persistence in Mutual Fund Performance	Journal of Finance 52, 1997, pg 57-82
Admati, Anat R. and Paul Pfeiderer	Does It All Add Up? Benchmarks And The Compensation Of Active Portfolio Managers	Journal of Business 70(July 3), 1997, pg 323-350

Step 4: Time Pickers

Professor H. Nejat Seyhun, University of Michigan	Stock Market Extremes and Portfolio Performance	© Copyright 1994, Towneley Capital Management, Inc.
Chua, J. H., R. S. Woodward. and E. C. To	Potential Gains From Stock Market Timing in Canada	Financial Analysts Journal 43(5), 1987, pg 50-56
Riepe, Mark, Peterson, James	The Costs and Benefits of Waiting to Invest	Schwab Center for Investment Research, Vol. III, Issue I, Jan 2000
Beebower, G. L., and A. -P. Varikooty	Measuring Market Timing Strategies	Financial Analysts Journal 47(6), 1991, pg 78-92

Name	Article	Source
William N. Goetzmann, Jonathan Ingersoll Jr., and Zoran Ivkovich	Monthly Measurement of Daily Timers (see abstract # 8)	Journal of Financial and Quantitative Analysis Vol. 35, No. 3, September 2000
Sharpe, William F.	Likely Gains from Market Timing	Financial Analysts Journal 31, 60-69, 1975
Merton, R. C	On Market Timing and Investment Performance: An Equilibrium Theory of Value for Market Forecasts	Journal of Business 54(3), 363-406, 1981
Chang, E. and Lewellen, W.	Market Timing and Mutual Fund Investment Performance	Journal of Business 57(1), 57-72, 1984
Henriksson, R. D	Market Timing and Mutual Fund Performance: An Empirical Investigation	Journal of Business 57(1), 73-96, 1984
Breen, W., R. Jagannathan, and Ofer, A. R.	Correcting for Heteroscedasticity in Tests for Market Timing Ability	Journal of Business 59(4(1)), 585-598, 1986
Jagannathan, R., and Korajczyk, R. A.	Assessing the Market Timing Performance of Managed Portfolios	Journal of Business 59(2(1)), 217-235, 1986
Grant, D	Portfolio Performance and the "Cost" of Timing Decisions	Journal of Finance 32(3), 837-838, 1977
Grant, D	Market Timing and Portfolio Management	Journal of Finance 33(4), 1119-1131, 1978
Alexander, Gordon, J. P., Benson, George and Eger, Carol E.	Timing Decisions and the Behavior of Mutual Fund Systematic Risk	Journal of Financial and Quantitative Analysis 17(4), 579-622, 1982
Kane, A and Marks, S. G.	Performance Evaluation of Market Timers: Theory and Evidence	Journal of Financial and Quantitative Analysis 23(4), 425-435, 1988
Cumby, R. E., and Modest, D. M.	Testing for Market Timing Ability	Journal of Financial Economics 19, 169-189, 1987
Vandell, R. F., and Steven, J. L.	Evidence of Superior Performance from Timing	Journal of Portfolio Management 15(3), 38-42, 1989
Larsen, Glen A., Jr. and Wozniak, Gregory D.	Market Timing Can Work in the Real World	Journal of Portfolio Management 21(3), 74-81, 1995
Viet, E. T., and Cheney, J. M.	Are Mutual Funds Market Timers?	Journal of Portfolio Management 8(2), 35-42, 1982
Admati Anat, Sudipto Bhattacharya, Paul Pfliederer, and Stephen Ross	On Timing and Selectivity	Journal of Finance 41(3), 715-730, 1986

Step 5: Manager Pickers

Kahn, Ronald N., & Rudd, A.	Does Historical Performance Predict Future Performance?	Financial Analysts' Journal, November/December 1995
Prem C. Jain; A. B. Freeman School of Business, Tulane University; Joanna Shuang Wu; William E. Simon Graduate School of Business Administration, University of Rochester	Truth in Mutual Fund Advertising: Evidence on Future Performance and Fund Flows	The Journal of Finance; Volume 55: Issue 2; pg 937 - 958, April, 2000
Brown, Stephen J. and William N. Goetzmann	Performance Persistence	Journal of Finance 50(2), 679-698, 1995
	Five Lies about Fund Manager Talent	July 17, 2000
Hendricks, Darryll, Jayendu Patel and Richard Zeckhauser	Hot Hands In Mutual Funds: Short-Run Persistence Of Relative Performance, 1974-1988.	Journal of Finance 48(1), 93-130, 1993

Step 6: Style Drifters

Name	Article	Source
Keith C. Brown, Department of Finance, University of Texas; W. V. Harlow, Fidelity Investments	Staying the Course: The Impact of Investment Style Consistency on Mutual Fund Performance	This Draft: March 8, 2002
Brown, Stephen J. and William N. Goetzmann	Mutual Fund Styles	Journal of Financial Economics 43(3,Mar), 373-399, 1995
Tierney, D. E., and K. Winston	Using Generic Benchmarks to Present Manager Styles	Journal of Portfolio Management 17, 33-36, 1991
Lucas, Lori and Riepe, Mark	The Role of Returns Based Style Analysis	Ibbotson Associates, May 9, 1996
Lebaron, Dean	Universal Model Of Equity Styles	Journal of Portfolio Management 21(1), 85-88, 1994
Clark, Davis and Rasmusen	Style Analysis: Easy to Use - and Misuse	Dimensional Fund Advisors, October, 2001
Gallo, John G. and Lockwood, Larry J.	Benefits Of Proper Style Classification of Equity Portfolio Managers.	Journal of Portfolio Management 23(3,Spring), 47-56, 1999
Gallo, John G. and Lockwood, Larry J.	Fund Management Changes and Equity Style Shifts	Financial Analysts Journal 55, 44-52, 1999

Step 7: Silent Partners

Name	Article	Source
Unkown	The Great Annuity Rip-off	Forbes.com, 1998
Davanzo, L. E., and S. L. Nesbitt	Performance Fees for Investment Management	Financial Analysts Journal 43(1), 14-20, 1987
Arnott, Robert, Andrew L. Berkin, Ph.D., and Jia Ye, Ph.D	Seven Articles on Tax Managed Investing	Various
Frank W. Stanton	An Unexpected Tax Bite from Barclays' iShares	Morningstar.com 12-22, 2000
Kritzman, M	Incentive Fees: Some problems and Some Solutions	Financial Analysts Journal 43(1), 21-26, 1987
Thelander	Netting Out Capital Gains and Losses on Schedule D	The MotleyFool, 2000
IRS	Wash Sale Rules	IRS, 2001
IRS	Capital Loss Carryforward	IRS Tax Tip 2003-29, Feb. 11, 2003
Grinold, R., and A. Rudd	Incentive fees: Who Wins? Who Loses?	Financial Analysts Journal 43(1), 27-38, 1987
Record, E. E. Jr., and M. A. Tynan	Incentive Fees: The Basic Issues	Financial Analysts Journal 43(1), 39-43, 1987
Ippolito, R. A., and J. A. Turner	Turnover, Fees and Pension Fund Performance.	Financial Analysts Journal 43(6), 16-26, 1987

Step 8: Riskese

Name	Article	Source
Able, Andrew B.	The Equity Premium Puzzle	Business Review, Federal Reserve Bank of Philadelphia, pg 1-14, Sept/Oct 1991

Name	Article	Source
Jensen, Michael	Risk, the Pricing of Capital Assets, and the Evaluation of Investment Performance	Journal of Business 42(2), 167-247, 1969
Kocherlakota, Narayana R.	The Equity Premium: It's Still a Puzzle	Journal of Economics Literature, 32, pg 42-71, March 1996
Robert D. Arnott and Peter L. Bernstein	What Risk Premium Is Normal?	First Quadrant's Reflections Investment Management Reflections, 2002
Chen, Nai-fu., Thomas E. Copeland, and David Mayers	A Comparison of Single and Multifactor Portfolio Performance Methodologies	Journal of Financial and Quantitative Analysis 22(4), 1987, pg 401-417
Mehra, Rajneesh, and Edward C. Prescott	The Equity Risk Premium: A Puzzle	Journal of Monetary Economics, 15, March , 1985, pg 145-161
Weil, Philippe	The Equity Premium Puzzle and the Risk-Free Rate Puzzle	Journal of Monetary Economics, 24, Nov 1989, pg 191-200
Siegel, Jeremy J.	Shrinking Equity Premium	Journal of Portfolio Management, Fall 1999 pg 10-17
Smith, Adam	Employment of Capitals	The Wealth of Nations, 1776
Fama, Eugene F., and French, Kenneth R.	The Cross-section of Expected Stock Returns	Journal of Finance, Vol. XLVII, No 2, June, 1992
Fama, Eugene F., and French, Kenneth R.	The Equity Premium	CRSP, 2001
Jim Davis, Fama, Eugene F., and French, Kenneth R.	Fama/French Three Factor Model in U.S., Characteristics, Covariances, and Average Returns: 1929-1997	unpublished research paper, February 1999
Conner, Gregory and Sehgal, Sanjay	Fama/French Three Factor Model in India	May, 2001, London School of Economics and Univ. of Dehli
Eugene Fama, Jr.	Asset Management: Engineering Portfolios for Better Returns	PCT Publishing, 1998
Yu Zhifeng Zeng	Fama/French Three Factor Model in China	School of Management Fudan University Shidian
Quigley, Garret, Sinquefield	Fama/French Three Factor Model in England, Performance of UK Equity Unit Trusts	Journal of Asset Management, Vol 1,1, 2000
Roger J. Bos, CFA, Senior Index Analyst Standard & Poor's, Michele Ruotolo Domestic Index Manager Standard & Poor's	General Criteria for S&P U.S. Index Membership	© 2000 The McGraw-Hill Companies
Fama, Eugene F., and French, Kenneth R.	Industry Costs of Equity	Economics, 1997
Chen, S. N. and C. F. Lee	The Sampling Relationship Between Sharpe's Performance Measure and its Risk Proxy: Sample Size, Investment Horizon and Market Conditions	Management Science 27(6), 1981, pg 607-618

Step 9: History

Roger G. Ibbotson, Yale University, Peng Chen Ibbotson Associates, Inc.	The Supply of Stock Market Returns	Yale International Center for Finance, 1976
Ibbotson, Roger G., and Rex Sinquefield	Stocks, Bonds and Bills, and Inflation: Simulations of the Future, 1976-2000	Journal of Business, 1976
Ibbotson, Roger G., and Rex Sinquefield	Stocks, Bonds and Bills, and Inflation: Year-by-Year Historical Returns (1926-74)	Journal of Business, 49, Jan 1976, pg 313-338
G. William Schwert	Indexes of United States Stock Prices from 1802 to 1987	Journal of Business 63, 1990, pg 399-426

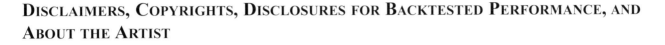

Appendix D

DISCLAIMERS, COPYRIGHTS, DISCLOSURES FOR BACKTESTED PERFORMANCE, AND ABOUT THE ARTIST

- **Dalbar, Inc**. is an independent third party not associated with Index Funds Advisors, Inc. The studies referred to in this book by DALBAR were performed by and obtained from DALBAR, Inc. The information is believed to be reliable but accuracy and completeness cannot be guaranteed. It is for informational purposes only and is not a solicitation to buy or sell securities. Use of information from DALBAR does not necessarily constitute agreement by DALBAR, Inc., of any investment philosophy or strategy presented in this book.

- **©2007 Morningstar, Inc. All rights reserved.** Morningstar, Inc is an independent investment research firm not associated with Index Funds Advisors, Inc. The information contained herein: (1) is proprietary to Morningstar and/or its content providers; (2) may not be copied or distributed; (3) does not constitute investment advice offered by Morningstar; and (4) is not warranted to be accurate, complete or timely. Neither Morningstar nor its content providers are responsible for any damages or losses arising from any of this information. Past performance is no guarantee of future results. Use of information from Morningstar does not constitute agreement by Morningstar, Inc. of any investment philosophy or strategy presented in this publication.

- **All Standard & Poor's 500 Index Data ©Copyright 2007 The McGraw-Hill Companies, Inc. Standard & Poor's including its subsidiary corporations ("S&P") is a division of The McGraw-Hill Companies, Inc.** Reproduction in any form is prohibited without S&P's prior written permission. Neither S&P, its affiliates nor any of their third-party licensors: (a) guarantee the accuracy, completeness or availability of the S&P Data, or (b) make any warranty, express or implied, as to the results to be obtained by the Publisher or any other person from the use of the S&P Data or any other data or information included therein or derived therefrom, or (c) make any express or implied warranties, including any warranty of merchantability or fitness for the particular purpose or use, or (d) shall in any way be liable to the Publisher or any recipient of the Materials for any inaccuracies, errors, or omissions, regardless of cause, in the S&P Data or for any damages, whether direct or indirect or consequential, punitive or exemplary resulting therefrom.

Quotations and portraits:

- Quotes contained in this book are for illustrative purposes only, and in no way imply any endorsements of the goods and services of Mr. Hebner, Index Funds Advisors, Inc. or any affiliates thereof.

Data and Charts:

- Data and charts are copyright of their respective owners and reproduced as supportive research data and not as an endorsement of their respective owners to the content contained herein.

- **Index Funds Advisors, Inc.**: THERE ARE NO WARRANTIES, EXPRESSED OR IMPLIED, AS TO ACCURACY COMPLETE-

NESS, OR RESULTS OBTAINED FROM ANY INFORMATION IN THIS BOOK. Nothing in this book should be interpreted to state or imply that past results are an indication of future performance. This book does not constitute a complete description of Index Funds Advisors, Inc., (IFA) services and is for information purposes only. It is in no way a solicitation or an offer to sell securities or investment advisory services except, where applicable, in states where IFA is registered, or where an exemption of such registration exists. Information throughout this book whether stock quotes, charts, articles, or any other statements regarding market or other financial information, is obtained from sources which IFA and and its suppliers believe reliable, but IFA does not warrant or guarantee the timeliness or accuracy of this information. Neither IFA or its information providers shall be liable for any errors or inaccuracies, regardless of cause, or the lack of timeliness of, or for any delay or interruption in the transmission thereof to the user. All investments involve risk, including foreign currency exchange rates, political risks, different methods of accounting and financial reporting, and foreign taxes.

DISCLOSURE FOR BACKTESTED PERFORMANCE INFORMATION ON THE SIMULATED STRATEGIES OF INDEX PORTFOLIOS (see ifa.com/btp for updates)

1. Index Funds Advisors, Inc. (IFA) was incorporated in March 1999 and placed its first independent client investments in early 2000. The performance information presented in the charts or tables of this book represents backtested performance based on combined simulated index data and live (or actual) mutual fund results from Jan 1, 1927 to period ending date shown using the strategy of buying, holding and annual rebalancing globally diversified portfolios of index funds. Backtested performance is hypothetical (it does not reflect trading in actual accounts) and is provided for informational purposes to indicate historical performance had the Index Portfolios been available over the relevant period. IFA did not offer the Index Portfolios until November 1999. Prior to 1999, IFA did not manage client assets. The IFA indexing investment strategy is based on the principles of the Modern Portfolio Theory and the Fama and French Three Factor Model for Equities and Two Factor Model for Fixed Income. The Index Portfolios are designed to provide substantial global diversification (approximately 16,000 companies in 40 countries) in order to reduce investment concentration and the resulting increased risk caused by the volatility of individual companies, indexes, or asset classes. Client portfolios are monitored and rebalanced, taking into consideration risk exposure consistency, transaction costs, and tax ramifications to maintain target asset allocations as shown in the 20 Index Portfolios.

2. A review of the IFA Index Data Sources and Time Series Construction in Appendix B is an integral part of and should be read in conjunction with this explanation of backtested performance information. For detailed descriptions and definitions of the underlying criteria and data used to construct backtested performance, Data Sources and IFA Indexes Time Series Construction in Appendix B. Simulated index data is based on the performance of indexes as described in Appendix B. The index mutual funds used in IFA's 20 Index Portfolios are IFA's best estimate of a mutual fund that will come closest to the index data provided in the simulated indexes. Simulated index data is used for the period prior to the inception of the relevant live mutual fund data. An equivalent mutual fund expense ratio is deducted from both live and simulated data. Live (or actual) mutual fund per-

formance is used after the inception date of each mutual fund. Backtested performance is calculated by using a computer program and monthly returns data set that starts with the first day of the given time period and evaluates the returns of simulated indexes and index mutual funds, as seen in Appendix B.

The IFA Indexes Times Series Construction goes back to Jan. 1927 and consistently reflects a tilt towards small and value equities over time, with an increasing diversification to international markets and the real estate index as data became available. In Jan. 1927, there are five equity indexes and two bond indexes. In Feb. 1955, there are a total of 10 indexes. There are 15 indexes from March 1998 to the present. If the original 5 equity indexes from 1927 are held constant through December 2006, the annualized rate of return is 11.80%, after the deduction of a 0.9% IFA advisor fee and a standard deviation of 25.81%. The evolving IFA Indexes over the same period have a 12.14% annualized return after the same IFA fees and a 24.85% standard deviation. The value of having a longer time series exceeds the concerns of index substitutions over the 1927 to present period. Due to the very high standard deviations of returns (25%), a 60-year or more sample size of data is recommended to reduce the standard error of the mean. In other words, smaller sample sizes introduce larger errors than the errors introduced by stitching together indexes over time. This is the advice IFA provides to it's clients. (See Appendix B for the Time Series Construction.)

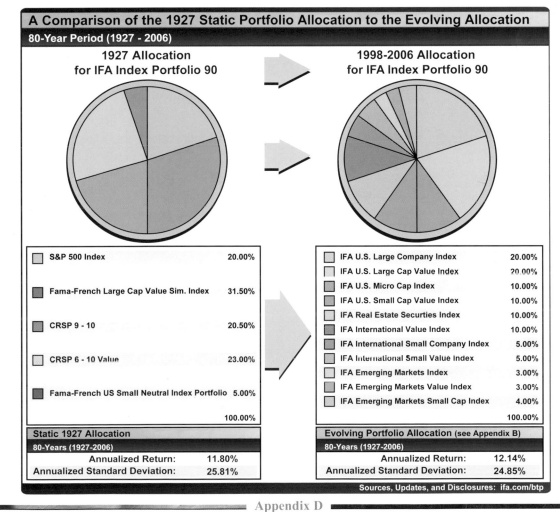

A Comparison of the 1927 Static Portfolio Allocation to the Evolving Allocation
80-Year Period (1927 - 2006)

1927 Allocation for IFA Index Portfolio 90

S&P 500 Index	20.00%
Fama-French Large Cap Value Sim. Index	31.50%
CRSP 9 - 10	20.50%
CRSP 6 - 10 Value	23.00%
Fama-French US Small Neutral Index Portfolio	5.00%
	100.00%

Static 1927 Allocation
80-Years (1927-2006)

Annualized Return:	11.80%
Annualized Standard Deviation:	25.81%

1998-2006 Allocation for IFA Index Portfolio 90

IFA U.S. Large Company Index	20.00%
IFA U.S. Large Cap Value Index	20.00%
IFA U.S. Micro Cap Index	10.00%
IFA U.S. Small Cap Value Index	10.00%
IFA Real Estate Securties Index	10.00%
IFA International Value Index	10.00%
IFA International Small Company Index	5.00%
IFA International Small Value Index	5.00%
IFA Emerging Markets Index	3.00%
IFA Emerging Markets Value Index	3.00%
IFA Emerging Markets Small Cap Index	4.00%
	100.00%

Evolving Portfolio Allocation (see Appendix B)
80-Years (1927-2006)

Annualized Return:	12.14%
Annualized Standard Deviation:	24.85%

Sources, Updates, and Disclosures: ifa.com/btp

Backtested performance is calculated by using a computer program and monthly returns data set that starts with the first day of the given time period and evaluates the returns of simulated indexes and index mutual funds, see Data Sources. In 1999, tax-managed funds became available for many different index funds. IFA uses tax-managed funds in taxable accounts. The tax-managed funds are consistent with the indexing strategy, however, they should not be expected to track the performance of corresponding taxable funds in the same or similar indexes. As such, the performance of portfolios using tax-managed funds will vary from portfolios that do not utilize these funds.

3. Backtested performance does not represent actual performance and should not be interpreted as an indication of such performance. Actual performance for client accounts may be materially lower than that of the Index Portfolios.

Backtested performance results have certain inherent limitations. Such results do not represent the impact that material economic and market factors might have on an investment adviser's decision-making process if the adviser were actually managing client money. Backtested performance also differs from actual performance because it is achieved through the retroactive application of model portfolios (in this case, IFA's 20 Index Portfolios) designed with the benefit of hindsight. As a result, the models theoretically may be changed from time to time to obtain more favorable performance results.

4. History of Changes to the IFA Indexes:

1. 1991-1999: Index Portfolios 10, 30, 50, 70 and 90 were originally suggested by Dimensional Fund Advisors (DFA), merely as an example of globally diversified investments using their many custom index mutual funds, back in 1991 with moderate modifications in 1996 to reflect the availability of index funds that tracked the emerging markets asset class. Portfolios between each of the above listed portfolios were created by IFA in 1999 by interpolating between the above portfolios. Portfolios 5, 95 and 100 were created by Index Funds Advisors in 1999, as a lower and higher extension of the DFA 1991 risk and return line.

2. November 2002: Due to the high similarities of the 1999 versions of Index Portfolios 95 and 100 to index portfolio 90, the 95 and 100 portfolios were moderately modified in November 2002 to have higher exposure to small and value equities throughout the world. According to the extensive research of Eugene Fama, Kenneth French and Jim Davis, utilizing data from the Center for Research of Security Prices (CRSP) over a 68 year period from July 1929 to June 1997, this change has higher risk and return expectations than the previous versions of 95 and 100.

3. January 2004: IFA changed the computer program setting to calculate annual rebalancing on the various indexes in the Index Portfolios in January 2004. Previous to that they were rebalanced monthly. Annual rebalancing is closer to the actual rebalancing of client accounts, therefore it was adopted as the new method in January 2005.

4. June 2006: The historical monthly returns of the 15 IFA indexes and the 20 IFA Index Portfolios were reconstructed in June of 2006 to address the following issues:

A. The availability of new and better sources of data for historical returns.

B. The correction of errors in the prior data.

C. Changes to the substitution of U.S. index data for international indexes in years prior to the existence of international data.

The overall impact of these changes to the returns is small. To illustrate, the 79-year average annualized returns for Portfolios 5, 50, and 100 changed as follows:

Average Annualized Return from Jan. 1927 to Dec. 2005

	Portfolio 5	Portfolio 50	Portfolio 100
Old Return	5.66%	9.65%	12.58%
New Return	5.54%	9.58%	12.62%

5. Backtested performance results assume the reinvestment of dividends, ordinary and capital gains and annual rebalancing. The performance of the strategy reflects, and is net of, the effect of IFA's investment management fee of 0.9% per year, billed monthly. Monthly fee deduction is a requirement of our software used for backtesting. Actual IFA advisory fees are deducted quarterly, in advance. This fee is the highest fee IFA has ever charged. Depending on the size of your assets under management, your investment management fee may be less. Backtested risk and return data is a combination of live (or actual) mutual fund results and simulated index data, and mutual fund fees and expenses have been deducted from both the live (or actual) results and the simulated index data. More information about advisory fees, expenses, no-load mutual fund fees, prospectuses for no-load index mutual funds, brokerage and custodian fees can be found at www.ifa.com/Admin/fees.asp.

Although index mutual funds minimize tax liabilities from short and long term capital gains, any resulting tax liability is not deducted from performance results. Performance results also do not reflect transaction fees and other expenses charged by broker-dealers, which reduce returns.

IFA is not paid any brokerage commissions, sales loads, 12b1 fees, or any form of compensation from any mutual fund company or broker dealer. The only source of compensation from client investments is obtained from asset based advisory fees paid by the client.

More information about advisory fees, expenses, no-load mutual fund fees, prospectuses for no-load index mutual funds, brokerage and custodian fees can be found on www.ifa.com.

6. For all data periods, annualized standard deviation is presented as an approximation by multiplying the monthly standard deviation number by the square root of twelve. Please note that the number computed from annual data may differ materially from this estimate. We have chosen this methodology because Morningstar uses the same method. (See IFA Indexes Time Series Construction in Appendix B.)

7. Not all of IFA clients follow their recommendations and depending on unique and changing client and market situations, IFA may customize the construction and implementation of the Index Portfolios for particular clients, including the use of tax-managed mutual funds, tax-harvesting techniques and rebalancing frequency and precision. In taxable accounts, IFA uses tax-managed index funds to manage client assets. However, the tax-managed index funds are not used in calculating the backtested performance of the Index Portfolios, unless specified in the table or chart. Some clients substitute the mutual funds recommended by IFA with investment options available through their 401k or other accounts, thereby creating a custom asset allocation. The performance of custom asset allocations may differ materially from (and may be lower than) that of the Index Portfolios.

8. Performance results for clients that invested in accordance with the Index Portfolios will vary from the backtested performance provided in this book due to market conditions and other factors, including investments cash flows, mutual fund allocations, frequency and precision of rebalancing, tax-management strategies, cash balances, lower than 0.9% advisory fees, varying custodian fees, and/or the timing of fee deductions. As the result of these and potentially other variances, IFA clients have not and are not expected to have achieved the exact results shown since November 1999, when IFA first placed investments. Actual performance for client accounts may differ materially from (and may be lower than) that of the Index Portfolios. Clients should consult their account statements for information about how their actual performance compares to that of the Index Portfolios.

9. As with any investment strategy, there is potential for profit as well as the possibility of loss. IFA does not guarantee any minimum level of investment performance or the success of any index portfolio or investment strategy. All investments involve risk (the amount of which may vary significantly) and investment recommendations will not always be profitable.

10. Past performance does not guarantee future results.

11. Why go to all this trouble? Backtested performance data analysis is important because a shorter time-period introduces a large statistical sampling error for both risk and average returns. Past performance does not predict future performance, however, analyzing 30 years or more of simulated risk and return data is a more reliable source of information concerning the cost of capital for firms and their shareholders and the resulting expected returns for investors who

trade their cash for shares and bonds of those firms. That is the essence of capitalism.

The result of this data is a probability distribution with an average return and a standard deviation around the average, which best characterizes future random events that are totally unpredictable like the roll of the dice or flip of a coin. Yet, these random events over long time horizons, like 30 years or more, accumulate to new distributions. These distributions are, to varying degrees, similar to a large sample of previous distributions, such as 30 years. Shorter time horizons demand lower risk investments, while longer time horizons allow for regression to the mean. The "mean" refers to the average expected outcome of returns, which is also the most probable outcome. The distribution of historical market data is a leptokurtic distribution, meaning it is not conclusive in any way as to the limits of losses or gains. Dice rolls and coin flips do have limits, but the market does not. There is an unlimited risk on stock market investments that can not be clear in even very long-term historical data. For example, in the stock market crash of 1929, the market declined 89% and many investors had leveraged their capital and lost all of their investments. The stock market is a risky investment and investors can lose all, or nearly all of their money because of the risk of firms going out of business, general macroeconomic and political risks, and challenges to the ideas of capitalism, in general.

However, this analysis is far more useful than the traditional 1, 3, or 5 year returns and risk data used by the great majority of individual and professional investors. Without such longer-term analysis, investors would be merely speculating on the risks and expected returns of their investments with a statistically unacceptable sample, like a gambler in a casino hopelessly trying to beat the casino statistician, who may be referred to as the dice, card, and roulette wheel actuary. This is in fact what investors do and several studies have confirmed it is the source of their near zero average returns over the last 20 years, after inflation and taxes. As Louis Bachelier stated in the first published paper on the random character of stock market data, "The Theory of Speculation" (1900), "...the mathematical expectation of the speculator is zero." Statistically speaking, investors have a relatively high standard error of the mean (average return) with data of less than 30 years.

Because Index Funds Advisors, Inc. is recommending mutual funds that correlate to the investment criteria of the simulated index data, there is a greater chance that the data is useful to index funds advisors than it is to actively managed mutual fund advisors that do not replicate the index and therefore engage in style drift. Past performance for active managers is an especially poor indicator of future results, due to the relatively small number of years of performance data available for each active manager and the fact that even during that period they are style drifting.

This analysis and investment strategy is consistent with Modern Portfolio Theory, which is the term used to summarize the combined research of Harry Markowitz, William Sharpe and Merton Miller. They were awarded the Nobel Prize for Economics in 1990 for their efforts to describe how financial markets work and how to build efficient portfolios.

ABOUT THE ARTIST

LALA RAGIMOV

Lala Ragimov

I would like to extend a special thanks to artist, Lala Ragimov, who painted the 47 original and beautiful oil paintings that are located throughout the book. Lala, who was born in Moscow, draws her artistic inspiration from the art of the Renaissance and Baroque periods. She graduated from the world-renowned, California Institute of the Arts, located in Valencia, California. Today Lala works as an artist and illustrator for companies and private collectors.

INDEX

Y

Yale University, 26

Z

Zero sum game, 58
Zuckerman, Gregory, 79
Zuelauf, Felix, 78
Zutz, Robert J., 109
Zweig, Jason, 10, 91